MATHEMATICS OF FINANCE

Fourth Edition

Thomas Marshall Simpson

Zareh M. Pirenian

Bolling H. Crenshaw

John Riner

Prentice-Hall, Inc.,   Englewood Cliffs, N.J.

© 1930, 1936, 1951, and 1969 by
PRENTICE-HALL, Inc.
Englewood Cliffs, N.J.

Current printing (last digit):

10 9 8 7 6 5 4 3 2 1

Library of Congress Catalog Card No.: 74-76037
Printed in the United States of America

PREFACE TO THE
FOURTH EDITION

In this revision, we have attempted to make certain changes in the text without destroying those features that have made it outstanding for many years. Changes in Part I are intended to make the treatment of algebra more in keeping with the present day techniques. At the same time, the traditional treatment of the subject that has made the text so effective has not been disturbed.

The major change in Part II is the handling of various types of problems as special cases of a general problem. The traditional approach, however, is maintained and a dual treatment of the various problems is possible. New, modern day, problems have been added to this part and existing problems have been somewhat modified.

We have continued to base the problems in Chapter 18 on the American Experience Table of Mortality. For our purposes this table is as adequate as any, although the reader should probably be aware that other tables are more commonly used by insurance companies today.

The revision of a successful book is difficult. We feel honored to have been entrusted with the task. Our sincere thanks are given to Mr. Bert Waits and Mr. John White who helped with the new problems.

JOHN RINER

Columbus, Ohio

v

PREFACE TO THE
THIRD EDITION

An outstanding feature of this revision is the replacement of all problems by new ones. These are in greater variety, graded as to difficulty; and there are many more of them. The revision was undertaken in response to numerous requests from those who have used former editions. The authors are grateful for many helpful suggestions. For greater clarity and brevity many minor improvements have been made throughout the book. In particular, certain parts of Chapters 1, 2, and 4 have been rewritten. With an elaboration upon several articles, new material has been added to Chapter 18, where symbols conform to the notation approved recently by the International Congress of Actuaries.

To avoid extensive computations, special pains have been taken in many instances to reduce them to a minimum. This has been done by careful selection of data without sacrificing diversity of problem material. Interest rates in examples and exercises comply with recent trends. Problems involving chronological data, particularly those in bond valuation, have been brought up to date.

The authors have been encouraged by the generous reception accorded the book in all sections of the country. It is hoped that this revision is even more teachable. Deep appreciation is due the Publishers for their courtesy, efficiency, and cheerful cooperation in making a new edition available.

PREFACE TO THE
SECOND EDITION

This text is designed primarily for a three-hour one-year course for students of commerce and business administration. However, a study of the numerous applications to a great variety of financial problems arising in modern life would be profitable also to students of engineering, education, law, and liberal arts.

The authors have provided in Part I a sufficient review and drill in the essentials of elementary algebra to enable the student to pass naturally and easily to advanced chapters. Certain topics not immediately related to the purpose at hand are omitted, while other topics, such as the construction and interpretation of formulas, simple interest and discount, and equations of value are treated at length and with more than usual emphasis. Experience of years leads the authors to believe that the subject matter presented in Part I is a **more suitable and effective preparation** than college algebra for a course in compound interest and annuities.

Part II provides an introduction to the mathematical theory of compound interest, annuities, and life insurance, together with well chosen practical applications. To enable the student to master first the simple case in annuities, the general case is relegated to a separate chapter toward the end of the book.

The favorable reception accorded the original edition has led to the preparation of the present edition. The general plan of the first edition has been retained. However, many portions of the text have been rewritten after a careful study of suggestions by those who have used the book. Besides many minor alterations for the better, the following **improvements** are worthy of note. The **problems** are all **new,** are of great variety, and are much more numerous. Some of these were submitted to the authors for solution by individuals or by firms. The usefulness of the book has been enhanced

ix

by **enlarging** the **tables. A chapter** on **statistics** has been added because of the ever-increasing importance of this subject in many departments of knowledge. Certain chapters in Part II have been amplified to permit the inclusion of continuous conversion, force of interest, a more clarified treatment of equations of value and deferred annuities, a unifying summary of annuities certain together with a new diagram, and conventional practices and terminology in bond valuation. The majority of the problems in bond valuation contain data from actual cases. Chapter 17 provides a **new, simplified** treatment of general annuities, in connection with which Tables IX, X, and XI, heretofore unpublished, are particularly convenient. The symbols used in Chapter 18 conform to standard actuarial notation. The considerable additions to that chapter should give the student a still better insight into the beauty and power of mathematics as applied to long-term finance based upon single life contingencies.

No effort has been spared to secure the utmost accuracy throughout the book. The authors are of the opinion that errors, typographic or otherwise, have an undesirable effect upon many students. Special pains have been taken to utilize all space without introducing congestion, to adjust the paging to the reader's convenience without sacrificing lucidity, and to make the general appearance of the book pleasing to instructors and students alike. Certain other features are pointed out here:

1. **The illustrative example is used** not only to show the application of principles already developed but also to introduce new ideas. These examples are worked in detail, the reasons for all necessary steps being given. The aim of the authors is to provide a book that will teach itself without too much dependence on an instructor.

2. **The necessity of checking answers** is emphasized.

3. **The language is adapted to the training** expected of the students taking the course. Technical terms are avoided as far as possible. As new terms arise, they are defined clearly.

4. At the end of each chapter, a **miscellaneous exercise** is inserted dealing with the principles and methods in the chapter.

5. At the middle and at the end of the book, a **general review exercise** is placed. Together these exercises contain 295 problems covering all the material in the text.

6. In nearly every exercise, except in miscellaneous exercises, the **grouping of problems** is such that the instructor may designate either the **odd-numbered** or the **even-numbered** problems as a **complete assignment.** Answers to odd-numbered problems, except for miscellaneous exercises, are given at the end of the book. Answers not given in the text will be supplied by the publishers to instructors at their request.

The minimum prerequisite to the course should be one year of high school algebra. The student who has had more than one year of high school algebra should find himself especially well prepared.

Tables III, IV, V, VI, and VII of this text are taken from Glover's *Tables of Applied Mathematics*, a standard work of great value to students in this field. The authors are greatly indebted to Professor James W. Glover and his publisher, Mr. George Wahr, for their kind permission.

CONTENTS

Part TWO

Compound Interest, Annuities, and Life Insurance

Part ONE

Commercial Algebra

To the Student

Gradually, the technique of modern business is being placed upon a scientific basis and here, as in the pure sciences, mathematics plays an important role. In many industries and professions of today, it is of decided advantage to be able to understand symbols and formulas, to grasp the significance of graphs and statistics, and, in general, to think in terms of algebra. Mathematics is a system of thinking as well as a tool of great utility. As such, it is a most helpful part of your training for the future.

"Commercial Algebra," Part I of the authors' *Mathematics of Finance*, will give you a review of the essentials of elementary algebra, will teach you methods of applying algebra to problems arising in everyday affairs, and will finally introduce you to more advanced topics. Upon completing this work, if you wish to get acquainted also with the theory and important applications of compound interest, annuities, and life insurance, you will be prepared to pursue to advantage the course presented in Part II.

Chapter **ONE**

THE FUNDAMENTAL
OPERATIONS

1. Algebra

We are familiar with the ordinary processes of arithmetic. Thus we can add, subtract, and multiply any two real numbers and can divide any two real numbers where the divisor is not zero. Algebra (of real numbers) is concerned with arithmetic performed in a rather general fashion. Letters are used to represent arbitrary real numbers or to be replaced by numerals, and a letter so used is called a (real) **variable.** When we see $a + b$, we understand this to mean the sum of the numbers a and b. If we assigned specific values to a and b we could compute the sum. If a is 3 and b is 5, the symbol $a + b$ represents the number 8. Likewise, $a - b$; $a \cdot b$, or $a \times b$, or ab; $a \div b$, or a/b, or $\frac{a}{b}$ denote, respectively, the difference, product, and quotient of a and b.

The symbol $=$ (read "equals") inserted between symbols representing two real numbers means "is the same as" or "is." Thus the statement $(a + b)c = 10$ means that the number represented by $(a + b)c$ is the number 10.

Now there are certain rules that regulate the way we handle the operations on real numbers. Depending on what basic set of assumptions we make, these rules are either assumed or provable. We will throughout this chapter point out certain of these rules. In general, we will not prove them but assume them to hold. An example of one of these is the associative law for multiplication of real numbers. Given any three real numbers a, b, and c,

$$a \cdot (b \cdot c) = (a \cdot b) \cdot c.$$

This tells us, for instance, that

$$(26 \times 5) \times 2 = 26 \times (5 \times 2).$$

It is probably better to compute the product on the right, for this is 26×10 or 260. This is not an obvious law because, if the operation under consideration were subtraction, the insertion of parentheses in different order (i.e., the order in which we perform the operation) would change the result. For $(25 - 5) - 2 = 18$ while $25 - (5 - 2) = 22$. However, with this associative property we need not specify the manner in which to group and the representation $26 \times 5 \times 2$ of a real number is unambiguous.

Briefly, then, we list here certain basic rules which can be used to prove most of the rules we list throughout this chapter.

Associative Laws:

For any real numbers a, b, and c,

$$a + (b + c) = (a + b) + c$$

and

$$a \cdot (b \cdot c) = (a \cdot b) \cdot c.$$

(These can be extended to any finite set of real numbers.)

Commutative Laws:

For any real numbers a and b,

$$a + b = b + a$$

and

$$a \cdot b = b \cdot a$$

Zero Axiom:

There exists a real number 0 (zero) such that

$$a + 0 = 0 + a = a$$

for every real number a.

Unity Axiom:

There exists a real number 1 (one), different from 0, such that

$$a \cdot 1 = 1 \cdot a = a$$

for every real number a.

Subtraction Axiom:

Given any two real numbers a and b, there exists a unique number x such that $a + x = b$. x is called the **difference** of b and a and is denoted $b - a$. In particular, $-a$, called the **negative** of a, is the number x when $b = 0$.

Division Axiom:

Given any two real numbers a and b, $b \neq 0$, there exists a unique number x such that $bx = a$. x is called the **quotient** of a and b and is denoted $\frac{a}{b}$ or $a \div b$. In particular, when $a = 1$, x is called the **inverse** of b and is denoted by b^{-1} as well as by $\frac{1}{b}$. Note that division by zero is not defined.

Distributive Law:

(The axioms and laws listed thus far have kept separate the operations. The distributive law relates them.) For any real numbers a, b and c,

$$a(b + c) = ab + ac.$$

As stated earlier, the axioms and laws above constitute a basic set of assumptions which can be used to develop many of the other basic algebraic properties of real numbers. Keep in mind that, while we will not prove the other familiar properties, they are usually provable from the assumptions above.

2. Terminology in algebra

Two or more symbols for numbers combined by symbols of operations form an **algebraic expression,** and the parts separated by the plus and minus signs are the **terms** of the expression. An algebraic expression of one term is called a **monomial,** one of two terms a **binomial,** and one of three terms a **trinomial.** For example, $5ax$ is a monomial, $5ax + 2$ is a binomial, $ax^2 + bx + c$ is a trinomial. A binomial, trinomial, or any expression for the sum of two or more terms is called a **polynomial.**

If the product of two or more numbers is indicated, each number is called a **factor.** For example, in the binomial $2xy + 5a$, the first term, $2xy$, is the product of the three factors 2, x, and y, and the second term, $5a$, is the product of the two factors 5 and a. In the term $5a$, 5 is said to be the **numerical coefficient** of a, and a the **literal coefficient** of 5.

The product of two or more **equal** factors is called a **power** of the factor. The number of equal factors is indicated by the **exponent**. Thus, $a \cdot a \cdot a = a^3$; a has the exponent 3, and a^3 is the third power of a. For first powers, the exponent 1 is understood, and is not written. A second power is called a **square,** and a third power a **cube.**

Conversely, one of the equal factors is called a **root** of the product. Thus, a is a **cube** root of a^3, 4 is a **square** root of 16 or of 4^2. A square root is indicated by the **radical** sign $\sqrt{}$, a cube root by $\sqrt[3]{}$, etc. The number written in the upper left opening is the **index** of the radical. When no index is written, the square root is indicated.

3. Operations with positive and negative numbers

We have not thus far mentioned the concepts of positive and negative numbers. Our assumption here is that there is a subset of the real numbers called the set P of positive real numbers. A number in the set P is called a **positive number.** We make several basic assumptions about the set P.

1. Given any real number x, one and only one of the following alternatives hold:

(a) x is a positive number,
(b) $x = 0$,
(c) $-x$ is a positive number.

2. If x and y are positive, then $x + y$ and $x \cdot y$ are positive.

We normally denote the fact that x is positive by writing $x > 0$ (read "x is greater than zero") or $0 < x$ (read "0 is less than x"). We say that x is greater than y and write $x > y$ when $x - y > 0$. The symbol $y < x$ (read "y is less than x") means $x > y$. We define a number x to be **negative** and write $x < 0$ ("x is less than 0") when $-x > 0$.

In certain computations we deal with both positive and negative numbers. Certain rules apply which we list below. The concept of absolute value is helpful here. We define the **absolute value,** $|x|$, of a number x to be x, if $x > 0$ or if $x = 0$, and to be $-x$ if $x < 0$. Essentially this says the absolute value of a number is the "positive" value of the number. Thus, $|-2| = 2$ and $|-5| = 5$ while $|2| = 2$.

Rules of Operation With Numbers of Unlike Signs

(a) To add two numbers having like signs, add their absolute values, and prefix their common sign. To add two numbers having unlike signs, subtract the smaller absolute value from the greater, and prefix the sign of the numerically greater.

(b) To subtract one number from another, change the sign of the number to be subtracted and add it to the other number according to rule (a).

(c) To multiply one number by another, find the product of their absolute values; prefix the plus sign to this product when the numbers have like signs, but prefix the minus sign when the numbers have unlike signs.

(d) To divide one number by another, find the quotient of their absolute values; prefix the plus sign to this quotient if the numbers have like signs, but prefix the minus sign if the numbers have unlike signs.

Note. No two of the symbols $+$, $-$, $\times$, $\div$ should appear in succession. Thus, to indicate that 2 is to be multiplied by -3, write $2(-3)$ and not 2×-3. Also, recall that in algebra, when two or more letters are placed side by side, their product is indicated.

4. Zero in four operations

We here summarize the rules for operating with 0 in various computations.

(a) Zero added to any number leaves the value of that number unchanged. Thus, $0 + a = a + 0 = a$; $0 + 0 = 0$.

(b) Zero subtracted from any number leaves the value of that number unchanged. Thus, $a - 0 = a$; $0 - 0 = 0$.

Any number subtracted from zero keeps its absolute value, but changes its sign. Thus, $0 - a = -a$; $0 - (-a) = a$.

(c) Zero multiplied by any number, or any number multiplied by zero, is zero. Thus, $0 \times a = 0$; $a \times 0 = 0$; $0 \times 0 = 0$.

(d) Zero divided by any number, *except zero*, is zero. Thus, $0/a = 0$, when a is not equal to zero.

Finally, note that *division by zero is meaningless.* For, to divide a by b means to find a number c such that $b \times c = a$. Accordingly, $a/0$ would mean to find a number c such that $0 \times c = a$. If a is not zero, no such number

c exists; if $a = 0$, the relation $0 \times c = 0$ would be true for *any* value of c. Hence division by zero is *excluded* from our operations.

EXERCISE 1 (Oral)

In Problems 1–3, supply missing words or syllables.

1. $m - n$ is the ———— of m and n. 5 is the ———— of 13 and 8. pq is the ———— of p and q. $ax + b$ is the ———— of ax and b. h/k is the ———— of h and k. 36 is the ———— of 9 and 4.

2. $x^2 + 2xy - 5$ consists of three ————; hence it is a ———— nomial. The first term has ———— factors, which are ————; the second term has three ————, which are ————. In the middle term, 2 is the ———— of xy. Each term of the given trinomial is a ———— nomial.

3. 8 is the product of three equal ————; it is the ———— power of 2. n^2 means n times ————; it is the ———— power or the ———— of n. In the expression kr^3, k is the ———— of r^3, and 3 is the ———— of r. $\sqrt[3]{64}$ equals ————; here the number 3 is the ———— of the radical.

4. State the sum, the difference, the product, and the quotient of each pair of numbers: (a) $+6, +2$; (b) $+10, -5$; (c) $-12, +3$; (d) $-15, -5$; (e) $+4, -12$; (f) $-3, +6$; (g) $-2, -8$.

5. Give the value of each: 8^2, 5^3, 2^4, $(-4)^3$, $(-6)^2$, $\sqrt{49}$, $\sqrt[3]{64}$, $\sqrt[4]{16}$.

6. Find the value of each expression if $x = 3$, $y = -2$, and $z = 0$: (a) $x^2 - y$; (b) $5x + y^2$; (c) $2x + 3y$; (d) $4xy$; (e) $x + 2z$; (f) $z - y$; (g) xz; (h) $\dfrac{x - y}{x + y}$; (i) $\dfrac{xy}{x - y}$; (j) $\dfrac{z}{x}$; (k) $\dfrac{4x}{z}$; (l) $\dfrac{2x + 3y}{5}$; (m) $\dfrac{3x + 1}{-5y}$.

5. Addition of algebraic expressions

Two or more terms are said to be **like terms** if they have the same **literal** part, but not necessarily the same numerical coefficients. Thus, $6x^2y$ and $-13x^2y$ are like terms. Suppose now that we wish to add the like terms $2a$ and $3a$. The sum $2a + 3a$, by our distributive law, is the same as $(2 + 3)a$ or $5a$. In the same fashion, $2xy^2 + 2xy^2 = (2 + 2)xy^2$. In general, the sum of like terms is the sum of their coefficients multiplied by the common literal part. The sum of unlike terms is simply indicated. Thus, the sum of $2a$ and $3b$ is simply written $2a + 3b$.

6. Subtraction of algebraic expressions

To subtract a term from a like term, subtract the coefficient of the former from that of the latter, and multiply this difference by the common factor of the two. Thus, $7a - 4a = (7 - 4)a = 3a$; $x(a + b) - y(a + b) = (x - y)(a + b)$. Again these are simple applications of the distributive law. If the terms are unlike, the subtraction is simply indicated. Thus, $5a - 3b$ cannot be further simplified.

7. Symbols of grouping

Parentheses ( ), brackets [ ], and braces { } are symbols used for grouping terms that are to be treated as a single number. If from 9 we subtract 3 and then add 4 to this result, we get 10. But, if from 9 we subtract the sum of 3 and 4, we get 2. The first operation is indicated by $9 - 3 + 4 = 10$; the second by $9 - (3 + 4) = 2$.

A parenthesis inclosing a sum of several terms and preceded by the plus sign may be removed without changing the signs of the terms of the polynomial. A parenthesis enclosing a sum of several terms and preceded by the minus sign may be removed if we change the sign of each term of the sum.

EXERCISE 2

Add:

1. $7ab, 5ab, -2ab$.

2. $mn, 4mn, -8mn$.

3. $5x, -7x, 3x, -2x$.

4. $-6y, 2y, 8y, -y$.

5. $cd + 1, 4cd - d, 2d - 3$.

6. $5 - ab, a + 2, 6a + ab$.

7. $x^2 - 3x, 3 + 5x, 2 - 4x^2$.

8. $6y^2 + 1, 8y - 5, 3y - 5y^2$.

9. $3s^2 - 5st - 2s, 2s - 3s^2$.

10. $pq + 3p^2, 5p - 3pq - 4p^2$.

11. $6(a + b), -4(a + b)$.

12. $8(c + d), 5(c + d)$.

13. $a(x - y), b(x + y)$.

14. $c(u - v), -d(u - v)$.

15. $Ay^2 + By, ay^2 - by$.

16. $Mx^2 - Nx, mx^2 + nx$.

Subtract:

17. $2x - 3y$ from $5x + y$.

18. $2m + n$ from $5m - n$.

19. $a^2 + 3a$ from $9a - 6a^2$.

20. $4x - 7x^2$ from $x^2 + 3x$.

21. $y^2 - 4y + 3$ from $8 - 2y$.

22. $2 + 3c - c^2$ from $c^2 + 2$.

23. $4 - x^2$ from $3x + x^3$.   **28.** $-4(s - t)$ from $5(s - t)$.
24. $y^2 + 1$ from $y^3 - 5y$.   **29.** $r(x - y)$ from $s(x - y)$.
25. 5 from $10b - 5$.   **30.** $m(a + b)$ from $n(a + b)$.
26. -2 from $3a + 2$.   **31.** $at^2 - bt$ from $At^2 + Bt$.
27. $3(m + n)$f rom $7(m + n)$.   **32.** $Mx^2 + Nx$ form $mx^2 - nx$.

Remove all symbols of grouping and simplify:

33. $3a - (3a - b) + 2b$.   **37.** $4m - n + [3m + (n - 2m)]$.
34. $(c - 3d) - (d - 4c)$.   **38.** $p + 3q - [(p - q) + (p + q)]$.
35. $y^2 - [2y + (6y - 3)]$.   **39.** $x^2 - \{x^2 - (y^2 + z^2)\}$.
36. $3x - [(x^2 - 5) + 2x]$.   **40.** $\{(a^2 - b^2) - (a^2 + b^2)\} + c^2$.

8. Multiplication of algebraic expressions

The product of two or more monomials is equal to the product of their numerical coefficients times the product of their literal factors. Thus, $3a \times 2b \times c = (3 \cdot 2 \cdot 1)abc = 6abc$. This is an application of the commutative and associative laws for real numbers.

The product of a polynomial and a monomial is the algebraic sum of the products obtained by multiplying each term of the polynomial by the monomial. Thus, $(2a - 5b)4c = 8ac - 20bc$. (A direct application of the distributive law.)

The product of two polynomials is the algebraic sum of the products obtained by multiplying each term of one polynomial by each term of the other. This also can be justified by repeated applications of the distributive law.

In multiplying algebraic expressions, we use the law of exponents for multiplication: $a^m \times a^n = a^{m+n}$. (See Art. 49, page 101). Thus, $3x^2 \times 7x^3 = 3 \times 7 \times x^{2+3} = 21x^5$.

ILLUSTRATIVE EXAMPLE. Multiply $2a^3 + a^2 - 3$ by $6a^2 - 2a + 1$.

SOLUTION.

$$
\begin{array}{l}
2a^3 + a^2 - 3 \\
6a^2 - 2a + 1 \\
\hline
12a^5 + 6a^4 - 18a^2 \\
 - 4a^4 - 2a^3 + 6a \\
 + 2a^3 + a^2 - 3 \\
\hline
12a^5 + 2a^4 - 17a^2 + 6a - 3. \quad \textit{Ans.}
\end{array}
$$

CHECK. When $a = 2$, $(2a^3 + a^2 - 3)(6a^2 - 2a + 1) = (2 \cdot 8 + 4 - 3)$

$\times (6.4 - 2 \cdot 2 + 1) = (16 + 4 - 3)(24 - 4 + 1) = 17 \times 21 = 357;$
$12a^5 + 2a^4 - 17a^2 + 6a - 3 = 384 + 32 - 68 + 12 - 3 = 357.$ There-fore the answer is probably correct.

———

EXERCISE 3

Multiply:

1. xy^2 by $-4x^2y^3$.
2. $-2a^2b$ by $3ab^3$.
3. $-5m^2$ by $-7mn$.
4. $-6x^2$ by $-3xy^2$.
5. $14cd^2$ by $\frac{1}{2}d$.
6. $\frac{1}{3}m$ by $6m^2n$.
7. $2x - 5x^2$ by $3x$.
8. $7y$ by $y^2 + 2y$.
9. $4ab$ by $a + b^2$.
10. $x^2 - 3x$ by $-4x$.

11. $a^2 + 3a$ by $a + 2$.
12. $x^2 + 2x$ by $x - 3$.
13. $3s^2 - 2t$ by $3s + 3t$.
14. $p^2 - 3pq$ by $2p - q$.
15. $x^2 - 3x + 5$ by $x - 2$.
16. $y^2 + 2y - 4$ by $3y - 1$.
17. $4a - a^2 + 2$ by $2 - a$.
18. $5 - b^2 + b$ by $4 + 3b$.
19. $y^2 - 2y + 4$ by $y + 2$.
20. $x^2 + xy + y^2$ by $x - y$.

Multiply mentally and note the form of the product:

21. $(3x - 9)(3x + 9)$.
22. $(2y + 5)(2y - 5)$.
23. $(4a - 3b)(4a - 3b)$.
24. $(3x + 4y)(3x + 4y)$.
25. $(7x + 2)^2$.
26. $(2y - 3)^2$.
27. $(m + 5)(m - 2)$.
28. $(a - 4)(a + 3)$.

29. $(a^3 + 3b)(a^3 - 3b)$.
30. $(4m - n^2)(4m + n^2)$.
31. $xy(x^2 - 3x + 5y)$.
32. $a^2b(3a - b - b^2)$.
33. $x(2x - 1)(2x + 1)$.
34. $n(n - \frac{1}{2})^2$.
35. $(c + 3d)(2c - d)$.
36. $(5x - y)(2x + 3y)$.

9. Factoring

By actual multiplication, we get the following special type products:

$$a(x + y) = ax + ay. \tag{1}$$

$$(x + y)^2 = x^2 + 2xy + y^2. \tag{2}$$

$$(x - y)^2 = x^2 - 2xy + y^2. \tag{3}$$

$$(x + y)(x - y) = x^2 - y^2. \tag{4}$$

$$(ax + b)(cx + d) = acx^2 + (ad + bc)x + bd. \tag{5}$$

The right member of each is the **expanded** form and the left member is the **factored** form. If, then, an algebraic expression is given in the expanded form of any one of these type products, we should be able to write the corresponding simple factors at once. This process is called **factoring.**

Monomial factors can usually be detected by inspection. When one is detected, the given expression should be written as the product of this monomial and another factor, as in illustrative example 1. The polynomial factor thus obtained should then be expressed as the product of its simple factors, if any, according to type forms (2) to (5) above.

The right member of type form (2) or type form (3) is the **expanded square of a binomial.** The right member of type form (4) is the **difference of two squares;** this may be put in words thus, *The product of the sum and difference of two numbers is equal to the difference of their squares.* The right member of type form $ax^2 + bx + c$, as in (5), is called the **general trinomial** in one variable.

ILLUSTRATIVE EXAMPLE 1. Factor $5a^2 - 45b^2$.

SOLUTION.
$$5a^2 - 45b^2 = 5(a^2 - 9b^2)$$
$$= 5[(a)^2 - (3b)^2]$$
$$= 5(a + 3b)(a - 3b). \quad Ans.$$

CHECK. Multiply the factors and get $5a^2 - 45b^2$.

ILLUSTRATIVE EXAMPLE 2. Factor $4x^2 - 12x + 9$.

SOLUTION. By inspection,

$$4x^2 - 12x + 9 = (2x)^2 - 2 \cdot 2x \cdot 3 + (3)^2$$
$$= (2x - 3)^2. \quad Ans.$$

CHECK. Multiply $2x - 3$ by itself and get $4x^2 - 12x + 9$.

ILLUSTRATIVE EXAMPLE 3. Factor $6x^2 + 7x - 20$.

SOLUTION. By trial,

$$6x^2 + 7x - 20 = (3x - 4)(2x + 5). \quad Ans.$$

CHECK. Multiply $3x - 4$ by $2x + 5$ and get $6x^2 + 7x - 20$.

EXERCISE 4

Factor and check by multiplication:

1. $R - Rst$.
2. $P + Pni$.
3. $3kx - 6kx^2$.
4. $2ay + 4a^2y^2$.
5. $x^2 - 4y^2$.
6. $16c^2 - 25$.
7. $9y - y^3$.
8. $7u^2 - 28$.
9. $x^2 - 4x + 4$.
10. $9x^2 + 12xy + 4y^2$
11. $m^4 + 6m^2n + 9n^2$.
12. $c^2 - c + \frac{1}{4}$.
13. $e\pi R - e^2 R$
14. $\frac{1}{4}ah + \frac{1}{2}bh$.
15. $a^2 + 4a - 12$.
16. $n^2 - 2n - 8$.
17. $y^2 - 5y + 6$.
18. $y^2 - 7y + 12$.
19. $2y^2 + 5y - 3$.
20. $3p^2 - p - 2$.

21. $m^2 - 1$.
22. $9x^4 - 25$.
23. $a^2x^4 - y^4$.
24. $2a^4 - 32b^4$.
25. $x^3 + 3x + 2x$.
26. $6x + 5x^2 + x^3$.
27. $3y^2 + 5y - 2$.
28. $2m^2 - 7m - 15$.
29. $dr^3 - 2dr^2 + dr$.
30. $a^2x^2 - 2ab^2x + b^4$.
31. $P(1 + i) + Pi(1 + i)$.
32. $L(1 - r) - L(1 - r)^6$
33. $(a - b) + x(a - b)$
34. $a(m - n) + b(m - n)$.
35. $xy + x + y + 1$.
36. $m + bm - n - bn$.
37. $a^2 - 2ax + x^2 - y^2$.
38. $x^2 - 2xy + y^2 - z^2$.
39. $9c^2 - (a - b)^2$.
40. $16x^2 - (y + 5)^5$.

10. Division of algebraic expressions

To divide one monomial by another, we use the law of exponents for division: $a^m \div a^n = a^{m-n}$, $a \neq 0$. (See Art. 49.) Of course, a cannot be zero. Thus,

$$a^5 \div a^3 = a^{5-3} = a^2; \quad x^7y^5 \div x^3y^2 = x^{7-3}y^{5-2} = x^4y^3.$$

To divide a polynomial by a monomial, divide each term of the polynomial by the monomial. Thus,

$$(12x^3y + 9x^2y^2 - 3xy^4) \div 3xy = \frac{12x^3y}{3xy} + \frac{9x^2y^2}{3xy} - \frac{3xy^4}{3xy}$$
$$= 4x^2 + 3xy - y^3.$$

This is an application of the distributive law and the division axiom.

$$(a + b) \div c = (a + b) \cdot \frac{1}{c} = a \cdot \frac{1}{c} + b \cdot \frac{1}{c} = \frac{a}{c} + \frac{b}{c}.$$

To divide one polynomial in x (we might, of course, have selected any other letter) by another, first arrange the terms of both polynomials in descending powers of x, and then apply the method of the following:

___

ILLUSTRATIVE EXAMPLE. Divide $x^4 + 5x^3 - 2x^2 + 5x - 4$ by $x^2 + 3x - 1$.

SOLUTION.

$$
\begin{array}{r}
x^4 + 5x^3 - 2x^2 + 5x - 4 \\
x^4 + 3x^3 - x^2 \\
\hline
2x^3 - x^2 + 5x \\
2x^3 + 6x^2 - 2x \\
\hline
-7x^2 + 7x - 4 \\
-7x^2 - 21x + 7 \\
\hline
28x - 11 = \text{Remainder}
\end{array}
\quad
\begin{array}{l}
x^2 + 3x - 1 \\
\hline
x^2 + 2x - 7 = \text{Quotient}
\end{array}
$$

CHECK. Let $x = 2$, and show that the dividend = the quotient $\times$ the divisor + the remainder. Thus,

$$x^4 + 5x^3 - 2x^2 + 5x - 4 = 2^4 + 5 \cdot 2^3 - 2 \cdot 2^2 + 5 \cdot 2 - 4$$
$$= 16 + 40 - 8 + 10 - 4 = 54;$$
$$(x^2 + 2x - 7)(x^2 + 3x - 1) + (28x - 11)$$
$$= (2^2 + 2 \cdot 2 - 7)(2^2 + 3 \cdot 2 - 1) + (28 \cdot 2 - 11)$$
$$= (1)(9) + 45 = 9 + 45 = 54.$$

Therefore the answer is probably correct.

___

EXERCISE 5

Divide:

1. $3^4 \cdot 5^8$ by $3^2 \cdot 5^5$.
2. $9^{10} \cdot 4^2$ by $9^5 \cdot 4$.
3. $15x^3 y^2$ by $-3xy$.
4. $-12a^5 b^3$ by $3a^2 b^2$.
5. $-24m^7 n^8$ by $-4m^3 n^8$.
6. $-18x^4 y^9$ by $-6x^3 y^5$.
7. $10ay^4 - 15a^3 y$ by $4ay$.
8. $8b^3 x^3 + 20b^3 x^5$ by $4b^2 x$.

9. $-8m^3 + 4m^2 - 2m^2$ by m^2.
10. $6a^4 - 9a^2 + 12a$ by $-3a$.
11. $2.4x^7 - 0.3x^4$ by $0.6x^2$.
12. $0.8y^4 + 0.2y^2$ by $0.4y$.
13. $x^3 + 1$ by $x + 1$.
14. $a^3 + b^3$ by $a + b$.
15. $m^4 - n^4$ by $m - n$.
16. $1 - i^4$ by $1 + i$.

Perform the indicated divisions and check by letting $x = 2$:

17. $(x^4 + 4x^3 + 4x^2 + x) \div (x^2 + x)$.
18. $(4x^3 - 5x^2 + 3x - 2) \div (2x + 3)$.
19. $(x^4 - 3x^2 + 5x + 8) \div (x^2 - 2x + 3)$.
20. $(x^4 + 2x^3 - 3x - 4) \div (x^2 - x + 1)$.
21. $(x^5 + x^2 - x + 1) \div (x^3 - x + 1)$.
22. $(x^5 - 3x^3 + 10) \div (x^4 - 2x)$.
23. $(x^4 - 5x + 3) \div (x^2 - 1)$.
24. $(x^4 + 6x^2 - 7) \div (x^2 + 2)$.

11. Fractions

A **fraction** is the indicated quotient of one expression by another. Thus, the fraction a/b means the **numerator** a divided by the **denominator** b. The numerator and denominator are called the **terms** of the fraction (not to be confused with the terms in a sum).

In operations with fractions, it is important to know and to use the following fundamental principle: *Multiplying or dividing both numerator and denominator by the same number, except zero, does not change the value of the fraction.*

By the **sign of a fraction** is meant the plus or minus sign in front of the fraction. The student should take care to write the sign of a fraction *on a level* with the line of division. The following relations, resulting from the rule of signs for division given in Art. 3(d), should be carefully noted:

$$\frac{a}{-b} = \frac{-a}{b} = -\frac{a}{b}.$$

Thus,

$$\frac{12}{-4} = \frac{-12}{4} = -3; \quad -\frac{a^2 - b^2}{a + 3b} = \frac{b^2 - a^2}{a + 3b}.$$

12. Reduction of fractions

By applying the fundamental principle given in Art. 11, fractions can be reduced to either higher or lower terms. Thus,

$$\frac{3}{4} = \frac{3 \times 5}{4 \times 5} = \frac{15}{20}; \quad \frac{28}{12} = \frac{28 \div 4}{12 \div 4} = \frac{7}{3}.$$

Likewise, if $c \neq 0$,

$$\frac{a}{b} = \frac{ac}{bc}; \quad \text{and} \quad \frac{x^2y}{xy^2} = \frac{x^2y \div xy}{xy^2 \div xy} = \frac{x}{y} \qquad \text{(if } xy \neq 0\text{)}.$$

A fraction is **reduced** to its **simplest form** (or **lowest terms**) when its numerator and denominator have no common factor. Hence to reduce a fraction to its simplest form, divide both numerator and denominator by their highest common factor. This process is simplified by first factoring the numerator and denominator. In the final result, the numerator and denominator are usually left in factored form.

ILLUSTRATIVE EXAMPLE. Reduce $\dfrac{a^3x^2 - 9a^3}{ax^2 + 7ax + 12a}$ to its simplest form.

SOLUTION.

$$\frac{a^3x^2 - 9a^3}{ax^2 + 7ax + 12a} = \frac{a^3(x+3)(x-3)}{a(x+3)(x+4)} = \frac{a^2(x-3)}{x+4}.$$

Caution. We have seen that multiplying or dividing both numerator and denominator of a fraction by the same number other than zero does not change its value. On the other hand, if the same number be added to, or subtracted from, both numerator and denominator, the value of the fraction is, in general, *changed*. Thus, consider the fraction $\frac{3}{6}$, whose value we know is $\frac{1}{2}$. Add 4 to both numerator and denominator; the resulting fraction is $\frac{7}{10}$, which is certainly not equal to $\frac{1}{2}$. Or subtract 2 from both numerator and denominator; the resulting fraction is $\frac{1}{4}$; the value of the given fraction is again changed. As an algebraic example, consider the fraction $\dfrac{x+5}{y+5}$. This fraction is in its simplest form, and yet it is a frequent error for some students to "simplify" it into x/y. It is true that x/y looks simpler than the given fraction, but to produce this change in form, we must *subtract* 5 from both numerator and denominator. But that step is not permissible, since it changes the value of the given fraction.

13. Algebraic sum of fractions

The algebraic sum of two or more fractions *having a common denominator* is a fraction whose numerator is the algebraic sum of the numerators and whose denominator is the common denominator. That is,

$$\frac{a}{d} + \frac{b}{d} - \frac{c}{d} = \frac{a}{d} + \frac{b}{d} + \frac{-c}{d} = \frac{a+b-c}{d}.$$

If the given fractions do not have the same denominator, it is necessary before adding to change them to equivalent fractions with a common denominator as simple as possible. If the student is not familiar with the method for finding the **lowest common denominator** (L.C.D.), he should study the next paragraph carefully.

The L.C.D. of two or more fractions is the **lowest common multiple** (L.C.M.) of their denominators. A rule for finding the L.C.M. of two or more expressions is: Find the simple factors of each expression; take the product of all the *different* factors, each having the highest exponent with which it occurs in any one of the expressions; this product is the L.C.M.

While it is usually desirable in adding two fractions to use the L.C.D. it is certainly not essential. In fact, the general procedure in adding two fractions with different denominators is given by

$$\frac{a}{b} + \frac{c}{d} = \frac{ad + bc}{bd}, \qquad bd \neq 0.$$

This follows from the division axiom and the other rules we assumed. (It is, of course, enough to be able to add fractions two at a time.)

ILLUSTRATIVE EXAMPLE 1. Find the L.C.M. of 30, 36, and 40.

SOLUTION.

$$30 = 6 \times 5 = 2 \times 3 \times 5,$$
$$36 = 4 \times 9 = 2^2 \times 3^2,$$
$$40 = 8 \times 5 = 2^3 \times 5.$$

Hence

$$\text{L.C.M.} = 2^3 \times 3^2 \times 5 = 8 \times 9 \times 5 = 360. \quad Ans.$$

ILLUSTRATIVE EXAMPLE 2. Find the L.C.M. of $x^2 - 2xy + y^2$ and $x^2 - y^2$.

SOLUTION.

$$x^2 - 2xy + y^2 = (x - y)^2,$$
$$x^2 - y^2 = (x - y)(x + y).$$

Hence

$$\text{L.C.M.} = (x - y)^2(x + y). \quad Ans.$$

ILLUSTRATIVE EXAMPLE 3. Simplify: $\dfrac{2a}{3a-3b} + \dfrac{a^2+b^2}{a^2-b^2} - \dfrac{a-b}{a+b}$.

SOLUTION.

$$3a - 3b = 3(a - b),$$
$$a^2 - b^2 = (a + b)(a - b),$$
$$a + b = a + b.$$

Then,

$$\text{L.C.D.} = 3(a + b)(a - b).$$

Now, reducing each of the given fractions to an equivalent fraction with the L.C.D. for denominator, we have

$$\frac{2a}{3a-3b} = \frac{2a}{3(a-b)} = \frac{2a(a+b)}{3(a+b)(a-b)},$$
$$\frac{a^2+b^2}{a^2-b^2} = \frac{a^2+b^2}{(a+b)(a-b)} = \frac{3(a^2+b^2)}{3(a+b)(a-b)},$$
$$\frac{a-b}{a+b} = \frac{3(a-b)(a-b)}{3(a+b)(a-b)} = \frac{3(a^2-2ab+b^2)}{3(a+b)(a-b)}.$$

Hence

$$\frac{2a}{3a-3b} + \frac{a^2+b^2}{a^2-b^2} - \frac{a-b}{a+b}$$

$$= \frac{2a(a+b)}{3(a+b)(a-b)} + \frac{3(a^2+b^2)}{3(a+b)(a-b)} - \frac{3(a^2-2ab+b^2)}{3(a+b)(a-b)}$$

$$= \frac{2a^2 + 2ab + 3a^2 + 3b^2 - 3a^2 + 6ab - 3b^2}{3(a+b)(a-b)}$$

$$= \frac{2a^2 + 8ab}{3(a+b)(a-b)}. \quad \textit{Ans.}$$

CHECK. The student should check the result by letting $a = 2, b = 1$.

EXERCISE 6

Reduce each fraction to its simplest form:

1. $\dfrac{54}{18}$.

2. $\dfrac{36}{63}$.

3. $\dfrac{-35x}{49y}$.

4. $\dfrac{2.4a}{-0.8b}$.

5. $\dfrac{4x^2y^2}{12xy^3}$.

6. $\dfrac{15pq^2}{5p^3q}$.

7. $\dfrac{a^2}{a^2+ab}$.

8. $\dfrac{xy-y^2}{x^2-y^2}$.

9. $\dfrac{m^2(x-y)}{m(y-x)}$.

10. $\dfrac{(m-n)x^3}{(n-m)x}$.

11. $\dfrac{a^3(x+y)}{a(x+y)^3}$.

12. $\dfrac{r(u-v)^5}{r^2(u-v)^2}$.

13. $\dfrac{a^2-2ab+2b^2}{a^2-2ab+b^2}$.

14. $\dfrac{4x^2-9y^2}{2xy+3y^2}$.

15. $\dfrac{x^2-4}{x^2+x-6}$.

16. $\dfrac{a^2+6a+9}{a^2+2a-3}$.

17. $\dfrac{3m^2+m-2}{m^2+m}$.

18. $\dfrac{2x^4-x^3}{6x^2+x-2}$.

Find the L.C.M. of the two or more expressions in each problem:

19. 45, 72, 100.

20. 15, 40, 108.

21. $3x^2y,\ 2y^2z,\ 5xyz^3$.

22. $4c^3dy,\ 3cd^2y^2,\ 2c^2dy^3$.

23. $x-3,\ 3a-ax,\ a^2(x^2-9)$.

24. $2y+4,\ y^2-4,\ (y+2)^3$.

25. $x^2-1,\ x^2+3x+2$.

26. $b^2-4b+4,\ ab^2-4a$.

Combine into a single fraction in simplest form:

27. $\frac{9}{4}-2+\frac{5}{6}$.

28. $\frac{2}{3}+\frac{3}{4}-\frac{1}{2}$.

29. $4\frac{1}{2}-3\frac{1}{3}-1\frac{2}{3}$.

30. $7\frac{1}{6}-5\frac{3}{8}+3$.

31. $\dfrac{3x+2}{6}-\dfrac{4x-5}{9}$.

32. $\dfrac{8-y}{4}-\dfrac{5y+2}{6}$.

33. $\dfrac{a}{y}+\dfrac{b^2}{ay}$.

34. $\dfrac{b}{a^2}+\dfrac{c}{ax}$.

35. $\dfrac{x}{x-2}+\dfrac{3}{2-x}$.

36. $\dfrac{2x}{x-y}+\dfrac{y}{y-x}$.

37. $\dfrac{3}{a^2-9}-\dfrac{2}{a+3}$.

38. $\dfrac{m+3}{m^2+2m+1}-\dfrac{m}{m+1}$.

39. $\dfrac{y}{y+1}-\dfrac{2}{y-4}$.

40. $\dfrac{-2}{x-2}+\dfrac{3}{x+3}$.

41. $\dfrac{x}{x^2+1}-\dfrac{2}{x}+1$.

42. $\dfrac{4}{y^2+y}+\dfrac{3}{y+1}-2$.

14. Multiplication and division of fractions

The student will recall that the **reciprocal** of a nonzero number is 1 divided by the number. Thus, the reciprocal of x is $\dfrac{1}{x}$; that of $\dfrac{3}{4}$ is $\dfrac{1}{\frac{3}{4}}=\dfrac{4}{3}$.

The **product** of two or more fractions is expressible as a fraction whose numerator is the product of the numerators and whose denominator is the product of the denominators. Thus,

$$\frac{a}{b} \times \frac{c}{d} = \frac{ac}{bd}.$$

Before performing the indicated multiplication of two or more fractions, factor the numerators and denominators, when possible. The final result should be a single fraction in *lowest terms;* the numerator and denominator are usually left in factored form.

The **quotient** of two fractions is expressible as the product of the dividend and the *reciprocal* of the divisor fraction. Thus,

$$\frac{a}{b} \div \frac{c}{d} = \frac{a}{b} \times \frac{d}{c} = \frac{ad}{bc}; \quad c \neq 0, b \neq 0, d \neq 0.$$

In multiplying or dividing fractions, an **integer** (whole number) may be treated as a fraction whose numerator is itself and whose denominator is 1. Thus, $3 \times \frac{a}{b} = \frac{3}{1} \times \frac{a}{b} = \frac{3a}{b}$. (It is a common error to get $\frac{3a}{3b}$ for the product.) Likewise, if $b \neq 0$, $a \neq 0$,

$$3 \div \frac{a}{b} = \frac{3}{1} \div \frac{a}{b} = \frac{3}{1} \times \frac{b}{a} = \frac{3b}{a}.$$

$$\frac{a}{b} \div 3 = \frac{a}{b} \div \frac{3}{1} = \frac{a}{b} \times \frac{1}{3} = \frac{a}{3b}.$$

ILLUSTRATIVE EXAMPLE 1. $\dfrac{x^2 - y^2}{x^2 + 2xy + y^2} \times \dfrac{5x + 5y}{3x} = ?$

SOLUTION. $\dfrac{x^2 - y^2}{x^2 + 2xy + y^2} \times \dfrac{5x + 5y}{3x} = \dfrac{(x + y)(x - y)}{(x + y)(x + y)} \times \dfrac{5(x + y)}{3x}$

$$= \frac{x - y}{x + y} \times \frac{5(x + y)}{3x}$$

$$= \frac{5(x - y)(x + y)}{3x(x + y)} = \frac{5(x - y)}{3x}.$$

CHECK. The student should check the result by letting $x = 2$, $y = 1$.

ILLUSTRATIVE EXAMPLE 2. $\dfrac{a^2 - 2a - 3}{21a^2} \div \dfrac{a^2m - 9m}{3a} = ?$

SOLUTION. $\dfrac{a^2 - 2a - 3}{21a^2} \div \dfrac{a^2m - 9m}{3a} = \dfrac{a^2 - 2a - 3}{21a^2} \times \dfrac{3a}{a^2m - 9m}$

$$= \frac{3a(a - 3)(a + 1)}{3 \cdot 7 \cdot a^2 \cdot m(a + 3)(a - 3)} = \frac{a + 1}{7am(a + 3)}. \quad Ans.$$

CHECK. The student should check this result by letting $a = m = 1$.

---

15. Complex fractions

A **complex fraction** contains one or more fractions in either its numerator or denominator, or both. A **common fraction** has no fractions in either its numerator or denominator.

Complex fractions occur in certain types of problems. It is often desirable to simplify a complex fraction, that is, to change it to an **equivalent** common fraction. The following is a convenient method: Multiply both numerator and denominator of the given complex fraction by the L.C.D. of all the common fractions appearing in it.

ILLUSTRATIVE EXAMPLE 1. Simplify $\dfrac{\frac{5}{6}}{\frac{2}{3} + \frac{1}{2}}$.

SOLUTION. Multiply numerator and denominator of the complex fraction by 6 (why 6?), thus obtaining

$$\frac{\frac{5}{6}}{\frac{2}{3} + \frac{1}{2}} = \frac{6\left(\frac{5}{6}\right)}{6\left(\frac{2}{3} + \frac{1}{2}\right)} = \frac{5}{4 + 3} = \frac{5}{7}. \quad Ans.$$

ILLUSTRATIVE EXAMPLE 2. Simplify $\dfrac{\dfrac{2}{a + b} - 1}{\dfrac{1}{a - b}}$.

SOLUTION. Multiply numerator and denominator of the complex fraction by $(a + b)(a - b)$, thus obtaining

$$\frac{\frac{2}{a + b} - 1}{\frac{1}{a - b}} = \frac{(a + b)(a - b)\left(\frac{2}{a + b} - 1\right)}{(a + b)(a - b)\left(\frac{1}{a - b}\right)} = \frac{2a - 2b - a^2 + b^2}{a + b}. \quad Ans.$$

EXERCISE 7

Perform the indicated operations:

1. $6 \times \frac{5}{12} \times \frac{5}{12}$.

2. $\frac{3}{5} \times \frac{25}{18} \times 7$.

3. $22 \div 2\frac{3}{4}$.

4. $5\frac{1}{3} \div \frac{8}{9}$.

5. $\frac{3a}{2b} \times \frac{4b}{9} \times \frac{2b}{12ab}$.

6. $ax \times \frac{b^2}{a} \times \frac{x}{b}$.

7. $\frac{4m}{n} \div 12mn$.

8. $8y \div \frac{4}{3y}$.

9. $\left(\frac{3b}{x}\right)^2 \div \frac{6b}{ax^2}$.

10. $\frac{20y}{a} \div \left(\frac{2y}{a}\right)^2$.

11. $\frac{5m^2}{9 - m^2} \times \frac{m + 3}{m}$.

12. $\frac{a^2 + ab}{a^2 + b^2} \times \frac{ab - b^2}{a^2 - b^2}$.

13. $\frac{x^2 + 2xy + y^2}{x^2 + xy - 2y^2} \div \frac{(x + y)^3}{x^2 - y^2}$.

14. $\frac{m^2 + 6m + 9}{m - 2} \div \frac{m^2 + 5m + 6}{m^2 - 4}$.

15. $\left(\frac{x}{y} - \frac{y}{x}\right)\left(\frac{x^2y^2}{x + y}\right)$.

16. $\left(a + \frac{b^2}{a - 2b}\right)\left(1 - \frac{b}{a - b}\right)$.

17. $\left(\frac{1}{2m^2} + \frac{1}{2m}\right) \div \left(\frac{2}{m} + \frac{1}{m^2}\right)$.

18. $\left(2 + \frac{3}{x}\right) \div \left(2 + \frac{5}{x - 1}\right)$.

19. $\left(\frac{a + 2b}{b} + \frac{b}{a}\right) \div \left(\frac{a}{b} + 1\right)$.

20. $\frac{m^2 - m}{m^2 - 1} \div \left(m - \frac{m}{m + 1}\right)$.

Simplify the following complex fractions:

21. $\dfrac{\frac{2}{3} + \frac{3}{2}}{\frac{1}{2} - \frac{3}{4}}$.

22. $\dfrac{6 - \frac{1}{4}}{\frac{5}{8} + \frac{9}{4}}$.

23. $\dfrac{610}{1 + \frac{0.05}{3}}$.

24. $\dfrac{17}{85 \times \frac{3}{2}}$.

25. $\dfrac{2 + \frac{1}{x^2}}{\frac{3}{x} + \frac{2}{x^2}}$.

26. $\dfrac{m - \frac{1}{n}}{n - \frac{1}{m}}$.

27. $\dfrac{3y - 1}{\frac{3}{y} - \frac{1}{y^2}}$.

28. $\dfrac{a}{3b + \frac{2}{a}}$.

29. $\dfrac{1 + \frac{y}{x + y}}{\frac{x}{y + x} - 1}$.

30. $\dfrac{1 - \frac{3}{x + 3}}{\frac{x}{9 - x^2}}$.

31. $\dfrac{m + n}{\frac{1}{m} + \frac{1}{n}}$.

32. $\dfrac{y^2 - 6y + 9}{\frac{1}{y} - \frac{3}{y^2}}$.

MISCELLANEOUS EXERCISE 8
REVIEW OF CHAPTER 1

1. Substituting -3 for y in $y^2 - y - 2$, we get what result?

2. If $x = -3$, $y = 5$, then $x^2y - 4x = ?$

3. Show that $3 \times 4 \times 6$ and $(-4)(-3)(-1)$ are special examples of $x(x + 1)(x + 3)$. Write another example, taking $x = -10$.

4. Add $2 - x$ and $3x^2 + 3x + 4$ and subtract the sum from $6 + 2x$.

5. Multiply: (a) $-x$ by $2 - \dfrac{1}{x}$; (b) 4 by $\dfrac{3y}{2}$; (c) $1.15z$ by $1.5xz^2$.

6. In $(x + y)^2 = x^2 + 2xy + y^2$, substitute 20 for x and 7 for y and thus obtain the square of 27.

7. In $(x - y)^2 = x^2 - 2xy + y^2$, substitute 20 for x and 3 for y and thus obtain the square of 17.

8. Factor: (a) $2 - 3x + x^2$; (b) $4p^2 - 9q^2$; (c) $x^3 - 2x^2 + x$.

9. Find the L.C.M. of: (a) 7, 12, 14 (b) $x - y$, $x^2 - y^2$, $(x - y)^2$.

10. Write the square of: (a) $i + \frac{1}{2}j$; (b) $\frac{3}{2} - x$; (c) $0.01 + 2a$.

11. Subtract: (a) 7 from $y - 7$; (b) 4.1 from 0; (c) $b - a$ from a.

12. Divide: (a) 4 by $1 - \dfrac{1}{x}$; (b) 6 by $\dfrac{1}{3}z$; (c) $y - \dfrac{1}{y}$ by $y + 1$.

13. Write the sum, difference, product, and quotient of 0.12 and 0.021.

14. Multiply: (a) $6 - 3x$ by $-\frac{2}{3}$; (b) 7.36 by 0; (c) $\frac{1}{3}$ by 0.36.

15. Indicate by symbols that: (a) $x - y$ is to be subtracted from z; (b) $a - b$ is to be multiplied by -6; (c) m is to be divided by $x + 2y$.

16. Evaluate $4x^2 - \frac{1}{9} - (2x - \frac{1}{3})$ if $x = \frac{1}{4}$.

17. In $(x - y)(x + y) = x^2 - y^2$, substitute 20 for x and 1 for y and thus find the product of 19 and 21.

18. Combine into a single fraction: (a) $\frac{5}{6} - \frac{3}{4}$; (b) $\frac{1}{5} + \frac{2}{15} - \frac{3}{25}$.

19. Add: (a) $\dfrac{1}{3}$ and $\dfrac{2}{5}$; (b) $\dfrac{1}{x}$ and $\dfrac{1}{y}$; (c) $\dfrac{5}{a}$, $\dfrac{3}{-a}$, $\dfrac{-2}{a}$, and $-\dfrac{3}{a}$.

20. Three fractions have denominators $x^2 - 4$, $x^2 - 4x + 4$, and $x + 2$, respectively. Find the L.C.D.

21. Find the reciprocal of: (a) $4\frac{3}{4}$; (b) $p - q$; (c) $\dfrac{1}{r + s}$; (d) $1 + \dfrac{a}{b}$.

22. Combine into a single fraction: (a) $\dfrac{x}{x - y} - \dfrac{x - y}{x + y}$; (b) $2 - \dfrac{a - b}{a + b}$.

23. Simplify: (a) $2x - y - (3x - 2y)$; (b) $a + 2b - [a - (2a - b)]$.

24. Divide: (a) 4 by $\frac{1}{2}$; (b) $ab - b^2$ by b; (c) 0 by -15; (d) 9 by 0.

25. What is the remainder if $a^3 - 3a^2 - 4$ is divided by $a + 2$?

26. What number divided by 7 gives a quotient 5 and a remainder 2?

27. When $x^2 - 2x + 6$ is added to a certain expression, the sum is $6 - x - x^2$. What is the expression?

28. One factor of $a^3 - 2a + 1$ is $a - 1$; find another factor.

29. Enclose the last three terms of $a + 2b - 3x - y + z$ in parentheses preceded by the minus sign.

30. Two of the simple factors of $(3x - 6)(7x + 14)$ are 3 and $x + 2$. What are the other factors?

31. Multiply $x^2 + 2x + 4$ by $x - 2$. Check by letting $x = 5$.

32. Factor: (a) $6a - ay$; (b) $9 - 4x^2$; (c) $3y - 2 - y^2$; (d) $a^2b - b$.

33. Find the value of k if $x^2 - 3x + k$ is the square of a binomial.

34. Multiply: (a) $\dfrac{9}{32}$ by $\dfrac{4}{3}$; (b) $\dfrac{6x^2}{1 - y^2}$ by $\dfrac{y + 1}{3x}$; (c) pq by $\dfrac{1}{p} + \dfrac{1}{q}$.

35. Simplify $\dfrac{2\frac{1}{2}}{3\frac{2}{3}}$ by multiplying numerator and denominator by a number.

36. A certain expression is divided by $x + 2$. The quotient is $2x - 3$ and the remainder is 5. What is that expression?

37. Subtract $(x - 2y^2)$ from $[5x - 6y^2 - (4x - 4y^2)]$.

38. Note that $2 \times 4 - 5 = 8 - 5 = 3$, and that $8 - 2 \times 3 = 8 - 6 = 2$. The first is a special case of $xy - z$; the second, one of $a - bc$. Evaluate: (a) $5 \times 6 - 2$; (b) $4 \times 7 + 2$; (c) $10 - 2 \times 4$; (d) $6 + 2 \times 3$.

39. Reduce to lowest terms: (a) $\dfrac{x}{x^2 + x}$; (b) $\dfrac{a + ab}{ab}$; (c) $\dfrac{-a - b}{(a + b)^2}$.

40. Simplify: (a) $(\frac{1}{2} - \frac{1}{3}) \div (\frac{2}{3} - \frac{1}{4})$; (b) $0.8 \times \frac{5}{2} \div \frac{3}{4}$.

41. Indicate by symbols that the sum of x and y is to be subtracted from z, the result multiplied by k, and this result divided by m.

42. Divide: (a) $-15a^4b^8$ by $3a^2b$; (b) $3^5(a + b)^3$ by $3^3(a + b)^2$.

43. Subtract $x - y$ from $\frac{1}{2}(x + y)$. Check by letting $x = 2$, $y = 1$.

44. Find dividend if divisor $= x - 2$, quotient $= x + 3$, remainder $= 1$.

45. Evaluate $\frac{1}{2}x^3(y + 1) - 4y$ when $x = 4$ and $y = -2$.

46. Simplify $(a + b)^2 - 2b(a - b)$. Check by letting $a = 3$, $b = 2$.

47. Divide $2x^3 - x^2 + 6x - 3$ by $2x - 1$. Check by letting $x = 2$.

48. Factor: (a) $x^4 - 3x^2 - 4$; (b) $p^4 + 6p^2 + 9$; (c) $(x + 1)^2 - n^2$.

49. Apply $(x + y)(x - y) = x^2 - y^2$ to find the product of 54 and 46.

50. For what value of k will $x - 3$ be a factor of $x^2 + kx - 9$?

Chapter TWO

SIMPLE EQUATIONS

16. Fundamental concepts

An equation is a statement that one algebraic expression equals another. It is a statement usually involving variables and it always contains the symbol " = ". The statement may be true for some values of the variables involved and false for others. These two expressions, separated by the symbol = are the two **members** or **sides** of the equation.

If the two members are equal for *all* values of the letter or letters involved, the equation is said to be an **identity.** Thus, in the equation $3x + 2x = 5x$, the two members are equal when x is replaced by any number whatever; hence, this is an identity.

In order to verify the correctness of the solution of an equation, the value of the unknown, as found, must be substituted for the unknown in the original equation. If this value **satisfies** the equation, i.e., makes the equation a true statement, it *is* a **root**; if it fails to satisfy the equation, it *is not* a root.

Equivalent equations are those with the same set of solutions. It is possible to show that, given an equation, the following processes yield an equivalent equation:

(a) Adding the same number to or subtracting the same number from both members.

(b) Multiplying or dividing both members by the same number, other than zero.

17. Linear equations in one unknown

An equation containing the first, but no higher, power of a variable is called an **equation of the first degree,** or a **linear equation** in that variable.

To solve a linear equation in one unknown, take the following steps to obtain an equivalent equation.

I. Carry all terms involving the variable to the left member and all other terms to the right member, by adding the same expression to, or subtracting the same expression from, each member.

II. Collect the terms in each member, i.e., find their algebraic sum.

III. Divide each member by the coefficient of the variable obtaining an equation of the form $x = k$. (If the coefficient is 0, this division is not possible and there is no solution unless $k = 0$.) k is the solution.

IV. Check by substitution in the original equation.

———

ILLUSTRATIVE EXAMPLE. Solve for x: $5x + 7 - x = 2x + 1$.

SOLUTION. To rid the right member of $2x$, subtract $2x$ from each member, and get

$$5x + 7 - x - 2x = 1.$$

To rid the left member of 7, subtract 7 from each member, and get

$$5x - x - 2x = 1 - 7.$$

Collect terms in each member,

$$2x = -6.$$

Divide both members by 2,

$$x = -3.$$
$$-3 \quad Ans.$$

CHECK. Substitute -3 for x in the original equation, and get

$$5(-3) + 7 - (-3) = 2(-3) + 1,$$
$$-15 + 7 + 3 = -6 + 1,$$
$$-5 = -5.$$

Therefore -3 is the correct solution.

———

EXERCISE 9

(Problems 1 to 4, oral)

1. Tell whether the given equation is an identity or a conditional equation:

(a) $(x + 2)^2 = x^2 + 4x + 4$.　　　(d) $x^2 - 4 = (x - 2)(x + 2)$.

(b) $4 + 3x = 16$.　　　　　　　　(e) $3(x + 1) = 4x + 3 - x$.

(c) $6(y - 1) = 12$.　　　　　　　(f) $\frac{1}{2}(x + 8) = x + 4$.

2. Given the equation $x + 3 = 7$. (a) Under what condition is one member equal to the other? (b) What name is given to the process of finding the value of the unknown x? (c) What is the discovered value of x called? (d) How do you verify whether or not this value for x satisfies the given equation? (e) What is meant by "satisfying the equation"?

3. By use of the fundamental operations alone, solve the equation $3x - 7 = x + 3$. What is the first step? the second step? the third step? What root is obtained? Show that it satisfies the given equation.

4. Given the equation $\dfrac{x - 2}{x} = \dfrac{3}{x + 2}$. Is 2 a root of this equation? 4? 0? 1? −1? Answer without solving the equation; give reason in each case.

Solve the following equations for x and check:

5. $4x - 3 = 10$.

6. $5x = x + 8$.

7. $x - 8 = 3x$.

8. $7 - 2x = 9$.

9. $3x + 14 = 3 - 4x$.

10. $21 - 2x = 10 + 9x$.

11. $7x - 9 = 4x + 3$.

12. $5 + 6x = 2x - 3$.

13. $4x - 29 = 1 - x$.

14. $x + 13 = 2x + 7$.

15. $3x + 2 = 2.6 + x$.

16. $2.9x - 2.2 = 5.9 - 0.1x$.

17. $11 - 4x = 3x + 8\frac{1}{2}$.

18. $1 + 3x = x - \frac{1}{3}$.

19. $4x + 5 = 7x - 3\frac{1}{2}$.

20. $4x = 7x - 1$.

21. $5x = -x - 2$.

22. $2x - 9 = 5x$.

23. $7(x - 3) = -7 + 5x$.

24. $x(4x - 1) = 4(x^2 + 3)$.

25. $x(x + 1) = (x + 2)(x - 4)$.

26. $x^2 - 15 = x(x - 3)$.

27. $(2x - 3)(x + 2) = x(2x - 1)$.

28. $(x + 4)(x - 4) = x(x + 8)$.

29. $(x + 3)^2 = x^2 + 3$.

30. $(3x - 1)(x + 2)$
$= (3x + 1)(x - 2)$.

31. $3(x^2 - 2) = x(2 + 3x)$.

32. $(x - 5)^2 = (x + 2)^2 - 7$.

33. $8x = 2a + 6x$.

34. $4x + 6c = 7x$.

35. $3x - n = 4x - m.$

36. $b + 2x = x + a.$

37. $x(x - a) = (x - 4a)(x + 4a).$

38. $x^2 + 3k^2 = (x - 3k)^2.$

39. $m^2 - mx = m - x.$

40. $cx + d^2 = c^2 - dx.$

18. Fractional equations

A **fractional** equation contains one or more fractions. To solve such an equation, first *clear it of fractions* by multiplying both members by the L.C.D. of all the fractions in it; then proceed as in Art. 17.

It is important to note that, when both members of an equation are multiplied by an expression *involving the* variable, a root of the resulting equation may *not* satisfy the *original* equation. Such roots may be introduced through the process of clearing of fractions, if the L.C.D. involves the variable. They are called **extraneous** roots, and are discarded, since they are not roots of the original equation. Thus, this process does not necessarily yield an equivalent equation but one whose set of solutions includes the solution for the original equation.

ILLUSTRATIVE EXAMPLE 1. Solve for x: $5 - \dfrac{6}{x - 2} = \dfrac{5x - 8}{x + 2}.$

SOLUTION. Multiplying both members by $(x - 2)(x + 2)$,

$$5(x - 2)(x + 2) - \frac{6(x - 2)(x + 2)}{x - 2} = \frac{(5x - 8)(x - 2)(x + 2)}{x + 2}.$$

Simplifying the fractions,

$$5(x - 2)(x + 2) - 6(x + 2) = (5x - 8)(x - 2),$$
$$5x^2 - 20 - 6x - 12 = 5x^2 - 18x + 16,$$
$$12x = 48,$$
$$x = 4. \quad Ans.$$

CHECK. $5 - \dfrac{6}{4 - 2} = \dfrac{20 - 8}{4 + 2};\ 5 - 3 = 2;\ 2 = 2.$

Therefore $x = 4$ is the correct solution.

ILLUSTRATIVE EXAMPLE 2. Solve for x: $\dfrac{x}{x - 1} = 3 + \dfrac{1}{x - 1}.$

SOLUTION. Multiplying both members by $x - 1$,

$$x = 3(x - 1) + 1,$$
$$x = 3x - 3 + 1,$$
$$-2x = -2,$$
$$x = 1.$$

CHECK. $\dfrac{1}{1-1} = 3 + \dfrac{1}{1-1}; \dfrac{1}{0} = 3 + \dfrac{1}{0}.$

But, $\frac{1}{0}$ is not a number (why?). Therefore $x = 1$ is not a solution; the original equation has no root.

———

EXERCISE 10

1. In solving the equation $\dfrac{3x}{3} - \dfrac{x}{4} = 1$, a student got $12x - 3x = 1$ or $x = \frac{1}{9}$. Does this value of x satisfy the original equation? If not, why? What is the correct solution? Check by substitution.

2. Another student, solving the equation $x - \dfrac{x-2}{2} = 3$ in a recent test, got $2x - x - 2 = 6$, hence $x = 8$. Does $x = 8$ satisfy the given equation? Point out his error. Solve the equation and check.

Solve the following equations for x and check:

3. $\frac{1}{2}x + \frac{1}{3}x = x - 2$.

4. $x + 7 = \frac{1}{2}x - \frac{1}{5}x$.

5. $-\frac{1}{2}(x - 1) = x + 2$.

6. $2x - 5 = \frac{3}{4}(x + 5)$.

7. $x + \dfrac{9}{2} = \dfrac{3-x}{14}$.

8. $\dfrac{7x-1}{12} = \dfrac{3}{4} + x$.

9. $\dfrac{7}{6+x} = \dfrac{3}{8-x}$.

10. $\dfrac{x+4}{x} = \dfrac{x-2}{x-4}$.

11. $\dfrac{2x}{x-1} - 1 = \dfrac{x+1}{x}$.

12. $\dfrac{x+3}{x} - \dfrac{6}{x+3} = 1$.

13. $-1 + \dfrac{3}{x+2} = \dfrac{-x}{x-1}$.

14. $\frac{1}{5}(4x - 7) = \frac{2}{3}x - 1$.

15. $\frac{4}{5}x - 2 = \frac{3}{2}(x + 1)$.

16. $\frac{1}{4}(x - 1) - \frac{1}{2}(x + 1) = 2x$.

17. $\frac{3}{2}(1 + 2x) - 3 = \frac{3}{2}(1 - 2x)$.

18. $\dfrac{x+6}{2} + x = \dfrac{4x+3}{6}$.

19. $\dfrac{x}{x-4} + \dfrac{8}{x+6} = 1$.

20. $2 - \dfrac{x}{x-1} = \dfrac{x+1}{x}$.

21. $\dfrac{x+1}{x+3} - 1 = \dfrac{1}{(x-2)(x+3)}$.

22. $\dfrac{8}{x^2-1} + \dfrac{x}{x+1} = \dfrac{x}{x-1}$.

23. $\dfrac{6}{x^2-6x} + \dfrac{1}{x} = \dfrac{2}{x-6}$.

24. $\dfrac{2}{x-2} + \dfrac{5}{x} = \dfrac{4}{x^2-2x}$.

19. Algebraic language

Progress in this subject will depend largely on one's ability (a) to express ideas in the language of algebraic symbolism, and (b) to translate the meaning of algebraic expressions into word language. Later we shall have many occasions to express symbols as ideas. Our immediate concern is translation from word language into algebraic language—an important step in solving problems.

For example, if A can do a piece of work in x days, in one day he can do $\frac{1}{x}$ of it. Suppose that B can do the same work in y days. Then A and B together can do $\left(\frac{1}{x} + \frac{1}{y}\right)$ of it in one day.

The following table contains further examples of "translation."

Ideas Expressed in Word Language	In Algebraic Symbols
1. John is x years old.	
His age 5 years ago	$x - 5$ years
His age y years ago	$x - y$ years
His age 8 years from now	$x + 8$ years
His age m years from now	$x + m$ years
One-third of his present age	$\frac{x}{3}$ years
Twice his present age	$2x$ years
2. A stick is a feet long.	
Its length in yards	$\frac{a}{3}$ yards
Its length in inches	$12a$ inches
Its length in rods	$\frac{a}{16.5}$ rods
3. A and B together earn $300 a month; A's monthly salary is x.	
The amount B earns a month	$\$(300 - x)$
The amount B earns in a year	$\$12(300 - x)$
The amount A earns in a year	$\$12x$
Three-fourths of B's monthly salary	$\$\frac{3}{4}(300 - x)$
A's salary increased by $50	$\$(x + 50)$
B's salary diminished by $35	$\$(300 - x - 35)$
The amount A earns in n months	$\$nx$
4. Sugar costs m cents per pound.	
The cost of 6 lbs.	$6m$ cents
The cost of x lbs.	mx cents
The quantity 35 cents will buy	$\frac{35}{m}$ lbs.
The quantity $2 will buy	$\frac{200}{m}$ lbs.
The quantity a will buy	$\frac{100a}{m}$ lbs.
The cost of a pound in dollars	$\$0.01m$

EXERCISE 11 (Oral)

1. Translate into algebraic symbols: (a) 6 added to the square of n; (b) x diminished by 4; (c) 5 more than 3 times y; (d) 2 less than half of r; (e) the amount by which 23 exceeds twice an unknown number m.

2. State in algebraic symbols: (a) 7 subtracted from the cube of x; (b) y increased by 8; (c) 3 less than twice t; (d) 9 more than half of n; (e) p and q added, the sum squared and divided by the product of p and q.

3. Joe is n years old. State his age: (a) 1 year hence; (b) t years ago; (c) when he becomes twice as old; (d) when he was half as old.

4. A girl is x years old. State: (a) how long since she was 3 years old; (b) how long before she becomes 28 years old.

5. One bushel (60 lbs.) of wheat costs $\$x$. What is the cost of: (a) 8 bushels? (b) n bushels? (c) 5 lbs.? (d) 1 lb. if the price per bushel be increased by 20¢? Give last two answers in cents.

6. Rye weighs 56 lbs. per bushel and costs y¢ per lb. Find: (a) the cost of 3 lbs.; (b) the cost of 10 bushels in dollars; (c) how many bushels would cost $14.

7. A college had m students. The next year it had a decrease of one-sixth, and the following year an increase of 80. What was the enrollment for the third year?

8. Three boys of the same age weigh x, y, and z lbs., respectively. Find the average weight: (a) of the first two; (b) of all three.

9. A clerk earns $60 a week and spends $\$r$ a day on the average. How much does he save: (a) in 8 weeks? (b) in k weeks?

10. A bank pays $\$i$ interest per dollar per year. How much would be the interest per dollar: (a) for 3 months? (b) for 15 months?

11. A car runs x miles an hour. How far does it run in 4 hours? in t hours? in 20 minutes? How long will it take to run 120 miles?

12. The speed of a train is $v - 3$ miles an hour. How far does it run in k hours? How long will it take to run m miles?

13. Add 1 to i, square the sum, then subtract 1, then divide by i.

14. If a is half of b and b is a third of c, then a is how many times c?

15. A rectangle is 5 feet long, b inches wide. What is its area?

16. What is the area of a square whose perimeter is $20x$ feet?

17. Find the cost of n oranges if one dozen costs k¢.

18. If 25 is a square root of x, what is x?

19. The middle one of 3 consecutive integers is y. Find the others.

20. If $2n + 1$ is an odd number, what is the next larger odd number?

20. Solution of problems by translation

To solve a problem leading to a linear equation in one variable, take the following steps, after a careful analysis of the problem:

I. Represent one unknown quantity by a letter; express other unknowns, if any, in terms of the same letter.

II. From the given data, determine two quantities that are equal. Translate these quantities from words into algebraic expressions involving the letter used, and set up an equation.

III. Solve the equation for the variable.

IV. Check the value of the variable in the problem itself, and *not* in the equation set up.

———

ILLUSTRATIVE EXAMPLE 1. An article is sold for $112. The profit realized is $\frac{2}{5}$ of its cost. Find the cost of the article.

SOLUTION. I. Let $\$x$ = cost of article.

Then $\$\frac{2}{5}x$ = profit realized.

II. Now, we know that cost + profit = selling price.

Hence $x + \frac{2}{5}x = 112.$

III. Clearing of fractions,

$$5x + 2x = 560,$$

whence $x = 80$ = cost of article in dollars.   *Ans.*

IV. CHECK. The profit realized is $\frac{2}{5}$ of $80, or $32. Now, $32 + $80 = $112, which is the given selling price. Therefore the answer is correct.

———

ILLUSTRATIVE EXAMPLE 2. In a certain class, there are 36 students. The number of boys is one more than four times the number of girls. How many of each are there?

SOLUTION. I. Let x = number of girls.

$$4x + 1 = \text{number of boys.}$$

II. Number of children is

$$5x + 1 = 36.$$

III. Then

$$5x = 35.$$
$$x = 7 = \text{number of girls.}$$
$$4x + 1 = 29 = \text{number of boys.}$$

IV. CHECK. The number of students should be 36: $29 + 7 = 36$. The number of boys should be one more than four times the number of girls: $1 + (4 \times 7) = 29$. Therefore the solution is correct.

EXERCISE 12

1. Two numbers differ by 14. Their product is 8 more than the square of the smaller number. Find the numbers.

2. The sum of two numbers is 23. Four times the smaller number is 6 less than three times the larger number. What are the numbers?

3. A man is 4 times as old as his son. Six years ago he was 10 times as old as his son was then. How old is each now?

4. Roy is 9 years older than his sister. Five years from now he will be twice as old as she will be then. Find the present age of each.

5. Fred buys three pets for $60. The second costs $10 more than the first and the third three times as much as the first. Find the cost of each.

6. A and B make $68 in a certain transaction. By agreement, B is to get three-fifths as much as A. How much does each get?

7. How long will it take two machines to do a job together if the first alone can do it in 6 hrs. and the second in 3 hrs.?

8. A and B can paint a car together in 6 hrs. If A can paint it alone in 10 hrs., how long would it take B to paint it alone?

9. If each side of a square be increased by 3 ft., the area would be increased by 33 sq. ft. Find the side of the original square.

10. A rectangle is 5 in. longer than wide. If each side were 1 in. shorter, the area would be decreased by 18 sq. in. Find the dimensions.

11. How many lbs. each of two kinds of tea, worth 50¢ and 75¢ a lb, must be used to get 20 lbs. of a mixture worth 55¢ a lb.?

12. How many lbs. of candy, worth 40¢ a lb., must be mixed with 10 lb. of candy, worth 25¢ a lb., to get mixed candy worth 30¢ a lb?

13. B hikes to his cabin at the rate of 5 mi./hr. He could reach there in $3\frac{1}{2}$ hrs. less time by driving 40 mi./hr. How far is his cabin?

14. A tourist estimated that his supply of gas would last 7 hr. But the actual consumption was $\frac{1}{3}$ gal./hr. more than he expected, and the gas lasted only 6 hrs. How much gas did he have?

15. A freight train running 25 mi./hr. leaves Chicago 3 hrs. ahead of a passenger train averaging 40 mi./hr. How soon will the passenger train overtake the freight train?

16. Two cars, starting from Atlanta, go east and west, respectively. In 6 hrs., they are 420 mi. apart. Find the average speed of each, if the second car goes on the average $\frac{2}{3}$ as fast as the first.

17. Work Problem 9 if the increase in the area is m sq. ft.

18. Work Problem 10 if the decrease in the area is n sq. in.

21. Simultaneous linear equations

If an equation has two variables, a **solution** consists of a pair of values for the variables which satisfy the equation.

Thus, a solution of the linear equation $x + y = 5$ is: $x = 1$, $y = 4$. Other solutions are: $x = 3$, $y = 2$; $x = -1$, $y = 6$; $x = \frac{7}{2}$, $y = \frac{3}{2}$, etc. The number of solutions is unlimited, since the equation is satisfied by any pair of numbers whose sum is 5.

Consider another linear equation in two unknowns: $x - y = 1$. Some solutions are: $x = 7$, $y = 6$; $x = 3$, $y = 2$; $x = \frac{3}{2}$, $y = \frac{1}{2}$, etc.

Do the two equations have a *common* solution? In general, a solution of one equation is not a solution of the other. But $x = 3$, $y = 2$ occurs in the set of solutions of either equation and is the only pair of values satisfying *both* equations.

Two linear equations in two variables are said to be **independent simultaneous** equations, or simply **independent** equations, if they have one and only one *common* solution, that is, if both equations are satisfied by one and only one pair of values. An example of this definition is furnished by the two equations considered above.

Two linear equations in two variables are **inconsistent** if they have no common solution. Thus, $x + y = 3$ and $x + y = 7$ are inconsistent equations, since there is no pair of numbers whose sum is 3 and also 7.

In case every solution of one equation is also a solution of the other, the two equations are **dependent.** Thus, $x + y = 2$ and $3x + 3y = 6$ are dependent equations. Dividing both sides of the second equation by 3 we get the first. Hence, any pair of values satisfying the first will also satisfy the second.

22. Solution by elimination

Methods for solving two independent linear equations have a common feature: that of combining the two equations so as to obtain a single equation in one unknown, the other unknown being eliminated. The following example illustrates two different methods: (a) **elimination by addition or subtraction,** and (b) **elimination by substitution.**

ILLUSTRATIVE EXAMPLE. Solve the pair of equations

$$2x + 3y = 5, \tag{1}$$

$$3x - 2y = -12. \tag{2}$$

(a) SOLUTION BY ELIMINATION BY ADDITION OR SUBTRACTION. We may select the variable y for elimination. To make the coefficients of y numerically equal, multiply (1) by 2 and (2) by 3, and get

$$4x + 6y = 10 \tag{1'}$$

$$9x - 6y = -36 \tag{2'}$$

Adding, $13x \qquad = -26$, or $x = -2.$

Substituting $x = -2$ in (1), we have

$$-4 + 3y = 5,$$
$$3y = 9, \text{ or } y = 3.$$

That is, $x = -2$, $y = 3$ is the solution.

CHECK. Substituting $x = -2$, $y = 3$ in (1) and (2) in order,

$$2(-2) + 3(3) = 5; \qquad -4 + 9 = 5.$$
$$3(-2) - 2(3) = -12; \qquad -6 - 6 = -12.$$

Note. Instead of y, the variable x could have been eliminated as follows: Multiply (1) by 3 and (2) by 2; from the first new equation subtract the second; this gives a single equation in y alone.

(b) SOLUTION BY ELIMINATION BY SUBSTITUTION. To eliminate y, proceed as follows: First solve one of the equations for y, that is, express y in terms of x. Thus, from (1),

$$3y = 5 - 2x$$
$$y = \frac{5 - 2x}{3}. \tag{1''}$$

Then substitute this value of y in (2):

$$3x - 2 \cdot \frac{5 - 2x}{3} = -12,$$
$$9x - 10 + 4x = -36,$$
$$13x = -26, \text{ or } x = -2.$$

Now, substitute -2 for x in (1''), and get

$$y = \frac{5 - 2(-2)}{3} = \frac{5 + 4}{3} = \frac{9}{3} = 3.$$

That is, $x = -2$, $y = 3$ is the solution.

Note. Instead of y, x could have been eliminated as follows: Solve one of the two original equations for x; substitute this value of x in the other; this gives a single equation in y alone.

EXERCISE 13

Solve for x and y by elimination by addition or subtraction; check.

1. $x - 2y = -3,$
    $2x + 3y = 8.$

2. $5x - 3y = 1,$
    $x + 2y = 8.$

3. $4x + 5y = 2,$
    $6x + 7y = 4.$

4. $3x + 2y = 5,$
    $8x - 3y = -20.$

5. $x - 4y = 7,$
    $4x - 3y = 2.$

6. $4x - 3y = 10,$
    $8x - 5y = 17.$

7. $3x + 7y = 8,$
    $6x + 4y = 11.$

8. $7x - 2y = 1,$
    $5x + 6y = 10.$

9. $0.6x + 0.5y = -2,$
    $0.2x - 1.5y = 4.$

10. $1.3x - 0.6y = -7,$
    $0.1x - 1.2y = -4.$

11. $\frac{2}{3}x - \frac{3}{4}y = 1,$
    $\frac{1}{4}x + \frac{5}{8}y = 4.$

12. $\frac{1}{2}x + \frac{4}{9}y = 5,$
    $\frac{7}{4}x - \frac{1}{3}y = \frac{1}{2}.$

13. $x + 3y = ab,$
    $x - 3y = b.$

14. $ax - by = a^2,$
    $x - y = b.$

Solve for x and y by elimination by substitution and check.

15. $3x + y = 5,$
    $2x - 3y = 18.$

16. $x + 4y = 2,$
    $3x - y = -7.$

17. $3x - 4y = 1,$
    $x - 2y = 0.$

18. $2x + 3y = 11,$
    $5x + y = 8.$

19. $4x - 2y = -1,$
    $8x + 3y = 5.$

20. $x - 6y = 0,$
    $4x + 3y = 9.$

21. $2x + 4y = 3,$
    $2x - y = 8.$

22. $3x + 5y = 6,$
    $5x - 3y = -7.$

23. $-3x + 2 = y,$
    $x - 2 = 0.$

24. $y + 7 = 0,$
    $2y + 17 = x.$

25. $\frac{1}{2}(x + y) = 5,$
    $\frac{3}{4}(2x - y) = 4.$

26. $\frac{1}{4}x - y = 4,$
    $x - \frac{1}{2}y = 9.$

27. $x - y = a + b,$
    $bx - ay = 2ab.$

28. $x + y = 2m,$
    $nx + my = m^2 + n^2.$

State in each case whether the equations are inconsistent or dependent:

29. $5x - 7y = 9,$
    $10x - 14y = -3.$

30. $3x - 5y = 3,$
    $9x - 15y = 9.$

31. $4x + 8y = 12,$
    $x + 2y = 3.$

32. $x - 3y = 5,$
    $3y - x = 7.$

23. Problems involving two variables

Problems involving two variables can be solved by translating the given data from word language into algebraic symbols, as discussed in Art. 20. But here we shall use two letters and set up two independent equations.

———

ILLUSTRATIVE EXAMPLE 1. A man bought a hat and a jacket for $31. If he had paid $5 more for the hat, its price would have been one-half of the price of the jacket. How much did he pay for each?

SOLUTION. I. Let $x = $ price of hat,

and $y = $ price of jacket.

II. Then $$x + y = 31. \tag{1}$$

Furthermore, price of hat + $5 = one-half of price of jacket.

Hence $$x + 5 = \tfrac{1}{2}y,$$
or $$2x - y = -10. \tag{2}$$

III. Solve (1) and (2) by an elimination method and get

$$x = 7 = \text{price of hat in dollars.}$$
$$y = 24 = \text{price of jacket in dollars.}$$

IV. CHECK. (a) Did he pay $31 for the hat and jacket? $24 + $7 = $31. (b) Adding $5 to the price of the hat, do we get one-half of the price of the jacket? $7 + $5 = $\tfrac{24}{2}$. Therefore the solution is correct.

———

ILLUSTRATIVE EXAMPLE 2. A chemist has two acid solutions, one containing 45% by weight of the pure acid, and the other 25%. He wants to prepare a solution of 100 lbs. that would contain 40% of the pure acid. How many lbs. of each should he use?

SOLUTION. I. Let x lbs. $=$ weight of the first solution used,

and y lbs. $=$ weight of the second solution used.

II. Then $$x + y = 100. \tag{1}$$

Furthermore, amount of pure acid in the first solution + amount of pure acid in the second solution = amount of pure acid in the final solution.

That is,   45% of x + 25% of y = 40% of 100,

or $0.45x + 0.25y = 40.$ (2)

III. Solve (1) and (2) by elimination and get $x = 75$, $y = 25$. Therefore he should use 75 lbs. of the 1st solution and 25 lbs. of the 2nd solution.

IV. CHECK. (a) Do the amounts add up to 100 lbs.? $75 + 25 = 100$. (b) Do the amounts of pure acid from the two solutions give the amount of pure acid expected to be present in the final solution? 45% of 75 lbs. = 33.75 lbs.; 25% of 25 lbs. = 6.25 lbs.; 40% of 100 lbs. = 40 lbs.; and $33.75 + 6.25 = 40$. Therefore the solution is correct.

EXERCISE 14

1. Find the fraction which equals $\frac{1}{7}$ when 3 is subtracted from the numerator, but equals 1 when 3 is added to the denominator.

2. The sum of two numbers is 4. Twice the larger number exceeds the smaller by 14. Find the numbers.

3. Admissions to a certain play were: children, $1.60; adults, $2.35. The receipts from 200 tickets totaled $425. How many of each were sold?

4. To pay $3.95 for a new pen, John gave 26 coins consisting of dimes and quarters. How many of each were there?

5. B is 15 years older than A. Five years ago, B was twice as old as A was then. Find the present age of each.

6. The sum of the present ages of a boy and his sister is 24. Three years ago, he was twice as old as she was then. How old is each?

7. The perimeter of a triangle is 60 in. The first side is twice as long as the third side. The second side is 10 in. shorter than the first side. Find the length of each side.

8. The perimeter of a rectangle is 40 ft. If the length is increased by 4 ft. and the breadth is decreased by 2 ft., the area will remain unchanged. Find the dimensions of the original rectangle.

9. A druggist receives an order for 20 gallons of 85% alcohol. He has two kinds in stock: One is 70% pure, the other 90% pure. How many gallons of each should he mix to fill the order?

10. Pure gold is 24 karats fine. A goldsmith wishes to melt 12-karat gold with 18-karat gold to make 36 ounces of 14-karat gold. How many ounces of each kind should he use?

11. A dealer wishes to produce 40 gallons of oil worth 80¢ a gallon by mixing two grades of oil worth 75¢ and 83¢ a gallon, respectively. How many gallons of each grade of oil should he use?

12. How many bushels each of barley and wheat should be mixed to form a 35-bushel mixture worth $2.00 per bushel, if barley is worth $1.60 per bushel and wheat is worth $2.30 per bushel?

13. The tens' digit of a two-digit number exceeds its units' digit by 4. Find the number if it is 10 times the sum of its digits.

14. A positive integer consists of two digits whose sum is 11. If the digits be reversed, the new number will be 45 less than the given number. Find the original number.

15. Two trains, 160 mi. apart, start at the same time and meet in $2\frac{1}{2}$ hrs. Find their speeds if one runs 8 mi./hr. faster than the other.

16. Two cars, 50 mi. apart, start at the same time and run in opposite directions. At the end of 5 hrs., the distance between them is 400 mi. Find their speeds if one runs $\frac{3}{4}$ times as fast as the other.

24. Formulas

A **formula** is a rule expressed in symbols. It usually takes the form of an equation showing a definite relation between two or more quantities. Thus, in plane geometry we meet the formula $A = lw$ for a rectangle, where A stands for the area of the rectangle, and l and w represent its length and width, respectively. This formula implies that the area of a rectangle is equal to the product of its length and width. Hence it is a rule, expressed in algebraic symbols, for finding the area of a rectangle.

Similarly, as will appear later, the formula $I = Pni$ occurs in problems dealing with simple interest. The interest yield I from a principal of $\$P$, loaned at simple interest for n years at an annual rate i is found by taking the product of P, n, and i. Thus, the simple interest on $200 for 3 years at 6% is equal to $\$200 \times 3 \times 0.06 = \$36$.

Sometimes it is desirable to change the *form* of a formula for convenience. In the preceding example, the formula can be solved for P; that is, the value of P can be expressed in terms of I, n, and i. Divide both members of $I = Pni$ by ni and get $P = I/ni$. This form is more desirable in case we wish to find the principal $\$P$ that would yield $\$I$ of interest in n years at the annual rate i.

ILLUSTRATIVE EXAMPLE. Solve the formula $pq = r(p + q)$ for p.

SOLUTION. Performing the indicated multiplication,

$$pq = pr + qr.$$

Since this is to be solved for p, get all terms involving p on one side and the remaining terms on the other side. Thus,

$$pq - pr = qr.$$

Factoring, $\qquad p(q - r) = qr.$

Whence $\qquad\qquad p = \dfrac{qr}{q - r}.$ *Ans.*

Note 1. If two letters can be interchanged in one form of a formula without affecting it, they can be interchanged in any other form. Thus, since interchanging p and q does not alter the formula $pq = r(p + q)$, we may interchange p and q in the form $p = \dfrac{qr}{q - r}$ and get $q = \dfrac{pr}{p - r}$. From the solution for p we may thus obtain a solution for q by inspection.

Note 2. In algebra a letter always represents a number. A device for increasing available letters is the use of **subscripts,** which are especially convenient in denoting magnitudes of related quantities. Thus, we might represent the heights of three men by h_1, h_2, h_3, and their respective weights by w_1, w_2, w_3. These are read "h sub 1, h sub 2," and so on. Subscripts should not be confused with exponents.

EXERCISE 15

Solve each formula for the letter or letters indicated:

1. $v = gt$ for g.
2. $f = ma$ for m.
3. $A = \frac{1}{2}bh$ for b; for h.
4. $E = \frac{1}{2}mv^2$ for m; for v^2.
5. $v = V + at$ for V; for a.
6. $H = b^2 - 4ac$ for b^2; for c.
7. $t^2 = \dfrac{2s}{a}$ for s; for a.
8. $h = \dfrac{v^2}{2g}$ for v^2; for g.

9. $S = \dfrac{a}{1-r}$ for a; for r.

10. $i = \dfrac{d}{1-nd}$ for n; for d.

11. $f = \dfrac{mn}{m+n}$ for m; for n.

12. $I = \dfrac{2E}{2R+r}$ for E; for R.

13. $A = \pi r(s+r)$ for s.

14. $A = 2\pi r(r+h)$ for h.

15. $S = P(1+ni)$ for n.

16. $P = S(1-nd)$ for d.

17. $P(V-b) = RT$ for b.

18. $l = a + (n-1)d$ for n.

19. $p = \dfrac{a}{a+b}$ for a.

20. $q = \dfrac{b}{a+b}$ for b.

21. $d = \dfrac{i}{1+i}$ for i.

22. $S = \dfrac{a-rl}{1-r}$ for r.

23. $s = \dfrac{H}{t_2 - t_1}$ for t_2.

24. $x = \dfrac{x_1 + kx_2}{1+k}$ for k.

25. Is it possible to solve the formula in Problem 10 for n by merely interchanging n and i in the solution for i? Give reason.

26. Is the formula in Problem 12 altered by interchanging R and r?

27. Using the formula in Problem 9, find r if $S = 4$, $a = 6$.

28. Using the formula in Problem 10, find d if $i = 0.025$, $n = \frac{5}{3}$.

29. A rental library charges 30¢ per book for the first 5 days, plus 2¢ for each extra day. Write a formula for the charge C cents for d days.

30. The parcel post rate in Zone 6 is 12¢ for the first lb., plus 7¢ for each additional lb. (a) Write a formula for the postage P cents on a parcel weighing n lbs. (b) Find the value of n when $P = 75$.

31. To find the area A of a trapezoid, we add the two bases b_1 and b_2, then multiply this sum by one-half the altitude h. Write a formula for this area.

32. To find the lateral area A of a right circular cone, we take the square root of the sum of the squares of the altitude h and the base radius r, and multiply it by πr. Write a formula for this area.

MISCELLANEOUS EXERCISE 16
REVIEW OF CHAPTER 2

1. Solve for x: (a) $3x - 9 = 5x$; (b) $\dfrac{x}{3} + 7 = 9$; (c) $\dfrac{3}{2x} = \dfrac{7}{31}$.

2. Solve for y: (a) $\frac{1}{2}(y+2) = 2(y+\frac{1}{2})$; (b) $\frac{4}{5}(10-y) = 2-y$.

3. If one-third of x equals one-fourth of 21, then $x = $?

4. Find x if twice the cube of x is $\frac{1}{9}$.

5. Write a formula for the number n of ft. in y yds. and i in.

6. Express as a formula: The value of K is found by multiplying 180 by 2 less than n and subtracting the result from T.

7. Is $x^2 - (x - 3)^2 = 6x - 9$ an identical or a conditional equation?

8. Is $2 + 5x = 7x$ an identical or a conditional equation?

9. If the perimeter of a square is $16m$ ft., what is its area?

10. A rectangle is x in. long, y in. wide. If the length is decreased by 3 in., the new rectangle has: (a) what area? (b) what perimeter?

11. Given the equation: $\dfrac{x}{x - 2} = \dfrac{3}{x} - 1$. Clear it of fractions and get a simple equation whose right member is zero. Do not solve for x.

12. Solve for x: (a) $\dfrac{x^2}{x^2 - 4} - 1 = \dfrac{4}{x + 2}$; (b) $\dfrac{3}{x} - \dfrac{1 - 2x}{2} = x$.

13. A car runs m mi. in h hrs. What is its average speed?

14. John is 12 yrs. old. Twice his age of m yrs. ago is what?

15. An automobile cost $2890. It depreciated on the average by $\$x$ per month for 24 months and sold for $1800. Find x.

16. Southern Produce Co. bought x crates of oranges at $\$b$ per crate; y crates spoiled and were thrown away. Selling price was $\$s$ per crate. What was the profit P on the transaction?

17. Solve the equation $6x - 3y = 9$: (a) for x; (b) for y.

18. Solve $C(m - n) = Kmn$: (a) for K; (b) for m; (c) for n.

19. A man owns 20 more shares of stock A than of stock B. The annual dividends are $4 and $5 per share, respectively. If his annual income is $1160, how many shares of each does he own?

20. Mr. Jones thought he had fuel in his car to last $5\frac{1}{2}$ hrs. But his motor consumed $\frac{3}{4}$ gallons more per hour than he expected and the gasoline lasted 4 hours. How many gallons did he have?

21. In $9x - 10y = 8$, replace x by $\frac{3}{5}(2y - 1)$; then solve for y.

22. In $2x - y = -6$, replace x by $4 - 3y$; then solve for y.

23. One-third of what number is 42 less than the number itself?

24. A can do a piece of work in 10 days. B can do the same work in 15 days. How long will it take the two to do the work together?

25. Solve for x and y by elimination by addition or subtraction:
   (a) $3x + 5y = 4$, $2x - y = 3$; (b) $ax + y = b$, $cx - y = d$.

26. Solve for x and y by elimination by substitution:
   (a) $8x - y = 1$, $2x + 3y = 10$; (b) $x + by = a$, $ax + y = b$.

27. What amounts of silver 70% pure and 82% pure must be mixed to get six ounces of silver 75% pure?

28. An automobile radiator contains 20 quarts of a mixture of glycerine and water, 25% being glycerine. How much should be drawn off and replaced by glycerine to have 40% glycerine in the radiator?

29. Solve $w = x(1 - yz)$ for y. Is it legitimate to interchange y and z in the answer as a short cut to solving for z? Give reason.

30. Solve for r: $\dfrac{1}{r} = \dfrac{1}{p} + \dfrac{1}{q}$. Could we obtain a solution for p by merely interchanging r and p in the solution for r? Give reason.

31. Admissions to a theater were: children, 50¢; adults, $1.50. The receipts from 340 tickets totaled $390. How many of each were sold?

32. Two cars, 180 mi. apart, start at the same time and meet in 3 hrs. Find their speeds if one runs 10 mi./hr. faster than the other.

33. Solve for x and y by any method: $4x + y = 0$, $x - \frac{3}{4}y = -2$.

34. For what value of x will $x^3 - 4$ equal $x(x - 2)(x + 2)$?

35. Solve for n: $P_1(1 + n_1 i) + P_2(1 + n_2 i) = (P_1 + P_2)(1 + ni)$.

36. Solve for r: (a) $\dfrac{Q}{P} = \dfrac{2r}{r - s}$; (b) $C = \dfrac{nE}{R + nr}$.

37. Is the equation $x^3 - 5x = 2$ satisfied by $x = 2$? $x = -2$?

38. Express x in terms of y if: (a) $xy^2 = x + 1$; (b) $y(x - 1) = x$.

39. Find the value of k if 3 is a root of the equation $2kx = 27$.

40. Find the value of c if a solution of $x + cy = 1$ is $x = 2$, $y = 5$.

41. The parcel post rate in Zone 3 is 9¢ for the first lb., plus 2¢ for each additional lb. Find the postage y cents on a parcel weighing x lbs.

42. In a certain zone, the telegram rate is 40¢ for the first 10 words, plus 3¢ for each additional word. Write a formula for the charge C cents for a telegram of w words.

43. In Problem 41, find the value of y when $x = 19$.

44. In Problem 42, find the value of w when $C = 105$.

Chapter THREE

RATIO, PROPORTION,
AND PERCENTAGE

25. Ratio

The **ratio** of a number a to a second number b is a divided by b, written a/b or $a:b$. a and b are called the **terms** of the ratio. It follows from the definition that a ratio should be looked upon as a fraction. Hence the fundamental laws of fractions given in Art. 11 may be applied to ratios also; that is, multiplying or dividing both terms of a ratio by the same number (other than zero) leaves the ratio unchanged. Thus, dividing both terms of the ratio $12:16$ by 4 simplifies that ratio to the ratio $3:4$, or $\frac{3}{4}$, which equals $\frac{12}{16}$.

Frequently we speak of the ratio of a quantity to another quantity, as for example, the ratio of a side of a square to a diagonal. It should be emphasized, however, that a ratio is always the quotient of two numbers. Thus, the phrase "ratio of side to diagonal" really means "the number of units in the length of a side divided by the number of the same units in the length of a diagonal." Similarly, the ratio of 3 feet to 11 inches is the ratio of 36 inches to 11 inches, that is, $\frac{36}{11}$. Note that we do not speak of "the ratio of two numbers," but specifically the ratio of one number to another. For, in general, the ratio of a to b is not the same as the ratio of b to a.

26. Proportion

A **proportion** expresses the equality of two ratios. Thus, four numbers, a, b, c, and d, are **in proportion** if the ratio of a to b equals the ratio of c to d;

that is, if $\dfrac{a}{b} = \dfrac{c}{d}$. This is sometimes written $a : b = c : d$, but the first form is to be preferred. This proportion, written in either form, should be read "the ratio of a to b equals the ratio of c to d," or "a is to b as c is to d." a, b, c, and d are called the **terms** of the proportion; a and d, the first and fourth terms, are called the **extremes;** and b and c, the second and third terms, the **means** of the proportion.

If the two means of a proportion are equal, either is said to be a **mean proportional** between the two extremes. Thus, if $\dfrac{a}{m} = \dfrac{m}{b}$, then m is a mean proportional between a and b.

Since a proportion expresses the equality of two fractions, it is a simple form of fractional equation, and any operation which may be performed on an equation may be performed on a proportion as well. Thus, in the proportion $\dfrac{a}{b} = \dfrac{c}{d}$, we can multiply both members by bd (the L.C.D.) and get $ad = bc$. Translated into words, this equation gives the important rule: *In a given proportion, the product of the extremes equals the product of the means.* It would follow, then, that two ratios are not equal when the product of the extremes is not equal to the product of the means.

EXERCISE 17 (Oral)

1. Is a proportion an equation? What is another name for ratio?

2. Is the ratio $4 : 8$ changed by adding 2 to both terms? subtracting 2 from both terms? multiplying both terms by 2? dividing both terms by 2?

3. A student's annual income is $2400, of which amount he spends $360 for rent. What is the ratio of this expense to his income?

4. Muntz metal consists of 3 parts copper to 2 parts zinc. What is the ratio of zinc to copper? What part of this alloy is copper? zinc?

State, in simplest form, the ratio of:

5. 21 to 12.	**9.** 8 ft. to 4 yd.	**13.** $a^2 - 1$ to $a + 1$.
6. 18 to 30.	**10.** 20 da. to 2 wk.	**14.** $8x$ to $2x^2 - 2x$.
7. 0.8 to 4.	**11.** 9 qt. to $1\frac{1}{2}$ gal.	**15.** $9y$ to $3y^2 + 6y$.
8. $3\frac{1}{4}$ to $2\frac{1}{2}$.	**12.** 12 oz. to 1 lb.	**16.** $n - 3$ to $n^2 - 9$.

Find the value of x in each proportion:

17. $\dfrac{x}{4} = \dfrac{7}{2}$.   **18.** $\dfrac{3}{x} = \dfrac{2}{5}$.   **19.** $\dfrac{5}{8} = \dfrac{x}{6}$.   **20.** $\dfrac{4}{3} = \dfrac{3}{x}$.

Insert the symbol $=$ or the symbol $\neq$ (meaning "does not equal") between the two ratios of each problem in order to make true statermuts.

21. $\dfrac{2}{3}$ $\dfrac{6}{9}$.   **22.** $\dfrac{-8}{12}$ $\dfrac{2}{3}$.   **23.** $\dfrac{7}{9}$ $\dfrac{\pi}{4}$.   **24.** $\dfrac{4}{7}$ $\dfrac{3}{5\frac{1}{4}}$.

EXERCISE 18

1. A manufactured article sold for $18. Materials cost $6, labor $8; the rest was profit. Find the ratio of total cost to selling price.

2. In Problem 1, find the ratio of profit to selling price.

3. To heat his store, a man spent $67.50 for oil when oil was selling for 9¢ a gal. Find the cost of the same amount of oil at 16¢ a gal.

4. B is taxed $58.50 on his real estate valued at $4500. Find the taxes at the same rate on a piece of property valued at $3000.

5. The scale of a certain map is $\frac{3}{8}$ of an inch to 100 miles. What distance is represented by $2\frac{1}{4}$ inches?

6. The vertical scale of a certain graph is $\frac{2}{3}$ of an inch to one million cars. How many cars would be represented by a length of $1\frac{3}{4}$ inches?

7. Carbon dioxide consists of carbon and oxygen in the ratio $3:8$ by weight. How many grams of each are present in 55 grams of the gas?

8. Mercuric iodide consists of mercury and iodine in the ratio $15:19$ by weight. How much of each is found in 17 grams of the iodide?

9. In 1960, New York City had a population of 7,780,000. The birth rate was 23.7 per 1000 population. How many were born in 1960?

10. The population of Chicago was 3,550,000 in 1960. The number of deaths was 36,300. Find the death rate per 1000 population.

11. Find the value of x if 6 is a mean proportional between 8 and x.

12. Find n if it is a mean proportional between $n + 4$ and $n - 3$.

13. What is the value of c if $(c + 4):c = (c - 2):(c + 2)$?

14. Evaluate x if $x:(x - 3) = (x - 3):(x - 5)$.

15. Separate $170 into two parts whose ratio is $3:7$. [*Hint.* Let x be one part; then $(170 - x)$ is the other; hence, $x:(170 - x) = 3:7$.]

16. Find two numbers whose sum is 91 and which are in the ratio $8:5$.

17. Two numbers are in the ratio $9:4$. Adding 2 to the first and multiplying the second by 2 changes the ratio to $5:4$. Find the numbers.

18. What number must be added to each of the numbers 11, 7, 2, and 0 to get four new numbers which will be in proportion?

19. A boy $5\frac{1}{4}$ ft. tall casts a shadow $4\frac{2}{4}$ ft. long at the same time that a building casts a shadow 36 ft. long. Find the height of the building.

20. Standing 30 ft. from a lamp post, John casts a shadow 10 ft. long. If he is 4 ft. tall, how high above ground is the light on the post?

21. If $x:y = (x+z)^2 : (y+z)^2$, prove that $x = z^2/y$.

22. If $x^2:y^2 = (x-z):(y-z)$, prove that $xy = z(x+y)$.

27. Percentage

The phrase **per cent** is abbreviated from the Latin *per centum*, meaning *in the hundred*, or *hundredths;* the symbol for it is $\%$. **Percentage** refers to calculations in which hundredths are used as a basis of comparison. Hence it involves no new mathematical principles, but applications of the student's work in fractions. Thus, 5% of 40 means $\frac{5}{100}$ of 40, which is 2. Again, $33\frac{1}{3}\% = 0.33\frac{1}{3} = \frac{1}{3}$. Problems in percentage can often be conveniently solved by algebra.

———

ILLUSTRATIVE EXAMPLE 1. If 12% of a number is 30, what is the number?

SOLUTION.   Let $x =$ the number.

Then 12% of $x = 30$.

That is, $0.12x = 30$

or $12x = 3000$.

Whence $x = 250$.   *Ans.*

CHECK. 12% of $250 = 0.12 \times 250 = 30$.

———

ILLUSTRATIVE EXAMPLE 2. What per cent of 900 is 315?

SOLUTION.   Let $x =$ the number of per cent.

Then $\qquad x\%$ of $900 = 315.$

That is, $\qquad \dfrac{x}{100} \times 900 = 315$

or $\qquad 900x = 31{,}500.$

Whence $\qquad x = 35.$

Therefore $\quad$ 315 is 35% of 900. $\qquad$ *Ans.*

CHECK. $\qquad$ 35% of $900 = 0.35 \times 900 = 315.$

ILLUSTRATIVE EXAMPLE 3. In 1968 the total enrollement in a certain college was 1614, while in 1969 it was 1723. What was the per cent increase of 1969 over 1968?

SOLUTION. The increase was 109 students. The problem is to find what per cent of 1614 is 109.

Let $\qquad x =$ the number of the per cent increase.

Then $\qquad x\%$ of $1614 = 109.$

That is, $\qquad \dfrac{x}{100} \times 1614 = 109$

or $\qquad 1614x = 10{,}900.$

Whence $\qquad x = 6.75$ (approximately).

Therefore the increase was about 6.75%. $\qquad$ *Ans.*

CHECK. $\qquad 0.0675 \times 1614 = 109; \; 1614 + 109 = 1723.$

ILLUSTRATIVE EXAMPLE 4. A dealer's profit for 1969 was \$3480, which was 13% less than his profit for 1968. What was his profit for 1968?

SOLUTION. $\qquad$ Let \$$x =$ profit for 1968.

Then $\qquad x - 0.13x = 3480,$

$\qquad 0.87x = 3480.$

Whence $$x = \frac{3480}{0.87} = 4000.\qquad Ans.$$

CHECK. $0.13 \times \$4000 = \$520;\ \$4000 - \$520 = \$3480.$

Note. When a number x is increased by 5% of itself, the result is $x + .05x = x(1 + .05) = 1.05x$. Thus, *to increase x by 5% of itself, multiply x by 1.05.* Similarly, when y is diminished by 3% of y, we have $y - 0.03y = y(1 - 0.03) = 0.97y$. Hence, *to decrease y by 3% of itself, multiply y by 0.97.*

Sometimes this process is repeated. For example, if P is increased by 4% of P, we have $1.04P$. To increase this result by 4% of itself, multiply $1.04P$ by 1.04 and get $(1.04)(1.04P) = (1.04)^2 P$.

EXERCISE 19 (Oral)

Read each in per cent form:

1. 0.7.   **3.** $\frac{1}{4}$.   **5.** 0.23.   **7.** $\frac{2}{3}$.   **9.** 0.591.   **11.** $\frac{4}{5}$.

2. 0.04.   **4.** $\frac{1}{5}$.   **6.** 1.16.   **8.** $\frac{3}{4}$.   **10.** 0.004.   **12.** $\frac{7}{4}$.

Read each as a decimal fraction:

13. 65%.   **14.** 8%.   **15.** $18\frac{1}{2}$%.   **16.** $5\frac{3}{4}$%.   **17.** 3.47%.   **18.** $1\frac{1}{2}$%.

Read each as a common fraction:

19. 25%.   **20.** 5%.   **21.** $87\frac{1}{2}$%.   **22.** $6\frac{1}{4}$%.   **23.** 120%.   **24.** $16\frac{2}{3}$%.

Give the value of each:

25. 40% of 75.   **27.** 8% of 350.   **29.** $\frac{1}{4}$% of 800.

26. 75% of 40.   **28.** $2\frac{1}{2}$% of 400.   **30.** 1.4% of 800.

Give the value of x in each case if:

31. 5% of x is 20.   **33.** $66\frac{2}{3}$% of x is 6.   **35.** x% of 200 is 4.

32. 75% of x is 48.   **34.** x% of 51 is 17.   **36.** x% of 50 is 40.

37. Adding 8% of n to n is equivalent to multiplying n by what?

38. Subtracting 5% of x from x is the same as multiplying x by what?

39. In a class of 75 students, 12% received a grade of A. How many in the class received grades lower than A?

40. A man is taxed $80 on his real estate. Find the valuation of the real estate if the tax rate is 2%.

EXERCISE 20

1. A bicycle bought for $36.00 is sold for $40. The profit is what per cent of the purchase price? of the selling price?

2. A corporation pays an income tax of $1221 on its net income of $7400. What is the rate of taxation based upon net income?

3. The average retail price of eggs per doz. in the U.S. was 32¢ in 1939 and $54 in 1965. Find the per cent of increase in price.

4. On Jan. 1, 1947, there were 1424 municipal airports in the U.S., 95 of them in Mich. What per cent of the airports were in Mich.?

5. A shipping clerk receives a 20% reduction in salary, which is thus reduced to $3800. What was his previous salary?

6. The 1960 population of a college town is 4648, which is 66% more than that for 1950. What was the 1950 population?

7. Freezing of water is accompanied by an expansion of 9% of its volume. How much water is needed to make 400 cu. ft. of ice?

8. Green coffee loses 15% of its weight when roasted. How much green coffee should be used to obtain 300 lbs. of roasted coffee?

9. In 1967 the number of Sunday newspapers in the United States was 22 more than in 1958—an increase of 4%. Find the number of Sunday papers in 1958.

10. To pay a debt of $350, Mr. Jones adds $133 to the $3\frac{1}{2}$% dividend due him on a certain investment. Find the size of the investment.

11. If x exceeds y by 25%, then y is what per cent less than x?

13. If a is 25% less than b, then b exceeds a by what per cent?

13. How should two partners, A and B, divide a profit of $5000 if A's share is to exceed B's share by 50% of B's share?

14. Work Problem 13 if A's share is to be 30% less than B's.

15. A man invests $2000, part at 3% and part at 5%, getting an average of $3\frac{1}{2}$% on the total. How much is each investment?

16. C buys two lots for $2200. He sells the first at 10% profit, the second at 5% loss, thus netting $100. Find what he paid for each lot.

17. B invests part of $2000 at 6% and the rest at 4%. Find each part if the annual income from the first is $30 less than that from the second.

18. What is the capital of a person whose annual return is $150, when he has $\frac{2}{5}$ of it invested at 6%, $\frac{1}{3}$ at 5%, and the remainder at $3\frac{1}{2}$%?

19. Nickel coinage is composed of copper and nickel in the ratio 3 : 1. How much copper should be melted with 20 lbs. of a copper-nickel alloy containing 60% copper to obtain the alloy for nickel coinage?

20. How much silver should be melted with 6 lbs. of an alloy containing 50% silver to bring it up to the 90% standard used for coinage?

MISCELLANEOUS EXERCISE 21
REVIEW OF CHAPTER 3

1. If the ratio of a to b is $\frac{5}{7}$ and b is 28, then a has what value?

2. Find the ratio of: (a) $13\frac{1}{2}$ hrs. to 3 days; (b) 5 lbs. to 12 oz.

3. If m is a mean proportional between 4 and 25, m has what value?

4. Find x if it is a mean proportional between $x - 1$ and $x - 2$.

5. Subtracting 7% of x from x is the same as multiplying x by what?

6. We add 3% of N to N; then we add 3% of the result to the result. The final answer is N multiplied by what number?

7. When x is increased by 16% of itself, the result is 145. Find x.

8. When 85 is diminished by r% of itself, there remains 68. Find r.

9. If $x : y = 11 : 6$, find the value of $(x + y) : (x - y)$.

10. What is the ratio of a to b if $(a - b):(a + b) = 3:8$?

11. $2\frac{1}{4}$ lbs. of butter and 2 doz. eggs cost $3.30, of which amount 40% was for eggs. What did butter cost per lb.?

12. On Jan. 1, 1968, Pennsylvania had bank deposits of (approximately)

$24.6 billion, or 6% of the national total. Find the amount deposited in the remaining states.

13. B received a check for $84, representing a dividend of 18% on his claim against a bank in receivers' hands. What was his total claim?

14. A salesman's salary is $9000 plus 95% of a special fund of x. 4% of his salary is $367.60. Find x.

15. Find two numbers in the ratio $4:3$ and differing by 14.

16. Two numbers are in the ratio $3:5$. By adding 42 to each, we get two new numbers in the ratio $5:6$. Find the original numbers.

17. A dealer raises the price of a $2000 piano by 20%. To restore the previous price, he must reduce the new price by what per cent?

18. Mr. Jones gave his bank a note for $1200. After deducting interest, the banker gave him $1179. What per cent of $1200 was deducted?

19. Goods costing $300 were sold partly at a 6% loss and partly at a 12% profit. Proceeds were $309. Find the cost of each part.

20. How many gal. of milk testing 4% butterfat should be added to 200 gal. testing $4\frac{1}{2}\%$ to produce a mixture testing $4\frac{2}{5}\%$?

21. Separate N into two parts such that one is $r\%$ of the other.

22. If there are y units of vitamin A in x cc. of milk testing $p\%$ butterfat, and if the vitamin A content of milk is entirely in butterfat, how many units of vitamin A does 1 cc. of butterfat contain?

23. If $a:b = c:d$, prove that $(a + b):(c + d) = b:d$.

24. Given that m is a mean proportional between x and y. Prove that: (a) $m:(x + m) = (m - y):(x - y)$; (b) $x^2:(x^2 - m^2) = m^2:(m^2 - y^2)$.

Chapter FOUR

APPLICATIONS TO

COMMERCIAL PROBLEMS

A. Simple Interest

28. Interest

A consideration or payment for the use of invested or loaned capital is called **interest.** It is convenient and customary to express both capital and interest in units of money.

Three elements are involved in interest transactions: **principal, rate of interest,** and **time.** The principal is the capital originally invested. The rate of interest is the per cent of the principal which is paid as interest for its use for one **period of time.** The time is the **number of periods** during which the principal is used. One year is generally taken as the unit period of time. We shall use the word **amount** to denote the sum of the principal and the interest.

There are two kinds of interest. If interest is computed on the original principal only, it is called **simple interest.** But when principal is increased by interest at the end of each period and interest is thus computed on a principal which grows periodically, we are dealing with **compound interest.** A fuller discussion of compound interest is reserved for Chapter 11 in Part II.

29. Formulas for simple interest

The simple interest on a given principal at a given rate for a given time is the product of three factors: the principal, the rate of interest per unit of time, and the number of units of time. If we let P denote the principal in dollars, i the annual rate of interest, n the time in years, I the total interest in dollars, and S the amount in dollars at the end of n years, we may write the formulas for simple interest as follows:

$$I = Pni, \tag{1}$$

and since, by definition, $S = P + I$, it follows that

$$S = P + Pni = P(1 + ni). \tag{2}$$

ILLUSTRATIVE EXAMPLE 1. What is the simple interest on $500 for 3 years at 4%? What is the amount?

SOLUTION. Here, $P = 500$, $n = 3$, $i = 0.04$. Substituting in formula (1), we have

$$I = Pni = 500 \times 3 \times 0.04 = \$60. \quad \text{Interest.}$$

And

$$S = P + I = 500 + 60 = \$560. \quad \text{Amount.}$$

ILLUSTRATIVE EXAMPLE 2. Find the time required for $2000 to yield $150 in simple interest at 5%.

SOLUTION. Noting that in formula (1) we know all the quantities except n, we solve this formula for n as follows: Divide each member by Pi, and obtain $\dfrac{I}{Pi} = n$, or $n = \dfrac{I}{Pi}$. Now, $I = 150$, $P = 2000$, and $i = 0.05$. Substituting these values in the above formula, we have

$$n = \frac{I}{Pi} = \frac{150}{2000 \times 0.05} = \frac{150}{100} = 1.5 \text{ (years).}$$

CHECK. 5% interest on $2000 for $1\frac{1}{2}$ years is: $2000 \times \frac{3}{2} \times 0.05 = \$150$.

ILLUSTRATIVE EXAMPLE 3. What principal will amount to $784 in two years at 6% simple interest?

SOLUTION. Noting that in formula (2) we know all the quantities except P, we solve this formula for P by dividing both members by $1 + ni$, and get $P = \dfrac{S}{1 + ni}$. Substituting $S = 784$, $n = 2$, and $i = 0.06$ in this formula, we have

$$P = \frac{S}{1 + ni} = \frac{784}{1 + (2 \times 0.06)} = \frac{784}{1.12} = \$700. \text{ Principal.}$$

CHECK. In 2 years $700 amounts at 6% to: 700[1 + 2(0.06)] = \$784.

_____

ILLUSTRATIVE EXAMPLE 4. At what rate will $450 yield $27 in simple interest in 9 months?

SOLUTION. Noting that in formula (1) we know all the quantities except i, we solve this formula for i by dividing both members by Pn, and get $i = \frac{I}{Pn}$. Substituting $I = 27$, $P = 450$, and $n = \frac{3}{4}$, we have

$$i = \frac{I}{Pn} = \frac{27}{450 \times \frac{3}{4}} = \frac{4 \times 27}{450 \times 3} = \frac{4}{50} = 0.08 = 8\%. \quad \text{Rate.}$$

CHECK. 8% interest on $450 for $\frac{3}{4}$ years is: $I = 450 \times \frac{3}{4} \times 0.08 = \$27$.

_____

EXERCISE 22

1. Find the simple interest and amount of a principal of (a) $1200 for $1\frac{1}{3}$ years at 5%; (b) $1600 for 9 months at $6\frac{1}{2}$%.

2. Find the simple interest and amount of a principal of (a) $1800 for 10 months at $4\frac{1}{2}$%; (b) $800 for $1\frac{1}{2}$ years at 3%.

3. At what rate will $1500 yield (a) $25 simple interest in 8 months? (b) $127.50 simple interest in 2 years?

4. Find the rate of simple interest if a principal of $720 amounts to (a) $782.10 in $1\frac{1}{2}$ years; (b) $741 in 5 months.

5. Find the principal amounting at 4% simple interest to (a) $1284 in 3 months; (b) $484 in 15 months.

6. What sum will yield in 4 months (a) $7 at 6%? (b) $14 at $3\frac{1}{2}$%?

7. In how many years will $560 (a) amount to $618.80 at 6% simple interest? (b) yield $12.60 simple interest at $4\frac{1}{2}$%?

8. How long will it take $3000 (a) to yield $17.50 simple interest at $3\frac{1}{2}$%? (b) to amount to $3300 at 4% simple interest?

9. A bank pays $1\frac{1}{2}\%$ on time deposits and loans money at 8%. What profit does it make by lending \$150,000, on the average, for a year?

10. To make an annual profit of \$8250, the bank in Problem 9 should lend money at what rate?

11. John gives a check for \$337.84 to a friend in settlement of a loan and $4\frac{1}{2}\%$ interest on it for 8 months. How much had he borrowed?

12. Work Problem 11 assuming that interest was at 6%.

30. Exact and ordinary interest

In practice, most business transactions in simple interest involve periods of time less than a year. Interest computed by considering each day to be $\frac{1}{365}$ of a year is called **exact simple interest.** Interest computed by assuming each day to be $\frac{1}{360}$ of a year is called **ordinary simple interest.** The relation between the two can be established as follows. Let I_0 denote the ordinary simple interest for t days, and I_e the exact simple interest for the same number of days. Then, by substituting $t/360$ and $t/365$, respectively, for n in formula (1), Art. 29, we have

$$I_0 = \frac{Pti}{360}. \tag{3}$$

$$I_e = \frac{Pti}{365}. \tag{4}$$

Dividing (3) by (4), member by member, we have

$$\frac{I_0}{I_e} = \frac{Pti}{365} \times \frac{365}{Pti} = \frac{365}{360} = \frac{73}{72},$$

whence

$$I_0 = \tfrac{73}{72} I_e = I_e + \tfrac{2}{72} I_e$$

In words, *ordinary interest is equal to exact interest increased by $\frac{1}{72}$ of itself.*

Similarly, dividing (4) by (3), member by member, we have

$$\frac{I_e}{I_0} = \frac{Pti}{365} \times \frac{360}{Pti} = \frac{72}{73},$$

whence

$$I_e = \tfrac{72}{73} I_0 = I_0 - \tfrac{1}{73} I_0.$$

In words, *exact interest is equal to ordinary interest decreased by* $\frac{1}{73}$ *of itself.*

31. Computing time

In some problems involving simple interest, it is necessary to compute the time between two given dates. The method is explained by an example.

ILLUSTRATIVE EXAMPLE 1. Find the time from April 17 to June 26.

SOLUTION. Number of days remaining in April .13
Number of days in May 31
Number of days in June to be counted 26
Total number of days 70

It should be noted that the first day, April 17, was not included, but the last day, June 26, was counted. This is the most general custom.

ILLUSTRATIVE EXAMPLE 2. Find the ordinary interest and exact interest on $2400 at 6% from April 17 to June 26.

SOLUTION. As computed above, the time is 70 days. Applying formula (3), we have

$$I_0 = \frac{Pti}{360} = \frac{2400 \times 70 \times 0.06}{360} = \$28.00.$$

Applying formula (4), we have

$$I_e = \frac{Pti}{365} = \frac{2400 \times 70 \times 0.06}{365} = \$27.62.$$

EXERCISE 23

Using formulas (3) and (4), find the ordinary and exact interest on:

1. $476 at 4% from May 12 to October 4.

2. $4300 at 3% from April 14 to August 9.

3. $1500 at $2\frac{1}{2}$% from June 3 to December 17.

4. $12,000 at $1\frac{1}{2}\%$ from March 25 to November 12.

5. $1255 at 6% from April 1 to June 17.

6. $6000 at $4\frac{1}{2}\%$ from July 10 to October 1.

7. $10,000 at $3\frac{1}{2}\%$ from August 20 to November 1.

8. $840 at 5% from September 1 to December 2.

9. $753 at $6\frac{1}{2}\%$ from November 8, 1968 to March 4, 1969.

10. $1000 at 7% from December 13, 1963 to April 2, 1969.

11. $1200 at 8% from September 3, 1969 to January 11, 1970.

12. $2000 at $5\frac{1}{2}\%$ from October 18, 1969 to February 6, 1970.

13. Give the ratio of exact interest to ordinary interest.

14. Exact interest is what per cent of ordinary interest?

15. If the ordinary interest is $105.12, find the exact interest.

16. $105.12 exact interest corresponds to what ordinary interest?

32. Short cuts in computing ordinary interest

When the rate of interest is 6%, the ordinary interest on $$P$ for 60 days is $$(0.01)P$. This result can be readily found by applying formula (3) of Art. 30:

$$I_o = \frac{Pti}{360} = \frac{P \times 60 \times 0.06}{360} = \frac{P \times 0.06}{6} = P(0.01).$$

Since 0.01 of a number is found by moving the decimal point two places to the left, we have the following simple rule: *To find the sixty-day 6% ordinary interest on $$P$, move the decimal point in P two places to the left.*

Similarly, the ordinary interest on $$P$ at 6% for 6 days is $$(0.001)P$. Hence, *to find the six-day 6% ordinary interest on $$P$, move the decimal point in P three places to the left.*

These two rules, combined with *mental* operations of addition, subtraction, multiplication, and division, enable us to find the ordinary interest on $$P$ at any given rate and for any number of days.

_____

ILLUSTRATIVE EXAMPLE 1. Find the ordinary interest on $4324 at 6% for 75 days.

SOLUTION.

a. Interest at 6% for 60 days = $43.240
b. Interest at 6% for 15 days =   10.810   (Divide *a* by 4)
c. Interest at 6% for 75 days = $54.050   (Add *a* and *b*)

Therefore the required interest is $54.05.   *Ans.*

———

ILLUSTRATIVE EXAMPLE 2. Find the ordinary interest on $782.80 at 5% for 93 days.

SOLUTION.

a. Interest at 6% for 60 days = $7.828
b. Interest at 6% for 30 days =   3.914   (Divide *a* by 2)
c. Interest at 6% for 3 days =   0.391   (Divide *b* by 10)
d. Interest at 6% for 93 days = $12.133   (Add *a*, *b*, and *c*)
e. Interest at 1% for 93 days =   2.022   (Divide *d* by 6)
f. Interest at 5% for 93 days = $10.111   (Subtract *e* from *d*)

Therefore the required interest is $10.11.   *Ans.*

———

ILLUSTRATIVE EXAMPLE 3. Find the ordinary interest on $6758 at $3\frac{3}{4}$% for 37 days.

SOLUTION.

a. Interest at 6% for 6 days = $6.758
b. Interest at 6% for 36 days =   40.548   (Multiply *a* by 6)
c. Interest at 6% for 1 day =   1.126   (Divide *a* by 6)
d. Interest at 6% for 37 days = $41.674   (Add *b* and *c*)
e. Interest at 3% for 37 days =   20.837   (Divide *d* by 2)
f. Interest at $\frac{3}{4}$% for 37 days =   5.209   (Divide *e* by 4)
g. Interest at $3\frac{3}{4}$% for 37 days = $26.046   (Add *e* and *f*)

Therefore the required interest is $26.05.   *Ans.*

———

33. Short cuts in computing exact interest

There are no satisfactory short cuts in computing exact interest. However, since exact interest is equal to ordinary interest decreased by $\frac{1}{73}$ of itself, it is quite possible to use this relation for computing exact interest, after ordinary interest has been found by the method of Art. 32.

ILLUSTRATIVE EXAMPLE. Find the exact interest on $6758 at $3\frac{3}{4}\%$ for 37 days.

SOLUTION. The ordinary interest on this principal is $26.05. (See illustrative example 3, Art. 32.)   Now,

$$I_e = I_o - \tfrac{1}{73} I_o = 26.05 - \tfrac{26.05}{73} = 26.05 - 0.36 = \$25.69. \quad Ans.$$

EXERCISE 24

In each case find the ordinary and exact interest by Arts. 32 and 33:

Prob.	Principal	Rate	Time (days)	Prob.	Principal	Rate	Time (days)
1.	$ 590.23	6%	72	9.	$ 541.00	$5\frac{5}{8}\%$	84
2.	436.88	6%	54	10.	913.00	4%	93
3.	1600.00	3%	45	11.	75.27	7%	132
4.	2800.00	3%	90	12.	68.50	$7\frac{1}{2}\%$	150
5.	651.17	$4\frac{1}{2}\%$	69	13.	4000.00	2%	210
6.	503.63	5%	36	14.	4200.00	$3\frac{3}{8}\%$	192
7.	675.00	8%	105	15.	824.00	$4\frac{1}{4}\%$	50
8.	860.00	$6\frac{3}{4}\%$	120	16.	580.00	5%	40

B. Discount

34. Introduction

A **discount** is a deduction allowed on a financial obligation. In business transactions, there exist different kinds of discounts, each depending upon the method by which it is computed or the reason for which it is allowed. We shall consider four classes: **simple discount, bank discount, cash discount,** and **trade discount.**

35. Present value at simple interest

The **present value, at the interest rate** i, of an amount S due in n years is that principal P which, invested now at the rate i, will amount to S in n years. Thus, the present value, at 5% simple interest, of $105 due in a year is $100, since $100 will amount to $105 in a year at 5% simple interest.

In general, since a principal P will amount to $P(1 + ni)$ in n years at the rate i, present value P and amount due S are related by the formula $S = P(1 + ni)$. Hence the present value, at the interest rate i, of S due in n years is

$$P = \frac{S}{1 + ni} \tag{5}$$

$S - P$, the difference between the amount due and its present value at simple interest, is called the **simple discount** on S and is denoted by D_s. The simple discount on S is the same as the simple interest on P.

If money earns interest at the rate i, we shall frequently say that money is **worth** i. Thus, the expression "money is worth 5%" refers to an interest rate of 5%.

Caution. In speaking of a sum of money, it is absolutely essential to know *the time connected with that sum.* Manifestly, the enthusiasm with which we would receive the promise, "I will give you $100," would be dampened if the promiser immediately added the words "50 years from now." In this book *the time connected with a stated sum will be specified.* In particular, the words "$5000 due in 3 months without interest," or the words "$5000 due in 3 months," shall mean that the $5000 will be $5000 at the end of 3 months. Consequently, under business conditions, it would not be worth $5000 today.

ILLUSTRATIVE EXAMPLE 1. What is the present value of $100 due in 1 year if money is worth 5%? What is the simple discount?

SOLUTION. Substitute the known quantities $S = 100$, $n = 1$, and $i = 0.05$ in formula (5):

$$P = \frac{S}{1 + ni} = \frac{100}{1 + (1)(0.05)} = \frac{100}{1.05} = \$95.24$$

And

$$D_s = 100 - 95.24 = \$4.76.$$

This means that a principal of $95.24 will earn $4.76 of interest in 1 year at 5%.

CHECK. $0.05 \times 95.24 = \$4.76$. It should be noted carefully that the *discount* on $100 is the *interest* on $95.24.

———

ILLUSTRATIVE EXAMPLE 2. A debt of $5000 is due 3 months hence. Allowing interest at 8%, find the present value of the debt. What is the discount if the debt is settled now?

SOLUTION. The problem is to find that principal which, placed at 8% simple interest, will amount to $5000 in 3 months. Substitute the known quantities $S = 5000$, $n = \frac{1}{4}$, $i = 0.08$ in (5):

$$P = \frac{S}{1 + ni} = \frac{5000}{1 + (\frac{1}{4})(0.08)} = \frac{5000}{1.02} = \$4901.96.$$

$$D_s = 5000 - 4901.96 = \$98.04.$$

This means that $4901.96 *today* is as good as $5000 *three months hence.* Computing the interest on $4901.96 at 8% for 3 months, we have $I = 4901.96 \times \frac{1}{4} \times 0.08 = \$98.04$. Adding this to $4901.96, we get $5000. Note that the *simple discount* on $5000 is the *simple interest* on $4901.96.

———

36. Present value of an interest-bearing debt

The cases discussed in Art. 35 involve debts that do not bear interest. There are cases, however, in which the debt bears interest, and the **maturity value** of the debt is different from the **face value.** The situation may be made clear by using an illustration. Suppose A borrows $100 from B, promising to pay it in a year with 4% simple interest. The face value of A's debt is $100, while the maturity value of his debt is $104. However, if A has a debt of $100, due in a year with no interest, the face value and the maturity value of his debt are identical; that is, $100.

The present value (at a given interest rate) of a debt bearing the same rate of interest is, of course, the face value of the debt. Thus, the present value at 8% of a debt of $100 due in a year and bearing interest at 8% is $100. However, in case the interest rate used in finding the present value is different from the rate of interest borne by the debt, two steps are necessary in solving the problem:

I. Find the *maturity value* of the debt, by adding the interest for the period to the face value of the debt.

II. Find the present value of the *maturity value* of the debt, using the interest rate given for determining the present value.

———

ILLUSTRATIVE EXAMPLE.   A grocer owes $1200 to a wholesaler, his debt maturing in 4 months and bearing $7\frac{1}{2}\%$ interest. Find the present value of the grocer's debt at the rate of 6%.

SOLUTION. I. Find the maturity value of the debt. That is, $1200 will amount to what sum of money in 4 months at $7\frac{1}{2}\%$ simple interest? Substituting the known quantites $P = 1200$, $n = \frac{1}{3}$, $i = 0.075$ in formula (2) of Art. 29:

$$S = P(1 + ni) = 1200[1 + (\tfrac{1}{3})(0.075)] = 1200 \times 1.025 = \$1230.00.$$

II. Now, find the present value of $1230.00 at 6%. Substituting the known quantities $S = 1230.00$, $n = \frac{1}{3}$, $i = 0.06$ in formula (5) of Art. 35:

$$P = \frac{S}{1 + ni} = \frac{1230.00}{1 + (\tfrac{1}{3})(0.06)} = \frac{1230.00}{1.02} = \$1205.88. \quad Ans.$$

———

Note that, in problems of this type, P in the first step is different from P in the second step; also, i in the first step is not the same as i in the second step.

EXERCISE 25

Assume a day to be $\frac{1}{360}$ of a year, and a month to be $\frac{1}{12}$ of a year.

1. Find P and D_s if $S = \$1200$, $n = \frac{1}{3}$, and $i = 0.05$.

2. How much is D_s in the illustrative example of Art. 36?

3. What is the present value at 6% of a debt of $500 due in 6 months?

4. Find the present value at 3% of a debt of $700 due in 8 months.

5. Mr. James has bond coupons for $1000 falling due on Sept. 15. What is the value of these coupons on Aug. 1 if money is worth 5%?

6. Henry is to receive a trust fund of $10,000 on his twenty-first birthday. Find the value of the fund 6 months before that if money is worth 8%.

7. A mortgage will have a maturity value of $800. Find its value 4 months before maturity, assuming that money is worth $4\frac{1}{2}\%$.

8. A widow expects to receive a $600 dividend on July 16. The dividend has what value on May 5? Assume money to be worth 5%.

9. The purchaser of a lot may pay either $900 now or $1100 in a year. What does he save now by the first plan if money is worth 8%?

10. From the standpoint of present value, which is the better offer for the buyer of a house: To pay $2000 down and $3000 in 6 months, or to pay $3000 down and $2000 in a year? Assume money to be worth 6%.

11. Work Problem 3 if the debt bears 4% interest for 6 months.

12. Work Problem 4 if the debt bears 6% interest for 8 months.

13. A note of $400 bearing 7% interest is due in 90 days. What is the present value at 8%? How much is the simple discount?

14. Find the present value at 4% of a debt of $900 due in 60 days with interest at 6%. Find also the simple discount.

15. B holds A's note for $500 due in 6 months with interest at 5%. Four months before the due date C buys the note so as to realize 3% interest on his investment. What does C pay to B?

16. Among the assets of a bankrupt firm is a 1-year note for $2000 bearing interest at 6%. Three months before maturity an investor buys the note so as to realize 8% interest. What does he pay for it?

17. Mr. Long has bond coupons which will be worth $1000 at maturity. When do they mature if their present value at 6% is $982.80?

18. Four months before the maturity date of a 6-month 8% interest-bearing note of $500, Mr. Moore paid $509.80 for it. At what rate of interest was this present value computed?

19. Using the definition for D_s, show that $D_s = Pni$.

20. Since $D_s = S - P$, prove that $D_s = Sni/(1 + ni)$.

37. Present value at discount rate

The topics discussed in Art. 35 and Art. 36 are helpful in studying Chapter 11 in Part 2. However, present value at simple interest is seldom used in actual practice. In making loans or discounting notes, bankers compute **present value at a discount rate.** Suppose a man requests a loan from a banker, promising to pay $100 in a year in settlement of this obligation. If the bank charges 5% annual discount, the banker computes the present value of $100 (due in a year) to be $95; that is, he deducts 5% of $100 from $100 and pays only $95 to the borrower. This deduction is called **bank discount.** The sum of money which the borrower actually receives on the day the loan is granted is called **proceeds.** In the above example, the bank discount is $5 and the proceeds are $95, although the borrower is said to have obtained a $100 loan.

Bank discount may be regarded as interest *paid in advance.* Thus, the above transaction may be described as follows: The borrower receives $100 but immediately returns $5 to the bank as 5% interest (paid in advance) on $100. Below are defined the more common instruments giving rise to bank discount.

A **promissory note** is an unconditional, written promise, made by one person to another and signed by the maker, to pay on demand or at a fixed or determinable future time a certain sum of money to order or to bearer. The term of a note is the length of time from date of the note to the due date.

A **draft** is an unconditional, written order, signed by the drawer, requiring the drawee to pay on demand or at a fixed or determinable future time a certain sum of money to order or to bearer. The drawer sends it to the drawee for acceptance. If the latter is willing to pay, he writes "Accepted" across the face of the draft, signs, and returns it to the drawer. In an "after date" draft, the term begins with the date of the draft; in an "after sight" draft, it begins with the date of acceptance indicated by the drawee on the accepted draft.

A **trade acceptance** is a draft arising from the sale of merchandise and drawn by the seller of merchandise on the purchaser.

A note may or may not bear interest; a trade acceptance or draft bears none. A form of each is shown on pages 72 and 73.

38. Formulas for bank discount and proceeds

Bank discount is the product of three factors: **maturity value, period of discount,** and **discount rate.** The maturity value of a non-interest-bearing note is the same as its face value. The maturity value of an interest-bearing note is its face value plus the interest on it for the term and at the rate stated in the note. If the term is given in days, use a 360-day year to compute interest; if in months, use a 12-month year. Thus, whether a 3-month or a 90-day note, the interest is for $\frac{1}{4}$ year.

The period of discount is the length of time from the date of discount to the due date (or maturity date). If this period is stated in days, assume a 360-day year to compute bank discount; if in months, assume a 12-month year. In most problems, however, the period of discount is not given, but is to be determined by *first finding the due date* and then computing the number of days (see Art. 31) from date of discount to due date. If the term of the note is given in days, count the actual number of days to find the due date. But if the term is given in months, we shall agree that a month after a given day expires on the corresponding day of the following month. Thus, 30 days after July 17 is August 16; 1 month after July 17 is August 17; 3 months after March 7 is June 7, but 90 days after March 7 is June 5; 3 months after March 31 is June 30, since June has no 31st day.

The discount rate is the per cent of the maturity value charged as bank discount for a discount period of unit length of time. One year is generally taken as the unit length of time.

Denoting bank discount by D_b, maturity value by S, the period of discount (in years) by n, and the annual discount rate by d, we have, by definition,

$$D_b = Snd. \tag{6}$$

The value of n in formula (6) is usually a fraction, since the term of a note and hence also the period of discount are seldom longer than a year. $S - D_b$, the difference between maturity value and bank discount, is the proceeds, denoted by P_b. Then, it follows by use of (6) that

$$P_b = S - Snd = S(1 - nd). \tag{7}$$

ILLUSTRATIVE EXAMPLE 1. A 3-month non-interest-bearing note of $1200, dated March 12, was discounted on May 7 at $6\frac{1}{2}\%$. Find the proceeds.

SOLUTION. 3 months after March 12 is June 12 (due date). From May 7 to June 12 is 36 days (period of discount).

$$S = 1200; \quad n = \tfrac{36}{360} = 0.1; \quad d = 0.065.$$

Now, since

$$D_b = Snd = 1200 \times 0.1 \times 0.065 = \$7.80,$$

it follows that

$$P_b = 1200 - 7.80 = \$1192.20. \quad \text{Proceeds.}$$

ILLUSTRATIVE EXAMPLE 2. A 60-day 5% interest-bearing note of $2700, dated September 1, was discounted on October 16 at 6%. Find the proceeds.

SOLUTION. First, find the maturity value of the note, by adding to $2700 its interest at 5% for 60 days. Substitute the known quantities $P = 2700$, $n = \frac{60}{360} = \frac{1}{6}$, and $i = 0.05$ in formula (1) of Art. 29:

$$I = Pni = 2700 \times \tfrac{1}{6} \times 0.05 = \$22.50.$$

The maturity value of the note, then, is

$$S = 2700 + 22.50 = \$2722.50.$$

Next, proceed as in the preceding example:

60 days after September 1 is October 31 (due date).
From October 16 to October 31 is 15 days (period of discount).
$S = 2722.50$; $n = \frac{15}{360} = \frac{1}{24}$; $d = 0.06$.

Now, since

$$D_b = Snd = 2722.50 \times \tfrac{1}{24} \times 0.06 = \$6.81,$$

it follows that

$$P_b = 2722.50 - 6.81 = \$2715.69. \quad \text{Proceeds.}$$

ILLUSTRATIVE EXAMPLE 3. A non-interest-bearing note was discounted at 8% 30 days before maturity. The proceeds were $1442.32. What was the face value of the note?

SOLUTION. Since the maturity value of a non-interest-bearing note is equal to its face value, here the unknown quantity is S, while P_b, n, and d are known. Solving formula (7) for S, and substituting $P_b = 1442.32$. $n = \frac{30}{360} = \frac{1}{12}$, $d = 0.08$, we have

$$S = \frac{P_b}{1 - nd} = \frac{1442.32}{1 - \dfrac{0.08}{12}} = \frac{1442.32}{1 - \dfrac{0.02}{3}} = \frac{1442.32}{\dfrac{2.98}{3}}$$

$$= \frac{1442.32 \times 3}{2.98} = \$1452.00. \quad \text{Face value.}$$

EXERCISE 26

In each of Problems 1–16, find the proceeds.

Problem	Face Value of Note	Date of Note	Term of Note	Interest Rate	Date of Discount	Discount Rate
1.	$2000.00	April 23	3 months	—	May 30	$6\frac{1}{2}\%$
2.	2500.00	Oct. 12	2 months	—	Nov. 2	8%
3.	680.00	Dec. 30	45 days	—	Jan. 11	5%
4.	400.00	May 7	90 days	—	May 25	$7\frac{1}{2}\%$
5.	1100.00	Sept. 19	4 months	6%	Dec. 5	8%
6.	720.00	Jan. 28	1 month	$4\frac{1}{2}\%$	Feb. 8	6%
7.	450.00	March 5	60 days	8%	April 10	$5\frac{1}{2}\%$
8.	4000.00	June 20	6 months	5%	Oct. 1	7%
9.	1500.00	July 17	5 months	4%	Aug. 31	6%
10.	960.00	Nov. 8	30 days	5%	Dec. 2	$7\frac{1}{2}\%$
11.	2400.00	Aug. 25	90 days	$6\frac{1}{2}\%$	Sept. 24	4%
12.	1200.00	Feb. 7	4 months	7%	April 20	7%
13.	600.00	Oct. 10	2 months	6%	Nov. 13	6%
14.	600.00	Sept. 29	60 days	5%	Oct. 19	6%
15.	1600.00	April 4	90 days	$4\frac{1}{2}\%$	April 4	8%
16.	3200.00	June 16	45 days	5%	June 16	7%

17. Don Kelly holds a 1-year non-interest-bearing note for $1500. When should he discount it at 6% to receive $1450 as proceeds?

18. Solve Problem 17 if the note bears interest at 4%.

19. A received $2982.50 as the proceeds of a non-interest-bearing note for $3000 discounted 42 days before maturity. Find the discount rate.

20. B received $2516.58 by discounting a 60-day note 15 days before maturity. The face value was $2500, and the bank discount was $8.42. Find the interest rate of the note and the bank's discount rate.

21. A 6-month 6% interest-bearing note is discounted at 6% 60 days before maturity. Find the face value of the note if the discount is $8.61.

22. Mr. Day wishes to receive $600 as the proceeds of a 90-day loan. If the bank's discount rate is 8%, what loan should he request?

23. A bill broker discounts at $6\frac{1}{2}\%$ a non-interest-bearing note for $8000 brought to him 51 days before maturity. Find his profit if he rediscounts the note immediately at a bank whose discount rate is 5%.

24. The Pacific Bank discounts at 6% a non-interest-bearing note for $4000, due in 45 days. Find the bank's profit if the note is rediscounted at 4% the same day at a Federal Reserve Bank. (In rediscounting notes for member banks, Federal Reserve Banks use a 365-day year.)

25. Who is the maker of the note in Fig. 1? the holder? What is the face value? the term? the due date? the interest rate? the maturity value?

$ *2000.00*   New York, *July 10,*   *1969*

_____*Three months*_____after date_____*I*_____promise to pay

to the order of_____*Henry B. Lee*_____

Two Thousand and $\frac{00}{100}$ ⁓⁓⁓⁓⁓⁓⁓⁓⁓⁓⁓⁓⁓⁓ Dollars

Payable at *New York City*

Value received with interest at___*6*___per cent.

                                        Oliver C. Gates

Fig. 1. A promissory note.

26. If Mr. Lee discounts the note in Fig. 1 at a bank on July 25, the period of discount begins and ends on what dates? Who pays the proceeds to whom? Who holds the note thereafter? On the due date, who pays, how much, and to whom?

27. Find the proceeds if Mr. Lee discounts the note shown in Fig. 1 on Sept. 10 at a bank charging 6% discount.

28. Suppose that, on Aug. 26, Mr. Lee discounts the note shown in Fig. 1 at a bank whose discount rate is 5%. What are the proceeds?

29. Who is the drawer of the draft in Fig. 2? the drawee? What is the face value? the term? the interest rate? the maturity value? How long is the discount period if Mr. Adams discounts it on May 13?

30. If Mr. Barnes accepts the draft in Fig. 3 on June 24, the term begins on what date? What is the due date? the maturity value?

31. The draft in Fig. 2 is duly accepted by O.P. Thompson and returned to F.B. Adams, who discounts it at 6% on June 16. Find the proceeds.

32. What are the proceeds if Mr. Adams discounts the draft shown in Fig. 2 on May 22 at a bank whose discount rate is $4\frac{1}{2}$%?

$ 800.00   Atlanta, Ga., *May 2,*   1969
            Sixty days   after   *date*   Pay to
the order of   *myself*
Eight Hundred and $\frac{00}{100}$ ～～～～～～～～～～～～ Dollars
Value received and charge the same to account of
To   *O. P. Thompson*
            Mobile, Ala.   *Frank B. Adams*

Fig. 2. An "after date" draft.

$ 340.00   Los Angeles, Calif., *June 21,*   1969
            Thirty days   after   *sight*   Pay to
the order of   *myself*
Three Hundred Forty and $\frac{00}{100}$ ～～～～～～～～ Dollars
Value received and charge same to account of
To   *A. H. Barnes*
            Houston, Tex.   *R. L. Fisher*

Fig. 3. An "after sight" draft.

No.   Jacksonville, Fla., *March 15,*   1969 $ *1436.50*
        Two months   after date pay to the order of OURSELVES
Fourteen Hundred Thirty-six and $\frac{50}{100}$ ～～～～～～～ Dollars

THE OBLIGATION OF THE ACCEPTOR HEREOF ARISES OUT OF THE
PURCHASE OF GOODS FROM THE DRAWER. THE ACCEPTOR MAY
MAKE THE ACCEPTANCE PAYABLE AT ANY BANK, BANKER OR TRUST
COMPANY IN THE UNITED STATES WHICH HE MAY DESIGNATE.

To   *M. P. Warren*   *Simmons Hardware Co.*
            Columbia, S. C.   *By H. E. Allen, Manager*

Fig. 4. A trade acceptance.

33. The drawee accepts the draft in Fig. 3 on June 29. What are the proceeds if the drawer discounts it at 7% on July 4?

34. Suppose that Mr. Barnes accepts the draft in Fig. 3 on June 23 and Mr. Fisher discounts it at $6\frac{1}{2}$% on June 26. Find the proceeds.

35. On March 31, the Simmons Hardware Co. discounts at 8% the trade acceptance in Fig. 4. What are the proceeds?

36. The trade acceptance in Fig. 4 is discounted by the drawer on April 9 at a bank charging 6% discount. Find the proceeds.

39. Comparison of simple discount and bank discount

It is rather important to understand fully the distinction between simple discount and bank discount, and hence the distinction between present value at an interest rate and present value at a discount rate. As shown in Art. 35 and Art. 37, there are two essentially different methods of deciding the present value of a debt due in the future.

Suppose a debt of $1000 is due in 1 year without interest. At a *simple interest rate* of 7%, the present value is that principal which, invested now at 7% simple interest, will amount to $1000 in a year. The answer, $934.58, is found by the formula $P = S/(1 + ni)$, where $S = \$1000$, $n = 1$, $i = 0.07$. Hence the simple discount is $1000 - \$934.58 = \$65.42$.

On the other hand, if a bank charges 7% annual discount, the banker computes the present value of this debt by use of a *discount rate* of 7%. The bank discount is $70, found by the formula $D_b = Snd$, where $S = 1000$, $n = 1$, $d = 0.07$. Hence, at a discount rate of 7%, the present value of $1000 due in a year is $930; that is, the proceeds are $930.

Summarizing, $D_s = \$65.42$, while $D_b = \$70$; and $P = \$934.58$, while $P_b = \$930$. Note that $65.42, the simple discount, is 7% of $934.58 (present value, at simple interest, of $1000); while $70, the bank discount, is 7% of $1000.

As the above example shows, bank discount can be computed much more easily than simple discount. Furthermore, a given discount rate insures a somewhat larger income to a lending agency than does an equal interest rate used in arriving at simple discount. This may explain the adoption of bank discount by banks and like institutions.

40. Interest rate corresponding to a given discount rate, and vice versa

In discounting a note at a given discount rate d, a bank virtually lends P_b (the proceeds) and collects S (the maturity value of the note) at the end of n years, thereby earning interest on $\$P_b$ at a rate higher than d. Suppose we wish to determine the interest rate i **corresponding** to the given discount rate d. In other words, at what rate of interest would the proceeds $\$P_b$ amount to $\$S$ in n years?

From formula (7) of Art. 38, $S = \dfrac{P_b}{1 - nd}$. If $\$P_b$ amount to $\$\dfrac{P_b}{1 - nd}$ in n years, the interest earned on $\$P_b$ in n years is

$$\frac{P_b}{1 - nd} - P_b = \frac{P_b - P_b(1 - nd)}{1 - nd} = \frac{P_b nd}{1 - nd}.$$

It follows that the interest earned on $\$P_b$ in one year is

$$\frac{P_b nd}{1 - nd} \div n = \frac{P_b d}{1 - nd}$$

and the interest earned on $\$1$ in one year is

$$\frac{P_b d}{1 - nd} \div P_b = \frac{d}{1 - nd}.$$

But the interest on $\$1$ for 1 year is the annual rate of interest. Hence, the interest rate i corresponding to the discount rate d is given by the formula

$$i = \frac{d}{1 - nd}. \tag{8}$$

It is left as an exercise for the student to solve formula (8) for d and thus to show that the discount rate d corresponding to a given interest rate i is given by

$$d = \frac{i}{1 + ni}. \tag{9}$$

———

ILLUSTRATIVE EXAMPLE 1. A bank discounts a 90-day note at 8%. What is the corresponding interest rate earned by the bank?

SOLUTION. Substitute the known quantities $d = 0.08$, $n = \frac{1}{4}$ in formula (8):

$$i = \frac{d}{1 - nd} = \frac{0.08}{1 - (\frac{1}{4})(0.08)} = \frac{0.08}{1 - 0.02} = \frac{0.08}{0.98}$$
$$= 0.0816 = 8.16\%. \quad Ans.$$

———

ILLUSTRATIVE EXAMPLE 2. A bank wishes to earn 6% interest in discounting a 2-month note. At what rate should the note be discounted?

SOLUTION. Substitute the known quantities $i = 0.06$, $n = \frac{1}{6}$ in formula (9):

$$d = \frac{i}{1 + ni} = \frac{0.06}{1 + (\frac{1}{6})(0.06)} = \frac{0.06}{1.01} = 0.0594 = 5.94\%. \quad Ans.$$

_____

EXERCISE 27

In Problems 1–6, find the rate of interest earned by a bank:

1. In discounting a note for 6 months at the discount rate 8%.

2. In discounting a note for 1 year at the discount rate 5%.

3. In charging 8% interest *payable in advance* for a 60-day loan.

4. In collecting 6% interest *in advance* for a 90-day loan.

5. In discounting a note for 3 months at the discount rate 6%.

6. In discounting a note for 45 days at the discount rate 6%.

In Problems 7–12, find the rate of discount charged by a bank if:

7. It earns interest at 5% in discounting a note for 1 year.

8. It earns interest at 6% in discounting a note for 90 days.

9. In granting a 6-month loan, it earns interest at 4%.

10. In discounting a note for 60 days, it earns interest at 8%.

11. It earns interest at 8% in discounting a note for 45 days.

12. It earns interest at $4\frac{1}{2}\%$ in discounting a note for 2 months.

13. Using formula (8), find i if $d = 0.04$ and $n = \frac{1}{2}$.

14. Apply formula (9) to find d if $i = 0.06$ and $n = \frac{1}{3}$.

15. By use of formula (9), show that $n = (i - d)/id$.

16. Solve formula (8) for d.

17. Show that, for $n = 1$, formula (8) becomes

$$i = \frac{d}{1 - d} = d + d^2 + d^3 + d^4 + \cdots.$$

18. Show that, for $n = 1$, formula (9) becomes

$$d = \frac{i}{1 + i} = i - i^2 + i^3 - i^4 + \cdots.$$

19. Using the result of Problem 15, find n if $d = .05$, $i = .085$.

20. Work Problem 2 by using the first three terms of the expression obtained in Problem 17.

41. Cash discount

Cash discount is an amount deducted from the invoice price of merchandise as an inducement for immediate payment or for payment before the ultimate date assigned for settling the account. The deduction is a certain per cent of the amount of the bill. The conditions of payment are called the **terms** of the sale. We shall denote cash discount by D_c.

Cash discounts are expressed in various ways. "Net 30, cash 8%" means that the bill will be due 30 days after the sale, but that a deduction of 8% is allowed for immediate payment. *Net 30* is sometimes written n/30. On a billhead, "Terms: Cash 5, 3/10, 1/30, n/60" means that a deduction of 5% is allowed for immediate payment; if paid within 10 days, the deduction allowed will be 3%; if payment is made after the tenth but not later than the thirtieth day, 1% will be allowed; after the thirtieth day, no discount is allowed and the full amount is due not later than the sixtieth day.

ILLUSTRATIVE EXAMPLE 1. An invoice of $500 carries terms as follows: "Cash 5, 3/10, 1/30, n/60." To what discount is the purchaser entitled if he pays (a) immediately? (b) on the 10th day? (c) on the 30th day?

SOLUTION.   (a) $D_c = 500 \times 0.05 = \$25.00.$
            (b) $D_c = 500 \times 0.03 = \$15.00$
            (c) $D_c = 500 \times 0.01 = \$\ 5.00.$

Comment. In the above example, the sale of goods has given rise to a debt of $500 which is not due until 60 days after the sale. However, a 5% cash discount is offered for immediate payment. The buyer may thus settle the account by paying $475 at once. In that case, he virtually lends $475 for 60 days to the seller and receives credit for $25 as interest on $475 for 60 days. The second offer amounts to letting the buyer receive $15 interest on $485 for 50 days; and the third offer is equivalent to paying the buyer $5 interest on $495 for 30 days.

By use of the formula $I = Pni$, the annual interest rate equivalent to a cash discount may be found. Interest rates thus obtained are usually higher than those met in actual loans. But cash discounts are offered because they tend to reduce losses arising from bad debts.

––––––

ILLUSTRATIVE EXAMPLE 2. Find the annual interest rate equivalent to each offer of discount in Illustrative example 1, and thus determine which one of the three is the most advantageous to the buyer.

SOLUTION. Since i is unknown, solve $I = Pni$ for i.

(a) $i = \dfrac{I}{Pn} = \dfrac{25}{475 \times \frac{60}{360}} = \dfrac{1}{19 \times \frac{1}{6}} = \dfrac{6}{19} = 0.3158 = 31.58\%.$

(b) $i = \dfrac{I}{Pn} = \dfrac{15}{485 \times \frac{50}{360}} = \dfrac{3}{97 \times \frac{5}{36}} = \dfrac{108}{485} = 0.2227 = 22.27\%.$

(c) $i = \dfrac{I}{Pn} = \dfrac{5}{495 \times \frac{30}{360}} = \dfrac{1}{99 \times \frac{1}{12}} = \dfrac{12}{99} = 0.1212 = 12.12\%.$

Hence an immediate payment is the most advantageous to the buyer.

––––––

EXERCISE 28

1. Home Grocery buys goods for $600 on the terms 4/5, n/30. Find the discount if the bill is paid on the 4th day.

2. A merchant buys merchandise for $650 on the terms 2/7, n/30. Find the discount if the bill is paid on the 5th day.

3. Quotation on lawn chairs is $8.50, subject to the terms cash 6, 4/10, n/30. Find the cost of a lawn chair on the 6th day.

4. In Problem 3, find the discount on the price of a lawn chair if payment is made on the 4th day.

5. An invoice for $1400 carries terms: 5/10, n/45. A payment of $760 is made on the 8th day. Find amount due on the 45th day.

6. A dealer buys goods for $1500 on the terms 4/5, n/15. He pays $1200 on the 5th day. How much more is due on the 15th day?

7. A druggist gets a bill for $400 marked: "Terms: Cash 5, 3/10, n/30." Find the annual interest rate equivalent to each offer.

8. An invoice for $600 is marked: "Terms: Cash 6, 4/15, 2/30, n/90." What is the annual interest rate equivalent to each offer?

9. A salesman claims that the discount offered by the terms 4/20, n/60 is equivalent to $\frac{360}{20} \times 4\% = 72\%$ annual interest rate. Explain the error and find the correct interest rate. [*Hint.* Assume a $1 invoice.]

10. From one firm a purchaser can obtain terms 4/10, n/30. From another firm he can obtain terms cash 5, n/30. Which is better for the purchaser if he can take advantage of cash discounts? [*Hint.* Assume a $1 invoice and compare the equivalent interest rates.]

11. A dealer buys goods amounting to $3000 on the terms cash 5, n/90. He gives a 90-day non-interest-bearing note for $3000 to a bank charging 8% bank discount and, from the proceeds, pays the bill at once. How much does he save by thus taking advantage of the cash discount?

12. Charging 6% discount, a certain bank grants loans to merchants wishing to take advantage of cash discounts, provided they save by so doing. Should the bank grant a 60-day loan to enable a merchant to pay cash for goods bought on the terms cash 2, *n*/60? Compare the interest rates equivalent to the bank discount and the cash discount involved.

13. Suppose that the amount of an invoice is payable net in t days, and let x be the rate of cash discount allowed for immediate payment. If the purchaser chooses to pay cash, show that the equivalent annual interest rate is $i = \dfrac{360x}{t(1-x)}$.

14. Find the value of i in Problem 13 if $x = 4\%$, $t = 30$.

15. Solve the formula in Problem 13 for x.

16. Solve the formula in Problem 13 for t.

42. Commercial terms in common use

The **net cost** of merchandise bought is the actual purchase price before buying expenses, such as transportation, are added. **Gross cost** includes net cost plus all buying expenses.

List price is the price of goods sold as given in a printed list or catalogue. For our purpose, the meaning of **marked price** is identical with that of list price, since it refers to the price marked by dealers but not given in a printed catalogue.

Net selling price is the price at which goods are actually sold, after all discounts are deducted.

Selling expenses include insurance, taxes, advertising, salesman's commission and traveling expenses, and the like. **Overhead expenses** include general and administrative expenses, such as salaries of officers and office employees, office supplies and expenses, bad debts, rent, and depreciation.

Gross profit is net selling price minus gross cost. **Net profit** is gross profit less selling and overhead expenses. If a profit is a negative number, it is a loss. A modern tendency is to express profits as a per cent of *net sales.*

43. Trade discount

A **trade discount** is expressed as a certain per cent of list price. It is a deduction from list price for some reason *other than* to induce payment within a specified time. Reasons for allowing trade discounts are: (a) to adjust list prices to prevailing market prices; (b) to secure the trade of an especially desirable customer; (c) to attract wholesalers or jobbers who buy in large quantities. To save time and money, merchants and manufacturers usually publish, for a season or a longer period, a single edition of their catalogue containing uniform list prices for all customers. Then they offer varying discounts to different customers.

After a trade discount has already been quoted, it may become necessary to offer one or several more discounts, on account of further declines in market prices or for some other reasons. These successive trade discounts are known as **discount series** or **chain discounts.** Later, if it should become necessary to increase selling prices, one or more of the discounts may be withdrawn.

44. Single discount rate equivalent to a series

In a discount series, the several rates *cannot* be added to compute the total discount. Each discount is computed as a per cent of the amount left after deducting the previous discount.

ILLUSTRATIVE EXAMPLE 1. An article listed at $100 is bought at 20%, 10%, and 3% discount. Find the equivalent single rate of discount.

SOLUTION.

$100.00 = list price.
  20.00 = 20% discount on $100.00
$80.00 = 1st reduced price.
   8.00 = 10% discount on $80.00
$72.00 = 2nd reduced price.
   2.16 = 3% discount on $72.00
$69.84 = net price.

Since the total discount on $100 is $30.16, the equivalent single rate of discount is 30.16%, which is *not* the sum of 20%, 10%, and 3%.

The single discount rate equivalent to a discount series may also be found by formula (11) below, derived as follows:

Let $\qquad\qquad L =$ list price,

$\qquad r_1, r_2, r_3 =$ 1st, 2nd, 3rd discount rates, respectively,

$\qquad N_1, N_2, N_3 =$ 1st, 2nd, 3rd reduced prices, respectively.

Then

$$N_1 = L - Lr_1 = L(1 - r_1),$$
$$N_2 = N_1 - N_1 r_2 = L(1 - r_1) - L(1 - r_1)r_2 = L(1 - r_1)(1 - r_2),$$
$$N_3 = N_2 - N_2 r_3 = L(1 - r_1)(1 - r_2) - L(1 - r_1)(1 - r_2)r_3$$
$$= L(1 - r_1)(1 - r_2)(1 - r_3).$$

If there are only three discounts in the series, N_3 is, of course, the net price. Extending the idea to any number n of discounts in a series, the net price N is given by

$$N = L(1 - r_1)(1 - r_2)(1 - r_3) \ldots (1 - r_n).$$

Let r be the single discount rate equivalent to the series of rates r_1, r_2, $r_3, \ldots, r_n$. Then,

$$N = L - Lr = L(1 - r). \tag{10}$$

Equating the two expressions found for N and solving for r, we have

$$r = 1 - [(1 - r_1)(1 - r_2)(1 - r_3) \ldots (1 - r_n)]. \tag{11}$$

Since the product of the factors inclosed in brackets in formula (11) is the same regardless of the order in which they are multiplied, the order of the several rates in a discount series is immaterial.

Note that trade discount is based upon the *list price*, whereas cash discount is based upon the *net selling price*. Denoting trade discount by D_t, we have the simple relation

$$D_t = L - N = Lr. \tag{12}$$

ILLUSTRATIVE EXAMPLE 2. By use of formula (11), find the single rate of trade discount equivalent to the series 20%, 10%, and 3%.

SOLUTION. Here $r_1 = \frac{20}{100} = \frac{1}{5}$, $r_2 = \frac{10}{100} = \frac{1}{10}$, $r_3 = \frac{3}{100}$.   By (11),

$$r = 1 - (1 - \tfrac{1}{5})(1 - \tfrac{1}{10})(1 - \tfrac{3}{100})$$
$$= 1 - \tfrac{4}{5} \times \tfrac{9}{10} \times \tfrac{97}{100} = 1 - \tfrac{3492}{5000} = \tfrac{1508}{5000} = 30.16\%. \quad Ans.$$

Compare this result with that of illustrative example 1.

ILLUSTRATIVE EXAMPLE 3. A manufacturer's list price of a machine is $125. He sells it to a jobber subject to a discount of $33\frac{1}{3}\%$ and 10%, with terms: "Cash 3, 2/10." Find: (a) the manufacturer's net selling price; (b) the total trade discount; (c) the price actually paid for the machine by the jobber if he settles the account on the seventh day.

SOLUTION. The single discount rate equivalent to $33\frac{1}{3}\%$ and 10% is

$$r = 1 - (1 - \tfrac{1}{3})(1 - \tfrac{1}{10}) = 1 - \tfrac{2}{3} \times \tfrac{9}{10} = 1 - \tfrac{3}{5} = \tfrac{2}{5} = 40\%.$$

(a) $N = L(1 - r) = 125 \times \tfrac{3}{5} = \$75.$ $Ans.$
(b) $D_t = L - N = 125 - 75 = \$50.$ $Ans.$
(c) $D_c = 75 \times 0.02 = \$1.50.$

Hence the price actually paid by the jobber is $75 - 1.50 = \$73.50.$ $Ans.$

ILLUSTRATIVE EXAMPLE 4. An article is to be sold for $48.45. At what price should it be listed so as to allow a discount series of 25%, 20%, and 5%?

SOLUTION. The given chain discount is equivalent to the single rate

$$r = 1 - (1 - \tfrac{1}{4})(1 - \tfrac{1}{5})(1 - \tfrac{1}{20}) = 1 - \tfrac{57}{100} = 43\%.$$

Solving formula (10) for L and substituting the known quantities,

$$L = \frac{N}{1 - r} = \frac{48.45}{1 - 0.43} = \frac{48.45}{0.57} = \$85.00. \quad Ans.$$

EXERCISE 29

Find the single discount rate equivalent to each series:
1. 20% and 5%.   2. 10% and 15%.

3. 20%, $16\frac{2}{3}$%, and 5%.

4. $33\frac{1}{3}$%, 10%, and 5%.

5. 20%, $12\frac{1}{2}$%, 10%, and 5%.

6. 10%, 10%, 20%, and $8\frac{1}{3}$%.

7. A jobber buys hats at $6 less 10% and sells at $8 less $12\frac{1}{2}$%. Buying expense is 12¢ per hat; overhead and selling expenses, 22¢. Find: (a) the net cost of a hat; (b) the gross cost; (c) the net selling price; (d) the gross profit per hat; (e) the net profit.

8. Work Problem 7 if the jobber buys the hats at $6.50 less 20% and sells at $8 less 15%, all else remaining unchanged.

9. In Problem 7 find per cent of net profit based on net selling price.

10. What cash payment will settle a bill for 500 bags of coffee at $26 per bag less 20% and 5%, terms: Cash 3, n/30?

11. A plumber pays $32.40 net per bathtub bought at a trade discount of 20% and 10%. Find the list price.

12. Two competing firms have the same list price for electric irons. One allows a trade discount of 35% and 5%; the second, 20% and 20%. Which discount series is more advantageous to the purchaser?

13. A jeweler gets an invoice showing a list price of $90 for a watch and a net price of $63 after a dicount series of 10% and another rate which is illegible. What is the second discount rate?

14. To meet a drop in prices, an article listed at $40 was sold at a discount of 25% and 10%. Then there was a 20% rise in prices. If the two discounts be now withdrawn, what single discount should be allowed to readjust the list price to prevailing market prices?

15. A wholesaler buys bicycles at $50 less 20% and 5%. At what price should he list them if he wishes to gain $12\frac{1}{2}$% of his net purchase price after allowing a trade discount of 15% to his own customers?

16. Typewriters are bought by a dealer at $100 less 10% and 20%. Find his own selling price if it is to cover overhead expenses of 10% and to yield a net profit of 15%, both based on the selling price.

17. The Modern Furniture Co. buys radios at $100 less $12\frac{1}{2}$% and 10%, paying $1.90 per radio for transportation. Find the company's selling price if 18% of it is to be the gross profit.

18. A manufacturer pays $48.80 for the raw material needed to make a refrigerator, and $70 for labor, overhead, etc. At what price should he list it so as to be able to allow a trade discount of $16\frac{2}{3}\%$ and 10% and still make a net profit of 12% based on his net selling price?

C. Partial Payments and Equation of Payments

45. Partial payments

If a note is payable on or before a certain date, the debtor may make equal or unequal payments on the note, at regular or irregular intervals. Such payments are known as **partial payments.** The debtor should receive credit for interest on each payment made before the final date of settlement. Consequently, it is necessary to determine the amount of indebtedness at a given time. There are two methods of applying partial payments to the reduction of indebtedness: (a) the **Merchant's Rule,** a method more or less prevalent among business men; (b) the **United States Rule,** a method made legal by statute in nearly every state, and so named because of its being in accordance with a ruling of the United States Supreme Court.

Under the *Merchant's Rule*, the principal draws interest from the date of indebtedness to the date of final settlement, and interest is allowed on each partial payment from the date of payment to the date of final settlement. On the date of final settlement, the balance due is the unpaid portion of the principal, plus the difference between the interest on the principal and the sum of interests on the partial payments.

The *United States Rule* specifies that the first partial payment must be applied to the payment of the interest due on the principal from the date of indebtedness to the date of first partial payment, and the excess over this interest item is to be applied to the reduction of the principal. The second partial payment is applied to the interest due on the reduced principal from the date of the first partial payment to the date of the second partial payment, and the excess is used to further reduce the principal, and so on. In case a partial payment is less than the interest due at the time of such payment, there will be no reduction of principal until this payment and subsequent payments exceed the accumulated interest.

ILLUSTRATIVE EXAMPLE. A 6% interest-bearing note for $4000, dated March 17, 1968, had the following indorsement: Received on this note —April 1, 1968, $800; June 30, 1968, $40; August 5, 1968, $2100. Find the balance due September 13, 1968, by both methods.

(a) Solution by Merchant's Rule

Original debt, March 17, 1968...............		$4000.00
Interest on $4000 for 180 days—from March 17 to September 13........................		120.00
Value of note on September 13..............		$4120.00
First payment, April 1.....................	$800.00	
Interest on $800 for 165 days—from April 1 to September 13	22.00	
Second payment, June 30..................	40.00	
Interest on $40 for 75 days—from June 30 to September 13	0.50	
Third payment, August 5..................	2100.00	
Interest on $2100 for 39 days—from August 5 to September 13........................	13.65	2976.15
Balance due on September 13, 1968..........		$1143.85 *Ans.*

(b) Solution by United States Rule

Original debt, March 17, 1968..............		$4000.00
Interest on $4000 for 15 days—from March 17 to April 1..............................		10.00
Amount due on April 1....................		$4010.00
Deduct first payment, April 1...............		800.00
Balance due on April 1....................		$3210.00
Interest on $3210 for 90 days, from April 1 to June 30, $48.15. Since second payment is less than $48.15, principal remains unchanged.		
Interest on $3210 for 126 days—from April 1 to August 5...........................		67.41
Amount due on August 5..................		$3277.41
Deduct:		
Second payment, June 30................	$40.00	
Third payment, August 5................	2100.00	2140.00
Balance due on August 5..................		$1137.41
Interest on $1,137.41 for 39 days—from August 5 to September 13.......................		7.39
Balance due on September 13, 1968..........		$1144.80 *Ans.*

EXERCISE 30

In each case, find the balance due by both methods unless otherwise directed (the short cuts in Art. 32 may be used for interest computations).

1. Note for $4000; dated Feb. 8; interest, 6%. Partial payments: May 9, $500; Nov. 5, $200. Date of final settlement, Dec. 5.

2. Note for $6000; dated Jan. 12; interest, 6%. Partial payments: March 13, $50; July 11, $1000. Date of final settlement, Sept. 9.

3. Note for $1000; dated Aug. 5, 1968; interest, 8%. Partial payments: Nov. 5, 1968, $200; Feb. 5, 1969, $200; May 5, 1969, $200. Date of final settlement, Aug. 5, 1969. (Use a 12-month year for interest computations; thus, from Aug. 5 to Nov. 5 is 3 months, etc.)

4. Note for $2000; dated April 1; interest, 4%. Partial payments: $500 each on June 1, Aug. 1, and Oct. 1. Date of final settlement: Dec. 1. (See directions in Problem 3 for interest computations.)

5. A 4 months' 6% interest-bearing note for $800, dated June 6, has the indorsement: Received on this note—June 30, $300; Aug. 14, $200; Sept. 13, $300. How much is due at the maturity date of the note?

6. A 90-day 6% interest-bearing note for $1200, dated July 21, has the indorsement: Received on this note—Aug. 11, $500; Sept. 10, $400; Oct. 4, $300. Find balance due at the end of 90 days.

7. A piano sells for $1400 cash. The purchaser pays $300 cash and agrees to make bimonthly payments of $200 each, the first due 2 months after purchase date. Using the Merchant's Rule, find the balance due just after the 4th payment of $200 if $7\frac{1}{2}$% interest is charged.

8. An automobile sells for $2450 cash. A customer receives $650 credit on his old car and agrees to make monthly payments of $60 each, the first due 1 month after purchase date. If 9% interest is charged, find by the Merchant's Rule the amount due just after the 5th payment.

9. Work Problem 7 by the United States Rule.

10. Find amount due in Problem 8 by the United States Rule.

11. The cash price of a lot is $1200. A purchaser pays $400 cash and $100 a month for 5 months starting 1 month after purchase date. If interest is at 6%, find by the United States Rule how large a payment at the end of the 6th month would close the account.

12. A man makes a down payment of $2000 on a house whose cash price is $13,000. Then he pays $800 at the end of each quarter for 4 quarters. If interest is at 8%, find by the United States Rule the amount still due at the end of the year.

13. Work Problem 11 by the Merchant's Rule.

14. Find the amount due in Problem 12 by the Merchant's Rule.

46. Commuting obligations. Equation of value

A given sum of money has different values at different times. Let a non-interest-bearing debt of $x be due at some specified time. Its value at the due date is of course $x. If not paid at that time and if money is worth i, the value of the debt n years *after* the due date is more than x and is found by *multiplying* x by $1 + ni$. But its value n years *before* the due date is less than x and is found by *dividing* x by $1 + ni$.

———

ILLUSTRATIVE EXAMPLE 1. A debt of $100 is due 5 months hence. Assuming money to be worth 8%, find the value of this obligation: (a) 11 months hence; (b) 2 months hence; (c) 5 months hence.

SOLUTION. (a) The debt is due 5 months hence. Its value 11 months hence, that is, 6 months *after* the due date, is found by *multiplying* 100 by $1 + ni$, where $n = \frac{6}{12}$, $i = 0.08$. Therefore, the required value is

$$100[1 + \tfrac{6}{12}(0.08)] = 100 \times 1.04 = \$104. \quad Ans.$$

(b) The value of this obligation 2 months hence, that is, 3 months *before* the due date, is found by *dividing* 100 by $1 + ni$, where $n = \frac{3}{12}$, $i = 0.08$. Therefore, the required value is

$$\frac{100}{1 + \tfrac{3}{12}(0.08)} = \frac{100}{1.02} = \$98.04. \quad Ans.$$

(c) The debt is due 5 months hence; its value at that time is $100.

———

ILLUSTRATIVE EXAMPLE 2. A debt of $1000 is due 3 months hence with 5% interest for 3 months. Assuming money to be worth 6%, find the value of this obligation: (a) 7 months hence; (b) 1 month hence.

SOLUTION. (a) The face value $1000 and the rate 5% are used here only to find the maturity value, which is $1000[1 + \tfrac{3}{12}(0.05)] = 1000 \times 1.0125 = \$1012.50$. Then the value of $1012.50 4 months *after* the due date is

$$1012.50[1 + \tfrac{4}{12}(0.06)] = 1012.50 \times 1.02 = \$1032.75. \quad Ans.$$

(b) The value of $1012.50 2 months *before* the due date is

$$\frac{1012.50}{1 + \frac{2}{12}(0.06)} = \frac{1012.50}{1.01} = \$1002.48. \quad Ans.$$

_____

Two sums of money are **equivalent at a certain date** if their values at that date are equal. Thus, in illustrative example 1, $100 (5 months hence) and $104 (11 months hence) are equivalent 11 months hence; similarly, $100 (5 months hence) and $98.04 (2 months hence) are equivalent 2 months hence.

To **commute** one set of obligations into another means to exchange one set of obligations due at various times for another set due at various other times. The two sets are equivalent at a given date, called the **focal date,** if the sum of the values (at the focal date) of the obligations in one set equals the corresponding sum of values (at the focal date) for the other set. The equation expressing the equivalence of the two sets at the focal date is called the **equation of value.** We shall consider here only short-term obligations and use an equation of value *based upon simple interest*, which makes the equivalence dependent upon the focal date selected.

_____

ILLUSTRATIVE EXAMPLE 3. A man owes $1000 due in 1 month, $500 due in 4 months, and $900 due in 6 months. He wishes to discharge his obligations by making two equal payments, due in 4 months and 10 months, respectively. Assume money to be worth 6%, and find the size of the installments in such a way as to make the two sets equivalent 10 months hence.

SOLUTION. The given focal date is 10 months hence. Now, if the two sets are to be equivalent at that date, the sum of values (at the focal date) of the debts in one set must equal the corresponding sum of values (at the focal date) for the other set. Let $x = each of the two equal installments. Prepare a table of values for both sets as follows:

FOCAL DATE: 10 MONTHS HENCE

Original Set of Obligations	Value of Each at Focal Date	New Set of Obligations	Value of Each at Focal Date
$1000 due in 1 mo.	$1000[1 + \frac{9}{12}(0.06)]$	$x due in 4 mos.	$x[1 + \frac{6}{12}(0.06)]$
$500 due in 4 mos.	$500[1 + \frac{6}{12}(0.06)]$	$x due in 10 mos.	x
$900 due in 6 mos.	$900[1 + \frac{4}{12}(0.06)]$		

The equation of value is

$$1000(1.045) + 500(1.03) + 900(1.02) = 1.03x + x,$$
$$1045 + 515 + 918 = 2.03x,$$
$$x = 1220.69. \quad Ans.$$

Therefore the original debts may be commuted into two installments of \$1220.69 each, payable 4 and 10 months hence, respectively. Note that the two sets of obligations are equivalent only at the focal date used. Varying that date somewhat would give a slightly different value to x.

ILLUSTRATIVE EXAMPLE 4. How large should the two equal installments in illustrative example 3 be to make the 2 sets equivalent 4 months hence?

SOLUTION. Prepare a table of values, using the new focal date.

FOCAL DATE: 4 MONTHS HENCE

Original Set of Obligations	Value of Each at Focal Date	New Set of Obligations	Value of Each at Focal Date
\$1000 due in 1 mo. \$500 due in 4 mos. \$900 due in 6 mos.	$1000[1 + \frac{3}{12}(0.06)]$ 500 $\dfrac{900}{1 + \frac{2}{12}(0.06)}$	\$x due in 4 mos. \$x due in 10 mos.	x $\dfrac{x}{1 + \frac{6}{12}(0.06)}$

The equation of value is

$$1000(1.015) + 500 + \frac{900}{1.01} = x + \frac{x}{1.03},$$
$$1015 + 500 + 891.09 = x + 0.970874x,$$
$$1.970874x = 2406.09,$$
$$x = 1220.82. \quad Ans.$$

Note that a change of 6 months in the focal date caused an increase of only 13¢ in the answer.

EXERCISE 31

Unless otherwise stated, obligations bear no interest.

1. A debt of \$800 is due 4 months hence. Assuming money to be worth

4%, what is the value of this obligation (a) 1 month hence? (b) 4 months hence? (c) 10 months hence?

2. A debt of $200 is due 9 months hence. Assuming money to be worth 6%, what is the value of this obligation (a) 3 months hence? (b) 9 months hence? (c) 12 months hence?

3. Answer the questions in Problem 1 if the debt of $800 bears 6% interest for 4 months.

4. Answer the questions in Problem 2 if the debt of $200 bears 8% interest for 9 months.

5. How large should the two equal installments in illustrative example 3 be to make the two sets equivalent 8 months hence, if the first sum due in one month is $2000?

6. Solve illustrative example 3, assuming that money is worth 8% and that the two sets are to be equivalent 7 months hence.

7. Commute a debt of $1200 due 2 months hence into three equal payments due 3, 6, and 9 months hence, money being worth 8%. The original debt and the new set are to be equivalent 9 months hence.

8. Money being worth 6%, commute debts of $900 and $600, due in 2 and 4 months, respectively, into three equal installments due in 4, 6, and 8 months, so as to make the two sets equivalent 8 months hence.

9. What single payment 5 months hence will discharge debts of $200 and $500 due 2 and 11 months hence, money being worth 4%? The single payment is to be equivalent to the original set 8 months hence.

10. Work Problem 9, taking 2 months hence for focal date.

11. Commute two debts of $400 each, due 2 and 5 months hence, into two payments due 3 and 9 months hence, the second being $100 more than the first. Assume money worth 6% and take 9 months hence for focal date. [*Hint.* If the first payment is x, the second is $x + 100$.]

12. Work Problem 11 if the second payment is twice the first.

13. A man was to pay $800 in 8 months with 5% interest for 8 months. He arranges to pay $200 in 2 months and the balance in 5 months. Money being worth 8%, how much is this balance if the original debt and the new set are to be equivalent 5 months hence?

14. B borrows $900 promising to pay $300 in 2 months and $600 in 8 months, both with 8% interest. What single payment 6 months hence is equivalent at that date to the original set? Assume money worth 6%.

15. Debts of $300 and $500 are due in 3 and 6 months. Find what money is worth if a single payment of $830 in 12 months is equivalent at that date to the original set.

16. A payment of $600 due in x months is equivalent 8 months hence to the two payments: $200 due in 2 months and $420 due in 10 months. Find x if money is worth 6%. (Note that x is less than 6.)

47. Equation of accounts

In the general case of commuting obligations as presented in Art. 46, the sum of the values of the obligations at their respective *due dates* in one set is unequal to the corresponding sum for the other set. We shall now treat the special case where the two sums in question are equal. We shall again consider only short-term obligations and use an equation of value based on simple interest.

Equation of accounts is the process of finding the date, called the **equated date,** at which (a) a set of obligations due at different times can be equitably discharged by a single payment *equal* to the sum of all the obligations, or (b) an account having both debits and credits can be equitably settled by a single payment *equal* to the balance of the account.

Case (a)

Suppose debts of P_1, P_2, P_3, due, respectively, n_1, n_2, n_3 years hence, are to be discharged by a single payment $P = P_1 + P_2 + P_3$. Let n denote the unknown number of years in the **equated time,** that is, the time extending from the present to the equated date. Then n is to be so determined that the single payment P (due n years hence) and the set consisting of P_1, P_2, P_3 (due n_1, n_2, n_3 years hence) will be *equivalent* at a given focal date; in other words, n must be such that the value (at the focal date) of the single payment will *equal* the sum of the values (at the focal date) of the debts in the original set. We take for focal date the *latest* of all the dates at which the debts are due. Suppose this latest date is n_3 years hence. As in Art. 46, we may prepare a table of values at the focal date, assuming money to be worth i.

FOCAL DATE: n_3 YEARS HENCE

Original Set of Obligations	Value of Each at Focal Date	Single Payment	Value at Focal Date
P_1 due in n_1 years P_2 due in n_2 years P_3 due in n_3 years	$P_1[1 + (n_3 - n_1)i]$ $P_2[1 + (n_3 - n_2)i]$ P_3	P due in n years	$P[1 + (n_3 - n)i]$

We selected the *latest* of all dates as focal date because the number in parentheses, $n_3 - n_1$, $n_3 - n_2$, $n_3 - n$, must be positive to make the argument valid. The equation of value is

$$P_1[1 + (n_3 - n_1)i] + P_2[1 + (n_3 - n_2)i] + P_3 = P[1 + (n_3 - n)i],$$

where $P = P_1 + P_2 + P_3$. It is left as an exercise to show that by expanding, collecting terms, and solving for n, we get

$$n = \frac{P_1 n_1 + P_2 n_2 + P_3 n_3}{P_1 + P_2 + P_3}. \tag{13}$$

Note that formula (13) is independent of the interest rate. For short-term obligations, n, n_1, n_2, and n_3 are fractions of a year. Since multiplying both members of (13) by 12 or 360 does not destroy the equality, these letters may also represent number of months or number of days, *provided* the same unit of time is used throughout the formula.

Case (b)

Suppose debts of P_1, P_2, P_3 are due in n_1, n_2, n_3 years and the debtor arranges for payments C_1, C_2 in m_1, m_2 years to apply on these debts. By a reasoning similar to that used in case (a), it can be shown that the equated time n for settling this account by a single payment equal to the balance $P_1 + P_2 + P_3 - (C_1 + C_2)$ is given by

$$n = \frac{P_1 n_1 + P_2 n_2 + P_3 n_3 - (C_1 m_1 + C_2 m_2)}{P_1 + P_2 + P_3 - (C_1 + C_2)}. \tag{14}$$

The remarks made in connection with formula (13) apply also to formula (14). If n is negative, count backward from the present. For convenience, we assumed three P's in both cases and two C's in case (b). The reasoning and steps in derivation are essentially the same for a different number of P's or C's or both. Hence formula (13) may be extended to any number of P's; (14), to any number of P's and C's.

ILLUSTRATIVE EXAMPLE 1. Find the equated date for discharging by a single payment debts of $600, $400, and $1000 due in 30, 45, and 90 days.

SOLUTION. Here $P_1 = 600$, $n_1 = 30$, $P_2 = 400$, $n_2 = 45$, $P_3 = 1000$, $n_3 = 90$. Substituting these in (13), we have

$$n = \frac{(600 \times 30) + (400 \times 45) + (1000 \times 90)}{600 + 400 + 1000} = \frac{126000}{2000} = 63.$$

Therefore the single payment of $2000 should be made 63 days hence.

_____

ILLUSTRATIVE EXAMPLE 2. Merchandise bought: March 16, $2000; April 20, $1200. Payments made: March 25, $1000; April 15, $500; April 30, $200. Find the equated date for the payment of the balance.

SOLUTION. For convenience, let the earliest date (March 16) be the present. Then $P_1 = 2000$, $n_1 = 0$, $P_2 = 1200$, $n_2 = 35$; $C_1 = 1000$, $m_1 = 9$, $C_2 = 500$, $m_2 = 30$, $C_3 = 200$, $m_3 = 45$. Substitution in an *extension* of (14) gives:

$$n = \frac{(2000 \times 0) + (1200 \times 35) - [(1000 \times 9) + (500 \times 30) + (200 \times 45)]}{2000 + 1200 - (1000 + 500 + 200)}$$

$$= \frac{42000 - 33000}{3200 - 1700} = \frac{9000}{1500} = 6.$$

Hence the equated date is 6 days after March 16, or March 22. Note that an account becomes interest-bearing *at* the equated date. It is possible that the above account was equated some time in May. Then the debtor should pay not only the balance of $1500, but also interest on $1500 from March 22 to the date of paying the balance.

_____

EXERCISE 32

1. Find equated date for paying in one sum a debt of $150 due in 30 days, one of $200 due in 45 days, and one of $300 due in 60 days.

2. Find equated date for paying in one sum 4 successive monthly install-ments of $200, $500, $800, and $900, the first due in 1 month.

3. In Illustrative example 1, show that a $2000 payment in 63 days and the 3 debts are equivalent 90 days hence. (Use any i; e.g., 6%.)

4. In Illustrative example 2, show that the set of payments (including $1500 on March 22) and the set of debts are equivalent on April 30.

5. Find equated date for paying in one sum 4 successive monthly intall-ments of $600, $500, $400, and $300, the first due in 3 months.

6. What is the equated date for discharging by a single payment debts of $300, $500, and $700 due in 10, 30, and 60 days?

7. A grocer buys merchandise on 10 days' credit as follows: Sept. 18, a bill for $560; Oct. 8, a bill for $240; Nov. 19, a bill for $400. What is the equated date for a single payment of $1200? (Find due dates first.)

8. A dealer buys goods as follows: May 5, $360, $n/10$; June 9, $440, $n/15$. Find equated date for a single payment of $800. (Use due dates.)

9. If the payment in Problem 7 is made on Dec. 15 instead of at the equated date, how large should it be? Assume money worth 6%.

10. If the payment in Problem 8 is made on July 21 instead of at the equated date, how large should it be? Assume money worth 6%.

11. Debit: May 13, $2500. Credits: June 2, $800; July 2, $500; July 22, $200. Find equated date for payment of balance.

12. Merchandise bought: Aug. 3, $600; Sept. 7, $400; Oct. 2, $800. Payments made: Sept. 22, $500; Oct. 12, $700. What is the equated date for settling this account in a single sum?

13. For goods bought, a merchant owes $750 on April 5 and $550 on April 21. On May 16 he accepts a 5-day "after sight" draft for $800 and pays it on time. How much interest at 3% should he pay in addition to the $500 balance if the account is settled on June 8?

14. To apply on a debt of $1000 due Aug. 1, a man pays $300 on July 15 and $400 on Aug. 16. How much interest at 5% should he pay in addition to the $300 balance if the account is settled on Sept. 5?

15. Solve, for n, the equation preceding formula (13), showing all steps. Examining these steps carefully, show that, although independent of interest rate, formula (13) does not hold when $i = 0$.

16. To apply on a debt of P due in m years, a payment of C will be made in k years, where $m > k$. Find the equated time n for the balance $P - C$ by taking m years hence for focal date. Do not use (14), but show details of reasoning and all steps.

MISCELLANEOUS EXERCISE 33
REVIEW OF CHAPTER 4

1. If interest at 6% is $54.48, what would it be (a) at 6%? (b) at 7%? (c) at $6\frac{3}{4}$%? (d) at $4\frac{1}{4}$%?

2. If interest for 60 days is $79.20, find it (a) for 80 days; (b) for 45 days; (c) for 69 days; (d) for 18 days.

3. If interest on $800 is $15.60, what would it be on $1000?

4. Find by formula the simple interest and amount of a principal of (a) $1250 for 8 months at $4\frac{1}{2}\%$; (b) $720 for 5 months at 7%.

5. What sum will yield in 3 months (a) $9 at 6%? (b) $4 at 3.2%?

6. In what length of time will $5400 yield $63 interest at $3\frac{1}{2}\%$?

7. At what interest rate will $400 amount to $405 in 90 days?

8. Find the number of days: (a) from Sept. 30 to Dec. 20; (b) from May 1 to Aug. 12; (c) from Nov. 13, 1968, to March 5, 1969.

9. Find by short cut the ordinary interest at 4% on $780 for 70 days.

10. How much is the exact interest in Problem 9?

11. What exact interest corresponds to $94.23 ordinary interest?

12. What ordinary interest corresponds to $14.40 exact interest?

13. A tax bill is subject to a 4% discount if paid in November, no discount if paid in January. What interest rate is equivalent to the saving effected by paying the bill on Nov. 30 instead of Jan. 31?

14. A bank allows ordinary interest at the annual rate of 1% on a depositor's daily balances. Find the interest due July 1 on the following account. Deposits: Jan. 2, $1200; March 3, $450; May 2, $600. Withdrawals: April 2, $200; June 1, $300.

15. Prove that a sum, invested at the simple interest rate i, doubles itself at the end of $1/i$ years.

16. Prove that a sum doubles itself at the end of n years if invested at the simple interest rate $1/n$.

17. "The present value, at 6% interest rate, of $200 due in 4 months is $196.08." Tell what is meant by this and check by multiplication.

18. John is to receive a $500 bequest 18 months hence. How much is the bequest worth now if money earns simple interest at 7%?

19. A debt of $1000 is due in 6 months with interest at 8%. Find the present value (a) at 6% discount rate; (b) at 6% interest rate.

20. A $300 debt due in 3 months may be settled now for $250 at what discount rate? Find the corresponding interest rate.

21. Interest paid in advance is the same as what kind of discount?

22. How does a promissory note differ from a draft?

23. A 2-month 6% interest-bearing note for $1000, dated May 24, has what value on May 24 if money is worth 3%?

24. If the note described in Problem 23 is discounted at a bank on June 5, find the number of days in the period of discount.

25. A man requests a 90-day, $600 loan from a bank charging 5% discount. How much will he pay to the bank at the end of 90 days?

26. In Problem 25, find the bank discount and the proceeds.

27. A 90-day 8% interest-bearing note for $1200, dated Oct. 1, is discounted at 6% on Nov. 10. How much does the holder receive?

28. In Problem 27, what does the original maker pay at the due date?

29. A non-interest-bearing note was discounted at 7% 60 days before maturity. Find the face value of the note if the discount was $12.

30. Mr. Hill wishes to receive $800 as the proceeds of a 90-day loan. If the bank's discount rate is 6%, what loan should he request?

31. A 60-day trade acceptance for $630, dated June 7, is discounted at 4% on June 17. Find the proceeds.

32. In making 3-month loans, a money-lender collects 8% interest at the end of 3 months. This corresponds to what discount rate?

33. At what rate does a bank earn interest in discounting a note: (a) for 120 days at $7\frac{1}{2}$%? (b) for 45 days at 8%?

34. A 60-day draft, dated Aug. 15 and accepted on Aug. 20, is discounted on Sept. 12. How long is the period of discount if the draft is (a) "after sight"? (b) "after date"?

35. A 2-month 5% interest-bearing note for $3600, dated March 8, is discounted at 7% on April 2. Find the proceeds.

36. Prove that: (a) $(1 - nd)(1 + ni) = 1$; (b) $P_b ni = D_b(1 - nd)$.

37. Let P be the present value at the interest rate r of a debt S due in n years, and let P_b be the present value of S at the discount rate r. Prove that P and P_b are related by: $P_b = P(1 - n^2 r^2)$.

38. In Problem 37 show that $D_b = D_s(1 + nr)$.

39. What annual interest rate is equivalent to (a) $6\frac{1}{2}\%$ cash discount on a 30-day bill? (b) 4% cash discount on a 15-day bill?

40. On Aug. 7 a dealer buys goods for $750 from a firm offering terms: "cash 3, n/30" and charging 8% interest for delinquency. What does he pay if he settles the bill on: (a) Aug. 7? (b) Sept. 1? (c) Sept. 30?

41. A dealer buys merchandise for $4000 on the terms 6/10, n/60. He pays $2540 on the 8th day. How much more is due on the 60th day?

42. Electric appliances are purchased on the terms 4/5, 2/15, n/45. What is the annual interest rate equivalent to each offer?

43. Find the single discount rate equivalent to each series: (a) 12% and 10%; (b) 20%, 20%, and 10%; (c) 10%, 10%, 15%, and 20%.

44. After discounts of 20% and 10%, the net price of a ring was $34. Find: (a) the list price; (b) the ratio of net price to list price.

45. Dining room furniture is sold to a jobber at $800 per set less 25% and 15%. To gain 20% of his net purchase price after allowing a 10% trade discount to his customers, at what price should he list a set?

46. A wholesaler buys rugs at $400 less 10% and $16\frac{2}{3}\%$. Find his own selling price if it is to cover overhead expenses of 5% and to yield a net profit of 15%, both based on his selling price.

47. A student borrows $300 at 8% on May 19. He pays $100 on each of the following dates: July 18, Sept. 1, and Oct. 1. Find the balance due on Nov. 15 by the Merchant's Rule.

48. Work Problem 47 by the United States Rule.

49. The trustees of a church borrow $3000 at 6% and agree to make a $400 payment at the end of each month. How much is still due at the end of the 6th month by the United States Rule?

50. Work Problem 49 by the Merchant's Rule.

51. A non-interest-bearing debt of $1000 is due 8 months hence. Assuming money worth 6%, what is the value of this obligation: (a) 5 months hence? (b) 8 months hence? (c) 1 year hence?

52. Work Problem 51 if the debt bears $7\frac{1}{2}\%$ interest for 8 months.

53. Money being worth 8%, commute a debt of $600 due 6 months hence into two payments due 3 and 12 months hence, the first being twice as large as the second. Take 12 months hence for focal date.

54. Work Problem 53 if the second payment is $55 less than the first.

55. Work Problem 53, taking 6 months hence for focal date.

56. A man owes two debts of $400 and $800 due 2 and 6 months hence. He wishes to pay $600 4 months hence and the balance 8 months hence. If money is worth 6%, so determine this balance as to make the two sets equivalent: (a) 4 months hence; (b) 6 months hence; (c) 8 months hence.

57. Find the equated date for paying in one sum a debt of $300 due in 30 days, one of $100 due in 60 days, and one of $400 due in 90 days.

58. Find the equated date for paying in one sum 4 successive monthly installments of $300, $350, $400, and $450, the first due in 1 month.

59. Debits: April 18, $700; July 5, $200. Credits: May 1, $500; June 15, $100. Find the equated date for paying the $300 balance.

60. Merchandise bought: Aug. 1, $700; Oct. 5, $400; Nov. 1, $100. Paid: Oct. 10, $700. Find the equated date for paying the $500 balance.

61. A contract calls for 7 monthly payments of $100 each, the first due now. Find the equated date for a single payment of $700.

62. If money is worth 6%, what single payment 4 months hence is equivalent to 6 monthly payments of $100 each, the first due now? Take 4 months hence for focal date.

63. A man is obligated to pay $1000 6 months hence. He arranges to pay $100 now and $200 2 months hence. Find the equated date for paying the balance of $700.

64. A 75-day 5% interest-bearing note for $750 is discounted at a bank 30 days before maturity. The proceeds are $758.08. Find the bank's discount rate.

65. The bank discount is $1.35 and the proceeds are $201.65 when a 90-day interest-bearing note for $200 is discounted 30 days before due date. Find the interest rate of the note and the bank's discount rate.

66. A money-lender deducts $6 interest in advance on a 3-month loan of $100. This is equivalent to what interest rate?

67. $500 is due 6 months hence. If money is worth 8%, the present value of this obligation is what per cent of its value 1 year hence?

68. The equated date for paying in one sum a debt of $200 due in 20 days and one of $X due in 60 days is 50 days hence. Find X.

69. Let x denote a $100 payment now; y, a $106 payment 6 months hence. If money is worth 6%, x and y are equivalent at what two dates? Is there any other date at which x and y are equivalent?

70. In formula (13) of Art. 47, let $P_2 = 2P_1$ and $P_3 = 3P_1$. For this special case, show that $n = \frac{1}{6}(n_1 + 2n_2 + 3n_3)$.

71. In formula (11) of Art. 44, let $n = 2$ and $r_2 = r_1$. For this special case, show that $r = r_1(2 - r_1)$.

72. Let i be the interest rate corresponding to the discount rate d. Show that the ratio of i to d is $1 + ni$.

73. Let d be the discount rate corresponding to the interest rate i. Show that the ratio of d to i is $1 - nd$.

74. Prove that $P: S = d:i$ if P is the present value, at the interest rate i, of S due in n years; d, the corresponding discount rate.

75. One payment of $P = P_1 + P_2 + P_3$ is to discharge debts of P_1, P_2, P_3 due n_1, n_2, n_3 years hence, where $n_2 > n_1$, $n_2 > n_3$. Find the equated time n for P by taking n_2 years hence for focal date.

Chapter FIVE

EXPONENTS AND RADICALS

48. Importance of the chapter

A good working knowledge of exponents is one of the essentials in the study of the mathematics of finance. Such topics as compound interest, annuities, bond valuation, and depreciation require computations which would be exceedingly long and difficult by ordinary arithmetic methods. These computations can be made rather easily by means of logarithms and a number of tables. But logarithms themselves are exponents, and will be considered in Chapter 9.

The meaning of integral exponents was given in Chapter 1. Two simple laws of exponents were also given. The present chapter will give the student a review of, and an extension to, his previous knowledge.

49. Operations with exponentials

An **exponential** is the expression of an indicated power of a given number. In the exponential a^x, a is the **base** and x the **exponent.** The exponentials a^x, a^{2x}, a^y, and a^z have **like** bases, a. The exponentials a^x, b^x, and c^x have **like** exponents, x, and **unlike** bases, a, b, c, when a, b, and c are distinct numbers. A word of caution is perhaps necessary here: *An exponent belongs only to the number or quantity to which it is attached.* Thus, $3 \cdot 4^2$ means $3 \cdot 16 = 48$; while $(3 \cdot 4)^2$ means $12^2 = 144$. Similarly, -4^2 means -16, while $(-4)^2 = +16$. Again, $P(1 + i)^3$ means $P(1 + i)(1 + i)(1 + i)$, and *not* the cube of $P(1 + i)$.

Operations with exponentials are governed by the following five **laws of exponents,** which we state without proof.

Multiplication and Division of Exponentials with Like Bases

I. $a^x \cdot a^y = a^{x+y}$.

II. $\dfrac{a^x}{a^y} = a^{x-y}$, $a \neq 0$.

Multiplication and Division of Exponentials with Like Exponents

III. $a^x \cdot b^x = (ab)^x$, $x \neq -1$ if $ab = 0$.

IV. $\dfrac{a^x}{b^x} = \left(\dfrac{a}{b}\right)^x$, $b \neq 0$.

Raising an Exponential to a Required Power

V. $(a^x)^p = a^{px}$.

It is left as an exercise to translate the above five laws from algebraic symbols into word language, and to establish their validity when the exponents x, y, and p are *positive whole numbers*, and in Law II when x is greater than y.

ILLUSTRATIVE EXAMPLES

1. $3^m \cdot 3^n = 3^{m+n}$.

2. $\dfrac{5^m}{5^n} = 5^{m-n}$.

3. $(x^4)^2 = x^{4 \cdot 2} = x^8$.

4. $\left(\dfrac{x^2}{y}\right)^4 = \dfrac{(x^2)^4}{y^4} = \dfrac{x^8}{y^4}$.

5. $(3ab)^d = 3^d a^d b^d$.

6. $3^m + 3^n$.   Cannot be simplified.

7. $5^m - 5^n$.   Cannot be simplified.

8. $\left(\dfrac{r^2 s}{rs^2}\right)^5 = \left(\dfrac{r}{s}\right)^5 = \dfrac{r^5}{s^5}$.

9. $\left(\dfrac{-2x^2 y}{a^3}\right)^5 = \dfrac{-32x^{10} y^5}{a^{15}}$.

10. $(3 + a - b)^d$.   Cannot be simplified.

EXERCISE 34

Perform indicated operations and simplify when possible.

1. $b^5 \cdot b^3$.

2. $m^3 \cdot m^4$.

3. $a^4 \cdot b^2$.

4. $p^3 \cdot q^3$.

5. $2^6 \cdot 2^3$.

6. $3^2 \cdot 4^2$.

7. $8^3 \div 4^3$.

8. $5^5 \div 5^3$.

9. $c^2 \div c^4$.

10. $r^7 \div s^7$.

11. $x^n \cdot x^{2n+1}$.

12. $b^{2n-1} \cdot b^2$.

13. $(-a)^2 \cdot (-a)^5$.

14. $(-a)^5 \cdot (-a)$.

15. $(a-b)^3 \cdot (a-b)^2$.

16. $(a+b)^3 \cdot (a-b)^3$.

17. $(1+i)^5 \div (1+i)^4$.

18. $(3x+y)^7 \div (3x+y)^3$.

19. $(a-b)^3 \div (b-a)^2$.

20. $(m^2-n^2) \div (m-n)^2$.

21. $(x^4)^3 - (x^3)^4$.

22. $(2x^6)^2 + (x^4)^3$.

23. $(-xy^2)^3 \div (-x^2y)^3$.

24. $(-a^2b)^5 \div (a^2b)^2$.

25. $(\frac{2}{3})^4 \cdot (\frac{3}{2})^2$.

26. $(1 - \frac{1}{2})^3 \cdot (1 + \frac{1}{2})^3$.

27. $(-2abc)^3 \div (2abc)$.

28. $(m^2n)^3 \div (-mn^2)^2$.

29. $(\frac{1}{4})^m \cdot (\frac{1}{2})^{3n}$.

30. $(\frac{8}{3})^m \cdot (\frac{3}{4})^m$.

31. $\left(\frac{-2x}{3y^2}\right)^4$.

32. $\left(\frac{-pq^2}{2rs}\right)^3$.

33. $\frac{(2a-b)^m}{2a-b}$.

34. $x^{3n} \cdot x^{2n} \cdot x^n$.

35. $\frac{64a^3b^4c^5}{16ab^3c^2}$.

36. $\frac{(3x^2y)^4}{(3xy^2)^3}$.

37. $\frac{P(1+i)^{3n}}{(1+i)^{n-1}}$.

38. $(-3)^2 \cdot (-2)^3$.

39. $\frac{(a^2)^4}{a^8b^2}$.

40. $\frac{P(1+i)^{2n}}{(1+i)^{n+1}}$.

41. $\frac{(2\frac{1}{2})^3 \cdot (\frac{2}{5})^3}{(\frac{1}{2})^3}$.

42. $(ax^2)(ax)^2 \div a^2x$.

50. Roots. Classification of numbers

A **root** of a number is one of the equal factors whose product is the given number. Thus, 5 is a cube root of 125, because $125 = 5 \cdot 5 \cdot 5$.

Either a positive or a negative number raised to an even power is equal to a *positive* number. Hence, in the ordinary sense, a *negative* number cannot have an *even* root. Such roots are merely indicated and are called **imaginary numbers.** Thus, the square root of -4 is neither $+2$ nor -2, since $(+2)(+2) = 4$, and $(-2)(-2) = 4$. Hence, $\sqrt{-4}$ is an imaginary number. Other examples are: $\sqrt{-1}$, $\sqrt[4]{-3}$, $\sqrt[6]{-10}$, and so on. But note that $\sqrt[3]{-8} = -2$, since $(-2)(-2)(-2) = -8$. In this case we have an *odd* root of a negative number. In our particular work, there is no need for imaginary numbers, but they are of great importance in other branches of mathematics, pure and applied. We deal here with real numbers only.

A **real number** is any number that is a whole number or is expressible by use of decimals. Thus, 5, -3, $\sqrt{13}$, and $\sqrt[3]{-15}$ are real numbers.

A **rational number** is any real number that can be expressed as the quotient of two whole numbers. 8, -9, $\frac{2}{3}$, $\sqrt{4}$, and 0.063 are examples of rational numbers. An **irrational number** is any real number that is not rational. For example, $\sqrt{3}$, $\sqrt[3]{5}$, $-7\sqrt{5}$, and $\sqrt{\frac{2}{3}}$ are irrational numbers.

It is shown in higher algebra that every real number has n distinct nth roots; none, some, or all of which may be imaginary numbers. Thus, 4 has two square roots, $+2$ and -2; -27 has three cube roots, -3, and two others that are imaginary; 81 has four fourth roots, $+3$, -3, and two others that are imaginary; -16 has two square roots, both imaginary.

If a number has *only one real root*, positive or negative, we shall call this its **principal root.** Thus, the principal cube root of -8 is -2, and the principal cube root of $+8$ is $+2$. If a number has *two real roots*, one positive and one negative, its **principal root** will be the positive one. Thus, the principal square root of 9 is $+3$.

We shall agree that *the radical sign indicates the principal root.* Thus, $\sqrt{9} = +3$, and not -3. To indicate the negative square root of 9, we shall write $-\sqrt{9} = -3$. To indicate both roots, we shall write $\pm\sqrt{9} = \pm3$.

51. Fractional, zero, and negative exponents

It should be observed that the meaning of a *positive* integral exponent *cannot* apply to other types of exponents. Thus, in 4^3, the exponent shows that 4 is taken three times as a factor, giving $4 \times 4 \times 4 = 64$. According to this definition of an exponent, such expressions as 4^0, 4^{-3}, and $4^{1/3}$ would be absurd, since the exponents 0, -3, and $\frac{1}{3}$ cannot show how many times 4 is taken as a factor. However, exponentials similar to the above are not to be discarded as useless or meaningless. Indeed, by broadening the definition of an exponent, the use of fractional numbers, zero, and negative numbers as exponents can be of great convenience in mathematical work. For the sake of consistency, it is natural to define these new kinds of exponents in such a way that the laws for positive integral exponents will hold also for them.

(a) Meaning of a Fractional Exponent

If $a^{1/2}$ is to obey Law I of Art. 49, then $a^{1/2} \cdot a^{1/2} = a^{1/2+1/2} = a^1 = a$. Since $a^{1/2}$ is one of the two equal factors whose product is a, we shall take $a^{1/2}$ to mean the principal square root of a, that is $a^{1/2} = \sqrt{a}$. Again, $a^{5/3} \cdot a^{5/3} \cdot a^{5/3} = a^{5/3+5/3+5/3} = a^{15/3} = a^5$. Since $a^{5/3}$ is one of the three equal factors whose product is a^5, we shall take $a^{5/3}$ to mean $(\sqrt[3]{a})^5$. In general, we shall define

$$a^{p/q} = (\sqrt[q]{a})^p.$$

In fractional exponents, then, the numerator of the exponent indicates the power to which the base is to be raised, and the denominator indicates the root to be extracted. These are inverse operations, and if p/q is a fraction in lowest terms and if real numbers and principal roots only are considered, then $\sqrt[q]{a^p} = (\sqrt[q]{a})^p$. That is, in this case, the operation may be performed in either order.

(b) Meaning of a Zero Exponent

If a^0 is to obey Law I of Art. 49, then $a^0 \cdot a^x = a^{0+x} = a^x$. Hence, by definition,

$$a^0 = 1, \qquad a \neq 0.$$

In words, *any number, except* 0, *raised to the zero power is equal to* 1. Thus, $5^0 = 1$, $(-3)^0 = 1$, $(0.059)^0 = 1$.

(c) Meaning of a Negative Exponent

If a^{-x}, where x is a positive number, is to obey Law I of Art. 49, then $a^{-x} \cdot a^x = a^{-x+x} = a^0 = 1$. Hence, by definition,

$$a^{-x} = \frac{1}{a^x}, \qquad a \neq 0.$$

In words, *a number raised to a negative power is equal to* 1 *divided by the same number raised to the* **corresponding positive power.** Thus,

$$2^{-3} = \frac{1}{2^3} = \frac{1}{8}; \quad a^{-4} = \frac{1}{a^4}; \quad 8^{-2/3} = \frac{1}{8^{2/3}} = \frac{1}{4}.$$

It can be shown that the meanings for fractional, zero, and negative exponents are consistent with the other laws of exponents also, but the proof is beyond the scope of this book.

EXERCISE 35

Problems 1 to 6, oral.

1. Tell the value of each indicated principal root: $\sqrt{16}$, $\sqrt[5]{-32}$, $\sqrt[4]{1}$, $\sqrt[3]{-1}$, $\sqrt{100}$, $\sqrt[4]{81}$, $\sqrt[3]{-8}$, $\sqrt[4]{16}$, $\sqrt[3]{64}$, $\sqrt{49}$.

2. Tell whether the given number is real rational, real irrational, or imaginary: $\sqrt{3}$, $\sqrt{-3}$, -3, $\sqrt[3]{-3}$, $\sqrt[4]{-1}$, π, 3.1, $\frac{2}{3}$, $\sqrt{-9}$, $\sqrt{2}$.

3. Give the meaning of: $a^{3/2}$, $b^{2/3}$, $(x+y)^{1/4}$, $x^{4/5}$, $a^{1/3}$, $b^{1/2}$.

4. Give the meaning of: x^{-2}, y^{-1}, $a^{-1/2}$, $(1+i)^{-12}$, $b^{-2/3}$, $c^{-3/4}$.

5. Tell the value of: $8^{1/3}$, $(-8)^{2/3}$, $16^{3/2}$, $(2.25)^{1/2}$, 6^{-1}, $(-7)^0$, $1^{1/2}$.

6. Tell the value of: -7^0, $9^{-1/2}$, $16^{3/4}$, $(1.2)^{-2}$, $(\frac{3}{2})^{-3}$, $81^{-3/4}$, $(\frac{2}{5})^{-1}$.

Express with radical signs:

7. $9b^{1/2}$.   **11.** $(9b)^{1/2}$.   **15.** $2bc^{1/3}$.   **19.** $(a^2+b^2)^{1/2}$.

8. $ax^{1/2}$.   **12.** $(4xy)^{3/2}$.   **16.** $xy^{-1/2}z$.   **20.** $(m^3-n^3)^{1/3}$.

9. $xy^{3/2}$.   **13.** $(2bc)^{2/3}$.   **17.** $3ax^{-1/2}$.   **21.** $(1+i)^{1/6}$.

10. $8b^{2/3}$.   **14.** $(8b)^{2/3}$.   **18.** $5(8x)^{2/3}$ **22.** $(1+i)^{-3/4}$.

Express with fractional exponents:

23. $a\sqrt{b}$.   **27.** $\sqrt{(x-y)^3}$.   **31.** $4\sqrt[5]{(m+n)^3}$.

24. $\sqrt{ab}$.   **28.** $\sqrt[3]{(a-b)^2}$.   **32.** $\sqrt{(p-q)^m}$.

25. $\sqrt[4]{xy^3}$.   **29.** $\sqrt[5]{(1+i)^3}$.   **33.** $x\sqrt{y}\cdot\sqrt[4]{a+b}$.

26. $x\sqrt[3]{y^2}$.   **30.** $\sqrt[5]{(1+i)^2}$.   **34.** $\sqrt{x-y}\cdot a\sqrt[3]{b}$.

Express with positive exponents:

35. $(x+y)^{-3/2}$.   **39.** $\sqrt{(1+i)^{-3}}$.   **43.** $15^{-1/2}$.

36. $x+y^{-3/2}$.   **40.** $\sqrt[3]{(1+i)^{-4}}$.   **44.** $2a^{-1/2}$.

37. $a^{-1/3}+b^{-1/2}$.   **41.** $\sqrt{x^2+y^3}$.   **45.** $4\sqrt[5]{c^{-2}}$.

38. $a^{-2}+a^{1/2}$.   **42.** $\sqrt[3]{x^3+y^3}$.   **46.** $p^{-3}+q^{-3}$.

Express without fractions and without radicals:

47. $\dfrac{x}{y^2}$.   **51.** $\dfrac{\sqrt{xy}}{z}$.   **55.** $\dfrac{\sqrt{m-n}}{x^2}$.   **59.** $a^{-1}+\dfrac{1}{a}$.

48. $\dfrac{x^2}{y}$.   **52.** $\dfrac{3a}{\sqrt{b}}$.   **56.** $\dfrac{\sqrt[3]{a-b}}{x^{-1/2}}$ **60.** $\sqrt{ab}-\dfrac{1}{\sqrt{ab}}$.

49. $\dfrac{a^3}{4ab}$.   **53.** $\dfrac{\sqrt[3]{pq}}{\sqrt[3]{x^2}}$.   **57.** $\dfrac{1}{\sqrt{x^2+y^3}}$.   **61.** $\dfrac{(1+i)^8-1}{(1+i)^8}$.

50. $\dfrac{5a}{b^2}$.   **54.** $\dfrac{\sqrt[3]{x^2}}{\sqrt{pq}}$.   **58.** $\dfrac{1}{x^{-2}+y^{-2}}$.   **62.** $\dfrac{1-(1+i)^{-8}}{(1+i)^{-8}}$.

Find the value of each expression by simplifying the terms or factors involved and then performing the indicated operations:

63. $25^{1/2} + 8^{1/3} - 3\sqrt[4]{16}.$

64. $\sqrt{144} - \sqrt[3]{64} + 9^{3/2}.$

65. $\sqrt{64} + \sqrt{49} \cdot \sqrt[3]{27} - \sqrt{36}.$

66. $(-8)^{2/3} \cdot \sqrt{25} + 8^0 - 1^{-2}.$

67. $13^0 \cdot (169)^{1/2} \cdot 4^{-1/2}.$

68. $6^{-1} \cdot (216)^{1/3} \cdot (36)^{3/2}.$

69. $4(64)^{2/3} \div [4^0 + \sqrt[4]{81}].$

70. $[49^{1/2} - 7^0] \div 7^{-1}.$

71. $(1 - r)^{3/2},$ when $r = 0.19.$

72. $(3 + x)^{2/3},$ when $x = \frac{3}{8}.$

52. Operations involving fractional, zero, and negative exponents

Fractional, zero, and negative exponents are defined in such a way that they obey the five laws of exponents. Hence we can operate with them in the same way as we operate with positive integral exponents.

ILLUSTRATIVE EXAMPLES

1. $x^{-3} \cdot x^8 = x^{-3+8} = x^5.$

2. $a^7 \div a^{-2} = a^{7-(-2)} = a^9.$

3. $(m^{-3})^{2/3} = m^{-3 \cdot 2/3} = m^{-2} = \dfrac{1}{m^2}.$

4. $(a + b)^{5/4} \div (a + b)^{1/4} = (a + b)^{5/4-1/4} = (a + b)^1 = a + b.$

5. $\left(\dfrac{x^2 y}{d}\right)^{3/2} = \dfrac{(x^2 y)^{3/2}}{d^{3/2}} = \dfrac{x^3 y^{3/2}}{d^{3/2}}.$

6. $p^{5/2} \cdot p^{-1/2} = p^{5/2-1/2} = p^2.$

7. $(x^{-1} + y^{-1})^2 = x^{-2} + 2x^{-1}y^{-1} + y^{-2} = \dfrac{1}{x^2} + \dfrac{2}{xy} + \dfrac{1}{y^2}.$

8. $\dfrac{3a^{-4}}{b^{-3}} = \dfrac{3a^{-4}}{b^{-3}} \cdot \dfrac{a^4 b^3}{a^4 b^3} = \dfrac{3a^0 b^3}{a^4 b^0} = \dfrac{3b^3}{a^4}.$

9. $(x^{1/4} + 1 + x^{-1/2})x^{3/4} = x^{1/4+3/4} + x^{3/4} + x^{-1/2+3/4}$
$$= x + x^{3/4} + x^{1/4}.$$

10. $\dfrac{c^{-2} + b^{-2}}{d} = \dfrac{\dfrac{1}{c^2} + \dfrac{1}{b^2}}{d} = \dfrac{b^2 c^2 \left(\dfrac{1}{c^2} + \dfrac{1}{b^2}\right)}{b^2 c^2 d} = \dfrac{b^2 + c^2}{b^2 c^2 d}$

53. Operations with radicals

A **radical** is an indicated root of a number or algebraic expression. The number or expression under the radical sign is called the **radicand.** The index of the radical gives the **order** of the radical. Thus, $\sqrt[3]{a^2x}$ is a radical of the third order, and a^2x is the radicand; $\sqrt{a+b}$ is a radical of the second order with radicand $a + b$ Radicals can often be simplified by using the relation

$$\sqrt[n]{ab} = (ab)^{1/n} = a^{1/n} \cdot b^{1/n} = \sqrt[n]{a} \cdot \sqrt[n]{b}.$$

Thus, $\sqrt{x^2y} = \sqrt{x^2} \cdot \sqrt{y} = x\sqrt{y}$; $\sqrt[3]{16} = \sqrt[3]{8 \cdot 2} = \sqrt[3]{8} \cdot \sqrt[3]{2} = 2\sqrt[3]{2}$.

Two or more radicals are said to be **similar** if they have the same order and the same radicand when simplified. Thus, $3\sqrt{5}$ and $-2\sqrt{5}$ are similar.

To add or subtract radicals, simplify each radical, when possible, and combine *only* the similar radicals.

To multiply radicals of the same order, multiply the radicands and write the product under the common radical sign; and then take the product of the coefficients of the radical factors for the coefficient of the resulting radical.

An important process in connection with *division of radicals of the second order* is to **rationalize** the denominator of a fraction, that is, to rid the denominator of irrational numbers, without changing the value of the fraction.

ILLUSTRATIVE EXAMPLE 1. Simplify $5\sqrt{18} - 4\sqrt{2} + \sqrt{3}$.

SOLUTION. $5\sqrt{18} - 4\sqrt{2} + \sqrt{3} = 5\sqrt{9 \cdot 2} - 4\sqrt{2} + \sqrt{3}$
$$= 15\sqrt{2} - 4\sqrt{2} + \sqrt{3}$$
$$= (15 - 4)\sqrt{2} + \sqrt{3}$$
$$= 11\sqrt{2} + \sqrt{3}. \quad Ans.$$

ILLUSTRATIVE EXAMPLE 2. Simplify $(\sqrt{8} - 5\sqrt{3})\sqrt{2}$.

SOLUTION. $(\sqrt{8} - 5\sqrt{3})\sqrt{2} = \sqrt{8} \cdot \sqrt{2} - 5\sqrt{3} \cdot \sqrt{2}$
$$= \sqrt{16} - 5\sqrt{6} = 4 - 5\sqrt{6}. \quad Ans.$$

ILLUSTRATIVE EXAMPLE 3. Rationalize the denominator of $\dfrac{5}{\sqrt{3}}$.

SOLUTION. $\dfrac{5}{\sqrt{3}} = \dfrac{5}{\sqrt{3}} \cdot \dfrac{\sqrt{3}}{\sqrt{3}} = \dfrac{5\sqrt{3}}{3}. \quad Ans.$

ILLUSTRATIVE EXAMPLE 4. Rationalize the denominator of $\dfrac{5}{6 - \sqrt{2}}$.

SOLUTION. $\dfrac{5}{6 - \sqrt{2}} = \dfrac{5}{6 - \sqrt{2}} \cdot \dfrac{6 + \sqrt{2}}{6 + \sqrt{2}} = \dfrac{5(6 + \sqrt{2})}{(6 - \sqrt{2})(6 + \sqrt{2})}$

$$= \dfrac{30 + 5\sqrt{2}}{36 - 2} = \dfrac{30 + 5\sqrt{2}}{34}. \quad Ans.$$

ILLUSTRATIVE EXAMPLE 5. Solve $(1 + i)^{1/2} - 1 = S$ for i.

SOLUTION. Adding 1 to each member,

$$(1 + i)^{1/2} = S + 1;$$

squaring each member,

$$1 + i = S^2 + 2S + 1.$$

Whence $\qquad\qquad i = S^2 + 2S = S(S + 2). \quad Ans.$

EXERCISE 36

Perform indicated operations and express with positive exponents:

1. $(x^{-3})^{-2}$.

2. $(x^{-1/3})^6$.

3. $(n^{-2/3})^3$.

4. $(n^{-1/2})^{-8}$.

5. $a^6 \div a^{-2}$.

6. $a^{-2} \cdot a^{5/2}$.

7. $\dfrac{(x^2 + y)^{-1}}{(x + y^2)^{-2}}$.

8. $\dfrac{u^2 + v^2}{(uv)^{-2}}$.

9. $(pq^{-2}r^{-1})(pq^2r^{10})$.

10. $pq^2(p^{-1} - q^{-1})$.

11. $(a^{-3} + b^{-2})a^3b^2c$.

12. $(a^{-1} - b)(a^{-1} + b)$.

13. $[(x + y)^{-2/3}]^3$.

14. $[(x - y)^8]^{1/4}$.

15. $\dfrac{a^{2/3} - b^{2/3}}{a^{1/3} - b^{1/3}}$.

16. $\dfrac{a^{-3} - b^{-3}}{a^{-3}b^{-3}}$.

17. $(a^2 + b^{1/2})(a^2 - b^{1/2})$.

18. $a^2b^2(a^{-2} + b^{-2})$.

19. $(x^{-2} + y^{-4}) \div x^{-2}$.

20. $(x^{-3} - 1) \div x^{-5}$.

21. $(\frac{9}{4})^{3/2} \div (\frac{9}{4})^4$.

22. $8^{-4/3} \cdot 8^2 \cdot 8^0$.

23. $\dfrac{(1 + i)^n - 1}{(1 + i)^{-n}}$.

24. $\dfrac{(2^{-1} + 3^{-1})^2}{2^{-2} + 3^{-2}}$.

Simplify:

25. $\sqrt{49} + 3\sqrt{12} - 2\sqrt{18}$.

26. $\sqrt{200} + \sqrt{45} - 2\sqrt{32}$.

27. $\sqrt{150} - 2\sqrt{24} - \sqrt{6}$.

28. $3\sqrt{20} - \sqrt{125} + \sqrt{45}$.

29. $\sqrt[3]{27} + 2\sqrt[3]{108} - 3\sqrt[3]{54}$.

30. $4\sqrt[3]{24} - \sqrt[3]{81} + \sqrt[3]{135}$.

31. $2\sqrt{8} \cdot \sqrt{6} \cdot \sqrt{3}$.

32. $4\sqrt{5} \cdot \sqrt{15} \cdot \sqrt{12}$.

33. $(\sqrt{6} + \sqrt{3})(\sqrt{6} - \sqrt{3})$.

34. $(\sqrt{7} - 2)(2 + \sqrt{7})$.

35. $(2 - \sqrt{3})(3 + \sqrt{3})$.

36. $(1 + \sqrt{2})(3 - \sqrt{8})$.

Rationalize the denominator:

37. $\dfrac{2}{\sqrt{5}}$.   **40.** $\dfrac{5}{2\sqrt{2}}$.   **43.** $\dfrac{1}{\sqrt{2}+1}$.   **46.** $\dfrac{6}{\sqrt{2}-\sqrt{5}}$.

38. $\dfrac{2}{\sqrt{6}}$.   **41.** $\dfrac{2}{3\sqrt{5}}$.   **44.** $\dfrac{2}{3-\sqrt{5}}$.   **47.** $\dfrac{1}{\sqrt{7}+\sqrt{2}}$.

39. $\dfrac{\sqrt{2}}{2\sqrt{3}}$.   **42.** $\dfrac{6\sqrt{2}}{\sqrt{6}}$.   **45.** $\dfrac{5+\sqrt{4}}{\sqrt{4}-1}$.   **48.** $\dfrac{\sqrt{5}-1}{\sqrt{3}+\sqrt{2}}$.

Solve the following for each letter appearing in the right member:

49. $y = 2(1-x)^3$.   **50.** $S = P(1+i)^7$.   **51.** $r = (1+i)^9 - 1$.

52. $S = \dfrac{p^3 - 1}{i}$.   **53.** $A = \dfrac{1-v^5}{2i}$.   **54.** $y = \dfrac{4}{x^{1/2}-1}$.

55. $x = (1 + \tfrac{1}{4}j)^4$.   **56.** $V = C(1-r)^8$.   **57.** $y = (3+x)^2 - 18$.

58. $p^2 = q^{-1/2} + 3$.   **59.** $s^3 = (t+1)^{-1/2}$.   **60.** $u^{1/2} = (v-4)^{-2}$.

MISCELLANEOUS EXERCISE 37
REVIEW OF CHAPTER 5

1. Simplify: (a) $2^x \cdot 2^{3y}$; (b) $5^{4x} \div 5^{x+1}$; (c) $(x^{3/2})^3$; (d) $2^x \cdot 3^x$.

2. Express with radical signs: (a) $5y^{3/4}$; (b) $(ab)^{2/3}$; (c) $S(1+i)^{-1/2}$.

3. Rewrite with fractional exponents: (a) $\sqrt[3]{64xy^2}$; (b) $\sqrt{(a-b)^3}$.

4. Simplify: (a) $\sqrt[3]{16}$; (b) $2\sqrt{27} + 3\sqrt{12}$; (c) $\sqrt{3}\,(5\sqrt{3} - \sqrt{12})$.

5. Solve for x: (a) $x^5 = 243$; (b) $6^{x+4} = 1$; (c) $x^{1/3} = 8$; (d) $16^x = 3$.

6. Tell whether the given number is real rational, real irrational, or imaginary: (a) -9; (b) $\sqrt{-64}$; (c) $\sqrt[3]{-2}$; (d) $\tfrac{4}{3}$; (e) $\sqrt[4]{-16}$; (f) $\tfrac{1}{2}\pi$.

7. Given $\sqrt{3} = 1.73205$. Evaluate to 4 decimals: (a) $\sqrt{48}$; (b) $\sqrt[4]{144}$; (c) $\dfrac{1}{\sqrt{3}}$; (d) $\dfrac{24}{\sqrt{12}}$; (e) $\dfrac{1}{2-\sqrt{3}}$. (The last two without long division.)

8. Solve for n: (a) $4^{2n+1} = 16$; (b) $3 \cdot 8^n = 6$; (c) $x^{-2} \cdot x^{1/2} \cdot x^0 = x^n$.

9. Express with positive exponents and, where possible, simplify: (a) $\dfrac{(x+y)^{2/3}}{(x+y)^{-4/3}}$; (b) $\dfrac{a^{-2}-b^{-2}}{a^{-1}-b^{-3}}$; (c) $\dfrac{1-(1.05)^{-n}}{0.05}$; (d) $\dfrac{(x+y)^2}{xy^{-1}}$; (e) $\dfrac{a^{-2}b}{a+b}$.

10. If $x = 9$, $y = 8$, evaluate: (a) $(4x)^{1/2} - 5y^{1/3}$; (b) $3x^{-1} + (2y)^0$.

11. Solve for m: (a) $(r^m)^2 = r^9$; (b) $4^m \cdot 3^m = 12^{1/2}$; (c) $m^5 \cdot m^2 = 10^7$.

12. Express without a denominator: (a) $\dfrac{a}{x^2 y}$; (b) $\dfrac{S}{(1.01)^{-n}}$; (c) $\dfrac{k}{\sqrt{x^2 + y^2}}$.

13. Given $x^{-1/2} = 5$. Find the value of: (a) $x^{1/2}$; (b) x^{-1}; (c) x^2.

14. Solve for x: (a) $x^5 \div x^{-3} = 7^8$; (b) $6^x \div 2^x = 3^{-5}$; (c) $h^{-x} = 1/h^2$.

15. Rationalize the denominator: (a) $\dfrac{5}{\sqrt{2}}$; (b) $\dfrac{7}{2\sqrt{3}}$; (c) $\dfrac{4}{3 - \sqrt{5}}$.

16. Find the square of: (a) $x^{3/2}$; (b) y^{-4}; (c) $x^{-1} - x$; (d) $3^x + 3^{-x}$.

17. Solve for x: (a) $2\sqrt{3x} = 3$; (b) $(6x)^{2/3} = 4$; (c) $\sqrt{1 - 2x} = 2$.

18. Evaluate: (a) $9^{3/2} - (\tfrac{1}{3})^{-1} + (-8)^{1/3}$; (b) $(\tfrac{1}{2})^{-3} \div (8^{1/3} \cdot 9^0)$.

19. If $i = e^{.05} - 1$, then $(1 + i)^4 = e^x$ where x equals what?

20. Solve for r: (a) $P = S(1 + r)^{-2}$; (b) $x = (1 + 2r)^{1/2} - 1$.

21. Evaluate $P(1 + i)^n$, when $P = 400$, $i = 0.21$, $n = \tfrac{1}{2}$.

22. Find k if the product of $(1.01)^n$ and $1 - (1.01)^{-n}$ is $(1.01)^n - k$.

23. If $210 = 70 (1 + i)^{40}$, then $i = \sqrt[n]{3} - 1$ where n equals what?

24. Solve for n: (a) $2^{15} = 8^n$; (b) $9^{1/8} = 3^n$; (c) $4^n \cdot 2^{-5} = 2^5$.

25. Show that $a^x \cdot a^y = a^{x+y}$ when x and y are positive integers.

26. Prove that $(a^x)^p = a^{px}$ when x and p are positive integers.

Chapter SIX

QUADRATIC EQUATIONS

54. Introduction

An equation that contains the second, but no higher, power of a single variable is called a **quadratic equation** in one variable. Thus, $3x^2 + x = 10$ is a quadratic equation in x.

A quadratic equation is said to be in the **standard form,** if the right member is zero and the left member is arranged in order of descending powers of the unknown. The general quadratic equation, arranged in the standard form, is

$$ax^2 + bx + c = 0,$$

where a may have any real value other than zero, and b and c may have any real values including zero.

A **root** of a quadratic equation is a value of the unknown which satisfies the equation. A quadratic equation in one unknown has two and only two roots. **To solve** a quadratic equation means to find both of its roots. We consider only the cases with real coefficients.

55. Solution by factoring

The left member of a quadratic equation in standard form can sometimes be readily factored into two linear factors. If such is the case, the solution is obtained at once by placing each factor in turn equal to zero. The process is based upon the principle that if the product of two factors is *zero*, one or the other must be equal to zero. This is an important algebraic property

111

of real numbers. It is usually stated as: For any real numbers a and b, $a \cdot b = 0$ if and only if $a = 0$ or $b = 0$.

_____

ILLUSTRATIVE EXAMPLE 1. Solve $x^2 - 5x = 0$.

SOLUTION. Factoring the left member, $x(x - 5) = 0$.
Placing each factor in turn equal to zero, we have

$$x = 0, \text{ or } x - 5 = 0.$$

Hence $x = 0$ or 5 is the solution of the given equation.   *Ans.*

CHECK. Substitute each value separately in the *original* equation:

When $x = 0$, $(0)^2 - 5(0) = 0$; $0 = 0$.
When $x = 5$, $(5)^2 - 5(5) = 0$; $25 - 25 = 0$.

Therefore $x = 0$ or 5 is the correct solution.

_____

ILLUSTRATIVE EXAMPLE 2. Solve $3x^2 + 8x = 3$.

SOLUTION. Arrange the equation in standard form:

$$3x^2 + 8x - 3 = 0.$$

Factor the left member, $(3x - 1)(x + 3) = 0$.
Equate each factor in turn to zero and solve for x:

$$3x - 1 = 0, \text{ or } x + 3 = 0.$$
$$x = \tfrac{1}{3} \text{ or } -3. \quad \textit{Ans.}$$

CHECK. $3(\tfrac{1}{3})^2 + 8(\tfrac{1}{3}) = 3$; $\tfrac{1}{3} + \tfrac{8}{3} = 3$.
      $3(-3)^2 + 8(-3) = 3$; $27 - 24 = 3$.

_____

EXERCISE 38

Solve for x by factoring, and check:

1. $x^2 - 9x + 20 = 0$.   3. $x^2 + 4x = 0$.
2. $x^2 + 5x + 6 = 0$.   4. $x^2 - x = 0$.

5. $x^2 + 6x + 8 = 0.$

6. $x^2 - 7x + 12 = 0.$

7. $3x^2 - 48 = 0.$

8. $4x^2 - 100 = 0.$

9. $5x^2 - 5x = 60.$

10. $3x^2 + 9x = 30.$

11. $2x^2 + 5x - 3 = 0.$

12. $3x^2 - x - 2 = 0.$

13. $3x^2 + x - 10 = 0.$

14. $4x^2 + 5x - 6 = 0.$

15. $9x^2 - 24x + 16 = 0.$

16. $4x^2 + 4x + 1 = 0.$

17. $x^2 + 0.08 = 0.6x.$

18. $x^2 + 0.2x = 0.15.$

19. $x + 6 = 12x^2.$

20. $6x^2 + 4 = 11x.$

21. $x^2 + ax - 12a^2 = 0.$

22. $x^2 - 3bx - 4b^2 = 0.$

23. $3b^2x^2 - 2bx - 8 = 0.$

24. $6a^2x^2 + 5ax - 4 = 0.$

Clear of fractions, solve for x by factoring, and check:

25. $x - 2 + \dfrac{1}{x + 3} = \dfrac{1}{x + 3}.$

26. $\dfrac{x^2 - 3}{x} = \dfrac{2x}{3}.$

27. $\dfrac{3x}{x - 1} - \dfrac{8}{x} = 2.$

28. $\dfrac{4x}{x + 3} - \dfrac{5}{x} = 3.$

29. $\dfrac{x + 2}{x} + \dfrac{12}{x - 2} = -5.$

30. $\dfrac{x - 2}{x - 3} + \dfrac{4}{x} = 3.$

31. $\dfrac{3}{x} - \dfrac{2x}{x + 1} = 2.$

32. $\dfrac{x - 1}{x} + \dfrac{8}{x + 1} = 4.$

33. $\dfrac{x + 1}{x - 1} + \dfrac{x - 1}{x + 1} = 1.$

34. $\dfrac{6x + 5}{2x + 1} - \dfrac{x + 1}{x} = 1.$

56. Solution by formula

Given the general quadratic equation (with real coefficients) $ax^2 + bx + c = 0$. Subtracting c from each member,

$$ax^2 + bx = -c.$$

Dividing each member by a,

$$x^2 + \frac{b}{a}x = -\frac{c}{a}.$$

To make the left member the square of a binomial, we add to both members the square of half the coefficient of x:

$$x^2 + \frac{b}{a}x + \frac{b^2}{4a^2} = \frac{b^2}{4a^2} - \frac{c}{a}.$$

Expressing the left member as the square of a binomial, and combining the two fractions in the right member, we have

$$\left(x + \frac{b}{2a}\right)^2 = \frac{b^2 - 4ac}{4a^2}.$$

If we equate the square roots of each member, each should have the double sign; but since all possible results are obtained by giving the double sign to one member only, we take

$$x + \frac{b}{2a} = \pm\frac{\sqrt{b^2 - 4ac}}{2a}.$$

Solving for x,

$$x = \frac{-b \pm \sqrt{b^2 - 4ac}}{2a}. \qquad \textbf{(F)}$$

The roots of any quadratic equation may be found either by the process of **completing the square** shown above, or, more conveniently, by use of the **quadratic formula** (F). Notice that in (F) the expression $b^2 - 4ac$ under the radical sign must be nonnegative in order that x be a real number. If $b^2 - 4ac < 0$, x is not a real number. If $b^2 - 4ac = 0$, there is only one solution, $x = -\frac{b}{2a}$. If $b^2 - 4ac > 0$, there are two distinct real solutions to our equations.

ILLUSTRATIVE EXAMPLE 1. Solve $3x^2 = 10x + 8$ by the formula.

SOLUTION. Rewriting the equation in standard form, $3x^2 - 10x - 8 = 0$. Here $a = 3$, $b = -10$, and $c = -8$. Substituting these values in (F),

$$x = \frac{-b \pm \sqrt{b^2 - 4ac}}{2a} = \frac{10 \pm \sqrt{100 - 4(3)(-8)}}{6}$$

$$= \frac{10 \pm \sqrt{196}}{6} = \frac{10 \pm 14}{6} = \frac{5 \pm 7}{3} = 4 \text{ or } -\frac{2}{3}. \quad Ans.$$

CHECK.
When $x = 4$, $3(4)^2 = 10(4) + 8$, $48 = 40 + 8$.
When $x = -\frac{2}{3}$, $3(-\frac{2}{3})^2 = 10(-\frac{2}{3}) + 8$; $3 \cdot \frac{4}{9} = -\frac{20}{3} + 8$; $\frac{4}{3} = \frac{4}{3}$.

ILLUSTRATIVE EXAMPLE 2. Solve $x^2 - 4x + 1 = 0$ by the formula.

SOLUTION. Substitute $a = 1$, $b = -4$, $c = 1$ in (F):

$$x = \frac{4 \pm \sqrt{16 - 4(1)(1)}}{2} = \frac{4 \pm \sqrt{12}}{2} = \frac{4 \pm 2\sqrt{3}}{2} = 2 \pm \sqrt{3}. \quad \textit{Ans.}$$

CHECK.
$$(2 \pm \sqrt{3})^2 - 4(2 \pm \sqrt{3}) + 1 = 0,$$
$$4 \pm 4\sqrt{3} + 3 - 8 \mp 4\sqrt{3} + 1 = 0; \quad 0 = 0.$$

EXERCISE 39

Solve by the formula, and check:

1. $5x^2 = 4x + 2.$
2. $2x^2 - 5x = 3.$
3. $4x^2 - 2 = 7x.$
4. $3x^2 + 2x = 1.$
5. $4x = 4 - 15x^2.$
6. $5x^2 + 6x + 1 = 0.$
7. $6x^2 + 5x + 1 = 0.$
8. $4x^2 + 3 = 8x.$
9. $r^2 + 2r - 1 = 0.$
10. $t^2 + 6t + 4 = 0.$
11. $x^2 + 4x - 2 = 0.$
12. $x^2 + 6x - 3 = 0.$

13. $2x^2 - 6x + 2 = 0.$
14. $3x^2 - 4x - 1 = 0.$
15. $4s^2 + 12s + 7 = 0.$
16. $2y^2 - 4y + 1 = 0.$
17. $m^2 - 4m - 2 = 0.$
18. $n^2 + 2n - 5 = 0.$
19. $9x^2 - 12x + 4 = 0.$
20. $16x^2 + 24x + 9 = 0.$
21. $4x^2 + 20x + 10 = 0.$
22. $25x^2 - 40x + 16 = 0.$
23. $x^2 - 2px + q = 0.$
24. $4x^2 - 4mx - n = 0.$

25. The square of what number exceeds half of the number by 14?

26. Find the number which is 6 less than twice its square.

27. A rectangle is 1 foot longer than it is wide. An increase of 6 feet in each dimension would double its area. Find its dimensions.

28. Shortening each leg of a right triangle by 2 feet would halve its area. Find the area if the legs differ in length by 7 feet.

29. Going from P to Q, a distance of 240 miles, a train travels the first 100 miles at schedule speed and the remaining distance at 15 miles per hour less, arriving at Q 40 minutes late. What is the schedule speed?

30. B walks 3 miles at a certain rate and then 6 miles farther at a rate 1 mile per hour less. Had he walked the 9 miles at the greater rate, his time would have been one-half hour less. Find the greater rate.

31. Find two numbers which differ by $\frac{1}{12}$ and whose product is $\frac{1}{2}$.

32. Find three consecutive *even* integers such that the product of the last two equals three times the square of the first.

MISCELLANEOUS EXERCISE 40
REVIEW OF CHAPTER 6

1. In using (F) to solve $5x - x^2 = 5$, $a = ?$ $b = ?$ $c = ?$

2. Solve by factoring: (a) $p^2 + 3p = 4$; (b) $3x^2 - x = 2$; (c) $3t = t^2$.

3. Substitute $3 + \sqrt{2}$ for x in $x^2 - 6x + 7$, and simplify.

4. For what values of r will $2r$ equal $3r^2$?

5. Solve by the formula: (a) $x^2 - 4 = 2x$; (b) $2y^2 = 2 - 9y$.

6. Evaluate $x^2 - 2x - 5$ if x equals: (a) $3\frac{1}{2}$; (b) $2\sqrt{3}$; (c) $1 + \sqrt{6}$.

7. If $-b = 2 - \sqrt{3}$, then $2b = ?$ $(2 + b)^2 = ?$

8. Solve for x: (a) $(x + 2)(x - 5) = 0$; (b) $(x - 3)(x + 2) = 6$.

9. Find the value of p if $3x^2 + px = 8$ is satisfied by $x = -2$.

10. What values of x will give $x^2 + x$ half the value it has for $x = 3$?

11. Solve by completing the square: (a) $2x^2 - 1 = x$; (b) $x^2 + 3x = 4$.

12. Show that the sum of the two roots of $ax^2 + bx + c = 0$ is $-b/a$.

13. Prove that the product of the roots of $ax^2 + bx + c = 0$ is c/a.

14. Solve by factoring: (a) $4x^2 + 9 = 12x$; (b) $3x^2 + x - 10 = 0$.

15. If 3 is a root of $x^2 + kx = 9$, find the other root.

16. What is another root of $x^2 + 3x = c$ if one root is 2?

17. Solve $2x^2 - x = 3$ by: (a) factoring; (b) formula.

18. What number is 45 less than twice its square?

19. A regular octagon of side 9 inches is to be obtained by cutting a triangle from each corner of a square of side x inches. Find x.

20. Solve $3x^2 + 4x = 2$ by: (a) formula; (b) completing the square.

21. Solve and check: (a) $\sqrt{5x + 6} = x + 2$; (b) $2\sqrt{x} + 8 = x$.

22. If a train traveled 10 miles an hour faster, it would take 1 hour less to go 300 miles. Find the speed of the train.

23. The denominator of a certain fraction exceeds its numerator by 5. If the numerator is increased by 6 and the denominator by 7, the resulting fraction will be twice the original fraction. Find the original fraction.

24. Solve and check: (a) $\dfrac{x}{x-2} - 2 = \dfrac{3}{x}$; (b) $\dfrac{2x}{x-1} - \dfrac{x+1}{x} = \dfrac{5}{2}$.

25. If a, b, c are real numbers and $a \neq 0$, show that the roots of the equation $ax^2 + bx + c = 0$ are (a) real and unequal when $b^2 - 4ac > 0$; (b) real and equal when $b^2 - 4ac = 0$; (c) imaginary when $b^2 - 4ac < 0$.

26. For the equation given in Problem 25 show that (a) the two roots are numerically equal but opposite in sign when $b = 0$, $c \neq 0$; (b) one root is zero when $b \neq 0$, $c = 0$; (c) both roots are zero when $b = 0$, $c = 0$.

Chapter SEVEN

SERIES—BINOMIAL THEOREM

57. Definition and terminology

A **series** is the indicated sum of a succession of numbers. The successive numbers are called the **terms** of the series.

If $t_1, t_2, t_3, t_4, \ldots, t_n$ denotes the 1st 2nd, 3rd, 4th, $\ldots$, nth term, respectively, the sum of the first n terms is written as follows:

$$t_1 + t_2 + t_3 + t_4 + \cdots + t_n.$$

We agree that $S_1 = t_1$ and that S_2 denotes the sum of the first two terms, S_3 the sum of the first three terms, etc., then S_n denotes the sum of a series of n terms. For example, in a series of 8 terms, S_5 denotes the sum of the first five terms and S_8 the sum of the series. In general, a series need not have a last term.

58. Arithmetic series

If, in a series, the difference between any term (after the first) and the preceding term is constant, the series is an **arithmetic series** (frequently written A.S.), and this difference is called the **common difference.** When the common difference is positive, the series is called an **increasing** series; and when the common difference is negative, the series is called a **decreasing** series.

Now if t_1 denotes the first term of an arithmetic series, n the number of terms, t_n the nth term, and d the common difference, the series may be written thus,

$$t_1 + (t_1 + d) + (t_1 + 2d) + (t_1 + 3d) + \cdots + [t_1 + (n - 1)d].$$

Plainly, then, the formula for the nth term may be written as,

$$t_n = t_1 + (n - 1)d. \tag{1}$$

To obtain a formula for the sum, S_n, of an arithmetic series, write the series twice, first beginning with t_1 and then beginning with t_n, thus,

$$S_n = t_1 + (t_1 + d) + (t_1 + 2d) + \cdots + t_n \tag{a}$$
$$S_n = t_n + (t_n - d) + (t_n - 2d) + \cdots + t_1 \tag{b}$$

Adding (a) and (b), we get

$$2S_n = (t_1 + t_n) + (t_1 + t_n) + (t_1 + t_n) + \cdots + (t_1 + t_n).$$

Since there are n equal terms $(t_1 + t_n)$ in the right member,

$$2S_n = n(t_1 + t_n).$$

Whence

$$S_n = \frac{n}{2}(t_1 + t_n). \tag{2}$$

With formulas (1) and (2) we can find any two of the five quantities t_1, t_n, n, d, and S_n, if the other three are given.

ILLUSTRATIVE EXAMPLE 1. Given $t_1 = -\frac{7}{2}$, $d = \frac{5}{2}$, $S_n = \frac{33}{2}$; find n and t_n.

SOLUTION. Substitute the given values in formulas (1) and (2), and get

$$t_n = -\frac{7}{2} + (n - 1)(\tfrac{5}{2}), \tag{1'}$$

$$\frac{33}{2} = \frac{n}{2}\left(-\frac{7}{2} + t_n\right). \tag{2'}$$

Simplifying (1') and (2'), we have

$$5n - 2t_n = 12, \tag{1''}$$

$$2nt_n - 7n = 66. \tag{2''}$$

From (1''),
$$t_n = \frac{5n - 12}{2}. \tag{3}$$

Substituting this value of t_n in (2''), we have

$$2n\left(\frac{5n - 12}{2}\right) - 7n = 66,$$

or
$$5n^2 - 19n - 66 = 0.$$

Factoring,
$$(n - 6)(5n + 11) = 0.$$

Whence
$$n = 6 \text{ or } -\tfrac{11}{5}.$$

We discard the value $-\tfrac{11}{5}$, since n must be a positive integer. Now, substitue $n = 6$ in (3), and we obtain

$$t_n = \frac{30 - 12}{2} = \frac{18}{2} = 9.$$

Thus,
$$n = 6 \text{ and } t_n = 9. \quad \textit{Ans.}$$

CHECK. Form the series and sum up the terms, giving

$$S_n = -\tfrac{7}{2} - 1 + \tfrac{3}{2} + \tfrac{8}{2} + \tfrac{13}{2} + \tfrac{18}{2} = \tfrac{33}{2}.$$

Therefore the answer is correct.

———

ILLUSTRATIVE EXAMPLE 2. Given $n = 5$, $d = 2$, $t_n = \tfrac{26}{3}$; find t_1 and S_n.

SOLUTION. Substitute the given values in formula (1), and get

$$\tfrac{26}{3} = t_1 + (5 - 1)(2).$$

Whence
$$t_1 = \tfrac{2}{3}.$$

Now, substitute $n = 5$, $t_1 = \tfrac{2}{3}$, $t_n = \tfrac{26}{3}$ in formula (2), and get

$$S_n = \tfrac{5}{2}(\tfrac{2}{3} + \tfrac{26}{3}) = \tfrac{5}{2}(\tfrac{28}{3}) = \tfrac{70}{3}.$$

Thus,
$$t_1 = \tfrac{2}{3} \text{ and } S_n = \tfrac{70}{3}. \quad \textit{Ans.}$$

CHECK. Form the series and sum up the terms, giving

$$S_n = \tfrac{2}{3} + \tfrac{8}{3} + \tfrac{14}{3} + \tfrac{20}{3} + \tfrac{26}{3} = \tfrac{70}{3}.$$

——————

EXERCISE 41

1. Given $t_1 = 2$, $d = 3$, $n = 10$. Find t_n and S_n.

2. Given $t_1 = 6$, $d = -2$, $t_n = -16$. Find n and S_n.

3. Given $t_n = -11$, $d = -4$, $n = 7$. Find t_1 and S_n.

4. Given $t_1 = 4$, $d = 3$, $n = 11$. Find t_n and S_n.

5. Given $t_1 = 3$, $t_n = 9$, $n = 7$. Find S_n and d.

6. Given $t_n = 8$, $d = \tfrac{3}{4}$, $n = 9$. Find S_n and t_1.

7. Given $t_1 = -3$, $d = 0.4$, $t_n = 3$. Find n and S_n.

8. Given $t_1 = -5$, $t_n = 11$, $n = 21$. Find d and S_n.

9. Given $d = -3$, $n = 16$, $S_n = 16$. Find t_1 and t_n.

10. Given $n = 18$, $t_n = -45$, $S_n = -198$. Find t_1 and d.

11. Given $t_1 = -8\tfrac{1}{2}$, $n = 27$, $S_n = 297$. Find d and t_n.

12. Given $d = \tfrac{5}{3}$, $n = 31$, $S_n = 0$. Find t_1 and t_n.

13. Given $t_1 = 7$, $t_n = 77$, $S_n = 420$. Find n and d.

14. Given $d = 3$, $t_1 = -13$, $S_n = 22$. Find n and t_n.

15. Given $t_1 = 13$, $d = -3$, $S_n = 20$. Find n and t_n.

16. Given $t_n = -4$, $d = -\tfrac{3}{2}$, $S_n = 18$. Find n and t_1.

17. What is the sum of all **odd** integers from 15 to 219 inclusive?

18. Find the sum of all **even** integers from 18 to 180 inclusive.

19. In drilling a well, the cost is 55¢ for the first foot; for each succeeding foot, the cost is 10¢ more than that for the preceding foot. How deep a well may be drilled at a cost of $100?

20. A ball loosed at the top of an incline 400 feet long rolls 4 feet in the first second, and, in each succeeding second, x feet more than in the preceding. If it reaches the bottom in 10 seconds, find x.

21. $1520 is put in 8 envelopes so that each, after the first, contains $4 less than the preceding. How much is in the first envelope?

22. In Problem 21, find the contents of the last envelope.

23. A man borrows $1000, agreeing to reduce the principal by $40 at the end of each month and to pay 6% interest on all unpaid balances. Find the sum of all interest payments.

24. A boy buys 75¢ worth of savings stamps the first week and, each week after that, 25¢ worth more than the week before. In how many weeks will he accumulate enough stamps to exchange for a bond costing $18.75?

25. If a, b, c are successive terms of an A.S., b is called the **arithmetic mean** of a and c. Show that $b = \frac{1}{2}(a + c)$. [*Hint.* First tell why $b - a = c - b$; then solve for b.]

26. If the **reciprocals** of a, b, c are successive terms of an A.S., b is called the **harmonic mean** of a and c. Show that $b = 2ac/(a + c)$. [*Hint.* Explain first why $\dfrac{1}{b} - \dfrac{1}{a} = \dfrac{1}{c} - \dfrac{1}{b}$; then solve for b.]

27. Find the arithmetic mean of 8 and 14; 4 and -12; $\frac{1}{2}$ and $\frac{9}{2}$.

28. Find the harmonic mean of 2 and 8; 9 and 3; $\frac{3}{2}$ and $\frac{3}{4}$; 1 and x.

59. Geometric series

If, in a series, the ratio of any term (after the first) to the preceding term is constant, the series is a **geometric series** (frequently written G.S.), and this ratio is called the **common ratio.**

Now, if, in a geometric series, t_1 denotes the first term, n the number of terms, r the common ratio, and t_n the nth, or last, term, the series may be written thus,

$$t_1 + t_1r + t_1r^2 + t_1r^3 + \cdots + t_1r^{n-1}.$$

Plainly, then, the formula for the last term may be written

$$t_n = t_1r^{n-1}. \tag{1}$$

To obtain the formula for the sum, S_n, of a G.S., write

$$S_n = t_1 + t_1r + t_1r^2 + \cdots + t_1r^{n-1}.$$ (a)

Multiplying each member of (a) by r, we have

$$rS_n = t_1r + t_1r^2 + \cdots + t_1r^{n-1} + t_1r^n.$$ (b)

Subtracting (b) from (a), we get

$$S_n - rS_n = t_1 - t_1r^n.$$

Whence $$S_n = \frac{t_1 - t_1r^n}{1-r} = \frac{t_1(1-r^n)}{1-r}, \qquad r \neq 1.$$ (2)

If $r = 1$, then every term of the series is the same and, in fact, is t_1. Thus for $r = 1$, the sum of a geometric series of n terms is given by

$$S_n = t_1 + t_1 \cdot 1 + t_1 \cdot 1^2 + \cdots + t_1 \cdot 1^{n-1} = n \cdot t_1.$$

With formulas (1) and (2), we can find any two of the quantities t_1, t_n, n, r, and S_n, if the other three are given.

———

ILLUSTRATIVE EXAMPLE 1. Given $t_1 = 1$, $r = \frac{1}{2}$, and $n = 5$; to find t_n and S_n.

SOLUTION. Substitute the given values in formula (1), and get

$$t_n = (1)(\tfrac{1}{2})^{5-1} = (\tfrac{1}{2})^4 = \tfrac{1}{16}.$$

Now, in formula (2), substitute $t_1 = 1$, $r = \frac{1}{2}$, $t_n = \frac{1}{16}$, and get

$$S_n = \frac{(1)[1 - (\tfrac{1}{2})^5]}{1 - \tfrac{1}{2}} = \frac{1 - \tfrac{1}{32}}{1 - \tfrac{1}{2}} = \frac{32 - 1}{32 - 16} = \frac{31}{16}.$$

Thus, $$t_n = \tfrac{1}{16}, \quad S_n = \tfrac{31}{16}. \quad Ans.$$

CHECK. Form the series and sum up the terms, giving

$$S_n = 1 + \tfrac{1}{2} + \tfrac{1}{4} + \tfrac{1}{8} + \tfrac{1}{16} = \tfrac{31}{16}.$$

Therefore the answer is correct.

———

ILLUSTRATIVE EXAMPLE 2. Given $t_1 = 9$, $t_n = -\frac{8}{3}$, $S_n = \frac{13}{3}$; to find r and n.

SOLUTION. Substitute the given values in formulas (1) and (2), and get

$$-\tfrac{8}{3} = 9r^{n-1} \tag{1'}$$

$$\frac{13}{3} = \frac{9(1-r^n)}{1-r}. \tag{2'}$$

Simplifying (1') and (2'), we have

$$r^{n-1} = -\tfrac{8}{27}, \tag{1''}$$

$$27r^n - 13r = 14. \tag{2''}$$

Factoring the left member of (2''),

$$r(27r^{n-1} - 13) = 14.$$

Substituting $-\tfrac{8}{27}$ for r^{n-1} in this equation,

$$r[27(-\tfrac{8}{27}) - 13] = 14,$$
$$r(-8 - 13) = 14.$$

Whence $\qquad\qquad\qquad r = -\tfrac{2}{3}.$

Now, substitute $r = -\tfrac{2}{3}$ in (1''), and get

$$(-\tfrac{2}{3})^{n-1} = -\tfrac{8}{27} = (-\tfrac{2}{3})^3.$$

Hence $\qquad\qquad\qquad n - 1 = 3,$

whence $\qquad\qquad\qquad n = 4.$

Thus, $\qquad\qquad\qquad r = -\tfrac{2}{3}, n = 4.$ *Ans.*

CHECK. Form the series and sum up the terms, obtaining

$$S_n = 9 - 6 + 4 - \tfrac{8}{3} = \tfrac{13}{3}.$$

Therefore the answer is correct.

———

ILLUSTRATIVE EXAMPLE 3. Find S_5 in the G.S. $1.2 + 1.44 + 1.728 + \cdots$.

SOLUTION. Here $t_1 = 1.2$, $n = 5$, and, from the definition of a G.S.,

$$r = \frac{1.44}{1.2} = 1.2, \text{ or } r = \frac{1.728}{1.44} = 1.2.$$

Substituting $t_1 = 1.2$, $n = 5$, $r = 1.2$, in formula (2), we have

$$S_5 = \frac{1.2[1 - (1.2)^5]}{1 - 1.2} = \frac{1.2(1 - 2.48832)}{-0.2} = 8.92992. \quad Ans.$$

CHECK. Form the series and sum up the terms, giving

$$S_5 = 1.2 + 1.44 + 1.728 + 2.0736 + 2.48832 = 8.92992.$$

EXERCISE 42

1. Given $t_1 = 5$, $r = 2$, $n = 12$. Find t_n and S_n.

2. Given $t_1 = 4$, $r = 3$, $n = 7$. Find t_n and S_n.

3. Given $t_1 = 12$, $r = \frac{1}{2}$, $t_n = \frac{3}{8}$. Find n and S_n.

4. Given $t_1 = 27$, $t_n = \frac{32}{9}$, $n = 6$. Find r and S_n.

5. Given $r = 10$, $t_n = 2000$, $n = 8$. Find t_1 and S_n.

6. Given $t_1 = \frac{3}{2}$, $r = -2$, $t_n = 96$. Find n and S_n.

7. Given $t_1 = 2$, $t_n = 162$, $S_n = 122$. Find r and n.

8. Given $t_1 = -1$, $r = -3$, $S_n = 182$. Find n and t_n.

9. Given $r = \frac{3}{2}$, $n = 4$, $S_n = 422$. Find t_1 and t_n.

10. Given $t_n = 96$, $r = 2$, $S_n = 189$. Find t_1 and n.

11. In a certain G.S., $t_2 = \frac{7}{4}$, $t_5 = 14$. Find t_{10}.

12. In a certain G.S., $t_3 = 36$, $t_6 = \frac{4}{3}$. Find t_8.

13. Find S_{15} if $t_1 = 1.03$, $r = 1.03$; given $(1.03)^{16} = 1.6047$.

14. Find S_{10} if $t_1 = 1$, $r = (1.05)^{-1}$; given $(1.05)^{-9} = 0.6446$.

15. An elastic ball, dropped from a height of 160 feet, rebounds after each fall to half the height from which it last fell. Find the total distance traversed when it strikes the ground the sixth time.

16. A's first gift to a charity is $320; after that, each succeeding gift is 50% more than the preceding. Find the sum of the first eight gifts.

17. In Problem 16, tell the ratio of the 7th gift to the 4th.

18. The 4th gift in Problem 16 is what per cent of the 6th?

19. Show that a, b, c are successive terms of a G.S. if b is the **geometric mean** of a and c; that is, if $b = \sqrt{ac}$ or if $b = -\sqrt{ac}$, according as a and c are both positive or both negative.

20. Find the geometric mean of 16 and 8; -8 and -2; $\frac{7}{3}$ and $\frac{3}{14}$.

60. Binomial theorem

The symbolic expression for a binomial raised to a given power is $(a + b)^n$, where a denotes the first term of the binomial, b the second term, and n the exponent of the binomial. Let $n = 2, 3, 4$, and 5, in order, and obtain the following identities by actual multiplication.

$$(a + b)^2 = a^2 + 2ab + b^2,$$
$$(a + b)^3 = a^3 + 3a^2b + 3ab^2 + b^3,$$
$$(a + b)^4 = a^4 + 4a^3b + 6a^2b^2 + 4ab^3 + b^4,$$
$$(a + b)^5 = a^5 + 5a^4b + 10a^3b^2 + 10a^2b^3 + 5ab^4 + b^5.$$

The right member of each of these identities is called the **expansion** of the left member. Note that, if $n = 2, 3, 4$, or 5, the expansion of $(a + b)^n$ has the following properties:

I. The total number of terms in the expansion is $n + 1$.

II. In any term the sum of the exponents of a and b is n.

III. The exponent of a is n in the first term, and decreases by 1 in each succeeding term.

IV. b appears first, with an exponent 1, in the second term; and its exponent increases by 1 in each succedding term.

V. The coefficient of the first term is 1; that of the second term is n.

VI. The coefficient of any term after the second is equal to the coefficient of the preceding term multiplied by the exponent of a in that term, and divided by the number of that term.

The student can easily verify the truth of properties I to VI for the above expansions where $n = 2, 3, 4$, or 5. These properties, proved in higher algebra to be true for *any* positive integer n, may be expressed in compact form by the following general formula, known as the **binomial theorem:**

$$(a + b)^n = a^n + na^{n-1}b + \frac{n(n-1)}{1 \cdot 2}a^{n-2}b^2 + \frac{n(n-1)(n-2)}{1 \cdot 2 \cdot 3}a^{n-3}b^3 + \cdots,$$

where the final dots indicate that the terms are to be supplied up to and including the $(n + 1)$th term.

We will assume without proof that, under certain conditions, not here stated, the binomial theorem is valid for fractional or negative values of n. By this we mean the following:

As the number of terms in the expansion is increased indefinitely, their sum approaches the value of $(a + b)^n$ more and more nearly; and by adding a sufficiently large number of terms, beginning with the first, in the expansion, we can obtain a sum as close as we please to the value of $(a + b)^n$.

ILLUSTRATIVE EXAMPLE 1. Expand $(x - 2y)^7$ and simplify.

SOLUTION. Applying the binomial theorem, we obtain

$$(x - 2y)^7 = x^7 + 7x^6(-2y) + \frac{7 \cdot 6}{1 \cdot 2}x^5(-2y)^2 + \frac{7 \cdot 6 \cdot 5}{1 \cdot 2 \cdot 3}x^4(-2y)^3$$

$$+ \frac{7 \cdot 6 \cdot 5 \cdot 4}{1 \cdot 2 \cdot 3 \cdot 4}x^3(-2y)^4 + \frac{7 \cdot 6 \cdot 5 \cdot 4 \cdot 3}{1 \cdot 2 \cdot 3 \cdot 4 \cdot 5}x^2(-2y)^5$$

$$+ \frac{7 \cdot 6 \cdot 5 \cdot 4 \cdot 3 \cdot 2}{1 \cdot 2 \cdot 3 \cdot 4 \cdot 5 \cdot 6}x(-2y)^6 + (-2y)^7$$

$$= x^7 - 14x^6y + 84x^5y^2 - 280x^4y^3 + 560x^3y^4 - 672x^2y^5$$

$$+ 448xy^6 - 128y^7. \quad Ans.$$

CHECK. The student should verify the expansion by letting $x = y = 1$.

ILLUSTRATIVE EXAMPLE 2. Expand $(1 - 3y^2)^{3/2}$ to 5 terms and simplify.

SOLUTION. Applying the binomial theorem, we obtain

$$(1 - 3y^2)^{3/2} = (1)^{3/2} + \tfrac{3}{2}(1)^{1/2}(-3y^2) + \tfrac{3}{8}(1)^{-1/2}(-3y^2)^2$$

$$- \tfrac{1}{16}(1)^{-3/2}(-3y^2)^3 + \tfrac{3}{128}(1)^{-5/2}(-3y^2)^4 + \cdots$$

$$= 1 - \tfrac{9}{2}y^2 + \tfrac{27}{8}y^4 + \tfrac{27}{16}y^6 + \tfrac{243}{128}y^8 + \cdots. \quad Ans.$$

CHECK. Verify this approximate result by letting y equal such a value that $3y^2$ will be less than 1 in absolute value (say $y = 0.1$).

Note. Observe that in illustrative example 1, we first wrote the coefficients in factored form. But, in illustrative example 2, we obtained them by a somewhat shorter method as follows: By property V, the coefficient of the 2nd term is $\tfrac{3}{2}$; then, by property VI,

$$\text{coefficient of 3rd term} = \frac{(\tfrac{3}{2})(\tfrac{1}{2})}{2} = \frac{3}{8};$$

$$\text{coefficient of 4th term} = \frac{(\frac{3}{8})(-\frac{1}{2})}{3} = -\frac{1}{16};$$

$$\text{coefficient of 5th term} = \frac{(-\frac{1}{16})(-\frac{3}{2})}{4} = \frac{3}{128}.$$

ILLUSTRATIVE EXAMPLE 3. Evaluate $(1.02)^{-7}$ to 4 decimal places.

SOLUTION. This does *not* mean to expand to 4 terms. The number of terms needed is determined as shown below. By the binomial theorem,

$$(1.02)^{-7} = (1 + 0.02)^{-7} = (1)^{-7} - 7(1)^{-8}(0.02) + 28(1)^{-9}(0.02)^2$$
$$- 84(1)^{-10}(0.02)^3 + 210(1)^{-11}(0.02)^4$$
$$- 462(1)^{-12}(0.02)^5 + \cdots .$$

Note that 1 raised to *any* power equals 1, but $(0.02)^2 = 0.0004$, $(0.02)^3 = 0.000008$, etc. Performing the multiplications indicated in the expansion,

$$(1.02)^{-7} = 1 - 0.14 + 0.0112 - 0.000672 + 0.0000336 - \cdots .$$

The 6th term in the expansion, -0.0000014784, has 5 zeros between the decimal point and the first significant digit, and hence cannot affect the value of $(1.02)^{-7}$ in the first 4 decimal places. Thus the 6th and all further terms may be omitted, since the number of zeros to the right of the decimal point becomes still larger in subsequent terms. For 4-place accuracy, we need not retain digits beyond the 5th decimal place in the terms to be summed up. Rounding these off to 5 decimal places, we write

1.00000	−0.14000
0.01120	−0.00067
0.00003	−0.14067
1.01123	

Since $1.01123 - 0.14067 = 0.87056$, where the last digit is somewhat doubtful, the value of $(1.02)^{-7}$, correct to 4 decimal places, is 0.8706. *Ans.*

Note. The binomial theorem is used in Part II mainly to expand powers of $1 + i$. To evaluate $(1 + i)^n$ to r decimal places, write the first few terms of the expansion and compute each to $r + 1$ decimal places. Continue this until you get a term having $r + 1$ zeros between the decimal point and the first significant digit. Then sum up and round off to r decimal places.

EXERCISE 43

Expand (in Problems 9 to 16, only to 5 terms) and simplify:

1. $(2x + y)^5$.

5. $(\frac{1}{2} + 2y)^5$.

9. $(1 - 2y)^{-5}$.

13. $(4 - x)^{3/2}$.

2. $(x + 2y)^6$.

6. $(\frac{1}{3} - 3y)^6$.

10. $(1 + 3x)^{-3}$.

14. $(x^2 - 2)^{1/2}$.

3. $(x - 2y)^6$.

7. $(x - y^2)^4$.

11. $(x + y^2)^{-2}$.

15. $(1 + i)^{-2/3}$.

4. $(2x - y)^7$.

8. $(x^2 + y)^5$.

12. $(x^2 - y)^{-4}$.

16. $(1 + i)^{-3/4}$.

Evaluate to four decimal places:

17. $(1.03)^4$.

21. $(1.05)^{-2}$.

25. $(1.06)^{1/6}$.

29. $(1.015)^{-1/2}$.

18. $(1.01)^7$.

22. $(1.04)^{-2}$.

26. $(1.05)^{1/3}$.

30. $(1.02)^{-1/4}$.

19. $(1.03)^{10}$.

23. $(1.02)^{-5}$.

27. $(1.04)^{1/3}$.

31. $(1.01)^{-1/12}$.

20. $(1.04)^4$.

24. $(1.03)^{-3}$.

28. $(1.03)^{3/4}$.

32. $(1.005)^{-1/2}$.

MISCELLANEOUS EXERCISE 44
REVIEW OF CHAPTER 7

1. Solve for t_1: (a) $S_n = \frac{1}{2}n(t_1 + t_n)$; (b) $t_n = t_1 r^{n-1}$.

2. Find the value of n if (a) $\frac{8}{27} = (\frac{2}{3})^{n-1}$; (b) $-\frac{1}{8} = (-\frac{1}{2})^{n-2}$.

3. According as the given series is an A.S. or a G.S., find d or r:
(a) $8 + 2 - 4 - \cdots$; (b) $8 + 2 + \frac{1}{2} + \cdots$; (c) $1 - x^2 + x^4 - \cdots$;
(d) $\frac{5}{6} + \frac{2}{3} + \frac{1}{2} + \cdots$; (e) $\frac{1}{3} + \frac{1}{6} + \frac{1}{12} + \cdots$.

4. By inspection, write the next two terms in each series of Problem 3.

5. Given the series $2 + 1 + \frac{1}{2} + \frac{1}{4} + \cdots$. Find: (a) S_{n+2}; (b) t_9.

6. Given the series $1 + 5 + 9 + \cdots$. Find: (a) t_{n-1}; (b) S_{30}.

7. Find the sum of the first 45 terms of the series $i + 4i + 7i + \cdots$.

8. What is t_n in the series $(1 + i)^3 + (1 + i)^5 + (1 + i)^7 + \cdots$?

9. Find S_7 in each: (a) $2 + \frac{7}{2} + 5 + \cdots$; (b) $2 + 3 + \frac{9}{2} + \cdots$.

10. Find the arithmetic, geometric, and harmonic means of 4 and 12.

11. Let A, G, and H denote, respectively, the arithmetic, geometric, and harmonic means of p and q. Show that $A \cdot H = G^2$.

12. Find x if $x - 1$, x^2, 16 are successive terms of an A.S.

13. If $2x$, 6, $x + 7$ are successive terms of a G.S., find x.

14. Find an A.S. of three terms, whose sum is 36, such that if the first term is increased by 2, the series becomes a G.S.

15. B invests \$800 at the beginning of each year for 15 years at 5% simple interest. Find the total interest earned in 15 years.

16. A's annual salary, \$4000 in the first biennium, is increased by 10% in each biennium. Find his salary in the 7th biennium.

17. Expand to 4 terms and simplify: (a) $(x^2 - \frac{1}{2}y)^8$; (b) $(1 + 2x)^{-4}$.

18. Evaluate to 4 decimal places: (a) $(1.02)^{-3}$; (b) $(1.04)^{3/4}$.

19. Find $\sqrt{15}$ to 3 decimal places by expanding $(16 - 1)^{1/2}$.

20. Find $\sqrt[3]{9}$ to 3 decimal places by expanding $(8 + 1)^{1/3}$.

21. Evaluate $(1.03)^{-1}$ to 4 decimals; as a check, divide 1 by 1.03.

22. Expand to 4 terms and simplify: (a) $(\frac{1}{2} + 2y)^7$; (b) $(4 - x)^{1/2}$.

23. Evaluate to 4 decimal places: (a) $(1.01)^8$; (b) $(1.03)^{-2/3}$.

24. For what values of x is the expansion of $(1 - 4x^2)^{2/3}$ valid?

25. The equation $1^2 + 2^2 + 3^2 + \cdots + n^2 = \frac{1}{6}n(n + 1)(2n + 1)$ is proved in higher algebra. Verify it for the case $n = 7$.

26. The equation $1^3 + 2^3 + 3^3 + \cdots + n^3 = \frac{1}{4}n^2(n + 1)^2$ is proved in algebra. Verify this equation for the case $n = 8$.

Chapter EIGHT

ELEMENTARY FUNCTIONS

AND GRAPHS

61. Graphic representation of simple statistics

A **graph** may be considered a "picture of figures," since (in the tabular case) it is the pictorial representation of a table made up of columns of figures. Such a graph cannot supply any more information than the tabulated data from which it is prepared, but it visualizes significant facts within a minimum time and portrays important trends vividly.

The student has undoubtedly seen graphs of various kinds in newspapers, magazines, and books. Accountants, advertising men, statisticians, and scientists make wide use of them, because a picture is effective and universal in its appeal. The graphic representation of statistical data is perhaps one of the most remarkable developments in modern commercial work.

62. Bar graphs and broken-line graphs

For an illustration, we shall take the graphic representation of the annual income of an American company for a 10-year period as tabulated on the next page.

Figure 5 is drawn to a convenient scale. The height of each bar represents the total income, or "income before taxes," for the year indicated. The diagram thus obtained is called a **bar graph.** In the same figure, the height of the shaded part of each bar represents the net income, or "income after

131

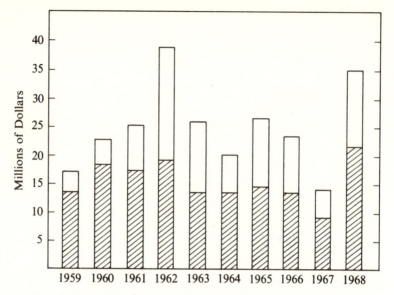

Fig. 5. Comparative bar graph of annual income, total and net.

taxes," for the corresponding year. The graph as a whole is called a **comparative bar graph,** because it shows net income as compared to total income for each year in the period under consideration.

| Year | ANNUAL INCOME | |
	Total	Net
1959	$16,900,000	$13,600,000
1960	22,800,000	18,300,000
1961	25,400,000	17,500,000
1962	39,000,000	18,800,000
1963	25,800,000	13,300,000
1964	20,200,000	13,300,000
1965	26,500,000	14,500,000
1966	23,200,000	13,300,000
1967	14,000,000	8,800,000
1968	35,400,000	21,800,000

Since the distance of the top of a bar from the base is a measure of annual income, we may place a dot at the top of each bar and do away with the bars. In order to assist the eye to follow the changes in annual income, we may then connect the dots by a series of straight lines. This has been done in Fig. 6, using the same scale as in Fig. 5. The resulting graph is called a **broken-line graph.** The upper part of the graph, composed of full lines, represents total income. The lower part, made up of dotted lines, exhibits net income. The graph as a whole is a **comparative broken-line graph.**

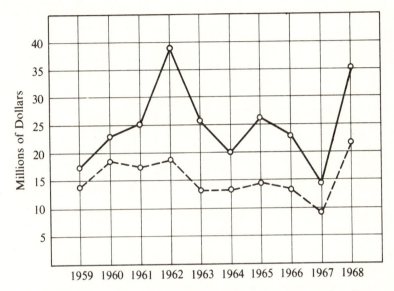

Fig. 6. Comparative broken-line graph of annual income, total and net.

It is important to be able to interpret a graph. Problems 1 and 2 of Exercise 45 contain questions suggestive of this.

63. Directed-number graph

In the graphs of Art. 62, we used numbers constituting the **arithmetic scale,** that is, numbers which represent *magnitude* only. Not infrequently we have to deal with **directed numbers,** that is, positive and negative numbers showing not only magnitude but also *one of two opposite directions* from some arbitrary point or line of reference marked 0. Thus, if we agree to indicate by 0° a certain temperature chosen arbitrarily, a temperature of +20° means 20 degrees above 0°, and a temperature of −20° means 20 degrees below 0°. Directed numbers constitute the **algebraic scale.** The yardstick is an example of arithmetic scale; the thermometer, one of algebraic scale. The significance of directed numbers can be brought out by means of graphic representation.

The following temperature readings, taken in a northern city on a winter's day, are exhibited graphically in Fig. 7.

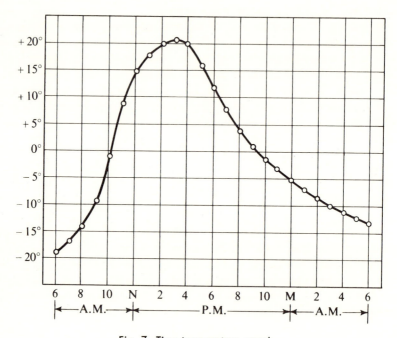

Fig. 7. Time-temperature graph.

Hour	Temp.	Hour	Temp.	Hour	Temp.
6 A.M.	−19°F	3 P.M.	+21°F	11 P.M.	−3°F
7 A.M.	−17	4 P.M.	+20	Midnight	−5
8 A.M.	−14	5 P.M.	+16	1 A.M.	−7
9 A.M.	−9	6 P.M.	+12	2 A.M.	−9
10 A.M.	−1	7 P.M.	+8	3 A.M.	−10
11 A.M.	+9	8 P.M.	+4	4 A.M.	−11
Noon	+15	9 P.M.	+1	5 A.M.	−12
1 P.M.	+18	10 P.M.	−1	6 A.M.	−13
2 P.M.	+20				

The temperature was 9° at 11 A.M. and rose to 15° at noon. Evidently this change was not abrupt, but the temperature passed gradually through the entire range of degrees between 9° and 15°. We may say, for all practical purposes, that the temperature was probably about 12° at 11:30 A.M., as approximated on the graph. This process of approximation is called **interpolation.** Note that interpolation cannot be applied to the graph in Fig. 6, since the magnitude of income, in varying from year to year, does not pass through all intervening values. In brief, we may think of temperature variations as a **continuous process;** but changes in such quantities as annual income may be called a **discontinuous process.**

A process or phenomenon of the discontinuous type is represented graphically by means of a *broken-line graph,* merely as an aid to the eye. There is no reason to assume that the fluctuations take place in any regular fashion; and, in some cases, no meaning can be attached to points between those located from the table of data. But in case the varying quantity represents a continuous process or phenomenon, it is permissible to join the located points in a smooth *curve.* This explains the use of a curved line in Fig. 7.

64. Construction of a graph

No detailed instructions can conveniently be given for the construction of a graph. The scale used will depend upon the magnitude of the varying quantity; hence, the student should use his judgment in selecting a suitable scale. It is a good practice to give a title to the graph. The work should be neat and the graph large enough to bring out the important facts. The illustrative graphs will give the student an idea about these points.

EXERCISE 45

1. Refer to Fig. 5: (a) In what year is the total income the greatest? smallest? (b) Answer same questions for the net income. (c) Is the ratio of net income to total income about the same each year? (d) What is represented by the unshaded part of each bar?

2. Refer to Fig. 7: (a) At about what different times was the temperature 5°? 0°? −5°? (b) About what was the temperature at 8:30 A.M.? 8:30 P.M.? (c) What was the minimum temperature for the day? maximum? (d) What was the total range of temperature (difference between maximum and minimum)? (e) Temperature rose from minimum to maximum in how many hours? (f) What was the average hourly rise in temperature during that period?

3. Draw a bar graph of lowest recorded temperatures for Denver: Jan., −29°; Feb., −25°; March, −11°; Apr., 4°; May, 19°; June, 32°; July, 42°; Aug., 40°; Sept., 21°; Oct., −2°; Nov., −18°; Dec., −25°.

4. The mean number of inches of total snowfall in Des Moines is Oct., 0.3; Nov., 2.2; Dec., 7.1; Jan., 8.5; Feb., 7.3; March, 5.4; Apr., 1.1. Draw a broken-line graph of these data.

5. Draw a solubility curve of copper sulfate if the extent to which it will dissolve in 100 grams of water at various temperatures is as follows:

Temp. (Deg. C)	0°	10°	20°	30°	40°	50°	60°	70°	80°	90°	100°
Grams of Sulfate	14	17	21	25	29	33	40	47	55	64	75

6. The table below shows the production (in thousands of bales) of cotton in Alabama. Exhibit this information by a bar graph.

Year	1959	1960	1961	1962	1963	1964	1965	1966
Production	720	760	625	695	880	895	845	463

7. Draw a bar graph of the production (in millions of boxes) of grapefruit in Southern City, U.S.A., as tabulated below.

Year	1960	1961	1962	1963	1964	1965	1966	1967
Production	24.6	19.2	27.3	31.0	22.3	32.0	29.0	33.0

In Problems 8–11, use the following table, which gives the Negro and total population (in millions) of continental United States:

Year	POPULATION		Year	POPULATION		Year	POPULATION	
	Negro	Total		Negro	Total		Negro	Total
1830	2.3	12.9	1880	6.6	50.2	1930	11.9	122.8
1840	2.9	17.1	1890	7.5	62.9	1940	12.9	131.7
1850	3.6	23.2	1900	8.8	76.0	1950	15.0	150.7
1860	4.4	31.4	1910	9.8	92.0	1960	18.9	179.3
1870	4.9	38.6	1920	10.5	105.7			

8. Draw a comparative bar graph of population.

9. Exhibit population by a comparative broken-line graph.

10. Draw a curve showing growth of *total* population.

11. Represent by a broken-line graph the variation in the percentage of Negro population based on the corresponding total population.

12. Using the table below, draw a curve showing how the freezing point of a solution of glycerine (antifreeze) and water varies with the percentage composition of the solution.

% Glycerine (by Weight)	10	20	30	40	50	60	70	80	90
Freezing Point (Deg. F)	29°	23°	15°	4°	−9°	−31°	−38°	−6°	29°

13. Exhibit by a comparative bar graph the following information concerning the production (in tens of thousands of tons) of sugar in the United States:

Year	1959	1960	1961	1962	1963	1964	1965	1966
Beet Sugar	1701	1642	1770	1825	2333	2339	2092	2026
Cane Sugar	1099	1124	1316	1278	1670	1735	1587	1641

14. Draw a comparative broken-line graph of the data in Problem 13.

15. Draw a curve of the range of visibility (in nautical miles) for objects of various heights (in feet) above sea level, as tabulated.

Height	10	20	30	40	50	60	70	80	90	100
Range	3.6	5.1	6.3	7.2	8.1	8.9	9.6	10.3	10.9	11.5

16. The table gives the expected future lifetime in United States for white males at various ages. Exhibit the data by a broken-line graph.

At Age	10	15	20	25	30	35	40	45	50
Future Lifetime	59.7	54.9	50.2	45.6	40.9	36.3	31.7	27.3	23.2

65. Locating points by the rectangular coördinates

The location of a point in a plane may be readily described by giving its distances relative to some convenient units of measurement from two mutually perpendicular lines, called the **axes of reference.** For convenience, we take a horizontal and a vertical line for axes of reference. The horizontal line, denoted by OX (Fig. 8), is called the **X-axis;** the vertical line, denoted

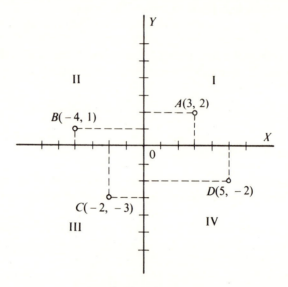

Fig. 8. Plotting points.

by OY, is called the **Y-axis.** The point of intersection, O, is the **origin.** The distance of a point from the Y-axis is called the **abscissa** of the point, and is designated by x. The distance from the X-axis is called the **ordinate** of the point, and is designated by y. Now, if the "foot of the ordinate" be defined as the point on the X-axis from which the ordinate is drawn, the distance from the origin to the foot of the ordinate may be taken as the abscissa. Likewise, the ordinate may be measured on the Y-axis. The abscissa and ordinate of a point are called its **coördinates.** They are written in a parenthesis, separated by a comma, with the abscissa always first. To specify on which side of each axis the point is located, we shall agree that the abscissa is *positive* for points on the *right* of the Y-axis, and *negative* for points on the *left;* similarly, the ordinate is *positive* for points *above* the X-axis, and *negative* for points *below.*

This process of taking a horizontal and vertical line and choosing a common unit of measurement is called *introducing a Cartesian coördinate system in a plane.* It is, in fact, a way of assigning to every point in the plane a unique ordered pair of real numbers. (The pairs (2, 3) and (3, 2) are distinct *ordered* pairs of real numbers.)

Thus, in Fig. 8, for the point A, $x = 3$ and $y = 2$; for the point B, $x = -4$ and $y = 1$; for the point C, $x = -2$ and $y = -3$; for the point D, $x = 5$ and $y = -2$. The point A is then designated by $(3, 2)$, B by $(-4, 1)$, C by $(-2, -3)$. and D by $(5, -2)$. The two axes divide the plane into four **quadrants,** I, II, III, and IV, as shown in the figure.

To **plot** a point is to mark with a dot its location as determined by its coördinates.

This is reversing the procedure of finding the coördinate of a point. This allows us to give a geometric interpretation to problems dealing with pairs of numbers.

66. Graph of a linear equation

A line, straight or curved, is said to be the **graph of an equation,** if it contains all points, and no others, the coördinates of which satisfy the equation.

We shall assume, without proof, that the graph of an equation of the *first degree* in one or two variables is a *straight line*. Hence the alternative name "linear equation" for a first degree equation.

It follows from the definition of a graph that to represent an equation graphically we must, in general, plot a representative number of points *whose coördinates satisfy the equation*, and then join these points in a straight line or a curved line, as the case may be. In particular, since the graph of a first degree equation is a straight line, and since a straight line is always determined by two points, only two points are necessary in graphing a first degree equation. The two points selected should be sufficiently far apart to determine the direction of the line accurately. It is well to plot a third point and see if it is in line with the first two.

ILLUSTRATIVE EXAMPLE. Draw the graph of $y = \frac{1}{2}x + 1$.

SOLUTION. We can find as many as we wish of the unlimited number of pairs of values for x and y that will satisfy this equation by assigning values to x and finding, by substitution in the equation, the corresponding values of y. The work is usually arranged in a **table of values,** as shown below.

When $x =$	-4	-3	-2	-1	0	1	2	3	4
then $y =$	-1	$-\frac{1}{2}$	0	$\frac{1}{2}$	1	$\frac{3}{2}$	2	$\frac{5}{2}$	3

Each pair of values in the table represents a point. Plot all the points and draw a straight line through them, as in Fig. 9. We have taken a rather large number of points merely to illustrate the fact that all of them lie in the same straight line, which represents the graph of the given first degree equation. The line may be drawn by using only two points.

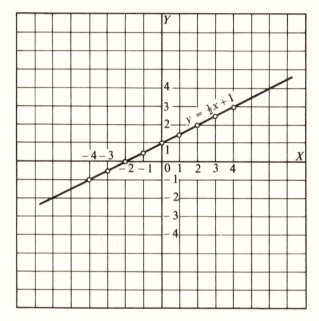

Fig. 9. Graph of $1/2x + 1$.

Note. As a matter of convenience, an equation like $2x + 3y = 6$ should first be solved for y, giving $y = -\frac{2}{3}x + 2$.

EXERCISE 46

1. Draw a triangle whose vertices are $(3, -1)$, $(-1, 4)$, $(-3, 0)$.

2. Three vertices of a rectangle are $(0, 2)$, $(-5, 2)$, $(-5, -4)$. Draw the the rectangle and give the coördinates of the fourth vertex.

3. Give the coördinates of the origin; of a point on the X-axis 6 units to the left of the origin; of a point on the Y-axis 5 units above the origin.

4. In which quadrant does a point lie if its coördinates are (a) both positive? (b) both negative? (c) of unlike signs?

5. Find the distance from the point $(2, -1)$ to the point $(6, 1)$.

6. How far is the point $(-2, 8)$ from the point $(3, -4)$?

7. Describe the locus of points for which (a) $x = 2$; (b) $x = -2$; (c) $y = 0$; (d) $x = 0$; (e) $y = x$; (f) $y = -x$.

8. Give the equation of a line (a) parallel to the X-axis and 4 units below it; (b) parallel to the Y-axis and passing through $(1, 0)$.

Draw the graph of each equation:

9. $y = 2x - 1$.	**15.** $5y = 2x - 10$.	**21.** $x - 2y = 0$.
10. $y = 3x + 2$.	**16.** $3y = 3 - 2x$.	**22.** $2x + y = 0$.
11. $3x + y = 3$.	**17.** $5x + 2y = 2$.	**23.** $x + 3 = 0$.
12. $2x - y = 4$.	**18.** $6x - 2y = 3$.	**24.** $y - 2 = 0$.
13. $4x - 3y = 12$.	**19.** $2y = 5 - 4x$.	**25.** $2x - 8 = 0$.
14. $3x + 2y = 6$.	**20.** $x + 4y = 6$.	**26.** $3y + 3 = 0$.

67. Graphic solution of two linear equations

Various methods were given in Chapter 2 for the solution of a pair of simultaneous linear equations in two unknowns. We shall now discuss a graphical method.

Suppose we wish to solve two given linear equations simultaneously. Each of the two can be represented graphically by a straight line. The x and y of any point on the first line will satisfy the corresponding first equation; likewise, the x and y of any point on the second line will satisfy the second equation. It is obvious that, if the two lines have a *point in common*, the x and y of this particular point will satisfy both equations. Now, since two straight lines have, in general, only one point in common, the corresponding linear equations have only one pair of values of the unknowns in common. Hence the required solution is obtained by measuring the x and y of the point of interesection.

It must be noted that the accuracy of the solution so obtained is not very great. For the process of drawing the graph is itself subject to inaccuracy. The process of "drawing" the lines in question with a pencil is at best very crude.

Two special cases arise. (a) If the graphs of the two equations are parallel lines, they have no point in common and there is no solution; the equations are **inconsistent** (see Art. 21). (b) If the graphs of the two equations are coincident lines, they have an unlimited number of points in common, and every solution of either equation is also a solution of the other; the equations are **dependent** (see Art. 21).

ILLUSTRATIVE EXAMPLE. Solve graphically $2x - y = -4$,   (1)

$$x + 3y = 5.$$ (2)

SOLUTION. Solve each equation for y and get

$$y = 2x + 4,$$ (1′)

$$y = \tfrac{1}{3}(5 - x).$$ (2′)

Prepare a table of three pairs of values for each.

TABLE I. $y = 2x + 4$

When $x =$	-2	0	1
then $y =$	0	4	6

TABLE II. $y = \tfrac{1}{3}(5 - x)$

When $x =$	-4	0	5
then $y =$	3	$\tfrac{5}{3}$	0

Plot the points of Table I, join them by a straight line, and thus get the graph of equation (1). Plot the points of Table II, join them by a straight

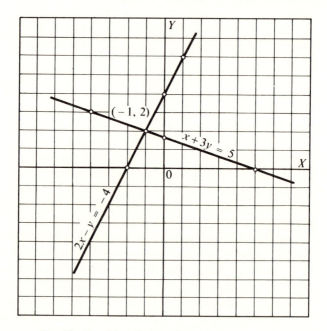

Fig. 10. Graphic solution of two linear equations.

line, and thus get the graph of equation (2). As seen from Fig. 10, these lines intersect in the point $(-1, 2)$. Verify that these coördinates *satisfy both equations*. The solution is $x = -1$ and $y = 2$.   *Ans.*

___

EXERCISE 47

Solve graphically:

1. $x - y = 4$,
   $x + y = 6$.

2. $x + y = 5$,
   $x - y = -3$.

3. $x - 2y = -4$,
   $2x + y = 7$.

4. $2x - y = 5$,
   $x - 3y = 0$.

5. $x - 2y = 4$,
   $5x + 2y = 8$.

6. $3x + 2y = 2$,
   $2x - 3y = -16$.

7. $5x + 3y = 7$,
   $4x - 2y = -1$.

8. $7x + 4y = 8$,
   $3x + 2y = 3$.

9. $3x - 4y = 5$,
   $2x + 3y = -8$.

10. $7x - 2y = 1$,
    $2x + y = -6$.

11. $4x + y = 0$,
    $2x + 3y = 5$.

12. $5y - x = 10$,
    $y - 3x = 9$.

13. $x - y = 5$,
    $x - 2 = 0$.

14. $3x + y = 1$,
    $y + 2 = 0$.

15. $2x + 6 = 0$,
    $3y - 6 = 0$.

16. Show graphically that the equations $x + 2y = 2$ and $x + 2y = 6$ are inconsistent.

17. Show graphically that the equations $x + 2y = 3$ and $2x + 4y = 6$ are dependent.

68. The idea of a function

In nature and in our everyday affairs there are countless examples of the dependence of one quantity upon one or more others. The volume of a gas at constant temperature depends upon the pressure upon it; that is, a change in pressure results in a corresponding change in volume. Volume and pressure are two varying quantities, called **variables.** We say that the volume of a gas is a **function** of the pressure upon it. Again, the distance traveled by a man depends upon how long he travels and his speed. We think of distance, one variable, as being a function of time and speed, two other variables. Likewise, the area of a circle is a function of its radius; the volume of a cube is a function of its edge; the interest on a given principal is a function of time and interest rate. It is not always possible to determine a definite relation between two variables. But in mathematical work we deal with cases in which, for any value of one variable, the corresponding value of the other variable can be readily determined.

A **constant** is a quantity whose value does not change.

69. Definition of a function; functional notation

The idea of a function is a very important concept in mathematics. It is difficult to give an accurate definition of function with the tools we have available. For our purposes the following will suffice.

Let A and B be sets of real numbers. A function from A into B is a rule of correspondence that assigns to every number in A a number in the set B.

Now at times the rule might be very explicit and these are the functions that we usually deal with. For example, if A is the set of nonzero real numbers and if B is the set of all real numbers, we can consider the rule: Assign to every element in A its reciprocal less 3. Thus, since 5 is a number in A, we know the number assigned to be $\frac{1}{5} - 3$. In general, if x is any number in A, the number assigned to x is $\frac{1}{x} - 3$.

We usually use letters, like f or g to denote functions. The symbol $f(x)$ (read f of x and called the **value of the function f at** x) is used to denote the number assigned to x by the function f. Thus, in the example of the preceding paragraph, if we denote the function by g, $g(5) = \frac{1}{5} - 3$ and $g(x) = \frac{1}{x} - 3$. Frequently we use this notation to describe a given function. For to know a function, we need to know the value of the function for each of the various numbers of the set A. So, if we tell one that $g(x) = \frac{1}{x} - 3$, and if one knows the x's under consideration, then it is possible to determine the functional value for any x. As we noted in our example, $g(5) = -2\frac{4}{5}$. We can compute $g(\frac{1}{5})$ for $g(x) = \frac{1}{x} - 3$. Since $\frac{1}{5}$ is in our set A, we replace x by $\frac{1}{5}$ and get $g(\frac{1}{5}) = \frac{1}{\frac{1}{5}} - 3 = 2$.

ILLUSTRATIVE EXAMPLE 1. The expression $2x - 3$ is a function of x, because when x is given any value, the value of $2x - 3$ is fixed. Thus, when $x = -1$, $2x - 3 = -5$; when $x = 0$, $2x - 3 = -3$; when $x = 2$, $2x - 3 = 1$. These facts can be stated in compact form by using the symbols $f(x)$, $f(-1)$, $f(0)$, $f(2)$; where, if $f(x)$ denotes the given function of x, then $f(-1)$, $f(0)$, $f(2)$ means the corresponding values of $f(x)$ when

$-1, 0, 2$ are substituted for x. Thus, if $f(x) = 2x - 3$, then

$$f(-1) = 2(-1) - 3 = -5,$$
$$f(0) = 2(0) - 3 = -3,$$
$$f(2) = 2(2) - 3 = 1.$$

ILLUSTRATIVE EXAMPLE 2. Since $t^2 + 3t$ depends for its value upon the value of t, we may write $f(t) = t^2 + 3t$. Then

$$f(-2) = (-2)^2 + 3(-2) = -2,$$
$$f(0) = (0)^2 + 3(0) = 0,$$
$$f(1) = (1)^2 + 3(1) = 4,$$
$$f(10) = (10)^2 + 3(10) = 130,$$
$$f(a^2) = (a^2)^2 + 3(a^2) = a^4 + 3a^2.$$

EXERCISE 48

1. If $f(x) = 2x + 4$, find $f(-2), f(4), f(0), f(x^2), [f(x)]^2, f(k)$.

2. If $f(r) = r^2 - r$, find $f(0), f(4), f(-2), f(\frac{1}{2}), f(x), f(2x)$.

3. If $f(t) = \dfrac{t-1}{t+2}$, find $f(1), f(0), f(-2), f\left(\dfrac{3}{4}\right), f\left(\dfrac{p}{q}\right), f(\sqrt{3})$.

4. If $f(y) = \dfrac{4-y^2}{y^3}$, find $f,(0)\ f(2), f(\frac{1}{2}), f(\sqrt{2}), f(2a), 2f(a)$.

5. The simple interest for 6 months on a given principal is a function of the rate of interest. Symbolically, $I = f(i)$. If the principal is \$400, what is the particular form of $f(i)$? Find $f(0.03), f(0.02), f(0.015)$.

6. The bank discount at the discount rate 6% on a given amount is a function of the time. Symbolically, $D_b = f(n)$. If the amount is \$500, what is the particular form of $f(n)$? Find $f(\frac{1}{6}), f(\frac{1}{3}), f(\frac{1}{4})$.

70. Graph of a function

A function may be represented graphically with reference to two mutually perpendicular axes. The graph shows pictorially the values of $f(x)$

corresponding to the values of x. It gives a convenient means of studying the behavior and properties of a function.

The method of graphing a conveniently smooth function is very similar to that used in Art. 66. Values of x are laid off horizontally and the corresponding values of $f(x)$ are laid off vertically, i.e., suitable points $(x, f(x))$ are plotted. The horizontal axis is referred to as the X-axis again, but we shall call the vertical axis the **function axis** and denote it by OF.

___

ILLUSTRATIVE EXAMPLE 1. Graph the function $\frac{1}{2}x + 1$.

SOLUTION. Let $f(x) = \frac{1}{2}x + 1$. The graph is made up of points whose abscissas are assigned values of x and whose ordinates are the corresponding values of $f(x)$. Assigning different values to x and computing corresponding values of $f(x)$, we get the following table of values:

When $x =$	-4	-3	-2	-1	0	1	2	3	4
then $f(x) = \frac{1}{2}x + 1 =$	-1	$-\frac{1}{2}$	0	$\frac{1}{2}$	1	$\frac{3}{2}$	2	$\frac{5}{2}$	3

Note that the work is identical with drawing the graph of the equation $y = \frac{1}{2}x + 1$. We have merely replaced y by $f(x)$ in this example. Hence the graph of the equation $y = \frac{1}{2}x + 1$ (see Fig. 9) is also the graph of the function $\frac{1}{2}x + 1$, except that the vertical axis should be labeled with OF instead of OY. Just as $y = \frac{1}{2}x + 1$ is called a linear equation, the function $\frac{1}{2}x + 1$ is called a **linear function** of x. The graph of every linear function in one variable is a straight line.

___

ILLUSTRATIVE EXAMPLE 2. Draw the graph of the function $x^2 - 3x - 4$.

SOLUTION. Let $f(x) = x^2 - 3x - 4$. Prepare a table of values as follows:

When $x =$	-3	-2	-1	0	1	$\frac{3}{2}$	2	3	4	5	6
then $f(x) =$	14	6	0	-4	-6	$-\frac{25}{4}$	-6	-4	0	6	14

Plotting the points corresponding to the pairs of values in the table, and joining them by a smooth curve, we obtain the curve in Fig. 11.

The expression $x^2 - 3x - 4$ is called a **quadratic function** of x. The graph of a quadratic function in one variable is a curve, called a **parabola,** whose general shape is that shown in Fig. 11.

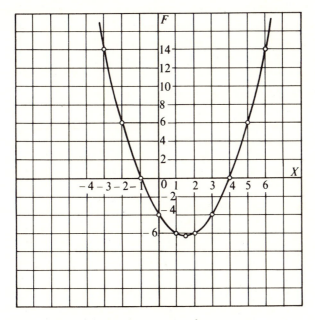

Fig. 11. Graph of $f(x) = x^2 - 3x - 4$.

ILLUSTRATIVE EXAMPLE 3. Represent the function $x^3 - x^2 - 10x + 12$ graphically.

SOLUTION. Let $f(x) = x^3 - x^2 - 10x + 12$. Prepare a table of values as follows:

When $x =$	-4	$-3\frac{1}{2}$	-3	-2	$-1\frac{1}{2}$	-1	0	1	$1\frac{1}{2}$	2	$2\frac{1}{2}$	3	$3\frac{1}{2}$	4
then $f(x) =$	-28	$-8\frac{1}{8}$	6	20	$21\frac{3}{8}$	20	12	2	$-1\frac{7}{8}$	-4	$-3\frac{5}{8}$	0	$7\frac{5}{8}$	20

Plotting the points corresponding to the pairs of values in the table, we obtain the curve in Fig. 12. The expression $x^3 - x^2 - 10x + 12$ is called a **cubic function** of x.

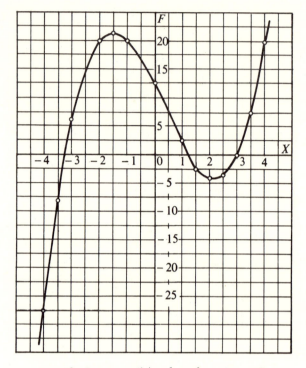

Fig. 12. Graph of $f(x) = x^3 - x^2 - 10x + 12$.

71. Extent of the graph of a function

The graphs in Figs. 9, 11, and 12 give only a partial view of the relation between the value of the function and the value of x. We might have inserted many more pairs of values in the respective tables. In fact, there is no limit to the extent of these tables in either positive or negative direction. We have represented, in each case, an essential portion of the curve. As will be seen from Art. 72, we are especially interested in that part of the graph that includes the points at which the function is zero.

In preparing a table of values, only two pairs are necessary for a linear function. Many more pairs are needed for quadratic, cubic, or higher functions. Efficacy in graphing a function is gained through experience. The student is advised to prepare a table of a sufficient number of pairs, using integral values of x, say from -5 to $+5$, and to plot the corresponding points. An inspection of these plotted points may show just where the graph makes sharp turns or curves rapidly. For such portions of the graph, the points should be closer. He should accordingly extend the table and take as many fractional values of x as would appear to be expedient.

It is not necessary to use the same scale on both axes. But if different scales are used the graph fails to be Cartesian. By inspecting the table of values, the student should be able to select the proper scale for each axis in order that the graph may show clearly the relation of the function to the variable.

72. Graphic solution of an equation

The problem of solving an equation in one unknown, say x, is closely connected with the problem of representing graphically the relation between the value of $f(x)$ and the value of x.

Suppose we wish to solve (to find the roots of) an equation $f(x) = 0$. At any point where the graph crosses the X-axis, the value of $f(x)$ is zero. The abscissa of this point represents, then, a value of x for which $f(x) = 0$. But to solve the equation $f(x) = 0$ is to find the value or values of x that satisfy the equation $f(x) = 0$. Hence *the abscissas of the points where the graph of $f(x)$ crosses the X-axis are the real roots of the equation $f(x) = 0$.* It should be said in passing that the graphic method gives only the *real* roots.

The student is already familiar with the algebraic solution of linear equations and quadratic equations in one unknown. There is no simple algebraic method for the solution of cubic and higher equations, in general. For this reason, the graphic method is very valuable for *approximating* the real roots of an equation of degree higher than the second. The accuracy is, of course, not necessarily very great.

———

ILLUSTRATIVE EXAMPLE 1. Solve $\frac{1}{2}x + 1 = 0$ graphically.

SOLUTION. Draw the graph of $f(x) = \frac{1}{2}x + 1$ (see Fig. 9). The graph of the function crosses the X-axis at $x = -2$. Hence $x = -2$ is the solution of the given equation. Verify this answer (a) by substituting -2 for x in the given equation, and (b) by solving the equation algebraically.

———

ILLUSTRATIVE EXAMPLE 2. Solve $x^2 - 3x - 4 = 0$ graphically.

SOLUTION. Draw the graph of $f(x) = x^2 - 3x - 4$ (see Fig. 11). The graph of the function crosses the X-axis at $x = -1$ and $x = 4$. Hence $x = -1$ or 4 is the required solution. Verify each answer as in Example 1.

ILLUSTRATIVE EXAMPLE 3. Solve $x^3 - x^2 - 10x + 12 = 0$ graphically.

SOLUTION. Draw the graph of $f(x) = x^3 - x^2 - 10x + 12$ (see Fig. 12). The graph of the function crosses the X-axis at $x = -3.2$, $x = 1.2$, and $x = 3$. (The first and second are approximations to one decimal place.) Hence the roots of the given equation are $x = -3.2$ (approximately), $x = 1.2$ (approximately), and $x = 3$. Check each by substitution.

EXERCISE 49

Represent each function graphically:

1. $f(x) = 2x - 3$. **6.** $f(x) = x^2 + x$. **11.** $f(x) = x^3 + x - 3$.

2. $f(x) = \frac{1}{2}x + 4$. **7.** $f(x) = 2x - x^2$. **12.** $f(x) = x^3 - x^2 - 2x$.

3. $f(x) = x^2 - 1$. **8.** $f(x) = 5x - x^2$. **13.** $f(x) = x^3 + x^2 - 3x$.

4. $f(x) = \pm 2\sqrt{x}$. **9.** $f(x) = 2^x$. **14.** $f(x) = \pm\sqrt{16 - x^2}$.

5. $f(x) = \dfrac{4}{x}$. **10.** $f(x) = \dfrac{2x}{x - 1}$. **15.** $f(x) = \pm\dfrac{3}{2}\sqrt{4 - x^2}$.

Find the real roots of each equation graphically:

16. $2x - 3 = 0$. **21.** $x^2 + x = 2$. **26.** $x^3 - 7x = 6$.

17. $2x + 4 = 0$. **22.** $x^2 - x = 2$. **27.** $2x^3 + x^2 + 7 = 0$.

18. $\frac{1}{4}x + 1 = 0$. **23.** $x^2 - 2x = 4$. **28.** $x^3 + 3x^2 + x = 2$.

19. $2 - \frac{1}{2}x = 0$. **24.** $2x^2 + 3x = 1$. **29.** $x^4 + 2x^3 - 2x - 1 = 0$

20. $x^2 - 2x = 0$. **25.** $x^2 - 2x = 15$. **30.** $x^4 - 6x^2 - 3x = 1$.

MISCELLANEOUS EXERCISE 50
REVIEW OF CHAPTER 8

1. Find the area of the triangle with vertices $(-3, 0)$, $(5, 0)$, $(-2, 1)$.

2. Draw a graph of: (a) $3x - y = 6$; (b) $2x = 5y$; (c) $x - 2 = 0$.

3. Solve graphically the equations $2x + 5y = 4$, $x + 2y = 1$.

4. If $f(x) = 5x - x^2$, find: (a) $f(-3)$; (b) $f(5)$; (c) $f(\frac{1}{2})$; (d) $f(a^2)$.

5. If $f(r) = r^{-1} + r^{1/2}$, then $f(\frac{1}{4})$ divided by $f(8)$ equals what?

6. Find the distance from the point $(-3, 1)$ to the point $(2, 4)$.

7. Describe the locus of points for which (a) $x = 3$; (b) $y = -2$.

8. Solve graphically the equations $y = 3x - 1$, $x + 2 = 1$.

9. A circle with center at $(4, 1)$ is tangent to the line $y = -2$. Find: (a) its radius; (b) its circumference; (c) its area.

10. For a given time the discount rate d corresponding to the interest rate i is a function of i. What is the form of $f(i)$ if the time is $\frac{1}{2}$ year?

11. Solve graphically: (a) $x^2 - x = 3$; (b) $x^3 + 2x = 5$; (c) $x^3 = 27$.

12. Graph: (a) $f(x) = 4^x$; (b) $f(x) = \pm\sqrt{9 - x^2}$; (c) $f(x) = 6/x$.

13. Grades on a certain test were as follows: 11% received A, 16% B, 40% C, 20% D, and 13% E. Illustrate these data by a bar graph.

14. In 1966 age distribution in the United States was: Under 10 years, 20.7% of population; 10 to 19, 19.0%; 20 to 29, 13.0%; 30 to 39, 11.5% 40 to 49, 12.2%; 50 to 59, 10.2%; 60 to 69, 7.3%; 70 years and over, 6.1%. Draw a broken-line graph of these data.

15. The interest on $1 for 10 years, at various rates compounded annually, is: At 1%, 10¢; at 2%, 22¢; at 3%, 34¢; at 4%, 48¢; at 5%, 63¢; at 6%, 79¢; at 7%, 97¢. Exhibit these data by a curve.

16. Read the interest at $6\frac{1}{2}$% from the graph of Problem 15.

17. From the graph of Problem 15, read the rate if interest is 25¢.

18. World War II peak strength of armed forces (in millions) was: U.S.S.R., 12.5; U.S., 12.4; Germany, 10.0; Japan, 6.1; France, 5.0; China, 5.0; U.K., 4.7; Italy, 4.0. Draw a bar graph of these data.

Refer to the curve $y = x^2 - x - 20$; answer without a graph:

19. If the abscissa of a point on the curve is 5, the ordinate = ?

20. If the ordinate of a point on the curve is 6, the abscissa = ?

21. In what points does the curve intersect the X-axis?

22. In what point does the curve intersect the Y-axis?

23. At what points is the ordinate 4 times the abscissa?

24. At what points is the abscissa 3 more than the ordinate?

Chapter NINE

LOGARITHMS

73. Definition

The **logarithm** of a positive number N to a given positive base a ($\neq$ 1) is the exponent of the power to which the base a must be raised to produce the number N. Thus, if $a^x = N$, the logarithm of N to the base a is x. This is expressed symbolically thus: $\log_a N = x$. The symbol **log,** which stands for the words "the logarithm of," is written without a capital and without a period.

From the above definition, we see that the statement

$$\log_2 32 = 5 \quad \text{is equivalent to} \quad 2^5 = 32,$$
$$\log_3 81 = 4 \quad \text{is equivalent to} \quad 3^4 = 81,$$
$$\log_5 625 = 4 \quad \text{is equivalent to} \quad 5^4 = 625,$$
$$\log_{10} 1000 = 3 \quad \text{is equivalent to} \quad 10^3 = 1000.$$

It should be evident, then, that any positive number other than 1 may be used as the base of a system of logarithms.

74. Common logarithms

The system whose base is 10 is known as the **Common,** or **Briggs',** system of logarithms; and since, in the mathematics of finance, logarithms are used merely to shorten the labor of computations with numbers, and since common logarithms are best adapted to this purpose, we shall, in the following pages, use this system exclusively. Thus, for example, instead of writing $\log_{10} 763$, we shall write $\log 763$, and read "the logarithm of 763," with the agreement that, when so written, the base 10 is understood.

The following relations between exponentials and logarithms are evident:

$$10^3 \ = 1000 \text{ is equivalent to } \log 1000 = 3;$$
$$10^2 \ = 100 \ \text{ is equivalent to } \log 100 = 2;$$
$$10^1 \ = 10 \ \ \text{ is equivalent to } \ \log 10 = 1;$$
$$10^0 \ = 1 \ \ \ \text{ is equivalent to } \ \ \log 1 = 0;$$
$$10^{-1} = 0.1 \ \ \text{ is equivalent to } \ \log 0.1 = -1;$$
$$10^{-2} = 0.01 \ \text{ is equivalent to } \log 0.01 = -2;$$
$$10^{-3} = 0.001 \text{ is equivalent to } \log 0.001 = -3.$$

Note. In this article, a "decimal" means a positive decimal fraction less than 1. We assume that a number is expressed as the sum of an integer and a decimal. The **significant digits** of a number are those preceded and followed by no digits other than zeros; thus, the four significant digits of either 706300 or 0.07063 are 7, 0, 6, and 3.

We consider the logarithm of a number to be the value of a function. For this discussion let us use the letter h to denote this function. Then $h(x) = \log_{10} x = \log x$. We will assume that this function is defined for all positive real numbers. Thus, given any positive number x, $h(x)$ is a real number. Now, as noted, we realize that the value of the function, $h(x)$, is easily discoverable for numbers x written in the form 10^k. This is because, from our definition, the logarithm of 10^k is k. Thus

$$h(100) = h(10^2) = \log 10^2 = 2.$$

Similarly,

$$h(0.0001) = h(10^{-4}) = \log 10^{-4} = -4.$$

But, given an arbitrary positive number, it is difficult to write this number in the form 10^k. That is, it is difficult to find its logarithm. Fortunately, we have available tables that give us approximate values of $\log x$ for x satisfying $1 \leq x < 10$. We also are able to use a property of this function to reduce the problem of finding the logarithm of any positive number to that of finding the logarithm of a number x, $1 \leq x < 10$.

The property needed is

$$h(xy) = h(x) + h(y)$$

or

$$\log xy = \log x + \log y.$$

We will prove this property in Art. 77. At this time we note how this property allows us to make the reduction indicated. Consider $x = 2734$. This is *not* a number between 1 and 10 and thus log x cannot be found in our tables. We may, however, write 2734 as 2.734×10^3. Then, using our property,

$$\begin{aligned}
\log 2734 &= \log (2.734 \times 10^3) \\
&= \log 2.734 + \log 10^3 \\
&= (\log 2.734) + 3.
\end{aligned}$$

We can find log 2.734 in our table.

In general, if N is a positive number whose logarithm we wish to find, we write N as

$$N = 10^c \cdot M$$

where c is an integer and where M satisfies $1 \leq M < 10$. Then

$$\begin{aligned}
\log N &= \log (10^c \cdot M) \\
&= \log 10^c + \log M \\
&= c + \log M,
\end{aligned}$$

where c is called the **characteristic** of log N, and log M, available in the table, is called the **mantissa** of log N. We should note that log M satisfies

$$0 \leq \log M < 1.$$

In brief, the logarithm of any positive number other than an integral power of 10 is an integer plus a decimal. The integer is called the characteristic and the decimal is called the mantissa. The characteristic depends upon the position of the decimal point, and is independent of the value of the individual digits; whereas the mantissa depends upon the sequence of digits, and is independent of the decimal point.

If one is given to the use of rules, the following will serve the purpose of yielding the characteristics of logarithms. They are not needed if one chooses to use the above procedure.

Rule 1

The characteristic of the logarithm of a number greater than 1 is positive, and its numerical value is one unit less than the number of digits to the left of the decimal point.

Rule 2

The characteristic of the logarithm of a positive number less than 1 is negative, and its numerical value is one unit more than the number of zeros between the decimal point and the first significant digit.

Note in particular the following: The logarithm of 1 is zero; the logarithm of any number greater than 1 is *positive;* the logarithm of any positive number less than 1 is *negative;* a negative number has no (real) logarithm, since the base 10 raised to any (real) power gives a positive number.

The mantissas of exact numbers except when they are zero, cannot be expressed as exact numbers, nor can they be obtained by inspection; they can, however, be computed to any required decimal place by methods too difficult for explanation here. When so computed, they are tabulated for convenient reference.

75. Tables of mantissas

Table I, found on pages 441–455 and called a **six-place** table, gives the mantissas of numbers from 1 to 9999, computed to six decimal places. Table II, found on pages 456–457 and called a **seven-place** table, gives the mantissas of numbers from 10,000 to 11,009, computed to seven decimal places. The former table is for computations with numbers in general, and the latter for computations in problems involving interest. The student should note that these tables contain the mantissas only, and that the decimal point must be placed before the first digit.

ILLUSTRATIVE EXAMPLE 1. Find log 643.7, using the six-place table.

SOLUTION. Since there are three digits to the left of the decimal point, the characteristic is 2 (see Rule 1 of Art. 74). To find the mantissa, disregard the decimal point and consider the number as if it were 6437. Now, on page 450, in the six-place table, look down the column of numbers headed *N*, for 643, the first three digits of the given number; then, opposite this number and in the column headed 7, the fourth digit of the given number, we find the mantissa .808684. This is the mantissa of 643.7. Therefore

$$\log 643.7 = 2.808684. \quad Ans.$$

ILLUSTRATIVE EXAMPLE 2. Find log 0.006437, using the six-place table.

SOLUTION. Since $0.006437 = 6.437 \times 10^{-3}$ the characteristic is -3 (see Rule 2 of Art. 74), which is written in the more convenient form $7 - 10$. Now, if we disregard the decimal point, the number is 6437, as in illustrative example 1; hence its mantissa is .808684 as before. Therefore

$$\log 0.006437 = 7.808684 - 10. \quad Ans.$$

Note. There is nothing particularly mysterious about representing -3 as $7 - 10$. The reason for doing this is that in many computations it is convenient to do so, as we shall see.

ILLUSTRATIVE EXAMPLE 3. Find log 1.0695, using the seven-place table.

SOLUTION. The characteristic is 0 (Rule 1 of Art. 74). For the mantissa, on page 459, in the seven-place table and in the column headed N, we find the number 1069, the first four digits of the given number; then, in this line and in the column headed 5 we find *1808; the asterisk indicates that the first three digits of the mantissa are 029 instead of 028. Thus, the mantissa of 1.0695 is .0291808. Therefore

$$\log 1.0695 = 0.0291808. \quad Ans.$$

ILLUSTRATIVE EXAMPLE 4. Given $\log x = 1.673557$; to find x to four significant digits, using the six-place table.

SOLUTION. Since the characteristic is 1, there will be two digits to the left of the decimal point. Since the six-place table contains the mantissas of all numbers of four digits or less, we may take directly from the table that number whose mantissa is nearest the given mantissa .673557. Mantissas whose first two digits are 67 are found on page 450, and we now find the mantissa nearest the given mantissa to be .673574. Since this mantissa is opposite the number 471 and in the column of 6, it is the mantissa of 4716. Placing the decimal point to the right of the second digit, we have

$$x = 47.16 \quad \text{Correct to four significant digits.} \quad Ans.$$

ILLUSTRATIVE EXAMPLE 5. Given $\log x = 0.0382613$; to find x to five significant digits, using the seven-place table.

SOLUTION. On page 457, in the seven-place table, we find the mantissa .0382624, which is the mantissa nearest to the given mantissa; hence the number 10921, corresponding to this mantissa, is the required number of five digits. Placing the decimal point to the right of the first digit (Rule 1 of Art. 74), we have

$$x = 1.0921. \quad \text{Correct to five significant digits.} \quad Ans.$$

———

EXERCISE 51

Using Table I, find the logarithm of each number:

1. 52.	**4.** 6.18.	**7.** 3687.	**10.** 0.0084.	**13.** 75.64.
2. 4300.	**5.** 62.3.	**8.** 85.49.	**11.** 0.1917.	**14.** 0.05612.
3. 0.042.	**6.** 0.618.	**9.** 3.166.	**12.** 32.08.	**15.** 0.00981.

Using Table II, find the logarithm of each number:

16. 1.025.	**19.** 10.473.	**22.** 0.0011.	**25.** 10.312.	**28.** 110.07.
17. 1.0138	**20.** 1069.4.	**23.** 0.0105.	**26.** 1.0426.	**29.** 10.012.
18. 0.107.	**21.** 1.0125.	**24.** 10285.	**27.** 103250.	**30.** 10.352.

Using Table I, find x to four significant digits if log x equals:

31. 3.851747.	**35.** 2.535674.	**39.** 1.733278.	**43.** 6.003029 − 10.
32. 2.531607.	**36.** 1.941213.	**40.** 4.823018.	**44.** 9.505693 − 10.
33. 0.016179.	**37.** 2.034378.	**41.** 1.040444.	**45.** 8.035510 − 10.
34. 0.342817.	**38.** 3.865755.	**42.** 1.572872.	**46.** 7.438226 − 10.

Using Table II, find x to five significant digits if log x equals:

47. 2.0062521.	**50.** 1.0151082.	**53.** 2.0125840.	**56.** 7.0146045 − 10.
48. 4.0318930.	**51.** 3.0357098.	**54.** 0.0201955.	**57.** 8.0110195 − 10.
49. 0.0269827.	**52.** 2.0174090.	**55.** 4.0239517.	**58.** 8.0037190 − 10.

76. Interpolation.

We will now show how to obtain from Table I the approximate mantissa of *any* number, and, also, how to obtain the number of five or, possibly, six significant digits corresponding to any given mantissa, by the method of (linear) **interpolation**. This method assumes that the number and its mantissa have the same rate of change. This is not true, of course, but with the following limitations is sufficiently accurate for small differences: Either the sixth significant digit of a number or the sixth digit of a mantissa obtained by interpolation in the six-place table is of uncertain accuracy; any further digits are meaningless and should not be written.

___

ILLUSTRATIVE EXAMPLE 1. Find log 374.587, using the six-place table.

SOLUTION. The characteristic is 2 (Rule 1 of Art. 74). To find the mantissa, disregard the decimal point and consider the number as if it were 374587. Now this number lies between the numbers 374500 and 374600; hence its mantissa lies between the mantissas of these two numbers. On page 445 we find the mantissas of these two numbers to be .573452 and .573568, respectively (the annexed ciphers do not affect the mantissa); the significant difference, as given in the last column, headed D, is 116, the last digit being in the sixth decimal place. More clearly,

$$\text{mantissa of } 374600 = .573568 \tag{1}$$

$$\text{mantissa of } 374587 = .\underline{\hspace{1.5cm}} \tag{2}$$

$$\text{mantissa of } 374500 = .573452 \tag{3}$$

Subtract (3) from (2), denoting the significant difference by a, thus getting

significant difference for $87 = a$.

Subtract (3) from (1), getting

significant difference for $100 = 116$.

Now, assuming that these differences are proportional, we have

$$\frac{a}{116} = \frac{87}{100}.$$

Whence $a = 100.92$, which we round off to 101.

Hence the significant difference for 87 is 101. Adding .000101 to .573452, the mantissa of 374500, we have .573553, which is the required mantissa.

Therefore   log 374.587 = 2.573553.   *Ans.*

___

ILLUSTRATIVE EXAMPLE 2. Given log $x = 2.252265$; to find x to six significant digits, using the six-place table.

SOLUTION. Since the given mantissa .252265 lies between the mantissas .252125 and .252368 (see table, page 000), which are the mantissas of

1787 and 1788, respectively, the required number lies between these numbers. Arranging the numbers with six digits, we have

$$\text{mantissa of } 178800 = .252368 \tag{1}$$

$$\text{mantissa of } \quad x \quad = .252265 \tag{2}$$

$$\text{mantissa of } 178700 = .252125 \tag{3}$$

Subtract (3) from (2), designating the difference of the numbers by a, and we have

significant difference for $a = 140$.

Subtract (3) from (1), and we have

significant difference for $100 = 243$.

Then, $$\frac{a}{100} = \frac{140}{243}.$$

Whence $$a = 57.6^{+}, \text{ which we round off to } 58.$$

Adding 58 to 178700, we have 178758. Placing the decimal point after the third digit, since the characteristic is 2, we have $x = 178.758$.   *Ans.*

ILLUSTRATIVE EXAMPLE 3. Given $\log x = 4.0351695$; to find x to seven significant digits, using the seven-place table.

SOLUTION. The given mantissa lies between the mantissas .0351495 and .0351895 (see table, page 459), which are the mantissas of 10843 and 10844 respectively; hence the required number lies between these numbers. Arranging the numbers with seven digits, we have

$$\text{mantissa of } 1084400 = .0351895 \tag{1}$$

$$\text{mantissa of } \quad x \quad = .0351695 \tag{2}$$

$$\text{mantissa of } 1084300 = .0351495 \tag{3}$$

Subtract (3) from (2), denoting the significant difference by a, and we have

significant difference for $a = 200$.

Subtract (3) from (1), and we have

significant difference for $100 = 400$.

Then
$$\frac{a}{100} = \frac{200}{400}.$$

Whence
$$a = 50.$$

Adding 50 to 1084300, we have the seven digits 1084350. Placing the decimal point after the fifth digit (Rule 1 of Art. 74) gives $x = 10843.50$.

EXERCISE 52

Using Table I, find the logarithm of each number:

1. 27.003.	**5.** 238.71.	**9.** 0.21461.	**13.** 295.11.	**17.** 0.25113.
2. 5623.7.	**6.** 12659.	**10.** 3.14426.	**14.** 413.766.	**18.** 0.0031812.
3. 89256.	**7.** 6504.8.	**11.** 281.932.	**15.** 59.3617.	**19.** 0.0047634.
4. 41.862.	**8.** 2.7531.	**12.** 0.51234.	**16.** 708345.	**20.** 0.069458.

Using Table II, find the logarithm of each number:

21. 10.6705.	**23.** 1080.33.	**25.** 104.201.	**27.** 0.0103062.
22. 105.864.	**24.** 1.02625.	**26.** 0.106727.	**28.** 11000.8.

Using Table I, find x to six significant digits if log x equals:

29. 1.392175.	**33.** 2.366805.	**37.** 1.355839.	**41.** 8.423084 − 10.
30. 4.331219.	**34.** 0.679231.	**38.** 3.992660.	**42.** 9.829234 − 10.
31. 3.892026.	**35.** 4.678814.	**39.** 2.058126.	**43.** 8.730364 − 10.
32. 2.056085.	**36.** 1.634317.	**40.** 1.894081.	**44.** 6.558392 − 10.

77. Applications of logarithms

Logarithms can be used in computations to shorten the processes of multiplication, division, raising to powers, and extracting roots.

Law I. MULTIPLICATION

The logarithm of the product of two or more numbers is equal to the sum of their logarithms.

PROOF:

If
$$x = \log M, \text{ and } y = \log N,$$

then $\qquad\qquad 10^x = M$, and $10^y = N$.

Taking the product of these last two equations, we have

$$10^x \times 10^y = MN,$$

or $\qquad\qquad 10^{x+y} = MN;$

expressed as a logarithm, this gives

$$\log (MN) = x + y.$$

Substituting the values of x and y, we have

$$\textbf{log } (MN) = \textbf{log } M + \textbf{log } N. \qquad\qquad (1)$$

This law can be extended to any number of factors.

Law II. DIVISION

The logarithm of a common fraction is equal to the logarithm of the numerator minus the logarithm of the denominator.

PROOF:

If $\qquad\qquad x = \log M$, and $y = \log N,$

then $\qquad\qquad 10^x = M$, and $10^y = N.$

Taking the quotient of these last two equations, we have

$$\frac{10^x}{10^y} = \frac{M}{N},$$

or $\qquad\qquad 10^{x-y} = \frac{M}{N};$

expressed as a logarithm, this gives

$$\log \left(\frac{M}{N}\right) = x - y.$$

Substituting the values of x and y, we have

$$\textbf{log } \left(\frac{M}{N}\right) = \textbf{log } M - \textbf{log } N. \qquad\qquad (2)$$

Law III. POWERS AND ROOTS

The logarithm of the power of a number is equal to the exponent times the logarithm of the number.

PROOF:

If
$$x = \log M,$$

then
$$10^x = M.$$

Raising each member of this equation to the pth power, we have

$$(10^x)^p = M^p,$$

or
$$10^{px} = M^p;$$

expressed as a logarithm, this gives

$$\log (M^p) = px.$$

Substituting the value of x, we have

$$\log (M^p) = p \times \log M. \qquad (3)$$

This formula holds true for all real values of p.

———

ILLUSTRATIVE EXAMPLE 1. Evaluate 2.567×13.748 to four significant digits.

SOLUTION. Let $2.567 \times 13.748 = x$. Applying Law I of logarithms, we have

$$\log 2.567 + \log 13.748 = \log x.$$

Arranging in column and using the six-place table, we have

$$\log 2.567 = 0.409426$$
$$\log 13.748 = 1.138240$$

Adding, $\log x = 1.547666.$
Whence $x = 35.29.$ *Ans.*

———

ILLUSTRATIVE EXAMPLE 2. Evaluate $\dfrac{26.375}{0.8537}$ to five significant digits.

SOLUTION. Let $\dfrac{26.375}{0.8537} = x$. Applying Law II of logarithms, we have

$$\log 26.375 - \log 0.8537 = \log x.$$

Arranging in column and using the six-place table, we have

$$\log 26.375 = 11.421193 - 10$$
$$\log 0.8537 = \;\;9.931305 - 10$$

Subtracting, $$\log x = \;\;1.489888.$$
Whence $$x = 30.895. \quad Ans.$$

ILLUSTRATIVE EXAMPLE 3. Evaluate $(1.02125)^{5/2}$ to six significant digits.

SOLUTION. Let $(1.02125)^{5/2} = x$. Applying Law III of logarithms and using the *seven-place* table, we have

$$\log x = \tfrac{5}{2} \times \log 1.02125 = \tfrac{5}{2}(0.0091321) = 0.0228303.$$

Whence $x = 1.05398. \quad Ans.$

ILLUSTRATIVE EXAMPLE 4. Evaluate $\dfrac{(1.045)^{20} - 1}{0.045}$ to five significant digits.

SOLUTION. We cannot evaluate this fraction at once by the use of logarithms, since we cannot take the logarithm of the numerator until the indicated subtraction has been performed. We can, however, find log $(1.045)^{20}$ from the *seven-place* table by applying Law III, thus:

$$\log (1.045)^{20} = 20 \times \log 1.045 = 20 \times 0.0191163 = 0.382326.$$

Whence $(1.045)^{20} = 2.41172.$ (Using the *six-place* table)

Now, substituting this value in the original fraction, we have

$$\frac{(1.045)^{20} - 1}{0.045} = \frac{2.41172 - 1}{0.045} = \frac{1.41172}{0.045} = 31.372. \quad Ans.$$

ILLUSTRATIVE EXAMPLE 5. Given $1795 = 980(1 + i)^{12}$; to find i.

SOLUTION. Divide each member by 980, and get

$$\frac{1795}{980} = (1 + i)^{12}.$$

Applying logarithms, we have

$$\log 1795 - \log 980 = 12 \times \log (1 + i).$$

Arranging in column, we have

$$\log 1795 = 3.254064$$
$$\log 980 = 2.991226$$

Subtracting, we have $12 \times \log(1 + i) = 0.262838,$

and $\qquad\qquad \log(1 + i) = 0.021903.$

Whence $\qquad\qquad 1 + i = 1.0517.$

Therefore $\qquad\qquad i = 0.0517.$ *Ans.*

ILLUSTRATIVE EXAMPLE 6. Given $320.71 = 100(1.06)^n$; to find n.

SOLUTION. Applying logarithms, we have

$$\log 320.71 = \log 100 + n \times \log 1.06.$$

Solving for n, we get

$$n = \frac{\log 320.71 - \log 100}{\log 1.06} = \frac{2.506113 - 2}{0.025306} = \frac{0.506113}{0.025306}$$

Applying logarithms, we have

$$\log 0.506113 - \log 0.025306 = \log n.$$

Arranging in column and performing the indicated subtraction,

$$\log 0.506113 = 9.704247 - 10$$
$$\log 0.025306 = 8.403224 - 10$$
$$\log n = 1.301023.$$

Whence $\qquad\qquad n = 20.00.$ (To 4 significant digits)   *Ans.*

EXERCISE 53

Compute by logarithms to four significant digits:

1. $(1.231)^4$.	**5.** $(1.035)^6$.	**9.** $(1.112)^3$.	**13.** $(135)^{1/2}$.
2. $(5.086)^4$.	**6.** $(0.563)^2$.	**10.** $(6.247)^3$.	**14.** $(0.156)^{5/2}$.
3. $\sqrt{873}$.	**7.** $\sqrt[5]{0.247}$.	**11.** $\sqrt[3]{60.12}$.	**15.** $(0.092)^{3/2}$.
4. $\sqrt[3]{6291}$.	**8.** $\sqrt[4]{71.08}$.	**12.** $\sqrt{0.065}$.	**16.** $(102.3)^{3/4}$.

17. 3.123×25.06.

18. 632.4×4.87.

19. $(3.65)^2 \div 521$.

20. $75.8\sqrt[3]{210}$.

21. $\dfrac{37(23.3)(2.11)^2}{\sqrt{111.3}}$.

22. $72.2 \div 0.0063$.

23. $4.853 \div 61.39$.

24. $(0.234)^2(4.72)^3$.

25. $1212 \div \sqrt{86.21}$.

26. $\dfrac{540 \times 0.06 \times 71}{365}$.

27. 85×34.

28. $85 \div 34$.

29. $(\log 84) \div (\log 31)$.

30. $(\log 85) \times (\log 34)$.

31. $\sqrt[3]{\dfrac{6034 \times 0.4185}{1.507}}$.

Compute by logarithms to five significant digits:

32. $256(1.0277)^{10}$.

33. $84.35(1.035)^{40}$.

34. $\dfrac{1 - (1.04)^{-8}}{0.04}$.

35. $6325(1.062)^{-60}$.

36. $4136(1.053)^{-50}$.

37. $\dfrac{(1.025)^{30} - 1}{0.025}$.

38. $5[(1.04)^{1/5} - 1]$.

39. $3[(1.06)^{1/3} - 1]$.

40. $\dfrac{(1.035)^{20} - 1}{0.035}$.

Compute by logarithms to six significant digits:

41. 2.1136×43.21.

42. 3.1416×210.4.

43. $3500(1.03)^{12}$.

44. $2760(1.02)^{15}$.

45. $38.6 \div 235.89$.

46. $708.53 \div 394.4$.

47. $35.42 \div \sqrt[3]{608}$.

48. $\sqrt{1564} \div 0.765$.

49. $825(1.02)^{1/12}$.

50. $7540(1.06)^{-20}$.

51. $4680(1.05)^{-10}$.

52. $375(1.03)^{5/2}$.

Solve each equation for the unknown (omit interpolation):

53. $50(1.035)^n = 200$.

54. $(1.0463)^{-n} = 0.3826$.

55. $(1.02)^n - 1 = 0.5314$.

56. $35(1 + i)^8 = 49$.

57. $(1 + i)^{-10} = 0.9490$.

58. $(1 + i)^{1/4} = 1.0113$.

MISCELLANEOUS EXERCISE 54
REVIEW OF CHAPTER 9

1. Tell the significant digits of: (a) 6.008; (b) 4500; (c) 0.00531.

2. Graph $y = \log x$ from $x = 1$ to $x = 10$ at intervals of $\frac{1}{2}$.

3. From Table I find: (a) log 405.3; (b) log 0.0073; (c) log 23.6.

4. From Table II find: (a) log 1053.8; (b) log 0.1045; (c) log 10.385.

5. (Table II) Find r if log r equals: (a) 2.0152759; (b) 0.0113621.

6. (Table I) Find x is log x equals (a) 3.861116; (b) 8.416141 − 10.

7. (No tables) Given log 621 = 2.7931, find: (a) log 6210; (b) log 6.21; (c) log 0.00621; (d) x if log x = 4.7931; (e) y if log y = 9.7931 − 10.

8. (No tables) Given $\log 258 = 2.4116$ and $\log 259 = 2.4133$, find: (a) $\log 25.88$; (b) $\log 0.02583$; (c) x to 4 digits if $\log x = 0.4126$.

9. Write in logarithmic form: (a) $y = 2^x$; (b) $r = 10^n$; (c) $q = a^{t^2}$.

10. Write in exponential form: (a) $x = \log_6 y$; (b) $s = \log_e t$.

11. Find x if: (a) $\log_3 x = 2$; (b) $\log_x 4 = \frac{1}{2}$; (c) $\log_2 32 = x + 1$.

12. Find y if: (a) $\log y = \log 6 + \log 4$; (b) $\log y = \log 12 - \log 3$.

13. Interpolate in Table I to find: (a) $\log 456.82$; (b) $\log 0.061276$.

14. Interpolate in Table II to find: (a) $\log 10361.8$; (b) $\log 1.05173$.

15. From Table I find N to 5 significant digits if $\log N = 1.876917$.

16. Find x if: (a) $\log_2 x = -3$; (b) $\log_3 \frac{1}{9} = x$; (c) $\log_4 (x - 2) = 0$.

17. Find y if: (a) $\log y = 2 \log 7$; (b) $\log y = 3 \log 2 - \frac{1}{2} \log 36$.

18. If we write $\log 25000 = 3 + n \log 5$, then $n = $?

19. Compute to 4 significant digits: (a) 386×2.457; (b) $59.4 \div 716$.

20. Compute to 5 significant digits: (a) $(1.013)^5$; (b) $25[(1.04)^{10} - 1]$.

21. Compute to 6 significant digits: (a) $(18.21)^3$; (b) $2650(1.024)^{-8}$.

22. Compute to 4 significant digits: (a) $\sqrt[3]{765.8}$; (b) $\sqrt{63.2} \div 32.15$.

23. If $(1 + i)^{-10} = 0.5513$, find i to 3 significant digits.

24. Find n to 4 significant digits if $(1.0325)^n = 1.782$.

25. Find x to 2 decimal places if: (a) $3^x = 12$; (b) $265 = (x - 3)^4$.

26. Given $a = v^2/R$. Express $\log a$ in terms of $\log v$ and $\log R$.

27. Find $\frac{1}{3} \log x$ if $\log x = 8.4732 - 10$. [*Hint.* Since 10 is not exactly divisible by 3, first add and subtract 20, rewriting $\log x = 28.4732 - 30$.]

28. If $\log x = 1.8034$ and $\log y = 8.7542 - 10$, find: (a) $\log x^{3/2}$; (b) $\log x^3 y$; (c) $\log y^2$; (d) $\log y^{1/3}$; (e) $\log (1/x)$; (f) $\log (x/y)$; (g) $\log y^{-1}$.

29. Evaluate $(1.02)^{-4}$ to 4 decimal places by logarithms.

30. Evaluate $(1.02)^{-4}$ to 4 decimal places by the binomial theorem.

Chapter TEN

STATISTICS

78. Introduction

In attacking any problem, the usual method of science is to begin by collecting facts, called **data.** Such data may result from measurements and be exhibited to the eye as a set of numbers. For example, the count of bacteria in water from each city in a state, the population of a state arranged by towns and cities, the incomes of farmers, the daily total sales on the New York Stock Exchange, the heights or weights of freshmen in a college, a count of the visible stars in a sector of the sky, and so on, indefinitely.

Originally statistics meant data collected in the interest of the state. Today statistics refers to the collection, classification, and mathematical analysis of any sort of data. The subject is of increasing importance. It has an enormous literature; the student who desires acquaintance with it is advised to read the article "Statistics" in the *Encyclopaedia Britannica* or in the *International*. Here we can do no more than touch upon a few significant features.

79. Measurements

If a single quantity such as the length of a field be measured many times, it is probable that these measurements, though made with the greatest care, are not all alike. All measurements, except the simple counting of a finite set of objects, are inaccurate. Even in the simple problem of grading a mathematics examination paper, frequently it happens that two teachers assign two different grades. Suppose ten teachers grade the paper. Which

167

grading is the best? To this question there is no easy answer, yet it is an axiom in statistical study that ten careful measurements are better than one. So it is desirable to have some one numerical answer which is indicative of the results obtained, or which, *in a certain sense*, is the *best fit.*

80. Averages

When some quantity varies in magnitude from one individual to another, or from one measurement to another, if a value can be chosen in some reasonable manner which may serve as a summarizing representative of the entire set, such a value is called an **average.**

That an average is a matter of choice may be illustrated by the problem of grading a class in mathematics. If there are 30 students in the class and the final examination is scored as a per cent, what one score will be in any sense representative? No one can answer this question with any degree of finality or by any fixed mathematical law. Mathematics can be of assistance, but one of the chief problems in statistical work is the problem of interpretation, which is a matter of judgment rather than of rule. One could add the grades and divide by 30. One could arrange the grades in order of magnitude and select the middle score. One could choose as the most representative score that received by the largest number of students.

Many other ways of selection could be devised. The results obtained by the three methods described above may be three different numbers. They are among the more common types of average and are called, respectively, the **arithmetic mean,** the **median,** and the **mode.** The arithmetic mean is often referred to as the **average,** or the **mean.**

81. The arithmetic mean

By the **arithmetic mean** or the **average** is meant the sum of the measurements divided by the number of measurements. Thus, suppose ten teachers grade an examination paper and assign grades shown in the following table.

TABLE 1

Teacher No.	1	2	3	4	5	6	7	8	9	10
Grade Assigned	82	80	84	79	83	85	78	81	80	82

Then the arithmetic mean is

$$(82 + 80 + 84 + 79 + 83 + 85 + 78 + 81 + 80 + 82) \div 10 = 81.4.$$

In general, if there are n measurements, $x_1, x_2, x_3, \ldots, x_n$, the arithmetic mean M is given by the formula

$$M = \frac{x_1 + x_2 + x_3 + \cdots + x_n}{n} = \frac{\sum x}{n}, \tag{1}*$$

where the sum of the x's in the numerator is abbreviated by $\sum x$, the Greek Σ (capital sigma) indicating summation.

A measurement may occur more than once. In Table 1 the grades 80 and 82 occur twice. The average may be written

$$(2 \times 82 + 2 \times 80 + 84 + 79 + 83 + 85 + 78 + 81) \div 10 = 81.4.$$

Then 82, likewise 80, is said to have a **frequency** or **weight** of 2. In general, if a measurement occurs f times in a tabulation we say that it has a frequency or weight of f. We are led, then, to the idea of a **weighted arithmetic mean.** The formula for this is given below. Here $f_1, f_2, \ldots, f_n$ denote, respectively, the frequency or weight of $x_1, x_2, \ldots, x_n$.

$$M_w = \frac{x_1 f_1 + x_2 f_2 + \cdots + x_n f_n}{f_1 + f_2 + \cdots + f_n} = \frac{\sum xf}{\sum f}. \tag{2}*$$

If each weight is equal to 1, M_w reduces to M.

ILLUSTRATIVE EXAMPLE 1. A man invests \$100 at 5%, \$200 at 4%, \$600 at 3%, and \$100 at 2%. Find his average rate of return.

SOLUTION. Since \$1 at 5% earns \$0.05 a year, \$100 earns \$0.05 × 100. We may thus regard the sums as weights or frequencies and get by (2)

$$M_w = \frac{0.05 \times 100 + 0.04 \times 200 + 0.03 \times 600 + 0.02 \times 100}{1000} = 0.033.$$

ILLUSTRATIVE EXAMPLE 2. A student makes a grade of 90 in a 2-hour course, 85 in a 3-hour course, 80 in a 5-hour course. If the hours count equally, what is his average grade?

*The notation $\sum x$ is an abbreviation for $\sum_{i=1}^{n} x_i$ which in turn is an abbreviation for $x_1 + x_2 + \cdots + x_n$. When $\sum x$ is used, the subscripts or indices are understood as well as the number of terms in the sum it represents.

SOLUTION. By formula (2) we have

$$M_w = \frac{90 \times 2 + 85 \times 3 + 80 \times 5}{10} = 83.5.$$

ILLUSTRATIVE EXAMPLE 3. Refer to formula (13) in Art. 47. n is in effect a weighted mean. The frequency or weight of n_1 is P_1, of n_2 is P_2, and so on. The results shows that n years hence is the "average due date."

EXERCISE 55

1. The table below gives the marriage rate per 1000 population in the United States for the years 1955–1964. Find the average for these years.

Year	1955	1956	1957	1958	1959	1960	1961	1962	1963	1964
Rate	9.3	9.5	8.9	8.4	8.5	8.5	8.5	8.5	8.8	9.0

2. The table below gives the birth rate per 1000 population in the United States for the years 1937–1946. Find the average for these years.

Year	1937	1938	1939	1940	1941	1942	1943	1944	1945	1946
Rate	24.6	24.9	25.0	24.3	24.1	23.7	23.3	22.4	21.7	21.0

3. In Problem 1, find the mean rate for the first 5 years and that for the last 5. Then determine the average of these two mean rates. Compare it with the answer to Problem 1. What does this illustrate?

4. In Problem 2, obtain the mean rate for the first 5 years and that for the last 5. Then find the average of these two mean rates. Compare it with the answer to Problem 2. What does this illustrate?

5. In Problem 1, obtain the mean rate for the first 6 years and that for the last 4. Then find the average of these two mean rates. Compare it with the answer to Problem 1. Explain.

6. In Problem 2, find the mean rate for the first 3 years and that for the last 7. Then determine the average of these two mean rates. Compare it with the answer to Problem 2. Explain.

7. Five different teachers grade a test paper. Because of differences in training and experience, it is agreed that the respective scores be weighted as shown below and that the final grade be the mean weighted score. Find the final grade. (This illustrates how weights are often assigned for various reasons, although somewhat arbitrarily.)

Teacher No.	1	2	3	4	5
Score	82	81	81	84	85
Weight	2	3	1	2	1

8. The geometry test scores of a pupil were: 68 on a $\frac{1}{2}$-hour test; 75 and 88 on two 1-hour tests, respectively; 81 on a 3-hour final test. Find his grade for the course if it is the weighted mean of the test scores, the weights being the lengths of the respective tests.

82. The median and quartiles

The **median** is simply the middle one of a set of measurements arranged in order of magnitude, or if there is no middle one it is such that there are as many measurements which exceed it as there are which fall below it.

Arranging the numbers in Table 1, Art. 81, in order of magnitude, we see that

78	79	80	80	81	82	82	83	84	85

we see that 81.5 could be taken as a median. As a matter of fact, so could 81.4 or any other number between 81 and 82. However, when there are two middle measurements, as in this case, the mean of these two is generally selected to be the median.

So for ungrouped data one finds the median as follows:

1. Arrange the n measurements in ascending order;

2. If n is odd, the $\frac{n+1}{2}$ item is the median;

3. If n is even, the mean of the $\frac{n}{2}$ and $\left(\frac{n}{2}+1\right)$ items is used as the median.

The median separates the set into two groups. The middle item of the lower group is called the **first quartile,** Q_1, and the middle item of the upper group is called the **third quartile,** Q_3. In the above table Q_1 may be taken as 80 and Q_3 as 83. If there is a small number of items, the median may be found by first arranging the items in order and then counting up to the middle. Another method of locating the median and quartiles will be found in Art. 88.

83. The mode

In a collection of measurements or numerical data if one item occurs more often than any other it is called the **mode,** meaning the "fashion."

On a psychological test given to 866 freshmen at the University of Florida, scores were made as indicated in the table below.

TABLE 2

Score	320– 349	290– 319	260– 289	230– 259	200– 229	170– 199	140– 169	110– 139	80– 109	50– 79	20– 49
Frequency	6	12	37	88	119	176	165	139	85	27	12

It is seen that the largest group, or 176 students, made a score between 170 and 199. This, however, does not enable us to locate a mode in the form of a single number, since apparently any number between 170 and 199 would serve equally well as a mode. Scores between 170 and 199 might be termed a "modal class."

84. Comparison and criticism of the three types of average

The most important average for a specified purpose is a matter for individual judgment and can only be decided for the particular purpose at hand after a careful study. The mean is based upon all the measurements. The mode indicates where the greatest frequency occurs. The median is a number such that there are as many measurements exceeding it as there are falling below it. The mean is generally more useful than either of the others. In some cases, as for example when the mean is unduly affected by the extreme measurements, the mode or the median may be preferred. As a general rule, however, all three of these averages are useful guides when taken in connection with each other and with a knowledge of the distribution as a whole.

For example, in selecting a locality in which to live, we may be more interested in the modal temperature than in the mean temperature. Or if the total annual rainfall is known, we could compute the mean daily rainfall, but we may prefer to know the distribution of rainy days in the year. Again, suppose two communities are of identical mean wealth; one may have a few individuals of great wealth and the rest in abject poverty; while in the other, everybody may be well to do, no one very rich or very poor. To a hat or a shoe merchant the most important measurement is the size that occurs most commonly, the mode. In studying the number of kilowatt hours of electricity consumed by a municipality, interest may lie in the mean consumption for the population, and also in the question of when a "peak load" occurs.

It is interesting to note how the three types of average are affected by an extreme measurement. If a millionaire joins the population in a small rural community, the mean income of that community would be increased considerably, the median income would be very little affected, if at all, and the mode not at all.

It has been pointed out that a chief problem in statistics is the *problem of interpretation*. This cannot be too strongly emphasized. It is to inadequate interpretations that we may attribute much of the unwarranted criticism leveled at statistical studies. It is not the fault of statistics if wrong conclusions are drawn. Such conclusions result from a failure to take into account the significance of all factors involved in the distribution.

EXERCISE 56

1. The table below gives the number of clear days in each month at Asheville, N.C. Find (a) the mean; (b) the median; (c) the mode.

Month	Jan.	Feb.	Mar.	Apr.	May	June	July	Aug.	Sept.	Oct.	Nov.	Dec.
Days	11	10	11	12	10	8	7	7	11	15	13	11

2. Average relative humidity for each month at Jacksonville, Fla., is shown below. Find (a) the mean; (b) the median; (c) the mode.

Month	Jan.	Feb.	Mar.	Apr.	May	June	July	Aug.	Sept.	Oct.	Nov.	Dec.
Humidity	74	72	69	67	69	72	74	75	77	75	74	76

3. Find the mean of the quartiles for the data of Problem 1.

4. What is the mean of the quartiles for the data of Problem 2?

5. If instead of the data of Problem 1, you were given that there are 12 items none of which is zero, and that the mean is 10, would it be possible for one of the items to be as large as 100? What is one disadvantage of the mean as a group representative?

6. If instead of the data of Problem 2, you were given that there are 12 items and that the median is 74 approximately, could you tell anything at all about the 1st and 12th items? What is one disadvantage of the median as a representative of the group?

7. In a certain arithmetic series, $t_1 = 4$, $d = 2$, and $n = 6$. Find: (a) the mean of the terms; (b) the median. Is there a mode?

8. In a certain geometric series, $t_1 = 3$, $r = 2$, and $n = 9$. Find: (a) the mean of the terms; (b) the median. Is there a mode?

9. Find a median of the coefficients in the expansion of $(a + b)^7$.

10. Find a median of the coefficients in the expansion of $(x + y)^9$.

11. The numbers 2, 2, 4, 3, 7, 6 form a set which has a mean $= 4$ and a mode $= 2$. Write 6 positive numbers which have a mean $= 2$ and a mode $= 4$. (Fractions may be necessary.)

12. For what integral values of x and y will the set 1, 2, 3, x, y have a mean $= 4$ and a median $= 3$ if $y > x > 3$?

13. What is the median for the data of Problem 1?

14. What is a median for the data of Problem 2?

15. Find the mean of Q_1 and Q_3 for the data of Problem 1.

16. Find the mean of Q_1 and Q_3 for the data of Problem 2.

85. Frequency distribution

All statistical investigations and, indeed, practically all scientific studies are concerned with *relationships* between variable quantities. For convenience, when a large number of statistical measurements are to be studied, it is customary to group them into **classes.** In practice, the measurements are represented by numbers. These are arranged on a scale, as for example in records of temperature or in grades of students. The subdivisions on the scale are called **class intervals.** Usually the class intervals are chosen to have the same lengths. Thus if the scale is to include real numbers between 1 and 100, the classes might be 1–10, 11–20, 21–30, etc. The length of the scale is the **range.** The set of numbers so classified is called a **frequency distribution** or **frequency table.** We may then make a graph in which the unit along the horizontal axis is the class interval, and class frequencies are laid off vertically.

The frequency distribution of Table 2, Art. 83, is graphed in Fig. 13. The range is 330 (from 20 to 349); the class interval, 30. The bar graph consisting of contiguous rectangles is called a **histogram.** The base of each rectangle

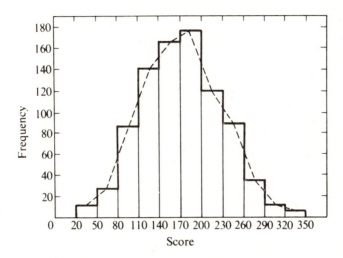

Fig. 13. Histogram and frequency polygon for Table 2.

is the class interval; heights of rectangles represent class frequencies. Connecting the midpoints of the tops of the bars by straight lines, we get a broken-line graph called a **frequency polygon.** This is shown by dotted lines in Fig. 13. Following a common practice, we have used midpoints of class intervals as abscissas. That is, all students with scores between 20 and 50 are classed as if their score were 35, all between 50 and 80 as if their score were 65, etc.

86. Class interval

One of the problems in making up a frequency table is the selection of a class interval. A proper selection makes the representation of the data more meaningful.

Table 2 of Art. 83, which is graphed in Fig. 13, shows that 12 received grades between 20 and 49, but does not tell how many had grades between

30 and 40. The class interval of length 30 was selected arbitrarily. Table 2 was condensed from a larger table partly reproduced here.

Score	340–9	330–9	320–9	310–9	300–9	290–9	etc.	20–9
Frequency	2	0	4	3	0	9	etc.	1

In this table the class interval is only 10 and there are 33 intervals. By grouping in threes we reduced the number of intervals to 11. On the other hand, the number of observations might have been extended to show the number of students who made scores of 1, 2, 3, ..., 349, respectively. Then the class interval would be 1 and the range 349. Since the scores in this test are recorded in whole numbers, the class interval could not be smaller than 1.

When data is placed in classes we say it is *grouped data*. In a sense, when we compute the weighted mean (2) in Article 81 we are working with grouped data. We have discussed finding the median for ungrouped data and it is appropriate now to note the procedure for finding the median for grouped data.

By a simple counting procedure we can find the class containing the median. Let us call the class C. If the class interval is c, if the frequency of the class is f, and if we need j more items to reach the median, we simply add $c \cdot \dfrac{j}{f}$ to the lower boundary L of the class C. Thus

$$M = L + c \cdot \frac{j}{f}.$$

For example, using the data of Table 2, Article 83, we know that we want the median between the 433rd and 434th measurement. Using the grouping of the data in the table we have that C has lower boundary 170 and that there are 428 items of data below this score. We need, then, $5\frac{1}{2}$ more items to reach the median. Note that $f = 176$, $j = 5.5$, $c = 30$ and $L = 170$. We can, then, compute M.

$$M = 170 + 30 \cdot \frac{5.5}{176}$$

(Here M is approximately 171.)

87. Frequency curve

A smooth curve through the vertices of a frequency polygon is called a **frequency curve.** Such a curve has many of the characteristic properties of the frequency polygon. For instance, the range is the same and the curve passes through the same plotted points. Figure 14 pictures a frequency curve for the data of Table 2. The student should compare it with the frequency polygon in Fig. 13.

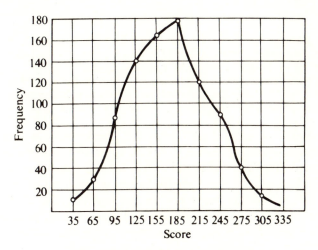

Fig. 14. Frequency curve for Table 2.

88. Cumulative frequency. Ogive

The table below gives the grades attained by 44 pupils on a test. The cumulative frequency row gives the sum of frequencies. Thus, 4 pupils had a grade of 2 or less, 8 pupils had a grade of 3 or less, etc. Plotting the cumulative frequencies as ordinates against the grades as abscissas, we have a **cumulative frequency curve,** or an **ogive,** shown in Fig. 15.

TABLE 3

Grade	1	2	3	4	5	6	7	8	9	10
Frequency	1	3	4	6	8	7	5	4	4	2
Cumul. Frequency	1	4	8	14	22	29	34	38	42	44

When frequencies greater than 1 occur, the ogive gives us a convenient method of locating the median and the quartiles. To find Q_1, take $\frac{1}{4}$ of the highest ordinate and locate the corresponding abscissa. Thus, since $\frac{1}{4} \cdot 44 = 11$, draw a horizontal line through the mark 11 on the vertical scale. From the

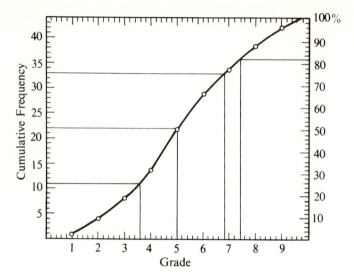

Fig. 15. Ogive for Table 3.

point in which this meets the curve drop a perpendicular to the axis of abscissas. The foot of this perpendicular locates Q_1. In Fig. 15, Q_1 appears to be 3.6. Similarly, to find the median, bisect the greatest ordinate and proceed in the same way. Q_3 may be located by taking $\frac{3}{4}$ of the largest ordinate and proceeding as before. Here the median appears to be 5 and Q_3 to be about 6.8.

Sometimes the range is divided into 100 equal parts called **percentiles.** The 25th percentile is Q_1. The method outlined above will serve to locate any desired percentile. Another convenient method is to divide the length of the highest ordinate into per cent divisions, as shown in Fig. 15. Thus, the 82nd percentile is about 7.4.

To draw an ogive for a cumulative frequency table which involves *class intervals*, ordinates should be erected from the bounds of the class intervals and not from the midpoints.

89. Normal frequency curve

The expansion of $(a + b)^6$ contains seven terms, with coefficients 1, 6, 15, 20, 15, 6, 1, respectively. If we regard these coefficients as frequencies and plot them as ordinates, using 1 as class interval and the midpoints of the class intervals as abscissas, we obtain a frequency polygon which may be smoothed into a symmetric frequency curve, as shown in Fig. 16. Much larger coefficients would appear in the expansions of higher powers of the binomial, but in each case the coefficients would show a symmetric frequency

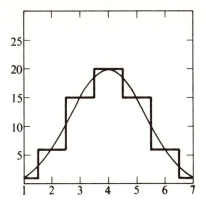

Fig. 16. Graphic representation of coefficients in the expansion of $(a + b)^6$.

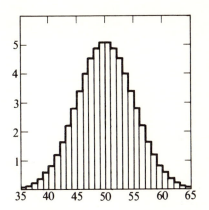

Fig. 17. Graphic representation of coefficients in the expansion of $(a + b)^{99}$.

distribution. Figure 17 shows a histogram for the distribution of the coefficients in the expansion of $(a + b)^{99}$. The two middle coefficients are approximately 5×10^{28}, marked 5 in the graph. The first 34 and last 34 coefficients are relatively so small that they have been omitted.

In order to avoid large coefficients, we may expand the **point binomial** $(\frac{1}{2} + \frac{1}{2})^n$. Thus

$$\left(\frac{1}{2} + \frac{1}{2}\right)^6 = \left[\frac{1}{2}(1 + 1)\right]^6 = \frac{1}{2^6}(1 + 1)^6$$

$$= \frac{1}{2^6} + \frac{6}{2^6} + \frac{15}{2^6} + \frac{20}{2^6} + \frac{15}{2^6} + \frac{6}{2^6} + \frac{1}{2^6} = 1.$$

Similarly, for positive integral values of n, the expansion of $(\frac{1}{2} + \frac{1}{2})^n$ contains $n + 1$ terms whose sum is 1. The graph obtained by plotting these terms as ordinates against any convenient lengths as class intervals along the axis of abscissas is a symmetric frequency polygon. A limit of these polygons, as n becomes infinite, with accompanying change of x-units is a smooth, bell-shaped curve, called a **normal frequency curve,** or a **normal distribution curve.** Its general form is exhibited in Fig. 18. Many statistical distributions are approximately represented by a curve of this sort. By a suitable choice of axes and by methods beyond the scope of this book, the equation of a normal frequency curve may be shown to be $y = Ce^{-h^2x^2}$, where $e = 2.718^+$, $C = $ ordinate of highest point on the curve, and h is a constant determining the steepness of the curve for a given C. Powers of e may be computed by logarithms.

Thus, since $e^{-1.6} = 1 \div e^{1.6}$ and $\log e = \log 2.718 = 0.4342$, we get $\log e^{-1.6} = \log 1 - 1.6 \log e = (10.0000 - 10) - 0.6947 = 9.3053 - 10$. Therefore $e^{-1.6} = 0.202$ (to 3 significant digits).

EXERCISE 57

1. Construct a histogram and a frequency polygon for the data in the table showing the distribution of pupils' scores on a test.

Score	5	10	15	20	25	30	35	40	45	50	55	60	65
Frequency	2	8	12	19	23	25	34	25	19	13	7	8	2

2. Construct a histogram and a frequency polygon for the data of Problem 14.

3. Draw a frequency curve for the data in the table of Problem 1.

4. Draw a frequency curve for the data of Problem 14.

5. Construct an ogive for the data in the table of Problem 1.

6. Construct an ogive for the data of Problem 14.

7. Refer to the ogive of Problem 5 to find: (a) the median score; (b) the quartiles; (c) the 45th percentile; (d) the percentage of pupils who made scores of 45 or more.

8. Refer to the ogive of Problem 6 to find: (a) the median age; (b) the quartiles; (c) the 60th percentile; (d) the percentage of persons under 25 years of age.

9. The table below, adapted from Pearl's *Studies in Human Biology*, gives the brain-weights (in grams) of 415 adult Swedish males. Construct a histogram and a frequency curve for these data.

Brain-weight	1100–1150	1150–1200	1200–1250	1250–1300	1300–1350	1350–1400	1400–1450	1450–1500	1500–1550	1550–1600	1600–1650	1650–1700
Frequency	1	9	21	45	53	86	72	61	28	25	13	3

10. Draw an ogive for the data of Problem 9. From the graph find: (a) the median brain-weight; (b) the quartiles; (c) the 80th percentile.

11. What is the modal class of brain-weights in Problem 9?

12. Using the data of Problem 9, find the mean brain-weight. [*Hint.* Brain-weights 1125, 1175, etc., may be taken as class representatives.]

13. The table gives a distribution of heads in tossing 7 coins 128 times. Draw a frequency curve for these data.

No. of Heads	0	1	2	3	4	5	6	7
No. of Tosses	1	7	21	22	35	31	7	1

14. The American Experience Table of Mortality gives the number of deaths at ages from 10 up to 95. A portion of the table appears below. Draw a frequency curve for these data. Does the distribution seem to fit a normal frequency curve approximately? (Take the "zero" level for ordinates as 2100, letting the first ordinate be 2158 − 2100 = 58 and the highest ordinate 2505 − 2100 = 405.)

Age	67	68	69	70	71	72	73	74	75	76	77	78	79
Deaths	2151	2243	2321	2155	2448	2487	2505	2490	2476	2431	2369	2291	2203

15. Draw a frequency curve showing the distribution of the coefficients in the expansion of $(a + b)^8$.

16. Draw a frequency curve showing the distribution of the coefficients in the expansion of $(a + b)^{10}$.

17. Graph $y = e^{-1/2x^2}$ from $x = -2$ to $x = +2$ at intervals of 0.4.

18. Graph $y = 2e^{-x^2}$ from $x = -1.5$ to $x = +1.5$ at intervals of 0.3.

90. Measures of dispersion

The various averages, arithmetic mean, median, mode, are sometimes called **measures of central tendency,** because in the type of distribution known as a normal distribution they coincide and the measurements tend to "heap up" about the average. Each of these measures is useful in its way. But a mere knowledge of an average is often insufficient and misleading.

Consider, for example, a hypothetical case in which each of two groups of ten people contributes $25 to a fund. In one group, eight members give $2.50 each, one gives $3.00, one gives $2.00. The average gift is $2.50. In the other group, seven give $1.00 each, and three give $6.00 each. Here also the average gift is $2.50. In the first instance, the individual items cluster closely about the average. In the second instance, the individual items are widely scattered or *dispersed* from the average.

Hence we desire some measure of the extent to which various individual measurements depart from an average. The differences between the individual measurements and the arithmetic mean are called **deviations.** A deviation is positive if the measurement exceeds the mean, negative if it is less than the mean. The average of the deviations from the mean is zero, so that such an average is no measure of dispersion. Common **measures of dispersion** are the quartile deviation, the mean deviation, and the standard deviation.

The **quartile deviation,** easy to compute, is defined by

$$Q = \frac{Q_3 - Q_1}{2}. \tag{3}$$

Since half of all measurements lie between Q_1 and Q_3, Q gives a measure of dispersion from the median. For a normal distribution, Q is also called the **probable deviation.**

The **mean deviation** is the average of the *absolute* values (see Art. 4) of the deviations. If $d_1, d_2, d_3, \ldots, d_n$ are the absolute values of the deviations of a set of measurements $x_1, x_2, x_3, \ldots, x_n$ from the arithmetic mean, then the mean deviation is given by

$$d = \frac{d_1 + d_2 + d_3 + \cdots + d_n}{n} = \frac{\sum d}{n}. \tag{4}$$

The **standard deviation** is the most important. It is designated by the Greek letter σ (sigma) and is computed in the following manner. First find the mean-square deviation, that is, the mean of the squares of the deviations. For a set of measurements in feet, this mean-square deviation is in square feet. Hence, to obtain a number of the same dimensions as the original, take the square root; the result is the standard deviation. Let $x_1, x_2, \ldots, x_n$ be a set of numbers and M their mean. Then the mean of the squares of the deviations is

$$\sigma^2 = \frac{(x_1 - M)^2 + (x_2 - M)^2 + \cdots + (x_n - M)^2}{n}.$$

Using the sign of summation, we may abbreviate

$$\sigma^2 = \frac{\sum (x - M)^2}{n}. \tag{5}$$

ILLUSTRATIVE EXAMPLE. Find the mean deviation, standard deviation, and quartile deviation for the distribution of grades in Table 3, Art. 88.

SOLUTION. The arithmetic mean of the 44 grades is $5\frac{7}{11}$, but we shall use the approximate mean 5.6. The table below shows the computations.

Grades	Frequencies f	Absolute Values of Deviations d	Weighted Values $f \times d$	Weighted Squares of Deviations $f \times d^2$
1	1	4.6	4.6	21.16
2	3	3.6	10.8	38.88
3	4	2.6	10.4	27.04
4	6	1.6	9.6	15.36
5	8	0.6	4.8	2.88
6	7	0.4	2.8	1.12
7	5	1.4	7.0	9.80
8	4	2.4	9.6	23.04
9	4	3.4	13.6	46.24
10	2	4.4	8.8	38.72
Totals	44		82.0	224.24

The total weighted absolute deviation from the mean is 82 and the total frequency 44. Hence the mean deviation is $82 \div 44 = 1.86$.

The sum of the squares of the deviations is 224 to 3 significant digits. Hence the mean-square deviation $\sigma^2 = 224 \div 44 = 5.09$, and $\sigma = 2.26$. Since $Q_3 = 6.8$, $Q_1 = 3.6$ (Art. 88), we have $Q = \frac{1}{2}(6.8 - 3.6) = 1.6$.

It should be observed that the use of formula (5) requires determining the mean of the numbers $x_1, \ldots, x_n$ and computing the deviations. It is possible to obtain the standard deviation without this computation.

Recall that

$$M = \frac{x_1 + x_2 + \cdots + x_n}{n} = \frac{\sum x}{n},$$

and that for any real number k,

$$\sum_{k=1}^{n} k = k + k + \cdots + k = n \cdot k.$$

Then notice that

$$\sigma^2 = \frac{\sum (x - M)^2}{n}$$

$$= \frac{\sum (x^2 - 2Mx + M^2)}{n}$$

$$= \frac{\sum x^2 - \sum 2Mx + \sum M^2}{n}$$

$$= \frac{\sum x^2}{n} - 2M \frac{\sum x}{n} + \frac{\sum M^2}{n}$$

$$= \frac{\sum x^2}{n} - 2M \frac{\sum x}{n} + \frac{n \cdot M^2}{n}$$

$$= \frac{\sum x^2}{n} - 2M \cdot M + M^2$$

$$= \frac{\sum x^2}{n} - M^2$$

$$= \frac{\sum x^2}{n} - \left(\frac{\sum x}{n}\right)^2.$$

So

$$\sigma^2 = \frac{n \sum x^2}{n^2} - \frac{(\sum x)^2}{n^2}$$

or

$$\sigma = \frac{1}{n}\sqrt{n(\sum x^2) - (\sum x)^2}. \tag{5'}$$

ILLUSTRATIVE EXAMPLE. Find the standard deviation for the data below using both formulas.

$$x_1 = 2, \quad x_2 = 3, \quad x_3 = 5, \quad x_4 = 7, \quad x_5 = 8$$

SOLUTION. Consider the following table.

x	x^2	$(x - M)^2 = (x - 5)^2$
2	4	9
3	9	4
5	25	0
7	49	4
8	64	9
25	151	26

By (5) $\sigma^2 = \frac{26}{5}$ or $\sigma = \sqrt{\frac{26}{5}} = \frac{1}{5}\sqrt{26 \times 5} = \frac{1}{5}\sqrt{130}$.

By (5') $\sigma = \frac{1}{5}\sqrt{5 \times 151 - 25^2} = \frac{1}{5}\sqrt{755 - 625} = \frac{1}{5}\sqrt{130}$.

91. Significance of measures of dispersion

It can be shown that, in the type of distribution called *normal*, the three measures of dispersion are connected by the equations:

$$d = 0.798\sigma = 1.18Q; \quad Q = 0.674\sigma = 0.845d.$$

The range is very nearly equal to 6σ or to $7\frac{1}{2}d$ or to $9Q$. That σ, d, and Q are significant measures of dispersion in a normal distribution is well brought out in the table below, which shows percentages of all measurements lying in stated intervals. Figure 18 shows a normal distribution curve with relative sizes of σ, d, and Q indicated.

Certain examples and problems in this chapter, inserted merely to illustrate methods, have been purposely chosen to shorten the labor of computations. The numerical results in such cases may have very little statistical significance *because of the small number of measurements involved.* In practical applications to specific fields of knowledge, particularly to biology, psychology, economics, and education, a *large* number of observations (measurements) may indicate an approximation to normal distribution,

INTERVAL		Per Cent
From	To	
$M - \sigma$	$M + \sigma$	68.3%
$M - 2\sigma$	$M + 2\sigma$	95.5
$M - 3\sigma$	$M + 3\sigma$	99.7
$M - d$	$M + d$	57.5%
$M - 2d$	$M + 2d$	89.0
$M - 3d$	$M + 3d$	98.3
$M - Q$	$M + Q$	50.0%
$M - 2Q$	$M + 2Q$	82.3
$M - 3Q$	$M + 3Q$	95.7

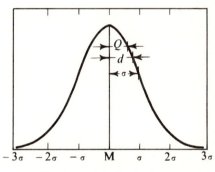

Fig. 18. A normal distribution curve.

or else a *definite* kind of departure from it. It is then that measures like σ, d, Q, and numerous others not discussed here acquire meaning and become valuable tools in the hands of the competent statistician.

92. Linear correlation

Consider a set of measurements represented by the numbers $x_1, x_2, \ldots,$ x_n, and a corresponding set represented by the numbers $y_1, y_2, \ldots, y_n$. Let M_x and M_y denote respectively the arithmetic means of the x's and the y's; and let σ_x and σ_y denote respectively the standard deviations of the x's and y's. Then, by (5),

$$\sigma_x^2 = \frac{(x_1 - M_x)^2 + (x_2 - M_x)^2 + \cdots + (x_n - M_x)^2}{n},$$

$$\sigma_y^2 = \frac{(y_1 - M_y)^2 + (y_2 - M_y)^2 + \cdots + (y_n - M_y)^2}{n}.$$

Abbreviate the deviations $x_1 - M_x, x_2 - M_x, \ldots, x_n - M_x$ by $X_1, X_2, \ldots, X_n,$ and the deviations $y_1 - M_y, y_2 - M_y, \ldots, y_n - M_y$ by $Y_1, Y_2, \ldots, Y_n.$ Thus

$$\sigma_x^2 = \frac{X_1^2 + X_2^2 + \cdots + X_n^2}{n} = \frac{\sum X^2}{n},$$

$$\sigma_y^2 = \frac{Y_1^2 + Y_2^2 + \cdots + Y_n^2}{n} = \frac{\sum Y^2}{n}.$$

Then the expression

$$r = \frac{X_1 Y_1 + X_2 Y_2 + \cdots + X_n Y_n}{n \sigma_x \sigma_y} = \frac{\sum XY}{n \sigma_x \sigma_y} \tag{6}$$

is called the **coefficient of correlation of x and y.** The value of r may be shown to lie between -1 and $+1.$ If $r = \pm 1,$ the correlation between the x's and y's is said to be **perfect.** Geometrically, this means that the pairs of numbers $(x_1, y_1), (x_2, y_2), \ldots, (x_n, y_n)$ plotted as shown in Art. 66 are points all lying on a straight line. If $r \neq \pm 1,$ the smaller its absolute value, the less the degree of correlation between the x's and y's.

In seeking to establish the existence of some degree of correlation between two sets of data, a set of values of x and a set of values of $y,$ the points should first be plotted, using the x's as abscissas and the y's as ordinates. If the points appear roughly to cluster about a straight line, that is, if there appears to be a **linear trend,** then the two sets may be thought of as "running along together" and the coefficient r may have some significance. A high degree of correlation between two sets does not necessarily indicate that there is a relation of cause and effect. It doubtless does suggest some, possibly unknown, common cause of both. For example, if the correlation between a boy's grades in English courses and in Latin courses is 0.98, that does not prove that Latin helps English, or vice versa, although this may be true in certain individual cases. The two sets of grades, if both good, may also result from natural ability or hard work or both.

ILLUSTRATIVE EXAMPLE. Show that $r = -1$ for the set: $x = 1, y = 1;$ $x = 2, y = 0; x = 3, y = -1.$

SOLUTION. Arrange the data in tabular array.

x	y	M_x	M_y	$x - M_x = X$	$y - M_y = Y$	XY	X^2	Y^2
1	1	2	0	-1	1	-1	1	1
2	0			0	0	0	0	0
3	-1			1	-1	-1	1	1
Totals						-2	2	2

By formula (5), $\sigma_x = \sqrt{\dfrac{\sum X^2}{n}} = \sqrt{\dfrac{2}{3}}$, $\sigma_y = \sqrt{\dfrac{\sum Y^2}{n}} = \sqrt{\dfrac{2}{3}}$.

Then, by formula (6), $r = \dfrac{\sum XY}{n\sigma_x\sigma_y} = \dfrac{-2}{3\sqrt{\frac{2}{3}}\sqrt{\frac{2}{3}}} = -1$.

Note. According as $r = +1$ or $r = -1$, the perfect correlation between x and y is called *positive* or *negative*. In the first case, y *increases* as x increases. In the second case, y *decreases* as x increases. In the above example, there is a perfect negative correlation between x and y. The points $(1, 1)$, $(2, 0)$, $(3, -1)$ lie on the straight line $x + y - 2 = 0$. Draw this line and note that y decreases as x increases.

93. Brief list of references

For supplementary reading in statistical analysis, reference is made to a few books:

(1) Croxton, Frederick E., and Cowden, Dudley J., *Practical Business Statistics*, 1960, 3rd Edition, Prentice-Hall, Englewood Cliffs, N.J.

(2) Dubois, Edward N., *Essential Methods in Business Statistics*, 1964, McGraw-Hill Book Company, New York.

(3) Ekeblad, Frederick A., *The Statistical Method in Business*, 1962, John Wiley & Sons, Inc., New York.

(4) Fisher, R. A., *Statistical Methods for Research Workers*, 1946, 12th Edition, Oliver and Boyd, London.

(5) Freund, John E, and Williams, Frank J., *Elementary Business Statistics*, 1964, Prentice-Hall, Englewood Cliffs, N.J.

(6) Garrett, Henry E., *Statistics in Psychology and Education*, 1958, Longmans, Green and Co., New York.

(7) Huff, Darrell, *How to Lie with Statistics*, 1954, W. W. Norton & Company, New York.

(8) Mainland, Donald, *Elementary Medical Statistics*, 1963, 2nd Edition, W.B. Saunders Company, Philadelphia.

(9) McNemar, Quinn, *Psychological Statistics*, 1955, 2nd Edition, John Wiley & Sons, Inc., New York.

(10) Mosteller, Frederick, Rourke, Robert E.K., and Thomas, George B., Jr. *Probability and Statistics*, 1961, Addison-Wesley Publishing Company, Reading, Mass.

(11) Netter, John and Wasserman, William, *Fundamental Statistics for Business and Economics*, 1961, 2nd Edition, Allyn and Bacon, Inc. Boston, Mass.

(12) Richmond, Samuel B., *Statistical Analysis*, 1964, 2nd Edition, The Ronald Press Company, New York.

(13) Schlaifer, Robert, *Probability and Statistics for Business Decisions*, 1959, McGraw-Hill Book Company, Inc., New York.

(14) Stockton, John R., *Business Statistics*, 1962, 2nd Edition, South-Western Publishing Company, Cincinnati, Ohio.

(15) Yamane, Taro, *Statistics, an Introductory Analysis*, 1964, Harper & Row Publishers, New York.

EXERCISE 58

1. Consider a normal distribution of 1000 measurements for which $M = 300$ and $Q = 20$. About how many of the measurements lie: (a) between 260 and 340? (b) between 240 and 360?

2. If $\sigma = 30$ for the distribution of Problem 1, how many of the measurements lie: (a) between 210 and 300? (b) between 270 and 330?

3. If $d = 24$ for the distribution of Problem 1, how many of the measurements lie: (a) between 228 and 372? (b) between 300 and 348?

4. The largest measurement in Problem 1 is of about what size?

5. The indexes of the retail cost of food for the first 9 months of 1967 were: 114.7, 114.2, 114.2, 113.7, 113.9, 115.1, 116.0, 116.6, 115.9. Find σ.

6. The cost-of-living indexes for the first 9 months of 1967 were: 114.7, 114.8, 115.0, 115.3, 115.6, 116.0, 116.5, 116.9, 117.1. Compute σ.

7. Find the quartile deviation and mean deviation in Problem 5.

8. Find the quartile deviation and mean deviation in Problem 6.

9. Find the coefficient of correlation between cost of food and cost of living for the first 9 months of 1967 (see Problems 5 and 6).

10. Do Problem 9, using the data for the first 6 months only.

11. Find the coefficient of correlation for the set: $x = 0$, $y = -3$; $x = 1$, $y = 0$; $x = 2$, $y = 1$; $x = 3$, $y = 2$; $x = 4$, $y = 5$.

12. Find the coefficient of correlation for the set: $x = -2$, $y = -3$; $x = 0$, $y = -1$; $x = 2$, $y = 4$; $x = 4$, $y = 7$; $x = 6$, $y = 8$.

13. For a set of data such as that in Problem 11 the line

$$y = \frac{r\sigma_y}{\sigma_x}x + \frac{\sigma_x M_y - r\sigma_y M_x}{\sigma_x}$$

is called "the line of best fit in the sense of least squares." Find the equation of this "line of best fit" for the set in Problem 11.

14. Find equation of "line of best fit" for the set in Problem 12.

15. In the equation of Problem 13, substitute M_x for x and M_y for y and show that the "average point" (M_x, M_y) lies on the "line of best fit."

16. Show that formula (6) may be written: $r = \dfrac{\Sigma\, XY}{\sqrt{\Sigma\, X^2}\sqrt{\Sigma\, Y^2}}$.

MISCELLANEOUS EXERCISE 59
REVIEW OF CHAPTER 10

1. The table gives the median age for the population of the United States for certain years. What is the median of the set of median ages?

Year	1900	1910	1920	1930	1940	1950	1960
Median Age	22.9	24.0	25.2	26.4	29.0	29.2	29.5

2. What is the mean of the median ages tabulated in Problem 1?

3. Find Q_1, Q_3, and Q for the median ages given in Problem 1.

4. Compute the weighted mean of the numbers 8, 6, 9, 10, 5 if the respective weights are 2, 1, 2, 3, 2.

5. The table below gives the annual expenditure for education per pupil enrolled in public schools, elementary and secondary. Construct a histogram and a frequency polygon of these data.

Year	1956	1958	1960	1962	1964	1966
Expenditure	$362	$405	$433	$480	$523	$649

6. Draw a frequency curve of the data tabulated in Problem 5.

7. Find the mean of the expenditures appearing in Problem 5.

8. Cost-of-living indexes for 1960–1966 were: 103, 104, 105, 107, 108, 110, 113. Find (a) the mean deviation; (b) the standard deviation.

9. In Problem 8, find: (a) the median; (b) Q_1 and Q_3; (c) Q.

10. Below is given a frequency table of state property taxes (in per cent) for 1967. Find: (a) the mode; (b) the mean. *Four states had no tax.*

Tax	2	$2\frac{1}{2}$	3	$3\frac{1}{2}$	4	$4\frac{1}{2}$	5
Frequency	7	1	26	2	5	2	3

11. Compute the mean deviation of the data of Problem 10.

12. Find the standard deviation of the data of Problem 10.

13. Draw an ogive for the data of Problem 10.

14. Refer to the ogive of Problem 13. (a) What is the median tax? (b) What are the quartiles? (c) What is the quartile deviation?

15. In a certain community, the death rates for male infants under 1 year were 45, 45, 44, 43, 38 for the years 1964–1968. For female infants under 1 year the corresponding rates were 36, 35, 35, 34, 30. Find the coefficient of correlation of the two sets.

16. Show that $n(\sigma^2 + M^2) = \sum x^2$.

GENERAL REVIEW
OF CHAPTERS 1-10

MISCELLANEOUS EXERCISE 60

1. Factor: (a) $x^2 - 5x + 4$; (b) $4m - mx^2$; (c) $y^4 + 2y^3 + y^2$.

2. Reduce to simplest form: (a) $\dfrac{2 - 7x + 3x^2}{3x - 1}$; (b) $\dfrac{n^2 - n}{n^2 + n - 2}$.

3. Evaluate $6x^2 + \dfrac{2}{x} - [3x - (4 - 2x)]$ if $x = \dfrac{1}{2}$.

4. Find the square of: (a) $3x - \frac{1}{3}$; (b) $4p + q$; (c) $x - y + z$.

5. One factor of $x^4 + 4x^3 + 5x^2 + 2x$ is $x + 1$; find the other 3 factors.

6. Find the L.C.M. of: $m^2x - 3m^2$, $mx^2 - 9m$, $x^2 + 6x + 9$.

7. Multiply the square of $x - y$ by the reciprocal of $x^2 - xy$.

8. Divide $x^3 - 4x^2 + 10$ by $x - 2$. Check by letting $x = 3$.

9. Subtract $\dfrac{x}{x - 1}$ from $\dfrac{2x + 1}{x^2 - x - 2}$. Check by letting $x = 3$.

10. Find the value of b if $x + 2$ is a factor of $x^2 + bx - 10$.

11. Add 1 to the reciprocal of $x - 1$; divide the sum by x; simplify.

12. Combine into one fraction in lowest terms: $\dfrac{9 - 4x^2}{x^2 - x} \div \left(\dfrac{1}{x - 1} - 2\right)$.

13. Find dividend if divisor $= x - 1$, quotient $= x + 1$, remainder $= 3$.

14. The sum of $3x^2 - 4ax + 5a^2$ and a certain other expression is $x^2 + ax - 2a^2$. What is that expression?

15. Solve the equation $4x - 3y = 7$: (a) for x; (b) for y.

16. Express the following as a formula: Add i to 1, indicate the cube of the sum, then subtract 1, then divide by i; all this gives the value of S.

17. For what value of x will $3x^2$ equal $(3x + 2)(x - 1)$?

18. Given the simultaneous equations: $x - 2y = 11$, $3x + y = 5$. Solve for x and y by elimination by addition or subtraction.

19. Do Problem 18 by elimination by substitution.

20. Does $x = 3$ satisfy the equation $x^2 = 6 - 5x$?

21. A dealer sold m desk lamps at x dollars each and thereby gained y dollars in all. What was the cost of one lamp?

22. Find the number whose half is 12 less than twice itself.

23. How many lbs. each of two kinds of nuts, worth 50¢ and 37¢ a lb., should be used to produce a 65-lb. mixture worth 45¢ a lb.?

24. John is n years old. Twice his age of 6 years ago is what?

25. Solve for x and check: (a) $2 - \dfrac{2x}{x+2} = \dfrac{3}{x}$; (b) $\dfrac{3x}{x-2} - 2 = \dfrac{x}{x+2}$.

26. Two cars, 360 mi. apart, start at the same time and meet in 5 hrs. Find the speed of each if one runs $\frac{4}{5}$ as fast as the other.

27. Solve for r: (a) $C = 2\pi r$; (b) $S = \dfrac{r}{a+r}$; (c) $I = \dfrac{E}{R+r}$.

28. In $3x - 2y = 7$, replace y by $3x - 2$; then solve for x.

29. Express y in terms of x if (a) $x^3y = 2y + 1$; (b) $xy - 3 = y$.

30. How long will it take two machines to do a job together if the first alone can do it in 30 hours and the second in 10 hours?

31. Find b if one solution of $3x + by = 4$ is $x = 1$, $y = 2$.

32. Write a formula for the number n of hours in p weeks and q days.

33. For what value of x will $x^3 + 2$ equal $x(x - 1)(x + 1)$?

34. A dealer's profit for 1968 was \$3124, which was 12% less than his profit for 1967. What was his profit for 1967?

35. Find two numbers whose sum is 78 and which are in the ratio 9:4.

36. How should two brothers, A and B, divide an inheritance of \$8600 if B's share is to exceed A's share by 15% of A's share?

37. Find x if it is a mean proportional between $x + 3$ and $x - 2$.

38. Adding 12% of x to x is equivalent to multiplying x by what?

39. If $(1 + x):(1 - x) = m:n$, express x in terms of m and n.

40. Lime consists of calcium and oxygen in the ratio 5:2 by weight. How much of each element is present in 35 grams of pure lime?

41. A corporation pays an income tax of $35,582 which is 31% of its net income. Find the amount of net income.

42. The population of Florida increased from 2,771,000 in 1950 to 4,952,000 in 1960. What is the per cent of increase?

43. A man invests $5000, part at $2\frac{1}{2}\%$ and part at 4%, getting an average of 3% on the total. How much is each investment?

44. An automobile radiator contains 4 gallons of a mixture of alcohol and water, 20% being alcohol. How much should be drawn off and replaced by alcohol to have 30% alcohol in the radiator?

45. Two numbers are in the ratio 3:4. Subtracting 25 from each, we get two new numbers in the ratio 4:7. Find the original numbers.

46. What is the ratio of x to y if $(x + y):(x - y) = 6:5$?

47. Find the ordinary interest at $3\frac{1}{2}\%$ on $800 for 70 days by formula.

48. Find the interest in Problem 47 by short cut.

49. How much is the exact interest in Problem 47?

50. Find the number of days from May 13 to Sept. 20.

51. In what length of time will $1200 yield $45 interest at $4\frac{1}{2}\%$?

52. What principal will amount in 9 months to $741.60 at 5%?

53. At what interest rate will $2000 amount to $2080 in 15 months?

54. What ordinary interest corresponds to $94 exact interest?

55. A $300 debt due in 4 months may be settled now for $295 at what discount rate? What is the corresponding interest rate?

56. A debt of $500 is due in 8 months with interest at 4%. Find the present value; (a) at $4\frac{1}{2}\%$ discount rate; (b) at $4\frac{1}{2}\%$ interest rate.

57. A man requests a 60-day, $800 loan from a bank charging 8% discount. Compute the bank discount and the proceeds.

58. A non-interest-bearing note was discounted at 5% 45 days before maturity. Find the face value of the note if the discount was $20.

59. A 20-day trade acceptance for $4080, dated July 6, is discounted at 6% on July 11. Find the proceeds.

60. A 90-day 6% interest-bearing note for $1500, dated Aug. 5, is discounted at 8% on Aug. 15. How much does the holder receive?

61. Find the rate of interest earned by a bank in discounting a note for 6 months at the discount rate 4%.

62. Compute the rate of discount charged by a bank if, in granting a 4-month loan, it earns interest at 6%.

63. What loan should a man request if he wishes to receive $1500 as the proceeds of a 120-day loan from a bank charging 6% discount?

64. A 60-day "after sight" draft for $2500, dated Apr. 8 and accepted on Apr. 14, is discounted at 8% on May 2. Find the proceeds.

65. Do Problem 64 assuming that the draft is "after date."

66. A is to receive a $1000 bequest 2 years hence. How much is the bequest worth now if money earns simple interest at 3%?

67. A 90-day 6% interest-bearing note for $1600 is discounted 60 days before maturity. The bank discount is $20.30. Find the proceeds.

68. Compute the rate of discount in Problem 67.

69. A dealer buys goods for $5000 on the terms 3/5, 2/10, n/30. He pays $1000 on the 10th day. How much is due on the 30th day?

70. In Problem 69 find the annual interest rate equivalent to each offer.

71. What single discount rate is equivalent to the series: (a) 6% and $12\frac{1}{2}$%? (b) 10%, 20%, and 25%? (c) 20%, 10%, and 10%?

72. After discounts of $12\frac{1}{2}$% and 20%, the net price of a rug was $210. Find: (a) the list price; (b) the ratio of net price to list price.

73. Filing cabinets are sold to a jobber at $80 less 20% and $5\frac{1}{2}$%. Find the jobber's marked price if he wishes to gain 25% of his net purchase price after allowing a trade discount of 10% to his own customers.

74. The cash price of a truck is $2400. The purchaser pays $800 down and $100 a month. If 9% interest is charged, find the balance due just after the 5th monthly payment by the United States Rule.

75. Work Problem 74 by the Merchant's Rule.

76. To apply on a debt of $800 due 8 months ago, the debtor has paid $300, 6 months ago; $200, 2 months ago. Assuming money worth 6%, find the balance due 4 months hence by the Merchant's Rule.

77. Work Problem 76 by the United States Rule.

78. A non-interest-bearing debt of $500 is due 5 months hence. Assuming money worth 4%, what is the value of this obligation: (a) 2 months hence? (b) 5 months hence? (c) 11 months hence?

79. Answer the questions in Problem 78 if the debt of $500 bears 6% interest for 5 months.

80. Money being worth 6%, commute a debt of $800 due 7 months hence into two payments due 1 month and 10 months hence, the first being $200 less than the second. Take 10 months hence for focal date.

81. Work Problem 80 if the first payment is twice the second.

82. Do Problem 80, taking 7 months hence for focal date.

83. Find the balance due in Problem 76 by use of an equation of value, taking the present for focal date.

84. Commute a debt of $1500 due 3 months hence into three equal payments due 3, 5, and 8 months hence, money being worth 8%. The original debt and the new set are to be equivalent 8 months hence.

85. Find the equated date for paying in one sum a debt of $300 due in 15 days, one of $200 due in 45 days, and one of $400 due in 90 days.

86. A man is obligated to pay $900 4 months hence. He arranges to pay $300 now and $400 3 months hence. Find the equated date for paying the balance of $200.

87. Merchandise bought: May 5, $500; July 14, $800. Paid: June 4, $300; July 24, $400. Find equated date for paying balance of $600.

88. The equated date for paying in one sum a debt of $200 due in 10 days and one of $300 due in x days is 50 days hence. Find x.

89. Express with radical signs: (a) $7x^{2/3}$; (b) $y^{-3/4}$; (c) $P(1 + i)^{1/3}$.

90. Given $\sqrt{5} = 2.23607$. Evaluate $\sqrt{45}$ to 4 decimal places.

91. Solve for n: (a) $\frac{1}{2}\sqrt{5n} = 5$; (b) $x^3 \cdot x^0 \div x^{-1} = x^n$; (c) $3^{4n} = 9$.

92. Write with positive exponents and simplify: $\dfrac{x^{-3}y}{xy^{-2}}$; $\dfrac{x^2 - y^{-2}}{xy - 1}$.

93. Given $3x^{1/2} = 2$. Find the value of: (a) x^2; (b) x^{-1}; (c) $x^{2/3}$.

94. Express with fractional exponents: (a) $\sqrt{4x^5y^3}$; (b) $\sqrt[3]{(a + b)^2}$.

95. Solve for m: (a) $16^m = 2$; (b) $3^m = \frac{1}{9}$; (c) $6^{m-3} = 1$.

96. Evaluate $(2x)^{3/2} + 6y^{-1/2} - 12x^0$ if $x = 8$ and $y = 9$.

97. Write without a denominator: (a) $\dfrac{x}{y^2z}$; (b) $\dfrac{mn}{\sqrt{m^2 - n^2}}$; (c) $\dfrac{S}{(1.03)^5}$.

98. Simplify: (a) $5\sqrt{18} + 3\sqrt{12} - \sqrt{50}$; (b) $7 \div (\sqrt{5} + 2)$.

99. Solve for n: (a) $n^4 \div n^{-2} = 7^6$; (b) $4^n \cdot 2^n = 8^{1/2}$; (c) $(x^3)^n = x^6$.

100. Evaluate: (a) $(\tfrac{1}{8})^{2/3} \cdot 9^{3/2}$; (b) $3^{-1} \cdot 6 \div 16^{1/2}$; (c) $100(1.01)^{-1}$.

101. Solve for x: (a) $x^4 \cdot x^2 = 5^6$; (b) $6^x \div 2^x = 3^{-4}$; (c) $a^x = 1/a^2$.

102. If $i = e^{i/2} - 1$, then: (a) $(1 + i)^6 = ?$ (b) $(1 + i)^{-2} = ?$

103. Evaluate $x^2 - 2x - 1$ if x equals: (a) $\tfrac{3}{2}$; (b) $3\sqrt{2}$; (c) $1 - \sqrt{3}$.

104. Solve by factoring: (a) $x^2 + x = 6$; (b) $n^2 = n$; (c) $2t^2 + t = 3$

105. The square of what number exceeds twice the number by 35?

106. What values of x will give $x^2 - x$ half the value it has for $x = 4$?

107. Solve by the quadratic formula: (a) $x^2 + 3x = 5$; (b) $3x^2 - x = -4$

108. The perimeter of a rectangular plot is 30 feet, and the plot is surrounded by a border $1\tfrac{1}{2}$ feet wide. Find the dimensions of the plot if its area is equal to the area of the border.

109. Solve by completing the square: (a) $x^2 + 2x = 1$; (b) $2x^2 + x = 2$.

110. Solve $3x^2 + 5x - 2 = 0$ by *three* different methods.

111. Find the diagonal of a rectangle if it is 1 inch longer than one dimension of the rectangle and 8 inches longer than the other.

112. Solve for x and check: (a) $3\sqrt{x} + 4 = x$; (b) $\dfrac{4x}{x - 1} = 3x - 2$.

113. The sum of a certain number and six times its reciprocal is 5. Find the number.

114. What is the sum of the roots of the equation $2x^2 - 6x = 3$?

115. Find value of k if $5x^2 - kx = 8$ is satisfied by $x = 2$.

116. Given the series $8 + 2 - 4 - \cdots$. Find: (a) t_{40}; (b) S_{40}.

117. Given the series $8 + 4 + 2 + \cdots$. Find: (a) t_{10}; (b) S_{10}.

118. Find the sum of all *even* integers from 30 to 300 inclusive.

119. What is the sum of the first n positive odd integers?

120. Find the arithmetic, geometric, and harmonic means of 5 and 20.

121. A man invests \$500 at the beginning of each year for 20 years at 4% simple interest. Find the total interest earned in 20 years.

122. In a certain G.S., $t_3 = \frac{1}{2}$, $t_5 = \frac{2}{9}$; write the intermediate term.

123. Given $(1.02)^{17} = 1.40024$. Find the sum of each G.S. to 4 places: (a) $1 + (1.02) + \cdots + (1.02)^{16}$; (b) $1 + (1.02)^{-1} + \cdots + (1.02)^{-16}$.

124. Given a series with $t_1 = x$, $t_2 = 2x - 2$, $t_3 = 4x - 7$. Find the value of x for which this series becomes: (a) an A.S., (b) a G.S.

125. The arc described by each swing of a certain pendulum bob is $\frac{4}{5}$ as long as the arc of the previous swing. If the arc of the first swing is 25 inches long, find the arc of the fifth swing.

126. Show that, in any A.S., (a) $t_{2n} = t_n + nd$; (b) $S_{2n} = 2S_n + n^2d$.

127. In a certain A.S., $t_1 = 1$, $t_7 = 5$; write the intermediate terms.

128. Find $\sqrt{17}$ to 3 decimal places by expanding $(16 + 1)^{1/2}$.

129. Find $\sqrt[3]{7}$ to 3 decimal places by expanding $(8 - 1)^{1/3}$.

130. Expand to 4 terms and simplify: (a) $(2x - y^2)^8$; (b) $(9 + x)^{-1/2}$.

131. Evaluate to 4 decimal places: (a) $(1.02)^{-5}$; (b) $(1.01)^{1/3}$.

132. For what values of x is the expansion of $(8 - x^3)^{2/3}$ valid?

133. Expand to 4 terms and simplify: (a) $(1 + i)^{-6}$; (b) $(x^2 - 2)^{2/3}$.

134. Solve graphically the equations $x - 2y = 12$, $2x + y = 6$.

135. If $f(x) = x^2/(x - 1)$, find $f(3)$, $f(1)$, $f(-2)$, $f(\frac{1}{2})$, $f(2a)$, $f(a^2)$.

136. A point on the curve $y = x^2 + x$ has ordinate 2; find its abscissa.

137. The curve $y = a + bx^2$ intersects the Y-axis in what point?

138. Graph: (a) $2x - y = 3$; (b) $y = 2 - x^2$; (c) $y = x^3 - 2x - 3$.

139. Solve graphically: (a) $x^2 + 2x = 5$; (b) $x^3 - 2x - 3 = 0$.

140. Exhibit by a comparative broken-line graph the following data for motor-vehicle production (in millions) in the United States:

Year	1925	1930	1935	1940	1945	1950	1955	1960
Passenger Cars	3.7	2.8	3.3	3.7	0.07	6.6	7.9	6.7
Total	4.3	3.4	4.0	4.5	0.7	8.0	9.2	7.9

141. Draw a comparative bar graph of the data in Problem 140.

142. In the table of Problem 140, use only the data for passenger cars to draw (a) a bar graph; (b) a broken-line graph.

143. Find the value of (a) $\log_{10} 0.001$; (b) $\log_2 16$; (c) $\log_6 36$.

144. Given $7 = 10^{.845}$ and $5 = 10^{.699}$. Express 35 as a power of 10.

145. Round off the value of $\pi = 3.14159$ to 3 significant digits.

146. If $\log x = 9.3058 - 10$ and $\log y = 2.1527$, find: (a) $\log x^3 y^2$; (b) $\log 1000x$; (c) $\log (y/x)$; (d) $\log (1/y)$; (e) $\log y^{0.3}$; (f) $\log x^{1/4}$.

147. Find the value of n if (a) $\log 9 = n \log 3$, (b) $\log \frac{1}{8} = n \log 2$.

148. Find x if (a) $\log 7 = \log x - \log 3$; (b) $\log_2 16 = x - 5$.

149. Solve $S = P(1 + i)^n$ for n by use of logarithms.

150. Compute to 4 significant digits: $43.68\sqrt{7.52} \div 226.4$.

151. Evaluate $(1.01)^{-3}$ to 4 decimal places by *three* different methods.

152. Compute to 5 significant digits: (a) $(1.048)^{20}$; (b) $1200\sqrt{\pi}$.

153. Find i to 3 significant digits if $(1 + i)^{40} = 4.3210$.

154. Compute to 6 significant digits: (a) $2500(1.02)^7$; (b) $\sqrt[3]{186,000}$.

155. Find n to 2 decimal places if (a) $4^n = 8$; (b) $(n + 1)^3 = 365$.

156. Solve for x: $10^{2x} - 5(10^x) + 6 = 0$.

157. Graph $y = 2 \log x$ from $x = 1$ to $x = 15$ at intervals of 1.

158. Graph $y = \log 2x$ from $x = \frac{1}{2}$ to $x = 5$ at intervals of $\frac{1}{2}$.

159. Taking $e = 2.718$, graph $y = \frac{1}{2}(e^x - e^{-x})$ from $x = -2$ to $x = +2$ at intervals of $\frac{1}{2}$.

160. The area of a triangle is given by: $A = \sqrt{s(s - a)(s - b)(s - c)}$, where a, b, and c are the lengths of the sides, and $s = \frac{1}{2}(a + b + c)$. Compute by logarithms, to the nearest square foot, the area of a triangular field whose sides are 125, 180, 145 ft., respectively.

161. The time (in seconds) for one oscillation of a pendulum of length l ft. is $T = \pi\sqrt{l/g}$, where $g = 32.2$. Find T when $l = 4.50$ ft.

162. Kepler's third law of planetary motion is $N = d^{3/2}$, where N is the time in years for one revolution of a planet about the sun, and d its distance from the sun taking $d = 1$ for the earth. If $d = 1.53$ for Mars, find N.

163. By use of Table I of six-place mantissas, find the average change in log N as N takes the successive values 401, 402, 403, ..., 410.

164. Find the mean and the median of passenger-car production tabulated in Problem 140.

165. Determine the quartiles and the quartile deviation for the data concerning all motor-vehicle production in the table of Problem 140.

166. The table gives a distribution of the (first) inauguration ages of the 37 presidents of the United States. (a) What is the "modal class?" (b) Find the mean inauguration age, using midvalues of class intervals.

Age	42–44	45–47	48–50	51–53	54–56	57–59	60–62	63–65	66–68
Frequency	2	2	4	5	11	5	5	2	1

167. Draw a histogram and a frequency polygon for the distribution shown in the table of Problem 166.

168. Construct a frequency curve for the data of Problem 166.

169. Draw an ogive for the data of Problem 166.

170. Refer to the ogive of Problem 169. (a) What is the median age at inauguration? (b) Find the quartiles. (c) Find the quartile deviation.

171. The table below gives the United States school attendance rates for 1940 per 100 children of each age shown. What is the "modal" rate?

Age	7	8	9	10	11	12	13	14	15
Rate	92	95	96	96	96	96	95	97	88

172. Find the mean deviation of the rates tabulated in Problem 171.

173. Find the standard deviation of the data in Problem 171.

174. Construct an ogive for the data of Table 2, Art. 83. From the graph find: (a) the median; (b) the quartiles; (c) the per cent of students who made scores of less than 200; (d) the 40th percentile.

175. The algebra grades of six students were: 78, 81, 83, 86, 90, 92. Later, the calculus grades of these students were, respectively: 76, 77, 83, 84, 88 94. Find the coefficient of correlation between the two sets.

176. If $y_1, y_2, \ldots, y_n$ are the deviations of the numbers $x_1, x_2, \ldots, x_n$ from an **assumed mean** M', and if M is the arithmetic mean of the x's, m the arithmetic mean of the y's, show that $M = M' + m$.

177. With the notation in Problem 176, show that $\sigma^2 = \dfrac{\Sigma y^2}{n} - m^2$.

178. Using the equations in Problems 176 and 177, compute M and σ for the set 1604, 1601, 1597, 1598, 1605. [*Hint.* Let $M' = 1600$.]

179. The number of employees in the four stores of a certain chain is: 10, 14, 16, and x. The mean weekly pay per employee is $62, $65, $70, and $73, respectively. The weighted mean weekly pay per employee for the entire chain is $68.50. Find x.

180. Given that the mean deviation of a set of six numbers is 4. The deviations of the numbers from the arithmetic mean of the set are: -5, -2, -1, 1, 7, and k, where k is a positive number. Find: (a) the value of k; (b) the standard deviation of the set.

Part TWO

Compound Interest

Annuities, and

Life Insurance

Introduction to Part Two

A general problem is encountered in various forms throughout the following chapters. This problem is as follows:

A fund has an initial **balance** of P dollars. At the end of regular intervals (periods) of time, a fixed amount, R dollars, is either added to or subtracted from the balance. (When this occurs we will say a **payment** is made) In any given situation we will either always add to or subtract from the balance. Now, in general, we will have the fund in an interest-bearing situation so that the balance at the end of each period, at the time the payment R is made, will be different from P.

The general problem is to find the balance at the end of n periods.

We will suppose that our balance draws interest at the rate of i per period (usually given in per cent). If, at the end of k periods, the balance is x_k, the balance at the end of $k + 1$ periods (after the payment R and after the addition of the interest earned) is given by:

$$(1) \quad x_{k+1} = x_k + ix_k + R$$
$$= x_k(1 + i) + R.$$

We have also that

$$(2) \quad x_0 = P.$$

In (1), if the payment is added to the balance, $R > 0$, and if the payment is subtracted from the balance, $R < 0$. It might also be the case that no payment is made, in which case $R = 0$.

Notice that

$$x_1 = x_0 + ix_0 + R$$
$$= (1 + i)x_0 + R$$

and

$$x_2 = (1 + i)x_1 + R$$
$$= (1 + i)[(1 + i)x_0 + R] + R$$
$$= (1 + i)^2 x_0 + (1 + i)R + R.$$

Continuing in this fashion we have that

$$x_n = (1 + i)^n x_0 + [(1 + i)^{n-1} + (1 + i)^{n-2} + \cdots + (1 + i) + 1] R.$$

Since

$$S_n = 1 + (1 + i) + \cdots + (1 + i)^{n-1}$$

represents the sum of the first n terms of a geometric series we have that

$$S_n = \frac{(1 + i)^n - 1}{i}.$$

Thus,

$$(M) \quad x_n = (1 + i)^n x_0 + \frac{R}{i}[(1 + i)^n - 1]$$
$$= \left(x_0 + \frac{R}{i}\right)(1 + i)^n - \frac{R}{i}$$
$$= \left(P + \frac{R}{i}\right)(1 + i)^n - \frac{R}{i}.$$

This development is a bit informal but it can be made rigorous using mathematical induction.

Now there are several variables involved in our formula and, given all but one, we can attempt to determine that one. As an example of how this formula can be used suppose that a person borrows $1000 at 6% interest compounded semiannually to be repaid in 20 installments at the end of each 6-month period. We would like to know the amount to be paid each 6 months. In this case the initial balance is $1000, and we want x_{20} to be zero dollars. We can list our values for this problem.

$$P = 1000, \quad i = 0.03, \quad n = 20, \quad \text{and } R \text{ is to be determined.}$$

Thus,

$$0 = \left(1000 + \frac{R}{0.03}\right)(1.03)^{20} - \frac{R}{0.03}$$

or

$$\frac{R}{0.03}[(1.03)^{20} - 1] = -1000(1.03)^{20}$$

or

$$R = -\frac{(0.03)(1000)(1.03)^{20}}{(1.03)^{20} - 1}.$$

On computing we get that

$$R = -\$67.22.$$

This means that the borrower should make 20 monthly payments of $67.22.

As another example, suppose that a debt of $1000 is to be paid off at the end of 5 years. The debtor decides to accumulate this amount by paying an unknown amount, R, into a savings account every 6 months. The account pays 3% interest compounded semiannually. We would like to know the amount of the payments necessary to accumulate the $1000. We assume the first payment to be made 6 months hence.

In this case the initial balance, R, is 0 dollars. We want x_{10} to be $1000. We have that $i = 0.015$, $n = 10$, $R = 0$ and that $x_n = \$1000$. Substituting into our formula we have

$$\$1000 = \left(0 + \frac{R}{0.015}\right)(1 + 0.015)^{10} - \frac{R}{0.015}.$$

Simplifying we get

$$\$1000 = R \cdot \frac{(1.015)^{10} - 1}{0.015}.$$

Solving for R, we have

$$R = \frac{(1000)(0.015)}{(1.015)^{10} - 1}$$
$$= \$93.45.$$

Now these are instances of the application of our formula

(M) $\quad x_n = \left(P + \frac{R}{i}\right)(1 + i)^n - \frac{R}{i},$

which also has the form

(M$_1$) $\quad x_n = (1 + i)^n P + \frac{R}{i}[(1 + i)^n - 1].$

In the following chapters we will look at various special applications of this formula.

Chapter ELEVEN

COMPOUND INTEREST AND
COMPOUND DISCOUNT

94. Compound amount and compound interest

In transactions involving simple interest, the principal on which the interest is computed remains unchanged throughout the term of the loan, and the interest becomes due either at the end of the term or at the end of stated intervals during the term of the loan. If not paid when due, the interest becomes simply a non-interest-bearing debt.

In transactions of other types, it is mutually agreed that the interest for each period, instead of being paid when due, shall be added to and become part of the principal. In other words, interest is computed upon a principal which increases periodically. Consequently, the interest for a given period is more than that of the preceding period. When interest is thus added to the principal at the end of each period, it is said to be **converted** into principal, or **compounded**, or **payable.** The total amount due at the end of the last period is called the **compound amount.** The difference between the compound amount and the original principal is called the **compound interest.**

95. The difference between compound interest and simple interest

This may be made clear by an illustration. The simple interest at 6% on $1000 for three years is three times the interest for one year, or 3 × $60 $180. However, if the 6% interest be converted annually, $1000 will amount in three years to $1191.02. The work is shown below.

205

```
Original principal  .............................$1000.00
    Add 6% interest ..............................    60.00
Principal at end of 1st year  .....................$1060.00
    Add 6% interest ..............................    63.60
Principal at end of 2nd year......................$1123.60
    Add 6% interest ..............................    67.42
Principal at end of 3rd year  .....................$1191.02
```

The compound interest is $1191.02 − $1000 = $191.02. The difference in this case between compound interest and simple interest is $11.02.

96. Conversion period and rate per period

The accumulation or growth of a principal at compound interest depends upon two elements: (a) the number of **conversion periods** over which the investment extends, and (b) **the interest rate per conversion period.**

Interest may be converted into principal annually, semiannually, quarterly, monthly, or at any other regular periods of time. The **frequency of conversion** is a number indicating how many times interest is compounded in one year. The time between two successive conversions of interest is called the **conversion period,** or **interest period.** Thus, if interest is compounded quarterly, the frequency of conversion is 4 and the conversion period is 3 months.

Regardless of the frequency of conversion, the rate of interest is usually expressed as an annual rate. When the conversion period is other than a year, the rate per conversion period is found by dividing the stated annual rate by the number of conversion periods in a year. Thus, if the quoted rate is 6% compounded semiannually, the rate per conversion period is 3%, or 0.03.

The time over which the investment extends is usually expressed in years, or years and months. It is necessary to change the given time into conversion periods. Thus, if interest is compounded quarterly and the investment runs over $3\frac{1}{2}$ years, the number of conversion periods is $4 \times 3\frac{1}{2}$, or 14.

ILLUSTRATIVE EXAMPLE. A certain principal is invested for 5 years and 7 months at 6% converted monthly. What is (a) the frequency of conversion? (b) the conversion period? (c) the total number of conversion periods? (d) the interest rate per conversion period?

SOLUTION. (a) The frequency of conversion is 12.

(b) The conversion period is 1 month.

(c) The total number of conversion periods is 67.

(d) The interest rate per conversion period is $\frac{1}{2}\%$.

EXERCISE 61

In each of Problems 1-6 state (a) the frequency of conversion; (b) the conversion period; (c) the total number of conversion periods; (d) the interest rate per conversion period.

Problem	Time	Rate Quoted
1.	15 years	$2\frac{3}{4}\%$ Compounded annually
2.	10 years and 6 months	$4\frac{1}{2}\%$ Compounded semiannually
3.	8 years and 3 months	5% Compounded quarterly
4.	7 years and 8 months	3% Compounded bimonthly
5.	5 years and 7 months	$7\frac{1}{2}\%$ Compounded monthly
6.	3 years and 2 months	6% Compounded semimonthly

7. Find the amount of $800 invested for $2\frac{1}{2}$ years (a) at 6% simple interest; (b) at 6% interest compounded semiannually.

8. Find the amount of $1000 invested for $1\frac{1}{2}$ years (a) at 4% simple interest; (b) at 4% interest compounded quarterly.

9. A principal of $2000 is invested for 21 months. Find (a) the simple interest at 8%; (b) the compound interest at 8% converted quarterly.

10. A principal of $1200 is invested for 5 years. Find (a) the simple interest at 3%; (b) the compound interest at 3% converted annually.

97. The meaning of certain expressions

To avoid confusion, attention is called to the meaning of certain expressions frequently used in succeeding discussions and problems.

(a) Unless simple interest is specified, the word "interest" will hereafter mean *compound interest*, and "amount" will mean *compound amount*.

(b) When the frequency of conversion is not stated, interest will be understood to be converted *annually*. Thus, the expression "interest at 5%" or "money worth 5%" will mean 5% converted annually.

(c) If a sum of money is stated to be due on a certain date, the given sum will be understood to be *due without interest*, unless specific mention is made that it is due with interest at a given rate. Thus, "$200 due in 3 years" will mean that the sum payable in 3 years is $200 with no interest.

98. Formula for compound amount

In Art. 95 an arithmetical method was used to compute compound amount. The method is tedious even in simple cases involving a comparatively small number of conversion periods. The larger the number of conversion periods, the longer becomes this arithmetical process. In actual practice, accountants and actuaries use much shorter methods based upon a general formula which we shall now derive.

What we encounter here is an application of our general formula, treated in the introduction to Part II, where the *initial balance* P is known, where the interest rate is known, and where the regular payment is $0. To know the balance at the end of n periods, we merely replace R by 0, and thus obtain

$$x_n = P(1 + i)^n.$$

This balance x_n, referred to as the **compound amount,** is usually denoted by S. Our formula, then, for finding the compound amount S is

$$S = P(1 + i)^n. \tag{1}$$

This formula is the key to all that we do in this chapter.

The quantity $1 + i$ in this formula is called the **ratio of increase,** because, as the student will observe in the foregoing derivation, the principal at the end of any period is $(1 + i)$ times the principal at the end of the preceding period.

To **accumulate** a principal means to find its compound amount at the end of a given number of periods. The quantity $(1 + i)^n$ in (1) is called the **accumulation factor,** because the compound amount of P is the product of P and $(1 + i)^n$. The accumulation factor is also called the **compound amount of 1,** because, as may be seen readily from (1), the compound amount of a principal of $1 is simply $(1 + i)^n$. Denoting by a small s the compound amount of 1 for n periods at the rate i per period, we have, then, as a special case of (1),

$$s = (1 + i)^n. \tag{1'}$$

99. Computation of compound amount by Table III

Formula (1) gives us a rule for finding the compound amount of P: *Multiply the original principal P by the compound amount of 1 for the given rate and time.*

To determine the compound amount of 1 by actual calculations requires considerable time. Much time may be saved by the use of a table, such as **Table III** on page 458, showing the compound amount of 1 for various rates and numbers of periods. The letter n at the top of the first column on each page refers to the number of conversion periods. The per cent that appears at the top of each of the remaining columns refers to the interest rate per period.

Table III gives values of $(1 + i)^n$ to 8 decimal places. However, it is unnecessary to use all of the decimal places in every problem. If the final results are to be determined to the nearest cent, read the entry to as many decimal places as there are digits in P expressed in dollars and cents. Thus, for a principal of $5000.00, read the proper entry only to 6 decimal places. Again, for a principal of $60.00, read the entry to 4 decimal places. This simple rule will eliminate unnecessary labor in multiplication.

———

ILLUSTRATIVE EXAMPLE 1. Find the compound amount of $2000 for 25 years at 6%.

SOLUTION. Here $P = 2000$, $i = 6\% = 0.06$, and $n = 25$. From Table III, $(1.06)^{25} = 4.291871$. Substituting these values in formula (1),

$$S = P(1 + i)^n = 2000 \times 4.291871 = \$8583.74. \quad Ans.$$

———

ILLUSTRATIVE EXAMPLE 2. Accumulate $750 for 10 years at $4\frac{1}{2}\%$ converted semiannually.

SOLUTION. Here $P = 750$, $i = 2\frac{1}{4}\% = 0.0225$, and $n = 20$. From Table II, $(1.0225)^{20} = 1.56051$. Hence

$$S = P(1 + i)^n = 750 \times 1.56051 = \$1170.38. \quad Ans.$$

_____

100. Time beyond table limit

When the value of n extends beyond the table limit, the compound amount of 1 may still be determined from Table III by a simple application of Law I of exponents, $a^x \cdot a^y = a^{x+y}$ (see Art. 49).

_____

ILLUSTRATIVE EXAMPLE. Accumulate \$300 for 125 years at 3%.

SOLUTION. No entry is found in the table for $n = 125$. However, we know that $(1 + i)^{100} \times (1 + i)^{25} = (1 + i)^{125}$. From Table III,

$$(1.03)^{100} = 19.21863, \text{ and } (1.03)^{25} = 2.093778.$$

Then

$$(1.03)^{125} = 19.21863 \times 2.093778 = 40.23955.$$

Hence

$$S = 300(1.03)^{125} = 300 \times 40.23955 = \$12,071.87. \quad Ans.$$

_____

EXERCISE 62

In each of Problems 1–10 state the ratio of increase and the accumulation factor; then look up the compound amount of 1.

	For	At	Converted		For	At	Converted
1.	$13\frac{1}{2}$ years	4%	Quarterly	**6.**	8 years	$3\frac{1}{2}\%$	Semiannually
2.	$12\frac{1}{2}$ years	6%	Monthly	**7.**	9 years	$7\frac{1}{2}\%$	Bimonthly
3.	10 years	5%	Annually	**8.**	5 years	6%	Semimonthly
4.	20 years	8%	Quarterly	**9.**	10 years	$5\frac{1}{2}\%$	Semiannually
5.	$6\frac{3}{4}$ years	4%	Monthly	**10.**	6 years	$4\frac{1}{2}\%$	Bimonthly

11. Accumulate \$2000 for 60 years (a) at $1\frac{1}{2}\%$; (b) at 3%; (c) at 6%. How much is the compound interest in each case?

12. Find the compound amount of $800 at 6% for (a) 5 years; (b) 10 years; (c) 20 years. Determine the compound interest in each case.

13. A savings deposit of $500 will amount in 10 years to what, if interest is at 2% converted (a) annually? (b) semiannually? (c) quarterly?

14. To what sum of money will $1000 accumulate in 15 years, if interest is at $3\frac{1}{2}$% converted (a) semiannually? (b) quarterly? (c) monthly?

15. A dividend of $40 is left with the Mutual Life Insurance Co. for accumulation at 3% converted quarterly. Find the amount in 20 years.

16. Compute the interest on $300 left with the Haven Savings Bank for 12 years if the bank pays interest at $2\frac{1}{2}$% converted semiannually.

17. A man's will dictates that his $100,000 estate be put in trust for 50 years. What is the amount of his estate at the end of that time if the principal is invested at 6% compounded semiannually?

18. $20,000 invested at 7% compounded monthly amounts to what at the end of 4 years?

19. X buys a lot for $1250, paying $250 cash. How much is due $3\frac{3}{4}$ years later if interest is at 6% compounded bimonthly?

20. A man borrows $500, agreeing to repay the principal with interest at 8% compounded quarterly. What does he owe at the end of 5 years?

21. Accumulate $2500 for 13 years at 7% compounded quarterly.

22. How many years will it take for $1000 to accumulate to $3869.68 if it is compounded annually at 7%?

23. Accumulate $1100 for 12 years at 5% converted monthly.

24. Accumulate $100 for 8 years at $5\frac{1}{4}$% converted bimonthly.

25. Benjamin Franklin bequeathed $5000 to the city of Boston. Assuming that the bequest was invested for 160 years at 4%, find its amount.

26. The Dutch bought Manhattan Island in 1626 for $24. If this sum had been invested then at 6%, to how much would it have accumulated in 1776?

27. If $(1 + i)^{85} = 10.0330$, then $(1 + i)^{170} = ?$

28. If $(1 + i)^{60} = 20.2500$, then $(1 + i)^{30} = ?$

29. Prove that $(1 + i)^n > 1 + ni$ for every integer $n > 1$. Hence compare amount at compound interest with amount at simple interest.

30. Draw a comparative graph of $S = P(1 + ni)$ and $S = P(1 + i)^n$ for integral values of n from 0 to 50, plotting points for every fifth period. Let P and i be given constants; for convenience, take $P = 1$ and $i = 0.05$.

31. Draw a comparative graph of $S = P(2 + i)^n$ and $S = (1 + i)^n$ for integral values of n from 0 to 50, plotting points for every fifth period. Let P and i be given constants; for convenience, take $P = 1$ and $i = 0.05$.

101. Compound amount at changing rates

Heretofore we have assumed a *constant rate of interest* for the entire duration of an investment. However, interest rates may change from time to time. Thus, a savings bank, which pays interest at 3% when a deposit is made, may, after a number of years, raise the rate to 4% and later on perhaps reduce it to $2\frac{1}{2}$%. The final compound amount is the product of the original principal and the two or more accumulation factors, each with its proper value for i and n.

———

ILLUSTRATIVE EXAMPLE. A man made a deposit of $250 in a savings bank. The deposit was left to accumulate at 3% compounded quarterly for the first 5 years and at 4% compounded semiannually for the next 8 years. Find the compound amount at the end of 13 years.

SOLUTION. For the first 5 years, $i = \frac{3}{4}\% = 0.0075$, $n = 20$. For the next 8 years, $i = 0.02$, $n = 16$. Hence the amount at the end of 13 years is

$$250(1.0075)^{20}(1.02)^{16} = 250 \times 1.16118 \times 1.37279 = \$398.52. \quad Ans.$$

———

102. Interest for fractional parts of conversion periods

In defining compound amount and deriving a formula for it, we assumed an integral number of conversion periods in the time. When it is desired to find the compound amount for a time involving a fractional part of a conversion period, the following method is used in practice: *Compute the compound amount by $S = P(1 + i)^n$ at the end of the last whole period contained in the given length of time; then, add to this amount the simple interest on it for the remaining fraction of a period.*

ILLUSTRATIVE EXAMPLE. To what sum of money does $6200 amount in 5 years and 8 months at 5% converted semiannually?

SOLUTION. The given time contains 11 whole periods and 2 months. Now, the compound amount at the end of the eleventh period is

$$S = 6200(1.025)^{11} = 6200 \times 1.312087 = \$8134.94.$$

The simple interest on $8134.94 for the remaining 2 months is

$$8134.94 \times \frac{2}{12} \times 0.05 = 8134.94 \times \frac{0.05}{6} = \$67.79.$$

Hence the amount at the end of 5 years and 8 months is

$$\$8134.94 + \$67.79 = \$8202.73. \quad Ans.$$

EXERCISE 63

1. Find the amount of $300 for 15 years if interest is at 6% for the first 7 years and at $4\frac{1}{2}$% for the last 8 years.

2. Find the amount of $400 for 12 years if interest is at $2\frac{1}{2}$% for the first 8 years and at 3% for the last 4 years.

3. Accumulate $100 for 20 years if interest is at $3\frac{1}{2}$% converted semiannually for 15 years and at 4% converted quarterly thereafter.

4. Accumulate $200 for 10 years at $4\frac{1}{2}$% converted quarterly for the first 4 years and at $3\frac{1}{2}$% converted monthly thereafter.

5. After 12 years a certain investment accumulated to $1121.33. Interest was at 4% compounded quarterly for the first 4 years and then 6% for the remaining time. How much was the original investment?

6. Find the amount of $1000 for $7\frac{1}{2}$ years at 3%.

7. In how many months will $5000 invested at 4% compounded semiannually amount to $6404.62?

8. Find the amount of $800 for $12\frac{1}{4}$ years at 4%.

9. Accumulate $500 for $5\frac{3}{4}$ years at 6% compounded semiannually.

10. Accumulate $1000 for $7\frac{2}{3}$ years at $4\frac{1}{2}$% compounded quarterly.

11. A deposit of $659.26 in a savings bank accumulates to what amount at $5\frac{1}{2}\%$ converted quarterly for the first 9 years, at 4% compounded semiannually for the next 8 years, and at $6\frac{1}{2}\%$ for the remaining 13 years?

12. In how many months will $1252.29 invested at 6% converted quarterly amount to $2719.46?

13. A man deposits $1000 in a savings bank on his son's natal day. Interest is at $2\frac{1}{2}\%$ for the first 8 years and at 2% converted quarterly thereafter. How much is accumulated when the boy is 21?

14. A student borrowed $600. He was to pay no interest for 3 years. After that he was to pay interest at 6% convertible annually. He made no payments for $4\frac{1}{2}$ years. What did he owe at the end of that time?

103. Nominal and effective rates of interest

When the conversion period is other than a year, the stated annual rate of interest is called the **nominal annual rate.** $100, invested at the nominal annual rate 6%, converted semiannually, amounts in 1 year to $100(1.03)^2 = \$106.09$. The interest actually earned on the original principal of $100 is $6.09, which represents an annual return of 6.09%. We say that the **effective annual rate** in this case is 6.09%. When the conversion period is a year, the effective annual rate is the same as the stated annual rate. Hereafter we shall abbreviate nominal annual rate and effective annual rate into **nominal rate** and **effective rate,** respectively.

Rates producing equal amounts in the same length of time on the same principal are called **equivalent,** or **corresponding, rates.** Thus, the nominal rate 6%, converted semiannually, is equivalent to, or corresponds to, the effective rate 6.09%. Let r denote the effective rate equivalent to a given nominal rate j converted m times a year. We shall use i exclusively for rate per conversion period. At the rate $i = j/m$, P amounts in 1 year to $P(1 + i)^m$. At the effective rate r, P amounts in 1 year to $P(1 + r)$. Since equivalent rates yield equal amounts in the same length of time,

$$P(1 + r) = P(1 + i)^m,$$

or

$$1 + r = (1 + i)^m,$$

whence

$$r = (1 + i)^m - 1. \tag{2}$$

By use of (2) we can find the effective rate r equivalent to the nominal rate $j = im$ converted m times a year, that is, equivalent to the rate $i = j/m$ per conversion period.

ILLUSTRATIVE EXAMPLE. Find the effective rate equivalent to the nominal rate 8% converted quarterly.

SOLUTION. Here $i = 0.02$ and $m = 4$. By substitution in (2), we have

$$r = (1 + i)^m - 1 = (1.02)^4 - 1 = 1.0824 - 1 = 0.0824.$$

Hence the effective rate in this case is 8.24%. This means that the rate 8.24% compounded *annually* yields the same interest as the nominal rate 8% compounded *quarterly* (or the rate 2% per quarter).

-----

104. Continuous conversion; force of interest

It is interesting to investigate how the effective rate r changes as interest is converted more and more frequently under the same nominal j; or, mathematically stated, how r changes as m increases and j remains constant. In (2), where $i = j/m$, let us for example take $j = 6\%$ and find successively the effective rates r equivalent to 6% converted annually, semiannually, quarterly, monthly, weekly, and daily. The results are given in the table below. The first two values of r are exact; the others are rounded off to five significant digits. Note that, although r increases as m does, the increase in r becomes less and less rapid. We could go further, passing from daily to hourly conversion; the first four digits in the value of r would remain unchanged, the increase being very slight. We could ultimately conceive of the rate 6% as being converted **continuously**. The value of r in this extreme case would be 6.1837%. See illustrative example 1 on page 216.

When $m =$	1	2	4	12	52	365
then $r =$	6%	6.09%	6.1364%	6.1678%	6.1800%	6.1831%

By (2), $r = \left(1 + \dfrac{j}{m}\right)^m - 1$. In the case of continuous conversion, m increases beyond all bounds. It can be shown that, as m becomes infinite,

$\left(1 + \dfrac{j}{m}\right)^m$ takes the *limiting* value e^j, where $e = 2.71828^+$. This means the following: As m increases indefinitely, the value of $\left(1 + \dfrac{j}{m}\right)^m$ approaches that of e^j more and more nearly; and the difference between the value of e^j and that of $\left(1 + \dfrac{j}{m}\right)^m$ can be made as small as we please by taking sufficiently large values of m. In the case of a nominal rate j converted continuously, we see therefore that the equivalent effective rate r is given by

$$r = e^j - 1. \tag{2'}$$

The nominal rate j converted continuously and equivalent to a given effective rate r is called the **force of interest** corresponding to the effective rate r.

ILLUSTRATIVE EXAMPLE 1. Find the effective rate equivalent to the nominal rate 6% converted continuously.

SOLUTION. Substituting $j = 0.06$ in (2') and adding 1 to both members, we get $1 + r = e^{0.06}$. Taking the logarithm of both members,

$$\log (1 + r) = 0.06 \times \log e = 0.06 \times 0.4342945 = 0.0260577.$$

$$\therefore \quad 1 + r = 1.061837 \text{ and } r = 6.1837\%. \quad \textit{Ans.}$$

Note. The value of e can be computed to any number of decimal places; see Problem 32, page 236. To 7 places, $e = 2.7182818$ and $\log e = 0.4342945$.

ILLUSTRATIVE EXAMPLE 2. Find the force of interest corresponding to the effective rate 6%.

SOLUTION. For a given r, the corresponding value of j (converted continuously) must be such as to satisfy equation (2'). Substituting $r = 0.06$ in (2') and adding 1 to both members, we get $1.06 = e^j$. Applying logarithms, $\log 1.06 = j \log e$. Hence

$$j = \frac{\log 1.06}{\log e} = \frac{0.0253059}{0.4342945} = 0.058269.$$

Here the force of interest is 5.8269%. This means that 5.8269% converted continuously and 6% effective are equivalent rates.

———

EXERCISE 64

1. Find the effective rate equivalent to 6% nominal converted (a) semiannually; (b) quarterly; (c) monthly; (d) continuously.

2. Find the effective rate equivalent to 8% nominal converted (a) semiannually; (b) monthly; (c) semimonthly; (d) continuously.

3. Which is a better yield rate: $5\frac{1}{2}\%$ converted semiannually or $5\frac{1}{4}\%$ converted bimonthly? [*Hint.* Compare the equivalent effective rates.]

4. Which yields more interest: $7\frac{1}{2}\%$ converted monthly or 8% effective?

5. Find the effective rate equivalent to $6\frac{1}{2}\%$ converted continuously.

6. What effective rate corresponds to 4% converted continuously?

7. What force of interest corresponds to $4\frac{1}{2}\%$ effective?

8. Find the force of interest corresponding to $6\frac{1}{2}\%$ effective.

9. Find the rate converted continuously equivalent to $7\frac{1}{2}\%$ effective.

10. What rate converted continuously is equivalent to 4% effective?

11. Express the right member of $r = (1 + i)^m - 1$ in another form, by expanding $(1 + i)^m$ by the binomial theorem.

12. Use the result of Problem 11 to evaluate $r = (1.006)^6 - 1$.

13. Evaluate $r = (1.003)^{12} - 1$ by use of logarithms.

14. Evaluate $r = (1.0275)^{76} - 1$.

15. Which yields more interest: 5% converted monthly or 5.12% effective?

16. Solve (a) $r = (1 + i)^m - 1$ for i; (b) $r = e^j - 1$ for j.

17. Compute the effective rate equivalent to a nominal rate of 2% converted continuously.

105. Present value at compound interest; compound discount

In finding the present value of a long-term obligation, it is customary to use a *compound interest rate.* If money is worth i per period, the **present value** of S due in n periods is that principal which, invested *now* at the rate i per period, will amount to S in n periods. The word "now," used here in a relative sense of time, refers to n periods before S is due.

We have already seen that a principal P will amount to $S = P(1 + i)^n$ in n periods at the rate i per period. It is evident, then, that P is the present value of S. Solving the formula for P by dividing both members by $(1 + i)^n$,

$$P = \frac{S}{(1 + i)^n} = S(1 + i)^{-n}. \tag{3}$$

It should be noted that P and S represent the value of the same obligation *at different dates.* P is the present value of a given obligation, while S is the future value of the same obligation. P (now) is just as good as S (n periods hence).

To **discount** a sum due in the future is to find its present value. By **compound discount** is meant the difference between the future value of a sum and its present value. The compound discount on S is the compound interest on P.

The quantity $(1 + i)^{-n}$ in (3) is called the **discount factor.** The discount factor is also called the **present value of 1 at compound interest,** because, as may be seen readily from (3), the present value of \$1 due n periods hence is simply $(1 + i)^{-n}$. Denoting the present value of 1 by v^n, so that $v = (1 + i)^{-1}$, we have, as a special case of (3),

$$v^n = (1 + i)^{-n}. \tag{3'}$$

106. Computation of present value by Table IV

Formula (3) gives a rule for finding the present value of S: *Multiply S by the present value of 1 for the given rate and time.*

In order to save time in calculations, we shall use **Table IV,** where the present value of 1 is shown for various rates and numbers of periods. If the final results are to be determined to the nearest cent, read the table to as many decimal places as there are digits in S expressed in dollars and cents.

———

ILLUSTRATIVE EXAMPLE 1. Find the present value of $5000 due in 15 years, if money is worth $5\frac{1}{2}\%$. What is the compound discount?

SOLUTION. Here $S = 5000$, $i = 5\frac{1}{2}\% = 0.055$, and $n = 15$. From Table IV, $(1.055)^{-15} = 0.447933$. Hence

$$P = S(1 + i)^{-n} = 5000 \times 0.447933 = \$2239.67. \quad Ans.$$

The present value of $5000 is $2239.67; that is, $2239.67 invested now at $5\frac{1}{2}\%$ would amount in 15 years to $5000. $2239.67 *now* and $5000 *fifteen years hence* are equally desirable; they represent the value of the same obligation at different dates.

CHECK. The reader may ask himself: Does $2239.67 actually amount to $5000 in 15 years at $5\frac{1}{2}\%$? Applying formula (1),

$$S = P(1 + i)^n = 2239.67 \times (1.055)^{15}$$
$$= 2239.67 \times 2.232477 = \$5000.01.$$

The compound discount on $5000 is $5000 - 2239.67 = \$2760.33$, which represents the compound interest on $2239.67 (the present value) for 15 years at $5\frac{1}{2}\%$.

———

ILLUSTRATIVE EXAMPLE 2. If money is worth $4\frac{1}{2}\%$ converted semiannually, find (a) the present value of $1500 due in 7 years, (b) the value of the same obligation 3 years before it is due.

SOLUTION. (a) Here $S = 1500$, $i = 0.0225$, and $n = 14$. From Table IV, $(1.0225)^{-14} = 0.732341$. Hence

$$P = S(1 + i)^{-n} = 1500 \times 0.732341 = \$1098.51. \quad Ans.$$

(b) In this case, $S = 1500$, $i = 0.0225$, and $n = 6$. From Table IV,

$(1.0225)^{-6} = 0.875024$. Hence

$$P = S(1 + i)^{-n} = 1500 \times 0.875024 = \$1312.54. \quad \textit{Ans.}$$

---

107. Present value of an interest-bearing debt

To find the present value of an interest-bearing debt, take the following two steps:

I. Find the amount of the debt *at maturity*.
II. Determine the present value of the compound amount found in I.

ILLUSTRATIVE EXAMPLE. A debt of $4500, bearing 5% interest converted semiannually, is due in 6 years. If money is worth $4\frac{1}{2}$% effective, find the present value of the debt.

SOLUTION. I. By formula (1), the maturity value of the debt is

$$S = 4500(1.025)^{12} = 4500 \times 1.344889 = \$6052.00.$$

II. By formula (3), the present value of this amount is

$$P = 6052.00(1.045)^{-6} = 6052.00 \times 0.767896 = \$4647.31.$$

Hence the present value of the debt is $4647.31. *Ans.*

EXERCISE 65

In Problems 1–10, tell the discount factor and look up its value.

	Due in	Money Worth	Converted		Due in	Money Worth	Converted
1.	40 years	$6\frac{1}{2}$%	Annually	**6.**	$11\frac{1}{2}$ years	5%	Semiannually
2.	15 years	$5\frac{1}{2}$%	Quarterly	**7.**	$8\frac{2}{3}$ years	3%	Bimonthly
3.	10 years	$7\frac{1}{2}$%	Monthly	**8.**	$5\frac{3}{4}$ years	6%	Semimonthly
4.	20 years	$3\frac{1}{3}$%	Annually	**9.**	$4\frac{1}{2}$ years	6%	Semiannually
5.	25 years	3%	Quarterly	**10.**	$14\frac{1}{3}$ years	4%	Bimonthly

11. Discount $100 for 8 years, assuming that money is worth (a) $1\frac{1}{2}\%$; (b) 3%; (c) 6%. How much is the compound discount in each case?

12. Assuming money to be worth $4\frac{1}{2}\%$, discount $1000 for (a) 10 years; (b) 20 years; (c) 40 years. Determine the compound discount in each case.

13. Find the present value of $2000, due in 5 years, if money is worth 4% compounded (a) annually; (b) semiannually; (c) quarterly; (d) monthly.

14. What sum will amount in 12 years to $3000 if invested now at 5% compounded (a) annually? (b) semiannually? (c) quarterly? (d) monthly?

15. At 3% converted monthly, what sum will amount in 5 years to $800?

16. Discount $500 for 7 years at 6% converted quarterly.

17. To discharge a debt, the debtor may pay $825 now or $1000 four years hence. Which plan should he accept if money is worth 5% to him?

18. Solve Problem 17 assuming that money is worth $4\frac{1}{2}\%$.

19. What is the present value at 3% of a debt of $1000 due in 6 years if the debt bears interest for 6 years (a) at 4%? (b) at 3%?

20. Find the present value at 4% of a note for $1000 due in 3 years if the note bears interest for 3 years (a) at 3%; (b) at 4%.

21. X signs a note promising to pay Y $2000 in 6 years with compound interest at 5%. Y sells the note to Z 3 years later. What does Z pay if Y and Z agree that money is worth 3% converted quarterly?

22. A student borrows $1000, agreeing to repay it in 6 years with accumulated interest at 4% *for the last* 3 *years only.* Four years later he wishes to settle the debt. What should he pay if money is worth 5%?

23. Find the present value at 4% converted semiannually of a debt of $3000 due in 6 years and 9 months. [*Hint.* Discount the debt for $6\frac{1}{2}$ years; then compute the present value of the result at simple interest.]

24. A debt of $2000 is due in 5 years. Find the present value (a) at 6% effective; (b) at 6% simple interest. Compare the two discounts.

25. The present value of a debt of $400 plus an unknown amount due in 10 years is $553.68. Find the unknown sum if money is worth 6% compounded semiannually.

26. A man borrowed $3000 due in 3 years at 6% simple interest to purchase a new car. A friend invests a certain sum at 4% compounded semiannually for 3 years to pay the man's debt. How much did the friend invest?

27. A father borrowed $5000 at 6% converted semiannually due in 10 years to pay for his son's college education. How much would he have invested at $4\frac{1}{2}\%$ compounded semiannually 20 years ago to pay his future obligation?

28. A debt of $6000 is due in 6 years at $5\frac{1}{2}\%$ effective. Find the discount factor if the present value of the debt is $6523.25.

29. How much was money worth in Problem 28 if interest was compounded semiannually?

30. A certain debt bearing 6% interest converted quarterly is due in 6 years. The present value of the debt is $10,629.15. Find the debt if the money is worth 5% compounded semiannually.

31. A certain debt at 7% compounded semiannually due in 10 years was cancelled after 4 years by a payment of $3922.35. If money was worth 4% compounded semiannually, find the debt.

32. Suppose the debt in Problem 31 was cancelled by a payment equal to the amount of the debt after 4 years plus the present value of the difference between the amount of the debt at maturity and the amount after 4 years. Find the payment.

33. Prove that, at the rate i, $v^{22}(1 + i)^{52} = (1 + i)^{30}$.

34. Look up values of v^{100} and v^{35}, both at 1%; then evaluate v^{135}.

35. Using Table III, evaluate $(1.04)^{-3}$; verify result from Table IV.

36. Evaluate $(1.01)^{-2}$ to 4 decimal places without using any table.

37. Prove that $\dfrac{1}{(1 + i)^n} < \dfrac{1}{1 + ni}$ for every integer $n > 1$. Hence compare present value at compound interest with that at simple interest.

38. Draw a comparative graph of $P = \dfrac{S}{1 + ni}$ and $P = S(1 + i)^{-n}$ for integral values of n from 0 to 40, plotting points for every fifth period. Let S and i be given constants; for convenience, take $S = 1$ and $i = 0.04$.

108. Further types of problems in compound interest

The fundamental formula, $S = P(1 + i)^n$, contains four quantities: S, P, i, and n. If any three of these are known, the fourth can be determined.

Methods have already been given for finding S, when P, i and n are known; also, for finding P, when S, i, and n are known. In the next two articles we shall consider the problem of finding n, when S, P, and i are given; and the problem of finding i, when S, P, and n are given.

109. Finding the time by tables

The method will be illustrated.

ILLUSTRATIVE EXAMPLE. How long will it take $1200 to amount to $2000 at 5% compounded quarterly?

SOLUTION. Placing $S = 2000$, $P = 1200$, $i = 0.0125$ in $S = P(1 + i)^n$,

$$2000 = 1200(1.0125)^n,$$

whence $\quad (1.0125)^n = \dfrac{2000}{1200} = 1.6667 \quad$ (to 4 decimal places).

The question here is: For what value of n is $(1.0125)^n$ equal to 1.6667? In the $1\frac{1}{4}\%$ column of Table III, we do not find the entry 1.6667, but one slightly less, and another slightly greater than 1.6667. For $n = 41$, the entry is 1.6642; for $n = 42$, the entry is 1.6850. The nearest time, then, is 41 quarterly periods, or 10 years and 3 months.

Comment on the solution. At the rate 5% compounded quarterly, $1200 will amount in 41 periods to $1200(1.0125)^{41} = 1200 \times 1.664165 = \$1997.00$. It is possible to compute the fraction of a period necessary for $1997 to amount to $2000 at 5% simple interest. However, we shall merely say that the nearest time is 41 quarterly periods.

110. Finding the rate by interpolation

The rate of interest may be found either by use of logarithms or by interpolation in interest tables. In this article, we shall show how the rate may be determined approximately by interpolation in Table III. The logarithmic method is illustrated in Art. 111.

ILLUSTRATIVE EXAMPLE 1. Find the amount of $750 for 5 years at 4.6% converted semiannually.

SOLUTION. We have of course in our formula (1), $P = \$750$, $i = 2.3\%$, $n = 10$. Thus

$$S = 750(1.023)^{10}.$$

From Table IV we have

$$(1.0225)^{10} = 1.24920343$$

and

$$(1.0250)^{10} = 1.28008454$$

Interpolating, we get as an approximation to $(1.0230)^{10}$ the value 1.25537965. Thus

$$S = (750)(1.25537965)$$
$$= \$941.53. \quad Ans.$$

While this is an approximation it compares favorably with the answer obtained using logarithms in the next section.

ILLUSTRATIVE EXAMPLE 2. At what nominal rate, convertible semiannually, will $840 amount to $2100 in 20 years?

SOLUTION. Substituting $S = 2100$, $P = 840$, $n = 40$ in $S = P(1 + i)^n$,

$$2100 = 840(1 + i)^{40},$$

whence $\qquad (1 + i)^{40} = \dfrac{2100}{840} = 2.5000.$

We must now determine that particular value of i for which $(1 + i)^{40}$ is equal to 2.5000. In Table III, we follow along the line $n = 40$ until we come to an entry slightly smaller than 2.5000 and one slightly greater. We record these entries and the corresponding values of i, as shown here.

$(1 + i)^{40}$	i
2.4352	0.0225
2.5000	?
2.6851	0.0250

It is sufficient to read the entries to the nearest fourth decimal figure. The answer cannot, in general, be made more accurate by using more than 4 decimals. We shall assume that for a small change in i, the change in the value of $(1 + i)^n$ is proportional to the change in i. Results obtained in this manner are sufficiently correct for ordinary purposes. It is evident from the tabulated data that the desired value of i is between 0.0225 and 0.0250. Now, for an increase of $2.6851 - 2.4352 = 0.2499$ in the value of $(1 + i)^{40}$, there is an increase of $0.0250 - 0.0225 = 0.0025$ in the value of i. Then, for an increase of $2.5000 - 2.4352 = 0.0648$ in $(1 + i)^{40}$, what is the corresponding increase in i? Denoting this by x, form the proportion:

$$0.2499 : 0.0025 = 0.0648 : x,$$

whence $$x = \frac{0.0648 \times 0.0025}{0.2499} = 0.00065.$$

Hence the desired $i = 0.0225 + 0.00065 = 0.02315 = 2.315\%$. Then the nominal rate, compounded semiannually, is $2i = 4.63\%$, approximately.

Note. In succeeding exercises, if a problem is numbered in brackets, as for example [7], *omit interpolation*. First find the two *successive* tabular rates between which the desired rate lies. Then bracket the nearer one. Thus, the answer to the example of Art. 110 may be written: $[2\frac{1}{4}\%] < i < 2\frac{1}{2}\%$; hence $[4\frac{1}{2}\%] < 2i < 5\%$.

EXERCISE 66

1. How long does it take $10 to amount to $35 at (a) $2\frac{1}{2}\%$? (b) 5%?

2. In how many years does $15 amount at 3% to (a) $50? (b) $100?

3. $250 amounts in 30 years to $900 at what rate?

4. Find the rate at which $500 amounts to $1200 in 25 years.

5. Find the nearest integral value of n if $(1.0225)^n = 2.7500$.

6. If $(1.01375)^x = 1.8500$, what is the nearest integral value of x?

[7]. At what rate converted monthly is a sum doubled in 15 years?

[8]. A sum is trebled in 20 years at what rate converted quarterly?

9. Evaluate i to 3 significant digits if $(1 + i)^{30} = 3.4925$.

10. Compute i to 4 significant digits if $(1 + i)^{100} = 1.5000$.

11. A principal of $2000 amounts in x years to $3450. Find x if the rate is (a) $5\frac{1}{2}\%$ converted semiannually; (b) 4% effective.

12. An investment of $500 amounts in m months to $800. Find m if the rate is (a) 3% converted monthly; (b) $4\frac{1}{2}\%$ converted quarterly.

[13]. Florida's population increased from 391,000 in 1890 to 4,952,000 in 1960. Find the average annual rate of growth for that interval.

[14]. Find the average biennial rate of growth in Problem 13.

15. A will dispersing an estate gave $200,000 to a nephew who invested it on June 4, 1938 at 3% converted semiannually. He withdrew it when it reached $213,682.11. On approximately what date did he withdraw it?

16. Solve Problem 15 if the rate is 7% converted quarterly.

17. A man leaves $60,000 to a college for a new building on condition that construction will not begin until his bequest, invested at $2\frac{1}{2}\%$, amounts to $100,000. How long before construction may begin?

18. Solve Problem 17 if the rate is $3\frac{1}{2}\%$.

19. Find the nearest integral value of x if $(1.04)^{3x} = 3(1.04)^x$.

20. Evaluate r to 3 significant digits if $17(1 + r)^5 = 5(1 + r)^{60}$.

111. Logarithmic solution of problems in compound interest

The use of logarithms in the solution of problems in compound interest is valuable in the following cases: (a) when the given rate is not found in the tables; (b) when it is desired to determine the unknown rate more accurately than is possible by interpolation in interest tables; (c) when no interest tables are available. To increase accuracy, we shall use the sevenplace table in finding the logarithm of $(1 + i)^n$.

———

ILLUSTRATIVE EXAMPLE 1. Find the amount of $750 for 5 years at 4.6% converted semiannually.

SOLUTION. Substituting $P = 750$, $i = 2.3\% = 0.023$, $n = 10$ in (1),

$$S = P(1 + i)^n = 750(1.023)^{10}.$$

Applying logarithms,

$$\begin{aligned}
\log 750 &= 2.875061 \\
\log (1.023)^{10} &= 0.098756 \qquad \text{(Using the \textit{seven-place} table)} \\
\log S &= 2.973817
\end{aligned}$$

$$\therefore \quad S = \$941.49. \quad \textit{Ans.}$$

_____

ILLUSTRATIVE EXAMPLE 2. Find the present value of $3200 due in 12 years, if money is worth 5.2%.

SOLUTION. Substituting $S = 3200$, $i = 5.2\% = 0.052$, $n = 12$ in (3),

$$P = S(1 + i)^{-n} = 3200(1.052)^{-12}$$

or
$$P = \frac{3200}{(1.052)^{12}}.$$

Applying logarithms,

$$\begin{aligned}
\log 3200 &= 3.505150 \\
\log (1.052)^{12} &= 0.264188 \qquad \text{(Using the \textit{seven-place} table)} \\
\log P &= 3.240962
\end{aligned}$$

$$\therefore \quad P = \$1741.66. \quad \textit{Ans.}$$

_____

ILLUSTRATIVE EXAMPLE 3. How long will it take $1200 to amount to $2000 at 5% converted quarterly?

SOLUTION. Placing $S = 2000$, $P = 1200$, $i = 1\frac{1}{4}\% = 0.0125$ in (1),

$$2000 = 1200(1.0125)^n,$$

whence
$$(1.0125)^n = \frac{2000}{1200}.$$

Taking the logarithm of both members,

$$\log (1.0125)^n = \log \frac{2000}{1200},$$

or $n \times \log 1.0125 = \log 2000 - \log 1200$.

Dividing both members by log 1.0125,

$$n = \frac{\log 2000 - \log 1200}{\log 1.0125}$$

$$= \frac{3.301030 - 3.079181}{0.005395} = 41.1. \quad Ans.$$

That is, the nearest number of quarterly periods is 41, or the time is $10\frac{1}{4}$ years. (See comment on solution, illustrative example, Art. 109).

ILLUSTRATIVE EXAMPLE 4. At what nominal rate, convertible semiannually, will $840 amount to $2100 in 20 years?

SOLUTION. Substituting $S = 2100$, $P = 840$, $n = 40$ in $S = P(1 + i)^n$,

$$2100 = 840(1 + i)^{40},$$

whence $\qquad (1 + i)^{40} = \frac{2100}{840}.$

Taking the logarithm of both members,

$$\log (1 + i)^{40} = \log \frac{2100}{840},$$

or $\qquad 40 \times \log (1 + i) = \log 2100 - \log 840.$

Dividing both members by 40,

$$\log (1 + i) = \frac{\log 2100 - \log 840}{40}$$

$$= \frac{3.322219 - 2.924279}{40} = 0.009949.$$

Since $\qquad \log (1 + i) = 0.009949,$

$$1 + i = 1.02317,$$

and $\qquad i = 0.02317.$

That is, the rate per conversion period is 2.317%. Hence, the nominal rate is $2i = 4.634\%$, compounded semiannually. (Compare with the illustrative example of Art. 110.)

_____

EXERCISE 67

Solve each problem by use of logarithms.

1. What sum invested now at $4\frac{1}{2}\%$ compounded semiannually will amount in 12 years to $100? Check by use of Table IV.

2. Find the amount of $40 for 10 years at $4\frac{1}{2}\%$ compounded semiannually. Check by use of Table III.

3. At what rate convertible quarterly will $2000 amount to $3200 in $7\frac{1}{2}$ years? Check by use of Table III.

4. In how many months will an investment of $1500 amount to $1800 at 3% converted monthly? Check by use of Table III.

5. Accumulate $420 for 5 years at 3.6% converted monthly.

6. Discount $3450 for 20 years assuming that money is worth 1.8%.

7. How long does it take $50 to amount to $120 at $4\frac{1}{4}\%$?

8. At what rate converted quarterly is a sum doubled in 15 years?

9. Find the effective rate equivalent to 2.4% converted monthly.

10. Accumulate $500 for $6\frac{3}{4}$ years at 2.8% converted semiannually.

11. An automobile company manufactured 1232 cars in 1938. In 1968 the company manufactured 9589 cars. What is the average annual rate of increase in production?

12. The present value of $3250 due in a certain number of months is $1935. If money is worth 5% compounded semiannually, find the number of months.

13. A debt of $5000 bearing 6% interest converted semiannually is due in 7 years. Find the effective interest rate involved if the present value of the debt is $6254.87.

14. At what nominal rate converted monthly is a sum doubled in 10 years?

15. Find the value of a note which is to be cancelled by a payment of $1195, 25 years hence. Money is worth 4.4% compounded semiannually.

16. A payment of what amount 25 years hence will cancel a debt of $10,000 at 4.7% effective?

17. On Aug. 1, 1968, a man wishes to pay a debt of $2150 due Aug. 1, 1973. To what discount is he entitled if money is worth $3\frac{1}{4}\%$?

18. Mr. Miller deposits $800 in a savings bank on his son's natal day. If the bank pays $1\frac{1}{2}\%$ compounded quarterly, what age will the boy have reached at the time this deposit amounts to $1000?

19. The population of a college town increased from 5121 in 1940 to 13,543 in 1960. Find the average annual rate of growth.

20. Find the average biennial rate of growth in Problem 19.

21. If the town of Problem 19 continues to grow at the same average annual rate, when will its population become 25,000?

22. Assuming that the town of Problem 19 has grown after 1960 at the previous average annual rate, find its population for 1970.

23. Solve $S = P(1 + i)^n$ for $\log (1 + i)$ by use of logarithms.

24. Using logarithms, solve $P = S(1 + i)^{-n}$ for n.

112. Equation of value on a compound-interest basis

A sum of money has different values at different times. Let a non-interest-bearing debt of $x be due at some specified time. Its value at the due date is of course $x. If not paid at that time and if money is worth i per period, the value of the debt n periods *after* the due date is more than x and is found by accumulating x for n periods, that is, by multiplying x by $(1 + i)^n$. But its value n periods *before* the due date is less than x and is found by discounting x for n periods, that is, by multiplying x by $(1 + i)^{-n}$.

ILLUSTRATIVE EXAMPLE 1. A debt of $100 is due 5 years hence. Assuming money to be worth 4% converted semiannually, find the value of this obligation (a) 11 years hence; (b) 2 years hence; (c) 5 years hence.

SOLUTION. (a) The debt is due 10 periods hence. Its value 22 periods hence, that is, 12 periods *after* the due date, is found by multiplying 100 by $(1 + i)^n$, where $i = 0.02$, $n = 12$. Therefore the required value is

$$100(1.02)^{12} = 100 \times 1.26824 = \$126.82. \quad Ans.$$

(b) The value of this obligation 4 periods hence, that is, 6 periods *before* the due date, is found by multiplying 100 by $(1 + i)^{-n}$, where $i = 0.02$, $n = 6$. Therefore the required value is

$$100(1.02)^{-6} = 100 \times 0.88797 = \$88.80. \quad Ans.$$

(c) The value of the debt at its due date is $100. *Ans.*

___

Recall that two sums of money are **equivalent at a certain date** if their values at that date are equal. Two sums equivalent *at simple interest* at one date may or may not be equivalent at another date. But it can be shown that if two sums are equivalent *at given compound interest* at one date, they are equivalent at any other date.

To **commute** one set of obligations into another means to exchange one set of obligations due at various times for another set due at various other times. The two sets are **equivalent** at a common date of comparison, called a **focal date,** if the sum of the values (at the focal date) of the obligations in one set equals the corresponding sum of values (at the focal date) for the other set. An equation expressing the equivalence of two sets at a focal date is called an **equation of value.** The equivalence of two sets *at compound interest* may be shown to be *independent* of the focal date selected. Here we shall deal with long-term obligations and use an equation of value *based on compound interest*.

___

ILLUSTRATIVE EXAMPLE 2. A debt of $200 due 2 years hence and another of $500 due 7 years hence are to be discharged by a single payment 3 years hence. If money is worth 5%, how much is this payment?

SOLUTION. Let the unknown payment be x. To shorten computations, let the focal date be 3 years hence, that is, the date connected with the unknown payment. An equation of value based on any other focal date would lead to the same final result. Prepare a table of values as follows:

FOCAL DATE: 3 YEARS HENCE

Original Set of Obligations	Value of Each at Focal Date	New Set of Obligations	Value of Each at Focal Date
$200 due in 2 years	(a) $200(1.05)^1$	x due in 3 years	(c) x
$500 due in 7 years	(b) $500(1.05)^{-4}$		

The sum of (a) and (b) must be equal to (c). Writing the equation of value,

$$200(1.05) + 500(1.05)^{-4} = x,$$

whence $\qquad x = (200 \times 1.05) + (500 \times 0.82270)$

$$= 210 + 411.35 = \$621.35. \quad Ans.$$

___

ILLUSTRATIVE EXAMPLE 3. A man owes $800 due in 2 years without interest and $300 due in 9 years with 6% interest. He wishes to pay these debts in two equal installments due 4 and 5 years hence, respectively. If money is worth 4% converted semiannually, how much should each installment be?

SOLUTION. Let 5 years hence be the focal date and x be each installment. Prepare a table of values.

FOCAL DATE: 5 YEARS HENCE

Original Set of Obligations	Value of Each at Focal Date	New Set of Obligations	Value of Each at Focal Date
$800 due in 2 years	$800(1.02)^6$	$x due in 4 years	$x(1.02)^2$
$300(1.06)^9$ due in 9 years	$300(1.06)^9(1.02)^{-8}$	$x due in 5 years	$x

The equation of value is

$$x(1.02)^2 + x = 800(1.02)^6 + 300(1.06)^9(1.02)^{-8},$$
$$1.0404x + x = (800 \times 1.12616) + (300 \times 1.68948 \times 0.85349),$$
$$2.0404x = 900.93 + 432.59.$$

Hence $\qquad x = \dfrac{1333.52}{2.0404} = \$653.56. \quad Ans.$

ILLUSTRATIVE EXAMPLE 4. Debts of $1000, $2000, and $5000, due in 3, 5, and 7 years, respectively, are to be discharged by a payment of $3000 one year hence and a second payment 4 years hence. If money is worth 6%, how large is the second payment?

SOLUTION. Let 4 years hence be the focal date and x be the second payment. Prepare a table of values.

FOCAL DATE: 4 YEARS HENCE

Original Set of Obligations	Value of Each at Focal Date	New Set of Obligations	Value of Each at Focal Date
$1000 due in 3 years $2000 due in 5 years $5000 due in 7 years	$1000(1.06)^1 $2000(1.06)$^{-1}$ $5000(1.06)$^{-3}$	$3000 due in 1 year x due in 4 years	$3000(1.06)^3 x

The equation of value is

$$x + 3000(1.06)^3 = 1000(1.06) + 2000(1.06)^{-1} + 5000(1.06)^{-3},$$
$$x + 3573.05 = 1060 + 1886.79 + 4198.10.$$

Hence $x = \$3571.84.$ *Ans.*

EXERCISE 68

1. A debt of $100 is due in 9 years. If money is worth 3% converted semiannually, what is the value of this debt (a) 12 years hence? (b) 9 years hence? (c) 7 years hence?

2. A debt of $100 is due in 6 years. If money is worth 4% converted quarterly, what is the value of this debt (a) 5 years hence? (b) 6 years hence? (c) 10 years hence?

3. Answer the questions of Problem 1 if the debt of $100 bears interest for 9 years at $4\frac{1}{2}\%$ effective.

4. Answer the questions of Problem 2 if the debt of $100 bears interest for 6 years at 5% effective.

5. What single payment 4 years hence will discharge debts of $800 and $500 due in 3 and 9 years, if money is worth 6% convertible monthly?

6. A debt of $200 3 years overdue and another of $600 due in 2 years may be discharged by what single payment now if money is worth $4\frac{1}{2}\%$?

7. Find the single payment of Problem 5, assuming that the first debt bears interest for 3 years at 5% effective, all else being unchanged.

8. Solve Problem 6 assuming that the second debt bears interest for 2 years at $3\frac{1}{2}\%$ converted semiannually, all else being unchanged.

9. Solve illustrative example 2, using 2 years hence as focal date.

10. Solve illustrative example 4, using 6 years hence as focal date.

11. A lot is sold for $600 cash and $200 a year for 3 years. If money is worth 6%, what single payment now is equivalent to these terms?

12. What 3 equal annual payments, the first due in 2 years, will discharge an obligation of $1000 due now? Money is worth 4%.

13. Solve Problem 12 if money is worth 6% converted annually.

14. Solve Problem 11, using the rate 6% converted monthly.

15. Money being worth $4\frac{1}{2}$%, commute debts of $400 and $600 due in 3 and 5 years into two equal payments due in 1 and 4 years, respectively.

16. Commute debts of $500 and $200 due in 2 and 3 years into two equal payments due in 2 and 3 years, respectively. Money is worth 5%.

17. Solve Problem 15 if the second payment is to be $300 more than the first. [*Hint.* If the first payment is x, then the second is $x + 300$.]

18. Solve Problem 16 if the second payment is to be twice as large as the first. [*Hint.* If the first is x, then the second is $2x$].

19. When will a payment of $200 cancel two debts of $100 each, one due now, the other in 4 years? Money is worth 8% converted monthly.

20. Find the effective rate at which a single payment of $750 now is equivalent to two payments of $300 and $500 due in 1 and 2 years.

MISCELLANEOUS EXERCISE 69
REVIEW OF CHAPTER 11

1. What sum will amount in 6 years to $50 at 3% converted quarterly?

2. At 3% converted quarterly, $50 will amount in 6 years to what?

3. Accumulate $1200 for $6\frac{2}{3}$ years at 6% converted semiannually.

4. Discount $800 for 5 years at $2\frac{3}{4}$% converted semiannually.

5. 6% converted monthly is equivalent to what effective rate?

6. What rate converted bimonthly is equivalent to 6% effective?

7. What is the value of i if $(1 + i)^{10} = 0.267(1 + i)^{40}$?

8. Find the nearest integral value of n if $(1.03)^{2n} = 5.72(1.03)^{n+1}$.

9. $1200 is due in 12 years. Find the difference between the present value at 5% effective and present value at 5% converted quarterly.

10. Find the amount at the end of 8 years if $100 is invested at 3% converted monthly for 3 years and at 2% effective thereafter.

11. A man with $1000 to invest for 20 years knows of the following two opportunities. Plan A: 6% simple interest for the first 10 years and then the principal plus interest after 10 years at 4% compounded semiannually. Plan B: 5% compounded semiannually for the first 10 years and then the amount after 10 years at $3\frac{1}{2}\%$ effective. Which plan should he choose?

12. In Problem 11 which plan is best at the end of 10 years? At the end of 17 years?

13. What constant effective rate r will produce at the end of 8 years the amount desired in Problem 10?

14. The Virgin Islands were bought for $25,000,000 March 31, 1917. Find the amount of this at 3% effective on March 31, 1962.

15. Do Problem 14 at the interest rate 3% compounded quarterly.

16. In 1797 a man left $100 to be invested at 6% compounded semi-annually. What would his investment be worth in 1970?

17. Find the nominal rate converted monthly equivalent to 31% effective.

18. What effective rate is equivalent to 3% converted continuously?

19. The present value at $5\frac{1}{2}\%$ compounded quarterly of debt of $2700 bearing interest of 6% was $2820.67. In how many years is the debt due?

20. Find the force of interest corresponding to 7% effective.

21. In 1957 a Central American country borrowed $3,452,400 at 5% interest from a New York bank for 5 years to purchase 20 jet fighter planes. Later there was a successful revolution and the new regime refused to pay the debt. Suppose money is worth $4\frac{1}{2}\%$ compounded semiannually, furthermore suppose that in 1976 the country decided to honor the debt. How much should the country pay the New York bank?

22. What single payment 4 years hence will discharge debts of $200 and $500 due in 2 and 5 years if money is worth 4% converted semiannually?

23. A man owes $1200 due in 10 years with $5\frac{1}{2}\%$ interest and another sum due in 7 years at 4% compounded semiannually. He discharges the debts in 5 years by a payment of $5432.29. If money is worth $4\frac{1}{2}\%$ effective, find the man's other debt.

24. Commute debts of $300 and $100 due in 2 and 5 years into two equal payments due in 3 and 4 years, respectively. Money is worth $4\frac{1}{2}\%$.

25. In how many years will $1000 amount to $3000 at 6% effective?

26. $3000 is due in 10 years with interest at 4.2% for 10 years. Find the value of this obligation 4 years hence if money is worth $3\frac{1}{4}\%$.

27. Find the rate converted continuously equivalent to 2.79% effective.

28. In how many months will money double itself at 3% converted bimonthly? Answer by use of (a) logarithms; (b) Table III.

29. A debt of $1600 due in 13 years with $5\frac{1}{2}\%$ interest and a debt of $950 due 20 years hence with no interest are to be canceled by payment of equal amounts 7 and 15 years hence. Find the payments, if money is worth $6\frac{1}{2}\%$ effective.

[30]. Ten years' interest on P is $\frac{1}{2}P$ at what rate converted monthly?

31. At what rate converted semiannually will $400 amount in 10 years to $700? Answer by use of (a) logarithms; (b) Table III.

32. In the infinite series $e^j = 1 + \dfrac{j}{1} + \dfrac{j^2}{1 \cdot 2} + \dfrac{j^3}{1 \cdot 2 \cdot 3} + \dfrac{j^4}{1 \cdot 2 \cdot 3 \cdot 4} + \cdots$, the dots indicate that more terms may be written in the manner shown. Substitute $j = 0.02$ and thus evaluate $e^{0.02}$ to 5 decimal places.

33. In the series for e^j let $j = 1$ and compute e to 3 decimal places.

34. Using logarithms, solve $r = (1 + i)^m - 1$ for m.

35. If D denotes compound discount, show that $D = S(1 - v^n)$.

36. If I denotes compound interest, show that $I = P[(1 + i)^n - 1]$.

Chapter **TWELVE**

ORDINARY ANNUITIES

113. Definitions

An **annuity** is a series of equal payments made at equal intervals of time. Annuities are of wide occurrence in our daily life. Some examples are: interest payments on bonds, premiums on life insurance, depreciation funds, sinking funds, and the like. The word "annuity" implies etymologically annual payments, but it is generally understood to apply to a series of equal payments at any equal intervals of time, whether they be made annually, semiannually, or otherwise.

The size of each payment is called the **periodic rent,** or **periodic payment.** By **rent period,** or **payment interval,** is meant the interval between two successive payments. The interval between the *beginning* of the first rent period and the *end* of the last rent period is called the **term** of the annuity.

The periodic payments of an **ordinary annuity** are made at the *end* of each rent period. Annuities of other types will be treated in Chapter 13. Unless otherwise stated or implied, annuities occurring in exercises and discussions of this book are *ordinary* annuities. Thus, "$100 a year for 5 years" means "$100 at the *end* of each year for 5 years."

Note that in Chapter 11 we considered a *single* sum of money at compound interest. In this chapter we shall consider a *series* of equal payments at compound interest.

114. Amount of an annuity

The **amount,** or **final value,** of an annuity is the sum of the compound amounts of all the payments accumulated to the end of the term.

237

Consider a simple case. Suppose a man deposits $100 at the end of each year for 5 years. If the bank pays $2\frac{1}{2}\%$ interest converted annually, to what sum of money will the deposits accumulate at the end of 5 years? The question is equivalent to: What is the amount of an annuity of $100 a year, payable annually for 5 years, the interest rate being $2\frac{1}{2}\%$?

The first deposit, made at the end of the first year, draws interest for 4 years; hence its compound amount is $100(1.025)^4$. The second deposit draws interest for 3 years and its compound amount is $100(1.025)^3$. Similarly, the next two deposits accumulate to $100(1.025)^2$ and $100(1.025)$, respectively. The last deposit, made at the end of the fifth year, draws no interest and its value is simply $100. Adding these five amounts, we get the sum of money to which the deposits will accumulate at the end of the fifth year. The work is shown below.

$$\begin{aligned}
\text{Amount of 1st payment} &= 100(1.025)^4 = \$110.381 \\
\text{Amount of 2nd payment} &= 100(1.025)^3 = \$107.689 \\
\text{Amount of 3rd payment} &= 100(1.025)^2 = \$105.063 \\
\text{Amount of 4th payment} &= 100(1.025) = \$102.500 \\
\text{Amount of 5th payment} & = \underline{\$100.000} \\
\text{Amount of annuity} & = \$525.63
\end{aligned}$$

Note. When we speak of an "annuity of R," we mean an annuity whose *periodic rent* is R.

EXERCISE 70

By the method of Art. 114, find the amount of an annuity of:

1. $1000 per annum for 5 years at 4% effective.

2. $800 a year for 4 years at $3\frac{1}{2}\%$ compounded annually.

3. $500 per quarter for 2 years at 6% converted quarterly.

4. $300 each half-year for $3\frac{1}{2}$ years at 6% converted semiannually.

5. $400 a year for 3 years at 5% *converted semiannually.*

6. $600 a year for 2 years at 2% *converted quarterly.*

115. Formula for the amount of an annuity

Consider an annuity whose periodic rent is R, the term is n periods, and each payment is accumulated at the rate i per period to the end of the term. It is important to note that we are assuming *the payment interval to coincide with the interest period.* Since there are n equal payments of $R each, it follows that *if these bore no interest* the total amount would be simply $nR. But actually each payment of $R bears interest at the rate i per period from the time the payment is made until the end of the term.

The reader probably realizes that the situation described can be treated by a special case of our formula M,

(M) $$X_n = \left(P + \frac{R}{i}\right)(1 + i)^n - \frac{R}{i}.$$

In this situation we have no initial balance so $P = 0$. The balance at the end of n periods is given, then, by

$$X_n = \frac{R}{i}(1 + i)^n - \frac{R}{i}$$

or, on reduction, by

$$X_n = R\frac{(1 + i)^n - 1}{i}$$

In this special situation, the regular payment is the periodic rent of $R and the amount of the annuity at the end of n periods is usually denoted by S_n. The quantity $\dfrac{(1 + i)^n - 1}{i}$ is called the *amount of an annuity of 1 per period* and is denoted by $s_{\overline{n}|i}$. Our basic formula, then, for the amount of an annuity of $R per period for n periods at the rate i per period is given by

$$S_n = R \cdot s_{\overline{n}|i} \tag{4}$$

where

$$s_{\overline{n}|i} = \frac{(1 + i)^n - 1}{i}. \tag{4'}$$

Caution. Beginning students sometimes speak of the "sum of an annuity." This erroneous expression has no meaning and should never be used. But the amount of an annuity has a definite meaning, as given in Art. 114.

Remark. Our formula (1) in various forms is the key to the various types of problems encountered in this chapter.

116. Finding the amount of an annuity

Formula (4) gives as a rule for finding the amount of an annuity: *Multiply the periodic rent by $s_{\overline{n}|i}$ (the amount of an annuity of 1 per period).* Since values of $s_{\overline{n}|i}$ for various rates and numbers of periods are tabulated in **Table V,** the amount of an annuity can be determined readily, without using the long method illustrated in Art. 114. When i is not found in Table V, logarithms may be used in conjunction with formulas (4) and (4′).

―――

ILLUSTRATIVE EXAMPLE 1. Find the amount of an annuity of $70 payable at the end of each 6 months for 15 years, if money is worth 4% compounded semiannually.

SOLUTION. Here $R = 70$, $n = 30$, and $i = 0.02$. From Table V, $s_{\overline{30}|.02}$ $= 40.5681$. Hence

$$S_n = R \cdot s_{\overline{30}|.02} = 70 \times 40.5681 = \$2839.77. \quad Ans.$$

Note that, *if the 30 payments bore no interest*, the total amount would be $30 \times 70 = \$2100$. The difference $2839.77 - 2100 = \$739.77$ represents the total compound interest on the 30 payments to the end of the term.

―――

ILLUSTRATIVE EXAMPLE 2. Find the amount of an annuity of $164.50 per annum for 10 years, if money is worth 3.6%.

SOLUTION. Since the rate 3.6% is not given in Table V, the problem may be solved by logarithms. Substituting the known quantities $R = 164.50$, $i = 0.036$, and $n = 10$ in (4) and (4′),

$$S_n = 164.50 \times \frac{(1.036)^{10} - 1}{0.036}.$$

First compute $(1.036)^{10}$ by logarithms:

$\log (1.036)^{10} = 0.153598.$ (Using the *seven-place* table)

Whence $(1.036)^{10} = 1.42429,$ (Using the *six-place* table)

and $(1.036)^{10} - 1 = 0.42429.$

Then $S_n = \dfrac{164.50 \times 0.42429}{0.036}.$

Applying logarithms,

$$\log 164.50 = 2.216166$$

$$\log 0.42429 = \underline{9.627663 - 10}$$

$$11.843829 - 10$$

$$\log 0.036 = \underline{8.556303 - 10}$$

That is, $\log S_n = 3.287526$

$$\therefore S_n = \$1938.77. \quad Ans.$$

———

EXERCISE 71

In each of Problems 1–6, find the amount of the given annuity.

1. \$300 a year for 10 years, interest at $3\frac{1}{2}\%$.

2. \$500 per annum for 8 years, interest at $3\frac{1}{2}\%$.

3. \$100 a month for 15 years, interest at 3% converted monthly.

4. \$200 each month for 12 years, interest at 5% converted monthly.

5. \$600 per quarter for 7 years, interest at 8% converted quarterly.

6. \$400 per quarter for 20 years, interest at 4% converted quarterly.

7. Mr. Hill saves \$500 each half-year and invests it at 3% converted semiannually. Find the amount of his savings at the end of 6 years.

8. Betty deposits \$60 semiannually in a bank whose rate is $2\frac{1}{2}\%$ converted semiannually. How much is to her credit at the end of 7 years?

9. To buy a new car in 4 years a man deposits \$300 quarterly in a bank paying $5\frac{1}{2}\%$ interest converted quarterly. How much will he have to buy the car?

10. To cancel a debt due in 10 years a man places \$99.23 monthly in a certain fund invested at 3% compounded monthly. How much is his debt?

11. A city places \$1000 quarterly in a special fund invested at $3\frac{1}{2}\%$ converted quarterly. What does the fund contain at the end of 4 years?

12. At 5% converted monthly, 36 monthly payments of $100 each are equivalent to what single payment at the end of 3 years?

13. Payments of $121.21 each year for 13 years will pay off a certain debt. After 4 years the amount of what equal annual investment at 4% will cancel the debt?

14. Find the amount of an annuity of $542.20 quarterly for 13 years if money is worth 13% converted quarterly.

15. At the end of each month, a college president invests one-fourth of his monthly salary of $1200. How much is accumulated in 10 years if the investment rate is 3% converted monthly?

16. Find the amount of $532 monthly for 16 years at 6% compounded monthly.

17. John will make quarterly payments of $300 for 4 years to purchase a new car valued at $4800. If money is worth 4% converted quarterly, what does the car ultimately cost John?

18. Fred's father deposits $30 per quarter in a fund invested at 4% converted quarterly. What will the fund contain just after Fred is 18 years old if the first deposit was made when he was 5 years old?

19. Eight annual payments of $150 each are equivalent to what single payment due at the end of 8 years? Money is worth 4%.

20. $250 is placed at the end of each year in a sinking fund accumulating at 3.7%. What will the fund contain at the end of 20 years?

21. 17 years ago Mr. Smith began semiannual deposits of $132 invested at $4\frac{1}{2}\%$ compounded semiannually to pay for his daughter's wedding. How much will he have if his daughter is to be married 4 years hence?

22. A man will pay $500 semiannually for 25 years to cancel a home mortgage of $15,000. How much would the man have now if 25 years ago he invested the payments at 4% compounded semiannually?

23. Show that (a) $s_{\overline{1}|i} + s_{\overline{2}|i} = 3 + i$; (b) $s_{\overline{3}|i} = 3 + 3i + i^2$.

24. In the tabular arrangement in Art. 115, write an expression for the amount of (a) the 4th payment; (b) the $(n-3)$rd payment.

25. Compute $s_{\overline{10}|.06}$ to 6 decimal places by use of Table III alone.

26. Show by direct reasoning that $s_{\overline{15}|i} \neq s_{\overline{9}|i} + s_{\overline{6}|i}$.

27. Prove algebraically that $s_{\overline{m+n}|i} = s_{\overline{m}|i} + (1+i)^m \cdot s_{\overline{n}|i}$.

28. Since m and n are interchangeable in the left member of the equation in Problem 27, write another expression for $s_{\overline{m+n}|i}$.

29. Using the equation in Problem 27, compute $s_{\overline{272}|i}$ if $i = \frac{7}{12}\%$.

30. Expand $(1 + i)^n$ by the binomial theorem. Then show that

$$s_{\overline{n}|i} = \frac{(1 + i)^n - 1}{i} = n + \frac{n(n - 1)}{1 \cdot 2}i + \frac{n(n - 1)(n - 2)}{1 \cdot 2 \cdot 3}i^2 + \cdots.$$

31. Using the expansion in Problem 30, compute $s_{\overline{6}|.01}$ to 4 decimals.

32. Denote by $s_{\overline{n}|i}$ the amount for an annuity of 1 per period for n periods and derive formula (4′) by direct reasoning. [*Hint.* Let a principal P be invested at the rate i per period for n periods. The interest payments Pi per period form an annuity whose amount is $Pis_{\overline{n}|i}$. This must equal the compound interest on P for n periods. Solve the equation for $s_{\overline{n}|i}$.]

117. Present value of an annuity and the corresponding formula

The **present value** of an annuity is that single sum of money which, invested now at a given rate, will amount at the end of the term of the annuity to the sum of the compound amounts of the payments. It may also be defined as the sum of the present values of all the payments of the annuity. The present value of an annuity is sometimes referred to as the "cash equivalent of the annuity."

Consider an annuity of $\$R$ per period for n periods, money being worth i per period. Denote the present value of the annuity by A_n. Now, by the first definition given above, A_n is that single sum of money which, invested at the periodic rate i for n periods, will amount to the final value of the annuity. This compound amount of A_n will be $A_n(1 + i)^n$. On the other hand, the amount, or final value, of the annuity has been shown in Art. 115 to be $R \cdot \frac{(1 + i)^n - 1}{i}$. Hence

$$A_n(1 + i)^n = R \cdot \frac{(1 + i)^n - 1}{i}.$$

To solve for A_n, we divide both members by $(1 + i)^n$:

$$A_n = R \cdot \frac{1 - (1 + i)^{-n}}{i}.$$

It is evident that when the periodic rent is \$1, the present value of the annuity is $\dfrac{1 - (1 + i)^{-n}}{i}$. This quantity is called the **present value of an annuity of 1 per period,** and is denoted by $a_{\overline{n}|i}$ (read: a sub n at the rate i). The present value of an annuity of \$$R$ per period is given, then, by

$$A_n = R \cdot a_{\overline{n}|i} \tag{5}$$

where

$$a_{\overline{n}|i} = \frac{1 - (1 + i)^{-n}}{i}. \tag{5'}$$

118. Finding the present value of an annuity

Formula (5) gives us a rule for finding the present value of an annuity: *Multiply the periodic rent by $a_{\overline{n}|i}$ (the present value of an annuity of 1 per period).* Values of $a_{\overline{n}|i}$ for various rates and numbers of periods are found in **Table VI.** When the given rate of interest is not found in Table VI, logarithms may be used in conjunction with formulas (5) and (5'). Finding the present value or cash equivalent of an annuity is an important phase of the mathematics of finance.

———

ILLUSTRATIVE EXAMPLE 1. Find the present value of an annuity of \$80 per annum for 35 years, if money is worth 6%.

SOLUTION. Here $R = 80$, $n = 35$, and $i = 0.06$. From Table VI we find that $a_{\overline{35}|.06} = 14.4982$. Hence

$$A_n = R \cdot a_{\overline{35}|.06} = 80 \times 14.4982 = \$1159.86. \quad Ans.$$

This means that \$1159.86 *now* is just as good as 35 annual payments of \$80 each, or just as good as the amount (final value) of the annuity 35 years hence.

CHECK. The single sum \$1159.86, invested at 6%, will amount in 35 years to $1159.86(1.06)^{35} = 1159.86 \times 7.686087 = \$8914.78$. On the other hand, the final value of this annuity is given by

$$S_n = 80 \times s_{\overline{35}|.06} = 80 \times 111.4348 = \$8914.78.$$

Therefore the determined present value of the annuity is correct.

———

ILLUSTRATIVE EXAMPLE 2. Find the cash equivalent of an annuity which pays $200 at the end of each 3 months for 10 years, assuming money to be worth 5% converted quarterly.

SOLUTION. The unknown quantity is A_n; $R = 200$, $n = 40$, and $i = 0.0125$. From Table VI, $a_{\overline{40}|.0125} = 31.32693$. Hence

$$A_n = R \cdot a_{\overline{40}|.0125} = 200 \times 31.32693 = \$6265.39. \quad Ans.$$

The result may be interpreted as follows: A payment of $6265.39 *now* is equivalent to 40 quarterly payments of $200 each for the next 10 years, assuming that money can earn interest at 5% converted quarterly.

CHECK. At the given rate, the single sum $6265.39 will amount in 10 years to $6265.39(1.0125)^{40} = 6265.39 \times 1.643619 = \$10,297.91$. On the other hand, the amount of this annuity is

$$S_n = 200 \times s_{\overline{40}|.0125} = 200 \times 51.48956 = \$10,297.91.$$

Therefore the computed present value of the annuity is correct.

———

ILLUSTRATIVE EXAMPLE 3. What is the present value of an annuity of $350 per annum, if the term of the annuity is 25 years and money is worth 4.3%?

SOLUTION. Substituting $R = 350$, $i = 0.043$, and $n = 25$ in (5) and (5'),

$$A_n = 350 \cdot \frac{1 - (1.043)^{-25}}{0.043}.$$

First compute $(1.043)^{-25} = \dfrac{1}{(1.043)^{25}}$ by logarithms:

$$\log 1 = 10.000000 - 10$$

From Table II, $\log (1.043)^{25} = \underline{\quad 0.457108}$

Subtracting, $\log (1.043)^{-25} = 9.542892 - 10.$

Whence $(1.043)^{-25} = 0.349054,$

and $1 - (1.043)^{-25} = 0.650946.$

Then $$A_n = \frac{350 \times 0.650946}{0.043}.$$

Applying logarithms,

$$
\begin{aligned}
\log 350 &= 2.544068 \\
\log 0.650946 &= 9.813545 - 10 \\
\hline
&\quad 12.357613 - 10 \\
\log 0.043 &= 8.633468 - 10 \\
\hline
\end{aligned}
$$

That is,
$$
\begin{aligned}
\log A_n &= 3.724145 \\
\therefore\ A_n &= \$5298.40. \quad Ans.
\end{aligned}
$$

EXERCISE 72

In Problems 1–4, assume an annuity of \$100 a year for 5 years, first payment due 1 year hence and money worth 4%. In each of Problems 5–10, find present value of given annuity.

1. By use of Table IV, discount each payment to the present and add. Then, from Table VI, find present value of annuity. Compare results.

2. Using Table III, accumulate each payment to end of term and add. Then, from Table V, find amount of annuity. Compare results.

3. Accumulate for 5 years the present value found in Problem 1.

4. Discount for 5 years the amount found in Problem 2.

5. \$600 per annum for 10 years, at $4\frac{1}{2}\%$.

6. \$500 a year for 8 years, at $2\frac{3}{4}\%$.

7. \$200 a month for 12 years, at 4% converted monthly.

8. \$100 each month for 15 years, at 5% converted monthly.

9. \$400 per quarter for 10 years, at 3% converted quarterly.

10. \$300 per quarter for 7 years, at 6% converted quarterly.

11. What does it cost to purchase an annuity of \$300 per half-year for 6 years if money is worth $4\frac{1}{2}\%$ converted semiannually?

12. A house sells for \$70 a month for 12 years "like paying rent." Find the equivalent cash price if money is worth 6% converted monthly.

13. If money is worth 5% to the buyer of a lot, which is better for him and by how much: To pay $2500 cash or $600 a year for 5 years?

14. What deposit in a trust bank will supply an income of $100 per quarter for 6 years if the bank's rate is 2% compounded quarterly?

15. If money is worth $2\frac{1}{2}$% converted semiannually, what single payment now is equivalent to 10 semiannual payments of $100 each?

16. Assuming money to be worth $3\frac{1}{2}$% converted semiannually, find the cash equivalent of 50 semiannual payments of $300 each.

17. Mr. Ivey holds a bond with attached coupons of $10 each, payable quarterly for 13 years. In addition he will receive $1010 in 13 years. What is the bond worth now on a basis of 4% converted quarterly?

18. A mine for sale will net $20,000 a year for 10 years. It is estimated that the property is disposable for $8000 at the end of 10 years. Find the present worth of the mine on a 5% basis.

19. A building is leased for 5 years at $200 per month. Find the cash equivalent of the lease at 4.2% converted monthly.

20. A contract calls for 20 semiannual payments of $500 each. Find the present value of the contract at 3.6% converted semiannually.

21. Compute $a_{\overline{10}|.03}$ to 6 decimal places by use of Table IV alone.

22. Show that $a_{\overline{2}|i} = (1 + i)^{-2}(2 + i)$.

23. Use the *second* definition in Art. 117 to derive formula (5). [*Hint.* Discount each R to the present and add the series.]

24. Denote by $a_{\overline{n}|i}$ the present value of an annuity of 1 per period for n periods and derive formula (5') by direct reasoning. [*Hint.* If money is worth i per period, a payment P *now* is equivalent to n payments of Pi per period and a single payment P in n periods. Hence $P =$ (present value of n periodic payments of Pi) + (present value of P due in n periods). But the present value of the n periodic payments is $Pia_{\overline{n}|i}$. Solve for $a_{\overline{n}|i}$.]

25. Prove algebraically that $a_{\overline{m+n}|i} = a_{\overline{m}|i} + (1 + i)^{-m} \cdot a_{\overline{n}|i}$.

26. Expand $(1 + i)^{-n}$ by the binomial theorem. Then show that
$$a_{\overline{n}|i} = \frac{1 - (1 + i)^{-n}}{i} = n - \frac{n(n + 1)}{1 \cdot 2}i + \frac{n(n + 1)(n + 2)}{1 \cdot 2 \cdot 3}i^2 - \cdots.$$

27. Use the equation in Problem 25 to compute $a_{\overline{145}|.04}$ to 4 decimals.

28. Use the expansion in Problem 26 to compute $a_{\overline{4}|.02}$ to 4 decimals.

119. Relation between $a_{\overline{n}|i}$ and $s_{\overline{n}|i}$

We shall now prove that the difference between the reciprocals of $a_{\overline{n}|i}$ and $s_{\overline{n}|i}$ is i. Since

$$a_{\overline{n}|i} = \frac{1 - (1 + i)^{-n}}{i} \quad \text{and} \quad s_{\overline{n}|i} = \frac{(1 + i)^n - 1}{i},$$

it follows that

$$\frac{1}{a_{\overline{n}|i}} = \frac{i}{1 - (1 + i)^{-n}} \quad \text{and} \quad \frac{1}{s_{\overline{n}|i}} = \frac{i}{(1 + i)^n - 1}.$$

Then

$$\frac{1}{a_{\overline{n}|i}} - \frac{1}{s_{\overline{n}|i}} = \frac{i}{1 - (1 + i)^{-n}} - \frac{i}{(1 + i)^n - 1}.$$

Multiplying both numerator and denominator of the first fraction in the right member by $(1 + i)^n$, we have

$$\frac{1}{a_{\overline{n}|i}} - \frac{1}{s_{\overline{n}|i}} = \frac{i(1 + i)^n}{(1 + i)^n - 1} - \frac{i}{(1 + i)^n - 1}$$

$$= \frac{i(1 + i)^n - i}{(1 + i)^n - 1} = \frac{i[(1 + i)^n - 1]}{(1 + i)^n - 1} = i.$$

Hence

$$\frac{1}{a_{\overline{n}|i}} - \frac{1}{s_{\overline{n}|i}} = i.$$

This relation may also be expressed in the form:

$$\frac{1}{s_{\overline{n}|i}} = \frac{1}{a_{\overline{n}|i}} - i. \tag{6}$$

120. Finding the periodic rent

Not infrequently the unknown quantity in annuity problems is the periodic rent. Since $A_n = R \cdot a_{\overline{n}|i}$ and $S_n = R \cdot s_{\overline{n}|i}$, it follows that

$$R = A_n \cdot \frac{1}{a_{\overline{n}|i}}, \qquad (7)$$

and

$$R = S_n \cdot \frac{1}{s_{\overline{n}|i}}. \qquad (8)$$

Formula (7) is used in case the *present value* of the annuity is known; formula (8), in case the *amount* is known.

It is evident that when the present value of an annuity is $1, the right member of (7) becomes $\frac{1}{a_{\overline{n}|i}}$. Hence this quantity is called the **periodic rent of an annuity whose present value is 1.** Similarly, when the amount of an annuity is $1, the right member of (8) becomes $\frac{1}{s_{\overline{n}|i}}$, which is called the **periodic rent of an annuity whose amount is 1.** Of course it is possible to compute values of these reciprocals from the corresponding values of $a_{\overline{n}|i}$ and $s_{\overline{n}|i}$ found in Tables VI and V. However, we shall use another table from which values of the *reciprocals themselves* may be obtained readily.

Table VII gives values of $\frac{1}{a_{\overline{n}|i}}$ for various rates and numbers of periods. From relation (6) of Art. 119, it is evident that values of $\frac{1}{s_{\overline{n}|i}}$ may also be obtained from Table VII by merely subtracting i from the corresponding values of $\frac{1}{a_{\overline{n}|i}}$.

ILLUSTRATIVE EXAMPLE 1. If money can be invested at 6% compounded quarterly, find the quarterly rent of an annuity for 15 years whose present value is $12,000.

SOLUTION. The *present value* of the annuity is given and the quarterly rent is desired. $A_n = 12,000$, $n = 60$, and $i = 0.015$. From Table VII, $\frac{1}{a_{\overline{60}|.015}} = 0.0253934$. Substituting these values in (7),

$$R = A_n \cdot \frac{1}{a_{\overline{60}|.015}} = 12,000 \times 0.0253934 = \$304.72. \quad Ans.$$

ILLUSTRATIVE EXAMPLE 2. How much must be set aside semiannually so as to have a fund of $8000 at the end of 12 years, interest being at the rate of 4% converted semiannually?

Solution. Here the *amount* of the annuity is known, and the semiannual payment is unknown. Hence we use formula (8). $S_n = 8000$, $n = 24$, and $i = 0.02$. From Table VII, $\dfrac{1}{a_{\overline{24}|.02}} = 0.052871$. To get the corresponding value of $\dfrac{1}{s_{\overline{n}|i}}$, i must be subtracted. Hence $\dfrac{1}{s_{\overline{24}|.02}} = 0.052871 - 0.02 = 0.032871$. Applying formula (8), we have

$$R = S_n \cdot \frac{1}{s_{\overline{24}|.02}} = 8000 \times 0.032871 = \$262.97 \quad Ans.$$

EXERCISE 73

1. A debt of $2000 is due now. Find the annual payment necessary to cancel it in (a) 4 years; (b) 8 years; (c) 16 years. Money is worth 6%.

2. What equal annual deposits for 15 years will accumulate to $3000 at the end of 15 years if interest is at (a) $1\frac{1}{2}\%$? (b) 3%? (c) $4\frac{1}{2}\%$?

3. What monthly deposits at 3% compounded monthly will cancel a debt of $7654.23 due in 12 years?

4. Twenty equal semiannual payments at 4.8% converted semiannually amounted to $1021. Find the payments.

5. The depreciation fund for a cotton mill is to contain $40,000 at the end of 20 years. What equal semiannual deposits must be made into this fund if deposits earn interest at $4\frac{1}{2}\%$ converted semiannually?

6. A certain amount due 13 years hence is worth $2000 now. Find equal annual payments which will cancel the debt if money is worth 5% effective.

7. Mrs. Boyd pays $150 down to buy a piano worth $990 and agrees to pay the balance, including interest at 8% converted monthly, in equal monthly installments for 2 years. Compute the monthly payment.

8. A paving assessment of $210, due now, is distributed over a 3-year period. If interest is at 7%, find the annual payment.

9. A $54,320 debt due in 19 years is to be repaid by $500 quarterly for the first 12 years and x quarterly for the remaining years. Find x if money is worth 6% compounded quarterly.

10. Mr. Hicks wishes to accumulate $10,000 in 10 years. How much should he invest each quarter at 4% compounded quarterly?

11. In Problem 9 what cash amount would cancel the debt at the end of 12 years?

12. Mr. Jones paid $482 semiannually for 25 years for his home. What was the original cost of the house if money is worth 5% converted semiannually?

13. By depositing $x at the end of each quarter, a man accumulates $6977 in 15 years. Find x if the bank paid 2% converted quarterly.

14. A man buys a car for $2500, agreeing to pay $700 cash and $y a month for 2 years. Find y if interest is at 8% converted monthly.

15. Mr. Jones agreed to pay $321 quarterly for 5 years to purchase a new car. If money is worth 4% converted quarterly, what was the original cost of the car?

16. For a certain loan at 6% converted monthly, a man makes $143.29 payments, monthly, for 20 years. Find the amount borrowed.

17. For a trip 4 years hence, a clerk wishes to accumulate $1000. What should he invest each half-year at 4% converted semiannually?

18. What semimonthly installments for 2 years will pay the $200 cash price of a set of books and interest at 6% converted semimonthly?

19. Four hundred seniors of a college agree to give $20,000 to their alma mater 10 years after graduation. How much should each contribute yearly to the fund if contributions are accumulated at $3\frac{1}{2}$%?

20. A corporation issues bonds for $100,000 and creates a sinking fund to redeem the bonds at the end of 20 years. If the fund earns 3% interest converted bimonthly, how much must be placed in it each 2 months?

21. The beneficiary of an insurance policy is given the option of $8000 cash or equal quarterly payments for 10 years. Find the quarterly payment on a basis of 6% compounded quarterly.

22. A fraternity buys a house for $36,000, agreeing to pay $6000 cash and to make 30 equal semiannual payments for the balance with interest at 6% converted semiannually. Find the semiannual payment.

23. Read the value of $0.03 \div [(1.03)^{50} - 1]$ from the tables.

24. Read the value of $0.045 \div [1 - (1.045)^{-20}]$ from the tables.

25. Using Table IV alone, compute $1 \div a_{\overline{10}|.07}$ to 5 decimal places.

26. Using Table III alone, compute $1 \div s_{\overline{10}|.08}$ to 5 decimal places.

27. A is to receive a $5000 bequest 3 years hence. He sells the equity to B who will pay $500 now and the balance in 36 equal monthly payments. Find the monthly payment at $3\frac{1}{2}\%$ converted monthly.

28. A loan of $2000 is to be repaid, principal and 6% interest converted monthly, by one payment of $500 in 5 years and 48 equal monthly payments, the first due in 1 month. Compute the monthly payment.

29. Show that $\dfrac{1}{a_{\overline{m+n}|i}} = \dfrac{(1+i)^m}{s_{\overline{m}|i} + a_{\overline{n}|i}}$.

30. Show that $\dfrac{1}{s_{\overline{m+n}|i}} = \dfrac{(1+i)^{-n}}{s_{\overline{m}|i} + a_{\overline{n}|i}}$.

31. Using the equation in Problem 29, compute $1 \div a_{\overline{113}|.0225}$.

32. Using the equation in Problem 30, compute $1 \div s_{\overline{113}|.0225}$.

121. Further types of annuity problems

Formula (4) for the amount of an annuity, $S_n = R \cdot s_{\overline{n}|i}$, contains four quantities: S_n, R, n, and i. If any three of these are known, the fourth can be determined. Similarly, formula (5) for the present value of an annuity, $A_n = R \cdot a_{\overline{n}|i}$, contains four quantities: A_n, R, n, and i. Any three being given, the fourth can be determined. In the next two articles we shall show how to find n when S_n (or A_n), R, and i are given; and how to find i when S_n (or A_n), R, and n are given.

122. Finding the term of an annuity

The following examples will illustrate the method.

ILLUSTRATIVE EXAMPLE 1. In how many years will an annuity of $300 per annum amount to $5500, if the interest rate is 6%?

SOLUTION. Since the *amount* of the annuity is given, use the formula $S_n = R \cdot s_{\overline{n}|i}$. Substituting $S_n = 5500$, $R = 300$, and $i = 0.06$,

$$5500 = 300 \times s_{\overline{n}|.06},$$

whence
$$s_{\overline{n}|.06} = \frac{5500}{300} = 18.3333.$$

Now, values of $s_{\overline{n}|.06}$ are found in the 6% column of Table V. There we find that the first entry greater than 18.3333 is 18.8821, and the corresponding value of n is 13. Since 18.8821 is somewhat greater than 18.3333, it is evident that 13 annual payments of $300 each will amount to more than $5500. We shall merely say, then, that the annuity will amount to somewhat more than $5500 at the end of the 13th year.

ILLUSTRATIVE EXAMPLE 2. A man borrows $3450, which he agrees to repay in installments of $250 at the end of each 6 months. How long will it take to pay the principal and interest at 7% compounded semiannually?

SOLUTION. The installments form an annuity whose *present value* is $3450. Substituting $A_n = 3450$, $R = 250$, and $i = 0.035$ in $A_n = R \cdot a_{\overline{n}|i}$,

$$3450 = 250 \times a_{\overline{n}|.035},$$

whence $$a_{\overline{n}|.035} = \frac{3450}{250} = 13.8000.$$

In the $3\frac{1}{2}$% column of Table VI, where values of $a_{\overline{n}|.035}$ are tabulated, we find that the first entry greater than 13.8000 is 14.2124, and the corresponding value of n is 20. It is evident that 20 semiannual payments of $250 each will have a present value somewhat greater than $3450. At present we shall merely say that the term of the annuity is 20 semiannual periods, the 20th payment being somewhat less than $250.

---

123. Finding the interest rate of an annuity

It is possible to find the interest rate of an annuity to a high degree of accuracy by methods which are beyond the scope of this book. However, interpolation in Tables V and VI gives the rate to a degree of accuracy sufficient for all practical purposes.

ILLUSTRATIVE EXAMPLE 1. At what rate, converted quarterly, will an annuity of $200 per quarter amount to $4542.34 in 5 years?

SOLUTION. Since the *amount* of the annuity is given, we use the formula $S_n = R \cdot s_{\overline{n}|i}$. Substituting $S_n = 4542.34$, $R = 200$, and $n = 20$,

$$4542.34 = 200 \times s_{\overline{20}|i},$$

whence $$s_{\overline{20}|i} = \frac{4542.34}{200} = 22.7117.$$

Since the unknown quantity is i, it is necessary in this case to follow the line $n = 20$ in Table V until we come to two successive values of $s_{\overline{20}|i}$, one slightly less than 22.7117 and the other slightly greater. We record these entries and the corresponding values of i as shown here. It is evident from the tabulated data that the desired value of i is between 0.0125

$s_{\overline{20}|i}$	i
22.5630	0.0125
22.7117	?
22.8412	0.01375

and 0.01375. Now for an increase of $22.8412 - 22.5630 = 0.2782$ in the value of $s_{\overline{20}|i}$, there is an increase of $0.01375 - 0.0125 = 0.00125$ in the value of i. Then, for an increase of $22.7117 - 22.5630 = 0.1487$ in the value of $s_{\overline{20}|i}$, what is the corresponding increase in the value of i? Denoting this by x, we form the proportion:

$$0.2782 : 0.00125 = 0.1487 : x,$$

whence $$x = \frac{0.1487 \times 0.00125}{0.2782} = 0.00067.$$

Hence the desired $i = 0.0125 + 0.00067 = 0.01317 = 1.317\%$. The nominal rate, converted quarterly, is $4i = 5.27\%$ approximately.

ILLUSTRATIVE EXAMPLE 2. The present value of an annuity of $500 per annum for 25 years is $8000. Find the interest rate.

SOLUTION. Since the *present value* is known, we use $A_n = R \cdot a_{\overline{n}|i}$. Substituting $A_n = 8000$, $R = 500$, and $n = 25$, we have

$$8000 = 500 \times a_{\overline{25}|i},$$

whence $$a_{\overline{25}|i} = \frac{8000}{500} = 16.0000.$$

Following the line $n = 25$ in Table VI, we come to two successive values of $a_{\overline{25}|i}$, one slightly greater than 16.0000 and the other slightly less. The

$a_{\overline{25}|i}$	i
$\begin{bmatrix} \begin{bmatrix} 16.4815 \\ 16.0000 \end{bmatrix} \\ 15.6221 \end{bmatrix}$	$\begin{bmatrix} \begin{bmatrix} 0.035 \\ ? \end{bmatrix} \\ 0.040 \end{bmatrix}$

work is arranged as before. Note that the value of $a_{\overline{25}|i}$ *decreases* as i *increases*. For a *decrease* of $16.4815 - 15.6221 = 0.8594$ in the value of $a_{\overline{25}|i}$, there is an *increase* of $0.040 - 0.035 = 0.005$ in the value of i. Then, for a *decrease* of $16.4815 - 16.0000 = 0.4815$ in the value of $a_{\overline{25}|i}$, what is the corresponding *increase* in the value of i? Denoting this by x, we form the proportion:

$$0.8594 : 0.005 = 0.4815 : x,$$

whence
$$x = \frac{0.4815 \times 0.005}{0.8594} = 0.0028.$$

Hence the desired $i = 0.035 + 0.0028 = 0.0378 = 3.78\%$ approximately.

Comment. If we wish to omit interpolation, the answer to this example would be written: $3\frac{1}{2}\% < i < [4\%]$. See **Note** on page 225.

EXERCISE 74

In Problems 1–6, find n corresponding to the first entry greater than the given number. In Problems 7–12, find i by interpolation.

1. $a_{\overline{n}|.02} = 30.5503$. **5.** $a_{\overline{n}|.01} = 32.1505$. **9.** $a_{\overline{12}|i} = 9.5326$.

2. $s_{\overline{n}|.01} = 55.1010$. **6.** $s_{\overline{n}|.05} = 11.8750$. **10.** $s_{\overline{15}|i} = 21.3100$.

3. $s_{\overline{n}|.04} = 18.0100$. **7.** $s_{\overline{8}|i} = 9.6000$. **11.** $s_{\overline{40}|i} = 48.1000$.

4. $a_{\overline{n}|.03} = 12.9170$. **8.** $a_{\overline{5}|i} = 4.2000$. **12.** $a_{\overline{60}|i} = 51.0000$.

13. The amount of an annuity of $700 a year for 10 years is $8000. Find the rate of interest by interpolation.

14. The present value of an annuity of $500 a year for 7 years is $3100. Use interpolation to find the rate of interest.

15. How many quarterly payments of $300 each are necessary to accumulate $15,000 if interest is at $2\frac{2}{3}\%$ compounded quarterly?

16. At the rate 3% compounded quarterly, how long will it take to accumulate $4500 by quarterly deposits of $75 each?

[17]. A farmer buys a freezer from a mail-order house, agreeing to pay $16.50 cash and $13.50 a month for 28 months. If the cash price is $285, he pays interest at what rate converted monthly?

[18]. A building and loan association advertises: Pay us $60 each half-year for $7\frac{1}{2}$ years and we will return $1000 at the end of $7\frac{1}{2}$ years. At what rate converted semiannually is interest allowed by the association?

19. How many quarterly installments of $200 each will pay a debt of $5000, due now, if interest is at 6% converted quarterly?

[20]. In return for 20 semiannual deposits of $50 each, a savings bank will pay the depositor $1075 at the end of 10 years. Find the nominal rate of interest converted semiannually.

21. A fraternity buys a chapter house for $40,000, paying $8500 down. How long will it take to pay the balance, principal, and 5% interest converted monthly, in monthly installments of $300 each?

22. A man deposits $4000 with a trust company to provide his mother with a monthly income of $50. If interest is allowed at $3\frac{1}{2}$% converted monthly, how many payments will she receive?

[23]. Work Problem [20] assuming that the bank will pay $1100.

24. Work Problem 21 if each monthly installment is $300.

25. How long will it take a YMCA to earn $50,000 for rebuilding if it can save $3000 quarterly at $4\frac{1}{2}$% converted quarterly?

26. At what bimonthly interest rate will $600 every 2 months for 10 years amount to $47,080?

27. How long will it take $200 invested semiannually at 3% converted semiannually to reach $5726.70?

28. If the present value of an annuity is $26,973 find the nominal rate, converted quarterly, when the premium is $600 per quarter for 15 years.

29. How many quarterly payments of $300 at 32% converted quarterly will buy an annuity whose present value is $3699.60?

30. What nominal interest rate converted every 4 months makes $250 payable three times a year equivalent to $7383.56, the present value of an annuity which runs for 11 years.

31. One hundred and four payments of $20 each at what interest rate per payment interval match an annuity whose present value is $1618.83?

32. A man pays $25 four times a year at $2\frac{1}{3}\%$ converted quarterly. How many payments are needed to amount to $260?

33. Find the annual interest rate for an annuity of $400 per year for 15 years if the amount of the annuity is $7304.71.

34. How many semiannual payments of $100 at 5% converted semiannually are necessary to pay for an annuity whose amount is $13,599.16?

35. Solve formula (5) for n and get $n = \dfrac{\log R - \log (R - iA_n)}{\log (1 + i)}$.

36. Solve formula (4) for n and get $n = \dfrac{\log (R + iS_n) - \log R}{\log (1 + i)}$.

MISCELLANEOUS EXERCISE 75
REVIEW OF CHAPTER 12

1. What is the present value of an annuity of $300 per quarter for 5 years if interest is at $3\frac{1}{2}\%$ compounded quarterly?

2. Find the amount of the annuity in Problem 1.

3. How many bimonthly payments of $150 each are necessary to accumulate $6000 if money is worth $3\frac{3}{4}\%$ converted bimonthly?

[4]. A sorority buys a radio with FM, paying $5 down and agreeing to pay $9.50 a month for 2 years. If the cash price of the radio is $214, interest is being charged at what rate converted monthly?

5. Annual deposits of $250 each are made into a trust fund invested at $3\frac{1}{4}\%$. Compute the size of the fund at the end of 15 years.

6. A garage is leased for 5 years at $600 per half-year. Find the cash equivalent of the lease on a basis of $4\frac{1}{2}\%$ compounded semiannually.

7. Determine i by interpolation if $s_{\overline{15}|i} = 16.7500$.

8. The beneficiary of a matured insurance policy is entitled to $8000. He prefers to receive $500 now and monthly payments of $60 each. If interest is at $3\frac{1}{2}\%$ converted monthly, how long will payments continue?

9. A buys furniture costing $890. He pays $90 down and agrees to pay the balance, with interest at 8% converted semimonthly, in 40 equal semimonthly installments. How large is each payment?

10. The Credit Union accumulates deposits at 4%. How much should a man deposit each year to have $5000 to his credit in 5 years?

11. Seventeen years ago, a foreign government placed certain equal semiannual payments in an investment fund paying 5% converted semiannually. Three years ago it invested at $3\frac{1}{2}$% effective, the accumulated amount which two years from now will amount to $20,542.21. Find the semiannual payment.

12. How much should a man pay quarterly to discharge a debt of $3000 due in 3 years at 6% simple interest if money is worth 4% converted quarterly.

13. A certain bank would require payments of $3540/12 = $295 quarterly for the loan in Problem 12. What actual effective rate would the man really pay?

14. Mr. Smith offered to loan Bill $1000 to be repaid by 7 annual payments of $200. Mr. Jones also offered to make the same $1000 loan to be canceled by a single payment of $1450 at the end of 5 years. If money is worth 5% effective, which offer should Bill take.

15. In Problem 14 what is the present value, at the end of five years, of the amount of the annuity involved at maturity?

16. A man wants to pay for a new house costing $20,595 by making equal quarterly payments for 25 years. How much should he pay quarterly if money is worth $5\frac{1}{2}$% converted quarterly?

17. What monthly sum should a man pay for 10 years to cancel a loan of $10,000 at 3% converted monthly?

18. To purchase a boat valued at $12,995 a man will pay $1000 down and $1199.50 each year for 11 years. What was the actual cost of the boat to the man if money is worth 5% effective?

19. A man offers to sell a $23,000 house for 20 equal annual payments of x dollars. Find x, if money is worth $5\frac{1}{2}$% effective.

20. Suppose a man accepts the offer in Problem 19. What cash payment 10 years hence would cancel the man's debt?

21. Find n from the tables if $a_{\overline{n}|.0275} = 33.0200$.

22. At what rate converted semiannually will 20 semiannual payments of $300 each amount to $7500 at the end of 10 years?

23. A will pay $x per month for 11 years to a building and loan association to accumulate $2945. Find x at 4% converted monthly.

24. What single payment now is equivalent to the 120 payments in Problem 23? Answer (a) by using the value of x; (b) without using x.

25. Look up the value of (a) $.04 \div (1.04^7 - 1)$; (b) $(1 - 1.01^{-8}) \div .01$.

26. Given $(1 + i)^m = 1.4221$ and $s_{\overline{m}|i} = 9.3800$. Find i and m.

27. Given $(1 + j)^{-n} = 0.6975$ and $a_{\overline{n}|j} = 24.3000$. Find j and n.

28. Draw a comparative graph of $s_{\overline{n}|.05}$ and $a_{\overline{n}|.05}$ for $n = 1, 2, \ldots, 9$.

29. Draw a comparative graph of $s_{\overline{9}|i}$ and $a_{\overline{9}|i}$ for $i = .01, .02, \ldots, .09$.

In each of Problems 30–35 prove the given equation by algebra.

30. $a_{\overline{1}|i} = (1 + i)^{-1}$.

31. $s_{\overline{n}|.01} = 100(1.01^n - 1)$.

32. $1 + i s_{\overline{n}|i} = (1 + i)^n$.

33. $1 - i a_{\overline{n}|i} = (1 + i)^{-n}$.

34. $(s_{\overline{n}|i})^2 = (s_{\overline{2n}|i} - 2s_{\overline{n}|i})/i$.

35. $(a_{\overline{n}|i})^2 = (2a_{\overline{n}|i} - a_{\overline{2n}|i})/i$.

Chapter THIRTEEN

FURTHER TYPES OF ANNUITIES

124. Three main classes of annuities

Annuities fall into three main classes: annuities certain, perpetuities, and contingent annuities. An annuity whose term begins and ends at fixed dates is called an **annuity certain.** An annuity in which the payments begin at a fixed date but continue forever is known as a **perpetuity.** When the date of either the first or the last payment of an annuity is uncertain, depending upon some event whose date of occurrence cannot be foretold, the annuity is called a **contingent annuity.** In the present chapter we shall consider only annuities certain and perpetuities. Certain contingent annuities will be considered in a later chapter in connection with the mathematics of life insurance.

125. Classification of annuities certain

Annuities certain may in turn be divided into three subgroups: ordinary annuities, annuities due, and deferred annuities.

An **ordinary annuity** is one in which the payments are made at the *end* of each rent period, the first payment being due one period hence. Ordinary annuities have already been discussed at length in Chapter 12.

An **annuity due** is one in which the payments are made at the *beginning* of each rent period, the first payment being due now.

A **deferred annuity** is an ordinary annuity whose term begins a given number of periods from now, the payments being made at the *end* of each period after the term begins.

126. The amount of an annuity due

The **term** of an annuity due begins at the time the first payment is made and ends one period after the last payment is made. The **amount** of an annuity due is the value of the annuity at the end of its term. Unless specific mention is made to the contrary, it is understood in this chapter also that *the payment interval coincides with the interest period.*

To obtain a formula for the amount of an annuity due, we may proceed as follows. Let us consider an annuity due of $R per period for n periods at the rate i per period. The first payment is due now, that is, at the beginning of the term. The nth, or last, payment is due at the beginning of the nth period, that is, one period before the end of the term. This annuity due is represented diagrammatically in the lower half of Fig. 19, where a cross

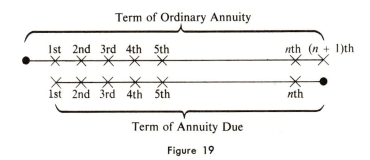

Figure 19

mark indicates payment of $R and the dot no payment. For the sake of comparison, we shall also consider an *ordinary* annuity of $n + 1$ payments of $R each, represented by the upper half of Fig. 19. The beginning of the term of the ordinary annuity is taken to be one period earlier than that of the annuity due, so that, beginning with the first, each payment of one annuity coincides with the corresponding payment of the other, except that the ordinary annuity has an additional payment of $R at the end of its term. Since the terms of the two annuities end at the same time, it is evident that the amount of the annuity due is $R less than that of the ordinary annuity. And, since the amount of an ordinary annuity for $n + 1$ periods is $R \cdot s_{\overline{n+1}|i}$, it follows that the amount of an annuity due for n periods is $R \cdot s_{\overline{n+1}|i} - R$. Hence, denoting the amount of an annuity due by $S_n(\text{due})$, we have

$$S_n(\text{due}) = R(s_{\overline{n+1}|i} - 1). \qquad (9)$$

ILLUSTRATIVE EXAMPLE. Find the amount of an annuity due of $300 per quarter for 15 years at 6% converted quarterly.

SOLUTION. Here $R = 300$, $i = 0.015$, and $n + 1 = 61$ (since $n = 60$). Substituting these values in formula (9), we have

$$S_n(\text{due}) = R(s_{\overline{n+1}|i} - 1) = 300(s_{\overline{61}|.015} - 1).$$

From Table V, $s_{\overline{61}|.015} = 98.65787.$

Hence $S_n(\text{due}) = 300(98.65787 - 1)$

$$= 300 \times 97.65787 = \$29,297.36. \quad Ans$$

127. The present value of an annuity due

The **present value** of an annuity due is the value of the annuity at the beginning of its term, including the initial payment. To obtain a formula for the present value of an annuity due, we shall use a diagram (Fig. 20) somewhat similar to Fig. 19. Here we have again an annuity due of R per

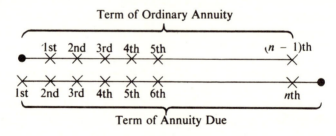

Figure 20

period for n periods at the rate i per period. We shall compare it with an ordinary annuity of $n - 1$ payments. The end of the term of the ordinary annuity is taken to be one period earlier than that of the annuity due, so that the payments of one coincide with those of the other, except that the annuity due has an additional payment of R at the beginning of its term. Since the terms of the two annuities begin at the same time, the present value of the annuity due is R more than that of the ordinary annuity. And, since the present value of an ordinary annuity for $n - 1$ periods is $R \cdot a_{\overline{n-1}|i}$, it follows that the present value of an annuity due for n periods is $R \cdot a_{\overline{n-1}|i} + R$. Hence, denoting the present value of an annuity due by A_n(due), we have

$$A_n(\text{due}) = R(a_{\overline{n-1}|i} + 1). \tag{10}$$

As an alternative to the above development we can, as in the case of ordinary annuities, ask what sum of money invested at i per period for n periods will yield S_n (due). Then, if we denote A_n (due) by B_n, we have that

$$B_n(1 + i)^n = R\left(\frac{(1 + i)^{n+1} - 1}{i} - 1\right).$$

Then

$$B_n = R(1 + i)^{-n}\left(\frac{(1 + i)^{n+1} - (1 + i)}{i}\right)$$

$$= R\left(\frac{(1 + i) - (1 + i)^{-(n-1)}}{i}\right)$$

$$= R\left(1 + \frac{1 - (1 + i)^{-(n-1)}}{i}\right)$$

$$= R(a_{\overline{n-1}|i} + 1).$$

This is, of course, our formula (10).

———

ILLUSTRATIVE EXAMPLE 1. At 4% converted semiannually, find the present value of an annuity due of $100 per half-year for $4\frac{1}{2}$ years.

SOLUTION. Here $R = 100$, $i = 0.02$, and $n - 1 = 8$ (since $n = 9$). Substituting these known quantities in formula (10),

$$A_n(\text{due}) = R(a_{\overline{n-1}|i} + 1) = 100(a_{\overline{8}|.02} + 1).$$

From Table VI, $a_{\overline{8}|.02} = 7.32548$.

Hence $A_n(\text{due}) = 100(7.32548 + 1)$
$$= 100 \times 8.32548 = \$832.55. \quad Ans.$$

———

ILLUSTRATIVE EXAMPLE 2. What is the annual rent of an annuity due whose present value is $7500, payable annually for 10 years; money worth 5%?

SOLUTION. It is given that $A_n(\text{due}) = 7500$, $i = 0.05$, and $n - 1 = 9$ (since $n = 10$); R is unknown. Substituting the known quantities in (10),

$$7500 = R(a_{\overline{9}|.05} + 1).$$

From Table VI, $a_{\overline{9}|.05} = 7.10782.$

Hence $7500 = R \times 8.10782.$

Solving for R, $R = 7500 \div 8.10782 = \$925.03.$ *Ans.*

EXERCISE 76

1. What is the present value, at 4% converted semiannually, of an annuity due of $400 payable semiannually for 12 years?

2. Determine the amount of the annuity in Problem 1.

3. Find the present value, at 2% converted quarterly for $21\frac{1}{2}$ years, of an annuity due of $50 each quarter.

4. Determine the amount of the annuity in Problem 3.

5. At $4\frac{1}{2}$% converted bimonthly, find the amount of an annuity due of $300 payable every   months for 15 years.

6. Compute the present value of the annuity in Problem 5.

7. Mr. Smith is saving to buy a $20,000 home for which he wants to pay cash. How much should he deposit each year, beginning now, at 4% annually for 10 years?

8. Work Problem 7 if the home costs $45,000.

9. Work Problem 7 if he deposits money quarterly at 6% converted quarterly.

10. What is the present value of an annuity due of $300 per quarter at 5%, converted quarterly for 5 years.

11. A theater is leased for 10 years at $2000 a year payable annually in advance. Find the cash equivalent of the lease on a 6% basis.

12. B paid 3 months ago the last of 60 quarterly life insurance premiums of $50 each. Had he been able to invest each payment at $3\frac{1}{2}$% converted quarterly, what would be the total amount now?

13. Mr. Abel is saving for 5 years to buy a $4500 automobile by depositing a sum in his bank each month, beginning now, at 4% converted monthly. How large is his deposit?

14. What single sum deposited now is equival nt to the annuity due in Problem 13?

15. The rent of a fashion shop on Broadway is $5400 for 3 years payable triennially in advance. What would be an equivalent monthly rent in advance if money is worth 7% compounded monthly?

16. A will need $600 six years hence. Beginning now, what should he deposit annually for 6 years in a bank that pays 2%?

17. A $2800 debt due in 7 years is to be discharged by 7 equal annual payments, the first due now. Find the annual payment on a 3% basis.

18. A color television set may be bought for 24 equal monthly payments, the first due at time of purchase. The cash price is $536.40 and interest is at 12% converted monthly. Compute the monthly payment.

19. Find n from the tables if $2520 = 120(a_{\overline{n-1}|.03} + 1)$.

20. Compute i by interpolation if $4900 = 200(s_{\overline{19}|i} - 1)$.

21. If interest is at 3% converted quarterly, how many quarterly payments of $15 each are necessary to have $600 accumulated 3 months after the last payment of $15?

22. A lot may be bought for either $1350 cash or 5 annual payments of $300 each, the first due at time of purchase. By choosing the second plan, the purchaser pays interest at what effective rate?

23. By placing $500 in a fund at the beginning of each half-year, it is desired to have $9000 in the fund at the end of 8 years. Each deposit must earn interest at what rate converted semiannually?

24. Given $4585 = 25(s_{\overline{n+1}|.005} - 1)$. Find n from the tables.

25. Compute i by interpolation from $1450 = 50 (a_{\overline{46}|i} + 1)$.

26. A trust fund of $10,000, drawing interest at 4% converted monthly beginning now, is to provide a chapel with a monthly income of $75, the first payment due now. Find the number of payments.

27. Derive formula (9) by use of a geometric series.

28. Derive formula (10) by use of a geometric series.

29. Using the lower half of Fig. 20, show that $A_n(\text{due}) = R(1 + i)a_{\overline{n}|i}$.

30. Using the lower half of Fig. 19, show that $S_n(\text{due}) = R(1 + i)s_{\overline{n}|i}$.

31. Prove algebraically that $(1 + i)s_{\overline{n}|i} = s_{\overline{n+1}|i} - 1$.

32. Prove algebraically that $(1 + i)a_{\overline{n}|i} = a_{\overline{n-1}|i} + 1$.

128. Deferred annuities

When the term of an ordinary annuity of n periods begins m periods hence, the annuity is said to be an annuity for n periods, **deferred** m periods. Such an annuity may be represented diagrammatically as in Fig. 21, where

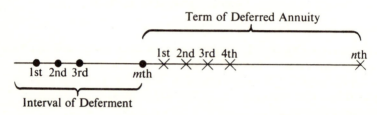

Figure 21

a cross mark indicates payment, and a dot no payment. The length of time between now and the beginning of the term of the deferred annuity is called the **interval of deferment,** which *ends one period before the first payment is due.* In other words, the first payment is due $m + 1$ periods hence, and the nth payment $m + n$ periods hence.

The **amount** of an annuity for n periods, deferred m periods, is the value of the annuity at the *end* of its term. This amount is that of an ordinary annuity for n periods, since no payments are made during the interval of deferment.

The **present value** of an annuity for n periods, deferred m periods, is the value of the annuity at the *beginning of the interval of deferment.* This is not the same as the value of an ordinary annuity for n periods at the beginning of its term. However, the deferred annuity may be thought of as an annuity for $m + n$ periods in which the first m payments are withheld. Hence the present value of the deferred annuity is equal to the present value of an ordinary annuity for $m + n$ periods diminished by the present value of an ordinary annuity for m periods. Let A_n(def.) denote the present value of the deferred annuity, and R the periodic rent. Then

$$A_n(\textbf{def.}) = R(a_{\overline{m+n}|i} - a_{\overline{m}|i}). \tag{11}$$

ILLUSTRATIVE EXAMPLE 1. At 4% converted semiannually, find the present value of 20 semiannual payments of $500 each, the first due in $7\frac{1}{2}$ years.

SOLUTION. Since the first payment is due in 15 periods, the term of the annuity begins 14 periods hence, that is, the annuity is deferred 14 periods. Substituting $R = 500$, $i = 0.02$, $m = 14$, $n = 20$ in (11),

$$A_n(\text{def.}) = R(a_{\overline{m+n}|i} - a_{\overline{m}|i}) = 500(a_{\overline{34}|.02} - a_{\overline{14}|.02}).$$

From Table VI, $a_{\overline{34}|.02} = 24.49859$ and $a_{\overline{14}|.02} = 12.10625$.

Hence $A_n(\text{def.}) = 500(24.49859 - 12.10625)$
$$= 500 \times 12.39234 = \$6196.17. \quad Ans.$$

ILLUSTRATIVE EXAMPLE 2. Find the term of an annuity, deferred 8 years, with present value = $450, $R = \$60$, $i = 5\%$ effective.

SOLUTION. Applying (11), $450 = 60(a_{\overline{8+n}|.05} - a_{\overline{8}|.05}).$

Dividing both members by 60, $7.5 = a_{\overline{8+n}|.05} - a_{\overline{8}|.05}.$

From Table VI, $a_{\overline{8}|.05} = 6.4632.$

Hence $a_{\overline{8+n}|.05} = 7.5 + 6.4632 = 13.9632.$

In the 5% column of Table VI, the first entry greater than 13.9632 is 14.0939, the corresponding number of periods being 25. Therefore $8 + n = 25$, or $n = 17$. That is, the annuity consists of 16 annual payments of $60 each and a 17th smaller payment (the 1st due in 9 years).

EXERCISE 77

1. At 6% converted semiannually, find the amount and present value of an annuity of $300 each half-year for 12 years, deferred 6 years.

2. At 3% converted quarterly, find the amount and present value of an annuity of $200 per quarter for 8 years, deferred $3\frac{1}{2}$ years.

3. A house sells for $2000 down and 20 annual payments of $500 each, the first due 3 years hence. Find the cash price on a 6% basis.

4. To buy a boat, Mr. Smith will make 5 annual payments of $953, the first due 4 years hence. If money is worth $5\frac{1}{2}\%$ effective, find the original price of the boat.

5. In Problem 4 what single payment 11 years hence would pay for the boat?

6. At 5% converted semiannually, what single payment now is equivalent to 15 semiannual payments of $200 each, the first due in 4 years?

7. A grove of tung trees is expected to yield $10,000 a year for 25 years after the trees come into full bearing. Find the present value of the entire expected yield at an interest rate of 5%, assuming the first income of $10,000 to be due at the end of 5 years.

8. A coal mine will yield $20,000 a year for 30 years. Production is to begin in 2 years and the first income of $20,000 is expected 3 years hence. Find the present value of the total yield on a $4\frac{1}{2}\%$ basis.

9. A $25,000 house can be purchased for what equal monthly payments for 11 years beginning 5 years hence at 6% converted monthly?

10. A loan of $2111.30 at 4% was canceled by n annual payments of $530 deferred 7 years. Find n.

11. When Jerry was born, his aunt invested $1000 at $3\frac{1}{2}\%$ converted quarterly, stipulating that this sum and interest thereon be returned to Jerry in 20 equal quarterly payments, the first due on the day he is 17 years old. Compute the quarterly payment.

12. A certain loan at $7\frac{1}{2}\%$ was canceled by 13 annual payments of $1350 which began 7 years after the original loan date. Find the original loan.

13. Find the present value of payments of $64 semiannually for 12 years, the first due $6\frac{1}{2}$ years hence. Money is worth 5% compounded semiannually.

14. A dealer borrows $3000, contracting to repay principal and interest at 6% converted monthly in 60 equal monthly installments, the first due 2 years hence. How large is each installment?

15. An insurance company gives a widow the option of $9000 cash or an annuity certain of $100 a month, the first payment due 15 months hence. Find the number of payments at $3\frac{1}{2}\%$ converted monthly.

16. Express $(1 + i)^{-n}$ in terms of A_n, R, and $a_{\overline{n}|i}$.

17. How much would a father have had to invest at 4% compounded semiannually 21 years ago so that the sum and interest thereon be returned to his son in 8 equal semiannual payments of $200 beginning now?

18. Given that $1500 = R(a_{\overline{40}|.02} - a_{\overline{8}|.02})$. Compute R.

19. Find n from the tables if $2500 = 125(a_{\overline{10+n}|.03} - a_{\overline{10}|.03})$.

20. An alumnus deposits $20,000 with a trust company, with the understanding that the company shall pay $500 per quarter to his alma mater, the first payment 8 years hence. How many payments will the college receive if the company allows 3% converted quarterly?

21. The present value of a deferred annuity of $200 quarterly for 13 years at $5\frac{1}{2}\%$ converted quarterly was $6451.20. How many quarters was the annuity deferred?

22. Suppose in Problem 21 the present value was $4585.30. Find how many quarters the annuity was deferred.

23. By trial and interpolation in Table VI, find i if $6 = a_{\overline{20}|i} - a_{\overline{5}|i}$.

24. By the method of Problem 23, find the rate at which a student is charged interest if he has agreed to repay a $500 loan in 6 annual installments of $100 each, beginning 4 years from date of loan.

25. Derive formula (11) by use of a geometric series.

26. Referring to Fig. 21, show that A_n (def.) $= Ra_{\overline{n}|i} (1 + i)^{-m}$.

27. Using Fig. 21, show that A_n (def.) $= Rs_{\overline{n}|i} (1 + i)^{-(m+n)}$.

28. Prove by algebra that $a_{\overline{n}|i} (1 + i)^{-m} = a_{\overline{m+n}|i} - a_{\overline{m}|i}$.

129. Perpetuities

A **perpetuity** is an annuity whose payments begin at a fixed date and continue forever. Some examples are: endowments of charitable institutions, interest payments on such perpetual bonds as the British consols, and dividends on preferred stock. The "amount" of a perpetuity is undefined, since it increases beyond all bounds as time goes on. In defining present value, we shall distinguish between two types of perpetuities.

Type I

Consider a perpetuity of R payable at the end of each period, the first payment due one period hence. Let money be worth i per period. We shall define the **present value**, denoted by A_∞ (read: A sub infinity), of this perpetuity to be that sum of money which, invested now at the rate i per period, will yield R at the end of each period forever, the original sum remaining intact. In other words, the interest on A_∞ for each period must be R;

or, $i \cdot A_{\infty} = R$. Dividing both members by i,

$$A_{\infty} = \frac{R}{i}. \tag{12}$$

Thus, $\$R/i$ is the cash equivalent of an unlimited number of periodic payments of $\$R$, the first due one period hence.

Type II

Consider a perpetuity of $\$W$ payable at the end of each k periods, the first payment due k periods hence. Let money be worth i per period. We shall define the **present value**, denoted by $A_{\infty, k}$, of this perpetuity to be that sum of money which, invested now at the rate i per period, will yield $\$W$ at the end of each k periods forever, the original sum remaining intact. Now, the interest on $A_{\infty, k}$ for one period is $I = i(A_{\infty, k})$. But payments of I at the end of each period for k periods form an annuity whose amount at the end of k periods is $I \cdot s_{\overline{k}|i} = i(A_{\infty, k})s_{\overline{k}|i}$. This amount must be equal to W due at that time; that is, $i(A_{\infty, k})s_{\overline{k}|i} = W$. Hence

$$A_{\infty, k} = \frac{W}{i} \cdot \frac{1}{s_{\overline{k}|i}}. \tag{13}$$

Thus, a payment of $\$A_{\infty, k}$ now is equivalent to payments of $\$W$ at the end of each k periods forever.

ILLUSTRATIVE EXAMPLE 1. At 6% converted quarterly, find the present value of a perpetuity of $300 payable at the end of each quarter.

SOLUTION. Here $R = 300$ and $i = 0.015$. Substituting in (12),

$$A_{\infty} = \frac{R}{i} = \frac{300}{0.015} = \$20,000. \quad Ans.$$

That is, at the given rate, $20,000 is the cash equivalent of a perpetual income of $300 per quarter, the first payment due 3 months hence.

ILLUSTRATIVE EXAMPLE 2. At 4% converted semiannually, find the present value of a perpetuity of $2000 at the end of each 3 years.

SOLUTION. Recognize that this is a perpetuity of type II, since payments occur at the end of each six conversion periods, and *not* at the end of each period. Here $W = 2000$, $i = 0.02$, $k = 6$. By (13),

$$A_{\infty, k} = \frac{2000}{0.02} \cdot \frac{1}{s_{\overline{6}|.02}} = 100,000 \left(\frac{1}{a_{\overline{6}|.02}} - 0.02 \right) = \$15,852.58. \quad Ans.$$

That is, an investment of $15,852.58 now would provide for an unlimited number of payments of $2000 each 3 years, the first due 3 years hence.

EXERCISE 78

1. Find the present value of a perpetuity of $3300 a year at $5\frac{1}{2}\%$.

2. What sum invested now at 4% converted semiannually will yield $200 biennally forever?

3. $25,000 invested now at 5% converted semiannually yields how much every five years forever?

4. Find the present value of a perpetuity of $400,000 a year at 6%.

5. If money is worth 4%, compare the present value of a perpetuity of $200 a year with that of an annuity of $200 a year for 100 years.

6. At 8% effective, compare the present value of a perpetuity of $100 a year with that of an annuity of $100 a year for 100 years.

7. If the cash equivalent of a perpetuity of $450 per half-year is $20,000, what is the interest rate convertible semiannually?

8. To secure a perpetual quarterly income for a clinic, a man invests $12,000 at $3\frac{1}{2}\%$ converted quarterly. Find the quarterly income.

9. At 8% converted monthly, what single payment now is equivalent to payments of $1500 at the end of each 10 years forever?

10. What sum of money invested at 4% converted semiannually will provide a perpetual income of $2000 at the end of each 5 years?

11. Do Problem 9 if the $1500 is due at the end of each 8 years.

12. Work Problem 10 if the rate is 3% convertible monthly.

13. To provide a sum of money payable triennially forever, $8000 is invested at 6% compounded quarterly. Find the triennial income.

14. Solve Problem 13 if the rate is 5% compounded semiannually.

15. Find x if, at 6% converted quarterly, $2875 is the present value of a perpetuity of $3000 payable at the end of each x years.

16. Do Problem 15 if the present value of the perpetuity is $15,336.

17. To establish a scholarship of $1200 to be awarded annually to a

deserving member, a fraternity must invest what sum of money at 4%
seven years before the first scholarship is awarded?

18. Work Problem 17 if $600 is to be awarded biennially.

19. At what rate converted semiannually will the present value of a
perpetuity of $1000 at the end of each 5 years be $5000? [*Hint.* Use the
formula in Problem 20 and interpolate in Table III for *i*.]

20. Do Problem 19 if the present value of the perpetuity is $6000.

21. If a farm will yield $3000 and $4000 in alternate years of each bien-
nium forever, find the present value of the yield at 4%. [*Hint.* Think
of a perpetuity of $3000 a year and another of $1000 each 2 years.]

22. Devise a modified form of formula (13) to give the present value of
a perpetuity of annual rents R, $\frac{3}{2}R$, $2R$, respectively, over each 3-year
interval, if money is worth *i* effective. See *Hint* in Problem 21.

23. Show that formula (13) reduces to formula (12) when $k = 1$.

24. Show that (13) may be written: $A_{\infty,k} = W \div [(1 + i)^k - 1]$.

25. Complete the following table:

	$A_{\infty,k}$	W	i	k
a.	$20,000	———	$3\frac{1}{2}\%$	6
b.	———	$ 400	2%	10
c.	$10,000	$1040.80	2%	———
d.	$5,000	———	$1\frac{3}{4}\%$	7
e.	$12,000	$2337.97	$2\frac{1}{4}\%$	———

130. Capitalized cost

The **capitalized cost** of an asset is the first cost plus the present value of
an unlimited number of future renewals. The costs of future renewals form
a perpetuity whose present value is given by formula (13) of Art. 129. Let C
denote the capitalized cost of an asset whose first cost is F and which must
be renewed at the end of each k interest periods at a cost of W. Then, from
the definition of capitalized cost and by formula (13),

$$C = F + \frac{W}{i} \cdot \frac{1}{s_{\overline{k}|i}}. \tag{14}$$

A special case arises when the cost of each renewal is equal to the first cost. Formula (14) still applies, of course. But it may be reduced to a simpler form to take account of this special case. Placing $F = W$ in (14),

$$C = W + \frac{W}{i} \cdot \frac{1}{s_{\overline{k}|i}}.$$

It is left as an exercise for the student to simplify the right member of this equation, and thus to show that

$$C = \frac{W}{i} \cdot \frac{1}{a_{\overline{k}|i}}. \tag{15}$$

ILLUSTRATIVE EXAMPLE 1. What sum of money set aside at 5% will provide for the construction of a railroad bridge at a cost of $25,000 and for its renewal every 30 years at a cost (a) of $20,000? (b) of $25,000?

SOLUTION. (a) Here $F = 25{,}000$, $W = 20{,}000$, $k = 30$, $i = 0.05$, and the unknown is the capitalized cost of the bridge. By formula (14),

$$C = 25{,}000 + \frac{20{,}000}{0.05} \cdot \frac{1}{s_{\overline{30}|.05}} = 25{,}000 + \frac{20{,}000}{0.05}\left(\frac{1}{a_{\overline{30}|.05}} - 0.05\right)$$
$$= 25{,}000 + 400{,}000(0.06505144 - 0.05) = \$31{,}020.58. \quad Ans.$$

(b) Since in this case $W = F = 25{,}000$, we use formula (15). Thus

$$C = \frac{25{,}000}{0.05} \cdot \frac{1}{a_{\overline{30}|.05}} = 500{,}000 \times 0.06505144 = \$32{,}525.72. \quad Ans.$$

ILLUSTRATIVE EXAMPLE 2. A certain machine, costing $80, must be replaced every 5 years. If money is worth 4%, how much could one afford to pay for a machine of a better grade that would last 8 years?

SOLUTION. This is a problem in determining the greatest amount which may be profitably expended on an article to extend its life a given number of years. The solution is based upon the assumption that if two different articles can be used for the same purpose, one is as economical as the other if their capitalized costs are equal.

By (15), the capitalized costs of the two machines are, respectively,

$$\frac{80}{0.04} \cdot \frac{1}{a_{\overline{5}|.04}} \quad \text{and} \quad \frac{W}{0.04} \cdot \frac{1}{a_{\overline{8}|.04}},$$

where W denotes the unknown cost of the second machine. Equating the two capitalized costs,

$$\frac{W}{0.04} \cdot \frac{1}{a_{\overline{8}|.04}} = \frac{80}{0.04} \cdot \frac{1}{a_{\overline{5}|.04}}.$$

Multiplying both members by $0.04 \cdot a_{\overline{8}|.04}$,

$$W = 80 \times a_{\overline{8}|.04} \times \frac{1}{a_{\overline{5}|.04}}$$
$$= 80 \times 6.73274 \times 0.224627 = \$120.99. \quad Ans.$$

<hr>

Comment on the solution. The capitalized cost of either machine is

$$C = \frac{80}{0.04} \cdot \frac{1}{a_{\overline{5}|.04}} = 2000 \times 0.224627 = \$449.25.$$

That is, \$449.25 invested at 4% would provide \$80 now and \$80 at the end of each 5 years, or \$120.99 now and \$120.99 at the end of each 8 years. Hence one could afford to expend as much as \$120.99 on the 8-year machine, instead of paying \$80 for the 5-year machine.

EXERCISE 79

1. \$20,000 worth of equipment of a telephone company must be replaced each 8 years at the same cost. Find the capitalized cost at 6%.

2. A \$3552.95 truck must be replaced every 3 years by a truck of similar cost. Find the capitalized cost of the truck at 4% converted semiannually if 3-year-old trucks are worth 13% of their original cost.

3. A householder must repaint his house every 2 years at a cost of \$242.50. Find the capitalized cost of painting the house at $3\frac{1}{2}$% converted quarterly.

4. The capitalized cost of a certain machine at $5\frac{1}{2}$% effective is \$3120. Find the cost of the original machine if a replacement, every 10 years, costs \$872.

5. An investment of \$102,000 at $4\frac{1}{2}$% converted semiannually will pay for a certain highway paving job and annual upkeep costing \$342. Find the cost of the paving job.

6. A taxicab company buys cabs for \$1850 each. Find the capitalized cost at 5% if the cabs must be replaced every 4 years at \$1400 each.

7. Work Problem 1 if the equipment is replaced each 12 years.

8. Find the capitalized cost in Problem 6 on a 7% basis.

9. A section of a city pavement costs $18,000. It is estimated that, at the end of each 20 years, $2000 will be needed for tearing it up and $18,000 for laying a new pavement. Find the capitalized cost at 7%.

10. What sum of money invested at $4\frac{1}{2}\%$ will finance the erection of a $27,000 dam and its reconstruction every 30 years at the same cost?

11. Compute the capitalized cost in Problem 9 on a 4% basis.

12. Do Problem 10 if the dam is to be reconstructed every 20 years.

13. If money is worth 4%, what endowment will provide for (a) the construction of a $50,000 library and its reconstruction each 40 years at the same cost, and (b) $2000 worth of books at the end of each year?

14. Our government purchases a certain lamp bulb, costing $32, which lasts for 10 years. If money is worth $4\frac{1}{2}\%$, how much could they pay for a lamp bulb lasting 25 years?

15. In Problem 14, how much should the government pay for a lamp bulb which lasts forever?

16. What is the capitalized cost at $3\frac{1}{2}\%$ converted quarterly of a $3500 machine which needs repair work of $500 annually plus parts worth $1500 every 2 years?

17. The capitalized cost at 4% of a taxicab fleet is $23,492. The fleet cost $7520 and must be replaced every 7 years. Find the replacement cost.

18. What sum of money invested at 4% will provide for (a) the construction of a $2000 tennis court and its reconstruction every 35 years at the same cost, and (b) its annual upkeep of $80?

19. A house can be painted for $200 with a cheap quality of paint that lasts 2 years. If money is worth $5\frac{1}{2}\%$, it is equally economical to spend how much on painting it with a better grade lasting 4 years?

20. A shingle roof that costs $600 will last 7 years. How much can one afford to spend on a 15-year asbestos roof if money is worth $3\frac{1}{2}\%$?

21. The steel stack of an industrial plant must be replaced each 12 years at a cost of $300. How much could one afford to spend on a brick stack needing renewal each 30 years? Assume an interest rate of 3%.

22. A bridge of a certain type will cost $8500 and will have to be partly rebuilt at the end of each 15 years at a cost of $4000. If money is worth 4%, a permanent bridge of what cost is equally economical?

23. A railroad company must either have a dangerous crossing guarded at an annual cost of $3000 or else build a $35,000 bridge over the track every 50 years spending $250 a year for upkeep. If money is worth 5%, what would be saved at the end of each year under the 2nd plan?

24. Chestnut poles for transmission lines must be replaced each 10 years at a cost of $24 each. If there are 40 poles per mile, what would be saved per mile at the end of each year by using creosoted pine poles which need renewal every 25 years at a cost of $30 each? Money is worth 6%.

25. Write formula (15) in a simple form for the special case $k = 1$.

26. Show how to obtain formula (15) as directed in Art. 130.

27. The capitalized cost at $5\frac{1}{2}\%$ effective of a $1,232,596 building was $1,541,723.91. The building must be replaced at a cost of $1,500,000 every x years. Find x.

28. Find an expression for $S_{\overline{k}|i}$ in terms of C, F, W and i.

131. Unifying summary of annuities certain

The classification of annuities certain into three types accords with business practice. However, for our purpose, a payment of $R at the *end of a period* is the same as a payment of $R at the *beginning of the following period*. From a broader point of view, each of the formulas (4), (5), (9), (10), and (11) gives the value of the same annuity *at a different date*. Referring to Fig. 22, consider n payments of $R per period, money being worth i per period. The value of this annuity

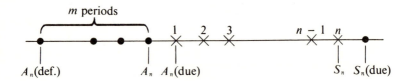

Figure 22

(a) $m + 1$ periods before the date of the first payment is given by the formula for $A_n(\text{def.})$;

(b) one period before the date of the first payment is given by the formula for A_n;

(c) on the day of the first payment is given by the formula for $A_n(\text{due})$;

(d) one period after the date of the nth payment is given by the formula for $S_n(\text{due})$;

(e) on the day of the nth payment is given by the formula for S_n. See also Problems 15 and 16 on page 281.

132. Collections of formulas; review of Chapters 11–13

Formulas used in previous work are collected on this page for convenient reference. To attain greater familiarity with principles and processes employed in Chapters 11–13, the student should pause here for a retrospect

Formula No.	Article No.	Formula	Table
		SIMPLE INTEREST	
(1)	29	$I = Pni$	
(2)	29	$S = P(1 + ni)$	
		COMPOUND INTEREST	
(1)	98	$S = P(1 + i)^n$	III
(2)	103	$r = (1 + i)^m - 1$	
(2')	104	$r = e^j - 1$	
(3)	105	$P = S(1 + i)^{-n}$	IV
		ORDINARY ANNUITIES	
(4)	115	$S_n = R \cdot s_{\overline{n}|i} = R \cdot \dfrac{(1 + i)^n - 1}{i}$	V
(5)	117	$A_n = R \cdot a_{\overline{n}|i} = R \cdot \dfrac{1 - (1 + i)^{-n}}{i}$	VI
(6)	119	$\dfrac{1}{s_{\overline{n}|i}} = \dfrac{1}{a_{\overline{n}|i}} - i$	VII
(7)	120	$R = A_n \cdot \dfrac{1}{a_{\overline{n}|i}}$	VII
(8)	120	$R = S_n \cdot \dfrac{1}{s_{\overline{n}|i}}$	VII
		OTHER ANNUITIES	
(9)	126	$S_n(\text{due}) = R(s_{\overline{n+1}|i} - 1)$	
(10)	127	$A_n(\text{due}) = R(a_{\overline{n-1}|i} + 1)$	
(11)	128	$A_n(\text{def.}) = R(a_{\overline{m+n}|i} - a_{\overline{m}|i})$	
(12)	129	$A_\infty = \dfrac{R}{i}$	
(13)	129	$A_{\infty,k} = \dfrac{W}{i} \cdot \dfrac{1}{s_{\overline{k}|i}}$	
		CAPITALIZED COST	
(14)	130	$C = F + \dfrac{W}{i} \cdot \dfrac{1}{s_{\overline{k}|i}}$	
(15)	130	$C = \dfrac{W}{i} \cdot \dfrac{1}{a_{\overline{k}|i}}$	

and solve the unclassified problems on pages 280–285. The following procedure will be helpful:

Read each problem with utmost care and decide whether it deals with a single payment, or an annuity, or a number of irregular payments. Draw a diagram whenever useful. If an annuity, determine the type: ordinary, due, deferred, or perpetual. If a number of irregular payments, use an equation of value (Art. 112), which is a powerful tool in such cases. Then make a systematic list of all given quantities and determine the exact nature of the unknown: amount, present value, rate, term or periodic rent. Finally turn to the proper formula or method and finish by use of tables when convenient.

MISCELLANEOUS EXERCISE 80
REVIEW OF CHAPTER 13

1. At 6% converted quarterly, what single payment now is equivalent to 32 quarterly payments of $100 each, the first due 4 years hence?

2. Do Problem 1 assuming the first $100 payment to be due now.

3. By investing $200 at the beginning of each half-year, how much is accumulated at the end of 7 years at 5% converted semiannually?

4. What sum set aside at $3\frac{1}{2}$% at the beginning of each year will provide for the replacement of a $10,000 engine at the end of 8 years?

5. At 6% converted monthly, a $4200 debt due now will be liquidated by 42 monthly payments of what size, the first due in 5 years?

6. How many payments of $50 at the beginning of each month will repay a $3000 loan with interest at 6% converted monthly?

7. Do Problem 6 assuming that the first $50 is due 3 years hence.

8. At 4% converted semiannually, what single payment now is equivalent to payments of $500 due at the end of each half-year forever?

9. Solve Problem 8 if $500 is due at the end of each 3 years.

10. The cash equivalent of a perpetuity of $300 per quarter is $24,000 at what rate of interest convertible quarterly?

[11]. Given that $1200 = 40(s_{\overline{23}|i} - 1)$. Determine i.

12. What equal payments at the beginning of each month for 7 years will pay for a $7000 house if interest is at 6% converted monthly?

13. A wooden bridge costing $5000 is to be rebuilt every 15 years at the same cost. Find the capitalized cost at 3%.

14. Instead of the wooden bridge of Problem 13, a 30-year steel bridge of what cost would be equally economical?

15. An endowment of $7500 invested at 3% converted quarterly will provide what income at the end of each 3 years forever?

16. In Problem 15, find equivalent perpetual income per quarter.

17. To buy a house, A agrees to make 15 annual payments of $1000 each, the first due now. Find the equivalent cash price on a 7% basis.

18. Do Problem 17 if the first $1000 is due 2 years hence.

19. If payments of $500 at the beginning of each year for 10 years will pay for a $4000 farm, interest is charged at what rate?

20. Find the present value of an annuity due of $200 semiannually at 3%, converted semiannually for 20 years.

21. Find the present value of an annuity of $200 semiannually at 3%, converted semiannually for 20 years, deferred for 2 years.

22. What size payments every three years forever will $3000, invested at 5% quarterly, give?

23. Do Problem 22 with payments every five years.

24. A farmer buys a tractor now and replaces it every 10 years at a cost of $4500. Find the capitalized cost at $4\frac{1}{2}$%.

25. Work Problem 24 replacing the tractor every 5 years.

26. A garage costs $30,000. Every five years $1500 repairs are done to the structure. At 6% effective, find the capitalized cost.

27. Work Problem 26 if repairs are done every 12 years at a cost of $3600.

28. Given that $a_{\overline{35}|i} - a_{\overline{11}|i} = 20$. Find i.

29. How many annual deposits of $300 each were made into a fund invested at 4% and containing $7235 one year after the last deposit?

30. In Problem 29, find size of fund just after the 8th deposit.

31. Show that the present value of the perpetuity of type I in Art. 129 is $R(1 + i)^{1-h} \div i$ if the first payment is due in h periods.

32. If the first payment is due in h periods, show that the present value of the perpetuity of type II in Art. 129 is $W(1 + i)^{k-h} \div is_{\overline{k}|i}$.

MISCELLANEOUS EXERCISE 81
REVIEW OF CHAPTERS 11-13

Assume ordinary annuities unless otherwise specified or implied.

1. A deposits $2000 in a bank paying 4% converted semiannually. What will he have to his credit at the end of 10 years?

2. B deposits $100 in the bank of Problem 1 each half-year for 10 years. How much will be to his credit at the end of 10 years?

3. An electric range is bought at an installment price of $15 down and $10 a month for 18 months. Compute the equivalent cash price if interest is at 9% converted monthly.

4. Accumulate $1000 for $8\frac{2}{3}$ years at 6% converted quarterly.

5. To liquidate a $10,000 debt with interest at 6% converted semiannually, the trustees of a church plan to make equal payments at the end of each half-year for 10 years. How large is each payment?

6. In buying a lot priced at $900 cash, Mr. Clark contracts to pay $100 down and $15 a month. Payments include interest at 6% converted monthly. How many are necessary?

7. A man pays $3.50 interest each month on a loan of $400. This is equivalent to paying interest at what rate compounded annually?

8. Which yields more: $6\frac{1}{2}$% converted continuously or $6\frac{3}{4}$% effective?

9. Accumulate $100 for 12 years if interest is at $3\frac{1}{2}$% compounded monthly for 5 years and at 4% compounded quarterly thereafter.

10. If money is worth $7\frac{1}{2}$% converted monthly, when would a single payment of $1000 be equivalent to 200 monthly payments of $5 each?

11. Mr. Parker has lived for 10 years in a house for which he has been paying $60 rent at the beginning of each month. These payments would have paid for a house of what cash price bought 10 years ago? Assume interest at 5% converted monthly.

12. If Mr. Parker of Problem 11 had invested $60 at the beginning of each month for 10 years at 3% compounded monthly, the accumulated sum would now be enough to pay cash for a house worth what?

13. $2500 is deposited with a trust company at 5% converted quarterly to provide a quarterly income of $100, the first payment due 8 years hence. How many payments will there be?

[14]. Instead of $50 a month rent in advance, an owner accepts $575 a year in advance; he allows interest at what rate converted monthly?

15. Show by direct reasoning that the value of the annuity in Art. 131, p periods after the date of the nth payment, is $R(s_{\overline{p+n}|i} - s_{\overline{p}|i})$.

16. Show by direct reasoning that the value of the annuity in Art. 131, on the date of the kth payment, is $R(s_{\overline{k}|i} + a_{\overline{n-k}|i})$, where $k < n$.

17. Discount $1000 for 5 years at 8% simple interest.

18. Look up values of v^{52} and v^{55}, both at 2%; then compute v^{107}.

19. A U.S. Savings Bond bought for $75 is redeemable at $100 in 10 years. Interest is earned at what rate converted quarterly?

20. Home Finance Co. uses a "6% per annum" time-payment plan. Thus, if the unpaid balance on a new car is $1500, 12% is added. Then the $1680 is divided by 24 and the buyer pays $70 a month for 24 months. He pays interest at what rate converted monthly?

21. A $400 assessment, due now, may be paid in 4 annual installments, the first due now. Find the annual payment on a 6% basis.

22. Jack borrows $400 from a friend. Five years later he returns $510. Find the effective rate by interpolation in the tables.

23. Solve Problem 22 by use of logarithms.

24. What is the annual rate of simple interest in Problem 22?

25. A firm advertises: Pay us $200 a year for 10 years and we will return you $2250 at the end of 10 years. Find the interest rate.

26. What sum invested at $3\frac{1}{2}$% will amount in 8 years to $1000?

27. Insurance premiums are payable in advance. Find the monthly premium equivalent at 6% converted monthly to a $60 annual premium.

28. Find the force of interest corresponding to $4\frac{1}{4}$% effective.

29. Mr. Jones was to pay $1000 at the end of each year for 5 years. Deviating from this schedule, he pays $2000 at the end of 2 years and $2000 at the end of 4 years. If money is worth 6%, what single payment at the end of 5 years will close the transaction?

30. How much should Mr. Ellis deposit at the end of each 6 months for 5 years in order to accumulate $4000 for a trip abroad? Interest on his deposits is at $2\frac{1}{2}\%$ compounded semiannually.

31. The widow of a man killed in an accident arranges to collect the equivalent of $5000 cash in 100 equal monthly payments, the first due in 2 years. At 6% converted monthly, find the monthly payment.

32. A college receives a legacy paying $10,000 a year for 15 years, the first payment due in 8 years. Being in urgent need of funds, the college discounts the legacy at an interest rate of 4%. What sum is realized?

33. B signs a note promising to pay A $600 in 5 years with interest at 4.2% compounded annually. Two years later A sells the note to C on a mutual agreement that money is worth $5\frac{1}{2}\%$. What does C pay?

34. An annuity of $100 a year for 12 years, with first payment due 4 years hence, is equivalent at 5% to what single payment due now?

Answer the question in Problem 34 if the single payment is due:

35. 3 years hence.   **37.** 10 years hence.   **39.** 17 years hence.

36. 4 years hence.   **38.** 15 years hence.   **40.** 20 years hence.

41. How long will it take a sum to double itself at 6% effective?

42. Which is the better: An investment yielding 4.2% converted semiannually, or one yielding 4% converted monthly?

43. A special district tax will be collected at the end of each year forever to provide for (a) building a $75,000 bridge now with an upkeep of $350 at the end of each year for 50 years and (b) rebuilding it each 50 years forever, cost and upkeep as in (a). Find the annual tax on a $3\frac{1}{2}\%$ basis.

44. Solve Problem 43 assuming the tax will be collected for only 50 years to provide for (a), with no provision for (b).

45. Commute two debts of $1000 each, due in 11 and 13 years, into 9 equal annual payments, the first due in 1 year. Money is worth $4\frac{1}{2}\%$.

46. A man earns $400 a month. What must he set aside at the end of each month to accumulate $4000 in 4 years at 4% converted monthly?

47. An income of $600 each half-year for 50 years is equivalent at 6% converted semiannually to what income each half-year forever?

48. A small house worth $4500 is to be "paid for like rent" in monthly installments of $50 each, the first due at time of purchase. If interest is at 6% converted monthly, determine the number of payments.

49. Accumulate $150 for 33 years at 3% compounded quarterly.

50. Florida was acquired in 1819 at a cost of $5,000,000. If this sum had been invested then at 4%, in 1969 it would amount to what?

51. What sum invested at 4% will provide a perpetual income of (a) $600 at the end of each 5 years? (b) $120 at the end of each year?

52. At $2\frac{3}{4}$% converted semiannually, how many semiannual payments of $300 each will amount to $16,600 six months after the last payment?

53. If roofing costing $10 a square lasts 15 years, how much could be spent on a better type lasting 30 years? Assume 6%.

54. At 3% converted quarterly, how much set aside at the beginning of each quarter for 5 years will amount to $500 at the end of 5 years?

55. Premium Oil Co. buys a chain of filling stations for $150,000, agreeing to pay $25,000 down and $2000 a month. Find the number of monthly payments if interest is at 6% converted monthly.

56. A scientific society receives a $5000 gift to provide for a prize 6 years hence and a like prize each 2 years thereafter. How large will each prize be if the gift yields 4% converted semiannually?

57. Intercity Transfer Co. buys vans at $6500 and replaces them every 5 years for $4000 each. Find the capitalized cost per van at 4%.

[58]. In offering $1200 loans for 5 years "at 5%," the E-Z Loan Co. uses the following method. First $300 is added to $1200. The $1500 is then divided into 60 monthly installments of $25 each to be paid by the borrower. Interest is charged at what rate converted monthly?

59. Using logarithms, discount $1500 for 10 years at $4\frac{1}{4}$%.

60. In how many years is a sum trebled at 7% converted monthly?

[61]. A dealer owes rent on his store for the past 18 months at $100 payable monthly in advance. In demanding $1900 for settlement, the landlord expects interest at what rate converted monthly?

62. B had arranged to pay a $5000 debt with interest at 5% in 10 equal annual installments. When time comes for the 7th payment, he offers to pay the equivalent of the remaining 4 payments. What should he pay?

63. Mr. Long obtains a $2000 loan at 6% converted quarterly. He contracts to pay $100 each 3 months for 5 years and after that $50 per quarter. Find the total number of quarterly payments.

64. To provide for an income of $1000 a year for 20 years starting on his 56th birthday, a man should set aside how much each year for 20 years beginning on his 36th birthday? Interest on his savings is at $3\frac{1}{2}\%$.

65. $100 is due at the end of each year for 10 years. Commute at $4\frac{1}{2}\%$ these 10 payments into 2 equal payments due in 7 and 15 years.

66. To secure for an orphanage a perpetual income of $2000 every 3 years, a man should deposit now what sum at 4% with a trust company if the first $2000 is payable 1 year hence?

67. In 1903 the Panama Canal Zone was ceded to the United States in perpetuity for $10,000,000 outright, plus $250,000 a year for 20 years, after that $430,000 a year forever. All this is equivalent to what equal annual payments forever starting in 1904? Assume 5%.

68. Find x if $s_{\overline{12}|i} - s_{\overline{11}|i} = (1 + i)^x$.

In each of Problems 69–76, prove the given equation by algebra. In doing Problems 77–80, tedious trials in tables or long computations may be avoided by use of the equations in Problems 71–74.

69. $s_{\overline{n+1}|i} - s_{\overline{n}|i} = (1 + i)^n$.

70. $a_{\overline{n}|i} - a_{\overline{n-1}|i} = (1 + i)^{-n}$.

71. $(1 + i)^n a_{\overline{n}|i} = s_{\overline{n}|i}$.

72. $(1 + i)^{-n} s_{\overline{n}|i} = a_{\overline{n}|i}$.

73. $(1 + i)^k s_{\overline{n}|i} = s_{\overline{n+k}|i} - s_{\overline{k}|i}$.

74. $(1 + i)^k a_{\overline{n}|i} = s_{\overline{k}|i} + a_{\overline{n-k}|i}$.

75. $(1 + i)^{-k} s_{\overline{n}|i} = s_{\overline{n-k}|i} + a_{\overline{k}|i}$.

76. $(1 + i)^{-k} a_{\overline{n}|i} = a_{\overline{n+k}|i} - a_{\overline{k}|i}$.

77. At what rate converted monthly will the amount of an annuity of $1 a month for 63 months be almost $1\frac{1}{2}$ times the present value?

78. Find n if, at 6% converted monthly, the present value of an annuity of $1 a month for n months is almost one-half the amount.

79. B deposits $100 a year for 5 years in a fund invested at $3\frac{1}{2}\%$. What does the fund contain 10 years after the last deposit?

80. A is to receive a legacy of $100 a year for 15 years. He discounts the legacy at an interest rate of 3% and invests the proceeds at 3%. How large is the investment at the end of 5 years?

81. Accumulate $1123 for 27 years at $5\frac{1}{2}\%$ converted semiannually.

82. Accumulate $63.95 for $17\frac{2}{3}$ years with interest at $6\frac{1}{2}\%$ effective for the first 7 years and then at $4\frac{1}{2}\%$ compounded semiannually for the remaining time.

83. Is 31.5775% effective equivalent to 27.6% compounded semiannually?

84. Find the present value of debt of $14,321 bearing interest of 6% converted monthly due 30 years hence, if money is worth 4% compounded semiannually.

85. How long will it take $1000 to amount to $10,000 at 4.7% interest converted semiannually?

86. A debt of $1200 bearing 3% effective interest due 7 years hence and another of $1700 with no interest due in 12 years are to be discharged by a single payment 10 years hence. Find the payment if money is worth 5% converted semiannually.

87. Seventeen semiannual payments of $62 at $4\frac{1}{2}$% converted semiannually are equivalent to what single payment at the end of $8\frac{1}{2}$ years?

88. A $12,000 loan is canceled by monthly payments of $97.37 for 16 years. Find the nominal interest rate converted monthly.

89. What equal monthly payments for 20 years will cancel a home mortgage of $10,000 at 6% compounded monthly?

90. A $23,000 home can be purchased for what equal monthly payments for 20 years at 6% converted monthly beginning now.

91. The present value of payments of x dollars annually at 6% effective for 12 years, deferred 6 years, is $3167.91. Find x.

92. What sum invested at 4% compounded semiannually will provide for semiannual payments of $100 forever?

93. A sum of $16,000 is invested at $3\frac{1}{2}$% converted quarterly to yield payments of x dollars every 5 years. Find x.

94. Find the capitalized cost of 4% compounded semiannually of a $2500 truck which is to be replaced every 5 years at a cost of $2000.

Chapter FOURTEEN

AMORTIZATION AND

SINKING FUNDS

133. Extinction of a debt by the method of amortization

An important application of annuities is found in the process of liquidating a long-term obligation by periodic payments, a process which is of frequent occurrence in financial transactions. There are two different methods in general use. We shall first consider the method of **amortization.**

The word "amortization" is of Latin origin (*ad mortem*, to death) and refers ordinarily to any method of extinguishing a debt. In this book, however, the **amortization** of an interest-bearing debt means the extinction of the debt, principal and interest on outstanding principal, by a series of equal payments at equal intervals. The periodic payments form an annuity whose present value is the principal of the debt.

The extinction of a debt by this method involves the following facts. (1) The periodic payment is greater than the interest for any period; hence part of the payment is applied to the reduction of the principal. (2) As the principal is thus reduced gradually, the interest per period decreases; hence, as time goes on, a larger portion of the periodic payment is applied to the reduction of the principal.

134. Finding the periodic payment and the outstanding principal

A common problem is to find the *periodic payment* when the principal of the debt, the interest rate, and the number of payments are known. Since the payments form an annuity whose present value is the principal of the debt, the unknown is the periodic rent of the annuity.

Another problem is to find the *outstanding principal* at any time. This information is necessary (a) in case the creditor and debtor agree to close the transaction before the time scheduled originally, and (b) for accounting purposes.

———

ILLUSTRATIVE EXAMPLE. A debt of $3000, bearing interest at 6%, is to be amortized by equal payments at the end of each year for 5 years.

(a) Find the annual payment.
(b) What is the principal outstanding just after the 2nd payment?
(c) How much of the original principal has been repaid just after the 2nd payment is made?
(d) How much of the 3rd payment is applied to payment of interest and how much to reduction of principal?

SOLUTION. (a) Here we have an ordinary annuity in which the present value is given and the periodic rent is unknown. Hence we use formula (7) of Art. 120. Substituting the known quantities $A_n = 3000$, $n = 5$, and $i = 0.06$ in $R = A_n \cdot \dfrac{1}{a_{\overline{n}|i}}$, we have

$$R = 3000 \times \frac{1}{a_{\overline{5}|.06}} = \$3000 \times 0.237396 = \$712.19. \quad Ans.$$

(b) The outstanding principal is obviously the value (*at the beginning of the 3rd year*) of the remaining 3 payments. The problem, then, is equivalent to finding the present value of an annuity of $712.19 per annum for 3 years. Here $R = 712.19$, $n = 3$, and $i = 0.06$. By formula (5)

$$A_n = R \cdot a_{\overline{n}|i} = \$712.19 \times a_{\overline{3}|.06} = \$712.19 \times 2.67301 = \$1903.69. \quad Ans.$$

That is, just after the 2nd regular payment is made, an additional payment of $1903.69 would close the transaction. Putting it in another way, a total payment of $712.19 + $1903.69 = $2615.88 at the end of the 2nd year would close the transaction.

(c) From (b) the outstanding principal is $1903.69 when the 2nd payment is made. Hence the original principal has been reduced by

$$\$3000 - \$1903.69 = \$1096.31. \quad Ans.$$

(d) From (b), the principal outstanding at the beginning of the 3rd year is $1903.69. Hence the interest due at the end of the 3rd year is

$$\$1903.69 \times 0.06 = \$114.22.$$

Then, $114.22 of the payment at the end of the 3rd year applies to paying the interest for the 3rd year; the remainder, $712.19 — $114.22 = $597.97, is applied to the reduction of the principal.

---

135. Amortization Schedule

For accounting purposes, it is desirable to prepare an amortization schedule showing, in tabular form, how each payment is distributed into interest payment and reduction of principal.

ILLUSTRATIVE EXAMPLE. Construct an amortization schedule for the debt of the illustrative example of Art. 134.

SOLUTION. In part (a) of the illustrative example of Art. 134, it was found that the necessary annual payment for this case is $712.19. The interest due at the end of the first year is $3000 × 0.06 = $180. Hence the principal is reduced by $712.19 — $180 = $532.19. The principal outstanding at the beginning of the 2nd year is $3000 — $532.19 = $2467.81, and the interest due at the end of the 2nd year is $2467.81 × 0.06 = $148.07. Hence the principal is reduced by $712.19 — $148.07 = $564.12. Continuing this process for the remaining three years, we obtain the following:

AMORTIZATION SCHEDULE

| (a) | (b) Outstanding Principal at Beginning of Year | (c) | (d) | (e) At End of Year Principal Reduced by |
Year	(b) — (e)	Interest Due at End of Year 0.06 × (b)	Annual Payment at End of Year	(d) — (c)
1	$3000.00	$180.00	$712.19	$532.19
2	2467.81	148.07	712.19	564.12
3	1903.69	114.22	712.19	597.97
4	1305.72	78.34	712.19	633.85
5	671.87	40.31	712.19	671.88
Totals	$9349.09	$560.94	$3560.95	$3000.01

Remarks about the Example. The student should verify the statements (1) and (2) at the end of Art. 133 from this schedule. The arithmetic involved in the construction of the schedule may be checked in various ways:

I. The last items of columns (b) and (e) should be equal; also, the total of column (e) should be equal to the principal of the debt. The discrepancy of 1 cent here is caused by the fact that we disregarded a fraction of a cent in the annual payment, which is $712.189 (to the nearest tenth of a cent).

II. The total of column (c) plus the total of column (e) should be equal to the total of column (d).

III. The total of column (c) should be 6% of the total of column (b).

IV. When the amortization involves a large number of payments, the entries in column (b) should be checked occasionally as one proceeds in the construction of the table. This particular check may be performed by the method shown in part (b) of the illustrative example of Art. 134. Thus, as it was found there, the principal outstanding at the beginning of the 3rd year is $1903.69, which agrees with the third entry in column (b).

136. Extinction of a bonded debt

To borrow money from investors, corporations sometimes issue bonds in such denominations as $10,000, $1000, $500, and $100. Arrangements are usually made to retire a certain number of bonds at the end of each period. The periodic payments for a bonded debt cannot be equal, since the principal repaid each time retires a whole number of outstanding bonds. However, these periodic payments are made as nearly equal as possible.

ILLUSTRATIVE EXAMPLE. Construct a schedule for the retirement of a debt of $20,000 by 6 annual payments as nearly equal as possible. The debt is in the form of $100 bonds bearing 5% interest payable annually.

SOLUTION. If all 6 payments were to be exactly equal, the annual payment would be, by the method of Art. 134,

$$R = 20,000 \times \frac{1}{a_{\overline{6}|.05}} = 20,000 \times 0.1970175 = \$3940.35.$$

The interest due at the end of the first year is $20,000 \times 0.05 = \$1000$. This would leave $3940.35 - \$1000 = \$2940.35$ to be applied to the repayment of principal. But the nearest number of $100 bonds that can be retired with $2940.35 is 29. Hence 29 bonds are retired at the end of the first year, making a total payment of $1000 + \$2900 = \$3900$.

The principal outstanding at the beginning of the 2nd year is $20,000 − $2900 = $17,100; and the interest due at the end of the 2nd year is 17,100 × 0.05 = $855. The sum to be used for retiring more bonds is $3940.35 − $855 = $3085.35. Hence 31 bonds are retired at the end of the 2nd year. The following schedule shows the progress of the retirement of bonds.

SCHEDULE FOR EXTINCTION OF BONDED DEBT

Year	Outstanding Principal at Beginning of Year	5% Interest Due at End of Year	Principal Reduced by	Bonds Retired at End of Year	Total Annual Payment
1	$20,000	$1,000	$ 2,900	29	$ 3,900
2	17,100	855	3,100	31	3,955
3	14,000	700	3,200	32	3,900
4	10,800	540	3,400	34	3,940
5	7,400	370	3,600	36	3,970
6	3,800	190	3,800	38	3,990
Totals	$73,100	$3,655	$20,000	200	$23,655

———

EXERCISE 82

1. A $1000 loan, with interest at 6% payable quarterly, will be amortized by 8 equal quarterly payments. Find the quarterly payment.

2. Six equal semiannual payments will amortize a $4000 loan with 6% interest payable semiannually. Find the semiannual payment.

3. Construct an amortization schedule for the loan in Problem 1.

4. Construct an amortization schedule for the loan in Problem 2.

5. A debt of $3000, with interest at 4% payable monthly, is being amortized by 20 equal monthly payments. Find (a) the monthly payment; (b) the principal outstanding just after the 11th payment.

6. Referring to Problem 5, determine the principal outstanding just after the 14th payment.

7. What part of the 12th payment in Problem 5 is interest?

8. In Problem 5, the 15th payment reduces principal by how much?

9. Construct a schedule for the retirement of a bonded debt of $100,000 by 5 annual payments as nearly equal as possible. The bonds are of $1000 denomination, bearing interest at 4% payable annually.

10. A debt of $50,000 in the form of $500 bonds bearing 4% interest payable semiannually will be retired in 6 semiannual payments as nearly equal as possible. Construct a schedule for its extinction.

11. Do Problem 10 if bonds bear 6% interest payable semiannually.

12. Do Problem 9 if bonds bear 5% interest payable annually.

13. A buys a house for $7000, paying $3000 cash. He will amortize the balance with interest at 6% payable monthly by 120 equal monthly payments. The first 40 payments will reduce the debt by how much?

14. To provide an invalid with a monthly income for 5 years, B deposits $6000 in a trust fund invested at 4% compounded monthly. Find what the fund contains just after the 36th payment.

15. Find the quarterly payment on a debt of $20,000 to be amortized by equal payments at the end of each quarter for 5 years. Interest is at 4% converted quarterly.

16. What is the outstanding principal on a debt of $5000, bearing interest at 3%, at the end of the 3rd payment? The debt is to be amortized by equal payments each year for 5 years.

17. What is the annual payment in Problem 16?

18. Construct an amortization schedule for the debt of Problem 16.

19. Find the annual payment on a debt of $10,000, to be amortized by equal quarterly payments for $4\frac{1}{2}$ years. Interest is 6%, converted quarterly.

20. What is the outstanding principal at the end of the 10th payment in Problem 19?

21. A college receives a $10,000 bequest. Principal and interest at $3\frac{1}{2}$% are to provide 35 equal annual scholarships beginning at the end of 6 years. How much is still available just after the 20th award?

22. A debt of $2520 on a church organ will be amortized at 5% payable quarterly by 30 equal quarterly payments, the first due now. The first 12 payments will cancel how much of the $2520?

23. A man borrows $10,000. The debt, principal and interest at 4%, is to be retired by a payment of $2000 at the end of 3 years and 7 equal annual payments after that. Find the annual payment.

24. Do Problem 23 if the number of equal annual payments is 12.

25. What equal annual payments for 12 years will repay a $3000 loan if interest is at 5% for the first 4 years and at 3% after that?

26. Do Problem 25 after interchanging the two interest rates.

137. Finding the number of payments

Circumstances may arise in which a debtor can pay only a given amount periodically to amortize his debt. It would be desirable then to find the number of payments necessary for amortization. The problem is equivalent to finding the term of an annuity whose present value, periodic rent, and interest rate are given.

ILLUSTRATIVE EXAMPLE. A debt of $3800, bearing interest at 8% payable quarterly, is to be discharged by payments of $400 at the end of each 3 months.

(a) Find the number of payments.
(b) Find the final payment.
(c) Construct the amortization schedule.

SOLUTION. (a) The problem is the same as that of finding the number n of periods in the annuity. Here $A_n = 3800$, $R = 400$, and $i = 0.02$. Substituting these in $A_n = R \cdot a_{\overline{n}|i}$, we have $3800 = 400 \cdot a_{\overline{n}|.02}$. Hence

$$a_{\overline{n}|.02} = \frac{3800}{400} = 9.5000.$$

From the 2% column of Table VI, we find

$$a_{\overline{10}|.02} = 8.9826 \qquad \text{(less than 9.5000)}$$
and
$$a_{\overline{11}|.02} = 9.7868 \qquad \text{(greater than 9.5000)}.$$

Hence the present value of 10 quarterly payments of $400 each is less than $3800, and the present value of 11 quarterly payments of $400 each is greater than $3800. It is evident, then, that the debtor must make 10 regular payments of $400 each and a final payment of somewhat less than $400 at the end of the 11th quarter. Of course another arrangement would be to make 10 regular payments of $400 each and a smaller payment along with the 10th regular payment. However, for the sake of uniformity, in problems of this type we shall always assume that *a final payment will be made one period after the last regular payment.*

(b) First find the principal outstanding just after the 10th payment. Note that the method used in part (b) of the illustrative example of Art. 134 cannot be applied here, since the final payment is unknown. However, the outstanding principal at any time can be found by a reasoning similar to the following: If no payments whatever be made, the original principal would amount in 10 quarterly periods to

$$3800(1.02)^{10} = 3800 \times 1.218994 = \$4632.18.$$

On the other hand, regular payments of $400, made at the end of each quarter for 10 quarters, will amount at the end of the 10th quarter to

$$400 \times s_{\overline{10}|.02} = 400 \times 10.94972 = \$4379.89.$$

Hence the outstanding principal is $4632.18 − $4379.89 = $252.29 just after the 10th payment. That is, the transaction would be closed if an additional payment of $252.29 were made at the end of the 10th quarter along with the regular payment of $400. However, since our understanding is to make a final payment one period after the last regular payment, the transaction would be closed by paying, at the end of the 11th quarter, $252.29 *plus the interest on it for* 3 *months*. Therefore the final smaller payment is

$$252.29 + (0.02 \times 252.29) = \$252.29 + \$5.05 = \$257.34. \quad Ans.$$

SOLUTION.

(c) AMORTIZATION SCHEDULE

(a) Quarterly Period	(b) Outstanding Principal at Beginning of Period (b) − (e)	(c) Interest Due at End of Period 0.02 × (b)	(d) Periodic Payment at End of Period	(e) At End of Period Principal Reduced by (d) − (c)
1	$ 3,800.00	$ 76.00	$ 400.00	$ 324.00
2	3,476.00	69.52	400.00	330.48
3	3,145.52	62.91	400.00	337.09
4	2,808.43	56.17	400.00	343.83
5	2,464.60	49.29	400.00	350.71
6	2,113.89	42.28	400.00	357.72
7	1,756.17	35.12	400.00	364.88
8	1,391.29	27.83	400.00	372.17
9	1,019.12	20.38	400.00	379.62
10	639.50	12.79	400.00	387.21
11	252.29	5.05	257.34	252.29
Totals	$22,866.81	$457.34	$4257.34	$3800.00

Note that the number of regular payments and the size of the final payment can be determined by the schedule, without the computations performed in the preceding parts of this illustrative example. However, these computations give us a check on the results found by the schedule, and they become necessary when no schedule is prepared.

The student should verify the accuracy of the above schedule by applying checks similar to those outlined after the illustrative example of Art. 135. Can check IV be applied in this case? Why? As one proceeds in the construction of the schedule, the principal outstanding at the beginning of a given period may be computed, as a check, by the method shown in part (b) of this illustrative example.

EXERCISE 83

In Problems 1 through 7, consider a debt of $25,000 with 6% interest payable monthly, being amortized by monthly payments of $200 each.

1. What is the last payment?

2. What is the outstanding principal just after the 59th payment?

3. What is the outstanding principal just after the 175th payment?

4. What part of the 60th payment is interest?

5. The 176th payment reduces the principal by how much?

6. What should the debtor pay to cancel the debt on the day of the 175th payment, if he fails to make the 11 payments preceeding it?

7. Just after what payment is the principal reduced by one-half or less for the first time?

8. To amortize a $12,000 loan at 9% converted monthly, a man will pay $250 monthly. Find the number of regular payments and the final payment.

9. To repay a loan of $800 with 5% interest, A will pay $200 a year. Find the number of regular payments and the final payment.

10. To amortize a $500 loan with 5% interest, B will pay $100 a year. Find the number of regular payments and the final payment.

11. Construct an amortization schedule for the loan in Problem 9.

12. Construct an amortization schedule for the loan in Problem 10.

In Problems 13–22 consider a debt of $10,000, with 6% interest payable monthly, being amortized by monthly payments of $100 each.

13. What is the principal outstanding just after the 38th payment?

14. Find the principal outstanding just after the 60th payment.

15. Determine what part of the 49th payment is interest.

16. The 61st payment reduces the principal by how much?

17. Just after making one half of the number of regular payments, the debtor has reduced the debt from $10,000 to what?

18. Compute what part of the $10,000 the debtor has paid just after making one third of the number of regular payments.

19. What should the debtor pay in all on the day of the 30th payment if he fails to make the 5 payments preceding it?

20. Suppose that the debtor omits the 6th, 7th, 8th, and 9th payments What should he pay altogether when time comes for the 10th payment?

21. Just after which payment is the principal of the debt reduced to $2500 or less for the first time?

22. Find k if, just after the kth payment, the principal of the debt is reduced to $7500 or less for the first time.

23. A $10,000 fund, invested at 3% converted semiannually, is to provide semiannual payments of $400 each. Find the final payment.

24. Air conditioning equipment is installed at a cost of $3500. The down payment is $500. The balance will be amortized at 8% payable quarterly by payments of $200 per quarter. Find the final payment.

25. Find size of fund in Problem 23 just after 12th payment.

26. Just before the 8th regular payment in Problem 24 how large a payment would cancel all remaining obligations?

27. To return a $1000 loan with interest at 6% converted monthly, a student will pay $500 at the end of 2 years and $20 a month after that. Find (a) number of $20 payments; (b) final payment.

28. To repay a $1059 loan at $4\frac{1}{2}$% effective, Mr. Smith will pay $200 annually for the first 3 years and then $50 annually. Find the number of $50 payments and the last payment.

29. To repay a certain loan at 4% converted semiannually, Mr. Jones will pay $500 semiannually for the first $3\frac{1}{2}$ years, then $100 semiannually for the next 16 years, and a final payment of $60.55 at the end of 20 years. Find the loan.

138. Extinction of a debt by the sinking fund method

In discharging an interest-bearing debt by the method of amortization, each periodic payment made to the creditor is used partly to pay the interest due at the end of the period and partly to reduce the principal. Some creditors object to this arrangement, since they would have to find ways of reinvesting a relatively smaller sum at the end of each period. Such creditors prefer a different arrangement whereby the entire principal of the debt is repaid at maturity in a single installment, the interest for each period being paid at the end of that period. Under this plan, the debtor pays the interest regularly as it falls due, and sets aside periodically sufficient funds to be able to repay the entire principal of the debt when due. Such a fund, accumulated for the purpose of paying an obligation due at some future date, is called a **sinking fund.**

The payments or deposits into a sinking fund may be unequal amounts and may be made at unequal intervals. For our purposes, unless mention is made to the contrary, we shall assume that (1) a sinking fund is created by equal payments at equal intervals; (2) the debtor invests each payment at once and lets it accumulate at a certain rate of interest until the obligation matures; (3) the equal periodic payments thus accumulated amount, at the maturity of the debt, to the original principal; (4) the periodic interest, if any, on the original principal is paid to the creditor as it falls due, but *not from the sinking fund;* (5) the periodic payment to the sinking fund is made on the same day that the periodic interest on the original principal is paid to the creditor.

139. Finding the periodic payment and the total periodic charge

It is important to bear in mind that, in extinguishing a debt by the sinking fund method, *the entire principal remains unpaid until its maturity.* The problem of finding the periodic payment to a sinking fund is that of finding the periodic rent of an annuity whose *amount* is known. **Total periodic charge,** an expression used in connection with this topic, is the sum of two items:

the periodic payment to the sinking fund and the periodic interest (if any) payable to the creditor.

_____

ILLUSTRATIVE EXAMPLE. A debt of $3000, due in 5 years, is to be discharged by the sinking fund method. The debtor will make equal payments at the end of each year for 5 years to a sinking fund invested at 6%. Find the annual payment to the sinking fund and the total annual charge.

(a) If the debt bears no interest.

(b) If the debt bears 6% interest payable annually.

(c) If the debt bears interest at 7% payable annually.

(d) Find the amount in the sinking fund at the end of the 3rd year.

(e) The **book value** of a debt at a given time is the difference between the principal of the debt and the amount in the sinking fund at that time. Find the book value of the debt at the end of the 3rd year.

SOLUTION. (a) The annual payments to the sinking fund must amount to $3000 at the maturity of the debt. Hence we find, at 6%, the annual rent of an annuity of 5 years whose *amount* is $3000. By formula (8),

$$R = S_n \cdot \frac{1}{s_{\overline{n}|i}} = 3000 \cdot \frac{1}{s_{\overline{5}|.06}} = 3000\left(\frac{1}{a_{\overline{5}|.06}} - 0.06\right)$$
$$= 3000(0.237396 - 0.06) = \$532.19. \quad Ans.$$

Since the debt bears no interest, the debtor makes no interest payments to the creditor, and the total annual charge is the same as the annual payment.

(b) The annual payment to the sinking fund is again $532.19. However, the debtor must pay 6% interest to the creditor at the end of each year. Hence the total annual charge is

$$532.19 + (0.06 \times 3000) = \$712.19. \quad Ans.$$

The student should note that this is the same as the annual payment for amortization found in part (a) of the illustrative example of Art. 134.

(c) As before, the annual payment to the sinking fund is $532.19. But the debtor must pay 7% interest. Hence the total annual charge is

$$532.19 + (0.07 \times 3000) = \$742.19. \quad Ans.$$

(d) Since the rate of interest borne by the debt has no relation to the rate at which the sinking fund is invested by the debtor, the sinking fund will be of the same size at the end of the 3rd year whether under (a) or (b) or (c). Its value will be the amount of an annuity of $532.19 per annum for 3 years at 6%, which is given by

$$532.19 \times s_{\overline{3}|.06} = 532.19 \times 3.18360 = \$1694.28. \quad Ans.$$

(e) By (d), the required book value of the debt is

$$\$3000 - \$1694.28 = \$1305.72. \quad Ans.$$

Note. The following schedule, showing how the sinking fund accumulates year by year, is self-explanatory.

SINKING FUND SCHEDULE

(a) At End of Year	(b) Annual Payment	(c) Interest Earned 0.06 × (e)	(d) Sinking Fund Increased by (b) + (c)	(e) Sinking Fund Contains (e) + (d)
1	$ 532.19		$ 532.19	$ 532.19
2	532.19	$ 31.93	564.12	1096.31
3	532.19	65.78	597.97	1694.28
4	532.19	101.66	633.85	2328.13
5	532.19	139.69	671.88	3000.01
Totals	$2660.95	$339.06	$3000.01	

EXERCISE 84

1. Construct a schedule for accumulating $3000 in a sinking fund in 4 years by equal payments at the end of each year. Interest is at 4%.

2. Construct a schedule for Problem 1 if interest is at 4%.

3. A $6000 debt, due in 7 years and bearing interest at 6% payable quarterly, will be retired by the sinking fund method. If the fund is invested at $4\frac{1}{2}\%$ converted quarterly, find the total quarterly charge.

4. A sinking fund is set up at 5% converted semiannually to pay the principal of a $7000 debt, due in 6 years and bearing 4% interest payable semiannually. Compute the total semiannual charge.

5. In Problem 3, find book value of debt at end of 4th year.

6. In Problem 4, find book value of debt at end of 5th year.

7. Find the annual payment to discharge a debt of $10,000 by the sinking fund method if the debtor makes equal annual payments for 7 years. The sinking fund is invested at 5%.

8. Find the total annual payment if the debt in Problem 7 bears interest at 7%.

9. Find the book value of the debt in Problem 7 at the end of the 4th payment.

10. Find the amount in a sinking fund set up to retire a debt of $2500 in 5 years at the end of the 3rd year. The fund is invested at $4\frac{1}{2}$%.

11. Find the book value of the debt in Problem 10 after the 3rd year.

12. Set up a sinking fund schedule finishing off the debt in Problem 10 after the third year.

13. To retire $100,000 worth of 20-year, 4% interest-bearing bonds at maturity, the Coast to Coast Airways accumulates a sinking fund at 3% by 20 equal annual payments. Find the total annual charge.

14. Union Hotel obtains a 7-year, $20,000 loan bearing interest at 5% payable annually. To pay the principal, 7 equal annual payments are made to a sinking fund invested at 4%. Find the total annual charge.

15. In Problem 13, find size of sinking fund at end of 6th year.

16. In Problem 14 find size of sinking fund at end of 4th year.

17. The loan of Problem 13 is financed at what effective rate?

18. At what effective rate is the loan of Problem 14 financed?

19. To retire certain bonds, the city of Bondville will need $10,000 a year for 5 years beginning 11 years hence. What equal annual payments for 10 years, the first 1 year hence, to a sinking fund accumulating at 6% will enable the city to retire the bonds as they fall due?

20. Do Problem 19 assuming 15 annual payments instead of 10.

MISCELLANEOUS EXERCISE 85
REVIEW OF CHAPTER 14

1. A sinking fund is being accumulated at 4% by payments of $200 a year. If the fund contains $4541 just after the mth payment, find its size just after the $(m + 1)$th payment. Use no tables.

2. A debt is being amortized at 6% by payments of \$700 a year. If the outstanding principal is \$6321.44 just after the kth payment, what was it just after the $(k-1)$th payment? Use no tables.

3. A debt of \$3595 bearing interest at 6% payable semiannually is to be amortized by equal semiannual payments for 7 years. Find the semiannual payment.

4. In Problem 3 what payment at the end of $3\frac{1}{2}$ years could close the transaction?

5. Construct a schedule for the amortization of a \$1000 debt, with interest at 6%, by equal payments at the end of each year for 3 years.

6. Do Problem 5 with payments at the beginning of each year.

7. If 400 bonds of \$500 denomination, bearing 5% interest payable annually, are to be retired by 10 annual payments as nearly equal as possible, how many should be retired at the end of the 2nd year?

8. A mine bought for \$50,000 will be exhausted in 15 years. What net annual income for 15 years will pay $5\frac{1}{2}\%$ effective on the investment?

9. A payment of \$1807.95 now will cancel a certain 5-year-old debt at 3% which was being amortized by annual payments of \$255. If the payments began 4 years ago, find the debt.

10. A debt of \$12,500 at $4\frac{1}{2}\%$ is to be retired by a payment of \$3000 at the end of 3 years and 17 equal annual payments after that. Find the annual payment.

11. A firm sets up a sinking fund at 4% converted monthly to pay the principal of a $2\frac{1}{2}$-year, \$10,000 loan bearing 6% interest payable monthly. (a) Find the total monthly charge. (b) What would the firm save per month if allowed to *amortize* the loan in 30 monthly installments?

12. Find book value of loan in Problem 11 at end of 7 months.

13. A debt of \$9875 at $5\frac{1}{2}\%$ is to be canceled by a payment of x dollars at the end of 6 years and 12 equal annual payments of \$1250 after that. Find x.

14. Consider a debt of \$12,500 with interest at 6% payable monthly, being amortized by monthly payments of \$150. Find the number of equal payments and the last payment.

15. In Problem 14 what principal is outstanding just after the 54th payment.

16. A certain debt at 6% payable monthly is to be amortized by monthly payments of $250. Thirteen years hence the transaction can be settled by a payment of $12,595.55. Find the debt.

17. A $3000 sinking fund is accumulated at $3\frac{1}{2}$% by 11 annual deposits of $200 each and what smaller deposit at the end of 12 years?

18. In Problem 17 find size of sinking fund at end of 5th year.

19. Construct a schedule for accumulating $4000 in a sinking fund in 5 years by equal payments at the end of each year. Interest is at 5%.

20. To repay a $7000 loan, which plan costs less to the borrower and by how much a year: (a) To amortize the loan at $5\frac{1}{2}$% in 8 equal annual installments, or (b) to pay 5% interest yearly and to accumulate a sinking fund at 3% by 8 equal annual payments to pay the principal?

21. Under plan (b) of Problem 20, interest at what effective rate is paid by the borrower for the privilege of the loan?

22. In Problem 20 (b), find book value of the loan at end of 6th year.

23. A sinking fund, to contain $5000 15 years hence, is accumulated at $4\frac{1}{2}$% converted semiannually by 20 semiannual payments of $100 each, followed by 10 semiannual payments of $x each. Compute x.

24. A debt of $11,550, due 11 years hence, is to be discharged by making annual payments of x dollars in a fund paying $6\frac{1}{2}$%. Find x.

25. The total annual charge of a debt, due 5 years hence, bearing interest at 11% payable annually, to be canceled by the sinking fund method, is $146.40. Find the debt and the payments to the sinking fund, if the fund pays $4\frac{1}{2}$% effective.

26. $300 is deposited annually in a sinking fund invested at 4% for 3 years and at 5% after that. Find size of fund at end of 10 years.

27. Consider 8 annual payments of $500 each, the first due in 3 years, and a $1000 payment due in 11 years. At the time of 4th payment, how much additional will close the transaction? Money is worth 4%.

28. Commute the 9 payments in Problem 27 to a lump sum due now.

To amortize a debt A, with interest at the rate i per period, let R be the periodic payment. Denote by P the outstanding principal just after the kth payment. Prove the equations in Problems 29–32.

29. $P = A(1 + i)^k - Rs_{\overline{k}|i}$.

30. $A - P = (R - Ai)s_{\overline{k}|i}$.

31. $A - P = (R - Pi)a_{\overline{k}|i}$.

32. $R - Pi = (R - Ai)(1 + i)^k$.

33. A sinking fund is set up at the rate i per period to retire a debt D due in n periods and bearing interest at the rate r per period. If C is the total periodic charge, show that $C = D\left(r - i + \dfrac{1}{a_{\overline{n}|i}}\right)$.

34. Verify the schedule below for the accumulation of a sinking fund, at the rate i per period, by n periodic payments of R each.

At End of Period	Periodic Payment	Interest Earned	Sinking Fund Increased by	Sinking Fund Contains
1	R		R	$R \cdot s_{\overline{1}|i}$
2	R	$R[(1 + i) - 1]$	$R(1 + i)$	$R \cdot s_{\overline{2}|i}$
3	R	$R[(1 + i)^2 - 1]$	$R(1 + i)^2$	$R \cdot s_{\overline{3}|i}$
...	...	...	...	...
n	R	$R[(1 + i)^{n-1} - 1]$	$R(1 + i)^{n-1}$	$R \cdot s_{\overline{n}|i}$
Totals	nR	$R(s_{\overline{n}|i} - n)$	$R \cdot s_{\overline{n}|i}$	$\dfrac{R}{i}[s_{\overline{n+1}|i} - (n + 1)]$

35. Verify the schedule below for amortizing a debt, with interest at the rate i per period, by n periodic payments of R each.

Period	Outstanding Principal at Beginning of Period	Interest Due at End of Period	Periodic Payment at End of Period	At End of Period Principal Reduced by
1	$R \cdot a_{\overline{n}|i}$	$R(1 - v^n)$	R	$R \cdot v^n$
2	$R \cdot a_{\overline{n-1}|i}$	$R(1 - v^{n-1})$	R	$R \cdot v^{n-1}$
3	$R \cdot a_{\overline{n-2}|i}$	$R(1 - v^{n-2})$	R	$R \cdot v^{n-2}$
...	...	...	...	...
n	$R \cdot a_{\overline{n}|i}$	$R(1 - v)$	R	$R \cdot v$
Totals	$\dfrac{R}{i}(n - a_{\overline{n}|i})$	$R(n - a_{\overline{n}|i})$	nR	$R \cdot a_{\overline{n}|i}$

Chapter FIFTEEN

VALUATION OF BONDS

140. Terminology

A **bond** is a written promise to pay (1) a specified sum, called the **redemption price,** at a fixed or determinable future date, and (2) equal **dividends,** at a specified rate, at equal intervals until the **redemption date.**

The dividend is periodic interest, always computed on the **face value** (or **par value**) of the bond at the rate specified in it. The par value is sometimes called the **denomination** of the bond. When the redemption price is repaid to the bondholder, the bond is surrendered to the issuing concern, and it is said to be **redeemed.** The redemption price is usually equal to the face value, in which case the bond is **redeemable at par.** Sometimes the redemption price is higher than the face value, to make the bond more attractive to investors; in this case, the bond is said to be **redeemable above par.**

Dates at which dividends are payable are called **dividend dates,** indicated by the initial letters of the months. Thus, M-S means that dividends are payable semiannually on March 1 and September 1. A given issue of bonds is usually designated by naming the issuing concern, the dividend rate, the redemption date, and the dividend dates. Thus, "Ala. Power $4\frac{1}{2}$s of '69, J-D" refers to bonds issued by the Alabama Power Company, redeemable in 1969, and bearing $4\frac{1}{2}\%$ dividends payable semiannually on June 1 and December 1.

141. Classification of bonds

The following classification, although far from being complete, may be of some interest to students not acquainted with this phase of the subject.

(a) *Classification as to Underlying Security*

A concern issuing bonds assumes the obligation of paying dividends periodically and the redemption price at maturity. As a protection to the bondholders, this obligation may be secured: (1) by the guarantee of a third party, as in the case of **guaranteed bonds;** (2) by collateral placed in the hands of a trustee, as in the case of **collateral trust bonds;** or, (3) by hypothecated property, the deed of trust being held by a trustee, as in the case of **mortgage**

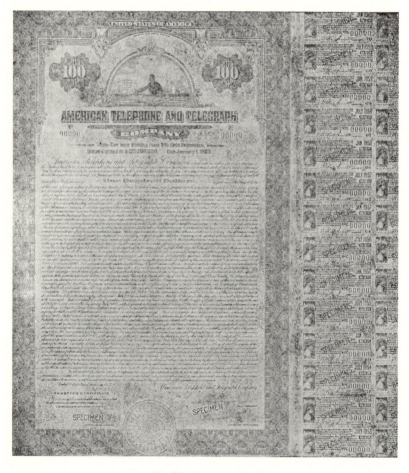

Fig. 23. A coupon bond.

bonds. An unsecured bond, pledged solely by the borrower's credit, is called a **debenture bond.**

(b) *Classification as to Method of Paying Dividends and Record of Ownership*

(1) A **coupon bond** has a detachable portion, called a coupon, for each dividend payment. On each dividend date, the bondholder detaches the proper coupon and presents it to a bank for collection. Coupon bonds may be transferred from one person to another without indorsement. Figure 23 shows an illustration of such a bond. (2) A bond is said to be **registered** if the holder's name is indorsed on the bond and recorded on the books of the issuing concern. A registered bond may be transferred to another person only with the holder's indorsement and through an official change in the records of the issuing concern. The redemption price is payable to the registered owner. A registered bond may be **fully registered,** in which case the dividends are paid by check to the holder; or, it may be **registered as to principal only,** in which case the dividends are paid as for coupon bonds.

(c) *Classification as to Payment of Redemption Price*

(1) The redemption price may be payable only at a specified redemption date. (2) The issuing concern may have the privilege of calling the bonds for payment before maturity, or the bondholder may have the privilege of presenting them for payment before maturity. (3) Bonds may be redeemable in series, or the face value and dividends may be payable in equal installments; these two forms will be discussed later. (4) There may be no redemption at all, the dividends forming a perpetuity; the British *consols* and the French *rentes* are examples.

142. Yield rate and purchase price

Bonds are bought in the open market at a price usually different from the redemption price or par value. This is due to the fact that the purchaser expects to realize an income from his investment at a rate, called the **yield rate,** which is usually either higher or lower than the dividend rate.

The purchaser of a bond pays the present value of the redemption price and that of all future dividends up to redemption date. The purchase price is thus the sum of (1) the present value of a single sum of money due in the future, and (2) the present value of the annuity formed by the periodic dividends, both computed *at the rate the purchaser expects to realize on his investment*, that is, *at the yield rate*, which is independent of the dividend rate.

143. Formula for purchase price

The following notation will be used in this chapter:

F = the face value.
C = the redemption price.
i = the yield rate per period.
n = the number of periods before redemption.
R = the periodic dividend payment.
V = the purchase price.

The redemption price C is a single sum due in n periods; its present value is therefore $C(1 + i)^{-n}$. The dividend payments of R at the end of each period for n periods form an ordinary annuity whose present value is $R \cdot a_{\overline{n}|i}$. Hence

$$V = C(1 + i)^{-n} + R \cdot a_{\overline{n}|i}. \tag{16}$$

In deriving formula (16) and, unless otherwise stated, in all problems and further discussions on bond valuation, we assume that (1) a bond is bought on a dividend date; (2) the purchaser holds the bond until maturity and receives the full redemption price at that time; (3) he receives each dividend in full as it falls due, beginning one period after purchase date until redemption date; (4) the conversion period of the yield rate coincides with the dividend period. With these assumptions, the purchase price may be seen from formula (16) to depend only upon redemption price, yield rate, number of periods before redemption, and size of periodic dividend.

―――――

ILLUSTRATIVE EXAMPLE 1. Find the purchase price of a \$500, 5% bond, dividends payable semiannually, redeemable 23 years hence at 108, if the yield rate is to be 6% compounded semiannually.

SOLUTION, "Redeemable at 108" means that the redemption price is 108% of the face value. Hence $C = 500 \times 1.08 = \$540$. "5% dividends, payable semiannually" means that the dividend payable at the end of each 6 months is $2\frac{1}{2}$% of the *face value*. Hence $R = 500 \times 0.025 = \$12.50$. Substituting $C = 540$, $R = 12.50$, $i = 0.03$, and $n = 46$ in formula (16),

$$V = 540(1.03)^{-46} + 12.50 \times a_{\overline{46}|\cdot 03}$$
$$= (540 \times 0.25674) + (12.50 \times 24.7754)$$
$$= \$138.64 + \$309.69 = \$448.33. \quad Ans.$$

Note. The present value (*at the yield rate*) of the redemption price is $138.64, while the present value (*at the yield rate*) of all future dividends is $309.69, the purchase price being the sum of these two present values.

ILLUSTRATIVE EXAMPLE 2. Find the purchase price of a $1000, 6% bond, dividends payable annually, redeemable at par 12 years hence, if the purchaser wishes a yield rate of $4\frac{1}{2}\%$.

SOLUTION. Here $C = 1000$, $R = 60$, $i = 0.045$, and $n = 12$. By (16),

$$V = 1000(1.045)^{-12} + 60 \times a_{\overline{12}|.045}$$
$$= \$589.66 + \$547.12 = \$1136.78. \quad Ans.$$

EXERCISE 86

In each of Problems 1–10, find the purchase price of the given bond.

Prob.	Face Value	Redeemable	Dividends at	Yield Rate	Converted
1.	$1000	at par in 30 yrs.	5%, Annually	$4\frac{1}{2}\%$	Annually
2.	100	at 105 in 25 yrs.	6%, Semiann.	4%	Semiann.
3.	500	at 102 in 13 yrs.	4%, Quarterly	3%	Quarterly
4.	1000	at par in 6 yrs.	$3\frac{1}{2}\%$, Annually	$4\frac{1}{2}\%$	Annually
5.	500	at 104 in 5 yrs.	6%, Semiann.	$3\frac{1}{2}\%$	Semiann.
6.	1000	at par in 20 yrs.	5%, Quarterly	3%	Quarterly
7.	100	at par in 8 yrs.	$2\frac{3}{4}\%$, Annually	$3\frac{1}{2}\%$	Annually
8.	500	at 108 in 15 yrs.	4%, Quarterly	$4\frac{1}{2}\%$	Quarterly
9.	100	at 110 in 40 yrs.	5%, Semiann.	3%	Semiann.
10.	100	at par in 9 yrs.	4%, Semiann.	5%	Semiann.

11. A $100 bond, redeemable at par by the American Telephone and Telegraph Co. on Jan. 1, 1970 has attached coupons which can be cashed for $2.50 on Jan. 1 and July 1 of each year. What purchase price on July 1, 1961, would yield 3% converted semiannually?

12. Do Problem 11 using a yield rate 4% converted semiannually.

13. A $500, 3% bond with annual dividends, redeemable in 12 years, is bought for $570.81 to yield 4%. What is the redemption price?

14. Find the redemption price of a $1000 bond with annual dividends at 3%, redeemable in 18 years, bought for $862.88 to yield $4\frac{1}{2}$%.

15. Compute the quarterly dividend of a $1000 bond, redeemable at 102 in 20 years, bought for $803.19 to yield 4% converted quarterly.

16. A $100 bond maturing at par in 20 years is bought for $115 to yield 3% converted quarterly. How large is the quarterly dividend?

17. Show from formula (16) that $V - C = (R - Ci)a_{\overline{n}|i}$.

18. As in Problem 17, show that $R - Vi = (R - Ci)(1 + i)^{-n}$.

19. A $100, 6% bond with semiannual dividends, redeemable at 105, is bought for $122.57 to yield 4% converted semiannually. Using the formula in Problem 17, find the number of years before redemption.

20. Employ the formula in Problem 18 to work Problem 19.

144. Premium and discount

Unless otherwise stated, it will be understood hereafter that *bonds are redeemable at par.* This assumption simplifies the work somewhat and covers a large number of cases on bond valuation in actual practice.

Consider the following three cases: (1) If the dividend rate is *greater* than the yield rate, the purchase price is *greater* than the face value, and the bond is said to be bought **at a premium,** *the premium being the difference between the purchase price and face value.* (2) If the dividend rate is *less* than the yield rate, the purchase price is *less* than the face value, and the bond is said to be bought **at a discount,** *the discount being the difference between the face value and purchase price.* (3) If the dividend rate is *equal* to the yield rate, the purchase price is *equal* to the face value, and the bond is bought **at par.**

145. Finding the premium or discount

Whether a bond is redeemable at par or above par, formula (16) gives the purchase price, from which the premium or discount may be found.

However, in the case of a bond *redeemable at par*, the premium or discount may be computed more readily. Let F be the face value of such a bond. Then $C = F$ and formula (16) becomes

$$V = F(1 + i)^{-n} + R \cdot a_{\overline{n}|i}.$$

Case (1) *Dividend Rate Greater than Yield Rate; Formula for Premium*

Let P = premium. By definition, $P = V - F$. Substituting in this the expression for V given above,

$$P = F(1 + i)^{-n} + R \cdot a_{\overline{n}|i} - F$$
$$= R \cdot a_{\overline{n}|i} - F + F(1 + i)^{-n}.$$

Factoring the last two terms,

$$P = R \cdot a_{\overline{n}|i} - F[1 - (1 + i)^{-n}].$$

Multiplying and dividing the last term by i,

$$P = R \cdot a_{\overline{n}|i} - Fi \cdot \frac{1 - (1 + i)^n}{i}.$$

But the fraction in the last term is the expression for $a_{\overline{n}|i}$. Hence

$$P = (R - Fi)a_{\overline{n}|i}. \tag{17}$$

Case (2) *Dividend Rate Less than Yield Rate; Formula for Discount*

Let D = discount. By definition, $D = F - V$. It is left as an exercise for the student to show that the formula for discount is given by

$$D = (Fi - R)a_{\overline{n}|i}. \tag{18}$$

ILLUSTRATIVE EXAMPLE 1. A $10,000, 5% bond, dividends payable semiannually, redeemable 17 years hence, is bought to yield 4% converted semiannually. Find the premium.

SOLUTION. Here $i = 0.02$, $n = 34$, $R = 10{,}000 \times 0.025 = 250$, and $Fi = 10{,}000 \times 0.02 = 200$. By formula (17),

$$P = (R - Fi)a_{\overline{n}|i} = (250 - 200)a_{\overline{34}|.02}$$
$$= 50 \times 24.4986 = \$1224.93. \quad Ans.$$

Hence the premium is $1224.93, which means that the purchase price $(V = F + P)$ is $10,000 + $1224.93 = $11,224.93.

ILLUSTRATIVE EXAMPLE 2. A $1000, 7% bond, dividends payable quarterly, redeemable 22 years hence, is bought to yield 8% convertible quarterly. Find the discount.

SOLUTION. Here $i = 0.02$, $n = 88$, $R = 1000 \times 0.0175 = 17.50$, and $Fi = 1000 \times 0.02 = 20$. By formula (18),

$$D = (Fi - R)a_{\overline{n}|i} = (20 - 17.50)a_{\overline{88}|.02}$$
$$= 2.50 \times 41.247 = \$103.12. \quad Ans.$$

Hence the discount is $103.12, which means that the purchase price $(V = F - D)$ is $1000 - $103.12 = $896.88.

---

146. Amortization of premium

When the dividend rate is greater than the yield rate, the bond is bought at a premium, that is, at a price greater than the face value. In this case, the bond may be thought of as having a periodically decreasing **book value,** approaching par at maturity. Since the periodic dividend is greater than the income expected for the period, the excess is applied periodically to the reduction of the book value from purchase price to face value, and hence to the reduction of the premium from its original size to zero. The student will understand the full significance of this process, called **amortization of premium,** in an accounting course. Here we shall merely illustrate the process itself.

Consider a $1000, 7% bond, dividends payable semiannually, redeemable 4 years hence, bought to yield 5% converted semiannually. By formula (17), the premium is found to be $71.70; hence the purchase price, which is the book value of the bond on the purchase date, is $1071.70. At the end of each period, a dividend of $35 is due; but the investor expects to realize only $2\frac{1}{2}\%$ of $1071.70, or $26.79, per period. The excess of $8.21 at the end of each period may be thought of as being set aside at once into an "amortization fund" accumulating at the yield rate ($2\frac{1}{2}\%$ per period). Thus, at the end of the first period, the amortization fund contains $8.21, and the book value of the bond is reduced to $1071.70 - $8.21 = $1063.49. At the end of the 2nd period, the fund is increased by $8.21 plus the interest on what it contained at the end of the preceding period; this interest is $8.21 \times 0.025 = $0.21. Hence the total addition to the fund at the end of the 2nd period is $8.42, and the book value of the bond is reduced to $1063.49 − $8.42 = $1055.07. Continuing the process for the remaining 6 periods, the book value of the bond should be reduced to $1000.

SCHEDULE FOR AMORTIZATION OF BOND PREMIUM

At End of Period	Amortization Payment	$2\frac{1}{2}\%$ Interest on Amort. Fund	Increase in Amort. Fund	Size of Amort. Fund	Book Value of Bond
0					$1071.70
1	$ 8.21		$ 8.21	$ 8.21	1063.49
2	8.21	$0.21	8.42	16.63	1055.07
3	8.21	0.42	8.63	25.26	1046.44
4	8.21	0.63	8.84	34.10	1037.60
5	8.21	0.85	9.06	43.16	1028.54
6	8.21	1.08	9.29	52.45	1019.25
7	8.21	1.31	9.52	61.97	1009.73
8	8.21	1.55	9.76	71.73	999.97
Totals	$65.68	$6.05	$71.73		

147. Accumulation of discount

When the dividend rate is less than the yield rate, the bond is bought at a discount and may be thought of as having a periodically increasing *book value*, approaching par at maturity. Since the periodic dividend is less than the income expected for the period, the deficit is applied periodically to raising the book value of the bond from purchase price to face value. This process, known as **accumulation of discount,** is illustrated on page 312.

Consider a $10,000, 5% bond, dividends payable semiannually, redeemable 5 years hence, bought to yield 6% convertible semiannually. By formula (18), the discount is $426.51; hence the purchase price is $9573.49. At the end of each period, a dividend of $250 is due; but the investor expects to realize 3% of $9573.49, or $287.20, per period. The deficit of $37.20 at the end of each period may be thought of as being borrowed at the yield rate (3% per period), the amounts borrowed and interest thereon building up a fictitious "accumulation fund." Thus, at the end of the first period, the fund contains $37.20 and the book value of the bond is raised to $9573.49 + $37.20 = $9610.69. At the end of the 2nd period, the fund is increased by $37.20 plus the interest on what is contained at the end of the preceding period; this interest is 37.20 × 0.03 = $1.12. Hence the total addition to the fund for the 2nd period is $38.32, and the book value is raised to $9610.69 + $38.32 = $9649.01. Continuing the process for the remaining 8 periods, the book value should be raised to $10,000. The work is arranged in tabular form in the following.

SCHEDULE FOR ACCUMULATION OF BOND DISCOUNT

At End of Period	Accumulation Payment	3% Interest on Accum. Fund	Increase in Accum. Fund	Size of Accum. Fund	Book Value of Bond
0					$9573.49
1	$ 37.20		$ 37.20	$ 37.20	9610.69
2	37.20	$ 1.12	38.32	75.52	9649.01
3	37.20	2.27	39.47	114.99	9688.48
4	37.20	3.45	40.65	155.64	9729.13
5	37.20	4.67	41.87	197.51	9771.00
6	37.20	5.93	43.13	240.64	9814.13
7	37.20	7.22	44.42	285.06	9858.55
8	37.20	8.55	45.75	330.81	9904.30
9	37.20	9.92	47.12	377.93	9951.42
10	37.20	11.34	48.54	426.47	9999.96
Totals	$372.00	$54.47	$426.47		

Note. The book value of a bond on any given dividend date is the purchase price of the bond if bought on that date just after the dividend is paid. This is a convenient check on *book value* entries in either schedule as one proceeds in the construction. The last entry in the last column of either schedule should equal the face value of the bond. A slight discrepancy may arise from writing results to two decimal places.

EXERCISE 87

Find the purchase price of each bond by use of formula (17) or (18).

Prob.	Face Value	Redeemable in	Dividends at	Yield Rate	Converted
1.	$1000	4 years	5%, Annually	5%	Annually
2.	500	4 years	5%, Annually	3%	Annually
3.	500	$3\frac{1}{2}$ years	5%, Semiann.	4%	Semiann.
4.	1000	$3\frac{1}{2}$ years	3%, Semiann.	4%	Semiann.
5.	500	10 years	$4\frac{1}{2}$%, Quarterly	4%	Quarterly
6.	100	12 years	$3\frac{1}{2}$%, Semiann.	$4\frac{1}{2}$%	Semiann.
7.	1000	35 years	3% Semiann.	$3\frac{1}{2}$%	Semiann.
8.	500	38 years	4%, Semiann.	2%	Semiann.
9.	1000	26 years	$3\frac{1}{2}$%, Annually	$4\frac{1}{2}$%	Annually
10.	1000	21 years	5%, Quarterly	3%	Quarterly

11. Prepare a schedule for accumulation of discount in Problem 1.

12. Construct a schedule for amortization of premium in Problem 2.

13. Construct a schedule for amortization of premium in Problem 3.

14. Prepare a schedule for accumulation of discount in Problem 4.

15. What is the purchase price for a $1500, 7% bond, dividends payable semiannually, redeemable 10 years hence, bought to yield 5% converted semiannually?

16. In Problem 15, construct a schedule for amortization of the bond premium. What is the premium?

17. A $1000, 5% Southern Railway Co. bond pays dividends on Jan. 1 and July 1 and is redeemable on July 1, 2013. What purchase price on July 1, 1969, would yield an investor 3% converted semiannually?

18. To realize $3\frac{1}{2}$% converted semiannually, what should a man pay on Dec. 1, 1968, for a $1000, $2\frac{1}{2}$%, Socony-Vacuum Oil Co. bond with dividend dates June 1 and Dec. 1 and maturing on June 1, 1992?

19. Compute the semiannual dividend of a $1000 Detroit Edison Co. bond if, 20 years before redemption, it is advertised to yield 4% converted semiannually at a price of $892.77.

20. A $1000, $3\frac{1}{2}$%, Jacksonville Terminal Co. bond with semiannual dividends is bought for $1200.50 to yield $2\frac{1}{2}$% converted semiannually. Determine the number of years before redemption.

21. A contract calls for 15 annual payments of $500 each, the first due Nov. 1, 1970, and an additional $10,000 payment on Nov. 1, 1984. At 3% effective, find the value of the contract as of Nov. 1, 1969.

22. A $5000 promissory note, with interest at 4% payable quarterly, matures Apr. 30, 1975. The holder wishes to sell it on Jan. 31, 1970, just after collecting the interest due at that time. What should an investor pay for it to realize 6% converted quarterly?

23. A $7000, $5\frac{1}{2}$% bond, dividends payable quarterly, redeemable 15 years hence, is bought to yield 6% converted quarterly. Find the purchase price and discount.

24. A $100,000, 6% bond, dividends payable annually, redeemable 25 years hence, is bought to yield 3% annually. Find the purchase price and premium.

25. A man wants a 10% yield, converted semiannually, on any short-term investment he makes. What price should he pay for a $25,000, $5\frac{1}{2}$% bond, dividends payable semiannually, redeemable 5 years hence?

26. Show that $R = P \cdot \dfrac{1}{a_{\overline{n}|i}} + Fi$ and $R = Fi - D \cdot \dfrac{1}{a_{\overline{n}|i}}$.

27. Show that $V = (F + Rs_{\overline{n}|i})(1 + i)^{-n}$ if $C = F$ in formula (16).

28. Derive (17) from the formula in Problem 17, page 308, if $C = F$.

29. What is the annual dividend of a \$5000 public works bond, if 17 years before redemption, it sold for \$6555.52. It was advertised to yield 6%.

30. A certain \$10,000 government bond, redeemable 25 years hence, sells for \$8750. What is the semiannual dividend, if the bond is to yield 5% converted semiannually?

31. Find the face value of a bond paying semiannual dividends of \$255, redeemable 12 years hence, bought to yield interest at 5% converted semiannually. The discount was \$1195.

32. Find the face value of a bond, paying quarterly dividends of \$100, redeemable 20 years hence, bought at a premium of \$1300 to yield 4% converted quarterly.

148. Annuity bonds

An **annuity bond** is a promise to pay an interest-bearing debt, principal and interest at the rate mentioned in the bond, in equal periodic installments.

———

ILLUSTRATIVE EXAMPLE. A 10-year annuity bond for \$10,000, with interest at 6% payable semiannually, is to be paid in 20 equal semiannual installments. Find the purchase price at the end of the 7th year, if the bond is bought to yield 5% convertible semiannually.

SOLUTION. Here we have an interest-bearing debt to be discharged by 20 equal semiannual installments. The periodic installment is

$$10,000 \times \frac{1}{a_{\overline{20}|.03}} = 10,000 \times 0.0672157 = \$672.16.$$

Now, since the bond is sold at the end of the 14th period, the purchaser must pay only for the right of receiving the remaining 6 payments, the first being due one period hence. In other words, the purchase price is the present value of an ordinary annuity which pays \$672.16 at the end of each semiannual period for 6 periods, *provided* this present value is determined at the *yield rate* ($i = 0.025$). Hence

$$V = 672.16 \times a_{\overline{6}|.025} = 672.16 \times 5.50813 = \$3702.34. \quad Ans.$$

149. Serial bonds

Sometimes a given set of bonds is issued with a provision for redemption at various dates, instead of a single redemption date for the entire issue. Bonds so redeemable are called **serial bonds.**

ILLUSTRATIVE EXAMPLE. A \$30,000 issue of 6% bonds, dividends payable semiannually, is to be redeemed by payments of \$10,000 at the end of each year for 3 years. Find the purchase price of the issue, if bought to yield 5% converted semiannually.

SOLUTION. This serial bond is equivalent to *three different bonds.* For each bond, $F = 10,000$, $R = 10,000 \times 0.03 = 300$, and $Fi = 10,000 \times 0.025 = 250$. The three bonds are redeemable 2, 4, and 6 periods hence, respectively. By formula (17), we may calculate the premium on each separately, and then add these to get the total premium. Thus,

$$P_1 = (300 - 250)a_{\overline{2}|.025} = 50 \times 1.9274 = \$\ 96.37$$
$$P_2 = (300 - 250)a_{\overline{4}|.025} = 50 \times 3.7620 = 188.10$$
$$P_3 = (300 - 250)a_{\overline{6}|.025} = 50 \times 5.5081 = \underline{275.41}$$
$$\text{Total premium} = P = \$559.88$$

Hence the purchase price for the issue is \$30,000 + \$559.88 = \$30,559.88.

EXERCISE 88

1. Find the purchase price of a \$1000, 16-year annuity bond, with 4% interest payable annually, bought at the end of 6 years to yield $2\frac{1}{2}$%.

2. Solve Problem 1 if the bond is bought at the end of 12 years.

3. A \$1000, 10-year annuity bond, with $2\frac{1}{2}$% interest payable semiannually, is being paid in 20 equal semiannual installments. What price at the end of 2 years will yield an investor 4% converted semiannually?

4. Do Problem 3 if the investor buys the bond at the end of $6\frac{1}{2}$ years.

5. A contract calls for the amortization of a $10,000 loan with 5% interest payable monthly, in 96 equal monthly installments. Just after receiving the 20th payment, the creditor sells the contract to yield a financier 4% converted monthly. What should the latter pay?

6. Do Problem 5 assuming sale of contract just after 9th payment.

7. Three $1000, 4%, municipal bonds with dividends payable March 1 and Sept. 1 are due serially on March 1, 1984–1986. Find the total price on Sept. 1, 1969, to yield 3% converted semiannually.

8. Four $3000, $2\frac{1}{2}$%, railroad bonds with dividend dates Jan. 1 and July 1 will mature serially on July 1, 1978–1981. What total price on Jan. 1, 1969, will yield $4\frac{1}{2}$% converted semiannually?

9. Solve Problem 8 with July 1, 1970, as date of purchase.

10. Work Problem 7 with March 1, 1970, as date of purchase.

11. On Oct. 1, 1969, A borrows $16,000 from B agreeing to pay on each Oct. 1, 1975–1977, $2000 of the principal plus 3% interest on unpaid balances. How much should C pay to B on Oct. 1, 1973, for the privilege of receiving all future payments if C is to realize 5%?

12. Do Problem 11 after interchanging the two rates.

13. Find the premium of a $500, 5% bond, dividends payable semiannually, redeemable 12 years hence, bought to yield $3\frac{1}{2}$% converted semiannually.

14. Find the purchase price in Problem 13.

15. Find the discount of a $10,000, $4\frac{1}{2}$% bond, dividends payable quarterly, redeemable in 20 years, bought to yield $5\frac{1}{2}$% converted quarterly.

16. Find the purchase price of the bond in Problem 15.

17. What is the purchase price at the end of the 24th payment of a $500 bond, with interest at 6% quarterly, redeemable in 10 years, and bought to yield 5% converted quarterly?

18. What is the purchase price of a series of four $500 bonds, with dividends payable annually, at $5\frac{1}{2}$%, redeemable 4 years hence, and bought to yield 4%?

150. Bonds purchased between dividend dates

So far we have confined our attention to the price of a bond purchased on a dividend date. However, bonds are most frequently bought between dividend dates. Several methods are available for finding the price of a bond purchased between dividend dates. We shall consider only the one used most commonly in actual practice. Take the following three steps:

I. Find the purchase price on the immediately preceding dividend date.

II. Find the ordinary simple interest (see Art. 30) on that price, *at the yield rate*, from the immediately preceding dividend date to the purchase date.

III. Add the results found in steps I and II.

ILLUSTRATIVE EXAMPLE. A $1000, 6% bond, dividends payable J-J, is redeemable on Jan. 1, 1978. It is bought on March 12, 1969, to yield 5% converted semiannually. Find the purchase price.

SOLUTION. I. The purchase price on Jan. 1, 1969, would be

$$V = F + P = 1000 + (30 - 25)a_{\overline{18}|.025}$$
$$= 1000 + (5 \times 14.353) = \$1071.77.$$

II. From Jan. 1, 1969, to March 12, 1969, is 70 days. The ordinary simple interest at 5% for 70 days on $1071.77 is

$$1071.77 \times \frac{70}{360} \times 0.05 = \$10.42.$$

III. The purchase price on March 12, 1969, is
$$\$1071.77 + \$10.42 = \$1082.19. \quad \textit{Ans.}$$

---

151. Conventional practices and terminology

In financial circles, the price actually to be paid for a bond is called the **flat price.** On a dividend date, the flat price is quoted. On other days, the price quoted in daily papers and elsewhere is not the flat price but a price presently to be defined, called the "and interest" price. We shall agree that the **accrued dividend** of a bond bought between dividend dates is the ordinary simple interest on the *face value* of the bond, *at the dividend rate*, from the immediately preceding dividend date to the purchase date. Then the **"and interest" price** is the flat price minus the accrued dividend.

ILLUSTRATIVE EXAMPLE 1. On March 12, 1969, at what "and interest" price should a bond house quote the bond of the foregoing illustrative example, if the yield is to be 5% converted semiannually?

SOLUTION. By definition, the accrued dividend on March 12, 1969, is

$$1000 \times \frac{70}{360} \times 0.06 = \$11.67.$$

As computed previously, the flat price on March 12, 1951, is $1082.19. Hence the "and interest" price on that day is

$$\$1082.19 - \$11.67 = \$1070.52. \quad Ans.$$

Note. The price actually to be paid for the bond is the flat price, that is, the quoted "and interest" price plus the accrued dividend. Thus on March 12, 1969, the purchaser will pay $1070.52 + $11.67 = $1082.19.

Dealers in bonds often arrive at the "and interest" price by a more direct method based upon interpolation, as shown in the next example.

ILLUSTRATIVE EXAMPLE 2. Solve the preceding example by interpolation.

SOLUTION. On Jan. 1, 1969 $V = 1000 + (30 - 25)a_{\overline{18}|.025} = \$1071.77.$

On July 1, 1969, $V = 1000 + (30 - 25)a_{\overline{17}|.025} = \$1068.56.$

In a period of 6 months, the value of V decreases by $3.21. Let x denote the corresponding decrease for 70 days. Then, $3.21 : 180 = x : 70$. Solving this proportion for x, we have $x = 1.25$. The corresponding value of V on March 12, 1969, is $1071.77 - $1.25 = $1070.52, which is the desired "and interest" price. Note that, when the "and interest" price is known, the flat price may be found by adding the accrued dividend.

EXERCISE 89

In each of Problems 1–12, find the flat price of the given bond.

Prob.	Face Value	Redemption Date	Purchase Date	Dividends	Nominal Yield Rate
1.	$ 500	Mar. 1, 1977	Sept. 19, 1969	5%, M-S	3%
2.	1000	Dec. 1, 1983	Dec. 31, 1970	3%, J-D	5%
3.	100	Jan. 1, 1994	Feb. 6, 1969	$2\frac{1}{2}\%$, J-J	$3\frac{1}{2}\%$
4.	100	Aug. 1, 2001	Dec. 14, 1969	4%, F-A	3%
5.	100	Apr. 1, 2010	May 31, 1970	3%, A-O	4%
6.	500	Nov. 1, 1979	June 10, 1969	$4\frac{1}{2}\%$, M-N	$2\frac{1}{2}\%$
7.	500	Feb. 1, 1987	Nov. 29, 1971	3%, F-A	2%
8.	1000	Sept. 1, 2012	Oct. 25, 1970	$3\frac{1}{2}\%$, M-S	$2\frac{1}{2}\%$
9.	200	May 1, 2006	Jan. 20, 1969	$4\frac{1}{2}\%$, M-N	$2\frac{1}{2}\%$
10.	500	July 1, 1992	Apr. 1, 1971	3%, J-J	4%
11.	500	June 1, 1985	July 16, 1970	4%, J-D	5%
12.	100	Oct. 1, 1981	Dec. 12, 1969	$2\frac{1}{2}\%$, A-O	$4\frac{1}{2}\%$

13. From the answer to Problem 3 find the "and interest" price.

14. From the answer to Problem 4 find the "and interest" price.

15. Suppose that the bond in Problem 1 is quoted on May 12, 1970, at the "and interest" price $561.09. A purchaser actually pays what?

16. If the bond in Problem 2 is quoted on Aug. 20, 1971, at an "and interest" price of $818.15, what does a purchaser actually pay?

17. A $12,000, 10% bond, dividends payable J-J, is redeemable on January 1, 1991. Find the purchase price, if the bond is to be bought on February 22, 1970, to yield $4\frac{1}{2}\%$ converted semiannually.

18. A $1250, $5\frac{1}{2}\%$ bond, dividends payable J-A-J-O, is redeemable on April 1, 1988. Find the purchase price of the bond if bought on June 27, 1969, to yield 6% converted quarterly.

19. A $2000, $3\frac{1}{2}\%$, power company bond, paying dividends J-J, will mature Jan. 1, 1988. By interpolation find what "and interest" price on Aug. 30, 1969, will yield $2\frac{1}{2}\%$ converted semiannually.

20. A $1000, 4%, airlines bond, paying dividends A-O, will mature Oct. 1, 1978. By interpolation find what "and interest" price on Aug. 14, 1970, will yield 5% converted semiannually.

21. From the answer to Problem 19 find the flat price.

22. From the answer to Problem 20 find the flat price.

23. A $7595 promissory note, with interest at 4% payable January 1st each year, matures January 1, 2006. Find the purchase price of the note, if bought on December 25, 1969, to yield $2\frac{1}{2}\%$.

24. On what day in 1970 was a $15,000, 5% bond, dividends payable January 1st each year, redeemable on January 1, 1987, bought, if its purchase price was $13,000.83, to yield $6\frac{1}{2}\%$?

25. The purchase price on February 1, 1970 of a $10,000, 5% bond, dividends payable J-J, redeemable January 1, 1990, is $8889.96. Find the yield rate on the bond, if the purchase price on January 1, 1970 is $8844.26.

26. A $50,000, 6% bond, dividends payable J-J, is redeemable at 110 on July 1, 1994. It is bought on November 3, 1969, to yield $5\frac{1}{2}\%$ converted semiannually. Find the purchase price.

27. What was the "and interest" price for a $1300, 5% bond, dividends payable F-A, redeemable February 1, 1981, if it was bought on April 9, 1969, to yield 4% converted semiannually?

28. In Problem 27, find the flat price of the accrued dividend.

152. Finding the approximate yield rate

Bond houses and other selling agencies often quote the price of a bond without stating the yield rate. It is important to the purchaser to know what yield to expect from his investment. When the purchase price is thus given, the yield rate may be determined approximately by interpolation.

ILLUSTRATIVE EXAMPLE. Find the nominal yield rate, convertible semiannually, of a \$100, 5% bond, dividends payable semiannually, redeemable at par in 10 years, if the quoted price is \$95.27.

SOLUTION. If the bond were sold at par (for \$100), the yield rate would be equal to the dividend rate. But since the quoted price is below par, the yield rate per period must be *greater* than $2\frac{1}{2}\%$ (the dividend rate per period). In Table VI, the next greater rate is $2\frac{3}{4}\%$. As a trial, compute the purchase price at the yield rate of $2\frac{3}{4}\%$ per period.

$$V = F - D = 100 - (2.75 - 2.50)a_{\overline{20}|.0275}$$
$$= 100 - (0.25 \times 15.227) = \$96.19.$$

Evidently the periodic yield is greater than $2\frac{3}{4}\%$. As a second trial, compute the purchase price at 3% per period.

$$V = F - D = 100 - (3 - 2.50)a_{\overline{20}|.03}$$
$$= 100 - (0.50 \times 14.887) = \$92.56.$$

Since the quoted price is \$95.27, the periodic yield must be between $2\frac{3}{4}\%$ and 3%. Arrange the results thus far obtained in tabular form as shown.

V	i
$\begin{bmatrix} 96.19 \\ 95.27 \\ 92.56 \end{bmatrix}$	$\begin{bmatrix} 0.0275 \\ ? \\ 0.03 \end{bmatrix}$

It is seen that for a *decrease* of 3.63 in the value of V, there is an *increase* of 0.0025 in the value of i; then, for a *decrease* of 0.92 in the value of V, what is the corresponding *increase* in the value of i? Denoting this by x,

$$3.63 : 0.0025 = 0.92 : x$$

whence $$x = \frac{0.0025 \times 0.92}{3.63} = 0.00063.$$

Therefore, the desired $i = 0.0275 + 0.00063 = 0.02813 = 2.813\%$, and the nominal yield rate converted semiannually is $2i = 5.63\%$ (approximately).

EXERCISE 90

In each case assume a $100 bond with purchase price and date given in last two columns and find its yield rate converted semiannually.

Prob.	Bond Issued by	Due	Dividends	Price	Date
1.	Pennsylvania R.R.	7/1/84	4%, J-J	$ 92	7/1/50
2.	Shell Union Oil Corp.	4/1/71	2½%, A-O	98½	4/1/50
3.	Ohio Edison Co.	9/1/74	3%, M-S	105	9/1/50
4.	Continental Baking Co.	7/1/65	3%, J-J	103	7/1/50
5.	Union Pacific R.R.	3/1/91	2¾%, M-S	95	9/1/50
6.	Atlantic Coast Line	6/1/64	4½%, J-D	103	6/1/50
7.	Chicago Great Western	1/1/88	4%, J-J	88	7/1/50
8.	Southern Railway	7/1/94	5%, J-J	113	7/1/50
9.	Bethlehem Steel Corp.	1/1/79	5%, J-J	105	7/1/50
10.	Illinois Central R.R.	8/1/66	4¾%, F-A	95	8/1/50
11.	Cleveland Union Term.	4/1/73	5%, A-O	107½	4/1/50
12.	Hudson Coal Co.	6/1/62	5%, J-D	90	6/1/50
13.	Niag. Falls Power Co.	3/1/66	3%, M-S	106	9/1/50
14.	State of Kentucky	7/1/71	2½%, J-J	104	7/1/50
15.	Southern Pacific Co.	5/1/81	4½%, M-N	93	5/1/50
16.	Western Union Tel. Co.	3/1/60	5%, M-S	97	9/1/50
17.	Australia	6/1/67	5%, J-D	97½	6/1/50
18.	U.S. Treasury	9/1/72	2½%, M-S	105	9/1/50
19.	Firestone T. &. R. Co.	5/1/61	3%, M-N	103½	5/1/50
20.	Universal Pictures Co.	3/1/59	3¾%, M-S	93	9/1/50

153. Bond tables

Extensive **bond tables** have been prepared to determine the purchase price of a bond (when the dividend rate, yield rate, and number of years before maturity are known), or to approximate the yield rate (when the other three quantities are known). However, a knowledge of the foregoing methods of bond valuation is useful when no bond tables are available. Furthermore, not every problem in bond valuation is solvable by these tables.

A small portion of a bond table is given on this page for illustrative purposes. The rates found horizontally across the top are nominal dividend rates, payable semiannually. The first column contains nominal yield rates, convertible semiannually. The remaining vertical columns give purchase prices of a $100 bond, redeemable in 10 years.

PURCHASE PRICE—10 YEARS BEFORE REDEMPTION

Nominal Yield Rate	Nominal Dividend Rate, Payable Semiannually						
	$3\frac{1}{2}\%$	4%	$4\frac{1}{2}\%$	5%	$5\frac{1}{2}\%$	6%	7%
3.50%	100.00	104.19	108.38	112.56	116.75	120.94	129.32
3.60	99.17	103.33	107.50	111.67	115.84	120.01	128.34
3.70	98.34	102.49	106.64	110.78	114.93	119.08	127.37
3.80	97.52	101.65	105.78	109.91	114.03	118.16	126.42
3.90	96.71	100.82	104.93	109.04	113.14	117.25	125.47
4.00	95.91	100.00	104.09	108.18	112.26	116.35	124.53
4.10	95.12	99.19	103.25	107.32	111.39	115.46	123.60
4.20	94.33	98.38	102.43	106.48	110.53	114.58	122.67
4.30	93.55	97.58	101.61	105.64	109.67	113.70	121.76
4.40	92.78	96.79	100.80	104.81	108.82	112.83	120.85
5.50	92.02	96.01	100.00	103.99	107.98	111.97	119.95
4.60	91.26	95.23	99.21	103.18	107.15	111.12	119.07
4.70	90.51	94.47	98.42	102.37	106.33	110.28	118.18
4.80	89.77	93.71	97.64	101.57	105.51	109.44	117.31
4.90	89.04	92.95	96.87	100.78	104.70	108.61	116.45
5.00	88.31	92.21	96.10	100.00	103.90	107.79	115.59
5.10	87.59	91.47	95.35	99.22	103.10	106.98	114.74
5.20	86.87	90.73	94.59	98.46	102.32	106.18	113.90
5.30	86.17	90.01	93.85	97.69	101.54	105.38	113.06
5.40	85.47	89.29	93.12	96.94	100.77	104.59	112.24
5.50	84.77	88.58	92.39	96.19	100.00	103.81	111.42
5.60	84.09	87.87	91.66	95.45	99.24	103.03	110.61
5.70	83.41	87.18	90.95	94.72	98.49	102.26	109.81
5.80	82.73	86.49	90.24	93.99	97.75	101.50	109.01
5.90	82.06	85.80	89.54	93.27	97.01	100.75	108.22
6.00	81.40	85.12	88.84	92.56	96.28	100.00	107.44
6.10	80.75	84.45	88.15	91.86	95.56	99.26	106.66

ILLUSTRATIVE EXAMPLE 1. Find the purchase price of a $100, 7% bond, dividends payable semiannually, redeemable in 10 years, bought to yield 5% convertible semiannually.

SOLUTION. The entry in the table, corresponding to 7% dividend rate and 5% yield rate, is 115.59. Hence the purchase price is $115.59.

———————

ILLUSTRATIVE EXAMPLE 2. By interpolation in the bond table, find the nominal yield rate, convertible semiannually, of a $100, 6% bond, dividends payable semiannually, redeemable in 10 years, if bought for $113.40.

SOLUTION. Since the given price is between the two entries 113.70 and 112.83 of the 6% column, the corresponding nominal yield rate must be between 4.30% and 4.40%. From the tabular arrangement below, form

V	$2i$
$\begin{bmatrix} \begin{bmatrix} 113.70 \\ 113.40 \end{bmatrix} \\ 112.83 \end{bmatrix}$	$\begin{bmatrix} \begin{bmatrix} 4.30\% \\ ? \end{bmatrix} \\ 4.40\% \end{bmatrix}$

the proportion $0.87 : 0.10 = 0.30 : x,$

whence $x = \frac{0.03}{0.87} = 0.03.$

Hence $2i = 4.30\% + 0.03\% = 4.33\%$ (approximate nominal yield rate).

———————

ILLUSTRATIVE EXAMPLE 3. Find the purchase price of a $100, 4% bond, dividends payable semiannually, redeemable in 10 years, bought to yield 5.25% convertible semiannually.

SOLUTION. The yield rate 5.25% is not found in the table. But, in the 4% column, the purchase prices corresponding to the nominal yield rates 5.20% and 5.30% are 90.73 and 90.01, respectively. By interpolation we find that the purchase price corresponding to 5.25% is $90.37.

———————

EXERCISE 91

In each case assume a $100 bond, due in 10 years, with semiannual dividends. From the bond table find the price in each of Problems 1–8 and the yield rate converted semiannually in Problems 9–16.

Prob.	Div. Rate	Yield Rate	Prob.	Div. Rate	Quoted Price
1.	4%	4.75%	9.	4%	$103.70
2.	$4\frac{1}{2}\%$	5.25%	10.	4%	102.75
3.	6%	4.62%	11.	$3\frac{1}{2}\%$	88.50
4.	5%	3.57%	12.	$4\frac{1}{2}\%$	92.00
5.	$3\frac{1}{2}\%$	4.30%	13.	7%	115.75
6.	$4\frac{1}{4}\%$	3.70%	14.	$3\frac{1}{2}\%$	97.25
7.	$4\frac{3}{4}\%$	4.10%	15.	4%	95.00
8.	$3\frac{5}{8}\%$	3.90%	16.	$5\frac{1}{2}\%$	107.50

MISCELLANEOUS EXERCISE 92
REVIEW OF CHAPTER 15

In each of Problems 1–10, consider a $1000, 5% bond, paying dividends A-O, and maturing Oct. 1, 1991.

1. Find price on Oct. 1, 1969, to yield 4% converted semiannually.

2. Solve Problem 1 assuming redemption at 103.

3. Prepare a 2-year schedule to find book value of bond on Apr. 1, 1972, if bought on Apr. 1, 1970, to yield 6% converted semiannually.

4. Do Problem 3 assuming yield at 4% converted semiannually.

5. Suppose that the bond is bought on Dec. 12, 1972, to yield 8% converted semiannually. Find the flat price without interpolation.

6. From the answer to Problem 5 find the "and interest" price.

7. By interpolation compute the "and interest" price on Nov. 30, 1973, to yield 3% converted semiannually.

8. From the answer to Problem 7 determine the flat price.

9. Find the yield if the bond is bought for $1080 on Apr. 1, 1975.

10. Find the yield if the bond is bought for $920 on Oct. 1, 1977.

11. Compute the price of a $100, 20-year annuity bond, with interest at 4%, payable annually, bought at the end of 7 years, to yield $3\frac{1}{2}\%$.

12 On April 1, 1969 a man pays $4327 for a $5000, 5% bond, due April 1, 1986, dividends semiannually. Find the yield rate.

13. Do Problem 12 for a $5000, $4\frac{1}{2}\%$ bond.

14. A $1000, 4% bond with semiannual dividends, redeemable in 13 years, is bought for $976.50 to yield 3%, converted semiannually. What is the redemption price?

15. Find the number of quarters before redemption at par of a $10,000, 5% bond with quarterly dividends, bought for $11,000, to yield 4% converted quarterly.

16. Find the purchase price in 4 years of a $10,000, 4% bond, dividends payable annually, redeemable at par, with yield rate of 5% annually.

17. Prepare a schedule for accumulation of discount in Problem 16.

18. Compute the semiannual dividend of a $1000 bond, redeemable at par, 18 years hence, if it is to yield 4% converted semiannually and is purchased at a price of $950.

19. A $100, 4%, Capital Airlines bond, maturing in 10 years and paying dividends A-O, was advertised on Oct. 1, 1950, to yield 3.52% converted semiannually. Find its price from the bond table.

20. On March 1, 1960, A pays $95 for a $100, 5%, Western Union bond due March 1, 1970, dividends M-S. Find the yield (bond table).

21. Compute the price of a $1000, 30-year annuity bond with interest at 3% payable annually, bought at the end of 10 years to yield 4%.

22. Four $1000, $2\frac{1}{2}$%, railway equipment bonds, paying dividends J-D 15, are due serially June 15, 1971–1974. What total price on Dec. 15, 1962 yielded $3\frac{1}{2}$% converted semiannually?

23. Compute the yield of a $100, 4%, *irredeemable* bond, dividends payable J-J, quoted at $102 on July 1, 1950.

24. Find the price on Jan. 5, 1952, of a £500, $2\frac{1}{2}$%, British consol, with perpetual dividends due J-A-J-O 5, to yield 4% converted quarterly.

25. A $100, 4%, union depot bond, with dividend dates A-O, bought for $104.97 on Oct. 1, 1944, was redeemed on Oct. 1, 1950. Find the redemption price if the yield was $2\frac{3}{4}$% converted semiannually.

26. Determine the quarterly dividend of a $100 bond bought 20 years before maturity for $115 to yield 3% converted quarterly.

27. When will the book value of the bond in Problem 26 be $110.90?

28. In formula (16), let $C(1 + i)^{-n} = K$ and $R = gC$, and obtain **Makeham's formula,** $V = K + \frac{g}{i}(C - K)$, requiring no annuity table.

Chapter SIXTEEN

MATHEMATICS OF DEPRECIATION

154. Terminology. Significance of depreciation

The fixed assets of a business enterprise, such as buildings, machinery, and equipment of all kinds, diminish in value as time goes on, on account of wear and tear, exposure, obsolescence, etc. That part of the decrease in value which cannot be made good by current repairs is called **depreciation.** The value of a depreciable asset at the end of its useful life is called the **scrap value.** The difference between the original cost and the scrap value is the **total depreciation** (or **wearing value**) of the asset.

According to a fundamental principle of economics, capital invested in a business enterprise should be kept intact. Consequently, in order to offset the gradual depreciation of fixed assets, a certain part of the profits obtained through the use of these assets must be transferred periodically (say annually) to a **depreciation fund.** By **annual contribution** we shall mean the sum of money placed annually in the depreciation fund. The **book value** of an asset on a given date is the difference between the original cost and the amount in the depreciation fund at that time. The difference between what the depreciation fund contains at the end of a given year and what it contains at the beginning of that year is called the **depreciation charge** for the year. As the student will see later, the annual depreciation charge may or may not be equal to the annual contribution.

155. Methods of computing the annual contribution

We shall consider three methods for computing a suitable annual contribution to the depreciation fund. These methods have a feature in common:

326

at the end of the useful life of the asset, the depreciation fund must contain an amount equal to the total depreciation of the asset. Hence the following must be taken into consideration: the original cost, the useful life, and the scrap value. The original cost of the asset is of course known definitely. The useful life and scrap value are ordinarily estimated by experts in engineering or in valuation.

The following notation will be used in connection with depreciation:

$C =$ the original cost.
$S =$ the (probable) scrap value.
$W =$ the total depreciation (or wearing value).
$n =$ the (probable) useful life in years.
$R =$ the annual contribution.

156. Straight line method

Consider an asset, costing C, which is estimated to have a scrap value of S at the end of n years. In calculating the annual contribution to the depreciation fund by the **straight line method,** it is assumed that the fund *earns no interest* and that *equal* contributions are to be made at the end of each year throughout the life of the asset. Since, at the end of n years, the depreciation fund must contain an amount equal to the total depreciation, the formula for the annual contribution is

$$R = \frac{C - S}{n} = \frac{W}{n}. \qquad (19)$$

ILLUSTRATIVE EXAMPLE. A machine costing $2000 has a probable life of 10 years. The estimated scrap value is $160. Using the straight line method, find the annual contribution to the depreciation fund and construct a schedule for depreciation.

SOLUTION. Here $C = 2000$, $S = 160$, $W = 2000 - 160 = 1840$, and $n = 10$. Hence

$$R = \frac{W}{n} = \frac{1840}{10} = \$184. \; Ans.$$

At the beginning of the first year, the book value of the machine is $2000. At the end of the first year, the depreciation fund contains $184; hence the depreciation charge for the first year is $184, and the book value is reduced to $2000 − $184 = $1816. At the end of the 2nd year, the depreciation fund contains $368; hence the depreciation charge is

$368 — $184 = $184, and the book value is reduced to $1816 — $184 = $1632. (It is evident that in the straight line method the annual depreciation charge is always equal to the annual contribution.) Thus, at the end of each year the fund is increased by $184, and the book value is reduced by $184, until, at the end of the 10th year, the depreciation fund contains $1840, and the book value is reduced to $160. These changes are shown in a convenient form in the following

DEPRECIATION SCHEDULE—STRAIGHT LINE METHOD

At End of Year	Annual Contribution	Depreciation Fund Contains	Book Value
0			$2000
1	$184	$ 184	1816
2	184	368	1632
3	184	552	1448
4	184	736	1264
5	184	920	1080
6	184	1104	896
7	184	1288	712
8	184	1472	528
9	184	1656	344
10	184	1840	160

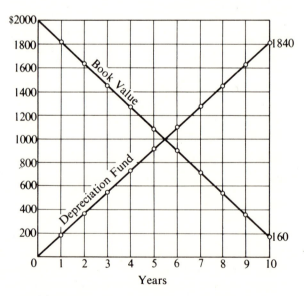

Fig. 24. Graphic representation of depreciation by the straight line method.

Plotting the entries in the last two columns against n, we may show graphically the increase in the depreciation fund and the decrease in the book value for the machine under consideration (see Fig. 24). The fact that the graphs are straight lines is the reason for the name of this method.

157. Sinking fund method

The depreciation fund under this plan is the exact analogue of a sinking fund. The n *equal* annual contributions to the fund *accumulate* at a given rate i, forming an ordinary annuity whose amount is W. By formula (8) of Art. 120, the annual contribution is

$$R = W \cdot \frac{1}{s_{\overline{n}|i}}. \tag{20}$$

___

ILLUSTRATIVE EXAMPLE. Using the sinking fund method and 5% interest, find the annual contribution to the depreciation fund for the machine of the illustrative example of Art. 156, and construct a depreciation schedule.

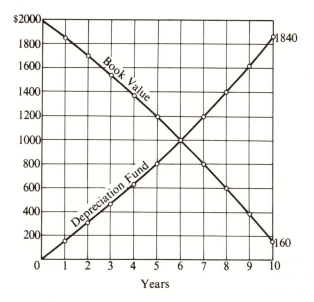

Fig. 25. Graphic representation of depreciation by the sinking fund method.

SOLUTION. By formula (20),

$$R = 1840 \times \frac{1}{s_{\overline{10}|.05}} = 1840 \times 0.079505 = \$146.29. \quad Ans.$$

'At the beginning of the first year, the book value of the machine is $2000. At the end of the first year, the depreciation fund contains $146.29, and the book value is reduced to $2000 − $ 146.29 = $1853.71. The interest on $146.29 for a year is 146.29 × 0.05 = $7.31; hence, at the end of the second year, the increase in the fund is $146.29 + $7.31 = $153.60. The depreciation charge for the second year is also $153.60, and the book value is reduced to $1853.71 − $153.60 = $1700.11. The schedule below shows the accumulation of the depreciation fund and the gradual reduction of the book value of the machine. The same changes are exhibited graphically in Fig. 25.

DEPRECIATION SCHEDULE—SINKING FUND METHOD

At End of Year	Annual Contribution	5% Interest on Fund	Increase in Fund	Fund Contains	Book Value
0					$2000.00
1	$146.29		$146.29	$ 146.29	1853.71
2	146.29	$ 7.31	153.60	299.89	1700.11
3	146.29	14.99	161.28	461.17	1538.83
4	146.29	23.06	169.35	630.52	1369.48
5	146.29	31.53	177.82	808.34	1191.66
6	146.29	40.42	186.71	995.05	1004.95
7	146.29	49.75	196.04	1191.09	808.91
8	146.29	59.55	205.84	1396.93	603.07
9	146.29	69.85	216.14	1613.07	386.93
10	146.29	80.65	226.94	1840.01	159.99

To find the book value at the end of a given year without preparing a schedule, compute the amount of the depreciation fund at the end of that year (see the illustrative example of Art. 139) and subtract it from the initial cost of the asset; the difference is the desired book value. Note that, under this plan, the annual contribution to the fund is a fixed amount, but the depreciation charge increases from year to year on account of interest earned on the fund. Since the depreciation charge for a given year is the difference between the amount of the depreciation fund at the end of that year and the amount at the end of the preceding year, it may be computed without preparing a schedule.

EXERCISE 93

1. A truck costs $2500 and will depreciate to a scrap value of $500 in 5 years. Using the straight line method, find the amount in the depreciation fund and the book value of the truck at the end of 3 years.

2. An asset costing $6500 is expected to have a scrap value of $900 in 8 years. Using the straight line method, find the amount in the depreciation fund and the book value of the asset at the end of 5 years.

3. Prepare a depreciation schedule for the truck of Problem 1.

4. Construct a depreciation schedule for the asset of Problem 2.

5. Use the schedule in Problem 3 to draw a graph similar to Fig. 24.

6. Draw a graph similar to Fig. 24 from the schedule in Problem 4.

7. An engine costing $1150 will be worth $50 as scrap in 5 years. Find the annual contribution to its depreciation fund invested at 3%.

8. A $4500 bus will have a scrap value of $500 in 6 years. Find the annual contribution to its depreciation fund accumulating at 4%.

9. Construct a depreciation schedule for the engine of Problem 7.

10. Prepare a depreciation schedule for the bus of Problem 8.

11. Draw a graph similar to Fig. 25 from the schedule in Problem 9.

12. Use the schedule in Problem 10 to draw a graph similar to Fig. 25.

13. Machinery costing $10,800 will depreciate to a scrap value of $800 in 12 years. A sinking fund earning interest at 8% will provide for its depreciation. Compute the annual contribution to the fund.

14. A small factory, built at a cost of $32,000, has a probable life of 25 years and a scrap value of $2000. To offset depreciation, a sinking fund is set up at $5\frac{1}{2}\%$. Compute the annual contribution.

15. Referring to Problem 13, determine (a) the amount in the sinking fund at the end of 8 years; (b) the book value of the machinery at that time; (c) the depreciation charge for the 8th year.

16. Referring to Problem 14, find (a) the size of the depreciation fund at the end of 15 years; (b) the book value of the factory at that time; (c) the depreciation charge for the 15th year.

17. A certain machine costs $11,595 and will depreciate to a scrap value of $1000 in 12 years. Find, by the straight line method, the annual contribution to its depreciation.

18. Prepare a depreciation schedule for the machine of Problem 17. What does the fund contain at the end of 7 years.

19. A truck valued at $3595 will be sold 7 years hence for $495. Find the annual contribution to its depreciation fund invested at $4\frac{1}{2}\%$.

20. Construct a depreciation schedule for the truck in Problem 19. What does the fund contain at the end of 4 years?

21. A jet aircraft costing $2,395,000 has scrap value 10 years hence of $650,000. To offset depreciation, a sinking fund is set up at $3\frac{1}{2}\%$. Find the annual contribution.

22. In Problem 21, find the book value of the aircraft and the amount in the sinking fund at the end of 5 years.

23. A certain piece of office equipment has a scrap value of $1.50 at the end of 15 years. The annual contribution to its depreciation fund, at $5\frac{1}{2}\%$, is $11.16. Find the book value of the piece of equipment when new.

24. A $4000 machine and a $3200 machine have scrap values of $100 and $12.50, respectively, 17 years hence. Find the annual contribution in a fund at 4% to offset their depreciation.

25. A certain building must be torn down, at a cost of $1950, and rebuilt, at a cost equal to the present value of the building, 59 years hence. A fund at $6\frac{1}{2}\%$ is to be set up to offset the above costs. Find the present value of the building, if the annual contribution to the fund will be $2000.

158. Constant percentage of book value method

Under **the constant percentage of book value method** the depreciation fund earns no interest and the annual contribution is a constant percentage of the book value at the end of the preceding year. This constant percentage must be determined so that at the end of the estimated life of the asset the book value is reduced to the scrap value.

Consider an asset, costing C, which is estimated to have a scrap value of S at the end of n years. Let r be the constant percentage, sometimes called the **rate of depreciation.** At the end of the first year, the contribution to the fund, or the depreciation, is Cr, and the book value is reduced to $C - Cr = C(1 - r)$. At the end of the second year, the contribution is $Cr(1 - r)$, and the book value is $C(1 - r) - Cr(1 - r) = C(1 - r)^2$. Similarly, at the end of n years, the book value is $C(1 - r)^n$, which must be equal to S. Hence

$$C(1 - r)^n = S.$$

Dividing both members by C,

$$(1 - r)^n = \frac{S}{C}. \tag{21}$$

———

ILLUSTRATIVE EXAMPLE. Given the machine of the illustrative example of Art. 156, find the rate of depreciation by the constant percentage of book value method, and construct a schedule for depreciation.

SOLUTION. It is given that $C = 2000$, $S = 160$, and $n = 10$. Substitute these values in formula (21) and get

$$(1 - r)^{10} = \frac{160}{2000}.$$

To evaluate r from this equation, take the logarithms of both members:

$$\log (1 - r)^{10} = \log \frac{160}{2000},$$

whence $10 \cdot \log (1 - r) = \log 160 - \log 2000.$

Divide both members by 10,

$$\log (1 - r) = \tfrac{1}{10} (\log 160 - \log 2000)$$
$$= \tfrac{1}{10}(8.903090 - 10) = 0.890309 - 1.$$

Therefore $1 - r = 0.7768,$

and $r = 0.2232 = 22.32\%$.   *Ans.*

DEPRECIATION SCHEDULE—CONSTANT PERCENTAGE METHOD

At End of Year	Annual Contribution	Depreciation Fund Contains	Book Value
0			$2000.00
1	$446.40	$ 446.40	1553.60
2	346.76	793.16	1206.84
3	269.37	1062.53	937.47
4	209.24	1271.77	728.23
5	162.54	1434.31	565.69
6	126.26	1560.57	439.43
7	98.08	1658.65	341.35
8	76.19	1734.84	265.16
9	59.18	1794.02	205.98
10	45.97	1839.99	160.01

———

Note. The annual contribution is a decreasing quantity under this plan, and the depreciation charge for a given year is the same as the contribution to the depreciation fund at the end of that year. Figure 26 illustrates graphically the increase in the depreciation fund and the decrease in the book value of the machine under consideration.

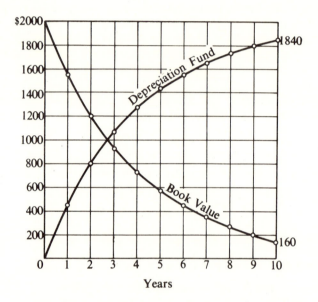

Fig. 26. Graphic representation of depreciation by the constant percentage method.

In the constant percentage method, the book value of the asset at the end of the kth year is $C(1 - r)^k$, as seen from the derivation of formula (21). The amount in the depreciation fund at the end of the kth year is the original cost of the asset minus its book value at the end of the kth year. The depreciation charge for the kth year, or the contribution to the depreciation fund at the end of the kth year, is the book value of the asset at the end of the $(k - 1)$th year minus the book value at the end of the kth year. When C and r are known, it is thus possible to compute book value, amount in depreciation fund, and depreciation charge without constructing a schedule.

159. Comments on the various methods

We have discussed only the mathematical aspects of the three methods presented in this chapter, and have omitted a number of other methods used to a limited extent. Of the three methods discussed here, the *straight line method* is probably used the most widely, on account of its simplicity. However, authorities on depreciation object to this method, because it fails to take interest into consideration. For this reason, the use of the *sinking fund method* is advocated by a number of accountants. In the *constant percentage method*, the depreciation charges are heavy for the first few years, but they grow lighter as the asset approaches the end of its useful life. This seems to be consistent with the fact that the value of an asset in general decreases rapidly during the earlier years of its useful life.

EXERCISE 94

1. An asset costing $421.40 will depreciate to a scrap value of $150 in 6 years. Find the rate of depreciation. [*Hint*. To divide the logarithm 9.551450 − 10 by 6, first rewrite it in the form 59.551450 − 60.]

2. After 7 years' use, a tractor bought for $850 has a value of $50. Compute the rate of depreciation. (See *Hint* in Problem 1.)

3. Construct a depreciation schedule for the asset in Problem 1.

4. Prepare a depreciation schedule for the tractor in Problem 2.

5. Draw a graph similar to Fig. 26 from the schedule in Problem 3.

6. Use the schedule in Problem 4 to draw a graph similar to Fig. 26.

7. Without using the schedule on page 333, find by logarithms the book value of the machine and amount in the fund at the end of 4 years.

8. Proceed as in Problem 7 to compute the book value of the machine and amount in the fund at the end of 7 years.

9. A rotary press costing $5000 depreciates at a constant rate of 12%. What is the depreciation charge for the 8th year?

10. An electric drill costs a garage $500. In 10 years its value is $125. Find the rate of depreciation.

11. Construct a depreciation schedule for the drill in Problem 10.

12. Draw a graph similar to Fig. 26, page 334, for the schedule in Problem 11.

13. Find the original cost of a machine which depreciates at a constant rate of 20% and at the end of 5 years is worth $1000.

14. A high-speed steam engine costing $3000 depreciates at a constant rate of $17\frac{1}{2}$%. The depreciation charge for the 7th year is what?

15. If the estimated useful life of the press in Problem 9 is 12 years, determine its scrap value.

16. Compute the scrap value of the engine in Problem 14 assuming that its useful life is 10 years.

160. Composite life

Consider a manufacturing plant consisting of various parts with different probable lives. Suppose the original cost, scrap value, and estimated life for each part are as shown in the second, third, and fourth columns, respectively, of the table below. Wearing values are entered in the fifth column. The student should verify the entries for annual contribution obtained by the sinking fund method at 4%.

Part	Original Cost	Scrap Value	Estimated Life	Wearing Value	Annual Contribution
A	$10,000	$2,000	18 years	$ 8,000	$ 311.95
B	6,000	1,500	10 years	4,500	374.81
C	4,000	500	7 years	3,500	443.13
Totals	$20,000	$4,000		$16,000	$1,129.89

The **composite life** of the plant is the time necessary for the total annual contribution to accumulate to the total wearing value at the given rate of interest, that is, the time necessary for annual payments of $1129.89 to amount at 4% to $16,000. Let the composite life be n years. Then

$$1129.89 \times s_{\overline{n}|.04} = 16,000;$$

whence

$$s_{\overline{n}|.04} = \frac{16,000}{1129.89} = 14.161.$$

From Table V, we find that the nearest value of n is 11. Hence the composite life of this plant is about 11 years.

A knowledge of the composite life of a plant is desirable in case a loan is secured by a mortgage on the plant as a whole. For safety's sake, the term of the loan should be for a time less than the computed composite life.

161. Valuation of mining property

Such assets as mines, timber tracts, and oil wells yield an income for a certain length of time and are eventually exhausted. As in depreciable assets, the capital invested should be kept intact. The net annual income should be used partly to pay the annual interest on the original investment and partly to build up a sinking fund which, at the exhaustion of the asset, will contain an amount equal to the original investment.

Consider a mine purchased now at the price V and estimated to yield a net annual income R for n years longer, at the end of which time it will be exhausted. Let i be the rate of interest expected on the purchase price; then the expected annual interest is Vi. Assuming that the sinking fund will accumulate at the rate r, the annual contribution to the sinking fund is $V \cdot \dfrac{1}{s_{\overline{n}|r}}$. Hence the net annual income is

$$R = Vi + V \cdot \frac{1}{s_{\overline{n}|r}} = V\left(i + \frac{1}{s_{\overline{n}|r}}\right).$$

Solving for V,

$$V = \frac{R}{i + \dfrac{1}{s_{\overline{n}|r}}}. \tag{22}$$

ILLUSTRATIVE EXAMPLE. A certain mine is expected to yield a net annual income of $20,000 for the next 25 years, at which time it will be exhausted. Find the present value of the mine, if the purchaser expects 8% on his investment and can invest the sinking fund at 5%.

SOLUTION. Here $R = 20{,}000$, $i = 0.08$, $r = 0.05$, and $n = 25$. Substituting these quantities in formula (22),

$$V = \frac{20{,}000}{0.08 + \dfrac{1}{s_{\overline{25}|.05}}} = \frac{20{,}000}{0.08 + 0.0209525} = \$198{,}113. \quad Ans.$$

EXERCISE 95

1. Find, at 8%, the composite life of a power plant consisting of: (a) Boiler-room equipment worth $22,000, life 20 years, scrap value $2000; (b) electric switching equipment worth $8500, life 12 years, scrap value $500; (c) turbine-room equipment worth $11,500, life 15 years, scrap value $1500; (d) building worth $33,000, life 35 years, scrap value $3000.

2. A plant consists of: (a) A building worth $24,000, with life 30 years and scrap value $4000; (b) machinery worth $11,000, with life 12 years and scrap value $1000; (c) tools worth $2300, with life 7 years and scrap value $300. Assuming interest at 5%, find the composite life.

3. Solve Problem 1 at 0% interest (straight line method).

4. Work Problem 2 at 0% interest (straight line method).

5. A quarry is estimated to yield $15,000 net annually for 12 years. Find the purchase price to yield 5% if the sinking fund will earn 3%.

6. Compute the value of a timber tract estimated to yield a net annual income of $8000 for the next 7 years, if the purchaser expects 6% on his investment and the sinking fund will accumulate at $3\frac{1}{2}$%.

7. How is the $15,000 annual income in Problem 5 distributed into interest on investment and annual contribution to sinking fund?

8. How much of the $8000 annual income in Problem 6 is interest on investment and how much is placed in the sinking fund?

9. A coal mine is expected to yield $25,000 a year net for 20 years. Find a purchase price to yield 8%, assuming a sinking fund at 4%.

10. Find the price of an oil well that will yield $10,000 a year net for 10 years. The investor expects 7%; the sinking fund can earn 5%.

11. A man pays $20,000 for the patent rights to an invention. If the rights expire in 10 years and a sinking fund can be accumulated at 4%, what net annual income will yield $7\frac{1}{2}$% on his investment?

12. Assuming that the patent will yield $3000 a year for 10 years, the man in Problem 11 will earn interst on his investment at what rate?

13. A certain factory has a total wearing value of $552,500. Find the composite life, at 6%, of the factory, if the annual total contribution to its depreciation fund is $2908.55.

14. In Problem 13, find the composite life, at $4\frac{1}{2}$%, of the factory, if the total annual contribution to its depreciation fund is $4205.50.

15. Find, at $5\frac{1}{2}$%, the composite life of a small factory consisting of: (a) machinery worth $14,500 with life 15 years, scrap value $1500; (b) miscellaneous equipment worth $27,500, with life 17 years, scrap value $550; (c) a building worth $25,000, with life 25 years, scrap value $11,000.

16. In Problem 15 find the composite life at 4%.

17. Find the purchase price of a gold mine, with expected net yield of $200,000 annually and expected life of 7 years. The investor expects 5%; and the sinking fund can earn 4%.

18. How is the $200,000 annual income in Problem 17 distributed into interest on investment and annual contribution to sinking fund?

19. Find the purchase price of a farm, with expected net annual yield of $5450, for 75 years, if the investor expects 4% and the sinking fund can be accumulated at $5\frac{1}{2}$%.

20. How much of the annual income in Problem 19 is interest on investment and how much is placed in the sinking fund annually?

21. An oil well, with expected life of 13 years, was purchased for $550,000 to yield 7%. Assuming a sinking fund at $3\frac{1}{2}$%, find the net annual yield of the well.

22. Find the expected net annual yield, for 33 years, of a coal mine, if the purchase price was $10,005.52, to yield $5\frac{1}{2}$%. Assume a sinking fund at 4%.

MISCELLANEOUS EXERCISE 96
REVIEW OF CHAPTER 16

1. A dynamo costing $7500 will depreciate to a scrap value of $300 in 15 years. Find the annual contribution by the straight line method.

2. Do Problem 1 by the sinking fund method with interest at 6%.

3. Using the constant percentage of book value method, determine the rate of depreciation for the dynamo in Problem 1.

4. Assuming a constant rate of depreciation of 15% for a Pullman car costing $30,000, compute its book value at the end of 10 years.

5. In Problem 4 find the depreciation charge for the 13th year.

6. Prepare the first 4 years' depreciation schedule for Problem 4.

7. To provide for the depreciation of air conditioning equipment worth $10,000, a company sets aside $400 a year in a sinking fund invested at 5%. Find the book value of the equipment at the end of 8 years.

8. In Problem 7 find the depreciation charge for the 8th year.

9. Prepare the first 2 years' depreciation schedule for Problem 7.

10. Find by the straight line method the book value, at the end of 5 years, of an asset with life 12 years, cost $5000, scrap value $500.

11. In Problem 10 find the depreciation charge for the 9th year.

12. Prepare the first 5 years' depreciation schedule for Problem 10.

13. Find the price of a copper mine that will yield $30,000 a year net for 20 years. The investor desires 7%; the sinking fund can earn $4\frac{1}{2}\%$.

14. An asset consists of part A, cost $9000, life 20 years, scrap value $1000; part B, cost $3500, life 10 years, scrap value $500. Find the total annual contribution by the sinking fund method at 7%.

15. Determine the composite life of the asset of Problem 14.

16. Name the method or methods discussed in this chapter under which (a) the depreciation fund earns no interest; (b) the annual depreciation is constant; (c) the annual contribution is constant; (d) the annual contribution for any year equals the depreciation charge for that year.

17. The three methods have what feature in common?

18. An asset costing C has a life of n years and a wearing value W. Prove the nine entries in the table below by algebraic methods.

At End of kth Year	Straight Line Method	Sinking Fund Method	Const. Percent. Method
Depr. fund contains	$kW \div n$	$Ws_{\overline{k}|i} \div s_{\overline{n}|i}$	$C[1 - (1 - r)^k]$
Book value of asset	$C - (kW \div n)$	$C - (Ws_{\overline{k}|i} \div s_{\overline{n}|i})$	$C(1 - r)^k$
Depreciation charge	$W \div n$	$W(1 + i)^{k-1} \div s_{\overline{n}|i}$	$Cr(1 - r)^{k-1}$

19. Find the present value of an asset which will yield $2000 a year for exactly 10 years, if the interest to be paid is 6% and the sinking fund is invested at 4%.

20. Find the annual contribution, by the sinking fund method, to the depreciation fund of an asset costing $10,000, which depreciates to a scrap value of $950 in 25 years. The sinking fund is invested at 6%.

21. A mine which is expected to yield $100,000 a year for 5 years is covered by a sinking fund invested at $4\frac{1}{2}\%$. Find the purchase price, if the investor expects to yield 7%.

22. An asset costing $2500 depreciates at a constant rate of 15%. What is the depreciation charge at the end of the 5th year by the constant percentage method?

23. Prepare a depreciation schedule for the asset in Problem 22 for the first 5 years of its life.

24. Graph the schedule in Problem 23.

25. If the scrap value of the asset in Problem 22 is $50 what is its approximate useful life?

26. A factory is composed of a building costing $30,000, with a life of 20 years and scrap value of $4500, and machinery costing $10,000 with life of 15 years and scrap value $2500. Find the total annual contribution to its depreciation fund by the sinking fund method at 5%.

Chapter SEVENTEEN

ANNUITIES: GENERAL CASE

162. Introductory remarks

The student should not get the impression that a large collection of formulas is *necessary* for the solution of varied types of problems in finance. Comprehensive treatises develop and explain many formulas, but they are a *convenience* rather than a necessity. The situation from a theoretical standpoint is simple. Two principal types of problems occur: the problem involving a *single payment* and the problem dealing with a *series of equal payments*. The first may be taken care of by the two formulas

$$S = P(1 + i)^n, \quad P = S(1 + i)^{-n};$$

the second, by the two formulas

$$S_n = R \cdot s_{\overline{n}|i} = R \cdot \frac{(1 + i)^n - 1}{i}, \quad A_n = R \cdot a_{\overline{n}|i} = R \cdot \frac{1 - (1 + i)^{-n}}{i}.$$

Indeed, the first two of the above formulas are sufficient, because with their aid a series of sums due on different dates may be accumulated or discounted to the same focal date, and then results added into a single sum which, on that focal date, is entirely equivalent to the series.

Up to this point in the discussion, i is the rate per interest conversion period and n is a *whole* number of such periods. The most frequent applications of annuities in ordinary commercial practice involve the **simple case,** that is, the case in which the payment interval coincides with the interest period. The annuity formulas given above are valid only in the simple case, n being either the number of interest periods or the number of payments, since these two numbers are equal in that case. Then n periodic payments

342

of R each are equivalent to a single payment of $R \cdot s_{\overline{n}|i}$ on the date of the nth payment, or to a single payment of $R \cdot a_{\overline{n}|i}$ one period before the date of the first payment.

EXERCISE 97 (Oral)

1. $(1.05)^{-4}$ is the _____ of _____ due _____ periods hence if money is worth _____ per _____.

2. $(1.02)^5$ is the _____ of _____ at compound interest for _____ periods at the rate _____ per _____.

3. $(1.04)^{-6}$ is the same as 1 divided by _____.

4. If money is worth 3%, the value of a \$1 debt, 4 years after the due date, is _____, and the value 3 years before the due date is _____.

5. Explain in terms of compound interest why $(1.06)^{-n}$ is less than 1 for *any* positive integral value of n.

6. Explain why $[(1.03)^{10} - 1] \div 0.03$ is larger than $(1.03)^{10}$.

7. Explain why $(1.04)^{-8}$ is less than $[1 - (1.04)^{-8}] \div 0.04$.

8. If the compound interest on \$1 at 5% per period for 6 periods is divided by 0.05, the result is $s_{\overline{x}|i}$. Find the values of x and i.

9. If the compound discount on \$1 at 3% per period for 12 periods is divided by 0.03, the result is $a_{\overline{k}|j}$. Find the values of k and j.

10. If n is kept fixed but i is increased, the value of $a_{\overline{n}|i}$ changes how?

11. Interpret the meaning of $50 \cdot s_{\overline{20}|.04}$.

12. Interpret the meaning of $100 \cdot a_{\overline{20}|.06}$.

163. Compound interest for fractional parts of conversion periods

If money is worth 6% compounded annually, the compound amount of \$1 for half a year seemingly has no meaning, because the phrase "compounded annually" signifies that interest is added to principal at the end of each year. Similarly, there is no apparent meaning in the phrase "compound amount of \$1 for 3 months, interest convertible semiannually"; and in a simple business transaction the expression would not be employed. Nevertheless, as the mathematics of finance has been called upon to develop formulas for computing the amounts and present values of complicated annuities, much labor is avoided by introducing a precise definition for the compound amount and the present value of $1 for a fractional part of an interest period. The formulas $s = (1 + i)^n$ and $v^n = (1 + i)^{-n}$ give the exact value of the compound amount and present value, respectively, of $1 for n periods at the rate i per period when n is a whole number. These facts have been rigorously proved.

Now, in case n is a fraction, these formulas will be taken as *definitions*. Observe that there is no pretense at proof here. It is simply agreed to compute amounts and present values by these formulas. Whether the results would be accepted or not in any given transaction would be a matter for the contracting parties to decide. It is worthy of note that the results obtained are reasonable, but little out of accord with computations based on simple interest for fractions of periods, and in many cases far easier to compute. The compound amount for any length of time less than an interest period is smaller than the amount at simple interest. On the other hand, present value, based on the new definition, is larger than present value based on simple interest if the time is less than an interest period.

ILLUSTRATIVE EXAMPLE 1. Find the compound amount of $1 for 3 months at 4% converted annually.

SOLUTION. We have immediately $s = (1.04)^{1/4}$. This may be computed by logarithms, or it may be found directly in **Table VIII**, or it may be computed by the binomial theorem. By the latter method, using the special

form of the theorem, $(1 + i)^n = 1 + ni + \dfrac{n(n-1)}{1 \cdot 2} i^2 + \dfrac{n(n-1)(n-2)}{1 \cdot 2 \cdot 3} i^3$

$+ \cdots$, and substituting 0.04 for i, and $\frac{1}{4}$ for n, we obtain

$$(1 + 0.04)^{1/4} = 1 + \tfrac{1}{4}(0.04) + \frac{(\frac{1}{4})(-\frac{3}{4})}{1 \cdot 2}(0.04)^2$$

$$+ \frac{(\frac{1}{4})(-\frac{3}{4})(-\frac{7}{4})}{1 \cdot 2 \cdot 3}(0.04)^3 + \cdots$$

$$= 1 + 0.01 - 0.00015 + 0.0000035 - \cdots = \$1.0098535^-.$$

This is correct to 5 decimal places. Hence a principal of $1000 would amount to $1009.85 under the same conditions.

ILLUSTRATIVE EXAMPLE 2. Find the present value of $1 due in $3\frac{3}{4}$ years, if money is worth 8% convertible annually.

SOLUTION. By definition, the answer is given by $v^n = (1.08)^{-15/4}$. According to the laws of exponents,

$$(1.08)^{-15/4} = (1.08)^{-4} \times (1.08)^{1/4}.$$

The first factor on the right is found in Table IV and the second factor in Table VIII. Substituting the values found in the tables, we get

$$(1.08)^{-15/4} = (1.08)^{-4} \times (1.08)^{1/4}$$
$$= 0.73502985 \times 1.01942655 = 0.74930898.$$

Under the same conditions an amount of $1000 would have a present value of $1000 \times 0.74930898 = \$749.31$.

EXERCISE 98

1. Compute $(1.02)^{1/2}$ to 5 decimal places by use of logarithms.

2. Using logarithms, evaluate $(1.02)^{1/3}$ to 5 decimal places.

3. Apply the binomial theorem to do the computation in Problem 1.

4. Do Problem 2 by use of the binomial theorem.

5. $(1.07)^{19/6}$ is the product of what two factors found in the tables?

6. Express $(1.05)^{9/4}$ as the product of two factors found in the tables.

7. Compute $(1.04)^{-8/3}$ from the tables. [*Hint.* If $(1.04)^{-8/3}$ is written equal to $(1.04)^{-3} \cdot (1.04)^x$, what is the value of x?]

8. Evaluate $(1.035)^{-23/12}$. (See *Hint* in Problem 7.)

9. Explain how to obtain the value of $(1.02)^{5/6}$ by use of Table VIII.

10. Explain how to obtain the value of $(1.03)^{2/3}$ by use of Table VIII.

11. Find the amount of $1000 for 3 months at 4% *simple interest* and compare the result with that obtained in illustrative example 1.

12. Discount $1000 for 3 years at 8% effective; discount the result for $\frac{3}{4}$ year at 8% *simple interest;* compare with illustrative example 2.

13. Find the amount of $10,000 for $4\frac{1}{2}$ years at 3% annually.

14. Express $(1.07)^{11/4}$ as a product of factors found in the tables.

15. Compute $(1.0225)^{-11/6}$.

16. Evaluate $(1.045)^{-7/4}$.

17. Find the amount of $2000 at 5% compounded semiannually for $9\frac{1}{4}$ years.

18. Find the present value of a debt of $1000, due in 1 year 10 months, at $5\frac{1}{2}$% interest.

19. Find the present value of a $5000 debt, due in 1 year 9 months, at $4\frac{1}{2}$% interest.

164. Equivalent rates

Consider a given interest rate i per conversion period. Let m be the number of such periods in a *year*. As shown in Art. 103, the rate r per *annual* conversion period, **equivalent** to the given rate i, is

$$r = (1 + i)^m - 1. \tag{2}$$

Consider next the number of original conversion periods in a *half-year*. Substitution of that number for m in (2) gives a different value for r, which is then the rate per *semiannual* conversion period, equivalent to the given rate i. In general, if we substitute for m the number of original conversion periods contained in a *new* conversion period of any length, the resulting value of r is the rate per *new* conversion period, equivalent to the given rate i. Note that m is *the length of the new conversion period* divided by *the length of the original conversion period*, both lengths being expressed in terms of the same unit of time. In view of the meaning assigned to compound interest for fractional periods, no complication is introduced when m is not an integer.

ILLUSTRATIVE EXAMPLE 1. Given the rate 4% converted quarterly. What is the corresponding rate per annual conversion period?

SOLUTION. Here the given interest rate per quarterly conversion period is 1%. The new conversion period is 12 months; the original conversion period is 3 months. Hence $m = 12 \div 3 = 4$. By (2),

$$r = (1.01)^4 - 1.$$

We may call the right member the *indicated value* of the new rate r. To obtain the value of r as a decimal fraction, we find in Table III $(1.01)^4$ = 1.040604. Hence $r = 0.040604 = 4.0604\%$. This means that increasing a principal by 1% at the end of each quarter is equivalent to increasing it by 4.0604% at the end of each year.

In this chapter it will usually be sufficient to leave the value of r in the form $(1 + i)^m - 1$, because of a device to be explained in Art. 165 which renders it unnecessary to evaluate r decimally.

ILLUSTRATIVE EXAMPLE 2. Given the rate 4% converted annually. What is the corresponding rate per quarterly conversion period?

SOLUTION. The given rate is 4% per annual conversion period. The new conversion period is 3 months; the original, 12 months. Hence $m = 3 \div 12 = \frac{1}{4}$. By (2), the indicated value of the new rate is

$$r = (1.04)^{1/4} - 1.$$

From Table VIII, $(1.04)^{1/4} = 1.00985341$. Hence $r = 0.9853\%$ (to 4 significant digits). Thus, increasing a principal by 4% annually is approximately the same as increasing it by 0.9853% quarterly.

ILLUSTRATIVE EXAMPLE 3. Indicate the value of the rate, per conversion period of 4 months, equivalent to 5% converted semiannually.

SOLUTION. The given rate per semiannual conversion period is $2\frac{1}{2}\%$. The new conversion period is 4 months; the original, 6 months. Hence $m = 4 \div 6 = \frac{2}{3}$. By (2),

$$r = (1.025)^{2/3} - 1.$$

EXERCISE 99

1. The rate 6% converted quarterly corresponds to what rate per conversion period of (a) 1 year? (b) 6 months? (c) 2 months? (d) $\frac{1}{2}$ month?

2. 6% converted semiannually corresponds to what rate per conversion period of (a) 2 years? (b) 1 year? (c) 4 months? (d) 1 month?

3. *Indicate* the value of the rate, per semiannual conversion period, equivalent to 5% converted (a) biennially; (b) annually; (c) quarterly.

4. *Indicate* the rate, per quarterly conversion period, equivalent to 4% converted (a) semiannually; (b) bimonthly; (c) monthly.

5. What rate, per conversion period of one month, is equivalent to 4.74% converted every 4 months?

6. What rate, per conversion period of 3 months, is equivalent to 12.78% converted every other month? What nominal rate?

165. A device for computation

Because of their importance in ensuing work, we group here certain annuity formulas which the student has used in the simple case.

$$s_{\overline{n}|i} = \frac{(1+i)^n - 1}{i}; \qquad \frac{1}{s_{\overline{n}|i}} = \frac{i}{(1+i)^n - 1}. \qquad (4'; 4'')$$

$$a_{\overline{n}|i} = \frac{1 - (1+i)^{-n}}{i}; \qquad \frac{1}{a_{\overline{n}|i}} = \frac{i}{1 - (1+i)^{-n}}. \qquad (5'; 5'')$$

Recall that the left members are convenient symbols abbreviating the algebraic expressions in the respective right members. *Even when n is fractional*, the right members will be abbreviated by the same symbols as are used when n is a whole number. In particular, if p is an integer,

$$s_{\overline{\frac{1}{p}}|i} = \frac{(1+i)^{1/p} - 1}{i}; \qquad \frac{1}{s_{\overline{\frac{1}{p}}|i}} = \frac{i}{(1+i)^{1/p} - 1}. \qquad (23; 23')$$

$$a_{\overline{\frac{1}{p}}|i} = \frac{1 - (1+i)^{-1/p}}{i}; \qquad \frac{1}{a_{\overline{\frac{1}{p}}|i}} = \frac{i}{1 - (1+i)^{-1/p}} \qquad (24; 24')$$

Note. Values of $s_{\overline{\frac{1}{p}}|i}$ and its reciprocal are given in **Tables IX** and **X**. Values of $a_{\overline{\frac{1}{p}}|i}$ are given in **Table XI**. Values of the reciprocal of $a_{\overline{\frac{1}{p}}|i}$ may be obtained by merely adding i to the corresponding entry in Table X. Thus, $\dfrac{1}{a_{\overline{\frac{1}{4}}|.03}} = \dfrac{1}{s_{\overline{\frac{1}{4}}|.03}} + 0.03 =$

$4.04472289 + 0.03 = 4.07472289.$

ILLUSTRATIVE EXAMPLE. Evaluate each fraction to six significant digits:

(a) $\dfrac{1 - (1.02)^{-32}}{(1.02)^4 - 1}$; (b) $\dfrac{(1.04)^3 - 1}{(1.04)^{1/3} - 1}$; (c) $\dfrac{(1.03)^{1/2} - 1}{1 - (1.03)^{-12}}$.

SOLUTION. (a) This may be computed directly by substituting the values of $(1.02)^{-32}$ and $(1.02)^4$ as found in the tables. Or, to avoid the long division involved, we may use the following device. Multiplying numerator and denominator by 0.02, we may write

$$\frac{1 - (1.02)^{-32}}{(1.02)^4 - 1} = \frac{1 - (1.02)^{-32}}{0.02} \cdot \frac{0.02}{(1.02)^4 - 1}$$

$$= a_{\overline{32}|.02} \cdot \frac{1}{s_{\overline{4}|.02}} \qquad \text{[By (5') and (4'')]}$$

$$= 23.46833 \times .2426238 \qquad \text{[By Tables VI and VII]}$$

$$= 5.69398. \quad Ans.$$

(b) $\dfrac{(1.04)^3 - 1}{(1.04)^{1/3} - 1} = \dfrac{(1.04)^3 - 1}{0.04} \cdot \dfrac{0.04}{(1.04)^{1/3} - 1} = s_{\overline{3}|.04} \cdot \dfrac{1}{s_{\overline{\frac{1}{3}}|.04}}$

$$= 3.121600 \times 3.039651 \qquad \text{[By Tables V and X]}$$

$$= 9.48857. \quad Ans.$$

(c) $\dfrac{(1.03)^{1/2} - 1}{1 - (1.03)^{-12}} = \dfrac{(1.03)^{1/2} - 1}{0.03} \cdot \dfrac{0.03}{1 - (1.03)^{-12}} = s_{\overline{\frac{1}{2}}|.03} \cdot \dfrac{1}{a_{\overline{12}|.03}}$

$$= .4963052 \times .1004621 \qquad \text{[By Tables IX and VII]}$$

$$= .0498599. \quad Ans.$$

EXERCISE 100

Express each as the product of two factors found in the tables.

1. $\dfrac{(1.03)^4 - 1}{(1.03)^{16} - 1}$.

2. $\dfrac{(1.045)^{1/3} - 1}{1 - (1.045)^{-12}}$.

3. $\dfrac{1 - (1.025)^{-6}}{(1.025)^{42} - 1}$.

4. $\dfrac{(1.07)^{1/4} - 1}{(1.07)^5 - 1}$.

5. $\dfrac{(1.035)^4 - 1}{1 - (1.035)^{-30}}$.

6. $\dfrac{1 - (1.02)^{-1/2}}{(1.02)^{36} - 1}$.

Use the tables to compute each to six significant digits.

7. $\dfrac{1 - (1.04)^{-15}}{1 - (1.04)^{-1/6}}$.

8. $\dfrac{1 - (1.005)^{-60}}{(1.005)^{12} - 1}$.

9. $\dfrac{1 - (1.06)^{-6}}{(1.06)^{1/12} - 1}$.

10. $\dfrac{(1.015)^{30} - 1}{1 - (1.015)^{-3}}$.

11. $\dfrac{(1.05)^{25} - 1}{1 - (1.05)^{-1/4}}$.

12. $\dfrac{1 - (1.01)^{-40}}{1 - (1.01)^{-4}}$.

166. General case: Reduction

When the payment interval of an annuity does not coincide with the interest period, the annuity is said to fall under the **general case**. A problem involving the general case may be solved by reducing it to the simple case and using the familiar annuity formulas (4) to (12) on page 277. To perform this reduction, think of a new conversion period, namely, the payment interval of the annuity. Then take three steps:

I. Indicate the value of the *rate r per payment interval*, equivalent to the given rate per interest period.

II. Select the proper formula coming under the simple case, rewrite it with the letter r in lieu of i, and replace abbreviating symbols by their algebraic expressions.

III. Substitute for r its value as indicated in step I and use the given numerical data for other substitutions.

_____

ILLUSTRATIVE EXAMPLE 1. A man buys a lot, agreeing to pay $175 at the end of each year for 8 years. Find the equivalent cash price if money is worth 8% converted quarterly.

SOLUTION. Since the payment interval does not coincide with the interest period, the annuity comes under the general case. To reduce to the simple case, write the rate per payment interval equivalent to the given rate 2% per interest period. The payment interval is 12 months; the interest period is 3 months. Hence $m = 12 \div 3 = 4$. By (2),

$$r = (1.02)^4 - 1 \quad \text{and} \quad 1 + r = (1.02)^4.$$

The unknown is the present value of an ordinary annuity. Hence we use formula (5) on page 277, with i replaced by r:

$$A_n = R \cdot a_{\overline{n}|r} = R \cdot \frac{1 - (1 + r)^{-n}}{r}.$$

Since the annuity is reduced to the simple case, n is the number of new conversion periods, or simply the number of payments. It is less confusing to think of n as the number of payments. Substituting $n = 8$, $R = 175$, and the values of r and $1 + r$ indicated above,

$$A_n = 175 \cdot \frac{1 - [(1.02)^4]^{-8}}{(1.02)^4 - 1} = 175 \cdot \frac{1 - (1.02)^{-32}}{(1.02)^4 - 1}$$
$$= 175 \times 5.69398 = \$996.45. \quad \textit{Ans.}$$

Refer to part (a), illustrative example, page 348, for details in finding the value of the above fraction to be 5.69398. Note that if the rate were 8% converted *annually*, we would have $A_n = 175 \cdot a_{\overline{8}|.08} = \$1005.66$.

_____

ILLUSTRATIVE EXAMPLE 2. $100 is placed at the end of each 4 months in a sinking fund accumulating at 4% converted annually. Find the amount in the fund at the end of 3 years.

SOLUTION. The payment interval is 4 months; the interest period is 12 months. Hence $m = 4 \div 12 = \frac{1}{3}$. The rate per payment interval equivalent to the given rate 4% per annual conversion period is

$$r = (1.04)^{1/3} - 1 \quad \text{and} \quad 1 + r = (1.04)^{1/3}.$$

The unknown is the amount of an ordinary annuity. Writing formula (4) on page 277, with i replaced by r,

$$S_n = R \cdot s_{\overline{n}|r} = R \cdot \frac{(1 + r)^n - 1}{r}.$$

Substituting $n = 9$, $R = 100$, and the above values of r and $1 + r$,

$$S_n = 100 \cdot \frac{[(1.04)^{1/3}]^9 - 1}{(1.04)^{1/3} - 1} = 100 \cdot \frac{(1.04)^3 - 1}{(1.04)^{1/3} - 1}$$

$$= 100 \times 9.48857 = \$948.86. \quad \textit{Ans.}$$

See (b), illustrative example, page 349, for details of computation.

––––––

ILLUSTRATIVE EXAMPLE 3. A house worth $12,000 is offered for sale for $2000 cash and 24 equal quarterly payments. Compute the quarterly payment if interest is at 6% converted semiannually.

SOLUTION. Payment interval, 3 months; interest period, 6 months. Placing $m = \frac{1}{2}$, $i = 0.03$ in (2), $r = (1.03)^{1/2} - 1$ and $1 + r = (1.03)^{1/2}$. We have an annuity with $A_n = 10,000$, $n = 24$, and R unknown. Write formula (7) with i replaced by r and substitute the known quantities.

$$R = A_n \cdot \frac{1}{a_{\overline{n}|r}} = A_n \cdot \frac{r}{1 - (1 + r)^{-n}} = 10,000 \cdot \frac{(1.03)^{1/2} - 1}{1 - (1.03)^{-12}}$$

$$= 10,000 \times .0498599 = \$498.60. \quad \textit{Ans.}$$

See (c), illustrative example, page 349, for computations.

––––––

EXERCISE 101

1. What single payment now is equivalent at 4% converted monthly to 25 semiannual payments of $100 each, the first due in 6 months?

2. Find the amount of the annuity of Problem 1 at the given rate.

3. A man deposits $1000 at the end of each 2 years in a bank paying 2% compounded quarterly. Compute the amount at the end of 12 years.

4. What is the equivalent cash price at 9% convertible semiannually if a man pays $500 cash and $100 a month for 18 months for a car?

5. At 6% converted quarterly, 60 monthly payments of $10 each are equivalent to what single payment at the end of 5 years?

6. Compute the present value of the annuity of Problem 5.

7. If A wishes to realize 7% effective, how much should he receive at the end of each month for 15 years for a house sold for $8000?

8. What sum invested at the end of each quarter for 10 years at 5% converted monthly will provide for the replacement of a $5000 engine?

9. B plans to accumulate $10,000 in 20 years. What should he invest at the end of each 6 months at 6% converted quarterly?

10. What equal payments at the end of each quarter for 5 years will amortize a $1000 loan bearing interest at 6% converted monthly?

11. Solve Problem 10 if the loan bears interest at 6% effective.

12. Do Problem 9 assuming the rate to be 4% effective.

13. Show that, at the rate j converted continuously, the amount of an ordinary annuity of R a year for n years is $S_n = R(e^{jn} - 1) \div (e^j - 1)$.

14. Show that, at the rate j converted continuously, the present value of the annuity of Problem 13 is $A_n = R(1 - e^{-jn}) \div (e^j - 1)$.

15. Compute the present value of an ordinary annuity of $200 a year for 8 years at 5% converted continuously.

16. Find the amount of the annuity of Problem 15 at the given rate.

In the following problems assume payments begin one period hence.

17. What will semiannual payments of $1200 amount to at the end of 13 years, assuming interest at 4% converted quarterly.

18. What amount 17 years hence would cancel a debt, at 6% converted quarterly, to be discharged by 17 annual payments of $595?

19. What cash amount would buy a house advertised for monthly payments of $125 for 10 years? Assume interest at $5\frac{1}{2}$% converted quarterly.

20. A man buys a boat for 10 annual payments of $529.50. Assuming interest at 5% converted semiannually, what cash amount would buy the boat?

21. A debt, at 4% converted semiannually, is to be discharged by quarterly payments of $159.20 for 13 years. Find the debt.

22. What sum deposited quarterly at 4% compounded semiannually will amount to $1200 7 years hence?

23. Mr. Smith wants $10,000 in his savings account 11 years hence. What monthly deposits should he make, if the savings bank pays $4\frac{1}{2}$% interest converted semiannually?

24. What monthly payments, for 20 years, will purchase a $25,000 house, if interest is 6% converted quarterly?

25. A debt of $5000, at 5% converted quarterly, is to be discharged by payments of x dollars, semiannually, for 7 years. Find x.

26. Find the number of annual deposits of $1000 which will amount to $100,000, at 4% compounded semiannually.

167. General case: Formulas

The general case presents no special difficulty, nor does it require new formulas. For a better insight into the theory of annuities certain, the student should master the *fundamental* method of reducing the general case to the simple case, as outlined and illustrated in Art. 166.

Below is given a set of general annuity formulas, merely for convenience in solving problems. By the reduction method of Art. 166, each of these formulas may be obtained from the corresponding formula for the simple case. It is left as an exercise to show that if

n = number of payments of an annuity,
R = size of each of the n payments,
i = interest rate per conversion period,
$$m = \frac{\text{number of months in payment interval}}{\text{number of months in interest period}},$$

then the **amount** of an **ordinary annuity** is

$$S_n = R \cdot s_{\overline{mn}|i} \cdot \frac{1}{s_{\overline{m}|i}}; \qquad (25)$$

the **present value** of an **ordinary annuity** is

$$A_n = R \cdot a_{\overline{mn}|i} \cdot \frac{1}{s_{\overline{m}|i}}; \tag{26}$$

the **amount** of an **annuity due** is

$$S_n(\text{due}) = R \cdot s_{\overline{mn}|i} \cdot \frac{1}{a_{\overline{m}|i}}; \tag{27}$$

the **present value** of an **annuity due** is

$$A_n(\text{due}) = R \cdot a_{\overline{mn}|i} \cdot \frac{1}{a_{\overline{m}|i}}; \tag{28}$$

the **present value** of an ordinary annuity, **deferred** k payment intervals, is

$$A_n(\text{def.}) = R(a_{\overline{m(k+n)}|i} - a_{\overline{mk}|i})\frac{1}{s_{\overline{m}|i}}. \tag{29}$$

It may similarly be shown that the **present value** of a **perpetuity** of payments of R at the end of each interval is

$$A_\infty = \frac{R}{i} \cdot \frac{1}{s_{\overline{m}|i}}, \tag{30}$$

where i and m are defined as above.

ILLUSTRATIVE EXAMPLE 1. What equal payments at the beginning of each quarter will amount at 4% effective to $1000 at the end of 5 years?

SOLUTION. Payment interval, 3 months; interest period, 12 months; $m = \frac{1}{4}$. The amount of an annuity due is given; R is unknown. Solving (27) for R and placing $S_n(\text{due}) = 1000$, $m = \frac{1}{4}$, $n = 20$, $i = 0.04$,

$$R = S_n(\text{due}) \cdot a_{\overline{m}|i} \cdot \frac{1}{s_{\overline{mn}|i}} = 1000 \cdot a_{\overline{\frac{1}{4}}|.04} \cdot \frac{1}{s_{\overline{5}|.04}}$$
$$= 1000 \times 0.24393 \times 0.18463 = \$45.04. \quad \text{[By Tables XI and VII]}$$

ILLUSTRATIVE EXAMPLE 2. A $6000 loan will be amortized by payments of $300 at the end of each 6 months. Find the number of payments, if interest on unpaid balances is at 6% convertible bimonthly.

SOLUTION. Payment interval, 6 months; interest period, 2 months; $m = 3$. The present value of an ordinary annuity is given; n is unknown.

Substituting $A_n = 6000$, $R = 300$, $m = 3$, and $i = 0.01$ in formula (26),

$$6000 = 300 \cdot a_{\overline{3n}|.01} \cdot \frac{1}{s_{\overline{3}|.01}}.$$

Hence $a_{\overline{3n}|.01} = 20 \cdot s_{\overline{3}|.01} = 20 \times 3.0301 = 60.6020.$

In the 1 % column of Table VI, the last entry less than 60.6020 is 60.3620, and the corresponding number in the column at the extreme left is 93. Hence $3n = 93$, or $n = 31$. That is, the amortization will require 31 semiannual payments of $300 each and a 32nd smaller payment.

ILLUSTRATIVE EXAMPLE 3. At what rate converted annually will an annuity of $200 per quarter amount to $4542.34 at the end of 5 years?

SOLUTION. When the unknown in a general annuity problem is the rate, we first solve a *different* problem in which the interest period coincides with the given payment interval. Since our example involves quarterly payments, we first ask: At what rate per *quarterly* conversion period will this annuity amount to $4542.34? By illustrative example 1, Art. 123, the answer is 1.317%. Next we compute the rate per *annual* conversion period, equivalent to the rate 1.317% per quarterly conversion period. Placing $i = 0.01317$ and $m = 4$ in formula (2), $r = (1.01317)^4 - 1$. Using logarithms, $(1.01317)^4 = 1.0537$. Hence $r = 0.0537 = 5.37\%$. *Ans.*

ILLUSTRATIVE EXAMPLE 4. Compute $a_{\frac{15}{4}|.08}$.

SOLUTION. Applying the definition and by illustrative example 2, page 344,

$$a_{\frac{15}{4}|.08} = \frac{1 - (1.08)^{-15/4}}{0.08} = \frac{1 - 0.74930898}{0.08} = 3.133638. \quad Ans.$$

Expressions of this sort may occur in problems with unusual data.

EXERCISE 102

1. What single payment now is equivalent at 4% converted quarterly to 10 annual payments of $200 each, the first due 1 year hence?

2. Do Problem 1 with first payment due 4 years hence.

3. B invests $1000 at the beginning of each quarter in a business yielding 7% effective. How much is to his credit at the end of 2 years?

4. Solve Problem 3 assuming payments at the *end* of each quarter.

5. To buy a house, A will pay $100 at the beginning of each month for 7 years. Find the equivalent cash price at 8% converted semiannually.

6. If a man wishes to accumulate $4000 in 10 years, what should he invest at the end of each quarter at 3% compounded monthly?

7. A $3000 loan will be amortized by 60 equal monthly payments, the first due 25 months hence. Find the monthly payment at 5% effective.

8. Work Problem 7 with first payment due 1 month hence.

9. A $6000 insurance policy carries the option of quarterly payments of $200 each beginning 3 months after the policy matures. Find the number of payments if the company allows 4% converted monthly.

10. Do Problem 9 if payments begin 2 years after maturity.

11. What equal deposits at the beginning of each month will amount at 4% compounded semiannually to $10,000 at the end of 10 years?

12. In buying a farm priced at $5000 cash, a farmer contracts to make 25 equal semiannual payments beginning on purchase date. Payments include interest at $5\frac{1}{2}$% effective. Compute the semiannual payment.

13. To retire a $5100 debt, a man will pay $600 at the end of each year for 10 years. Interest is at what rate converted quarterly?

14. At what effective rate will an annuity of $250 at the end of each 2 months amount to $6500 at the end of 4 years?

15. What sum of money invested at 6% convertible semiannually will provide a perpetual income of $120 at the end of each month?

16. Solve Problem 15 assuming the rate to be 6% effective.

17. Find the present value of a perpetuity of $300 every 4 months with interest at 4% converted annually.

18. A realtor agrees to accept payment of $500 per quarter, payable at the beginning of each quarter, to be invested at 6%. How much does he have at the end of 5 years?

19. Work Problem 18 if payment is made at the end of each quarter.

20. Find the present value of an ordinary annuity of $300 per quarter for 3 years at 5%.

21. Find the present value of an annuity due of $450 each half year for 10 years at 5% annually.

22. Find the present value of an annuity of $200 per quarter at $4\frac{1}{2}\%$ converted semiannually for 7 years, payments deferred for 8 payment intervals.

23. Let C = redemption price of a bond, R = size of each dividend, n = number of remaining dividends, i = yield rate per conversion period, m = (dividend payment interval) $\div$ (conversion period of yield rate). Show that the purchase price is $V = C(1 + i)^{-mn} + R \cdot a_{\overline{mn}|i} \cdot \dfrac{1}{s_{\overline{m}|i}}$.

24. Deduce $V = C + \left(R \cdot \dfrac{1}{s_{\overline{m}|i}} - Ci \right) a_{\overline{mn}|i}$ from formula in Problem 23.

25. Find the price of a $100, 4% bond with quarterly dividends, redeemable at 110 in 20 years, bought to yield 3% effective (see Problem 23).

26. Employ the formula in Problem 24 to work Problem 25.

MISCELLANEOUS EXERCISE 103
REVIEW OF CHAPTER 17

1. Indicate the rate, per semiannual conversion period, equivalent to 6% converted (a) monthly; (b) quarterly; (c) annually; (d) biennially.

2. Determine the value of n if $a_{\overline{5+3n}|.04} = 24.6532$.

3. Solve the example of Art. 102 using only *compound* interest.

4. $a_{\overline{kn}|i} \div s_{\overline{k}|i}$ abbreviates what fraction if $k = \frac{1}{4}$, $n = 18$, $i = 0.04$?

5. Explain how to compute $(1.06)^n$ from the tables when $n = -\frac{7}{4}$.

6. Indicate $[(1.02)^4 - 1] \div [1 - (1.02)^{-12}]$ in annuity symbols.

7. Compute $(1.01)^m$ to 5 decimal places by logarithms if $m = \frac{1}{6}$.

8. Apply the binomial theorem to do the computation in Problem 7.

9. Using no formulas from page 354, find at 4% converted monthly the amount of an annuity of $100 at the end of each quarter for 10 years.

10. Compute the present value of the annuity in Problem 9 as directed.

11. A $1000 payment due 4 years hence is equivalent at 4% effective to what 48 equal monthly payments, the first due 1 month hence?

12. Work Problem 11 if the first monthly payment is due now.

13. Do Problem 11 if the $1000 is due now, all else unchanged.

14. Solve Problem 11 if the $1000 is due 1 month hence.

15. Determine the price of a $100, 4% bond with semiannual dividends redeemable at par in 15 years, bought to yield $3\frac{1}{2}$% effective.

16. A $100, $5\frac{1}{2}$% bond with semiannual dividends costs $116.75 ten years before due. Using the bond table, find the effective yield rate.

17. How much invested now at 6% converted quarterly will provide 5 biennial payments of $2000 each, the first due 6 years hence?

18. Solve Problem 17 if the first $1000 is due 2 years hence.

19. Do Problem 17 assuming the first $2000 is due now.

20. If the payments of the perpetuity in Art. 173 are made at the beginning of each interval, show that the present value is $R \div i a_{\overline{m}|i}$.

21. A fraternity buys a $35,000 house on Sept. 1 with terms: $5000 cash and x on the first of each month except Aug. and Sept. for 15 years; interest on unpaid balances at 6% converted monthly. Find x. [*Hint.* 10 payments of x each are equivalent to payment of $x \cdot a_{\overline{10}|.005}$ on Sept. 1 preceding; think of an annuity due of $x \cdot a_{\overline{10}|.005}$ a year.]

22. If each of the time-payments in Problem 21 were $331.26, with no change in dates, how long would it take to cancel the obligation?

23. A $1000 payment due 5 years hence is equivalent at 6% converted quarterly to what 30 equal bimonthly payments, the first due now?

24. Do Problem 23 if the $1000 is due now, all else unchanged.

25. What nominal rate, converted every other month, corresponds to $3\frac{1}{2}$% converted semiannually?

26. Deposits of $55 monthly, at 4% compounded semiannually, will amount to what sum 5 years hence? Payments are to begin one month hence.

27. In Problem 26, what would the amount be, if the deposits were to begin immediately?

28. What cash amount, now, will buy a car offered for 8 semiannual payments of $350, beginning 6 months hence. Assume interest at 6% effective.

29. In Problem 28, what cash amount will buy the car, assuming that the payments were to begin immediately?

30. A certain debt, at 4% compounded quarterly, is to be discharged by semiannual payments of $500 for 12 years, beginning $4\frac{1}{2}$ years hence. Find the debt.

31. A loan of $5000 is to be amortized by payments of $100 monthly, beginning one month hence. Find the number of monthly payments, if interest is 6% converted quarterly.

32. What amount, invested at 4% converted semiannually, will provide for monthly payments of $100?

33. At what rate converted semiannually, will quarterly payments beginning 3 months hence of $150 amount to $2000 3 years hence?

34. What equal monthly payments beginning one month hence for 25 years should a man make to buy a $22,000 house, if interest is at 6% converted quarterly?

35. In Problem 34, what would the monthly payments be, if payments were to begin immediately?

Chapter EIGHTEEN

LIFE ANNUITIES AND
LIFE INSURANCE

A. Basic Principles and Processes

168. Probability

The mathematical definition of **probability,** which is fundamental in the theory of life annuities and insurance, is based upon a very simple principle. By way of illustration, suppose we have three letters and three envelopes. If the letters are put into the envelopes at random, what is the probability that all three get into the right envelopes? Denote the letters by A, B, C, and the envelopes by a, b, c. Denote by A_a the combination: letter A in envelope a, by A_c the combination: letter A in envelope c, etc. It is evident that only the following cases can occur:

1. A_a, B_b, C_c.   4. A_a, B_c, C_b.
2. A_b, B_c, C_a.   5. A_c, B_b, C_a.
3. A_c, B_a, C_b.   6. A_b, B_a, C_c.

There are 6 equally likely ways of placing the letters in the envelopes. Of these 6 ways, numbered 1 to 6 in the above table, number 1 indicates that the letters are in the correct envelopes. Numbers 2 and 3 show every letter in a wrong envelope. Numbers 4, 5, and 6 each show two letters wrongly placed, and one correctly placed. In one case, all are correct; in two cases, all are incorrect; in three cases, exactly one is correct.

Returning to the question of correct placing of all three letters, we see that all are correct in 1 case out of 6. Hence the probability that a random selection of letters and envelopes will be correct is $\frac{1}{6}$. This is in accordance with the following.

Definition

If each of the ways in which an event can happen or fail is equally likely, and if the event can happen in h ways and fail in f ways, then the **probability** of the event happening is

$$p = \frac{h}{h+f},\qquad(31)$$

and the probability of its failing is

$$q = \frac{f}{h+f}.\qquad(32)$$

Thus, each of the numbers p and q is less than 1 or, at most, equal to 1. Their sum is 1. The probability of an event failing is 1 minus the probability of its happening; in symbols, $q = 1 - p$. In the problem cited, $h + f$ is 6, the total number of ways of placing 3 letters in 3 envelopes. The definition given is useful only *if all the ways of happening (or failing) are equally likely*.

When the mathematical probability cannot be known, use is frequently made of probability determined by observed data and analysis. If, out of 10,000 pupils of approximately equal training and ability, 200 failed to solve a given problem, we might say that the probability of not finding the correct solution on an individual paper is $200 \div 10,000 = \frac{1}{50}$. Probability determined in this way is supposed to be more dependable as the number of observed happenings or failings of an event increases.

EXERCISE 104

In the problem of Art. 168, find the probability that the number of letters correctly placed is:

1. Exactly one.   **3.** At least one.   **5.** Zero.

2. More than one.   **4.** Exactly two.   **6.** One or zero.

7. If a card is drawn at random from a pack of 52 cards, what is the probability that it will be a king, queen, or ace?

8. The faces of a cubical die are numbered from 1 to 6. What is the probability that a number less than 3 will turn up in one throw?

9. What is the probability that a man selected at random in a large crowd was born in the second half of April? Assume 365 days in a year.

10. The probability that a man will die within 10 years is 0.15. What is the probability that he will live at least 10 more years?

11. If three coins are tossed once, find the probability that there will be (a) exactly one tail; (b) at least one tail; (c) no tail. (Let H stand for heads, T for tails; the 8 possibilities are: HHH, HHT, HTH, etc.)

12. If a coin is tossed three times, find the probability that it will fall heads (a) more than once; (b) each time; (c) exactly once.

13. What is the probability of drawing the queen of spades from a deck of 52 cards?

14. Out of 10 pupils, 5 got one problem right and 3 got another problem right. What is the probability of a student getting both problems-right?

15. What is the probability that the sum of the faces in two rolls of a die is less than 6?

16. What is the probability that the sum of the faces in two rolls of a die is equal to 6? Greater than 6?

17. What is the probability of drawing a spade from a deck of 52 cards?

169. Mortality table

In the American Experience Table of Mortality, **Table XII,** will be found five columns. The first column, headed x, gives the age in years from 10 to 95. The second column, headed l_x, gives the number of people alive at age x. The number dying between ages x and $x + 1$ is denoted by d_x, the probability that a person aged x will die within one year by q_x, and the probability that he will live at least one year by p_x. The manner in which l_x is found for the purpose of making the table will not concern us here. This column represents approximately the life record of a group of 100,000 alive at age 10. When l_x is known, the remainder of the table is easily constructed. Thus, d_x is the difference between l_x and l_{x+1}, or

$$d_x = l_x - l_{x+1}. \tag{33}$$

For example, $d_{15} = l_{15} - l_{16} = 96,285 - 95,550 = 735$.

The probability that a man aged x will die between age x and age $x + 1$ is by definition

$$q_x = \frac{d_x}{l_x}. \tag{34}$$

The probability that a person aged x will live at least one year is

$$p_x = 1 - q_x = \frac{l_{x+1}}{l_x}. \tag{35}$$

The probability that a man aged x will live at least n years, or what is the same thing, the probability that he will be alive at age $x + n$ is

$$_np_x = \frac{l_{x+n}}{l_x}. \tag{36}$$

The probability that he will die within n years is of course $1 - {}_np_x$ and is denoted by $_nq_x$, so that

$$_nq_x = 1 - {}_np_x = \frac{l_x - l_{x+n}}{l_x}. \tag{37}$$

Finally, the probability that he will die within the year after he reaches age $x + n$ is

$$_n|q_x = \frac{d_{x+n}}{l_x} = \frac{l_{x+n}}{l_x} - \frac{l_{x+n+1}}{l_x} = {}_np_x - {}_{n+1}p_x. \tag{38}$$

ILLUSTRATIVE EXAMPLE. Find the values of the following:

(a) The number dying between ages 30 and 31, or d_{30}.
(b) The probability that a man aged 30 will live at least a year, or p_{30}.
(c) The probability that a man aged 30 will die within the year, or q_{30}.
(d) The probability that a man aged 30 will live at least 5 years, or $_5p_{30}$.
(e) The probability that a man aged 30 will die within 5 years, or $_5q_{30}$.
(f) The probability that a man aged 30 will live 5 years and die the year following, or $_5|q_{30}$.

SOLUTION

(a) From the table, $d_{30} = 720.$
(b) From the table, $p_{30} = 0.991573.$
(c) From the table, $q_{30} = 0.008427.$

(d) By formula (36), $\qquad {}_5p_{30} = \dfrac{l_{35}}{l_{30}} = \dfrac{81{,}822}{85{,}441} = 0.95764.$

(e) By formula (37), $\qquad {}_5q_{30} = \dfrac{l_{30} - l_{35}}{l_{30}} = \dfrac{3619}{85{,}441} = 0.04236.$

(f) By formula (38), $\qquad {}_5|q_{30} = \dfrac{d_{35}}{l_{30}} = \dfrac{732}{85{,}441} = 0.00857.$

EXERCISE 105

Use results of above example to answer each question. What per cent of a large group of persons aged 30 now may be expected to die:

1. Within 2 years? **3.** After 5 years? **5.** During 4th year?

2. Within 5 years? **4.** After 1 year? **6.** After 6 years?

State in words the probability denoted by each and find its value:

7. q_{18}. **10.** ${}_{30}p_{40}$. **13.** $l_{37} \div l_{35}$. **16.** $d_{48} \div l_{40}$.

8. p_{21}. **11.** ${}_{20}|q_{50}$. **14.** $d_{29} \div l_{29}$. **17.** $(l_{50} - l_{80}) \div l_{50}$.

9. p_{80}. **12.** ${}_{15}q_{60}$. **15.** $l_{67} \div l_{52}$. **18.** $(l_{75} - l_{76}) \div l_{65}$.

Use symbols appearing in left members of formulas in Art. 169 to indicate the probability that a man aged 50 will live:

19. Less than 8 years. **21.** To be 52. **23.** To be 58 but not 59.

20. Less than 1 year. **22.** To be 58. **24.** To be 58 but not 65.

25. Show that $l_x = d_x + d_{x+1} + d_{x+2} + \cdots + d_{95}$.

26. Show that $l_x - l_{x+n} = d_x + d_{x+1} + d_{x+2} + \cdots + d_{x+n-1}$.

27. The **curtate expectation of life** for a man aged x is defined by $e_x = (l_{x+1} + l_{x+2} + \cdots + l_{95}) \div l_x$. Compute e_{90}.

28. The **complete expectation of life** for a man aged x is defined by: $\mathcal{E}_x = \frac{1}{2} + [(l_{x+1} + l_{x+2} + \cdots + l_{95}) \div l_x]$. Compute $\mathcal{E}_{90}$.

170. Present value of a contingent payment

Let S be a sum of money due n years hence. If S is *sure* to be paid, its present value at the effective rate i is Sv^n, where $v = (1 + i)^{-1}$. But if the payment of S is **contingent** on the occurrence of some event and p is the probability of that event happening, then the **present value** P of S is defined by $P = pSv^n$. P is often called the present value of the **expectation** of the person to whom S is promised conditionally. When n is nearly zero, we take $P = pS$ and speak of P as the value of the expectation, thus omitting the word "present." For example, if a man is to win \$20 in case a coin tossed once falls head up, the value of his expectation is $\frac{1}{2} \cdot 20 = \$10$.

In this chapter we shall deal mainly with payments contingent upon duration of human life. Suppose a person aged x is to receive \$$S$ at age $x + n$ if he is alive. The payment of \$$S$ will then depend on the occurrence of an event, namely, his survival. The probability that he will attain age $x + n$ is $_np_x$. As a special case of the above definition, the present value of this contingent payment S is

$$P = {_np_x} \cdot Sv^n = \frac{Sv^n l_{x+n}}{l_x}. \tag{39}$$

ILLUSTRATIVE EXAMPLE 1. A man is to receive \$30 if he throws an ace in a single throw with a die. Find the value of his expectation.

SOLUTION. The probability of throwing an ace in a single trial is $\frac{1}{6}$. By definition, $P = \frac{1}{6} \cdot 30 = \$5$. To grasp the significance of this, consider a hypothetical game paying \$30 to each person who throws an ace in the manner specified. If a *large* number of persons, say 60,000, were to engage in the "game," one-sixth of them, or 10,000, would be expected to throw an ace. To pay \$30 to each of the 10,000 winners, \$300,000 would be required. This sum could be realized if each player contributed \$5. In other words, the value of each person's expectation is the *net* fee for the privilege of engaging in the "game."

ILLUSTRATIVE EXAMPLE 2. A man aged 30 is to receive \$1000 if he lives to be 35. Find the present value, at $3\frac{1}{2}\%$, of his expectation.

SOLUTION. Here $S = 1000$, $i = 0.035$, $n = 5$, $x = 30$. By (39)

$$P = \frac{1000(1.035)^{-5} l_{35}}{l_{30}} = \frac{1000 \times 0.841973 \times 81822}{85441} = \$806.31. \quad Ans.$$

Note. Example 2 may be solved by the following **mutual fund** method. Suppose a group of l_{30} persons of age 30 agree to create a fund and to invest it at $3\frac{1}{2}\%$, with the understanding that (1) each member of the group shall contribute a single sum to the fund at age 30; (2) every individual of the group alive at age 35 shall receive $1000 from the fund. Since l_{35} members are expected to be alive at age 35, the fund must contain $1000l_{35}$ at the end of 5 years. The present value of this amount is $1000(1.035)^{-5}l_{35}$; that is, at the time of agreement, a total contribution of $1000(1.035)^{-5}l_{35}$ is needed. Hence each of the l_{30} persons should pay his share of $1000(1.035)^{-5}l_{35} \div l_{30} = \$806.31$. This may be interpreted in terms of a contract between a man aged 30 and an insurance company using the rate $3\frac{1}{2}\%$. If the man contracts to receive $1000 from the company at age 35 in case of survival, he should pay the company at least $806.31, the present value of his expectation.

EXERCISE 106

1. One automobile out of 250 is stolen in a certain city each year. What is the value of the expectation of an owner who carries theft insurance for one year on his car worth $2500?

2. Statistics show that one house out of 800 of a certain type is destroyed each year by fire. Find the value of the expectation of a man who carries $6000 insurance on such a house for one year.

3. Rain insurance of $8000 is taken out on a ball game. If, at this season, 3 days out of 20 are rainy, what is the value of the expectation?

4. One ship out of 3000 of a certain type is lost at sea. Find the value of the expectation of a man who insures such a ship for $75,000.

5. If alive 5 years hence, a girl now aged 13 will inherit an estate which will be worth $10,000 then. Compute the present value of her expectation assuming money to be worth $4\frac{1}{2}\%$.

6. A minor aged 12 will receive $1000 if he lives to be 21. At 3%, determine the present value of his expectation.

7. Do Problem 5 by the mutual fund method. (See above **Note.**)

8. Solve Problem 6 by the mutual fund method.

9. A man is to receive $3.00 if the face numbered 1 or 6 turns up in a single throw with a die. Find the value of his expectation.

10. Determine the value of a man's expectation if he is to win $2 in case a coin tossed three times falls heads each time.

11. The family of a man now aged 45 is to receive $10,000 twenty years hence if he dies any time before reaching age 65. Compute the present value of the promised contingent payment on a 5% basis.

12. Solve Problem 11 assuming that the $10,000 payment due twenty years hence is contingent on the man's death between ages 55 and 65.

13. What is the expectation if a game of chance pays $50 for drawing the queen of diamonds from a full deck of cards?

14. Would the establishment running the game in Problem 13 make money by charging $1.00 to play?

15. If alive in 10 years a man will receive $1000. What is the present value of his expectation if money is worth 5%. He is 42 now.

16. Do Problem 15 by the mutual fund method.

17. An indian chief is offered $5000 if he can make rain for a festival. If the area averages 10 days of rain each year (out of 365) what is his expectation?

18. Jones, who is 25 years old, will receive $10,000 at age 65. If money is worth 4% converted semiannually, find the present value of his expectation.

171. Commutation symbols

A number of mortality tables have been prepared from the experience of insurance companies. We shall use the well-known American Experience Table in this book. The *limiting* age of a mortality table is denoted by the Greek letter ω (omega). In the American Experience Table, $\omega = 95$.

For later use we introduce the **commutation symbols** C_x, D_x, M_x, and N_x, defined as follows:

$$C_x = v^{x+1}d_x. \tag{40}$$

$$D_x = v^x l_x. \tag{41}$$

$$M_x = C_x + C_{x+1} + C_{x+2} + \cdots + C_\omega. \tag{42}$$

$$N_x = D_x + D_{x+1} + D_{x+2} + \cdots + D_\omega. \tag{43}$$

Thus, $C_{40} = v^{41}d_{40}$; $C_{k-1} = v^k d_{k-1}$; $D_{21} = v^{21}l_{21}$; $D_{x+n} = v^{x+n}l_{x+n}$; $M_{65} = C_{65} + C_{66} + \cdots + C_\omega$; $N_{x+1} = D_{x+1} + D_{x+2} + \cdots + D_\omega$.

Note. Use of commutation symbols not only simplifies formulas in life annuities and insurance, but also lightens the labor of computations. *Unless otherwise stated, computations in this chapter will be based on the American Experience Table and interest at* $3\frac{1}{2}\%$. **Commutation columns** of **Table XIII** give values of C_x, D_x, M_x, and N_x on a basis of $v = (1.035)^{-1}$ and of mortality according to American Experience.

ILLUSTRATIVE EXAMPLE 1. Compute N_{93} at $i = 4\%$.

SOLUTION. Since interest is at 4%, Table XIII cannot be used. Apply (43), then (41), and use Tables IV and XII. Thus

$$N_{93} = D_{93} + D_{94} + D_{95} = (1.04)^{-93}l_{93} + (1.04)^{-94}l_{94} + (1.04)^{-95}l_{95}$$
$$= 79(0.02606) + 21(0.02505) + 3(0.02409) = 2.657. \quad Ans.$$

ILLUSTRATIVE EXAMPLE 2. Show that

$$C_x + C_{x+1} + \cdots + C_{x+n-1} = M_x - M_{x+n}.$$

SOLUTION. From (42), the expressions for M_x and M_{x+n} are:

$$M_x \quad = C_x + C_{x+1} + \cdots + C_{x+n-1} + C_{x+n} + C_{x+n+1} + \cdots + C_\omega,$$
$$M_{x+n} = \qquad\qquad\qquad\qquad\qquad\quad C_{x+n} + C_{x+n+1} + \cdots + C_\omega.$$

Subtracting the second equation from the first, we have

$$M_x - M_{x+n} = C_x + C_{x+1} + \cdots + C_{x+n-1}.$$

ILLUSTRATIVE EXAMPLE 3. Show that $D_x + N_{x+1} = N_x$.

SOLUTION. Since $N_{x+1} = D_{x+1} + D_{x+2} + \cdots + D_\omega$, we have

$$D_x + N_{x+1} = D_x + (D_{x+1} + D_{x+2} + \cdots + D_\omega) = N_x.$$

ILLUSTRATIVE EXAMPLE 4. Show that

$$D_{x+1} + D_{x+2} + \cdots + D_{x+n} = N_{n+1} - N_{x+n+1}.$$

SOLUTION. From (43), the expressions for N_{x+1} and N_{x+n+1} are:

$$N_{x+1} \quad = D_{x+1} + D_{x+2} + \cdots + D_{x+n} + D_{x+n+1} + \cdots + D_\omega,$$
$$N_{x+n+1} = \qquad\qquad\qquad\qquad\qquad\qquad\quad D_{x+n+1} + \cdots + D_\omega.$$

Subtracting the second equation from the first, we have

$$N_{x+1} - N_{x+n+1} = D_{x+1} + D_{x+2} + \cdots + D_{x+n}.$$

ILLUSTRATIVE EXAMPLE 5. Show that

$$\frac{v d_x + v^2 d_{x+1} + v^3 d_{x+2} + \cdots + v^{\omega-x+1} d_\omega}{l_x} = \frac{M_x}{D_x}.$$

SOLUTION. Multiplying both numerator and denominator of the left member by v^x, we have

$$\frac{v^{x+1} d_x + v^{x+2} d_{x+1} + v^{x+3} d_{x+2} + \cdots + v^{\omega+1} d_\omega}{v^x l_x}$$

$$= \frac{C_x + C_{x+1} + C_{x+2} + \cdots + C_\omega}{D_x} = \frac{M_x}{D_x}.$$

EXERCISE 107

Compute each to 4 significant digits:

1. D_{58} at $2\frac{1}{2}\%$.　**2.** C_{29} at $4\frac{1}{2}\%$.　**3.** M_{93} at 4%.　**4.** N_{93} at 3%.

Apply formula (40) or (41) to express each in another form:

5. D_{50}.　**6.** C_{36}.　**7.** C_{m-1}.　**8.** D_{m+1}.　**9.** $v^{12} l_{12}$.　**10.** $v^{48} d_{47}$.

Express each as a sum of C's or D's:

11. M_{60}.　**12.** N_{45}.　**13.** N_{x-2}.　**14.** M_{x-2}.　**15.** M_{k+1}.　**16.** N_{k+3}.

Express each in terms of M's or N's:

17. $D_{25} + D_{26} + \cdots + D_\omega$.　　**19.** $C_{53} + C_{54} + \cdots + C_{60}$.

18. $C_{32} + C_{33} + \cdots + C_\omega$.　　**20.** $D_{15} + D_{16} + \cdots + D_{21}$.

Use the tables to verify that:

21. $C_{86} = v^{87} d_{86}$.　　**23.** $D_{63} - N_{67} = D_{63} + D_{64} + D_{65} + D_{66}$.

22. $D_{72} = v^{72} l_{72}$.　　**24.** $M_{48} - M_{52} = C_{48} + C_{49} + C_{50} + C_{51}$.

Prove each relation:

25. $C_x = v\, D_x q_x.$ **26.** $D_{x+1} = v\, D_x p_x.$ **27.** $C_x = v\, D_x - D_{x+1}.$

28. $M_x = v N_x - N_{x+1}.$ [*Hint.* Use relation of Problem 27 to write also $C_{x+1} = v D_{x+1} - D_{x+2},\ C_{x+2} = v D_{x+2} - D_{x+3}$, etc.; add all.]

B. Life Annuities

172. Introduction

In an annuity certain, it is assumed that each payment is *sure* to be made when due. In a **life annuity,** each payment is *contingent* on the survival of a specified person, called an **annuitant,** to the payment date. Unless otherwise stated, we assume a life annuity to consist of *equal annual* payments. The **present value** of any life annuity is the sum of the present values of the payments. Since each payment is contingent on the survival to the date of each payment of the annuitant, its present value is given by (39). To express formula (39) in terms of D, multiply numerator and denominator of the right member by v^x; thus

$$P = \frac{v^x}{v^x} \cdot \frac{S v^n l_{x+n}}{l_x} = S \cdot \frac{v^{x+n} l_{x+n}}{v^x l_x} = S \cdot \frac{D_{x+n}}{D_x}.$$

Hence *the present value of a single sum* S, *payable at the end of* n *years if a person now aged* x *attains age* x + n, *is*

$$P = S \cdot \frac{D_{x+n}}{D_x}. \tag{44}$$

173. Whole life annuities

A life annuity whose payments continue as long as the annuitant lives is called a **whole life annuity.** Such an annuity may be classified as ordinary, due, or deferred, according to the time of the first payment with respect to the present age x of the annuitant. Consider a whole life annuity of \$1 per year under three cases:

Case (a)

Let the first \$1 be due at age $x + 1$ of the annuitant. The second is due at age $x + 2$, etc., as long as he lives. By successive use of (44), with $n = 1$,

2, etc., and $S = 1$, write the present values of the payments. Their sum is the present value a_x of an **ordinary** whole life annuity of $1 per year on a life now aged x. Thus

$$a_x = \frac{D_{x+1}}{D_x} + \frac{D_{x+2}}{D_x} + \cdots + \frac{D_\omega}{D_x} = \frac{D_{x+1} + D_{x+2} + \cdots + D_\omega}{D_x}.$$

By (43), the numerator is N_{x+1}. Hence

$$a_x = \frac{N_{x+1}}{D_x}. \tag{45}$$

Case (b)

Let the first payment be due at age x. Then the annuity is a whole life annuity **due** of $1 per year whose present value is denoted by the symbol $\ddot{a}_x$. The present value of the first payment is $1. The remaining payments form an ordinary whole life annuity with present value a_x. Hence

$$\ddot{a}_x = 1 + a_x = 1 + \frac{N_{x+1}}{D_x} = \frac{D_x + N_{x+1}}{D_x}.$$

By illustrative example 3, page 368, $D_x + N_{x+1} = N_x$. Thus

$$\ddot{a} = 1 + a_x = \frac{N_x}{D_x}. \tag{46}$$

Case (c)

Let the first payment be due at age $x + k$ of the annuitant if he is alive. When $k > 1$, the annuity is a **deferred** whole life annuity of $1 per year whose present value is denoted by $_k|\ddot{a}_x$. This annuity would be a whole life annuity due with respect to age $x + k$ of the annuitant; hence its value *then* would be $\ddot{a}_{x+k}$. To find the *present* value of the annuity, that is, the value at age x, apply formula (44) with $S = \ddot{a}_{x+k}$ and $n = k$. Thus

$$_k|\ddot{a}_x = \ddot{a}_{x+k} \cdot \frac{D_{x+k}}{D_x} = \frac{N_{x+k}}{D_{x+k}} \cdot \frac{D_{x+k}}{D_x}.$$

Therefore

$$_k|\ddot{a}_x = \frac{N_{x+k}}{D_x}. \tag{47}$$

If the annual payment of a life annuity is R, its present value A is R

times the present value of the corresponding life annuity of $1. Thus

Ord. whole life annuity: $\qquad A = R \cdot a_x = R \cdot \dfrac{N_{x+1}}{D_x}.$ $\qquad$ (48)

Whole life annuity due: $\qquad A = R \cdot \ddot{a}_x = R \cdot \dfrac{N_x}{D_x}.$ $\qquad$ (49)

Def. whole life annuity: $\qquad A = R \cdot {}_k|\ddot{a}_x = R \cdot \dfrac{N_{x+k}}{D_x}$ $\qquad$ (50)

Note. "Annuitant" usually refers to a person receiving an annuity. For our purpose, an annuitant is a person on whose survival the payments of an annuity are contingent, irrespective of who receives the annuity.

———

ILLUSTRATIVE EXAMPLE 1. Find the present value of a whole life annuity of $600 per year on the life of a man now aged 50, if the first payment is due when he attains (a) age 51; (b) age 65.

SOLUTION. (a) Table XIII gives values of $\ddot{a}_x = 1 + a_x$ on a $3\frac{1}{2}\%$ basis. Since $1 + a_{50} = 14.5346$, we have $a_{50} = 13.5346$. By (48),

$$A = 600 \cdot a_{50} = 600 \times 13.5346 = \$8120.76. \quad Ans.$$

(b) By use of formula (50) and Table XIII,

$$A = 600 \cdot \frac{N_{65}}{D_{50}} = \frac{600 \times 48616.4}{12498.6} = \$2333.85. \quad Ans.$$

———

ILLUSTRATIVE EXAMPLE 2. What annual income for life can a man aged 60 buy with $10,000, the first payment due at age 60?

SOLUTION. Here we have a whole life annuity due in which $A = 10,000$ and R is unknown. From (49), $R = A \div \ddot{a}_x$. Hence

$$R = 10,000 \div \ddot{a}_{60} = 10,000 \div 11.0324 = \$906.42. \quad Ans.$$

———

EXERCISE 108

1. How much should a man deposit at age 50 with an insurance company in order to receive $1000 at age 60 provided he is alive then?

2. A man aged 55 is to receive $1000 from an insurance company at age 65 if he is alive. Compute the present value of this sum.

3. Find the present value of a whole life annuity of $500 a year on the life of a man now aged 60 if the first payment is due at age 60.

4. How much should a man deposit at age 46 with an insurance company in order to receive $800 a year for life beginning at age 47?

5. Solve Problem 3 if the first payment is due age 63.

6. Do Problem 4 with annual payments beginning at age 46.

7. Work Problem 3 if annual payments begin at age 70.

8. Solve Problem 4 with first payment due at age 57.

9. A widow aged 41 is offered the option of $6000 cash or an annual life income. How large is each payment, the first due at age 50?

10. Do Problem 9 if the first payment is due at age 42.

11. How much should a man deposit with an insurance company, at age 49, to receive $10,000 at age 65, provided he is alive then?

12. Find the present value of a whole life annuity (ordinary) of $300 a year starting at age 40.

13. Find the present value of Problem 12 if it is an annuity due.

14. Work Problem 12 if the annuity is $1000 a year and Mr. Smith is 53 years old.

15. Compute the present value of a sum of $10,000 to go to a 45-year-old man at age 70.

16. How much should the man in Problem 15 deposit with an insurance company in order to receive $1000 a year beginning at age 65?

17. What is the present value of an ordinary whole life annuity of $500 a year beginning for a man aged 23?

18. Work Problem 17 if a sum of $20,000 is to be paid the man at age 65.

In each of Problems 19–28, express the given symbol in terms of N and D; describe the annuity whose present value it represents.

19. $\ddot{a}_{12}$.   **20.** a_{33}.   **21.** $_8|\ddot{a}_{45}$.   **22.** $\ddot{a}_{56}$.   **23.** a_{15}.   **24.** $_5|\ddot{a}_{60}$.

25. Prove: $a_x = v\,p_x(1 + a_{x+1})$.   **26.** Prove: $\ddot{a}_x = 1 + v\,p_x\,\ddot{a}_{x+1}$.

27. Write $a_{25} = N_{26} \div D_{25}$ in terms of v and l's, then divide numerator and denominator by v^{25}. Note labor of computations involved.

28. Proceed as in Problem 27 after changing a_{25} to $\ddot{a}_{25}$.

174. Temporary life annuities

A life annuity whose payments cease at a specified time, even though the annuitant continues to live, is called a **temporary life annuity,** which may be classified as ordinary, due, or deferred according to the time of the first payment with respect to the present age x of the annuitant. Consider a temporary life annuity of n annual payments of $1 each under three cases:

Case (a)

Let the first $1 be due at age $x + 1$ of the annuitant. The second is due at age $x + 2$, etc.; the nth, or last, payment is due at age $x + n$ if he survives to that age. By successive use of (44), with $n = 1, 2, \ldots, n$, and $S = 1$, write the present values of the payments. Their sum is the present value, denoted by $a_{x:\overline{n}|}$, of an **ordinary** temporary life annuity of n annual payments of $1 each on the life of an annuitant now aged x. Thus

$$a_{x:\overline{n}|} = \frac{D_{x+1}}{D_x} + \frac{D_{x+2}}{D_x} + \cdots + \frac{D_{x+n}}{D_x} = \frac{D_{x+1} + D_{x+2} + \cdots + D_{x+n}}{D_x}.$$

By illustrative example 4, page 368, the numerator of the last fraction is $N_{x+1} - N_{x+n+1}$. Hence

$$a_{x:\overline{n}|} = \frac{N_{x+1} - N_{x+n+1}}{D_x}. \tag{51}$$

Case (b)

Let the first payment be due at age x. Then the annuity is a temporary life annuity **due** of n annual payments of $1 each whose present value is denoted by $\ddot{a}_{x:\overline{n}|}$. The present value of the first payment is $1. The remaining $n - 1$ payments form an ordinary temporary life annuity with present value $a_{x:\overline{n-1}|}$. Hence

$$\ddot{a}_{x:\overline{n}|} = 1 + a_{x:\overline{n-1}|} = 1 + \frac{N_{x+1} - N_{x+n}}{D_x} = \frac{D_x + N_{x+1} - N_{x+n}}{D_x}.$$

By illustrative example 3, page 368, $D_x + N_{x+1} = N_x$. Thus

$$\ddot{a}_{x\,:\,\overline{n}|} = \frac{N_x - N_{x+n}}{D_x}. \tag{52}$$

Case (c)

Let the first payment be due at age $x + k$ of the annuitant if he is alive. When $k > 1$, the annuity is a **deferred** temporary life annuity of n annual payments of \$1 each whose present value is denoted by $_k|\ddot{a}_{x\,:\,\overline{n}|}$. This annuity would be a temporary life annuity due with respect to age $x + k$ of the annuitant; hence its value *then* would be $\ddot{a}_{x+k\,:\,\overline{n}|}$. To find the *present* value of the annuity, that is, at age x, apply (44) with $S = \ddot{a}_{x+k\,:\,\overline{n}|}$ and $n = k$. Thus

$$_k|\ddot{a}_{x\,:\,\overline{n}|} = \ddot{a}_{x+k\,:\,\overline{n}|} \cdot \frac{D_{x+k}}{D_x} = \frac{N_{x+k} - N_{x+k+n}}{D_{x+k}} \cdot \frac{D_{x+k}}{D_x}.$$

Therefore

$$_k|\ddot{a}_{x\,:\,\overline{n}|} = \frac{N_{x+k} - N_{x+k+n}}{D_x}. \tag{53}$$

If the annual payment is \$R\$ instead of \$1, the present value formulas may be written

Ord. temp. life annuity: $\quad A = R \cdot a_{x\,:\,\overline{n}|} = R \cdot \dfrac{N_{x+1} - N_{x+n+1}}{D_x}.$ (54)

Temp. life annuity due: $\quad A = R \cdot \ddot{a}_{x\,:\,\overline{n}|} = R \cdot \dfrac{N_x - N_{x+n}}{D_x}.$ (55)

Def. temp. life annuity: $\quad A = R \cdot {}_k|\ddot{a}_{x\,:\,\overline{n}|} = R \cdot \dfrac{N_{x+k} - N_{x+k+n}}{D_x}.$ (56)

Note. The student should understand clearly that the present value of a given *life annuity* depends ultimately upon formula (39) of Art. 170, which involves not only an interest rate but also a probability of survival; whereas the present value of a given *annuity certain* involves only an interest rate. It should also be emphasized that all life annuity and life insurance *formulas* in this chapter hold true *regardless of what mortality table or interest rate is assumed*. However, if a mortality different from American Experience or an interest rate different from $3\frac{1}{2}\%$ be assumed, Table XIII of this text cannot be used for computations.

ILLUSTRATIVE EXAMPLE 1. Find the present value of a temporary life annuity of 10 annual payments of \$600 each to a man now aged 50, if the first payment is due (a) at age 51; (b) at age 65.

SOLUTION. From (54) and (56), respectively, and using Table XIII:

(a) $A = 600 \cdot \dfrac{N_{51} - N_{61}}{D_{50}} = \dfrac{600 \times 95410.3}{12498.6} = \$4580.21;$

(b) $A = 600 \cdot \dfrac{N_{65} - N_{75}}{D_{50}} = \dfrac{600 \times 36887.5}{12498.6} = \$1770.80.$

In either case the number of $600 payments is 10 at most, no payment being due if the man dies before the date of the first payment.

ILLUSTRATIVE EXAMPLE 2. To buy a life insurance policy, a man aged 37 is offered the option of paying $2000 cash or the equivalent in 20 equal annual premiums beginning at once. Find the annual premium.

SOLUTION. The 20 equal annual premiums form a temporary life annuity due in which $A = 2000$ and R is unknown. By (55),

$$R = \frac{A \cdot D_x}{N_x - N_{x+n}} = \frac{2000 \cdot D_{37}}{N_{37} - N_{57}} = \frac{2000 \times 22501.4}{302911} = \$148.57.$$

EXERCISE 109

1. Find the present value of a 10-year life annuity of $1000 a year on the life of a man now aged 60 if the first payment is due at age 60.

2. What should a man deposit at age 46 with an insurance company to receive a 20-year life annuity of $800 a year beginning at age 47?

3. Solve Problem 1 if the first payment is due at age 61.

4. Do Problem 2 with annual payments beginning at age 46.

5. Work Problem 1 if annual payments begin at age 80.

6. Solve Problem 2 with first payment due at age 57.

7. A widow aged 41 is offered the option of $6000 cash or a 15-year life annuity. How large is each payment, the first due at age 48?

8. Do Problem 7 if the first payment is due at age 42.

9. A boy aged 12 is left $5000. If living, he is to receive annually the interest at 6% until he is 21, at which time he is to receive the principal. Compute the present value of the legacy at 4%.

10. A man aged 64 is granted a pension of $2000 a year for 6 years beginning at once and $1000 a year thereafter for the rest of his life. If all payments are contingent on his survival, find their present value.

11. A teacher aged 40 agrees to pay, if living, $1000 a year for 20 years beginning at once to an insurance company. This would entitle her to a whole life annuity of what annual payment beginning at age 60?

12. A policy will pay $500 a year for 8 years beginning at once to a girl aged 14 if she remains alive. Instead, she chooses to receive 4 annual payments beginning at age 17, if living. Find the annual payment.

13. A man 27 years old is to receive annual payments of $2500 for 3 years, if living. Find the present value of the payments, if payments are to begin at age 28.

14. In Problem 13, what is the present value, if payments are to begin at age 34?

15. A temporary life annuity with present value $11,000 will allow what annual payments for 17 years to a man 39 years old, if payments are to begin at age 40?

16. In Problem 15, what are the annual payments, if: (a) the payments are to begin at age 44? (b) the payments are to begin immediately?

17. A certain life insurance policy is offered to a man aged 20 for 40 equal annual premiums or the cash equivalent of $7550.59. Find the annual premium.

18. In Problem 17, find the annual premium, if payments are for 45 years, and they are to begin immediately.

19. A man aged 18 agrees to pay, if living, $300 a year for 47 years beginning at once to an insurance company. This would entitle him to a temporary life annuity of what annual payment for 15 years beginning at age 66?

20. In Problem 19, if the man pays $200 a year, he would be entitled to what annual payment for 20 years beginning at age 66?

In Problems 21–26 express the given symbol in terms of N and D; in Problems 27–32, write the given expression in terms of $\ddot{a}$ or a. In each case, describe the annuity whose present value is denoted.

21. a_{17}.   **22.** $\ddot{a}_{65}$.   **23.** $\ddot{a}_{25:\overline{8}|}$.   **24.** $a_{43:\overline{6}|}$.   **25.** $_4|\ddot{a}_{35}$.   **26.** $_5|\ddot{a}_{50:\overline{7}|}$.

27. $N_{33} \div D_{33}$.   **29.** $N_{51} \div D_{50}$.   **31.** $(N_{55} - N_{65}) \div D_{40}$.

28. $N_{45} \div D_{35}$.   **30.** $(N_{31} - N_{51}) \div D_{31}$.   **32.** $(N_{47} - N_{59}) \div D_{47}$.

33. Prove: $\ddot{a}_x = \ddot{a}_{x:\overline{n}|} + _n|\ddot{a}_x$.   **34.** Prove: $_k|\ddot{a}_x = _k|\ddot{a}_{x:\overline{n}|} + _{k+n}|\ddot{a}_x$.

C. Life Insurance

175. Introduction

In a scientific system of life insurance, individual losses caused by death are distributed by some principle of mutuality over a *large* group of persons. A **policy** is a written contract between an insurance company and the **insured,** or **policyholder.** The company agrees to pay, on the happening of specified events, the **face,** or **benefit** of the policy to the designated **beneficiary.** The insured agrees in turn to pay stated sums, called **gross premiums.** The contract takes effect on the **policy date,** after which each successive year is a **policy year.** An important item in determining premiums is the insured person's **age at issue,** that is, age on birthday *nearest to policy date.*

176. Net premiums

The **net single premium** for a policy is the value of the benefit on the policy date, assuming that: (1) Policyholders will die at the rate given by an adopted mortality table; (2) the company's funds will earn interest at an assumed rate; (3) the benefit will be paid at the end of the policy year in which it falls due; (4) there will be no expense in conducting the business. Under these assumptions, one could buy a policy by paying either a net single premium on the policy date or its equivalent in equal annual installments, called **net annual premiums** and due at the beginning of each policy year. Life insurance is seldom purchased by a single payment, but a knowledge of the net single premium enables us to find the net annual premium by use of the fundamental relation: *The present value of the net annual premiums equals the net single premium.*

Note. A death benefit is actually due immediately on proof of death. Moreover, the company must meet such expenses as commissions, medical fees, salaries, taxes, etc. To provide for expenses and unforeseen contingencies, the company adds to a net premium a certain amount, called the **loading.** The resulting sum is the **gross premium** actually paid by the insured. It is beyond the scope of this book to discuss methods used for loading. We shall deal with the basic problem of determining net premiums. In numerical computations, we shall assume the American Experience Table and interest at $3\frac{1}{2}\%$, unless otherwise stated.

177. Whole life insurance

A policy for whole life insurance or, briefly a **whole life policy,** provides for the payment of the benefit at the death of the insured. Let A_x denote the *net* single premium for a whole life policy of $1 on the life of a person aged x. We shall obtain an expression for A_x by the mutual fund method. Suppose that a company issues a whole life policy of $1 simultaneously to each of l_x persons, all of age x. The number of deaths during the first year is d_x, and the company must pay $$d_x$ in death benefits at the end of the first policy year; at an assumed rate i, the present value of $$d_x$ is $$vd_x$, where $v = (1 + i)^{-1}$. The number of deaths during the second year is d_{x+1}; at the end of that year the company must pay $$d_{x+1}$ in death benefits, whose present value is $$v^2d_{x+1}$, etc., to the end of the mortality table. The net single premium A_x for each of the l_x policies is the total present value of all death benefits divided by l_x. Thus

$$A_x = \frac{vd_x + v^2d_{x+1} + v^3d_{x+2} + \cdots + v^{\omega-x+1}d_\omega}{l_x}.$$

By illustrative example 5, page 369, we have

$$A_x = \frac{M_x}{D_x}. \tag{57}$$

A whole life policy calling for annual premiums payable throughout the life of the insured is an **ordinary life policy.** Let P_x denote the *net* annual premium for an ordinary life policy of $1 on the life of a person aged x. Payments of P_x to the company at the beginning of each policy year for life constitute a whole life annuity due. From formula (49), with $R = P_x$, the present value of this annuity is $P_x \cdot \ddot{a}_x$, which must be equal to the net single premium A_x for the policy. Thus, $P_x \cdot \ddot{a}_x = A_x$. Expressing $\ddot{a}_x$ and A_x in commutation symbols as given by (46) and (57),

$$P_x \cdot \frac{N_x}{D_x} = \frac{M_x}{D_x}.$$

Therefore

$$P_x = \frac{M_x}{N_x}. \tag{58}$$

A whole life policy calling for n annual premiums is an **n-payment life policy.** Let $_nP_x$ be the *net* annual premium for an n-payment life policy of $1 issued at age x. The premiums form a temporary life annuity due whose present value is $_nP_x \cdot \ddot{a}_{x:\overline{n}|}$, as obtained from (55) with $R = {_nP_x}$. Thus, $_nP_x \cdot \ddot{a}_{x:\overline{n}|} = A_x$. Or, by use of (52) and (57),

$$_nP_x \cdot \frac{N_x - N_{x+n}}{D_x} = \frac{M_x}{D_x}.$$

Therefore

$$_nP_x = \frac{M_x}{N_x - N_{x+n}}. \tag{59}$$

ILLUSTRATIVE EXAMPLE. A $1000 whole life policy is issued at age 30. Find (a) the net single premium; (b) the net annual premium, if payable for life; (c) the net annual premium, if payable for 15 years.

SOLUTION. Apply (57), (58), (59), and multiply the results by 1000.

(a) Directly from Table XIII, $A_{30} = .33702$; $1000 \cdot A_{30} = \$337.02$.

(b) $P_{30} = \dfrac{M_{30}}{N_{30}} = \dfrac{10259.0}{596804} = .01719$; $1000 \cdot P_{30} = \$17.19$.

(c) $_{15}P_{30} = \dfrac{M_{30}}{N_{30} - N_{45}} = \dfrac{10259.0}{343059} = .02990$; $1000 \cdot {_{15}P_{30}} = \$29.90$.

Note. In all three cases, insurance protection continues for life. In (c), the number of premium payments is 15 unless death occurs earlier.

EXERCISE 110

In Problems 1–12 assume a $1000 policy of the type specified.

1. Ordinary life, issued at age 30. Compute net annual premium.

2. Ordinary life, issued at age 45. Compute net annual premium.

3. Whole life, issued at age 25. Determine net single premium.

4. Whole life, issued at age 45. Determine net single premium.

5. Twenty-payment life, issued at age 30. Find net annual premium.

6. Twenty-payment life, issued at age 45. Find net annual premium.

7. Ordinary life, issued at age 40. Compute the net annual premium.

8. Whole life, issued at age 28. Determine the net single premium.

9. Twenty-payment life, issued at age 34. Find the net annual premium.

10. Ordinary life, issued at age 23. Compute the net annual premium.

11. Whole life, issued at age 39. Determine net single payment.

12. Twenty-payment life, issued at age 43. Compute the net annual premium.

13. Compute by the mutual fund method the net single premium for a $1000 whole life policy taken at age 93, assuming interest at 4%.

14. Do Problem 13 assuming interest at 3%.

15. Show that $A_x = v\ddot{a}_x - a_x = 1 - d\ddot{a}_x$, where $d = 1 - v$. [*Hint.* Substitute in (57) the expression for M_x in Problem 28, page 370.]

16. From $P_x = \dfrac{A_x}{\ddot{a}_x}$ and Problem 9, prove $P_x = \dfrac{1}{\ddot{a}_x} - d = \dfrac{dA_x}{1 - A_x}$.

178. Term insurance

A policy for an n-year term insurance or, briefly, an **n-year term policy,** promises the payment of the benefit at the death of the insured, provided death occurs within n years. Let $A^1_{x:\,\overline{n}|}$ be the net single premium for an n-year term policy of $1 issued at age x. We shall obtain an expression for $A^1_{x:\,\overline{n}|}$ by supposing, as in Art. 177, that a company issues an n-year term policy of $1 to each of l_x persons of age x. Note that, in this case, the *last* set of payments in death benefits is due at the end of the nth policy year. The amount needed at that time is d_{x+n-1}, since d_{x+n-1} deaths occur during the nth year. All the remaining policies expire after the term of n years. Dividing by l_x the sum of the present values of all death benefits for n years, we see that

$$A^1_{x:\,\overline{n}|} = \frac{vd_x + v^2 d_{x+1} + v^3 d_{x+2} + \cdots + v^n d_{x+n-1}}{l_x}.$$

Multiplying both numerator and denominator by v^x, then inserting the commutation symbols C and D,

$$A^1_{x:\,\overline{n}|} = \frac{C_x + C_{x+1} + C_{x+2} + \cdots + C_{x+n-1}}{D_x}.$$

By illustrative example 2, page 368, we then have

$$A^1_{x:\,\overline{n}|} = \frac{M_x - M_{x+n}}{D_x}. \tag{60}$$

Let $P^1_{x:\,\overline{n}|}$ be the net annual premium for an n-payment, n-year term policy of \$1 issued at age x. The premium payments form a temporary life annuity due with present value $P^1_{x:\,\overline{n}|} \cdot \ddot{a}_{x:\,\overline{n}|}$, so that $P^1_{x:\,\overline{n}|} \cdot \ddot{a}_{x:\,\overline{n}|} = A^1_{x:\,\overline{n}|}$. Or

$$P^1_{x:\,\overline{n}|} \cdot \frac{N_x - N_{x+n}}{D_x} = \frac{M_x - M_{x+n}}{D_x}. \qquad \text{[By formulas (52) and (60)]}$$

Therefore

$$P^1_{x:\,\overline{n}|} = \frac{M_x - M_{x+n}}{N_x - N_{x+n}}. \tag{61}$$

It is left as an exercise to show that the net annual premium $P^1_{x:\,\overline{n}|}$ for a t-payment, n-year term policy ($t < n$) of \$1 issued at age x is given by

$$_tP^1_{x:\,\overline{n}|} = \frac{M_x - M_{x+n}}{N_x - N_{x+t}}. \tag{62}$$

The net single premium at age n for a 1-year term policy is called the **natural premium** at age x. Setting $n = 1$ in (60), the natural premium c_x at age x for a \$1 policy is

$$c_x = \frac{M_x - M_{x+1}}{D_x} = \frac{C_x}{D_x}. \tag{63}$$

ILLUSTRATIVE EXAMPLE. A \$1000, 15-year term policy is issued at age 30. Find (a) the net single premium; (b) the net annual premium, if payable for 15 years; (c) the net annual premium, if payable for 5 years.

SOLUTION. Apply (60), (61), (62), and multiply the results by 1000.

(a) $A^1_{30:\,\overline{15}|} = \dfrac{M_{30} - M_{45}}{D_{30}} = \dfrac{3066.19}{30440.8} = 0.10073; \; 1000 \cdot A^1_{30:\,\overline{15}|} = \$100.73.$

(b) $P^1_{30:\,\overline{15}|} = \dfrac{M_{30} - M_{45}}{N_{30} - N_{45}} = \dfrac{3066.19}{343059} = 0.00894; \; 1000 \cdot P^1_{30:\,\overline{15}|} = \$8.94.$

(c) $_5P^1_{30:\,\overline{15}|} = \dfrac{M_{30} - M_{45}}{N_{30} - N_{35}} = \dfrac{3066.19}{139933} = 0.02191; \; 1000 \cdot {_5P^1_{30:\,\overline{15}|}} = \$21.91.$

Note. In all three cases, insurance protection is for 15 years, after which the policy has no force. In (b) and (c), premium payments cease in case the insured dies before the expiration of the premium payment period.

EXERCISE 111

Interpret each as a premium and express in commutation symbols:

1. $_{20}P_{30}$.   **2.** A_{28}.   **3.** $P^1_{57:\,\overline{5}|}$.   **4.** P_{35}.   **5.** $A^1_{35:\,\overline{8}|}$.   **6.** $_3P^1_{40:\,\overline{8}|}$.

In each of Problems 7–12, assume a $1000 policy issued at age 35.

7. Five-year term. Determine net single premium.

8. Ten-year term. Determine net single premium.

9. Ten-payment, 10-year term. Find net annual premium.

10. Ten-payment, 10-year term. Find net annual premium.

11. Three-payment, 5-year term. Compute net annual premium.

12. Six-payment, 10-year term. Compute net annual premium.

13. Find the natural premium at age 12 for a $10,000 insurance.

14. The natural premium at age 72 for a $1000 insurance is what?

In each of Problems 15 through 20, assume a $5000 policy issued at age 21.

15. Ten-year term. Determine net single premium.

16. Seventeen-year term. Determine net single premium.

17. Twenty-payment, 20-year term. Find net annual premium.

18. Seven-payment, 7 year term. Find net annual premium.

19. Five-payment, 10 year term. Find the net annual premium.

20. Seven-payment, 15 year term. Find the net annual premium.

21. Find the natural premium, at age 21, for a $5000 insurance policy.

22. In Problem 21, find the natural premium: (a) at age 65; and (b) at age 95.

23. Prove: $c_x = v\,d_x \div l_x = vq_x$.   **24.** Prove: $A^1_{x:\,\overline{2}|} = c_x + v^2\,_1|q_x$.

25. Show that $A_{x:\,\overline{n}|}^{1} = v\,\ddot{a}_{x:\,\overline{n}|} - a_{x:\,\overline{n}|}$. [*Hint.* Substitute in (60) the expressions for M_x and M_{x+n} obtained from Problem 28, page 370.]

26. From $P_{x:\,\overline{n}|}^{1} = \dfrac{A_{x:\,\overline{n}|}^{1}}{\ddot{a}_{x:\,\overline{n}|}}$ and Problem 25, prove $P_{x:\,\overline{n}|}^{1} = v - \dfrac{a_{x:\,\overline{n}|}}{\ddot{a}_{x:\,\overline{n}|}}$.

179. Pure endowment

An n-year **pure endowment** policy promises a certain sum at the end of an **endowment period** of n years, provided the policyholder is alive then; if death occurs earlier, the policy pays no benefit. The present value (net single premium at age x) of an n-year pure endowment of \$1 is denoted by ${}_nE_x$ or, for uniformity of symbols in Art. 180, by $A_{x:\,\overline{n}|}^{1}$. From (44), with $S = 1$, we have immediately

$$_nE_x = A_{x:\,\overline{n}|}^{\,1} = \frac{D_{x+n}}{D_x}. \tag{64}$$

Let $P_{x:\,\overline{n}|}^{\,1}$ be the net annual premium, if payable for n years, for an n-year pure endowment of \$1 to a person aged x; and ${}_tP_{x:\,\overline{n}|}^{\,1}$, the net annual premium if payable for t years ($t < n$). It is left as an exercise to show that

$$P_{x:\,\overline{n}|}^{\,1} = \frac{D_{x+n}}{N_x - N_{x+n}}, \tag{65}$$

$$_tP_{x:\,\overline{n}|}^{\,1} = \frac{D_{x+n}}{N_x - N_{x+t}}. \tag{66}$$

180. Endowment insurance

An n-year **endowment insurance** provides for (1) the payment of the benefit at the death of the insured if death occurs within the **endowment period** of n years, and (2) the payment of an equal benefit at the end of the endowment period if the insured is alive then. An n-year endowment insurance may thus be regarded as an n-year term insurance plus an n-year pure endowment. Let $A_{x:\,\overline{n}|}$ be the net single premium for an endowment policy of \$1 issued at age x; $P_{x:\,\overline{n}|}$, the net annual premium if payable for n years; ${}_tP_{x:\,\overline{n}|}$, the net annual premium if payable for t years ($t < n$). From the corresponding formulas for term insurance and pure endowment, it is seen that

$$A_{x:\,\overline{n}|} = A_{x:\,\overline{n}|}^{1} + A_{x:\,\overline{n}|}^{\,1} = \frac{M_x - M_{x+n} + D_{x+n}}{D_x}, \tag{67}$$

$$P_{x:\overline{n}|} = P^1_{x:\overline{n}|} + P_{x:\overline{n}|}^{1} = \frac{M_x - M_{x+n} + D_{x+n}}{N_x - N_{x+n}}, \tag{68}$$

$$_tP_{x:\overline{n}|} = {}_tP^1_{x:\overline{n}|} + {}_tP_{x:\overline{n}|}^{1} = \frac{M_x - M_{x+n} + D_{x+n}}{N_x - N_{x+t}}. \tag{69}$$

Note. The number of net annual premiums for an *n*-year endowment, pure endowment, or term policy is *n*, unless otherwise specified. In the symbols for net single or net annual premiums, a superscript "1" above *x* indicates that the benefit is payable only if the insured *dies* within *n* years (term insurance); when written above *n*, it indicates that the benefit is payable only if he *survives n* years (pure endowment); its omission implies a combination of the two benefits (endowment insurance).

EXERCISE 112

In each of Problems 1–14, assume a $1000 policy issued at age 35.

1. Twenty-year pure endowment. Compute net single premium.

2. Fifteen-year pure endowment. Compute net annual premium.

3. Twenty-year endowment. Determine net annual premium.

4. Twenty-year endowment. Determine net single premium.

5. Ten-payment, 15-year pure endowment. Find net annual premium.

6. Ten-payment, 20-year endowment. Find net annual premium.

7. Fifty-year endowment. Determine net annual premium.

8. Ordinary life. Find net annual premium (compare Problem 7).

9. Thirty-year pure endowment. Compute the net single premium.

10. Twenty-five-year endowment. Compute the net single premium.

11. Thirty-year pure endowment. Compute the net annual premium.

12. Twenty-five-year endowment. Compute the net annual premium.

13. Twenty-payment, 25-year endowment. Find the net annual premium.

14. Ten-payment, 15-year pure endowment. Find the net annual premium.

15. Prove $A_{x:\overline{n}|} = v\,\ddot{a}_{x:\overline{n}|} - a_{x:\overline{n-1}|} = 1 - d\,\ddot{a}_{x:\overline{n}|}$, where $d = 1 - v$.

16. From $P_{x:\overline{n}|} = \dfrac{A_{x:\overline{n}|}}{\ddot{a}_{x:\overline{n}|}}$ and Problem 15, prove $P_{x:\overline{n}|} = \dfrac{1}{\ddot{a}_{x:\overline{n}|}} - d$.

181. Deferred insurance

An insurance, taken out at age x, is **deferred** k years if the term of insurance begins at age $x + k$. Let $_k|A_x$ be the net single premium at age x for a \$1 whole life insurance deferred k years. Then $_k|A_x$ is the value at age x of the net single premium A_{x+k} due at age $x + k$. Setting $S = A_{x+k}$ and $n = k$ in formula (44),

$$_k|A_x = A_{x+k} \cdot \frac{D_{x+k}}{D_x} = \frac{M_{x+k}}{D_{x+k}} \cdot \frac{D_{x+k}}{D_x}. \quad \text{[By formula (57)]}$$

Hence

$$_k|A_x = \frac{M_{x+k}}{D_x}. \tag{70}$$

Similarly, the net single premiums at age x for an n-year term insurance of \$1 and for an n-year endowment insurance of \$1, both deferred k years, are given respectively by

$$_k|A^1_{x:\overline{n}|} = \frac{M_{x+k} - M_{x+k+n}}{D_x}, \tag{71}$$

$$_k|A_{x:\overline{n}|} = \frac{M_{x+k} - M_{x+k+n} + D_{x+k+n}}{D_x}. \tag{72}$$

182. Miscellaneous policies

A **miscellaneous policy** is a single contract combining features of life insurance and annuities or features of different types of life insurance.

———

ILLUSTRATIVE EXAMPLE 1. A policy issued at age 25 will pay \$1000 if the insured dies between ages 25 and 35; \$2000, if death occurs after age 35. Find the net annual premium P payable for life.

SOLUTION. The policy promises two benefits: (a) a 10-year term insurance of \$1000 whose present value (net single premium at age 25) is $1000 \cdot A^1_{25:\overline{10}|}$; (b) a whole life insurance of \$2000, deferred 10 years, whose present value (net single premium at age 25) is $2000 \cdot {}_{10}|A_{25}$. The premiums form a whole life annuity due with present value $P \cdot \ddot{a}_{25}$. This must equal the sum of the present values of the benefits. Thus

$$P \cdot \ddot{a}_{25} = 1000 \cdot A^1_{25:\overline{10|}} + 2000 \cdot {}_{10}|A_{25}$$

$$P\frac{N_{25}}{D_{25}} = 1000\frac{M_{25} - M_{35}}{D_{25}} + 2000\frac{M_{35}}{D_{25}}$$

$$P = \frac{1000(M_{25} - M_{35}) + 2000M_{35}}{N_{25}} = \frac{1000(M_{25} + M_{35})}{N_{25}} = \$26.91. \quad Ans.$$

ILLUSTRATIVE EXAMPLE 2. A policy issued at age 30 will pay \$5000 if the insured dies between ages 30 and 50; \$3000, if he dies between ages 50 and 65; a whole life annuity of \$1000 a year beginning at age 65 if he lives. Find the net annual premium P payable for 25 years.

SOLUTION. The policy promises: (a) a 20-year term insurance of \$5000 whose present value (net single premium at age 30) is $5000 \cdot A^1_{30:\overline{20|}}$; (b) a 15-year term insurance of \$3000, deferred 20 years, whose present value (net single premium at age 30) is $3000 \cdot {}_{20}|A^1_{30:\overline{15|}}$; (c) a whole life annuity of \$1000 a year, deferred 35 years, whose present value is $1000 \cdot {}_{35}|\ddot{a}_{30}$. Premiums form a temporary life annuity due with present value $P \cdot \ddot{a}_{30:\overline{25|}}$. This must equal the sum of the present values of the benefits. Thus

$$P \cdot \ddot{a}_{30:\overline{25|}} = 5000 \cdot A^1_{30:\overline{20|}} + 3000 \cdot {}_{20}|A^1_{30:\overline{15|}} + 1000 \cdot {}_{35}|\ddot{a}_{30}.$$

$$P\frac{N_{30} - N_{55}}{D_{30}} = 5000\frac{M_{30} - M_{50}}{D_{30}} + 3000\frac{M_{50} - M_{65}}{D_{30}} + 1000\frac{N_{65}}{D_{30}}.$$

$$P = \frac{5000(M_{30} - M_{50}) + 3000(M_{50} - M_{65}) + 1000N_{65}}{N_{30} - N_{55}} = \$161.70. \quad Ans.$$

Note. In the later years of a policy of the type just illustrated, the surrender value (see Art. 185) may exceed the death benefit. However, the policy usually provides that, if the insured dies during that period, the death benefit will be so increased as to make it equal to the surrender value at time of death.

EXERCISE 113

1. Find P in illustrative example 1 if it is payable for 30 years.

2. Compute P in illustrative example 2 if it is payable for life.

3. How large is the net single premium in illustrative example 1 ?

4. What is the net single premium in illustrative example 2?

5. A policy, issued at age 35 and calling for 20 annual premiums, provides for a death benefit of $1000 payable only if the insured dies after attaining age 50. Determine the net annual premium.

6. Solve Problem 5 assuming that the benefit is payable only if the insured dies between ages 45 and 65.

7. A policy issued at age 40 will pay either $1000 if the insured dies between ages 45 and 60 or a life annuity of $1000 a year for 10 years beginning at age 60 if he lives. Compute the net single premium.

8. In Problem 7 find the net annual premium payable for 20 years.

9. For a $1000 **modified** whole life policy issued at age 30, the net annual premium P for the first 5 years is one-half of the net annual premium after that for life. Compute P.

10. A **double endowment** policy issued at age 50 pays $1000 if the insured dies before age 65 and $2000 at age 65 if he survives to that age. Find the net annual premium payable for 15 years.

11. A special whole life policy of $3000 is issued to a student aged 20. The net annual premium for the first 4 years is that for a 4-year term policy issued at age 20. Thereafter the net annual premium is that for an ordinary policy issued at age 24. Find these premiums.

12. Do Problem 11 assuming that the first 4 net annual premiums are the *natural* premiums at ages 20 to 23, after which the net annual premium is that for a 30-payment life policy issued at age 24.

13. Find the net single premium for a $10,000 whole life insurance policy issued at age 21, deferred until age 30.

14. A $5000, 10-year term policy was issued to a man aged 25. Find the net single premium, if the policy was deferred 5 years.

15. Find the net single premium for a $2000, 15-year endowment insurance policy, deferred 7 years, issued to a man aged 32.

16. What is the net single premium in Problem 15, if the policy is deferred: (a) 1 year? (b) 10 years?

17. A policy issued at age 21 will pay $20,000 if the insured dies between the ages of 21 and 50; $2500 if death occurs after the age 50. Find the net annual premium payable for life.

18. In Problem 17, find: (a) the net annual premium payable for 44 years; (b) the net single premium.

19. A policy issued at age 13 will pay $500 if the insured dies between the ages of 13 and 20; $15,000 if the insured dies between the ages of 20 and 50; and a temporary life annuity of $5000 annually for 15 years beginning at the age of 50, if he lives. Find the net annual premium payable for life.

20. In Problem 19, find: (a) the net annual premium payable for 52 years; (b) the net single premium.

183. Reserve fund

By collecting the natural premium c_x (Art. 178) from each of l_x persons aged x, a company would have just sufficient on hand, under the assumptions of Art. 176, to pay $\$d_x$ in death claims at the end of one year. The natural premium is thus the net cost of a 1-year insurance. As age advances, the probability of death increases and hence the natural premium becomes greater. If insurance is for a term longer than a year and the net cost is payable by a sequence of **net level premiums** (equal annual premiums), each premium must exceed the natural premium for the earlier ages. The excess is used to build up a **reserve fund** to take care of increased cost at later ages.

Consider a whole life policy of $1000 issued at age 20. The insured pays annually throughout life a net level premium of $1000P_{20} = \$13.48$. The table below shows the natural premium for a $1000 policy from age 20 to age 75 at 5-year intervals. Note that, up to age 50, the net level premium ($13.48) exceeds the natural premium, that is, the net annual cost of insurance. The company places the excess for each year in an accumulating reserve fund. Beginning with age 51, the net level premium is less than the natural premium; withdrawals from the reserve fund take care of the gradually increasing deficiency.

x	20	25	30	35	40	45	50	55	60	65	70	75
$1000c_x$	$7.54	$7.79	$8.14	$8.64	$9.46	$10.79	$13.32	$17.94	$25.79	$38.77	$59.90	$91.18

184. Terminal reserves

The **rth terminal reserve** for a particular policy is the reserve on that policy at the end of the rth policy year, just before the next premium is paid.

Determining reserves is an important phase of actuarial work. Since the total policy reserve is a legal liability to policyholders, the company must have net assets equal in value to the total reserve.

Assume that each of $l_{45} = 74{,}173$ persons of age 45 takes out a $1000, 5-payment, 5-year endowment policy. By (68), the net annual premium is $185.01. At the beginning of the first year, the company receives 74,173 premiums of $185.01 each, or $13,722,747. This is increased by $480,296 (interest at $3\frac{1}{2}\%$) at the end of the year. Since $d_{45} = 828$ persons die during the year, $828,000 is paid in death benefits, leaving a balance of $13,375,043. This divided by $l_{46} = 73{,}345$ (number of survivors) is $182, the first terminal reserve per policy. At the beginning of the 2nd year, the company receives $l_{46} = 73{,}345$ premiums of $185.01 each, or $13,569,558. Add this to what the fund contained at the end of the first year, then compute the interest, etc. The table below shows the accumulation of the reserve fund. Note that the 5th terminal reserve per policy is $1000, so that the company pays $1000 to each survivor at the end of the 5th year, according to the terms of the endowment policy.

Year	Number Living at Beginning of Year	Premiums Received at Beginning of Year	Reserve Fund at Beginning of Year	Interest Earned at End of Year	Death Claims at End of Year	Reserve Fund at End of Year	Terminal Reserve per Policy
1	74,173	$13,722,747	$13,722,747	$ 480,296	$828,000	$13,375,043	$ 182
2	73,345	13,569,558	26,944,601	943,061	848,000	27,100,662	373
3	72,497	13,412,670	40,452,332	1,415,832	870,000	40,998,164	572
4	71,627	13,251,711	54,249,875	1,898,746	896,000	55,252,621	781
5	70,731	13,085,942	68,338,563	2,391,850	927,000	69,803,413	1000
6	69,804						

The table was made by a **retrospective method,** that is, by accumulating premiums received and deducting death claims paid. The underlying principle may be used to compute a terminal reserve without constructing a table. Or, we may determine a terminal reserve by the **prospective method,** that is, by reference to the future. Consider a policy issued at age x, promising certain benefits and calling for annual premiums. Then, by the prospective method,

$$\begin{bmatrix} r\text{th} \\ \text{terminal} \\ \text{reserve} \end{bmatrix} = \begin{bmatrix} \text{Value at} \\ \text{age } x + r \text{ of} \\ \text{future benefits} \end{bmatrix} - \begin{bmatrix} \text{Value at age } x + r \\ \text{of net premiums} \\ \text{yet to be paid} \end{bmatrix}. \qquad (73)$$

ILLUSTRATIVE EXAMPLE 1. Find the 2nd terminal reserve for a 5-payment, 5-year endowment policy of $1000 issued at age 45.

SOLUTION. By (68), the net annual premium is $1000 \cdot P_{45:\overline{5}|} = \$185.01$. At the end of the 2nd policy year, the insured is of age 47. At that time, the future benefit of the policy is a 3-year endowment insurance of $1000 for a person aged 47. By (67), the value (net single premium) at age 47 of this benefit is $1000 \cdot A_{47:\overline{3}|}$. The 3 premiums yet to be paid form a temporary life annuity due. By (55), the value of this annuity at age 47 is $185.01 \cdot \ddot{a}_{47:\overline{3}|}$. Let V be the 2nd terminal reserve. From (73),

$$V = 1000 \cdot A_{47:\overline{3}|} - 185.01 \cdot \ddot{a}_{47:\overline{3}|}$$

$$= \frac{1000(M_{47} - M_{50} + D_{50})}{D_{47}} - \frac{185.01(N_{47} - N_{50})}{D_{47}} = \$372.97. \quad Ans.$$

(Compare with the corresponding figure in the table, page 390.)

ILLUSTRATIVE EXAMPLE 2. Find the rth terminal reserve for an ordinary life policy of \$1 issued at age x.

SOLUTION. The net annual premium is P_x. At the end of the rth year, the insured is of age $x + r$ and the benefit is a whole life insurance of \$1 on a life aged $x + r$. By (57), the value (net single premium) at age $x + r$ of this benefit is A_{x+r}. The premiums yet to be paid form a whole life annuity due, whose value at age $x + r$ is $P_x \cdot \ddot{a}_{x+r}$. Let $_rV_x$ be the rth terminal reserve. Then, from (73),

$$_rV_x = A_{x+r} - P_x \cdot \ddot{a}_{x+r}. \quad Ans.$$

Note. The symbol for the rth terminal reserve for a \$1 policy is formed from the symbol for the net annual premium for the policy as follows. Replace the letter P by V and write r as a subscript on the left; if a subscript is already present on the left, write r on the left of that, inserting a colon between the two. Thus, if $_tP_{x:\overline{n}|}$ is the net annual premium, the rth terminal reserve is denoted by $_{r:t}V_{x:\overline{n}|}$.

185. Surrender options

The **surrender value** of a policy is the reserve on it less a small **surrender charge,** if any. In event of surrender or lapse of a policy after the first year or two, the policyholder may elect one of three options: (a) **Paid-up insurance,** or fully paid insurance of original type and for remainder of original term but its amount so reduced that the net single premium at attained age equals the surrender value; (b) **extended insurance,** or fully paid term insurance for original amount but its term so determined that the net single premium at attained age equals the surrender value; (c) **cash refund** of surrender value. Most policies provide that one of the options, usually (b), will apply if the policyholder elects none. The maximum **loan value** of a policy is its surrender value.

ILLUSTRATIVE EXAMPLE. A $1000 ordinary life policy issued at age 28 is discontinued at age 40. The 12th terminal reserve is $126; the surrender charge, $1. Determine surrender options (a) and (b).

SOLUTION. (a) Since the surrender charge is $1, the surrender value is $125. Let S be the amount of paid-up insurance. By (57),

$$S(M_{40} \div D_{40}) = 125; \qquad S = 125(D_{40} \div M_{40}) = \$304.85.$$

Thus, under option (a), the $125 is used as a single premium to buy at age 40 a whole life insurance of $304.85.

(b) Let a $1000, n-year term policy be issued at age 40. By (60),

$$1000(M_{40} - M_{40+n}) \div D_{40} = 125; \qquad M_{40+n} = 5622.99.$$

From Table XIII, $M_{54} = 5682.86$ and $M_{55} = 5510.54$. By interpolation, $40 + n = 54.347$. Hence $n = 14.347$. Thus, under option (b), the $125 is used as a single premium to buy at age 40 a term insurance of $1000 for 14 years and 127 days, assuming 365 days in a year.

Comment on Option (b) for an Endowment Policy. Consider an n-year endowment policy of $\$S$ issued at age x and surrendered at age $x + r$. Let $V =$ surrender value and $A =$ net single premium at age $x + r$ for a term insurance of $\$S$ for the remaining $n - r$ years. Two cases arise in applying option (b). *Case* I: $V < A$. The surrender value V is used solely as the net single premium at age $x + r$ for a term insurance of $\$S$ expiring in less than $n - r$ years. *Case* II: $V > A$. The surrender value V is used as the net single premium at age $x + r$ for a policy furnishing a term insurance of $\$S$ for $n - r$ years and a pure endowment maturing in $n - r$ years but of amount less than $\$S$. See Problem 18 on page 393.

EXERCISE 114

1. A certain policy is issued at age 35. At the end of the 15th policy year, the value of future benefits is $600. The net annual premium, payable for life, is $20. Compute the 15th terminal reserve.

2. A 20-payment policy is issued at age 31. At the end of the 8th policy year, the value of future benefits is $1600. Each of the remaining 12 net annual premiums is $100. Find the 8th terminal reserve.

3. A 10-year term policy of $1000, taken out at age 40, is fully paid for by a single premium at age 40. Find the 6th terminal reserve.

4. A $1000 whole life policy, taken out at age 45, is fully paid for by a single premium at age 45. Compute the 20th terminal reserve.

5. In illustrative example 1, page 386, find the 15th terminal reserve.

6. In illustrative example 2, page 387, find the 25th terminal reserve.

7. Refer to the policy of illustrative example 2, page 387. Write an expression in commutation symbols for the 30th terminal reserve.

8. Refer to the policy of illustrative example 1, page 386. Write an expression in commutation symbols for the 4th terminal reserve.

9. In illustrative example 1, page 390, find the 4th terminal reserve.

10. As in Problem 9, compute the 3rd terminal reserve.

11. Make a table (see page 390) showing the first 3 terminal reserves for a 20-payment life policy of $10,000 issued at age 39. Given $_{20}P_{39} = .03001$.

12. Make a table (see page 390) showing the first 3 terminal reserves for an ordinary life policy of $1000 taken at age 25. Given $P_{25} = .01510$.

13. Compute the 7th terminal reserve for the policy of Problem 11.

14. Compute the 35th terminal reserve for the policy of Problem 12.

15. The 5th terminal reserve for a $10,000, 20-payment life policy issued at age 40 is $1194.60. Assuming a surrender charge of $84.60, find the term of extended insurance at age 45 under option (b), page 391.

16. In Problem 15, find amount of paid-up insurance under option (a).

17. In illustrative example 1, page 390, assume a surrender charge of $12.97 and compute the amount of 3-year paid-up endowment insurance that the surrender value at age 47 will purchase.

18. A $1000, 15-year endowment policy is issued at age 35. *Case* I: If the surrender value at age 37 is $90, it will purchase a $1000 term insurance for how many years? *Case* II: If the surrender value at age 45 is $591.09, it will purchase a 5-year term insurance of $1000 and a 5-year pure endowment of what amount? See **Comment,** page 392.

19. Show that $_{r:n}V_x = A_{x+r} - {}_nP_x \cdot \ddot{a}_{x+r:\overline{n-r|}}$, if $r < n$.

20. Show that $_rV_{x:\overline{n|}} = A_{x+r:\overline{n-r|}} - P_{x:\overline{n|}} \cdot \ddot{a}_{x+r:\overline{n-r|}}$.

MISCELLANEOUS EXERCISE 115
REVIEW OF CHAPTER 18

1. A bag contains 7 black, 8 red, and 10 white balls. If a ball is drawn at random, what is the probability that it will not be white?

2. Find the probability that a man aged 63 will die (a) within 1 year; (b) within 10 years; (c) between ages 73 and 74; (d) after age 73.

3. What is the probability that: (a) In one throw of a die a 1 will turn up?; (b) In one throw of a die a number less than 6 will turn up?.

4. What is the probability that from a deck of 52 cards (a) a king or a jack of clubs will be drawn?; (b) if a pair of cards are drawn, one will be a king and the other, the jack of clubs?

5. One man out of 1200 dies each year from accident. Find the value of A's expectation if he carries $3000 insurance against such death.

6. B is promised a $1000 payment at age 32, if living. If his age is 22 now, find the present value of his expectation on a 5% basis.

7. A man is promised $100 if the Cardinals win the pennant. Find the value of his expectation, if the Cardinals are favored 7 to 1.

8. A boy, aged 10, is to receive $10,000 if he lives to the age of 21. Find the present value of his expectation at $4\frac{1}{2}\%$.

9. Express in terms of C's or D's: (a) $v^{18}d_{17}$; (b) N_{50}; (c) M_{x-1}.

10. Determine x if $N_{35} - N_x = D_{35} + D_{36} + \cdots + D_{50}$.

11. Prove that $v = \dfrac{C_x l_x}{d_x D_x}$.

12. Prove that $D_{x+1} = \dfrac{C_x p_x}{q_x}$.

13. A policy issued at age 35 calls for 25 annual premiums of $100 each. Compute the present value of the premiums.

14. Do Problem 13 assuming each premium is *certain* to be paid.

15. Find the present value of a life pension of $1000 a year to a man aged 65 with first payment due (a) at age 65; (b) at age 66; (c) at age 70.

16. What pure endowment maturing at age 60 can a man aged 40 buy for $1000 cash? Assume interest at 3% and disregard loading.

17. A man aged 50 pays $10,000 to buy a life annuity whose payments begin at age 60 and continue for life. Compute the annual payment.

18. Do Problem 17 assuming a life annuity with 20 payments.

19. Compute at $2\frac{1}{2}\%$ the natural premium at age 32 for a $1000 policy.

Assume that a beneficiary, entitled at age 40 to $10,000, is offered its equivalent in a series of annual payments of $R each, the first due at age 47. In Problems 20–25, find R if the annual payments form:

20. A whole life annuity.   **22.** A 20-year life annuity.

21. A 40-year life annuity.   **23.** A 20-year annuity certain.

24. A 10-year annuity certain followed by a 10-year life annuity.

25. A 10-year annuity certain followed by a whole life annuity.

In each of Problems 26–29, compute the net annual premium payable for 10 years for a policy issued at age 35, assuming that it provides for a death benefit of $1000 if death occurs:

26. Before age 45.   **28.** Between ages 45 and 60.

27. After age 45.   **29.** Any time after policy date.

30. A policy issued at age 40 provides for a $1000 death benefit if the insured dies between ages 45 and 65, and a $1000 cash payment at age 65 if he lives. Find the net annual premium payable for 15 years.

31. Compute the net single premium for the policy of Problem 30.

Compute the net single premium for each of the following $1000 policies issued at age 42:

32. Whole life.   **33.** 15-year term.   **34.** 10-year endowment.

Determine the net annual premium for each of the following $1000 policies issued at age 42:

35. Ordinary life.   **37.** 10-payment life.   **39.** 3-payment 10-year term.

36. 15-year term.   **38.** 20-payment life.   **40.** 10-year endowment.

Compute the 10th terminal reserve for each of the following $1000 policies issued at age 42:

41. Ordinary life.   **43.** 10-payment life.   **45.** 3-payment 10-year term.

42. 15-year term.   **44.** 20-payment life.   **46.** 10-year endowment.

47. A $1000 whole life policy issued at age 34 is fully paid for by a single premium at age 34. Find the 15th terminal reserve.

48. A certain whole life annuity will entitle a man aged 21 to annual payments of $5000. Find the present value, if payments are to begin immediately.

49. What annual payments beginning 3 years hence would a man aged 35 receive from a whole life annuity with present value $12,500.

50. Find the present value of a temporary life annuity of $10,000 annually for 15 years to a boy aged 11, if payments are to begin at age 21.

51. To purchase a certain life insurance policy a man is offered the option of paying $12,000 cash or the equivalent in 30 equal annual premiums beginning one year hence. Find the premium.

52. A policy issued at age 30 pays $10,000 if the insured dies between ages 30 and 55, and a whole life annuity of $1000 a year beginning at age 55 if he lives. Compute the net annual premium payable for 20 years.

53. Find the 20th terminal reserve for the policy of Problem 52.

54. The 12th terminal reserve for a $1000 ordinary life policy issued at age 40 is $205.10. Assuming a surrender charge of $5.10, compute the amount of paid-up insurance at age 52 under option (a), page 391.

55. In Problem 54 find term of extended insurance under option (b).

56. A man aged 32 takes a $1000 ordinary life policy. At the end of 12 years he wishes to convert it to a $1000, 20-payment life policy. He is to pay annually for 8 years the premium for a 20-payment life policy *taken at age* 32, plus a lump sum representing the differences in the net annual premiums for the first 12 years with interest at $3\frac{1}{2}\%$ effective from their respective due dates to the date of exchange. Find the lump sum due at the date of exchange. Given $P_{32} = 0.01819$ and $_{20}P_{32} = 0.02572$.

57. Compare the result obtained in Problem 56 with the difference between the 12th terminal reserves for the two policies. Explain.

Show that:

58. $_1|\ddot{a}_x = a_x.$ **60.** $a_{x:\overline{1}|} = v\,p_x.$ **62.** $_nE_x = {_n|}\ddot{a}_{x:\overline{1}|}.$

59. $_1E_x = v\,p_x.$ **61.** $c_x + {_1}E_x = v.$ **63.** $\ddot{a}_{x:\overline{2}|} = 1 + v\,p_x.$

64. $M_x = D_x - dN_x$, if $d = 1 - v.$ **65.** $a_x\,P_{x+1} = \ddot{a}_x\,P_x - c_x.$

66. $_rV_x = (P_{x+r} - P_x)\ddot{a}_{x+r} = (\ddot{a}_x - \ddot{a}_{x+r}) \div \ddot{a}_x.$

67. $_{r:n}V_x = (_{n-r}P_{x+r} - {_n}P_x)\ddot{a}_{x+r:\overline{n-r}|},$ if $r < n.$

68. $_rV_{x:\overline{n}|} = (P_{x+r:\overline{n-r}|} - P_{x:\overline{n}|})\ddot{a}_{x+r:\overline{n-r}|}.$

69. Find the net annual premium and the net single premium for a whole life policy of $10,000 issued to a man aged 23.

70. Find the net single premium and the net annual premium for a 25-payment, $5000 whole life insurance policy issued to a man aged 35.

71. A $15,000, 7-payment, 10-year term insurance policy was issued to a man aged 24. Find the net annual premium.

72. What amount of term insurance for 7 years will 7 annual premiums of $250 buy for a man aged 27.

73. Find the net annual premium for a 7-payment, 7-year, $13,000 pure endowment policy issued to a man aged 42.

74. Find the net annual premium payable for 5 years for a 10-year, $5000 endowment insurance policy issued to a man aged 60.

75. Find the net single premium for a $5000 whole life policy, deferred 7 years, issued to a boy 14 years old.

76. A policy issued at age 25 will pay $50,000 if the insured dies between the ages of 25 and 45; $2000 if death occurs between the ages of 45 and 65; a temporary life annuity of $3000 annually, beginning at age 66 and ending at age 86, if he lives. Find the net annual premium payable for 40 years.

77. Find the 16th terminal reserve for an ordinary life policy of $5000 issued at age 32.

78. Suppose the policy in Problem 77 is discontinued at age 48. If the surrender charge is $1.00, how much paid-up life insurance is the policyholder entitled to?

GENERAL REVIEW OF
CHAPTERS 11-18

MISCELLANEOUS EXERCISE 116

In problems involving annuities, assume ordinary annuities unless otherwise specified or implied. See **Note** on page 225 for problems numbered in brackets and **Note** on page 367 for numerical problems in life annuities and life insurance.

1. A $1000 payment due 7 years hence is equivalent at 5% to what payment due (a) 3 years hence? (b) 10 years hence?

2. A deposit of $2000 draws interest at 3% compounded quarterly. Compute the accumulated value at the end of $12\frac{1}{2}$ years.

3. A sum of money left in a bank paying $2\frac{1}{2}$% interest compounded semiannually accumulates to $415 in $7\frac{1}{2}$ years. Find the original sum.

4. How long will it take a sum to double itself at $6\frac{1}{2}$% effective?

5. Solve the equation $r = (1 + \frac{1}{4}j)^4 - 1$ for j.

6. A tax bill due April 1 is subject to a discount of 2% if paid by Dec. 1 preceding. Find the corresponding effective rate of interest.

7. The population of a town is 8830. At what annual rate of growth would it increase to 15,000 in 20 years? Solve by logarithms.

8. At the end of each month a man pays $3.50 interest on a loan of $600. This is equivalent to interest at what effective rate?

9. A owes $1000 plus interest for $5\frac{1}{2}$ years at 6% converted annually. What should he pay if simple interest is used for the last $\frac{1}{2}$ year?

10. Find the force of interest corresponding to 3.8% effective.

11. Determine i by interpolation if $(1 + i)^{30} = 2.7500$.

12. A house may be bought for $6000 cash or by monthly payments of $60 each for 12 years, the first due on purchase date. What would a buyer save under the first plan if money is worth 6% converted monthly?

13. Building and loan stock owned by Mr. Fisher pays a $20 dividend each 3 months. He deposits each dividend in a bank paying 2% converted quarterly. How much is to his credit just after the 30th deposit?

398

[14]. George borrows $500 from his brother. Five years later he returns $650, thus paying interest at what rate converted quarterly?

15. Discount $2000 for 7 years at 6% converted monthly.

16. What effective rate is equivalent to $7\frac{1}{2}\%$ converted bimonthly?

17. Commute two debts of $1000 each, due in 5 and 10 years, into a single payment due in 7 years. Money is worth 4%.

18. Commute two debts of $1000 each, due in 5 and 10 years, into 7 equal annual payments, the first due in 1 year. Money is worth 4%.

19. A trust fund of $15,000 is to provide an income of $100 a month. Find the number of payments if interest is at $3\frac{1}{2}\%$ convertible monthly.

20. What rate converted semiannually is equivalent to the rate $6\frac{1}{2}\%$ converted weekly? Assume 26 weeks in a half-year.

21. At the end of each quarter, a man receives a check for $60 from a certain source. He deposits each check at once in a bank whose rate is 2% compounded quarterly. When will he have $2000 to his credit?

22. Given that $s_{\overline{150}|.01} = 344.84229$. Compute $(1.01)^{150}$.

23. Given that $(1.01)^{-120} = 0.30299478$. Compute $a_{\overline{120}|.01}$.

[24]. A television set sells for $280 cash or $28 down and $15 at the end of each month for 18 months. If a customer chooses the time-payment plan, he pays interest at what rate compounded monthly?

25. The population of a city is 30,000. If it increases at the rate of $4\frac{1}{4}\%$ annually, what will be the population 10 years hence?

26. A house is sold for $1500 down and $60 a month for 15 years. Find the equivalent cash price if money is worth 5% converted monthly.

27. To redeem a $1,000,000 bond issue at the end of 20 years, a city sets up a sinking fund accumulating at 3% converted quarterly. How much should be placed in the fund at the end of each quarter?

28. What sum invested at $3\frac{1}{2}\%$ will provide an annual income of $1000 for 15 years beginning at the end of 5 years?

29. An oriental rug may be bought for either $900 cash or 24 monthly payments of $40 each, the first due on purchase date. By choosing the second plan, a buyer pays interest at what rate converted monthly?

30. A man buys furniture worth $1250. He pays $250 and agrees to pay the balance, with interest at 8% converted semimonthly, in 40 equal semimonthly installments. How large is each installment?

31. An annuity of $100 a year for 10 years, with first payment due 6 years hence, is equivalent at 6% to what single payment due now?

Answer the question in Problem 31 if the single payment is due:

32. 5 years hence.   **34.** 10 years hence.   **36.** 16 years hence.

33. 6 years hence.   **35.** 15 years hence.   **37.** 20 years hence.

38. A $1000 payment due now is equivalent at 4% converted quarterly to what 20 equal quarterly payments, the first due in 3 years?

Answer the question in Problem 38 if the $1000 payment is due:

39. 10 years hence.   **41.** $7\frac{3}{4}$ years hence.   **43.** 3 years hence.

40. 8 years hence.   **42.** 5 years hence.   **44.** $2\frac{3}{4}$ years hence.

45. Mr. Smith has three children aged 10, 14, and 17. He places $2424 with a trust company at 3%, so distributed that each child will receive the same amount at age 21. Compute that amount.

46. Find the original share allocated to each child in Problem 45.

47. At the birth of his son, a man establishes a trust fund of $1000 to provide for college expenses. The fund draws interest at 4% converted bimonthly for 7 years and at $3\frac{1}{2}$% effective after that. What is the amount when the boy is 17 years of age?

48. To secure a perpetual income of $1500 payable at the end of each year, what sum must be invested at 3% converted monthly?

49. Work Problem 48 using the rate 3% effective.

50. A piece of timberland will net $1000 per quarter for 5 years. The cleared land will be worth $2000 at the end of 5 years. What is the present value of the timberland on a basis of 6% converted quarterly?

51. Look up the value of $(1.035)^{-72}$ and compute $(1.035)^{-144}$.

52. Find the effective rate equivalent to $3\frac{1}{4}$% converted continuously.

53. $500 is due in 6 years with interest at $3\frac{3}{4}$% for 6 years. Find the value of this obligation 2 years hence if money is worth 5%.

54. A man pays $200 at the beginning of each quarter for 10 years to the Investors' Association. At the end of 10 years he has $9200 to his credit. Interest is allowed at what rate converted quarterly?

55. Do Problem 54 for $200 payments at the *end* of each quarter.

56. On March 1, 1968, a philanthropist places $50,000 with a trust company to provide a benevolent society with a monthly income of $500 beginning on March 1, 1973. Determine the number of monthly payments if the company allows interest at 3% convertible monthly.

57. If the philanthropist of Problem 56 specifies 120 monthly payments, what would be the size of each payment, all else unchanged?

58. Compute $(1.0025)^{270}$ from values of $(1.0025)^{164}$ and $(1.0025)^{106}$.

59. Instead of a $5000 payment in cash, the beneficiary of a matured policy will receive 60 equal monthly payments, the first due at once. Compute the monthly payment if interest is at $3\frac{1}{2}$% converted monthly.

60. At 4% converted semiannually, what equal payments at the beginning of each 6 months will amount to $3000 at the end of 12 years?

61. Six months ago, Mr. Jones paid the last of 30 semiannual life insurance premiums of $100 each. If he had invested each payment at $3\frac{1}{2}$% converted semiannually, what would be the total amount now?

62. In buying a lot priced at $1050 cash, Mr. Baker contracts to pay $25 a month beginning on purchase date. Payments include interest at 7% converted monthly. How many are necessary?

63. Obtain an approximate value of $a_{\overline{1000}|.04}$ by inspection.

64. Accumulate $100 for 10 years at $3\frac{1}{2}$% effective.

65. Accumulate $100 for 10 years at $3\frac{1}{2}$% converted continuously.

66. What sum invested at 4% will provide a perpetual income of $400 at the end of each year beginning at the end of the 10th year?

67. Solve Problem 66 using the rate 4% converted quarterly.

68. Given that $(1.09)^{-74} = 0.0017000$. Compute $(1.09)^{-73}$.

69. Find at 5% the capitalized cost of a highway bridge with initial cost $12,000, annual upkeep $1000, renewal cost $10,000 each 20 years.

70. Do Problem 69 assuming that each renewal cost is $12,000.

71. Composition roofing must be replaced each 3 years at a cost of $3 per 100 sq. ft. How much could one afford to spend per 100 sq. ft. of asphalt roofing that lasts 12 years? Money is worth $4\frac{1}{2}$%.

72. Determine n if $4500 = 75(s_{\overline{n+1}|.045} - 1)$.

73. Alfred Nobel bequeathed $9,000,000 in 1896 stipulating that the income each year forever be used for an annual award of 5 equal prizes in different fields. Assuming that the bequest was invested at 2.1 % effective 4 years before the first award, how large is each prize?

74. If money is worth 4%, an income of $1000 a year for 12 years is equivalent to an income of $500 a year for how many years?

75. Explain why $(a_{\overline{8}|i} - a_{\overline{3}|i})$ is greater than $(a_{\overline{12}|i} - a_{\overline{7}|i})$.

76. What value must x have if $a_{\overline{18}|i} - a_{\overline{17}|i} = (1 + i)^{-x}$?

77. A man deposits $50 at the end of each month for 10 years. Then he begins to withdraw $50 at the end of each month. How long can he withdraw at that rate? Interest is at $3\frac{1}{2}$% converted monthly.

78. If interest is at 7% for the first 5 years and at 5% after that, what equal annual payments for 10 years will repay a loan of $2000?

79. Do Problem 78 after interchanging the two interest rates.

80. Solve Problem 78 assuming a constant rate of 6%.

[81]. Given that $a_{\overline{25}|i} - a_{\overline{5}|i} = 12$. Find i.

82. The monthly rent for a store is $100 due at the beginning of each month. Assuming money is worth 6% converted monthly, compute the equivalent annual rent payable at the beginning of each year.

83. A debtor was to pay $100 at the end of each quarter for 6 years. After omitting the first 9 payments, he pays $1000 at the end of $2\frac{1}{2}$ years. If money is worth 8% converted quarterly, a second payment of what size at the end of 6 years will close the transaction?

84. Show that $s_{\overline{n}|i} - a_{\overline{n}|i} = i\, s_{\overline{n}|i}\, a_{\overline{n}|i}$.

85. Show that $s_{\overline{m+n}|i} = s_{\overline{m}|i} + s_{\overline{n}|i} + i\, s_{\overline{m}|i}\, s_{\overline{n}|i}$.

86. Show that $a_{\overline{m+n}|i} = a_{\overline{m}|i} + a_{\overline{n}|i} - i\, a_{\overline{m}|i}\, a_{\overline{n}|i}$.

87. A $10,000 bequest, invested at 4%, is to provide a scholarship of $x at the end of each year for 75 years. Compute x.

88. In Problem 87, how much remains unused after the 45th award?

89. How much of the last scholarship of Problem 87 is interest?

90. Construct a schedule for the amortization of a $1000 loan, with interest at 4%, by equal payments at the end of each year for 4 years.

91. $2000 will be accumulated in a sinking fund, invested at 5%, by deposits of $400 at the end of each year for 4 years and a smaller final deposit at the end of 5 years. How large is the final deposit?

92. Make a schedule showing the growth of the fund in Problem 91.

93. A man borrows $10,000. The debt, principal and interest at 5%, will be retired by a payment of $1025 at the end of 2 years and 10 equal annual payments after that. Compute the annual payment.

94. A contract calls for 30 quarterly payments of $100 each, the first due 3 months hence, and a payment of $1000 due 8 years hence. What additional payment together with the 20th quarterly payment would close the transaction? Money is worth 5% compounded quarterly.

95. A loan of $1000, bearing interest at 5% payable semiannually, will be amortized by payments of $100 at the end of each 6 months. Find the principal outstanding just after the 8th payment.

96. What part of the first payment in Problem 95 is interest?

97. Find the final payment for the loan of Problem 95.

98. What should the debtor of Problem 95 pay on the day of the 9th payment if he fails to make the 4 payments preceding it?

99. A firm sets up a sinking fund at 3% converted semiannually to pay the principal of a 6-year, $15,000 loan bearing 5% interest payable semiannually. How much should be placed in the fund each half-year?

100. Compute the total semiannual charge in Problem 99.

101. Referring to Problem 99, find (a) the amount in the fund at the end of 4 years; (b) the book value of the loan at that time.

102. What would the firm of Problem 99 save at the end of each half-year if allowed to *amortize* the loan in 12 equal semiannual installments?

103. A city issues 400 bonds of $1000 denomination paying interest annually at 3%. The debt will be retired by 10 annual payments as nearly equal as possible. At the beginning of the 7th year, 175 bonds will be outstanding. How many should be retired at the end of that year?

104. Home mortgage fund sources provided an average of $5256 for each mortgage given in 1950 for financing new homes or remodeling, refinancing, and the like. Assuming a 10-year plan of amortization at 6% converted monthly, the average American home mortgagor of 1950 paid how much a month for 10 years?

105. To retire certain bonds, a corporation will need $10,000 a year for 3 years beginning 10 years hence. What equal annual payments for 12 years, the first 1 year hence, to a sinking fund accumulating at 3% will enable the corporation to retire the bonds as they fall due?

106. A deposits $100 a year for 10 years in a fund invested at 3%. What does the fund contain 5 years after the last deposit?

107. To repay a $10,000 loan, which plan costs less to a borrower and by how much a year: (a) to amortize the loan at 6% in 10 equal annual installments, or (b) to pay $5\frac{1}{2}$% interest yearly and to accumulate a sinking fund at $3\frac{1}{2}$% by 10 equal annual payments to pay the principal?

108. Under plan (b) of Problem 107, at what effective rate does the borrower actually pay interest for the privilege of the loan?

109. A man buys a summer cottage for $3200 and pays $700 cash. He contracts to make equal quarterly payments for 7 years to amortize the balance at 6% converted quarterly. Find the quarterly payment.

110. Just after the 12th quarterly payment in Problem 109, a single payment of what size would cancel all remaining obligations?

111. Just after the 12th quarterly payment in Problem 109, suppose that the creditor reduces the interest rate to $4\frac{1}{2}$% converted quarterly for the remaining 4 years. Compute the new quarterly payment.

112. At the end of each quarter, $400 is deposited in a sinking fund invested at 4% for the first 3 years and at 3% after that, both rates converted quarterly. What does the fund contain at the end of 6 years?

113. Do Problem 112 using the constant rate $3\frac{1}{2}$% converted quarterly.

114. A sinking fund is accumulated at 3% by 3 annual payments of $1000 each followed by 7 annual payments of $R each. Compute R if the fund is to contain $10,000 at the end of 10 years.

115. The trustees of a hospital borrow $10,000 to build a nurses' home. The debt, principal and 5% interest payable semiannually, will be retired by 6 semiannual payments of $500 each followed by semiannual payments of $1000 each. Find the number of $1000 payments.

116. What final payment will close the transaction of Problem 115?

117. Assuming a constant semiannual payment of $750 in Problem 115, determine the number of $750 payments and the final payment.

118. The Empire State Building was erected at a cost of $52,000,000. Assuming that at the end of a useful life of 100 years the scrap value will be offset by the cost of demolishing, what net annual income for 100 years would yield 5% on the investment?

119. A water system is installed at a cost of $100,000. Assume that the operating expenses will be $20,000 annually and that the plant, mains, etc., will be worthless in 30 years. What total annual payment by consumers for 30 years will yield 8% on the original investment?

120. Compute the price of a $1000, 5% bond with annual dividends bought 5 years prior to redemption to yield 3%.

121. Make a schedule for amortization of premium in Problem 120.

122. Do Problem 120 after interchanging the two given rates.

123. Prepare a schedule for accumulation of discount in Problem 122.

124. A $1000, 30-year annuity bond paying interest annually at $2\frac{1}{4}\%$ is bought at the end of the 18th year to yield $2\frac{3}{4}\%$. Find the price.

125. A $1000, 3% bond with annual dividends, maturing at 102 in 12 years, is bought now to yield $2\frac{1}{2}\%$. What price is paid?

126. Find the book value of the bond in Problem 125 five years hence.

127. Compute the yield of a $100, 4%, Canadian Pacific Ry. perpetual bond, dividends payable J-J, quoted at $101.25 on Jan. 1, 1951.

128. Three $1000, 2%, Erie R.R. equipment bonds, paying dividends M-N 15, are due serially May 15, 1977–1979. What total price on May 15, 1971, will yield 3% converted semiannually?

129. Mr. Bell pays $1100 for a $1000 bond, with quarterly dividends of $10 each, redeemable at 105 in 10 years. Find the yield.

130. Mr. Bell of Problem 129 deposits each coupon as it falls due in a bank at 2% converted quarterly. At the end of 10 years, he withdraws the amount on deposit and surrenders the bond for $1050. At what rate converted quarterly did the entire transaction yield interest?

131. A $1000 Seaboard Air Line bond, paying $4\frac{1}{2}\%$ annual dividends on May 1, was quoted at $915 on Oct. 8, 1950. Find the flat price.

132. The flat price of a $1000, 4%, Northern Pacific Ry. bond, J-A-J-O, is $1095 on Dec. 12, 1970. Find the "and interest" price.

133. On March 1, 1949, a man paid $120 for a $100, 6%, Pennsylvania Gas & Electric Corp. bond, M-S, maturing at par on March 1, 1986. The bond was actually called for redemption at 105 on Sept. 1, 1960. What yield, converted semiannually, was obtained on the investment?

134. What would have been the yield of the bond in Problem 133 if the corporation had not exercised its right to redeem prior to maturity?

135. A $100 bond, paying annual dividends at 4% and maturing at par in 15 years, is to be replaced by a $100 bond, paying annual dividends at 3% and maturing in 15 years. Find the redemption price of the new bond if, at 3%, the present values of the two bonds are to be equal.

136. A $1000, Western Maryland Ry. Co. bond matures Oct. 1, 1979. Dividends were at $4\frac{1}{2}\%$ payable annually to Oct. 1, 1962; thereafter, at 4% payable semiannually, A-O. Thus, the last $45 dividend was due Oct. 1, 1962, and the first $20 dividend was due Apr. 1, 1963. Find the price on Oct. 1, 1959, to yield $3\frac{1}{2}\%$ converted semiannually.

137. Solve Problem 136 with Oct. 1, 1962, as date of purchase.

In each of Problems 138–149, assume a $100 bond paying semiannual dividends and compute the yield rate converted semiannually.

138. A 4% Delaware & Hudson Co. bond, dividends M-N, maturing on May 1, 1973; bought for $95.25 on Nov. 1, 1960.

139. A 5% Missouri Pacific R.R. bond, dividends F-A, maturing on Feb. 1, 1991; bought for $108.25 on Aug. 1, 1960.

140. A 3% American Tobacco Co. bond, dividends A-O 15, maturing on Apr. 15, 1972; bought for $103 on Oct. 15, 1960.

141. A $4\frac{1}{2}\%$ Southern Pacific Co. bond, dividends M-N, maturing on May 1, 1979; bought for $97.50 on Nov. 1, 1960.

142. A 4% Manati Sugar Co. bond, dividends M-N, maturing on Nov. 1, 1967; bought for $92.50 on Nov. 1, 1960.

143. A $3\frac{1}{2}\%$ Florida Power & Light Co. bond, dividends J-J and maturing on Jan. 1, 1984; bought for $107 on Jan. 1, 1961.

144. A 3% Southern Bell Tel. & Tel. Co. bond, dividends J-J and maturing on July 1, 1989; bought for $106 on Jan. 1, 1961.

145. A $3\frac{1}{2}\%$ Vanadium Corp. bond, dividends A-O and maturing on Oct. 1, 1975; bought for $104 on Oct. 1, 1960.

146. A 4% Atchison, Topeka & Santa Fe Ry. bond, dividends A-O, maturing on Oct. 1, 2005; bought for $127 on Oct. 1, 1960.

147. A $4\frac{1}{2}\%$ Lehigh Valley Ry. bond, dividends J-J, maturing on July 1, 1984; bought for $86 on Jan. 1, 1961.

148. A 3% Texas Corp. bond, dividends M-N 15, and maturing on May 15, 1975; bought for $105 on Nov. 15, 1960.

149. A 4% Walt Disney Productions bond, dividends J-J, maturing on July 1, 1970; bought for $85.50 on July 1, 1960. (Use bond table.)

150. To obtain a yield of 4% converted semiannually, what should a man pay on March 18, 1951, for a $1000, 3%, RKO Theatres bond with dividend dates F-A and maturing on Feb. 1, 1966?

151. Compute the flat price as of Jan. 9, 1951, for a $1000, $3\frac{1}{2}$%, Lehigh Coal & Navigation Co. bond, paying dividends A-O and maturing on Oct. 1, 1970. Yield is to be 3% converted semiannually.

152. A $1000, 5%, Pennsylvania R.R. bond, J-D, due on Dec. 1, 1968, is to yield 4% converted semiannually. Find the flat price on March 19, 1951. Use the result to find the "and interest" price.

153. Interpolate to find the "and interest" price on May 1, 1951, of a $1000, 4%, Baltimore & Ohio R.R. bond, J-J, due on July 1, 1985, to yield 5% converted semiannually. Then find the flat price.

154. A $100, 4% bond paying dividends semiannually costs $96.01 ten years before redemption. Use the bond table to find the yield rate converted semiannually; then compute the effective annual yield rate.

155. Find by the straight line method the book value, at the end of 7 years, of a sawmill with life 20 years, cost $25,000, scrap value $1000.

156. In Problem 155 find the depreciation charge for the 8th year.

157. Prepare the first 5 years' depreciation schedule for Problem 155.

158. Assuming a constant rate of depreciation of 12% for a steam pump worth $10,000, compute its book value at the end of 10 years.

159. In Problem 158 find the depreciation charge for the 11th year.

160. Prepare the first 4 years' depreciation schedule for Problem 158.

161. To provide for the depreciation of an electronic computing machine worth $75,000, each year $5000 is set aside in a sinking fund invested at 4%. Find the book value of the machine at the end of 6 years.

162. In Problem 161 find the depreciation charge for the 6th year.

163. Prepare the first 3 years' depreciation schedule for Problem 161.

164. An engine costing $4250 will depreciate to a scrap value of $250 in 12 years. Find the annual contribution by the straight line method.

165. Using the sinking fund method with 5% interest, find the annual contribution to a depreciation fund for the engine of Problem 164.

166. Employ the constant percentage of book value method to compute the rate of depreciation for the engine of Problem 164.

167. A peat bog is expected to yield $250 a month net for 10 years. Compute a purchase price to yield 6% if a sinking fund can be set up at 3% to restore the investment, both rates converted monthly.

168. How is the $250 monthly income in Problem 167 distributed into interest on investment and monthly contribution to sinking fund?

169. The net annual return from a patent expiring in 10 years is estimated to be $2000 for the first 4 years and $1000 for the last 6 years. Find the price of the patent to yield 8% to an investor who can accumulate a sinking fund at 3% to restore the investment.

170. A plant consists of part A, cost $12,000, life 15 years, scrap value $2000; part B, cost $7000, life 10 years, scrap value $1000; part C, cost $1100, life 5 years, scrap value $100. Find the total annual contribution to a depreciation fund by the sinking fund method at $4\frac{1}{2}\%$ interest.

171. Determine the composite life of the plant of Problem 170.

172. Compute $(1.03)^{1/5}$ to 5 decimal places by use of logarithms.

173. $(1.05)^{7/3}$ is the product of what two factors found in the tables?

174. Determine the value of n if $a_{\overline{8+4n}|.01} = 58.3400$.

175. Compute $(1.002)^{1/3}$ to 8 decimal places by the binomial theorem.

176. $s_{\overline{kn}|t} \div a_{\overline{k}|t}$ abbreviates what fraction if $k = \frac{1}{4}$, $n = 60$, $i = .05$?

177. Indicate $[1 - (1.03)^{-36}] \div [(1.03)^4 - 1]$ in annuity symbols.

178. A house is sold for $1500 down and $50 a month for 18 years. Compute the equivalent cash price if money is worth $4\frac{1}{2}\%$ effective.

179. To redeem a $1,000,000 bond issue at the end of 14 years, a city sets up a sinking fund accumulating at $2\frac{1}{2}\%$ compounded semiannually. How much should be placed in the fund at the end of each month?

180. A warehouse is leased for $3\frac{1}{2}$ years. The monthly rent is $100 due at the beginning of each month. Determine the cash equivalent of the lease on a basis of 4% converted quarterly.

181. What equal deposits at the beginning of each quarter will amount at $2\frac{1}{4}\%$ effective to $1000 at the end of 5 years?

182. To amortize a $3500 loan, a man will pay $250 at the end of each 2 months for $2\frac{1}{2}$ years. What effective rate is charged?

183. If interest is at $4\frac{1}{2}\%$ convertible at the end of each 8 months, find the present value of 10 biennial payments of $1000 each.

184. Quarterly payments of $1000 each are being made to a sinking fund. Compute the amount in the fund just before the 11th payment if the fund accumulates at 4% compounded semiannually.

185. What sum of money invested at $2\frac{1}{2}\%$ convertible annually will provide a perpetual income of $500 at the end of each 6 months?

186. Do Problem 185 assuming interest at $2\frac{1}{2}\%$ converted quarterly.

187. Compute the price of a $100, 4% bond with quarterly dividends, redeemable at par in 12 years, bought to yield 3% effective.

188. What single payment now is equivalent at 4% converted quarterly to payments of $1000 due at the end of each year for 9 years?

189. To build and equip a cafeteria, the trustees of a school obtain a $15,000 loan with interest at 3% converted monthly. Quarterly payments of $500 each will amortize the loan. Find the number of payments.

190. At $4\frac{1}{2}\%$ converted quarterly, what single payment now is equivalent to 15 annual payments of $1000 each, the first due 4 years hence?

191. To repay a loan secured by a mortgage, including principal and interest, a man agrees to pay $100 a month for 10 years. Just after the 42nd payment, the mortgagee assigns to an investor the right to receive all remaining payments in return for their cash equivalent at $5\frac{1}{2}\%$ converted semiannually. What does the investor pay?

192. B deposits $100 a month for 12 years in a trust fund invested at 3% effective. This will provide his niece with what equal monthly payments for 12 years beginning 1 month after the last deposit?

193. A $10,000 loan, with interest at $4\frac{1}{2}\%$ converted quarterly, will be repaid by equal monthly payments for 15 years, the first due 3 years and 1 month after date of loan. Find the monthly payment.

194. Do Problem 193 with first payment due on date of loan.

195. A city employee earning $2000 a year was killed at age 32 in the discharge of his duties. Bringing suit against the city, counsel established that at time of death he had a life expectancy of 33 years and claimed a compensation equal to the present value of $2000 at the end of each year for 33 years certain. Compute the sum claimed on a $3\frac{1}{2}\%$ basis.

196. Solve Problem 195 assuming that the sum claimed was the present value of a whole life annuity of $2000 a year to a man aged 32.

197. Solve Problem 195 assuming that the sum claimed was the present value of a 33-year life annuity of $2000 a year to a man aged 32.

198. Find the probability that a man aged 32 (a) will live to be 65; (b) will die before age 65; (c) will die between ages 65 and 66.

199. A person holds 5 tickets out of 1000 in a contest. One of the 1000 will win a car worth $2000. What is the value of his expectation?

200. The annual dues of a national society are $10 payable in advance. What payment at age 36 should entitle a man to life membership?

201. A minor aged 12 is promised a $1000 payment at age 25, if living. Find the present value of his expectation on a 4% basis.

202. Tell the probability denoted by (a) $_kq_{35}$; (b) $_{20}p_x$; (c) $_{15}|q_{30}$.

203. The family of a man aged 63 is to receive $1000 ten years hence if he dies any time before reaching age 73. Find by the mutual fund method the present value of this contingent payment on a 3% basis.

204. Express in terms of v and d's or l's: (a) C_{m-2}; (b) D_{k+3}.

205. Express in terms of C's or D's: (a) N_{x+2}; (b) M_{k-3}; (c) $v^{54}d_{53}$.

206. What pure endowment maturing at age 46 can a man aged 41 buy for $1000 cash? Disregard loading.

207. A policy taken at age 30 calls for 20 annual premiums of $100 each. Compute the present value of the premiums.

208. Do Problem 207 assuming each premium *certain* to be paid.

209. The 25-year-old beneficiary of an insurance policy is to receive the equivalent of $10,000 cash in the form of a 15-year life annuity, the first payment due at age 26. Compute the annual payment.

210. Do Problem 209 assuming annual payments for 15 years *certain*.

211. Do Problem 209 assuming annual payments for life.

212. What should a man pay at age 55 to an insurance company to buy a life annuity of $1000 a year for 15 years beginning at age 65?

213. Do Problem 212 if payments begin at age 65 and continue for life.

In each of Problems 214 to 218 express each in commutation symbols and describe in detail the life annuity whose present value is denoted:

214. $a_{38:\overline{5}|}$.　**215.** $_{10}|\ddot{a}_{40}$.　**216.** $\ddot{a}_{54:\overline{15}|}$.　**217.** a_{62}.　**218.** $_5|\ddot{a}_{50:\overline{20}|}$.

In each of Problems 219 to 223, express each in commutation symbols and describe in detail the life insurance whose net single or net annual premium is denoted:

219. $_{15}P_{40}$. **220.** $A_{52:\overline{20}|}$. **221.** $P^1_{47:\overline{10}|}$. **222.** A_{23}. **223.** $_{10}P_{35:\overline{15}|}$.

In each of Problems 224 to 226, compute the net single premium of a $1000 policy issued at age 46:

224. Whole life. **225.** 10-year term. **226.** 15-year endowment.

In each of Problems 227 to 232 determine the net annual premium of a $1000 policy issued at age 26:

227. Ordinary life. **229.** 10-payment life. **231.** 5-payment 10-year term.

228. 15-year term. **230.** 15-payment life. **232.** 15-year endowment.

In each of Problems 233 to 238, compute the 10th terminal reserve of a $1000 policy issued at age 26:

233. Ordinary life. **235.** 10-payment life. **237.** 5-payment 10-year term.
234. 15-year term. **236.** 15-payment life. **238.** 15-year endowment.

239. The 46-year-old widow of an insured person is entitled to $5000. She elects to receive equal annual payments for 15 years *certain* and thereafter for life, first payment due at once. Find the annual payment.

240. Assume that the widow of Problem 239 elects to leave enough of the $5000 with the company to buy a paid-up whole life policy of $5000 and to receive the balance in cash. Find the cash payment.

241. Find the natural premium at age 46 for a $5000 policy.

242. A $1000 whole life policy is issued at age 31. The net annual premium for the first 10 years is $\frac{1}{2}$ of the net annual premium for subsequent years. Compute the net annual premium for the first 10 years.

243. A policy issued at age 30 provides for $1000 payable in event of death after age 45. Find the net annual premium payable for 15 years.

244. Compute the net single premium for the policy of Problem 243.

245. Solve Problem 243 assuming the benefit to be payable only if the insured dies between ages 45 and 65.

246. A policy issued at age 40 pays $10,000 if the insured dies between ages 40 and 60, and a whole life annuity of $1000 a year beginning at age 60 if he lives. Find the net annual premium payable for 20 years.

247. Compute the net single premium for the policy of Problem 246.

248. Find the 20th terminal reserve for the policy of Problem 246.

249. A $1000 ordinary life policy issued at age 36 is discontinued at age 46. The 10th terminal reserve is $141.55. Assuming a surrender charge of $1.55, compute the amount of paid-up insurance at age 46.

250. Find the term of extended insurance at age 46 in Problem 249.

ANSWERS TO
ODD-NUMBERED PROBLEMS

EXERCISE 2

1. $10ab$.   **3.** $-x$.   **5.** $5cd + d - 2$.

7. $-3x^2 + 2x + 5$.,   **9.** $-5st$.   **11.** $2(a + b)$.

13. $x(a + b) - y(a - b)$ **15.** $(A + a)y^2 + (B - b)y$.   **17.** $3x + 4y$.

19. $6a - 7a^2$.   **21.** $5 + 2y - y^2$.   **23.** $x^3 + x^2 + 3x - 4$.

25. $10b - 10$.   **27.** $4(m + n)$.   **29.** $(s - r)(x - y)$.

31. $(A - a)t^2 + (B + b)t$.   **33.** $3b$.   **35.** $y^2 - 8y + 3$.

37. $5m - 2n$.   **39.** $y^2 + z^2$.

EXERCISE 3

PAGE 11

1. $-4x^3y^5$.   **3.** $35m^3n$.   **5.** $2c^2d$.   **7.** $6x^2 - 15x^3$.

9. $4a^2b + 4ab^3$.   **11.** $a^3 + 5a^2 + 6a$.   **13.** $9s^3 + 9ts^2 - 6ts - 6t^2$.

15. $x^3 - 5x^2 + 11x - 10$.   **17.** $a^3 - 6a^2 + 6a + 4$.   **19.** $y^3 + 8$.

21. $9x^2 - 81$.   **23.** $16a^2 - 24ab + 9b^2$.   **25.** $49x^2 + 28x + 4$.

27. $m^2 + 3m - 10$.   **29.** $a^4 - 9b^2$.   **31.** $x^3y - 3x^2y + 5xy^2$.

33. $4x^3 - x$.   **35.** $2c^2 + 5cd - 3d^2$.

413

EXERCISE 4

1. $R(1 - st)$.   **3.** $3kx(1 - 2x)$.   **5.** $(x + 2y)(x - 2y)$.
7. $y(3 - y)(3 + y)$.   **9.** $(x - 2)^2$.   **11.** $(m^2 + 3n)^2$.
13. $er(\pi - e)$.   **15.** $(a + 6)(a - 2)$.   **17.** $(y - 3)(y - 2)$.
19. $(2y - 1)(y + 3)$.   **21.** $(m + 1)(m - 1)$.
23. $(ax^2 + y^2)(ax^2 - y^2)$.   **25.** $x(x + 1)(x + 2)$.   **27.** $(3y - 1)(y + 2)$.
29. $dr(r - 1)^2$.   **31.** $P(1 + i)^2$.   **33.** $(a - b)(1 + x)$.
35. $(x + 1)(y + 1)$.   **37.** $(a - x - y)(a - x + y)$.
39. $(3c + a - b)(3c - a + b)$.

EXERCISE 5

1. 45.   **3.** $-6m^4$.   **5.** $6m^4n^5$.
7. $2y^3 - 3a^2$.   **9.** $-8m + 2$.   **11.** $4x^5 - 0.5x^2$.
13. $x^2 - x + 1$.   **15.** $m^3 + m^2n + mn^2 + n^3$.
17. $x^2 + 3x + 1$.   **19.** $x^2 + 2x - 2$; rem. $= -5x + 14$.
21. $x^2 + 1$.   **23.** $x^2 + 1$; rem. $= -5x + 4$.

EXERCISE 6

1. 3.   **3.** $\dfrac{-5x}{7y}$.   **5.** $\dfrac{x}{3y}$.   **7.** $\dfrac{a}{a + b}$.

9. $-m$.   **11.** $\dfrac{a^2}{(x + y)^2}$.   **13.** $\dfrac{a - 2b}{a - b}$.   **15.** $\dfrac{x + 2}{x + 3}$.

17. $\dfrac{3m - 2}{m}$.   **19.** 1800.   **21.** $30x^2y^2t^3$.   **23.** $a^2(x^2 - 9)$.

25. $(x - 1)(x + 1)(x + 2)$.   **27.** $\frac{13}{12}$.   **29.** $-\frac{1}{2}$.   **31.** $\dfrac{x + 16}{18}$.

33. $\dfrac{a^2 + b^2}{a}$.   **35.** $\dfrac{x - 3}{x - 2}$.   **37.** $\dfrac{27 + 3a - 2a^2}{a^2 - 9}$.   **39.** $\dfrac{y^2 - 6y - 2}{y^2 - 3y - 4}$.

41. $\dfrac{x^3 - x^2 + x - 2}{x(x^2 + 1)}$.

EXERCISE 7

PAGE 22

1. $\frac{25}{24}$. **3.** 8. **5.** $\frac{4b}{3a}$. **7.** $\frac{1}{3n^2}$.

9. $\frac{3ab}{2x}$. **11.** $\frac{5m}{3-m}$. **13.** $\frac{1}{x+2y}$. **15.** $xy(x-y)$.

17. $\frac{m+1}{2(2m+1)}$. **19.** $\frac{a+b}{a}$. **21.** $-\frac{26}{3}$. **23.** 600.

25. $\frac{2x^2+1}{3x+2}$. **27.** y^2. **29.** $\frac{x+2y}{y}$. **31.** mn.

EXERCISE 9

PAGE 28

5. $\frac{13}{4}$. **7.** -4. **9.** $-\frac{11}{7}$. **11.** 4. **13.** 10.
15. 0.3. **17.** $-\frac{5}{14}$. **19.** $\frac{17}{6}$. **21.** $-\frac{1}{3}$. **23.** 7.
25. $-\frac{8}{3}$. **27.** 3. **29.** -1. **31.** -3. **33.** a.
35. $m-n$. **37.** 16. **39.** m.

EXERCISE 10

PAGE 30

3. 12. **5.** -1. **7.** -4. **9.** $\frac{19}{5}$. **11.** -1.
13. $\frac{1}{4}$. **15.** -5. **17.** $\frac{1}{2}$. **19.** $\frac{2}{3}$. **21.** $-\frac{3}{2}$.
23. No solution.

EXERCISE 12

PAGE 34

1. 2; 6. **3.** 36; 9. **5.** \$10.00; \$20.00; \$30.00.
7. 2 hrs. **9.** 4 ft. **11.** 16 lbs. of 50¢; 4 lbs. of 75¢.

13. 20 mi. **15.** 5 hrs. **17.** $\frac{m-9}{-6}$ ft.

EXERCISE 13

1. $x = 1, y = 2.$ **3.** $x = 3, y = -2.$ **5.** $x = -1, y = -2.$
7. $x = \frac{3}{2}, y = \frac{1}{2}.$ **9.** $x = -1, y = \frac{-4.2}{1.5}.$ **11.** $x = 6, y = 4.$
13. $x = \dfrac{b(a + 1)}{2}, \ y = \dfrac{b(a - 1)}{6}.$ **15.** $x = 3, y = -4.$
17. $x = 1, y = \frac{1}{2}.$ **19.** $x = \frac{1}{4}, y = 1.$ **21.** $x = \frac{7}{2}, y = -1.$
23. $x = 2, y = -4.$ **25.** $x = 6, y = 4.$ **27.** $x = a, y = -b.$
29. Inconsistent.   **31.** Dependent.

EXERCISE 14

1. $\frac{4}{7}.$ **3.** 60 of 20¢; 140 of 45¢.   **5.** A, 20; B, 35.
7. 28 in., 18 in., 14 in.   **9.** 5 gals. of 70%; 15 gals. of 90%.
11. 15 gals. of 15¢; 25 gals. of 23¢.   **13.** 40.
15. 36 mi. per hr.; 28 mi. per hr.

EXERCISE 15

1. $g = \dfrac{v}{t}.$ **3.** $b = \dfrac{2A}{h}; h = \dfrac{2A}{b}.$ **5.** $V = v - at; a = \dfrac{v - V}{t}.$
7. $s = \dfrac{at^2}{2}; a = \dfrac{2s}{t^2}.$ **9.** $a = S(1 - r); r = \dfrac{S - a}{S}.$
11. $m = \dfrac{nf}{n - f}; n = \dfrac{mf}{m - f}.$ **13.** $s = \dfrac{A - \pi r^2}{\pi r^2}.$ **15.** $n = \dfrac{S - P}{Pi}.$
17. $b = \dfrac{PV - RT}{P}.$ **19.** $a = \dfrac{pb}{1 - p}.$ **21.** $i = \dfrac{d}{1 - d}.$
23. $t_2 = \dfrac{H + st_1}{s}.$ **25.** No.   **27.** $-\frac{1}{2}.$
29. $C = 30 + 2(d - 5),$ if $d > 5.$ **31.** $A = \frac{1}{2}h(b_1 + b_2).$

EXERCISE 18

PAGE 49

1. $\frac{7}{9}$.   **3.** $120.00   **5.** 600 mi.   **7.** 15 g. carbon; 40 g. oxygen.
9. 184,396.   **11.** 4.5.   **13.** $c = -1$ **15.** $51; $119.
17. 18, 8.   **19.** 42 ft.

EXERCISE 20

PAGE 53

1. $\frac{100}{9}\%$, 10%.   **3.** 71.9%.   **5.** $4750.   **7.** 366.97 cu. ft.   **9.** 550.
11. 20%.   **13.** A, $3000; B, $2000.   **15.** $500 at 5%; $1500 at 3%.
17. $500 at 6%; $1500 at 4%.   **19.** 12 lb.

EXERCISE 22

PAGE 58

1. (a) $80.00, $1280.00; (b) $178.00, $1678.00.   **3.** (a) $2\frac{1}{2}\%$; (b) $4\frac{1}{4}\%$.
5. (a) $1271.87; (b) $1460.95.   **7.** (a) $1\frac{3}{4}$ yr.; (b) $\frac{1}{2}$ yr.
9. $9750.00.   **11.** $328.00.

EXERCISE 23

PAGE 60

1. $8.04; $7.93.   **3.** $20.52; $20.24.   **5.** $16.11; $15.86.
7. $70.97; $70.00.   **9.** $15.77; $15.56.   **11.** $34.67; $34.19.
13. $\frac{72}{73}$.   **15.** $103.68.

EXERCISE 24

1. $7.08; $6.99.　　**3.** $6.00; $5.92.　　**5.** $5.62; $5.54.
7. $15.75; $15.53.　　**9.** $7.08; $6.99.　　**11.** $1.93; $1.90.
13. $46.67; $46.03.　　**15.** $4.86; $4.79.

EXERCISE 25

1. $1180.33; $19.67.　　**3.** $485.44.　　　**5.** $993.79.
7. $788.18.　　　　　　**9.** $118.52.　　　**11.** $495.15.
13. $399.02; $7.98.　　**15.** $507.43.　　　**17.** In 105 days.

EXERCISE 26

1. $1980.86.　　**3.** $676.88.　　**5.** $993.79.　　**7.** $454.33.
9. $1497.55.　　**11.** $2422.74.　　**13.** $603.27.　　**15.** $1585.64.
17. 200 days before maturity.　　**19.** 5%.　　**21.** $835.92.　　**23.** $17.00.
25. Maturity value $2030.00.　　**27.** $2029.80.
29. Discount period 49 days.　　**31.** $798.00.
33. $338.35.　　　　　　　　　**35.** $1422.13.

EXERCISE 27

1. $8\frac{1}{3}\%$.　　**3.** 8.11%.　　**5.** 6.09%.　　**7.** 4.76%.
9. 3.92%.　　**11.** 7.92%.　　**13.** 4.08%.　　**19.** $n = 28$.

EXERCISE 28

PAGE 78

1. $24.00.　　**3.** $8.16.　　**5.** $600.00.　　**7.** 63.16%; 55.67%.
9. 36%.　　　　**11.** $90.00.　　　　**15.** $x = \dfrac{it}{360 + it}$.

EXERCISE 29

PAGE 82

1. 24%.　　　　**3.** $36\frac{2}{3}$%.　　　　**5.** 40.15%.
7. (a) $5.40; (b) $5.52; (c) $7.00; (d) $1.48; (e) $1.26.　　**9.** 18%.
11. $45.00.　　**13.** 22.23%.　　**15.** $50.29.　　**17.** $100.81.

EXERCISE 30

PAGE 85

1. $3481.50; $3483.60.　　**3.** $456.00; $458.11.　　**5.** $8.21; $8.44.
7. $335.00.　　**9.** $335.87.　　**11.** $316.76.　　**13.** $316.50.

EXERCISE 31

PAGE 89

1. (a) $792.08; (b) $800.00; (c) $816.00.
3. (a) $403.96; (b) $408.00; (c) $416.16.　　**5.** $1730.76.
7. $410.46.　　**9.** $692.13.　　**11.** $355.67; $455.67.
13. $606.46.　　**15.** 6.32%.

EXERCISE 32

PAGE 93

1. 57 days hence. **5.** 4 mo. 7 days hence. **7.** Oct. 23.
9. $1210.60. **11.** March 19. **13.** $15.00.

EXERCISE 34

PAGE 101

1. b^8. **3.** $(a^{2b})^2$. **5.** 2^9. **7.** 8.
9. $1/c^2$. **11.** x^{3n+1}. **13.** $-a^7$. **15.** $(a-b)^5$.
17. $1+i$. **19.** $a-b$. **21.** 0. **23.** $\dfrac{y^3}{x^3}$.

25. $\frac{4}{9}$. **27.** $-4a^2b^2c^2$. **29.** $\dfrac{1}{2^{2m+3n}}$. **31.** $\dfrac{16x^4}{81y^8}$.

33. $(2a-b)^{m-1}$. **35.** $4a^2bc^3$. **37.** $P(1+i)^{2n+1}$. **39.** $\dfrac{1}{b^2}$.
41. 8.

EXERCISE 35

PAGE 104

7. $9\sqrt{b}$. **9.** $x\sqrt{y^3}$. **11.** $3\sqrt{b}$. **13.** $\sqrt[3]{(2bc)^2}$.
15. $2b\sqrt[3]{c}$. **17.** $\dfrac{3a}{\sqrt{x}}$. **19.** $\sqrt{a^2+b^2}$. **21.** $\sqrt[6]{1+i}$.
23. $ab^{1/2}$. **25.** $(xy^3)^{1/4}$. **27.** $(x-y)^{3/2}$. **29.** $(1+i)^{3/5}$.
31. $4(m+n)^{3/5}$. **33.** $xy^{1/2}(a+b)^{1/4}$. **35.** $\dfrac{1}{(x+y)^{3/2}}$. **37.** $\sqrt[1/3]{a}$.

39. $\dfrac{1}{(1+i)^{3/2}}$. **41.** $(x^2+y^3)^{1/2}$ **43.** $\dfrac{1}{15^{1/2}}$. **45.** $\dfrac{4}{c^{2/5}}$.
47. xy^{-2}. **49.** $a^2(3b)^{-1}$. **51.** $(xy)^{1/2}z^{-1}$. **53.** $(pq)^{1/3}x^{-2/3}$.
55. $(m-n)^{1/2}x^{-2}$. **57.** $(x^2+y^3)^{-1/2}$. **59.** $2a^{-1}$. **61.** $1-(1+i)^{-8}$.
63. 1. **65.** 23. **67.** $6\frac{1}{2}$. **69.** 16.
71. 0.729.

EXERCISE 36

PAGE 108

1. x^{16}.
3. $\dfrac{1}{n^2}$.
5. a^8
7. $\dfrac{(x+y^2)^2}{x^2+y}$.

9. $p^2 r^9$.
11. $c(a^3+b^2)$.
13. $\dfrac{1}{(x+y)^2}$.
15. $a^{1/3}+b^{1/3}$.

17. a^4-b.
19. $\dfrac{x^2+y^4}{y^4}$.
21. $(\tfrac{4}{9})^{5/2}$.
23. $(1+i)^{2n}-(1+i)^n$.

25. $7+6\sqrt{3}-6\sqrt{2}$.
27. 0.
29. $3+6\sqrt[3]{4}-9\sqrt[3]{2}$.
31. 24.

33. 3.
35. $3-\sqrt{3}$.
37. $\tfrac{2}{5}\sqrt{5}$.
39. $\tfrac{1}{6}\sqrt{6}$.

41. $\tfrac{2}{15}\sqrt{5}$.
43. $\sqrt{2}-1$.
45. 7.
47. $\tfrac{1}{5}(\sqrt{7}-\sqrt{2})$.

49. $x=1-\left(\dfrac{y}{2}\right)^{1/3}$.
51. $i=(1+r)^{1/9}-1$.

53. $i=\dfrac{1-v^5}{2A}$; $v=(1-2Ai)^{1/5}$.
55. $j=4(x^{1/4}-1)$.

57. $x=-3\pm\sqrt{y+18}$.
59. $t=s^{-6}-1$.

EXERCISE 38

PAGE 112

1. $4; 5$.
3. $0; -4$.
5. $-2; -5$.
7. ± 4.

9. $3; -2$.
11. $\tfrac{1}{2}; -3$.
13. $-\tfrac{5}{3}; -2$.
15. $\tfrac{4}{3}; \tfrac{4}{3}$.

17. $0.4; 0.2$.
19. $\tfrac{3}{4}; -\tfrac{2}{3}$.
21. $-4a; 3a$.
23. $-\dfrac{4}{3b}; \dfrac{2}{b}$.

25. $-3; 2$.
27. $2; 4$.
29. $-1; \tfrac{2}{3}$.
31. $1; -\tfrac{3}{4}$.

33. $\sqrt{3}; -\sqrt{3}$.

EXERCISE 39

PAGE 115

1. $1; -\tfrac{1}{3}$.
3. $2; -\tfrac{1}{4}$.
5. $-\tfrac{2}{3}; \tfrac{2}{5}$.
7. $-\tfrac{1}{2}; -\tfrac{1}{3}$.

9. $-1\pm\sqrt{2}$.
11. $-2\pm\sqrt{6}$.
13. $\dfrac{3}{2}\pm\dfrac{\sqrt{5}}{2}$.
15. $\tfrac{1}{2}(-3\pm\sqrt{2})$.

17. $1\pm\dfrac{\sqrt{6}}{2}$.
19. $\tfrac{2}{3}; \tfrac{2}{3}$.
21. $-\tfrac{5}{2}; \pm\tfrac{15}{2}$.
23. $p\pm\sqrt{p^2-q}$.

25. $-\frac{7}{2}$; 4.   **27.** 14 ft. by 15 ft.   **29.** 60 mi. per hr.
31. ($\frac{3}{4}$ and $\frac{2}{3}$) or ($-\frac{2}{3}$ and $-\frac{3}{4}$).

EXERCISE 41

PAGE 121

1. $t_n = 29$, $S_n = 155$.   **3.** $t_1 = 13$, $S_n = 7$.   **5.** $S_n = 42$, $d = 1$.
7. $n = 16$, $S_n = 0$.   **9.** $t_1 = 47/2$, $t_n = -43/2$.   **11.** $d = \frac{3}{2}$, $t_n = 30\frac{1}{2}$.
13. $n = 10$, $d = 70/9$.   **15.** $n = 8$, $t_n = -8$.   **17.** 12,051.
19. 40 ft.   **21.** \$204.   **23.** \$65.   **27.** 11; -4; 5/2.

EXERCISE 42

PAGE 125

1. $t_n = 10{,}240$, $S_n = 20{,}475$.   **3.** $n = 6$, $S_n = 23\frac{5}{8}$.
5. $t_1 = 0.002$, $S_n = 1111.12$.   **7.** $r = -3$, $n = 5$.
9. $t_1 = \frac{3376}{65}$; $t_n = \frac{11 \cdot 394}{65}$.   **11.** 448.
13. 19.157.   **15.** 470 ft.   **17.** $\frac{27}{8}$.

EXERCISE 43

PAGE 129

1. $32x^5 + 80x^4y + 80x^3y^2 + 40x^2y^3 + 10xy^4 + y^5$.
3. $x^6 - 12x^5y + 60x^4y^2 - 160x^3y^3 + 240x^2y^4 - 192xy^5 + 64y^6$.
5. $\frac{1}{32} + \frac{5}{8}y + 5y^2 + 20y^3 + 40y^4 + 32y^5$.
7. $x^4 - 4x^3y^2 + 6x^2y^4 - 4xy^6 + y^8$.
9. $1 + 10y + 60y^2 + 280y^3 + 1120y^4 + \cdots$.
11. $\dfrac{1}{x^2} - \dfrac{2y^2}{x^3} + \dfrac{3y^4}{x^4} - \dfrac{4y^6}{x^5} + \dfrac{5y^8}{x^6} - \cdots$.
13. $8 - 3x + \dfrac{3x^2}{16} + \dfrac{x^3}{128} + \dfrac{3x^4}{4096} + \cdots$.
15. $1 - \dfrac{2i}{3} + \dfrac{5i^2}{9} - \dfrac{40i^3}{81} + \dfrac{110i^4}{243} - \cdots$

17. 1.1255.   **19.** 1.3439.   **21.** 0.9070.   **23.** 0.9057.
25. 1.0098.   **27.** 1.0132.   **29.** 0.9926.   **31.** 0.9992.

EXERCISE 47

PAGE 143

1. $x = 5, y = 1$.   **3.** $x = 2, y = 3$.   **5.** $x = 2, y = -1$.
7. $x = \frac{1}{2}, y = \frac{3}{2}$.   **9.** $x = -1, y = -2$.   **11.** $x = -\frac{1}{2}, y = 2$.
13. $x = 2, y = -3$.   **15.** $x = -3, y = 2$.

EXERCISE 48

PAGE 145

1. $0, 12, 4,\ 2x^2 + 4,\ 4x^2 + 16x + 16, 2k + 4$.

3. $0, -\frac{1}{2}$, no answer, $-\frac{1}{11}$, $\dfrac{p - q}{p + 2q}$, $3\sqrt{3} - 5$.

5. $f(i) = 200i,\ f(.03) = 6,\ f(.02) = 4,\ f(.015) = 3$.

EXERCISE 49

PAGE 150

17. -2.   **19.** 4.   **21.** $1, -2$.   **23.** $-1.2, 3.2$.
25. $5, -3$.   **27.** -1.7.   **29.** $1, -1$.

EXERCISE 51

PAGE 157

1. 1.716003.   **3.** $8.623249 - 10$.   **5.** 1.794488.   **7.** 3.566673.
9. 0.500511.   **11.** $9.282622 - 10$.   **13.** 1.878752.   **15.** $7.991669 - 10$.
17. 0.0059523.   **19.** 1.0200711.   **21.** 0.0053950.   **23.** $8.0211893 - 10$.
25. 1.0133429.   **27.** 5.0138901.   **29.** 1.0005208.   **31.** 7108.
33. 1.038.   **35.** 343.3.   **37.** 10.82.   **39.** 54.11.

41. 10.98. **43.** 0.0001007. **45.** 0.01085. **47.** 101.45.
49. 1.0641. **51.** 1085 7. **53.** 102.94. **55.** 10567.
57. 0.010257.

EXERCISE 52

PAGE 160

1. 1.431412. **3.** 4.950637. **5.** 2.377871. **7.** 3.813234.
9. 9.331650 − 10. **11.** 2.496984. **13.** 5.982938. **15.** 1.773506.
17. 9.399899 − 10. **19.** 7.677917 − 10. **21.** 1.0281848. **23.** 3.0335565.
25. 2.0178719. **27.** 8.0130985 − 10. **29.** 24.6703. **31.** 7798.77.
33. 232.705. **35.** 47732.5. **37.** 26.6903. **39.** 114.321.
41. 0.0264901. **43.** 0.0537483.

EXERCISE 53

PAGE 164

1. 2.296. **3.** 29.55. **5.** 1.229. **7.** 0.7560.
9. 1.375. **11.** 3.917. **13.** 11.62. **15.** 0.02791.
17. 78.26. **19.** 0.02557. **21.** 363.8. **23.** 0.07905.
25. 130.05. **27.** 2890. **29.** 1.290. **31.** 11.88.
33. 333.96. **35.** 171.23. **37.** 43.903. **39.** 0.058839.
41. 91.3287. **43.** 4990.15. **45.** 0.163636. **47.** 4.18101.
49. 826.363. **51.** 2873.11. **53.** $n = 40.28$. **55.** 21.52.
57. $i = 0.005833$.

EXERCISE 55

PAGE 170

1. $M = 8.79$. **3.** $M = 8.79$. **5.** $M = 8.78$. **7.** $M_w = 82.33$.

EXERCISE 56

PAGE 173

1. (a) 10.5; (b) 11; (c) 11. **3.** 10.
5. Yes; the mean is unduly affected by the extreme measurements.
7. (a) 9; (b) 9; no mode. **9.** 14.
11. 4, 4, $\frac{5}{4}$, $\frac{3}{2}$, $\frac{3}{4}$, $\frac{1}{2}$. Many others. **13.** 12.1. **15.** 12.1.

EXERCISE 57

PAGE 180

7. (a) 34; (b) $Q_1 = 21$, $Q_3 = 41$; (c) 30; (d) 26%. **11.** 1350–1400.

EXERCISE 58

PAGE 188

1. (a) 823; (b) 957. **3.** (a) 983; (b) 445.
5. $\sigma = 0.960$. **7.** $Q = 0.85$; $d = 0.87$. **9.** $r = 0.835$.
11. $r = \dfrac{9}{\sqrt{85}} = 0.976$. **13.** $5y = 9x - 13$.

EXERCISE 61

PAGE 207

1. (a) 1; (b) 1 yr.; (c) 15; (d) $2\frac{3}{4}$%.
3. (a) 4; (b) 3 mo.; (c) 33; (d) $1\frac{1}{4}$%.
5. (a) 12; (b) 1 mo.; (c) 67; (d) $\frac{5}{8}$%.
7. (a) $920; (b) $927.42. **9.** (a) $280; (b) $297.37.

EXERCISE 62

PAGE 210

1. 1.01; $(1.01)^{62}$; 1.71141047.   **3.** 1.05; $(1.05)^{10}$; 1.62889463.
5. 1.0025; $(1.0025)^{81}$; 1.30937641.   **7.** 1.0125; $(1.0125)^{54}$; 1.95583279.
9. 1.0275; $(1.0275)^{14}$; 1.72042843.
11. (a) \$4886.44, \$2886.44; (b) \$11,783.21, \$9783.21;
     (c) \$65,975.38, \$63,975.38.   **13.** (a) \$731.40; (b) \$732.11; (c) \$732.47.
15. \$72.72.   **17.** \$1,921,863.20   **19.** \$12,516.21.
21. \$6162.11.   **23.** \$2001.83.   **25.** \$2,656,466.18
27. 100.661.

EXERCISE 63

PAGE 213

1. \$641.49.   **3.** \$205.33.   **5.** \$600.   **7.** 75 months.
9. \$702.50.   **11.** \$3355.18.   **13.** \$1579.16.

EXERCISE 64

PAGE 217

1. (a) 6.09%; (b) 6.1364%; (c) 6.1678%; (d) 6.1837%.
3. $5\frac{1}{2}\%$ converted semiannually.   **5.** 6.7159%.   **7.** 4.4017%.
9. 7.2321%.   **11.** $r = mi + \dfrac{m(m-1)}{1 \cdot 2} i^2 + \dfrac{m(m-1)(m-2)}{1 \cdot 2 \cdot 3} i^3 + \cdots$.
13. 3.6599%.   **15.** 5.12 effective   **17.** 2.02%.

EXERCISE 65

PAGE 220

1. $(1.065)^{-40}$; 0.08054075.   **3.** $(1.00\frac{5}{8})^{-120}$; 0.47347036.
5. $(100\frac{3}{4})^{-100}$; 0.47369033.   **7.** $(1.005)^{-52}$; 0.77155127.
9. $(1.03)^{-9}$; 0.76641673.

11. (a) $887.71, $112.29; (b) $789.41, $210.59; (c) $627.41, $372.59.
13. (a) $1643.25; (b) $1640.70; (c) $1639.09; (d) $1638.01.
15. $688.70.   **17.** Second plan, to save $2.30 now.
19. (a) $1059.69; (b) $1000.00.   **21.** $2450.23.   **23.** $2296.14.
25. $600.   **27.** $2356.30.   **29.** 4%/year
31. $2500.   **35.** 0.88899636.

EXERCISE 66

PAGE 225

1. (a) 50.73 yrs.; (b) 26.58 yrs.   **3.** 4.36%.   **5.** $n = 45$.
7. $4\% < 12i < [5\%]$.   **9.** 4.26%.   **11.** (a) 10^+; (b) 14^-.
13. 3.67%.   **15.** December 4, 1963.
17. 21^- yrs.   **19.** $x = 9$.

EXERCISE 67

PAGE 229

1. $58.62.   **3.** 6.32% converted quarterly.
5. $502.71.   **7.** 21^+ yrs.   **9.** 2.4264%.
11. 7.08%.   **13.** 2.75%.   **15.** $402.55.   **17.** $317.74.
19. 4.98%.   **21.** About 1973.   **23.** $\log (1 + i) = \dfrac{\log S - \log P}{n}$.

EXERCISE 68

PAGE 233

1. (a) $109.34; (b) $100.00; (c) $94.22.
3. (a) $1624.97; (b) $1486.10; (c) $1400.18.
5. $1220.03   **7.** $1437.41.   **9.** $621.35.   **11.** $1134.60.
13. $396.58.   **15.** $463.37.   **17.** First 207.32, 2nd 507.32.
19. 22^+ months hence.

EXERCISE 70

PAGE 238

1. $4416.32.   **3.** $4216.42.   **5.** $1261.78.

EXERCISE 71

PAGE 241

1. $3519.42.   **3.** $22,697.27.   **5.** $22,230.73.   **7.** $6520.61.
9. $5328.23.   **11.** $17,094.12.   **13.** $148.90.   **15.** $41,922.43.
17. $5177.36.   **19.** $1382.13.   **21.** $3507.54.   **25.** 13.180795.
29. 662.56317.   **31.** 6.1520.

EXERCISE 72

PAGE 246

1. $445.18.   **3.** $541.63.   **5.** $4747.63.   **7.** $22,843.35.
9. $23,997.78.   **11.** $17,094.12.
13. Paying $2500 cash is better for him by $62.17 now.
15. $934.55.   **17.** $1005.96.   **19.** $10,807 (to the nearest dollar).
21. 8.530203.   **27.** 24.9153.

EXERCISE 73

PAGE 250

1. (a) $577.18; (b) $322.07; (c) $197.90.
3. $44.23.   **5.** $627.10.   **7.** $37.99.
9. $44.87.   **11.** $500 + $1019.66.
13. $100.   **15.** $5792.62.   **17.** $116.51.
19. $4.26.   **21.** $267.42.   **23.** 0.00886550.
25. 0.142378.   **27.** $117.28.   **31.** 0.02448095.

EXERCISE 74

PAGE 255

1. 48.   **3.** 14.   **5.** 39.   **7.** 5.15%.
9. 3.7349%.   **11.** 0.921%.   **13.** 2.9325%.
15. 43 quarterly payments of $300 each and a smaller 44th payment.
17. $2\frac{1}{4}\% < i < [2\frac{1}{2}\%]$.
19. 31 quarterly payments of $200 each and a smaller 32nd payment.
21. $10 < n < [11]$.   **23.** $1\frac{3}{4}\% < 2i < [2\%]$.
25. 15^+ payments or $3^{3/4+}$ years.
27. 12 years.   **29.** 56.   **31.** 1/2%.   **33.** $2\frac{3}{4}\%$.

EXERCISE 76

PAGE 264

1. $6977.44.   **3.** $6342.74.   **5.** $38,651.43.
7. $1601.75.   **9.** $373.25.   **11.** $15,603.38.
13. $67.65.   **15.** $165.77.   **17.** $354.77.
19. 32.
21. 35 quarterly payments of $15 each and a smaller 36th payment.
23. $2\frac{1}{2}\% < 2i < [2\frac{3}{4}\%]$. **25.** 2.3392%.

EXERCISE 77

PAGE 267

1. $10,327.94; $3563.47.   **3.** $7104.09.
5. $6245.53.   **7.** $115,951.23.   **9.** $347.85.   **11.** $98.10.
13. $851.10.
15. 109 monthly payments of $100 each and a smaller 110th payment.
17. $650.52.   **19.** $7636.75.   **21.** 10.   **23.** 7.7299%.

EXERCISE 78

PAGE 271

1. $60,000   **3.** $7002.11.
5. $5000.00; $4901.00.   **7.** $4\frac{1}{2}\%$ converted semiannually.
9. $1229.87.   **11.** $2442.43.   **13.** $1564.95.   **15.** $x = 12$.
17. $23,709.44.   **19.** 3.68% converted semiannually. **21.** $87,254.90.
25. a. $4585.11. b. $1826.53. c. 5. d. $645.61. e. 8.

EXERCISE 79

PAGE 274

1. $53,678.65.   **3.** $3602.08.   **5.** $94,484.55.   **7.** $53,276.09.
9. $24,969.41.   **11.** $34,790.88.   **13.** $113,154.36.
15. The cost would be prohibitive.
17. $5046.07.   **19.** $379.69.   **21.** $590.73.   **23.** $832.81.
25. $C = \dfrac{W}{i}(1 + i)$.   **27.** $x = 33$.

EXERCISE 82

PAGE 290

1. $133.58.   **5.** (a) $155.31; (b) $1387.09.   **7.** $6.94.
9. Ann. payt. near $22,462.71.   **11.** Semiann. payt. near $9229.88.
13. $1077.85.   **15.** $1108.30.   **17.** $1091.77.   **19.** $638.06.
21. $6839.27.   **23.** $1540.91.   **25.** $321.85.

EXERCISE 83

PAGE 294

1. $131.28.   **3.** $4095.24.   **5.** $179.52.   **7.** 122nd.
9. 4; $115.90   **13.** $7913.23.   **15.** $36.48.   **17.** $5892.24.

19. $609.32. **21.** 113th payment. **23.** $227.93.
25. $6739.70. **27.** (a) 34; (b) $3.87. **29.** $5306.48.

EXERCISE 84

PAGE 298

1. $R = $706.47. **3.** $273.50. **5.** $2802.78. **7.** $1228.19.
9. $4706.35. **11.** $1066.44. **13.** $7721.57. **15.** $24,072.65.
17. 4.55%. **19.** $3195.83.

EXERCISE 86

PAGE 307

1. $1081.44. **3.** $573.70. **5.** $528.19. **7.** $94.84.
9. $149.45. **11.** $114.91. **13.** $688.50. **15.** $6.25.
19. $12\frac{1}{2}$ yrs.

EXERCISE 87

PAGE 312

1. $1000.00. **3.** $516.18. **5.** 520.52. **7.** $899.56.
9. $848.51. **15.** $1733.84. **17.** $1486.82. **19.** $16.08.
21. $12,387.59. **23.** $6655.42 and $344.58. **25.** $20,656.52.
29. $448.47. **31.** $12,872.62.

EXERCISE 88

PAGE 315

1. $751.10. **3.** $771.48. **5.** $8487.10. **7.** $3369.51.
9. $10,165.56. **11.** $7636.75. **13.** $72.98. **15.** $1208.41.
17. $240.96.

EXERCISE 89

PAGE 318

1. $567.57.	**3.** $83.72.	**5.** $80.66.	**7.** $570.14.
9. $298.62.	**11.** $450.47.	**13.** $566.09.	**15.** $1132.18.
17. $21,041.90.	**19.** $2292.68.	**21.** $2304.34.	**23.** $10,581.
25. 6%.	**27.** $1421.44.		

EXERCISE 90

PAGE 321

1. 4.4617%, using $R = 2.0$.		**3.** 2.72%.	**5.** 2.9644%.
7. 4.69%.	**9.** 4.6869%.	**11.** 4.48%.	**13.** 2.5307%.
15. 4.95%.	**17.** 5.2282%.	**19.** 2.63%.	

EXERCISE 91

PAGE 323

1. $94.09.	**3.** $110.95.	**5.** $93.55.	**7.** $105.29.
9. 3.5570%.	**11.** 4.97%.	**13.** 4.9814%.	**15.** 4.63%.

EXERCISE 93

PAGE 331

1. $1200.00; $1300.00.   **7.** $207.19.   **13.** $526.95.
15. (a) $5866.92; (b) $4933.08; (c) $891.30.
17. $882.92.   **19.** $386.57.   **21.** $148,746.19.   **23.** $251.58.
25. $1,231,290.36.

EXERCISE 94

PAGE 335

1. 15.81%.   **7.** $728.23; $1271.77.   **9.** $245.21.
13. $3051.76.   **15.** $711.21.

EXERCISE 95

PAGE 337

1. 20⁺ yrs.   **3.** 21⁺ yrs.   **5.** $124,520.50.
7. $6434.89; $8565.11.   **9.** $220,105.78.   **11.** $3165.82.
13. 43 years.   **15.** 18 years.   **17.** $1,132,441.21.
19. $132,894.35.   **21.** $72,633.86.

EXERCISE 98

PAGE 345

1. 1.01489.   **3.** 1.01489.   **5.** $(1.07)^3(1.07)^{1/6}$.
7. 0.90069503.   **9.** $(1.02)^{1/2}(1.02)^{1/3}$.   **11.** $1010.00.
13. $11,422.67.   **15.** .96002804.   **17.** $3158.07.
19. $4629.31.

EXERCISE 99

PAGE 347

1. (a) 6.1364%; (b) 3.0225%; (c) 1.0100%; (d) 0.2485%.
3. (a) $r = (1.10)^{1/4} - 1$; (b) $r = (1.05)^{1/2} - 1$; (c) $r = (1.0125)^2 - 1$.

EXERCISE 100

PAGE 349

1. $s_{\overline{4}|.03} \cdot \dfrac{1}{s_{\overline{16}|.03}}$. **3.** $a_{\overline{6}|.025} \cdot \dfrac{1}{s_{\overline{42}|.025}}$. **5.** $s_{\overline{4}|.035} \cdot \dfrac{1}{a_{\overline{30}|.035}}$.

7. 68.2584. **9.** 60.61353771. **11.** 196.838.

EXERCISE 101

PAGE 351

1. $1948.51. **3.** $6644.78. **5.** $697.17. **7.** $70.95.

9. $131.95. **11.** $58.06. **15.** $1286.02. **17.** $40,459.04.

19. $11,531.11. **21.** $6438.41. **23.** $58.83. **25.** $x = $428.15.

EXERCISE 102

PAGE 355

1. $1617.31. **3.** $8639.19. **5.** $6484.94. **7.** $62.25.

9. 35 quarterly payments of $200 each and a smaller 36th payment.

11. $67.81. **13.** 3.0298%. **15.** $24,298.28. **17.** $22,797.39.

19. $11,524.78. **21.** $7209.11. **25.** $121.08.

EXERCISE 104

PAGE 361

1. $\frac{1}{2}$. **3.** $\frac{2}{3}$. **5.** $\frac{1}{3}$. **7.** $\frac{3}{13}$.

9. $\frac{3}{13}$. **11.** (a) $\frac{3}{8}$; (b) $\frac{7}{8}$; (c) $\frac{1}{8}$. **13.** $\frac{1}{52}$.

15. $\frac{10}{36} = \frac{5}{18}$. **17.** $\frac{1}{4}$.

EXERCISE 105

PAGE 364

1. 1.6855%.   **3.** 95.764%.   **5.** 0.8497%.   **7.** 0.007727.
9. 0.855534.   **11.** 0.034253.   **13.** 0.982046.   **15.** 0.66761.
17. 0.792648.   **19.** $_8q_{50}$.   **21.** $_2p_{50}$.   **23.** $_8|q_{50}$.
27. 0.92.

EXERCISE 106

PAGE 366

1. $10.00.   **3.** $1200.00.   **5.** $7723.02.   **7.** $7910.47.
9. $1.00   **11.** $1261.77.   **13.** $.96.   **15.** $543.95.
17. $136.99.

EXERCISE 107

PAGE 369

1. 14.513.   **3.** 1.956.   **5.** $v^{51}l_{51}$.   **7.** $v^m d_{m-1}$.
9. D_{12}.   **11.** $C_{60} + C_{61} + \cdots + C_{\omega}$.
13. $N_{x-2} = D_{x-2} + D_{x-1} + D_x + D_{x+1} + \cdots + D_{\omega}$.
15. $C_{k+1} + C_{k+2} + \cdots + C_{\omega}$.   **17.** N_{25}.   **19.** $M_{53} - M_{61}$.

EXERCISE 108

PAGE 372

1. $588.20.   **3.** $5516.20.   **5.** $4104.83.   **7.** $1766.11.
9. $623.36.   **11.** $4023.02.   **13.** $5233.84.   **15.** $2200.30.
17. $9868.75.   **19.** $\dfrac{N_{12}}{D_{12}}$.   **21.** $\dfrac{N_{53}}{D_{45}}$.   **23.** $\dfrac{N_{16}}{D_{15}}$.

EXERCISE 109

PAGE 376

1. $7500.18.   **3.** $3486.13.   **5.** $547.48.   **7.** $764.34.
9. $5478.84.   **11.** $3243.40.   **13.** $6890.52.   **15.** $951.80.
17. $406.82.   **19.** $7729.68.   **21.** $\dfrac{N_{18}}{D_{17}}$.   **23.** $\dfrac{N_{25} - N_{33}}{D_{25}}$.
25. $\dfrac{N_{38}}{D_{35}}$.   **27.** $\ddot{a}_{33}$ **29.** a_{50}.   **31.** $_{15|}\ddot{a}_{40:\overline{10|}}$.

EXERCISE 110

PAGE 380

1. $17.19.   **3.** $308.73.   **5.** $24.71.   **7.** $23.50.
9. $26.81.   **11.** $401.63.   **13.** $950.36.

EXERCISE 111

PAGE 383

1. $\dfrac{M_{30}}{N_{30} - N_{50}}$.   **3.** $\dfrac{M_{57} - M_{62}}{N_{57} - N_{62}}$.   **5.** $\dfrac{M_{35} - M_{43}}{D_{43}}$.
7. $40.99.   **9.** $9.36.   **11.** $14.26.   **13.** $72.88.
15. $325.46.   **17.** $40.87.   **19.** $70.72.   **21.** $37.95.

EXERCISE 112

PAGE 385

1. $396.56.   **3.** $40.11.   **5.** $61.53.   **7.** $20.01.
9. $214.85.   **11.** $12.92.   **13.** $35.66.

EXERCISE 113

PAGE 387

1. $32.12.   **3.** $550.15.   **5.** $19.14.   **7.** $2926.01.
9. $10.20.   **11.** $22.84; $44.24.   **13.** $2298.64.
15. $919.87.   **17.** $156.86.   **19.** $561.69.

EXERCISE 114

PAGE 392

1. $309.31.   **3.** $44.28.   **5.** $350.59.

7. $\dfrac{3000(M_{60} - M_{65}) + 1000N_{65}}{D_{60}}$.   **9.** $781.00.   **13.** $1691.60.

15. 10 years 143 days.   **17.** $398.63.

Tables

CONTENTS

Table

440

TABLE I.—Six-place Mantissas

N.	0	1	2	3	4	5	6	7	8	9	D.
100	000000	000434	000868	001301	001734	002166	002598	003029	003461	003891	432
1	4321	4751	5181	5609	6038	6466	6894	7321	7748	8174	428
2	8600	9026	9451	9876	010300	010724	011147	011570	011993	012415	424
3	012837	013259	013680	014100	4521	4940	5360	5779	6197	6616	420
4	7033	7451	7868	8284	8700	9116	9532	9947	020361	020775	416
105	021189	021603	022016	022428	022841	023252	023664	024075	4486	4896	412
6	5306	5715	6125	6533	6942	7350	7757	8164	8571	8978	408
7	9384	9789	030195	030600	031004	031408	031812	032216	032619	033021	404
8	033424	033826	4227	4628	5029	5430	5830	6230	6629	7028	400
9	7426	7825	8223	8620	9017	9414	9811	040207	040602	040998	397
110	041393	041787	042182	042576	042969	043362	043755	044148	044540	044932	393
1	5323	5714	6105	6495	6885	7275	7664	8053	8442	8830	390
2	9218	9606	9993	050380	050766	051153	051538	051924	052309	052694	386
3	053078	053463	053846	4230	4613	4996	5378	5760	6142	6524	383
4	6905	7286	7666	8046	8426	8805	9185	9563	9942	060320	379
115	060698	061075	061452	061829	062206	062582	062958	063333	063709	4083	376
6	4458	4832	5206	5580	5953	6326	6699	7071	7443	7815	373
7	8186	8557	8928	9298	9668	070038	070407	070776	071145	071514	370
8	071882	072250	072617	072985	073352	3718	4085	4451	4816	5182	366
9	5547	5912	6276	6640	7004	7368	7731	8094	8457	8819	363
120	079181	079543	079904	080266	080626	080987	081347	081707	082067	082426	360
1	082785	083144	083503	3861	4219	4576	4934	5291	5647	6004	357
2	6360	6716	7071	7426	7781	8136	8490	8845	9198	9552	355
3	9905	090258	090611	090963	091315	091667	092018	092370	092721	093071	352
4	093422	3772	4122	4471	4820	5169	5518	5866	6215	6562	349
125	6910	7257	7604	7951	8298	8644	8990	9335	9681	100026	346
6	100371	100715	101059	101403	101747	102091	102434	102777	103119	3462	343
7	3804	4146	4487	4828	5169	5510	5851	6191	6531	6871	341
8	7210	7549	7888	8227	8565	8903	9241	9579	9916	110253	338
9	110590	110926	111263	111599	111934	112270	112605	112940	113275	3609	335
130	113943	114277	114611	114944	115278	115611	115943	116276	116608	116940	333
1	7271	7603	7934	8265	8595	8926	9256	9586	9915	120245	330
2	120574	120903	121231	121560	121888	122216	122544	122871	123198	3525	328
3	3852	4178	4504	4830	5156	5481	5806	6131	6456	6781	325
4	7105	7429	7753	8076	8399	8722	9045	9368	9690	130012	323
135	130334	130655	130977	131298	131619	131939	132260	132580	132900	3219	321
6	3539	3858	4177	4496	4814	5133	5451	5769	6086	6403	318
7	6721	7037	7354	7671	7987	8303	8618	8934	9249	9564	316
8	9879	140194	140508	140822	141136	141450	141763	142076	142389	142702	314
9	143015	3327	3639	3951	4263	4574	4885	5196	5507	5818	311
140	146128	146438	146748	147058	147367	147676	147985	148294	148603	148911	309
1	9219	9527	9835	150142	150449	150756	151063	151370	151676	151932	307
2	152288	152594	152900	3205	3510	3815	4120	4424	4728	5032	305
3	5336	5640	5943	6246	6549	6852	7154	7457	7759	8061	303
4	8362	8664	8965	9266	9567	9868	160168	160469	160769	161068	301
145	161368	161667	161967	162266	162564	162863	3161	3460	3758	4055	299
6	4353	4650	4947	5244	5541	5838	6134	6430	6726	7022	297
7	7317	7613	7908	8203	8497	8792	9086	9380	9674	9968	295
8	170262	170555	170848	171141	171434	171726	172019	172311	172603	172895	293
9	3186	3478	3769	4060	4351	4641	4932	5222	5512	5802	291
150	176091	176381	176670	176959	177248	177536	177825	178113	178401	178689	289
1	8977	9264	9552	9839	180126	180413	180699	180986	181272	181558	287
2	181844	182129	182415	182700	2985	3270	3555	3839	4123	4407	285
3	4691	4975	5259	5542	5825	6108	6391	6674	6956	7239	283
4	7521	7803	8084	8366	8647	8928	9209	9490	9771	190051	281
155	190332	190612	190892	191171	191451	191730	192010	192289	192567	2846	279
6	3125	3403	3681	3959	4237	4514	4792	5069	5346	5623	278
7	5900	6176	6453	6729	7005	7281	7556	7832	8107	8382	276
8	8657	8932	9206	9481	9755	200029	200303	200577	200850	201124	274
9	201397	201670	201943	202216	202488	2761	3033	3305	3577	3848	272
N.	0	1	2	3	4	5	6	7	8	9	D.

TABLE I.—Six-place Mantissas

N.	0	1	2	3	4	5	6	7	8	9	D.
160	204120	204391	204663	204934	205204	205475	205746	206016	206286	206556	271
1	6826	7096	7365	7634	7904	8173	8441	8710	8979	9247	269
2	9515	9783	210051	210319	210586	210853	211121	211388	211654	211921	267
3	212188	212454	2720	2986	3252	3518	3783	4049	4314	4579	266
4	4844	5109	5373	5638	5902	6166	6430	6694	6957	7221	264
165	7484	7747	8010	8273	8536	8798	9060	9323	9585	9846	262
6	220108	220370	220631	220892	221153	221414	221675	221936	222196	222456	261
7	2716	2976	3236	3496	3755	4015	4274	4533	4792	5051	259
8	5309	5568	5826	6084	6342	6600	6858	7115	7372	7630	258
9	7887	8144	8400	8657	8913	9170	9426	9682	9938	230193	256
170	230449	230704	230960	231215	231470	231724	231979	232234	232488	232742	255
1	2996	3250	3504	3757	4011	4264	4517	4770	5023	5276	253
2	5528	5781	6033	6285	6537	6789	7041	7292	7544	7795	252
3	8046	8297	8548	8799	9049	9299	9550	9800	240050	240300	250
4	240549	240799	241048	241297	241546	241795	242044	242293	2541	2790	249
175	3038	3286	3534	3782	4030	4277	4525	4772	5019	5266	248
6	5513	5759	6006	6252	6499	6745	6991	7237	7482	7728	246
7	7973	8219	8464	8709	8954	9198	9443	9687	9932	250176	245
8	250420	250664	250908	251151	251395	251638	251881	252125	252368	2610	243
9	2853	3096	3338	3580	3822	4064	4306	4548	4790	5031	242
180	255273	255514	255755	255996	256237	256477	256718	256958	257198	257439	241
1	7679	7918	8158	8398	8637	8877	9116	9355	9594	9833	239
2	260071	260310	260548	260787	261025	261263	261501	261739	261976	262214	238
3	2451	2688	2925	3162	3399	3636	3873	4109	4346	4582	237
4	4818	5054	5290	5525	5761	5996	6232	6467	6702	6937	235
185	7172	7406	7641	7875	8110	8344	8578	8812	9046	9279	234
6	9513	9746	9980	270213	270446	270679	270912	271144	271377	271609	233
7	271842	272074	272306	2538	2770	3001	3233	3464	3696	3927	232
8	4158	4389	4620	4850	5081	5311	5542	5772	6002	6232	230
9	6462	6692	6921	7151	7380	7609	7838	8067	8296	8525	229
190	278754	278982	279211	279439	279667	279895	280123	280351	280578	280806	228
1	281033	281261	281488	281715	281942	282169	2396	2622	2849	3075	227
2	3301	3527	3753	3979	4205	4431	4656	4882	5107	5332	226
3	5557	5782	6007	6232	6456	6681	6905	7130	7354	7578	225
4	7802	8026	8249	8473	8696	8920	9143	9366	9589	9812	223
195	290035	290257	290480	290702	290925	291147	291369	291591	291813	292034	222
6	2256	2478	2699	2920	3141	3363	3584	3804	4025	4246	221
7	4466	4687	4907	5127	5347	5567	5787	6007	6226	6446	220
8	6665	6884	7104	7323	7542	7761	7979	8198	8416	8635	219
9	8853	9071	9289	9507	9725	9943	300161	300378	300595	300813	218
200	301030	301247	301464	301681	301898	302114	302331	302547	302764	302980	217
1	3196	3412	3628	3844	4059	4275	4491	4706	4921	5136	216
2	5351	5566	5781	5996	6211	6425	6639	6854	7068	7282	215
3	7496	7710	7924	8137	8351	8564	8778	8991	9204	9417	213
4	9630	9843	310056	310268	310481	310693	310906	311118	311330	311542	212
205	311754	311966	2177	2389	2600	2812	3023	3234	3445	3656	211
6	3867	4078	4289	4499	4710	4920	5130	5340	5551	5760	210
7	5970	6180	6390	6599	6809	7018	7227	7436	7646	7854	209
8	8063	8272	8481	8689	8898	9106	9314	9522	9730	9938	208
9	320146	320354	320562	320769	320977	321184	321391	321598	321805	322012	207
210	322219	322426	322633	322839	323046	323252	323458	323665	323871	324077	206
1	4282	4488	4694	4899	5105	5310	5516	5721	5926	6131	205
2	6336	6541	6745	6950	7155	7359	7563	7767	7972	8176	204
3	8380	8583	8787	8991	9194	9398	9601	9805	330008	330211	203
4	330414	330617	330819	331022	331225	331427	331630	331832	2034	2236	202
215	2438	2640	2842	3044	3246	3447	3649	3850	4051	4253	202
6	4454	4655	4856	5057	5257	5458	5658	5859	6059	6260	201
7	6460	6660	6860	7060	7260	7459	7659	7858	8058	8257	200
8	8456	8656	8855	9054	9253	9451	9650	9849	340047	340246	199
9	340444	340642	340841	341039	341237	341435	341632	341830	2028	2225	198
N.	0	1	2	3	4	5	6	7	8	9	D.

TABLE I.—Six-place Mantissas

N.	0	1	2	3	4	5	6	7	8	9	D.
220	342423	342620	342817	343014	343212	343409	343606	343802	343999	344196	197
1	4392	4589	4785	4981	5178	5374	5570	5766	5962	6157	196
2	6353	6549	6744	6939	7135	7330	7525	7720	7915	8110	195
3	8305	8500	8694	8889	9083	9278	9472	9666	9860	350054	194
4	350248	350442	350636	350829	351023	351216	351410	351603	351796	1989	193
225	2183	2375	2568	2761	2954	3147	3339	3532	3724	3916	193
6	4108	4301	4493	4685	4876	5068	5260	5452	5643	5834	192
7	6026	6217	6408	6599	6790	6981	7172	7363	7554	7744	191
8	7935	8125	8316	8506	8696	8886	9076	9266	9456	9646	190
9	9835	360025	360215	360404	360593	360783	360972	361161	361350	361539	189
230	361728	361917	362105	362294	362482	362671	362859	363048	363236	363424	188
1	3612	3800	3988	4176	4363	4551	4739	4926	5113	5301	188
2	5488	5675	5862	6049	6236	6423	6610	6796	6983	7169	187
3	7356	7542	7729	7915	8101	8287	8473	8659	8845	9030	186
4	9216	9401	9587	9772	9958	370143	370328	370513	370698	370883	185
235	371068	371253	371437	371622	371806	1991	2175	2360	2544	2728	184
6	2912	3096	3280	3464	3647	3831	4015	4198	4382	4565	184
7	4748	4932	5115	5298	5481	5664	5846	6029	6212	6394	183
8	6577	6759	6942	7124	7306	7488	7670	7852	8034	8216	182
9	8398	8580	8761	8943	9124	9306	9487	9668	9849	380030	181
240	380211	380392	380573	380754	380934	381115	381296	381476	381656	381837	181
1	2017	2197	2377	2557	2737	2917	3097	3277	3456	3636	180
2	3815	3995	4174	4353	4533	4712	4891	5070	5249	5428	179
3	5606	5785	5964	6142	6321	6499	6677	6856	7034	7212	178
4	7390	7568	7746	7923	8101	8279	8456	8634	8811	8989	178
245	9166	9343	9520	9698	9875	390051	390228	390405	390582	390759	177
6	390935	391112	391288	391464	391641	1817	1993	2169	2345	2521	176
7	2697	2873	3048	3224	3400	3575	3751	3926	4101	4277	176
8	4452	4627	4802	4977	5152	5326	5501	5676	5850	6025	175
9	6199	6374	6548	6722	6896	7071	7245	7419	7592	7766	174
250	397940	398114	398287	398461	398634	398808	398981	399154	399328	399501	173
1	9674	9847	400020	400192	400365	400538	400711	400883	401056	401228	173
2	401401	401573	1745	1917	2089	2261	2433	2605	2777	2949	172
3	3121	3292	3464	3635	3807	3978	4149	4320	4492	4663	171
4	4834	5005	5176	5346	5517	5688	5858	6029	6199	6370	171
255	6540	6710	6881	7051	7221	7391	7561	7731	7901	8070	170
6	8240	8410	8579	8749	8918	9087	9257	9426	9595	9764	169
7	9933	410102	410271	410440	410609	410777	410964	411114	411283	411451	169
8	411620	1788	1956	2124	2293	2461	2629	2796	2964	3132	168
9	3300	3467	3635	3803	3970	4137	4305	4472	4639	4806	167
260	414973	415140	415307	415474	415641	415808	415974	416141	416308	416474	167
1	6641	6807	6973	7139	7306	7472	7638	7804	7970	8135	166
2	8301	8467	8633	8798	8964	9129	9295	9460	9625	9791	165
3	9956	420121	420286	420451	420616	420781	420945	421110	421275	421439	165
4	421604	1768	1933	2097	2261	2426	2590	2754	2918	3082	164
265	3246	3410	3574	3737	3901	4065	4228	4392	4555	4718	164
6	4882	5045	5208	5371	5534	5697	5860	6023	6186	6349	163
7	6511	6674	6836	6999	7161	7324	7486	7648	7811	7973	162
8	8135	8297	8459	8621	8783	8944	9106	9268	9429	9591	162
9	9752	9914	430075	430236	430398	430559	430720	430881	431042	431203	161
270	431364	431525	431685	431846	432007	432167	432328	432488	432649	432809	161
1	2969	3130	3290	3450	3610	3770	3930	4090	4249	4409	160
2	4569	4729	4868	5048	5207	5367	5526	5685	5844	6004	159
3	6163	6322	6481	6640	6799	6957	7116	7275	7433	7592	159
4	7751	7909	8067	8226	8384	8542	8701	8859	9017	9175	158
275	9333	9491	9648	9806	9964	440122	440279	440437	440594	440752	158
6	440909	441066	441224	441381	441538	1695	1852	2009	2166	2323	157
7	2480	2637	2793	2950	3106	3263	3419	3576	3732	3889	157
8	4045	4201	4357	4513	4669	4825	4981	5137	5293	5449	156
9	5604	5760	5915	6071	6226	6382	6537	6692	6848	7003	155
N.	0	1	2	3	4	5	6	7	8	9	D.

443

TABLE I.—Six-place Mantissas

N.	0	1	2	3	4	5	6	7	8	9	D.
280	447158	447313	447468	447623	447778	447933	448088	448242	448397	448552	155
1	8706	8861	9015	9170	9324	9478	9633	9787	9941	450095	154
2	450249	450403	450557	450711	450865	451018	451172	451326	451479	1633	154
3	1786	1940	2093	2247	2400	2553	2706	2859	3012	3165	153
4	3318	3471	3624	3777	3930	4082	4235	4387	4540	4692	153
285	4845	4997	5150	5302	5454	5606	5758	5910	6062	6214	152
6	6366	6518	6670	6821	6973	7125	7276	7428	7579	7731	152
7	7882	8033	8184	8336	8487	8638	8789	8940	9091	9242	151
8	9392	9543	9694	9845	9995	460146	460296	460447	460597	460748	151
9	460898	461048	461198	461348	461499	1649	1799	1948	2098	2248	150
290	462398	462548	462697	462847	462997	463146	463296	463445	463594	463744	150
1	3893	4042	4191	4340	4490	4639	4788	4936	5085	5234	149
2	5383	5532	5680	5829	5977	6126	6274	6423	6571	6719	149
3	6868	7016	7164	7312	7460	7608	7756	7904	8052	8200	148
4	8347	8495	8643	8790	8938	9085	9233	9380	9527	9675	148
295	9822	9969	470116	470263	470410	470557	470704	470851	470998	471145	147
6	471292	471438	1585	1732	1878	2025	2171	2318	2464	2610	146
7	2756	2903	3049	3195	3341	3487	3633	3779	3925	4071	146
8	4216	4362	4508	4653	4799	4944	5090	5235	5381	5526	146
9	5671	5816	5962	6107	6252	6397	6542	6687	6832	6976	145
300	477121	477266	477411	477555	477700	477844	477989	478133	478278	478422	145
1	8566	8711	8855	8999	9143	9287	9431	9575	9719	9863	144
2	480007	480151	480294	480438	480582	480725	480869	481012	481156	481299	144
3	1443	1586	1729	1872	2016	2159	2302	2445	2588	2731	143
4	2874	3016	3159	3302	3445	3587	3730	3872	4015	4157	143
305	4300	4442	4585	4727	4869	5011	5153	5295	5437	5579	142
6	5721	5863	6005	6147	6289	6430	6572	6714	6855	6997	142
7	7138	7280	7421	7563	7704	7845	7986	8127	8269	8410	141
8	8551	8692	8833	8974	9114	9255	9396	9537	9677	9818	141
9	9958	490099	490239	490380	490520	490661	490801	490941	491081	491222	140
310	491362	491502	491642	491782	491922	492062	492201	492341	492481	492621	140
1	2760	2900	3040	3179	3319	3458	3597	3737	3876	4015	139
2	4155	4294	4433	4572	4711	4850	4989	5128	5267	5406	139
3	5544	5683	5822	5960	6099	6238	6376	6515	6653	6791	139
4	6930	7068	7206	7344	7483	7621	7759	7897	8035	8173	138
315	8311	8448	8586	8724	8862	8999	9137	9275	9412	9550	138
6	9687	9824	9962	500099	500236	500374	500511	500648	500785	500922	137
7	501059	501196	501333	1470	1607	1744	1880	2017	2154	2291	137
8	2427	2564	2700	2837	2973	3109	3246	3382	3518	3655	136
9	3791	3927	4063	4199	4335	4471	4607	4743	4878	5014	136
320	505150	505286	505421	505557	505693	505828	505964	506099	506234	506370	136
1	6505	6640	6776	6911	7046	7181	7316	7451	7586	7721	135
2	7856	7991	8126	8260	8395	8530	8664	8799	8934	9068	135
3	9203	9337	9471	9606	9740	9874	510009	510143	510277	510411	134
4	510545	510679	510813	510947	511081	511215	1349	1482	1616	1750	134
325	1883	2017	2151	2284	2418	2551	2684	2818	2951	3084	133
6	3218	3351	3484	3617	3750	3883	4016	4149	4282	4415	133
7	4548	4681	4813	4946	5079	5211	5344	5476	5609	5741	133
8	5874	6006	6139	6271	6403	6535	6668	6800	6932	7064	132
9	7196	7328	7460	7592	7724	7855	7987	8119	8251	8382	132
330	518514	518646	518777	518909	519040	519171	519303	519434	519566	519697	131
1	9828	9959	520090	520221	520353	520484	520615	520745	520876	521007	131
2	521138	521269	1400	1530	1661	1792	1922	2053	2183	2314	131
3	2444	2575	2705	2835	2966	3096	3226	3356	3486	3616	130
4	3746	3876	4006	4136	4266	4396	4526	4656	4785	4915	130
335	5045	5174	5304	5434	5563	5693	5822	5951	6081	6210	129
6	6339	6469	6598	6727	6856	6985	7114	7243	7372	7501	129
7	7630	7759	7888	8016	8145	8274	8402	8531	8660	8788	129
8	8917	9045	9174	9302	9430	9559	9687	9815	9943	530072	128
9	530200	530328	530456	530584	530712	530840	530968	531096	531223	1351	128
N.	0	1	2	3	4	5	6	7	8	9	D.

TABLE I.—Six-place Mantissas

N.	0	1	2	3	4	5	6	7	8	9	D.
340	531479	531607	531734	531862	531990	532117	532245	532372	532500	532627	128
1	2754	2882	3009	3136	3264	3391	3518	3645	3772	3899	127
2	4026	4153	4280	4407	4534	4661	4787	4914	5041	5167	127
3	5294	5421	5547	5674	5800	5927	6053	6180	6306	6432	126
4	6558	6685	6811	6937	7063	7189	7315	7441	7567	7693	126
345	7819	7945	8071	8197	8322	8448	8574	8699	8825	8951	126
6	9076	9202	9327	9452	9578	9703	9829	9954	540079	540204	125
7	540329	540455	540580	540705	540830	540955	541080	541205	1330	1454	125
8	1579	1704	1829	1953	2078	2203	2327	2452	2576	2701	125
9	2825	2950	3074	3199	3323	3447	3571	3696	3820	3944	124
350	544068	544192	544316	544440	544564	544688	544812	544936	545060	545183	124
1	5307	5431	5555	5678	5802	5925	6049	6172	6296	6419	124
2	6543	6666	6789	6913	7036	7159	7282	7405	7529	7652	123
3	7775	7898	8021	8144	8267	8389	8512	8635	8758	8881	123
4	9003	9126	9249	9371	9494	9616	9739	9861	9984	550106	123
355	550228	550351	550473	550595	550717	550840	550962	551084	551206	1328	122
6	1450	1572	1694	1816	1938	2060	2181	2303	2425	2547	122
7	2668	2790	2911	3033	3155	3276	3398	3519	3640	3762	121
8	3883	4004	4126	4247	4368	4489	4610	4731	4852	4973	121
9	5094	5215	5336	5457	5578	5699	5820	5940	6061	6182	121
360	556303	556423	556544	556664	556785	556905	557026	557146	557267	557387	120
1	7507	7627	7748	7868	7988	8108	8228	8349	8469	8589	120
2	8709	8829	8948	9068	9188	9308	9428	9548	9667	9787	120
3	9907	560026	560146	560265	560385	560504	560624	560743	560863	560982	119
4	561101	1221	1340	1459	1578	1698	1817	1936	2055	2174	119
365	2293	2412	2531	2650	2769	2887	3006	3125	3244	3362	119
6	3481	3600	3718	3837	3955	4074	4192	4311	4429	4548	119
7	4666	4784	4903	5021	5139	5257	5376	5494	5612	5730	118
8	5848	5966	6084	6202	6320	6437	6555	6673	6791	6909	118
9	7026	7144	7262	7379	7497	7614	7732	7849	7967	8084	118
370	568202	568319	568436	568554	568671	568788	568905	569023	569140	569257	117
1	9374	9491	9608	9725	9842	9959	570076	570193	570309	570426	117
2	570543	570660	570776	570893	571010	571126	1243	1359	1476	1592	117
3	1709	1825	1942	2058	2174	2291	2407	2523	2639	2755	116
4	2872	2988	3104	3220	3336	3452	3568	3684	3800	3915	116
375	4031	4147	4263	4379	4494	4610	4726	4841	4957	5072	116
6	5188	5303	5419	5534	5650	5765	5880	5996	6111	6226	115
7	6341	6457	6572	6687	6802	6917	7032	7147	7262	7377	115
8	7492	7607	7722	7836	7951	8066	8181	8295	8410	8525	115
9	8639	8754	8868	8983	9097	9212	9326	9441	9555	9669	114
380	579784	579898	580012	580126	580241	580355	580469	580583	580697	580811	114
1	580925	581039	1153	1267	1381	1495	1608	1722	1836	1950	114
2	2063	2177	2291	2404	2518	2631	2745	2858	2972	3085	114
3	3199	3312	3426	3539	3652	3765	3879	3992	4105	4218	113
4	4331	4444	4557	4670	4783	4896	5009	5122	5235	5348	113
385	5461	5574	5686	5799	5912	6024	6137	6250	6362	6475	113
6	6587	6700	6812	6925	7037	7149	7262	7374	7486	7599	112
7	7711	7823	7935	8047	8160	8272	8384	8496	8608	8720	112
8	8832	8944	9056	9167	9279	9391	9503	9615	9726	9838	112
9	9950	590061	590173	590284	590396	590507	590619	590730	590842	590953	112
390	591065	591176	591287	591399	591510	591621	591732	591843	591955	592066	111
1	2177	2288	2399	2510	2621	2732	2843	2954	3064	3175	111
2	3286	3397	3508	3618	3729	3840	3950	4061	4171	4282	111
3	4393	4503	4614	4724	4834	4945	5055	5165	5276	5380	110
4	5496	5606	5717	5827	5937	6047	6157	6267	6377	6487	110
395	6597	6707	6817	6927	7037	7146	7256	7366	7476	7586	110
6	7695	7805	7914	8024	8134	8243	8353	8462	8572	8681	110
7	8791	8900	9009	9119	9228	9337	9446	9556	9665	9774	109
8	9883	9992	600101	600210	600319	600428	600537	600646	600755	600864	109
9	600973	601082	1191	1299	1408	1517	1625	1734	1843	1951	109
N.	0	1	2	3	4	5	6	7	8	9	D.

TABLE I.—Six-place Mantissas

N.	0	1	2	3	4	5	6	7	8	9	D.
400	602060	602169	602277	602386	602494	602603	602711	602819	602928	603036	108
1	3144	3253	3361	3469	3577	3686	3794	3902	4010	4118	108
2	4226	4334	4442	4550	4658	4766	4874	4982	5089	5197	108
3	5305	5413	5521	5628	5736	5844	5951	6059	6166	6274	108
4	6381	6489	6596	6704	6811	6919	7026	7133	7241	7348	107
405	7455	7562	7669	7777	7884	7991	8098	8205	8312	8419	107
6	8526	8633	8740	8847	8954	9061	9167	9274	9381	9488	107
7	9594	9701	9808	9914	610021	610128	610234	610341	610447	610554	107
8	610660	610767	610873	610979	1086	1192	1298	1405	1511	1617	106
9	1723	1829	1936	2042	2148	2254	2360	2466	2572	2678	106
410	612784	612890	612996	613102	613207	613313	613419	613525	613630	613736	106
1	3842	3947	4053	4159	4264	4370	4475	4581	4686	4792	106
2	4897	5003	5108	5213	5319	5424	5529	5634	5740	5845	105
3	5950	6055	6160	6265	6370	6476	6581	6686	6790	6895	105
4	7000	7105	7210	7315	7420	7525	7629	7734	7839	7943	105
415	8048	8153	8257	8362	8466	8571	8676	8780	8884	8989	105
6	9093	9198	9302	9406	9511	9615	9719	9824	9928	620032	104
7	620136	620240	620344	620448	620552	620656	620760	620864	620968	1072	104
8	1176	1280	1384	1488	1592	1695	1799	1903	2007	2110	104
9	2214	2318	2421	2525	2628	2732	2835	2939	3042	3146	104
420	623249	623353	623456	623559	623663	623766	623869	623973	624076	624179	103
1	4282	4385	4488	4591	4695	4798	4901	5004	5107	5210	103
2	5312	5415	5518	5621	5724	5827	5929	6032	6135	6238	103
3	6340	6443	6546	6648	6751	6853	6956	7058	7161	7263	103
4	7366	7468	7571	7673	7775	7878	7980	8082	8185	8287	102
425	8389	8491	8593	8695	8797	8900	9002	9104	9206	9308	102
6	9410	9512	9613	9715	9817	9919	630021	630123	630224	630326	102
7	630428	630530	630631	630733	630835	630936	1038	1139	1241	1342	102
8	1444	1545	1647	1748	1849	1951	2052	2153	2255	2356	101
9	2457	2559	2660	2761	2862	2963	3064	3165	3266	3367	101
430	633468	633569	633670	633771	633872	633973	634074	634175	634276	634376	101
1	4477	4578	4679	4779	4880	4981	5081	5182	5283	5383	101
2	5484	5584	5685	5785	5886	5986	6087	6187	6287	6388	100
3	6488	6588	6688	6789	6889	6989	7089	7189	7290	7390	100
4	7490	7590	7690	7790	7890	7990	8090	8190	8290	8389	100
435	8489	8589	8689	8789	8888	8988	9088	9188	9287	9387	100
6	9486	9586	9686	9785	9889	9984	640084	640183	640283	640382	99
7	640481	640581	640680	640779	640879	640978	1077	1177	1276	1375	99
8	1474	1573	1672	1771	1871	1970	2069	2168	2267	2366	99
9	2465	2563	2662	2761	2860	2959	3058	3156	3255	3354	99
440	643453	643551	643650	643749	643847	643946	644044	644143	644242	644340	98
1	4439	4537	4636	4734	4832	4931	5029	5127	5226	5324	98
2	5422	5521	5619	5717	5815	5913	6011	6110	6208	6306	98
3	6404	6502	6600	6698	6796	6894	6992	7089	7187	7285	98
4	7383	7481	7579	7676	7774	7872	7969	8067	8165	8262	98
445	8360	8458	8555	8653	8750	8848	8945	9043	9140	9237	97
6	9335	9432	9530	9627	9724	9821	9919	650016	650113	650210	97
7	650308	650405	650502	650599	650696	650793	650890	0987	1084	1181	97
8	1278	1375	1472	1569	1666	1762	1859	1956	2053	2150	97
9	2246	2343	2440	2536	2633	2730	2826	2923	3019	3116	97
450	653213	653309	653405	653502	653598	653695	653791	653888	653984	654080	96
1	4177	4273	4369	4465	4562	4658	4754	4850	4946	5042	96
2	5138	5235	5331	5427	5523	5619	5715	5810	5906	6002	96
3	6098	6194	6290	6386	6482	6577	6673	6769	6864	6960	96
4	7056	7152	7247	7343	7438	7534	7629	7725	7820	7916	96
455	8011	8107	8202	8298	8393	8488	8584	8679	8774	8870	95
6	8965	9060	9155	9250	9346	9441	9536	9631	9726	9821	95
7	9916	660011	660106	660201	660296	660391	660486	660581	660676	660771	95
8	660865	0960	1055	1150	1245	1339	1434	1529	1623	1718	95
9	1813	1907	2002	2096	2191	2286	2380	2475	2569	2663	95
N.	0	1	2	3	4	5	6	7	8	9	D.

TABLE I.—Six-place Mantissas

N.	0	1	2	3	4	5	6	7	8	9	D.
460	662758	662852	662947	663041	663135	663230	663324	663418	663512	663607	94
1	3701	3795	3889	3983	4078	4172	4266	4360	4454	4548	94
2	4642	4736	4830	4924	5018	5112	5206	5299	5393	5487	94
3	5581	5675	5769	5862	5956	6050	6143	6237	6331	6424	94
4	6518	6612	6705	6799	6892	6986	7079	7173	7266	7360	94
465	7453	7546	7640	7733	7826	7920	8013	8106	8199	8293	93
6	8386	8479	8572	8665	8759	8852	8945	9038	9131	9224	93
7	9317	9410	9503	9596	9689	9782	9875	9967	670060	670153	93
8	670246	670339	670431	670524	670617	670710	670802	670895	0988	1080	93
9	1173	1265	1358	1451	1543	1636	1728	1821	1913	2005	93
470	672098	672190	672283	672375	672467	672560	672652	672744	672836	672929	92
1	3021	3113	3205	3297	3390	3482	3574	3666	3758	3850	92
2	3942	4034	4126	4218	4310	4402	4494	4586	4677	4769	92
3	4861	4953	5045	5137	5228	5320	5412	5503	5595	5687	92
4	5778	5870	5962	6053	6145	6236	6328	6419	6511	6602	92
475	6694	6785	6876	6968	7059	7151	7242	7333	7424	7516	91
6	7607	7698	7789	7881	7972	8033	8154	8245	8336	8427	91
7	8518	8609	8700	8791	8882	8973	9064	9155	9246	9337	91
8	9428	9519	9610	9700	9791	9882	9973	680063	680154	680245	91
9	680336	680426	680517	680607	680698	680789	680879	0970	1060	1151	91
480	681241	681332	681422	681513	681603	681693	681784	681874	681964	682055	90
1	2145	2235	2326	2416	2506	2596	2686	2777	2867	2957	90
2	3047	3137	3227	3317	3407	3497	3587	3677	3767	3857	90
3	3947	4037	4127	4217	4307	4396	4486	4576	4666	4756	90
4	4845	4935	5025	5114	5204	5294	5383	5473	5563	5652	90
485	5742	5831	5921	6010	6100	6189	6279	6368	6458	6547	89
6	6636	6726	6815	6904	6994	7083	7172	7261	7351	7440	89
7	7529	7618	7707	7796	7886	7975	8064	8153	8242	8331	89
8	8420	8509	8598	8687	8776	8865	8953	9042	9131	9220	89
9	9309	9398	9486	9575	9664	9753	9841	9930	690019	690107	89
490	690196	690285	690373	690462	690550	690639	690728	690816	690905	690993	89
1	1081	1170	1258	1347	1435	1524	1612	1700	1789	1877	88
2	1965	2053	2142	2230	2318	2406	2494	2583	2671	2759	88
3	2847	2935	3023	3111	3199	3287	3375	3463	3551	3639	88
4	3727	3815	3903	3991	4078	4166	4254	4342	4430	4517	88
495	4605	4693	4781	4868	4956	5044	5131	5219	5307	5394	88
6	5482	5569	5657	5744	5832	5919	6007	6094	6182	6269	87
7	6356	6444	6531	6618	6706	6793	6880	6968	7055	7142	87
8	7229	7317	7404	7491	7578	7665	7752	7839	7926	8014	87
9	8101	8188	8275	8362	8449	8535	8622	8709	8796	8883	87
500	698970	699057	699144	699231	699317	699404	699491	699578	699664	699751	87
1	9838	9924	700011	700098	700184	700271	700358	700444	700531	700617	87
2	700704	700790	0877	0963	1050	1136	1222	1309	1395	1482	86
3	1568	1654	1741	1827	1913	1999	2086	2172	2258	2344	86
4	2431	2517	2603	2689	2775	2861	2947	3033	3119	3205	86
505	3291	3377	3463	3549	3635	3721	3807	3893	3979	4065	86
6	4151	4236	4322	4408	4494	4579	4665	4751	4837	4922	86
7	5008	5094	5179	5265	5350	5436	5522	5607	5693	5778	86
8	5864	5949	6035	6120	6206	6291	6376	6462	6547	6632	85
9	6718	6803	6888	6974	7059	7144	7229	7315	7400	7485	85
510	707570	707655	707740	707826	707911	707996	708081	708166	708251	708336	85
1	8421	8506	8591	8676	8761	8846	8931	9015	9100	9185	85
2	9270	9355	9440	9524	9609	9694	9779	9863	9948	710033	85
3	710117	710202	710287	710371	710456	710540	710625	710710	710794	0879	85
4	0963	1048	1132	1217	1301	1385	1470	1554	1639	1723	84
515	1807	1892	1976	2060	2144	2229	2313	2397	2481	2566	84
6	2650	2734	2818	2902	2986	3070	3154	3238	3323	3407	84
7	3491	3575	3659	3742	3826	3910	3994	4078	4162	4246	84
8	4330	4414	4497	4581	4665	4749	4833	4916	5000	5084	84
9	5167	5251	5335	5418	5502	5586	5669	5753	5836	5920	84
N.	0	1	2	3	4	5	6	7	8	9	D.

TABLE I.—Six-place Mantissas

N.	0	1	2	3	4	5	6	7	8	9	D.
520	716003	716087	716170	716254	716337	716421	716504	716588	716671	716754	83
1	6838	6921	7004	7088	7171	7254	7338	7421	7504	7587	83
2	7671	7754	7837	7920	8003	8086	8169	8253	8336	8419	83
3	8502	8585	8668	8751	8834	8917	9000	9083	9165	9248	83
4	9331	9414	9497	9580	9663	9745	9828	9911	9994	720077	83
525	720159	720242	720325	720407	720490	720573	720655	720738	720821	0903	83
6	0986	1068	1151	1233	1316	1398	1481	1563	1646	1728	82
7	1811	1893	1975	2058	2140	2222	2305	2387	2469	2552	82
8	2634	2716	2798	2881	2963	3045	3127	3209	3291	3374	82
9	3456	3538	3620	3702	3784	3866	3948	4030	4112	4194	82
530	724276	724358	724440	724522	724604	724685	724767	724849	724931	725013	82
1	5095	5176	5258	5340	5422	5503	5585	5667	5748	5830	82
2	5912	5993	6075	6156	6238	6320	6401	6483	6564	6646	82
3	6727	6809	6890	6972	7053	7134	7216	7297	7379	7460	81
4	7541	7623	7704	7785	7866	7948	8029	8110	8191	8273	81
535	8354	8435	8516	8597	8678	8759	8841	8922	9003	9084	81
6	9165	9246	9327	9408	9489	9570	9651	9732	9813	9893	81
7	9974	730055	730136	730217	730298	730378	730459	730540	730621	730702	81
8	730782	0863	0944	1024	1105	1186	1266	1347	1428	1508	81
9	1589	1669	1750	1830	1911	1991	2072	2152	2233	2313	81
540	732394	732474	732555	732635	732715	732796	732876	732956	733037	733117	80
1	3197	3278	3358	3438	3518	3598	3679	3759	3839	3919	80
2	3999	4079	4160	4240	4320	4400	4480	4560	4640	4720	80
3	4800	4880	4960	5040	5120	5200	5279	5359	5439	5519	80
4	5599	5679	5759	5838	5918	5998	6078	6157	6237	6317	80
545	6397	6476	6556	6635	6715	6795	6874	6954	7034	7113	80
6	7193	7272	7352	7431	7511	7590	7670	7749	7829	7908	79
7	7987	8067	8146	8225	8305	8384	8463	8543	8622	8701	79
8	8781	8860	8939	9018	9097	9177	9256	9335	9414	9493	79
9	9572	9651	9731	9810	9889	9968	740047	740126	740205	740284	79
550	740363	740442	740521	740600	740678	740757	740836	740915	740994	741073	79
1	1152	1230	1309	1388	1467	1546	1624	1703	1782	1860	79
2	1939	2018	2096	2175	2254	2332	2411	2489	2568	2647	79
3	2725	2804	2882	2961	3039	3118	3196	3275	3353	3431	78
4	3510	3588	3667	3745	3823	3902	3980	4058	4136	4215	78
555	4293	4371	4449	4528	4606	4684	4762	4840	4919	4997	78
6	5075	5153	5231	5309	5387	5465	5543	5621	5699	5777	78
7	5855	5933	6011	6089	6167	6245	6323	6401	6479	6556	78
8	6634	6712	6790	6868	6945	7023	7101	7179	7256	7334	78
9	7412	7489	7567	7645	7722	7800	7878	7955	8033	8110	78
560	748188	748266	748343	748421	748498	748576	748653	748731	748808	748885	77
1	8963	9040	9118	9195	9272	9350	9427	9504	9582	9659	77
2	9736	9814	9891	9968	750045	750123	750200	750277	750354	750431	77
3	750508	750586	750663	750740	0817	0894	0971	1048	1125	1202	77
4	1279	1356	1433	1510	1587	1664	1741	1818	1895	1972	77
565	2048	2125	2202	2279	2356	2433	2509	2586	2663	2740	77
6	2816	2893	2970	3047	3123	3200	3277	3353	3430	3506	77
7	3583	3660	3736	3813	3889	3966	4042	4119	4195	4272	77
8	4348	4425	4501	4578	4654	4730	4807	4883	4960	5036	76
9	5112	5189	5265	5341	5417	5494	5570	5646	5722	5799	76
570	755875	755951	756027	756103	756180	756256	756332	756408	756484	756560	76
1	6636	6712	6788	6864	6940	7016	7092	7168	7244	7320	76
2	7396	7472	7548	7624	7700	7775	7851	7927	8003	8079	76
3	8155	8230	8306	8382	8458	8533	8609	8685	8761	8836	76
4	8912	8988	9063	9139	9214	9290	9366	9441	9517	9592	76
575	9668	9743	9819	9894	9970	760045	760121	760196	760272	760347	75
6	760422	760498	760573	760649	760724	0799	0875	0950	1025	1101	75
7	1176	1251	1326	1402	1477	1552	1627	1702	1778	1853	75
8	1928	2003	2078	2153	2228	2303	2378	2453	2529	2604	75
9	2679	2754	2829	2904	2978	3053	3128	3203	3278	3353	75
N.	0	1	2	3	4	5	6	7	8	9	D.

TABLE I.—Six-place Mantissas

N.	0	1	2	3	4	5	6	7	8	9	D.
580	763428	763503	763578	763653	763727	763802	763877	763952	764027	764101	75
1	4176	4251	4326	4400	4475	4550	4624	4699	4774	4848	75
2	4923	4998	5072	5147	5221	5296	5370	5445	5520	5594	75
3	5669	5743	5818	5892	5966	6041	6115	6190	6264	6338	74
4	6413	6487	6562	6636	6710	6785	6859	6933	7007	7082	74
585	7156	7230	7304	7379	7453	7527	7601	7675	7749	7823	74
6	7898	7972	8046	8120	8194	8268	8342	8416	8490	8564	74
7	8638	8712	8786	8860	8934	9008	9082	9156	9230	9303	74
8	9377	9451	9525	9599	9673	9746	9820	9894	9968	770042	74
9	770115	770189	770263	770336	770410	770484	770557	770631	770705	0778	74
590	770852	770926	770999	771073	771146	771220	771293	771367	771440	771514	74
1	1587	1661	1734	1808	1881	1955	2028	2102	2175	2248	73
2	2322	2395	2468	2542	2615	2688	2762	2835	2908	2981	73
3	3055	3128	3201	3274	3348	3421	3494	3567	3640	3713	73
4	3786	3860	3933	4006	4079	4152	4225	4298	4371	4444	73
595	4517	4590	4663	4736	4809	4882	4955	5028	5100	5173	73
6	5246	5319	5392	5465	5538	5610	5683	5756	5829	5902	73
7	5974	6047	6120	6193	6265	6338	6411	6483	6556	6629	73
8	6701	6774	6846	6919	6992	7064	7137	7209	7282	7354	73
9	7427	7499	7572	7644	7717	7789	7862	7934	8006	8079	72
600	778151	778224	778296	778368	778441	778513	778585	778658	778730	778802	72
1	8874	8947	9019	9091	9163	9236	9308	9380	9452	9524	72
2	9596	9669	9741	9813	9885	3957	780029	780101	780173	780245	72
3	780317	780389	780461	780533	780605	780677	0749	0821	0893	0965	72
4	1037	1109	1181	1253	1324	1396	1468	1540	1612	1684	72
605	1755	1827	1899	1971	2042	2114	2186	2258	2329	2401	72
6	2473	2544	2616	2688	2759	2831	2902	2974	3046	3117	72
7	3189	3260	3332	3403	3475	3546	3618	3689	3761	3832	71
8	3904	3975	4046	4118	4189	4261	4332	4403	4475	4546	71
9	4617	4689	4760	4831	4902	4974	5045	5116	5187	5259	71
610	785330	785401	785472	785543	785615	785686	785757	785828	785899	785970	71
1	6041	6112	6183	6254	6325	6396	6467	6538	6609	6680	71
2	6751	6822	6893	6964	7035	7106	7177	7248	7319	7390	71
3	7460	7531	7602	7673	7744	7815	7885	7956	8027	8098	71
4	8168	8239	8310	8381	8451	8522	8593	8663	8734	8804	71
615	8875	8946	9016	9087	9157	9228	9299	9369	9440	9510	71
6	9581	9651	9722	9792	9863	9933	790004	790074	790144	790215	70
7	790285	790356	790426	790496	790567	790637	0707	0778	0848	0918	70
8	0988	1059	1129	1199	1269	1340	1410	1480	1550	1620	70
9	1691	1761	1831	1901	1971	2041	2111	2181	2252	2322	70
620	792392	792462	792532	792602	792672	792742	792812	792882	792952	793022	70
1	3092	3162	3231	3301	3371	3441	3511	3581	3651	3721	70
2	3790	3860	3930	4000	4070	4139	4209	4279	4349	4418	70
3	4488	4558	4627	4697	4767	4836	4906	4976	5045	5115	70
4	5185	5254	5324	5393	5463	5532	5602	5672	5741	5811	70
625	5880	5949	6019	6088	6158	6227	6297	6366	6436	6505	69
6	6574	6644	6713	6782	6852	6921	6990	7060	7129	7198	69
7	7268	7337	7406	7475	7545	7614	7683	7752	7821	7890	69
8	7960	8029	8098	8167	8236	8305	8374	8443	8513	8582	69
9	8651	8720	8789	8858	8927	8996	9065	9134	9203	9272	69
630	799341	799409	799478	799547	799616	799685	799754	799823	799892	799961	69
1	800029	800098	800167	800236	800305	800373	800442	800511	800580	800648	69
2	0717	0786	0854	0923	0992	1061	1129	1198	1266	1335	69
3	1404	1472	1541	1609	1678	1747	1815	1884	1952	2021	69
4	2089	2158	2226	2295	2363	2432	2500	2568	2637	2705	68
635	2774	2842	2910	2979	3047	3116	3184	3252	3321	3389	68
6	3457	3525	3594	3662	3730	3798	3867	3935	4003	4071	68
7	4139	4208	4276	4344	4412	4480	4548	4616	4685	4753	68
8	4821	4889	4957	5025	5093	5161	5229	5297	5365	5433	68
9	5501	5569	5637	5705	5773	5841	5908	5976	6044	6112	68
N.	0	1	2	3	4	5	6	7	8	9	D.

TABLE I. — Six-place Mantissas

N	0	1	2	3	4	5	6	7	8	9	D.
640	806180	806248	806316	806384	806451	806519	806587	806655	806723	806790	68
1	6858	6926	6994	7061	7129	7197	7264	7332	7400	7467	68
2	7535	7603	7670	7738	7806	7873	7941	8008	8076	8143	68
3	8211	8279	8346	8414	8481	8549	8616	8684	8751	8818	67
4	8886	8953	9021	9088	9156	9223	9290	9358	9425	9492	67
645	9560	9627	9694	9762	9829	9896	9964	810031	810098	810165	67
6	810233	810300	810367	810434	810501	810569	810636	0703	0770	0837	67
7	0904	0971	1039	1106	1173	1240	1307	1374	1441	1508	67
8	1575	1642	1709	1776	1843	1910	1977	2044	2111	2178	67
9	2245	2312	2379	2445	2512	2579	2646	2713	2780	2847	67
650	812913	812980	813047	813114	813181	813247	813314	813381	813448	813514	67
1	3581	3648	3714	3781	3848	3914	3981	4048	4114	4181	67
2	4248	4314	4381	4447	4514	4581	4647	4714	4780	4847	67
3	4913	4980	5046	5113	5179	5246	5312	5378	5445	5511	66
4	5578	5644	5711	5777	5843	5910	5976	6042	6109	6175	66
655	6241	6308	6374	6440	6506	6573	6639	6705	6771	6838	66
6	6904	6970	7036	7102	7169	7235	7301	7367	7433	7499	66
7	7565	7631	7698	7764	7830	7896	7962	8028	8094	8160	66
8	8226	8292	8358	8424	8490	8556	8622	8688	8754	8820	66
9	8885	8951	9017	9083	9149	9215	9281	9346	9412	9478	66
660	819544	819610	819676	819741	819807	819873	819939	820004	820070	820136	66
1	820201	820267	820333	820399	820464	820530	820595	0661	0727	0792	66
2	0858	0924	0989	1055	1120	1186	1251	1317	1382	1448	66
3	1514	1579	1645	1710	1775	1841	1906	1972	2037	2103	65
4	2168	2233	2299	2364	2430	2495	2560	2626	2691	2756	65
665	2822	2887	2952	3018	3083	3148	3213	3279	3344	3409	65
6	3474	3539	3605	3670	3735	3800	3865	3930	3996	4061	65
7	4126	4191	4256	4321	4386	4451	4516	4581	4646	4711	65
8	4776	4841	4906	4971	5036	5101	5166	5231	5296	5361	65
9	5426	5491	5556	5621	5686	5751	5815	5880	5945	6010	65
670	826075	826140	826204	826269	826334	826399	826464	826528	826593	826658	65
1	6723	6787	6852	6917	6981	7046	7111	7175	7240	7305	65
2	7369	7434	7499	7563	7628	7692	7757	7821	7886	7951	65
3	8015	8080	8144	8209	8273	8338	8402	8467	8531	8595	64
4	8660	8724	8789	8853	8918	8982	9046	9111	9175	9239	64
675	9304	9368	9432	9497	9561	9625	9690	9754	9818	9882	64
6	9947	830011	830075	830139	830204	830268	830332	830396	830460	830525	64
7	830589	0653	0717	0781	0845	0909	0973	1037	1102	1166	64
8	1230	1294	1358	1422	1486	1550	1614	1678	1742	1806	64
9	1870	1934	1998	2062	2126	2189	2253	2317	2381	2445	64
680	832509	832573	832637	832700	832764	832828	832892	832956	833020	833083	64
1	3147	3211	3275	3338	3402	3466	3530	3593	3657	3721	64
2	3784	3848	3912	3975	4039	4103	4166	4230	4294	4357	64
3	4421	4484	4548	4611	4675	4739	4802	4866	4929	4993	64
4	5056	5120	5183	5247	5310	5373	5437	5500	5564	5627	63
685	5691	5754	5817	5881	5944	6007	6071	6134	6197	6261	63
6	6324	6387	6451	6514	6577	6641	6704	6767	6830	6894	63
7	6957	7020	7083	7146	7210	7273	7336	7399	7462	7525	63
8	7588	7652	7715	7778	7841	7904	7967	8030	8093	8156	63
9	8219	8282	8345	8408	8471	8534	8597	8660	8723	8786	63
690	838849	838912	838975	839038	839101	839164	839227	839289	839352	839415	63
1	9478	9541	9604	9667	9729	9792	9855	9918	9981	840043	63
2	840106	840169	840232	840294	840357	840420	840482	840545	840608	0671	63
3	0733	0796	0859	0921	0984	1046	1109	1172	1234	1297	63
4	1359	1422	1485	1547	1610	1672	1735	1797	1860	1922	63
695	1985	2047	2110	2172	2235	2297	2360	2422	2484	2547	62
6	2609	2672	2734	2796	2859	2921	2983	3046	3108	3170	62
7	3233	3295	3357	3420	3482	3544	3606	3669	3731	3793	62
8	3855	3918	3980	4042	4104	4166	4229	4291	4353	4415	62
9	4477	4539	4601	4664	4726	4788	4850	4912	4974	5036	62
N.	0	1	2	3	4	5	6	7	8	9	D.

TABLE I.—Six-place Mantissas

N.	0	1	2	3	4	5	6	7	8	9	D.
700	845098	845160	845222	845284	845346	845408	845470	845532	845594	845656	62
1	5718	5780	5842	5904	5966	6028	6090	6151	6213	6275	62
2	6337	6399	6461	6523	6585	6646	6708	6770	6832	6894	62
3	6955	7017	7079	7141	7202	7264	7326	7388	7449	7511	62
4	7573	7634	7696	7758	7819	7881	7943	8004	8066	8128	62
705	8189	8251	8312	8374	8435	8497	8559	8620	8682	8743	62
6	8805	8866	8928	8989	9051	9112	9174	9235	9297	9358	61
7	9419	9481	9542	9604	9665	9726	9788	9849	9911	9972	61
8	850033	850095	850156	850217	850279	850340	850401	850462	850524	850585	61
9	0646	0707	0769	0830	0891	0952	1014	1075	1136	1197	61
710	851258	851320	851381	851442	851503	851564	851625	851686	851747	851809	61
1	1870	1931	1992	2053	2114	2175	2236	2297	2358	2419	61
2	2480	2541	2602	2663	2724	2785	2846	2907	2968	3029	61
3	3090	3150	3211	3272	3333	3394	3455	3516	3577	3637	61
4	3698	3759	3820	3881	3941	4002	4063	4124	4185	4245	61
715	4306	4367	4428	4488	4549	4610	4670	4731	4792	4852	61
6	4913	4974	5034	5095	5156	5216	5277	5337	5398	5459	61
7	5519	5580	5640	5701	5761	5822	5882	5943	6003	6064	61
8	6124	6185	6245	6306	6366	6427	6487	6548	6608	6668	60
9	6729	6789	6850	6910	6970	7031	7091	7152	7212	7272	60
720	857332	857393	857453	857513	857574	857634	857694	857755	857815	857875	60
1	7935	7995	8056	8116	8176	8236	8297	8357	8417	8477	60
2	8537	8597	8657	8718	8778	8838	8898	8958	9018	9078	60
3	9138	9198	9258	9318	9379	9439	9499	9559	9619	9679	60
4	9739	9799	9859	9918	9978	860038	860098	860158	860218	860278	60
725	860338	860398	860458	860518	860578	0637	0697	0757	0817	0877	60
6	0937	0996	1056	1116	1176	1236	1295	1355	1415	1475	60
7	1534	1594	1654	1714	1773	1833	1893	1952	2012	2072	60
8	2131	2191	2251	2310	2370	2430	2489	2549	2608	2668	60
9	2728	2787	2847	2906	2966	3025	3085	3144	3204	3263	60
730	863323	863382	863442	863501	863561	863620	863680	863739	863799	863858	59
1	3917	3977	4036	4096	4155	4214	4274	4333	4392	4452	59
2	4511	4570	4630	4689	4748	4808	4867	4926	4985	5045	59
3	5104	5163	5222	5282	5341	5400	5459	5519	5578	5637	59
4	5696	5755	5814	5874	5933	5992	6051	6110	6169	6228	59
735	6287	6346	6405	6465	6524	6583	6642	6701	6760	6819	59
6	6878	6937	6996	7055	7114	7173	7232	7291	7350	7409	59
7	7467	7526	7585	7644	7703	7762	7821	7880	7939	7998	59
8	8056	8115	8174	8233	8292	8350	8409	8468	8527	8586	59
9	8644	8703	8762	8821	8879	8938	8997	9056	9114	9173	59
740	869232	869290	869349	869408	869466	869525	869584	869642	869701	869760	59
1	9818	9877	9935	9994	870053	870111	870170	870228	870287	870345	59
2	870404	870462	870521	870579	0638	0696	0755	0813	0872	0930	58
3	0989	1047	1106	1164	1223	1281	1339	1398	1456	1515	58
4	1573	1631	1690	1748	1806	1865	1923	1981	2040	2098	58
745	2156	2215	2273	2331	2389	2448	2506	2564	2622	2681	58
6	2739	2797	2855	2913	2972	3030	3088	3146	3204	3262	58
7	3321	3379	3437	3495	3553	3611	3669	3727	3785	3844	58
8	3902	3960	4018	4076	4134	4192	4250	4308	4366	4424	58
9	4482	4540	4598	4656	4714	4772	4830	4888	4945	5003	58
750	875061	875119	875177	875235	875293	875351	875409	875466	875524	875582	58
1	5640	5698	5756	5813	5871	5929	5987	6045	6102	6160	58
2	6218	6276	6333	6391	6449	6507	6564	6622	6680	6737	58
3	6795	6853	6910	6968	7026	7083	7141	7199	7256	7314	58
4	7371	7429	7487	7544	7602	7659	7717	7774	7832	7889	58
755	7947	8004	8062	8119	8177	8234	8292	8349	8407	8464	57
6	8522	8579	8637	8694	8752	8809	8866	8924	8981	9039	57
7	9096	9153	9211	9268	9325	9383	9440	9497	9555	9612	57
8	9669	9726	9784	9841	9898	9956	880013	880070	880127	880185	57
9	880242	880299	880356	880413	880471	880528	0585	0642	0699	0756	57
N.	0	1	2	3	4	5	6	7	8	9	D

TABLE I.—Six-place Mantissas

N.	0	1	2	3	4	5	6	7	8	9	D.
760	880814	880871	880928	880985	881042	881099	881156	881213	881271	881328	57
1	1385	1442	1499	1556	1613	1670	1727	1784	1841	1898	57
2	1955	2012	2069	2126	2183	2240	2297	2354	2411	2468	57
3	2525	2581	2638	2695	2752	2809	2866	2923	2980	3037	57
4	3093	3150	3207	3264	3321	3377	3434	3491	3548	3605	57
765	3661	3718	3775	3832	3888	3945	4002	4059	4115	4172	57
6	4229	4285	4342	4399	4455	4512	4569	4625	4682	4739	57
7	4795	4852	4909	4965	5022	5078	5135	5192	5248	5305	57
8	5361	5418	5474	5531	5587	5644	5700	5757	5813	5870	57
9	5926	5983	6039	6096	6152	6209	6265	6321	6378	6434	56
770	886491	886547	886604	886660	886716	886773	886829	886885	886942	886998	56
1	7054	7111	7167	7223	7280	7336	7392	7449	7505	7561	56
2	7617	7674	7730	7786	7842	7898	7955	8011	8067	8123	56
3	8179	8236	8292	8348	8404	8460	8516	8573	8629	8685	56
4	8741	8797	8853	8909	8965	9021	9077	9134	9190	9246	56
775	9302	9358	9414	9470	9526	9582	9638	9694	9750	9806	56
6	9862	9918	9974	890030	890086	890141	890197	890253	890309	890365	56
7	890421	890477	890533	0589	0645	0700	0756	0812	0868	0924	56
8	0980	1035	1091	1147	1203	1259	1314	1370	1426	1482	56
9	1537	1593	1649	1705	1760	1816	1872	1928	1983	2039	56
780	892095	892150	892206	892262	892317	892373	892429	892484	892540	892595	56
1	2651	2707	2762	2818	2873	2929	2985	3040	3096	3151	56
2	3207	3262	3318	3373	3429	3484	3540	3595	3651	3706	56
3	3762	3817	3873	3928	3984	4039	4094	4150	4205	4261	55
4	4316	4371	4427	4482	4538	4593	4648	4704	4759	4814	55
785	4870	4925	4980	5036	5091	5146	5201	5257	5312	5367	55
6	5423	5478	5533	5588	5644	5699	5754	5809	5864	5920	55
7	5975	6030	6085	6140	6195	6251	6306	6361	6416	6471	55
8	6526	6581	6636	6692	6747	6802	6857	6912	6967	7022	55
9	7077	7132	7187	7242	7297	7352	7407	7462	7517	7572	55
790	897627	897682	897737	897792	897847	897902	897957	898012	898067	898122	55
1	8176	8231	8286	8341	8396	8451	8506	8561	8615	8670	55
2	8725	8780	8835	8890	8944	8999	9054	9109	9164	9218	55
3	9273	9328	9383	9437	9492	9547	9602	9656	9711	9766	55
4	9821	9875	9930	9985	900039	900094	900149	900203	900258	900312	55
795	900367	900422	900476	900531	0586	0640	0695	0749	0804	0859	55
6	0913	0968	1022	1077	1131	1186	1240	1295	1349	1404	55
7	1458	1513	1567	1622	1676	1731	1785	1840	1894	1948	54
8	2003	2057	2112	2166	2221	2275	2329	2384	2438	2492	54
9	2547	2601	2655	2710	2764	2818	2873	2927	2981	3036	54
800	903090	903144	903199	903253	903307	903361	903416	903470	903524	903578	54
1	3633	3687	3741	3795	3849	3904	3958	4012	4066	4120	54
2	4174	4229	4283	4337	4391	4445	4499	4553	4607	4661	54
3	4716	4770	4824	4878	4932	4986	5040	5094	5148	5202	54
4	5256	5310	5364	5418	5472	5526	5580	5634	5688	5742	54
805	5796	5850	5904	5958	6012	6066	6119	6173	6227	6281	54
6	6335	6389	6443	6497	6551	6604	6658	6712	6766	6820	54
7	6874	6927	6981	7035	7089	7143	7196	7250	7304	7358	54
8	7411	7465	7519	7573	7626	7680	7734	7787	7841	7895	54
9	7949	8002	8056	8110	8163	8217	8270	8324	8378	8431	54
810	908485	908539	908592	908646	908699	908753	908807	908860	908914	908967	54
1	9021	9074	9128	9181	9235	9289	9342	9396	9449	9503	54
2	9556	9610	9663	9716	9770	9823	9877	9930	9984	910037	53
3	910091	910144	910197	910251	910304	910358	910411	910464	910518	0571	53
4	0624	0678	0731	0784	0838	0891	0944	0998	1051	1104	53
815	1158	1211	1264	1317	1371	1424	1477	1530	1584	1637	53
6	1690	1743	1797	1850	1903	1956	2009	2063	2116	2169	53
7	2222	2275	2328	2381	2435	2488	2541	2594	2647	2700	53
8	2753	2806	2859	2913	2966	3019	3072	3125	3178	3231	53
9	3284	3337	3390	3443	3496	3549	3602	3655	3708	3761	53
N.	0	1	2	3	4	5	6	7	8	9	D.

TABLE I. — Six-place Mantissas

N.	0	1	2	3	4	5	6	7	8	9	D.
820	913814	913867	913920	913973	914026	914079	914132	914184	914237	914290	53
1	4343	4396	4449	4502	4555	4608	4660	4713	4766	4819	53
2	4872	4925	4977	5030	5083	5136	5189	5241	5294	5347	53
3	5400	5453	5505	5558	5611	5664	5716	5769	5822	5875	53
4	5927	5980	6033	6085	6138	6191	6243	6296	6349	6401	53
825	6454	6507	6559	6612	6664	6717	6770	6822	6875	6927	53
6	6980	7033	7085	7138	7190	7243	7295	7348	7400	7453	53
7	7506	7558	7611	7663	7716	7768	7820	7873	7925	7978	52
8	8030	8083	8135	8188	8240	8293	8345	8397	8450	8502	52
9	8555	8607	8659	8712	8764	8816	8869	8921	8973	9026	52
830	919078	919130	919183	919235	919287	919340	919392	919444	919496	919549	52
1	9601	9653	9706	9758	9810	9862	9914	9967	920019	920071	52
2	920123	920176	920228	920280	920332	920384	920436	920489	0541	0593	52
3	0645	0697	0749	0801	0853	0906	0958	1010	1062	1114	52
4	1166	1218	1270	1322	1374	1426	1478	1530	1582	1634	52
835	1686	1738	1790	1842	1894	1946	1998	2050	2102	2154	52
6	2206	2258	2310	2362	2414	2466	2518	2570	2622	2674	52
7	2725	2777	2829	2881	2933	2985	3037	3089	3140	3192	52
8	3244	3296	3348	3399	3451	3503	3555	3607	3658	3710	52
9	3762	3814	3865	3917	3969	4021	4072	4124	4176	4228	52
840	924279	924331	924383	924434	924486	924538	924589	924641	924693	924744	52
1	4796	4848	4899	4951	5003	5054	5106	5157	5209	5261	52
2	5312	5364	5415	5467	5518	5570	5621	5673	5725	5776	52
3	5828	5879	5931	5982	6034	6085	6137	6188	6240	6291	51
4	6342	6394	6445	6497	6548	6600	6651	6702	6754	6805	51
845	6857	6908	6959	7011	7062	7114	7165	7216	7268	7319	51
6	7370	7422	7473	7524	7576	7627	7678	7730	7781	7832	51
7	7883	7935	7986	8037	8088	8140	8191	8242	8293	8345	51
8	8396	8447	8498	8549	8601	8652	8703	8754	8805	8857	51
9	8908	8959	9010	9061	9112	9163	9215	9266	9317	9368	51
850	929419	929470	929521	929572	929623	929674	929725	929776	929827	929879	51
1	9930	9981	930032	930083	930134	930185	930236	930287	930338	930389	51
2	930440	930491	0542	0592	0643	0694	0745	0796	0847	0898	51
3	0949	1000	1051	1102	1153	1204	1254	1305	1356	1407	51
4	1458	1509	1560	1610	1661	1712	1763	1814	1865	1915	51
855	1966	2017	2068	2118	2169	2220	2271	2322	2372	2423	51
6	2474	2524	2575	2626	2677	2727	2778	2829	2879	2930	51
7	2981	3031	3082	3133	3183	3234	3285	3335	3386	3437	51
8	3487	3538	3589	3639	3690	3740	3791	3841	3892	3943	51
9	3993	4044	4094	4145	4195	4246	4296	4347	4397	4448	51
860	934498	934549	934599	934650	934700	934751	934801	934852	934902	934953	50
1	5003	5054	5104	5154	5205	5255	5306	5356	5406	5457	50
2	5507	5558	5608	5658	5709	5759	5809	5860	5910	5960	50
3	6011	6061	6111	6162	6212	6262	6313	6363	6413	6463	50
4	6514	6564	6614	6665	6715	6765	6815	6865	6916	6966	50
865	7016	7066	7117	7167	7217	7267	7317	7367	7418	7468	50
6	7518	7568	7618	7668	7718	7769	7819	7869	7919	7969	50
7	8019	8069	8119	8169	8219	8269	8320	8370	8420	8470	50
8	8520	8570	8620	8670	8720	8770	8820	8870	8920	8970	50
9	9020	9070	9120	9170	9220	9270	9320	9369	9419	9469	50
870	939519	939569	939619	939669	939719	939769	939819	939869	939918	939968	50
1	940018	940068	940118	940168	940218	940267	940317	940367	940417	940467	50
2	0516	0566	0616	0666	0716	0765	0815	0865	0915	0964	50
3	1014	1064	1114	1163	1213	1263	1313	1362	1412	1462	50
4	1511	1561	1611	1660	1710	1760	1809	1859	1909	1958	50
875	2008	2058	2107	2157	2207	2256	2306	2355	2405	2455	50
6	2504	2554	2603	2653	2702	2752	2801	2851	2901	2950	50
7	3000	3049	3099	3148	3198	3247	3297	3346	3396	3445	49
8	3495	3544	3593	3643	3692	3742	3791	3841	3890	3939	49
9	3989	4038	4088	4137	4186	4236	4285	4335	4384	4433	49
N.	0	1	2	3	4	5	6	7	8	9	D.

453

TABLE I.—Six-place Mantissas

N.	0	1	2	3	4	5	6	7	8	9	D.
880	944483	944532	944581	944631	944680	944729	944779	944828	944877	944927	49
1	4976	5025	5074	5124	5173	5222	5272	5321	5370	5419	49
2	5469	5518	5567	5616	5665	5715	5764	5813	5862	5912	49
3	5961	6010	6059	6108	6157	6207	6256	6305	6354	6403	49
4	6452	6501	6551	6600	6649	6698	6747	6796	6845	6894	49
885	6943	6992	7041	7090	7140	7189	7238	7287	7336	7385	49
6	7434	7483	7532	7581	7630	7679	7728	7777	7826	7875	49
7	7924	7973	8022	8070	8119	8168	8217	8266	8315	8364	49
8	8413	8462	8511	8560	8609	8657	8706	8755	8804	8853	49
9	8902	8951	8999	9048	9097	9146	9195	9244	9292	9341	49
890	949390	949439	949488	949536	949585	949634	949683	949731	949780	949829	49
1	9878	9926	9975	950024	950073	950121	950170	950219	950267	950316	49
2	950365	950414	950462	0511	0560	0608	0657	0706	0754	0803	49
3	0851	0900	0949	0997	1046	1095	1143	1192	1240	1289	49
4	1338	1386	1435	1483	1532	1580	1629	1677	1726	1775	49
895	1823	1872	1920	1969	2017	2066	2114	2163	2211	2260	48
6	2308	2356	2405	2453	2502	2550	2599	2647	2696	2744	48
7	2792	2841	2889	2938	2986	3034	3083	3131	3180	3228	48
8	3276	3325	3373	3421	3470	3518	3566	3615	3663	3711	48
9	3760	3808	3856	3905	3953	4001	4049	4098	4146	4194	48
900	954243	954291	954339	954387	954435	954484	954532	954580	954628	954677	48
1	4725	4773	4821	4869	4918	4966	5014	5062	5110	5158	48
2	5207	5255	5303	5351	5399	5447	5495	5543	5592	5640	48
3	5688	5736	5784	5832	5880	5928	5976	6024	6072	6120	48
4	6168	6216	6265	6313	6361	6409	6457	6505	6553	6601	48
905	6649	6697	6745	6793	6840	6888	6936	6984	7032	7080	48
6	7128	7176	7224	7272	7320	7368	7416	7464	7512	7559	48
7	7607	7655	7703	7751	7799	7847	7894	7942	7990	8038	48
8	8086	8134	8181	8229	8277	8325	8373	8421	8468	8516	48
9	8564	8612	8659	8707	8755	8803	8850	8898	8946	8994	48
910	959041	959089	959137	959185	959232	959280	959328	959375	959423	959471	48
1	9518	9566	9614	9661	9709	9757	9804	9852	9900	9947	48
2	9995	960042	960090	960138	960185	960233	960280	960328	960376	960423	48
3	960471	0518	0566	0613	0661	0709	0756	0804	0851	0899	48
4	0946	0994	1041	1089	1136	1184	1231	1279	1326	1374	48
915	1421	1469	1516	1563	1611	1658	1706	1753	1801	1848	47
6	1895	1943	1990	2038	2085	2132	2180	2227	2275	2322	47
7	2369	2417	2464	2511	2559	2606	2653	2701	2748	2795	47
8	2843	2890	2937	2985	3032	3079	3126	3174	3221	3268	47
9	3316	3363	3410	3457	3504	3552	3599	3646	3693	3741	47
920	963788	963835	963882	963929	963977	964024	964071	964118	964165	964212	47
1	4260	4307	4354	4401	4448	4495	4542	4590	4637	4684	47
2	4731	4778	4825	4872	4919	4966	5013	5061	5108	5155	47
3	5202	5249	5296	5343	5390	5437	5484	5531	5578	5625	47
4	5672	5719	5766	5813	5860	5907	5954	6001	6048	6095	47
925	6142	6189	6236	6283	6329	6376	6423	6470	6517	6564	47
6	6611	6658	6705	6752	6799	6845	6892	6939	6986	7033	47
7	7080	7127	7173	7220	7267	7314	7361	7408	7454	7501	47
8	7548	7595	7642	7688	7735	7782	7829	7875	7922	7969	47
9	8016	8062	8109	8156	8203	8249	8296	8343	8390	8436	47
930	968483	968530	968576	968623	968670	968716	968763	968810	968856	968903	47
1	8950	8996	9043	9090	9136	9183	9229	9276	9323	9369	47
2	9416	9463	9509	9556	9602	9649	9695	9742	9789	9835	47
3	9882	9928	9975	970021	970068	970114	970161	970207	970254	970300	47
4	970347	970393	970440	0486	0533	0579	0626	0672	0719	0765	46
935	0812	0858	0904	0951	0997	1044	1090	1137	1183	1229	46
6	1276	1322	1369	1415	1461	1508	1554	1601	1647	1693	46
7	1740	1786	1832	1879	1925	1971	2018	2064	2110	2157	46
8	2203	2249	2295	2342	2388	2434	2481	2527	2573	2619	46
9	2666	2712	2758	2804	2851	2897	2943	2989	3035	3082	46
N.	0	1	2	3	4	5	6	7	8	9	D.

TABLE I.—Six-place Mantissas

N.	0	1	2	3	4	5	6	7	8	9	D.
940	973128	973174	973220	973266	973313	973359	973405	973451	973497	973543	46
1	3590	3636	3682	3728	3774	3820	3866	3913	3959	4005	46
2	4051	4097	4143	4189	4235	4281	4327	4374	4420	4466	46
3	4512	4558	4604	4650	4696	4742	4788	4834	4880	4926	46
4	4972	5018	5064	5110	5156	5202	5248	5294	5340	5386	46
945	5432	5478	5524	5570	5616	5662	5707	5753	5799	5845	46
6	5891	5937	5983	6029	6075	6121	6167	6212	6258	6304	46
7	6350	6396	6442	6488	6533	6579	6625	6671	6717	6763	46
8	6808	6854	6900	6946	6992	7037	7083	7129	7175	7220	46
9	7266	7312	7358	7403	7449	7495	7541	7586	7632	7678	46
950	977724	977769	977815	977861	977906	977952	977998	978043	978089	978135	46
1	8181	8226	8272	8317	8363	8409	8454	8500	8546	8591	46
2	8637	8683	8728	8774	8819	8865	8911	8956	9002	9047	46
3	9093	9138	9184	9230	9275	9321	9366	9412	9457	9503	46
4	9548	9594	9639	9685	9730	9776	9821	9867	9912	9958	46
955	980003	980049	980094	980140	980185	980231	980276	980322	980367	980412	45
6	0458	0503	0549	0594	0640	0685	0730	0776	0821	0867	45
7	0912	0957	1003	1048	1093	1139	1184	1229	1275	1320	45
8	1366	1411	1456	1501	1547	1592	1637	1683	1728	1773	45
9	1819	1864	1909	1954	2000	2045	2090	2135	2181	2226	45
960	982271	982316	982362	982407	982452	982497	982543	982588	982633	982678	45
1	2723	2769	2814	2859	2904	2949	2994	3040	3085	3130	45
2	3175	3220	3265	3310	3356	3401	3446	3491	3536	3581	45
3	3626	3671	3716	3762	3807	3852	3897	3942	3987	4032	45
4	4077	4122	4167	4212	4257	4302	4347	4392	4437	4482	45
965	4527	4572	4617	4662	4707	4752	4797	4842	4887	4932	45
6	4977	5022	5067	5112	5157	5202	5247	5292	5337	5382	45
7	5426	5471	5516	5561	5606	5651	5696	5741	5786	5830	45
8	5875	5920	5965	6010	6055	6100	6144	6189	6234	6279	45
9	6324	6369	6413	6458	6503	6548	6593	6637	6682	6727	45
970	986772	986817	986861	986906	986951	986996	987040	987085	987130	987175	45
1	7219	7264	7309	7353	7398	7443	7488	7532	7577	7622	45
2	7666	7711	7756	7800	7845	7890	7934	7979	8024	8068	45
3	8113	8157	8202	8247	8291	8336	8381	8425	8470	8514	45
4	8559	8604	8648	8693	8737	8782	8826	8871	8916	8960	45
975	9005	9049	9094	9138	9183	9227	9272	9316	9361	9405	45
6	9450	9494	9539	9583	9628	9672	9717	9761	9806	9850	44
7	9895	9939	9983	990028	990072	990117	990161	990206	990250	990294	44
8	990339	990383	990428	0472	0516	0561	0605	0650	0694	0738	44
9	0783	0827	0871	0916	0960	1004	1049	1093	1137	1182	44
980	991226	991270	991315	991359	991403	991448	991492	991536	991580	991625	44
1	1669	1713	1758	1802	1846	1890	1935	1979	2023	2067	44
2	2111	2156	2200	2244	2288	2333	2377	2421	2465	2509	44
3	2554	2598	2642	2686	2730	2774	2819	2863	2907	2951	44
4	2995	3039	3083	3127	3172	3216	3260	3304	3348	3392	44
985	3436	3480	3524	3568	3613	3657	3701	3745	3789	3833	44
6	3877	3921	3965	4009	4053	4097	4141	4185	4229	4273	44
7	4317	4361	4405	4449	4493	4537	4581	4625	4669	4713	44
8	4757	4801	4845	4889	4933	4977	5021	5065	5108	5152	44
9	5196	5240	5284	5328	5372	5416	5460	5504	5547	5591	44
990	995635	995679	995723	995767	995811	995854	995898	995942	995986	996030	44
1	6074	6117	6161	6205	6249	6293	6337	6380	6424	6468	44
2	6512	6555	6599	6643	6687	6731	6774	6818	6862	6906	44
3	6949	6993	7037	7080	7124	7168	7212	7255	7299	7343	44
4	7386	7430	7474	7517	7561	7605	7648	7692	7736	7779	44
995	7823	7867	7910	7954	7998	8041	8085	8129	8172	8216	44
6	8259	8303	8347	8390	8434	8477	8521	8564	8608	8652	44
7	8695	8739	8782	8826	8869	8913	8956	9000	9043	9087	44
8	9131	9174	9218	9261	9305	9348	9392	9435	9479	9522	44
9	9565	9609	9652	9696	9739	9783	9826	9870	9913	9957	43
N.	0	1	2	3	4	5	6	7	8	9	D.

TABLE II.—Seven-place Mantissas

10000-10509

N.	0	1	2	3	4	5	6	7	8	9	D.
1000	000 0000	0434	0869	1303	1737	2171	2605	3039	3473	3907	434
1001	4341	4775	5208	5642	6076	6510	6943	7377	7810	8244	434
1002	8677	9111	9544	9977	*0411	*0844	*1277	*1710	*2143	*2576	433
1003	001 3009	3442	3875	4308	4741	5174	5607	6039	6472	6905	433
1004	7337	7770	8202	8635	9067	9499	9932	*0364	*0796	*1228	432
1005	002 1661	2093	2525	2957	3389	3821	4253	4685	5116	5548	432
1006	5980	6411	6843	7275	7706	8138	8569	9001	9432	9863	431
1007	003 0295	0726	1157	1588	2019	2451	2882	3313	3744	4174	431
1008	4605	5036	5467	5898	6328	6759	7190	7620	8051	8481	431
1009	8912	9342	9772	*0203	*0633	*1063	*1493	*1924	*2354	*2784	430
1010	004 3214	3644	4074	4504	4933	5363	5793	6223	6652	7082	430
1011	7512	7941	8371	8800	9229	9659	*0088	*0517	*0947	*1376	429
1012	005 1805	2234	2663	3092	3521	3950	4379	4808	5237	5666	429
1013	6094	6523	6952	7380	7809	8238	8666	9094	9523	9951	429
1014	006 0380	0808	1236	1664	2092	2521	2949	3377	3805	4233	428
1015	4660	5088	5516	5944	6372	6799	7227	7655	8082	8510	428
1016	8937	9365	9792	*0219	*0647	*1074	*1501	*1928	*2355	*2782	427
1017	007 3210	3637	4064	4490	4917	5344	5771	6198	6624	7051	427
1018	7478	7904	8331	8757	9184	9610	*0037	*0463	*0889	*1316	426
1019	008 1742	2168	2594	3020	3446	3872	4298	4724	5150	5576	426
1020	6002	6427	6853	7279	7704	8130	8556	8981	9407	9832	426
1021	009 0257	0683	1108	1533	1959	2384	2809	3234	3659	4084	425
1022	4509	4934	5359	5784	6208	6633	7058	7483	7907	8332	425
1023	8756	9181	9605	*0030	*0454	*0878	*1303	*1727	*2151	*2575	424
1024	010 3000	3424	3848	4272	4696	5120	5544	5967	6391	6815	424
1025	7239	7662	8086	8510	8933	9357	9780	*0204	*0627	*1050	424
1026	011 1474	1897	2320	2743	3166	3590	4013	4436	4859	5282	423
1027	5704	6127	6550	6973	7396	7818	8241	8664	9086	9509	423
1028	9931	*0354	*0776	*1198	*1621	*2043	*2465	*2887	*3310	*3732	422
1029	012 4154	4576	4998	5420	5842	6264	6685	7107	7529	7951	422
1030	8372	8794	9215	9637	*0059	*0480	*0901	*1323	*1744	*2165	422
1031	013 2587	3008	3429	3850	4271	4692	5113	5534	5955	6376	421
1032	6797	7218	7639	8059	8480	8901	9321	9742	*0162	*0583	421
1033	014 1003	1424	1844	2264	2685	3105	3525	3945	4365	4785	420
1034	5205	5625	6045	6465	6885	7305	7725	8144	8564	8984	420
1035	9403	9823	*0243	*0662	*1082	*1501	*1920	*2340	*2759	*3178	420
1036	015 3598	4017	4436	4855	5274	5693	6112	6531	6950	7369	419
1037	7788	8206	8625	9044	9462	9881	*0300	*0718	*1137	*1555	419
1038	016 1974	2392	2810	3229	3647	4065	4483	4901	5319	5737	418
1039	6155	6573	6991	7409	7827	8245	8663	9080	9498	9916	418
1040	017 0333	0751	1168	1586	2003	2421	2838	3256	3673	4090	417
1041	4507	4924	5342	5759	6176	6593	7010	7427	7844	8260	417
1042	8677	9094	9511	9927	*0344	*0761	*1177	*1594	*2010	*2427	417
1043	018 2843	3259	3676	4092	4508	4925	5341	5757	6173	6589	416
1044	7005	7421	7837	8253	8669	9084	9500	9916	*0332	*0747	416
1045	019 1163	1578	1994	2410	2825	3240	3656	4071	4486	4902	415
1046	5317	5732	6147	6562	6977	7392	7807	8222	8637	9052	415
1047	9467	9882	*0296	*0711	*1126	*1540	*1955	*2369	*2784	*3198	415
1048	020 3613	4027	4442	4856	5270	5684	6099	6513	6927	7341	414
1049	7755	8169	8583	8997	9411	9824	*0238	*0652	*1066	*1479	414
1050	021 1893	2307	2720	3134	3547	3961	4374	4787	5201	5614	413
N.	0	1	2	3	4	5	6	7	8	9	D.

TABLE II.—Seven-place Mantissas

10500-11009

N.	0	1	2	3	4	5	6	7	8	9	D.
1050	021 1893	2307	2720	3134	3547	3961	4374	4787	5201	5614	413
1051	6027	6440	6854	7267	7680	8093	8506	8919	9332	9745	413
1052	022 0157	0570	0983	1396	1808	2221	2634	3046	3459	3871	413
1053	4284	4696	5109	5521	5933	6345	6758	7170	7582	7994	412
1054	8406	8818	9230	9642	*0054	*0466	*0878	*1289	*1701	*2113	412
1055	023 2525	2936	3348	3759	4171	4582	4994	5405	5817	6228	411
1056	6639	7050	7462	7873	8284	8695	9106	9517	9928	*0339	411
1057	024 0750	1161	1572	1982	2393	2804	3214	3625	4036	4446	411
1058	4857	5267	5678	6088	6498	6909	7319	7729	8139	8549	410
1059	8960	9370	9780	*0190	*0600	*1010	*1419	*1829	*2239	*2649	410
1060	025 3059	3468	3878	4288	4697	5107	5516	5926	6335	6744	410
1061	7154	7563	7972	8382	8791	9200	9609	*0018	*0427	*0836	409
1062	026 1245	1654	2063	2472	2881	3289	3698	4107	4515	4924	409
1063	5333	5741	6150	6558	6967	7375	7783	8192	8600	9008	408
1064	9416	9824	*0233	*0641	*1049	*1457	*1865	*2273	*2680	*3088	408
1065	027 3496	3904	4312	4719	5127	5535	5942	6350	6757	7165	408
1066	7572	7979	8387	8794	9201	9609	*0016	*0423	*0830	*1237	407
1067	028 1644	2051	2458	2865	3272	3679	4086	4492	4899	5306	407
1068	5713	6119	6526	6932	7339	7745	8152	8558	8964	9371	406
1069	9777	*0183	*0590	*0996	*1402	*1808	*2214	*2620	*3026	*3432	406
1070	029 3838	4244	4649	5055	5461	5867	6272	6678	7084	7489	406
1071	7895	8300	8706	9111	9516	9922	*0327	*0732	*1138	*1543	405
1072	030 1948	2353	2758	3163	3568	3973	4378	4783	5188	5592	405
1073	5997	6402	6807	7211	7616	8020	8425	8830	9234	9638	405
1074	031 0043	0447	0851	1256	1660	2064	2468	2872	3277	3681	404
1075	4085	4489	4893	5296	5700	6104	6508	6912	7315	7719	404
1076	8123	8526	8930	9333	9737	*0140	*0544	*0947	*1350	*1754	403
1077	032 2157	2560	2963	3367	3770	4173	4576	4979	5382	5785	403
1078	6188	6590	6993	7396	7799	8201	8604	9007	9409	9812	403
1079	033 0214	0617	1019	1422	1824	2226	2629	3031	3433	3835	402
1080	4238	4640	5042	5444	5846	6248	6650	7052	7453	7855	402
1081	8257	8659	9060	9462	9864	*0265	*0667	*1068	*1470	*1871	402
1082	034 2273	2674	3075	3477	3878	4279	4680	5081	5482	5884	401
1083	6285	6686	7087	7487	7888	8289	8690	9091	9491	9892	401
1084	035 0293	0693	1094	1495	1895	2296	2696	3096	3497	3897	400
1085	4297	4698	5098	5498	5898	6298	6698	7098	7498	7898	400
1086	8298	8698	9098	9498	9898	*0297	*0697	*1097	*1496	*1896	400
1087	036 2295	2695	3094	3494	3893	4293	4692	5091	5491	5890	399
1088	6289	6688	7087	7486	7885	8284	8683	9082	9481	9880	399
1089	037 0279	0678	1076	1475	1874	2272	2671	3070	3468	3867	399
1090	4265	4663	5062	5460	5858	6257	6655	7053	7451	7849	398
1091	8248	8646	9044	9442	9839	*0237	*0635	*1033	*1431	*1829	398
1092	038 2226	2624	3022	3419	3817	4214	4612	5009	5407	5804	398
1093	6202	6599	6996	7393	7791	8188	8585	8982	9379	9776	397
1094	039 0173	0570	0967	1364	1761	2158	2554	2951	3348	3745	397
1095	4141	4538	4934	5331	5727	6124	6520	6917	7313	7709	397
1096	8106	8502	8898	9294	9690	*0086	*0482	*0878	*1274	*1670	396
1097	040 2066	2462	2858	3254	3650	4045	4441	4837	5232	5628	396
1098	6023	6419	6814	7210	7605	8001	8396	8791	9187	9582	395
1099	9977	*0372	*0767	*1162	*1557	*1952	*2347	*2742	*3137	*3532	395
1100	041 3927	4322	4716	5111	5506	5900	6295	6690	7084	7479	395
N.	0	1	2	3	4	5	6	7	8	9	D.

TABLE III.—Amount of 1 at Compound Interest

$$s = (1 + i)^n$$

n	$\frac{1}{4}\%$	$\frac{7}{24}\%$	$\frac{1}{3}\%$	$\frac{5}{12}\%$	n
1	1.0025 0000	1.0029 1667	1.0033 3333	1.0041 6667	1
2	1.0050 0625	1.0058 4184	1.0066 7778	1.0083 5069	2
3	1.0075 1877	1.0087 7555	1.0100 3337	1.0125 5216	3
4	1.0100 3756	1.0117 1781	1.0134 0015	1.0167 7112	4
5	1.0125 6266	1.0146 6865	1.0167 7815	1.0210 0767	5
6	1.0150 9406	1.0176 2810	1.0201 6741	1.0252 6187	6
7	1.0176 3180	1.0205 9618	1.0235 6797	1.0295 3379	7
8	1.0201 7588	1.0235 7292	1.0269 7986	1.0338 2352	8
9	1.0227 2632	1.0265 5834	1.0304 0313	1.0381 3111	9
10	1.0252 8313	1.0295 5247	1.0338 3780	1.0424 5666	10
11	1.0278 4634	1.0325 5533	1.0372 8393	1.0468 0023	11
12	1.0304 1596	1.0355 6695	1.0407 4154	1.0511 6190	12
13	1.0329 9200	1.0385 8736	1.0442 1068	1.0555 4174	13
14	1.0355 7448	1.0416 1657	1.0476 9138	1.0599 3983	14
15	1.0381 6341	1.0446 5462	1.0511 8369	1.0643 5625	15
16	1.0407 5882	1.0477 0153	1.0546 8763	1.0687 9106	16
17	1.0433 6072	1.0507 5732	1.0582 0326	1.0732 4436	17
18	1.0459 6912	1.0538 2203	1.0617 3060	1.0777 1621	18
19	1.0485 8404	1.0568 9568	1.0652 6971	1.0822 0670	19
20	1.0512 0550	1.0599 7829	1.0688 2060	1.0867 1589	20
21	1.0538 3352	1.0630 6990	1.0723 8334	1.0912 4387	21
22	1.0564 6810	1.0661 7052	1.0759 5795	1.0957 9072	22
23	1.0591 0927	1.0692 8018	1.0795 4448	1.1003 5652	23
24	1 0617 5704	1.0723 9891	1.0831 4296	1.1049 4134	24
25	1.0644 1144	1.0755 2674	1.0867 5344	1.1095 4526	25
26	1.0670 7247	1.0786 6370	1.0903 7595	1.1141 6836	26
27	1.0697 4015	1.0818 0980	1.0940 1053	1.1188 1073	27
28	1.0724 1450	1.0849 6508	1.0976 5724	1.1234 7244	28
29	1.0750 9553	1.0881 2956	1.1013 1609	1.1281 5358	29
30	1.0777 8327	1.0913 0327	1.1049 8715	1.1328 5422	30
31	1.0804 7773	1.0944 8624	1.1086 7044	1.1375 7444	31
32	1.0831 7892	1.0976 7849	1.1123 6601	1.1423 1434	32
33	1.0858 8687	1.1008 8005	1.1160 7389	1.1470 7398	33
34	1.0886 0159	1.1040 9095	1.1197 9414	1.1518 5346	34
35	1.0913 2309	1.1073 1122	1.1235 2679	1.1566 5284	35
36	1.0940 5140	1.1105 4088	1.1272 7187	1.1614 7223	36
37	1.0967 8653	1.1137 7995	1.1310 2945	1.1663 1170	37
38	1.0995 2850	1.1170 2848	1.1347 9955	1.1711 7133	38
39	1.1022 7732	1.1202 8648	1.1385 8221	1.1760 5121	39
40	1.1050 3301	1.1235 5398	1.1423 7748	1.1809 5142	40
41	1.1077 9559	1.1268 3101	1.1461 8541	1.1858 7206	41
42	1.1105 6508	1.1301 1760	1.1500 0603	1.1908 1319	42
43	1.1133 4149	1.1334 1378	1.1538 3938	1.1957 7491	43
44	1.1161 2485	1.1367 1957	1.1576 8551	1.2007 5731	44
45	1.1189 1516	1.1400 3500	1.1615 4446	1.2057 6046	45
46	1.1217 1245	1.1433 6010	1.1654 1628	1.2107 8446	46
47	1.1245 1673	1.1466 9490	1.1693 0100	1.2158 2940	47
48	1.1273 2802	1.1500 3943	1.1731 9867	1.2208 9536	48
49	1.1301 4634	1.1533 9371	1.1771 0933	1.2259 8242	49
50	1.1329 7171	1.1567 5778	1.1810 3303	1.2310 9068	50

TABLE III.—Amount of 1 at Compound Interest

$$s = (1 + i)^n$$

n	$\frac{1}{4}\%$	$\frac{7}{24}\%$	$\frac{1}{3}\%$	$\frac{5}{12}\%$	n
51	1.1358 0414	1.1601 3165	1.1849 6981	1.2362 2002	51
52	1.1386 4365	1.1635 1537	1.1889 1971	1.2413 7114	52
53	1.1414 9026	1.1669 0896	1.1928 8277	1.2465 4352	53
54	1.1443 4398	1.1703 1244	1.1968 5905	1.2517 3745	54
55	1.1472 0484	1.1737 2585	1.2008 4858	1.2569 5302	55
56	1.1500 7285	1.1771 4922	1.2048 5141	1.2621 9033	56
57	1.1529 4804	1.1805 8257	1.2088 6758	1.2674 4946	57
58	1.1558 3041	1.1840 2594	1.2128 9714	1.2727 3050	58
59	1.1587 1998	1.1874 7935	1.2169 4013	1.2780 3354	59
60	1.1616 1678	1.1909 4283	1.2209 9659	1.2833 5868	60
61	1.1645 2082	1.1944 1641	1.2250 6658	1.2887 0601	61
62	1.1674 3213	1.1979 0013	1.2291 5014	1.2940 7561	62
63	1.1703 5071	1.2013 9400	1.2332 4730	1.2994 6760	63
64	1.1732 7658	1.2048 9807	1.2373 5813	1.3048 8204	64
65	1.1762 0977	1.2084 1235	1.2414 8266	1.3103 1905	65
66	1.1791 5030	1.2119 3689	1.2456 2093	1.3157 7872	66
67	1.1820 9817	1.2154 7171	1.2497 7300	1.3212 6113	67
68	1.1850 5342	1.2190 1683	1.2539 3891	1.3267 6638	68
69	1.1880 1605	1.2225 7230	1.2581 1871	1.3322 9458	69
70	1.1909 8609	1.2261 3813	1.2623 1244	1.3378 4580	70
71	1.1939 6356	1.2297 1437	1.2665 2015	1.3434 2016	71
72	1.1969 4847	1.2333 0104	1.2707 4188	1.3490 1774	72
73	1.1999 4084	1.2368 9816	1.2749 7769	1.3546 3865	73
74	1.2029 4069	1.2405 0578	1.2792 2761	1.3602 8298	74
75	1.2059 4804	1.2441 2393	1.2834 9170	1.3659 5082	75
76	1.2089 6291	1.2477 5262	1.2877 7001	1.3716 4229	76
77	1.2119 8532	1.2513 9190	1.2920 6258	1.3773 5746	77
78	1.2150 1528	1.2550 4179	1.2963 6945	1.3830 9645	78
79	1.2180 5282	1.2587 0233	1.3006 9068	1.3888 5935	79
80	1.2210 9795	1.2623 7355	1.3050 2632	1.3946 4627	80
81	1.2241 5070	1.2660 5547	1.3093 7641	1.4004 5729	81
82	1.2272 1108	1.2697 4813	1.3137 4099	1.4062 9253	82
83	1.2302 7910	1.2734 5156	1.3181 2013	1.4121 5209	83
84	1.2333 5480	1.2771 6580	1.3225 1386	1.4180 3605	84
85	1.2364 3819	1.2808 9086	1.3269 2224	1.4239 4454	85
86	1.2395 2928	1.2846 2680	1.3313 4532	1.4298 7764	86
87	1.2426 2811	1.2883 7362	1.3357 8314	1.4358 3546	87
88	1.2457 3468	1.2921 3138	1.3402 3575	1.4418 1811	88
89	1.2488 4901	1.2959 0010	1.3447 0320	1.4478 2568	89
90	1.2519 7114	1.2996 7980	1.3491 8554	1.4538 5829	90
91	1.2551 0106	1.3034 7054	1.3536 8283	1.4599 1603	91
92	1.2582 3882	1.3072 7233	1.3581 9510	1.4659 9902	92
93	1.2613 8441	1.3110 8520	1.3627 2242	1.4721 0735	93
94	1.2645 3787	1.3149 0920	1.3672 6483	1.4782 4113	94
95	1.2676 9922	1.3187 4435	1.3718 2238	1.4844 0047	95
96	1.2708 6847	1.3225 9069	1.3763 9512	1.4905 8547	96
97	1.2740 4564	1.3264 4825	1.3809 8310	1.4967 9624	97
98	1.2772 3075	1.3303 1706	1.3855 8638	1.5030 3289	98
99	1.2804 2383	1.3341 9715	1.3902 0500	1.5092 9553	99
100	1.2836 2489	1.3380 8856	1.3948 3902	1.5155 8426	100

TABLE III.—Amount of 1 at Compound Interest

$$s = (1 + i)^n$$

n	¼%	⁷⁄₂₄%	⅓%	⁵⁄₁₂%	n
101	1.2868 3395	1.3419 9131	1.3994 8848	1.5218 9919	101
102	1.2900 5104	1.3459 0546	1.4041 5344	1.5282 4044	102
103	1.2932 7616	1.3498 3101	1.4088 3395	1.5346 0811	103
104	1.2965 0935	1.3537 6802	1.4135 3007	1.5410 0231	104
105	1.2997 5063	1.3577 1651	1.4182 4183	1.5474 2315	105
106	1.3030 0000	1.3616 7652	1.4229 6931	1.5538 7075	106
107	1.3062 5750	1.3656 4807	1.4277 1254	1.5603 4521	107
108	1.3095 2315	1.3696 3121	1.4324 7158	1.5668 4665	108
109	1.3127 9696	1.3736 2597	1.4372 4649	1.5733 7518	109
110	1.3160 7895	1.3776 3238	1.4420 3731	1.5799 3091	110
111	1.3193 6915	1.3816 5047	1.4468 4410	1.5865 1395	111
112	1.3226 6757	1.3856 8029	1.4516 6691	1.5931 2443	112
113	1.3259 7424	1.3897 2186	1.4565 0580	1.5997 6245	113
114	1.3292 8917	1.3937 7521	1.4613 6082	1.6064 2812	114
115	1.3326 1240	1.3978 4039	1.4662 3202	1.6131 2157	115
116	1.3359 4393	1.4019 1742	1.4711 1946	1.6198 4291	116
117	1.3392 8379	1.4060 0635	1.4760 2320	1.6265 9226	117
118	1.3426 3200	1.4101 0720	1.4809 4327	1.6333 6973	118
119	1.3459 8858	1.4142 2001	1.4858 7979	1.6401 7543	119
120	1.3493 5355	1.4183 4482	1.4908 3268	1.6470 0950	120
121	1,3527 2693	1.4224 8166	1.4958 0212	1.6538 7204	121
122	1.3561 0875	1.4266 3057	1.5007 8813	1.6607 6317	122
123	1.3594 9902	1.4307 9157	1.5057 9076	1.6676 8302	123
124	1.3628 9777	1.4349 6471	1.5108 1006	1.6746 3170	124
125	1.3663 0501	1.4391 5003	1.5158 4609	1.6816 0933	125
126	1.3697 2077	1.4433 4755	1.5208 9892	1.6886 1603	126
127	1.3731 4508	1.4475 5731	1.5259 6858	1.6956 5193	127
128	1.3765 7794	1.4517 7935	1.5310 5514	1.7027 1715	128
129	1.3800 1938	1.4560 1371	1.5361 5866	1.7098 1181	129
130	1.3834 6943	1.4602 6042	1.5412 7919	1.7169 3602	130
131	1.3869 2811	1.4645 1951	1.5464 1678	1.7240 8992	131
132	1.3903 9543	1.4687 9103	1.5515 7151	1.7312 7363	132
133	1.3938 7142	1.4730 7500	1.5567 4341	1.7384 8727	133
134	1.3973 5609	1.4773 7147	1.5619 3256	1.7457 3097	134
135	1.4008 4948	1.4816 8047	1.5671 3900	1.7530 0485	135
136	1.4043 5161	1.4860 0204	1.5723 6279	1.7603 0903	136
137	1.4078 6249	1.4903 3621	1.5776 0400	1.7676 4365	137
138	1.4113 8214	1.4946 8302	1.5828 6268	1.7750 0884	138
139	1.4149 1060	1.4990 4252	1.5881 3889	1.7824 0471	139
140	1.4184 4787	1.5034 1472	1.5934 3269	1.7898 3139	140
141	1.4219 9399	1.5077 9968	1.5987 4413	1.7972 8902	141
142	1.4255 4898	1.5121 9743	1.6040 7328	1.8047 7773	142
143	1.4291 1285	1.5166 0801	1.6094 2019	1.8122 9763	143
144	1.4326 8563	1.5210 3145	1.6147 8492	1.8198 4887	144
145	1.4362 6735	1.5254 6779	1.6201 6754	1.8274 3158	145
146	1.4398 5802	1.5299 1707	1.6255 6810	1.8350 4588	146
147	1.4434 5766	1.5343 7933	1.6309 8636	1.8426 9190	147
148	1.4470 6631	1.5388 5460	1.6364 2328	1.8503 6978	148
149	1.4506 8397	1.5433 4293	1.6418 7802	1.8580 7966	149
150	1.4543 1068	1.5478 4434	1.6473 5095	1.8658 2166	150

TABLE III.—Amount of 1 at Compound Interest

$$s = (1 + i)^n$$

n	$\frac{1}{4}\%$	$\frac{7}{24}\%$	$\frac{1}{3}\%$	$\frac{5}{12}\%$	n
151	1.4579 4646	1.5523 5889	1.6528 4212	1.8735 9591	151
152	1.4615 9132	1.5568 8660	1.6583 5160	1.8814 0256	152
153	1.4652 4530	1.5614 2752	1.6638 7943	1.8892 4174	153
154	1.4689 0842	1.5659 8169	1.6694 2570	1.8971 1358	154
155	1.4725 8069	1.5705 4913	1.6749 9045	1.9050 1822	155
156	1.4762 6214	1.5751 2990	1.6805 7375	1.9129 5580	156
157	1.4799 5279	1.5797 2403	1.6861 7566	1.9209 2645	157
158	1.4836 5268	1.5843 3156	1.6917 9625	1.9289 3031	158
159	1.4873 6181	1.5889 5253	1.6974 3557	1.9369 6752	159
160	1.4910 8021	1.5935 8697	1.7030 9369	1.9450 3821	160
161	1.4948 0791	1.5982 3493	1.7087 7067	1.9531 4254	161
162	1.4985 4493	1.6028 9645	1.7144 6657	1.9612 8063	162
163	1.5022 9129	1.6075 7157	1.7201 8146	1.9694 5264	163
164	1.5060 4702	1.6122 6032	1.7259 1540	1.9776 5869	164
165	1.5098 1214	1.6169 6274	1.7316 6845	1.9858 9893	165
166	1.5135 8667	1.6216 7888	1.7374 4068	1.9941 7351	166
167	1.5173 7064	1.6264 0878	1.7432 3215	2.0024 8257	167
168	1.5211 6406	1.6311 5247	1.7490 4292	2.0108 2625	168
169	1.5249 6697	1.6359 1000	1.7548 7306	2.0192 0469	169
170	1.5287 7939	1.6406 8140	1.7607 2264	2.0276 1804	170
171	1.5326 0134	1.6454 6672	1.7665 9172	2.0360 6645	171
172	1.5364 3284	1.6502 6600	1.7724 8035	2.0445 5006	172
173	1.5402 7393	1.6550 7928	1.7783 8862	2.0530 6902	173
174	1.5441 2461	1.6599 0659	1.7843 1658	2.0616 2347	174
175	1.5479 8492	1.6647 4799	1.7902 6431	2.0702 1357	175
176	1.5518 5488	1.6696 0350	1.7962 3185	2.0788 3946	176
177	1.5557 3452	1.6744 7318	1.8022 1929	2.0875 0129	177
178	1.5596 2386	1.6793 5706	1.8082 2669	2.0961 9921	178
179	1.5635 2292	1.6842 5518	1.8142 5411	2.1049 3338	179
180	1.5674 3172	1.6891 6760	1.8203 0163	2.1137 0393	180
181	1.5713 5030	1.6940 9433	1.8263 6930	2.1225 1103	181
182	1.5752 7868	1.6990 3544	1.8324 5720	2.1313 5483	182
183	1.5792 1688	1.7039 9096	1.8385 6539	2.1402 3547	183
184	1.5831 6492	1.7089 6094	1.8446 9394	2.1491 5312	184
185	1.5871 2283	1.7139 4541	1.8508 4292	2.1581 0793	185
186	1.5910 9064	1.7189 4441	1.8570 1240	2.1671 0004	186
187	1.5950 6836	1.7239 5800	1.8632 0244	2.1761 2963	187
188	1.5990 5604	1.7289 8621	1.8694 1311	2.1851 9683	188
189	1.6030 5368	1.7340 2909	1.8756 4449	2.1943 0182	189
190	1.6070 6131	1.7390 8667	1.8818 9664	2.2034 4474	190
191	1.6110 7896	1.7441 5901	1.8881 6963	2.2126 2576	191
192	1.6151 0666	1.7492 4614	1.8944 6352	2.2218 4504	192
193	1.6191 4443	1.7543 4811	1.9007 7840	2.2311 0272	193
194	1.6231 9229	1.7594 6496	1.9071 1433	2.2403 9899	194
195	1.6272 5027	1.7645 9673	1.9134 7138	2.2497 3398	195
196	1.6313 1839	1.7697 4347	1.9198 4962	2.2591 0787	196
197	1.6353 9669	1.7749 0522	1.9262 4912	2.2685 2082	197
198	1.6394 8518	1.7800 8203	1.9326 6995	2.2779 7299	198
199	1.6435 8390	1.7852 7393	1.9391 1218	2.2874 6455	199
200	1.6476 9285	1.7904 8098	1.9455 7589	2.2969 9565	200

461

TABLE III.—Amount of 1 at Compound Interest

$$s = (1 + i)^n$$

n	½%	⁷⁄₁₂%	⅝%	⅔%	n
1	1.0050 0000	1.0058 3333	1.0062 5000	1.0066 6667	1
2	1.0100 2500	1.0117 0069	1.0125 3906	1.0133 7778	2
3	1.0150 7513	1.0176 0228	1.0188 6743	1.0201 3363	3
4	1.0201 5050	1.0235 3830	1.0252 3535	1.0269 3452	4
5	1.0252 5125	1.0295 0894	1.0316 4307	1.0337 8075	5
6	1.0303 7751	1.0355 1440	1.0380 9084	1.0406 7262	6
7	1.0355 2940	1.0415 5490	1.0445 7891	1.0476 1044	7
8	1.0407 0704	1.0476 3064	1.0511 0753	1.0545 9451	8
9	1.0459 1058	1.0537 4182	1.0576 7695	1.0616 2514	9
10	1.0511 4013	1.0598 8865	1.0642 8743	1.0687 0264	10
11	1.0563 9583	1.0660 7133	1.0709 3923	1.0758 2732	11
12	1.0616 7781	1.0722 9008	1.0776 3260	1.0829 9951	12
13	1.0669 8620	1.0785 4511	1.0843 6780	1.0902 1950	13
14	1.0723 2113	1.0848 3662	1.0911 4510	1.0974 8763	14
15	1.0776 8274	1.0911 6483	1.0979 6476	1.1048 0422	15
16	1.0830 7115	1.0975 2996	1.1048 2704	1.1121 6958	16
17	1.0884 8651	1.1039 3222	1.1117 3221	1.1195 8404	17
18	1.0939 2894	1.1103 7182	1.1186 8053	1.1270 4794	18
19	1.0993 9858	1.1168 4899	1.1256 7229	1.1345 6159	19
20	1.1048 9558	1.1233 6395	1.1327 0774	1.1421 2533	20
21	1.1104 2006	1.1299 1690	1.1397 8716	1.1497 3950	21
22	1.1159 7216	1.1365 0808	1.1469 1083	1.1574 0443	22
23	1.1215 5202	1.1431 3771	1.1540 7902	1.1651 2046	23
24	1.1271 5978	1.1498 0602	1.1612 9202	1.1728 8793	24
25	1.1327 9558	1.1565 1322	1.1685 5009	1.1807 0718	25
26	1.1384 5955	1.1632 5955	1.1758 5353	1.1885 7857	26
27	1.1441 5185	1.1700 4523	1.1832 0262	1.1965 0242	27
28	1.1498 7261	1.1768 7049	1.1905 9763	1.2044 7911	28
29	1.1556 2197	1.1837 3557	1.1980 3887	1.2125 0897	29
30	1.1614 0008	1.1906 4069	1.2055 2661	1.2205 9236	30
31	1.1672 0708	1.1975 8610	1.2130 6115	1.2287 2964	31
32	1.1730 4312	1.2045 7202	1.2206 4278	1.2369 2117	32
33	1.1789 0833	1.2115 9869	1.2282 7180	1.2451 6731	33
34	1.1848 0288	1.2186 6634	1.2359 4850	1.2534 6843	34
35	1.1907 2689	1.2257 7523	1.2436 7318	1.2618 2489	35
36	1.1966 8052	1.2329 2559	1.2514 4614	1.2702 3705	36
37	1.2026 6393	1.2401 1765	1.2592 6767	1.2787 0530	37
38	1.2086 7725	1.2473 5167	1.2671 3810	1.2872 3000	38
39	1.2147 2063	1.2546 2789	1.2750 5771	1.2958 1153	39
40	1.2207 9424	1.2619 4655	1.2830 2682	1.3044 5028	40
41	1.2268 9821	1.2693 0791	1.2910 4574	1.3131 4661	41
42	1.2330 3270	1.2767 1220	1.2991 1477	1.3219 0092	42
43	1.2391 9786	1.2841 5969	1.3072 3424	1.3307 1360	43
44	1.2453 9385	1.2916 5062	1.3154 0446	1.3395 8502	44
45	1.2516 2082	1.2991 8525	1.3236 2573	1.3485 1559	45
46	1.2578 7892	1.3067 6383	1.3318 9839	1.3575 0569	46
47	1.2641 6832	1.3143 8662	1.3402 2276	1.3665 5573	47
48	1.2704 8916	1.3220 5388	1.3485 9915	1.3756 6610	48
49	1.2768 4161	1.3297 6586	1.3570 2790	1.3848 3721	49
50	1.2832 2581	1.3375 2283	1.3655 0932	1.3940 6946	50

TABLE III.—Amount of 1 at Compound Interest

$$s = (1 + i)^n$$

n	½%	⁷⁄₁₂%	⅝%	⅔%	n
51	1.2896 4194	1.3453 2504	1.3740 4375	1.4033 6325	51
52	1.2960 9015	1.3531 7277	1.3826 3153	1.4127 1901	52
53	1.3025 7060	1.3610 6628	1.3912 7297	1.4221 3713	53
54	1.3090 8346	1.3690 0583	1.3999 6843	1.4316 1805	54
55	1.3156 2887	1.3769 9170	1.4087 1823	1.4411 6217	55
56	1.3222 0702	1.3850 2415	1.4175 2272	1.4507 6992	56
57	1.3288 1805	1.3931 0346	1.4263 8224	1.4604 4172	57
58	1.3354 6214	1.4012 2990	1.4352 9713	1.4701 7799	58
59	1.3421 3946	1.4094 0374	1.4442 6773	1.4799 7918	59
60	1.3488 5015	1.4176 2526	1.4532 9441	1.4898 4571	60
61	1.3555 9440	1.4258 9474	1.4623 7750	1.4997 7801	61
62	1.3623 7238	1.4342 1246	1.4715 1736	1.5097 7653	62
63	1.3691 8424	1.4425 7870	1.4807 1434	1.5198 4171	63
64	?.3760 3016	1.4509 9374	1.4899 6881	1.5299 7399	64
65	1.3829 1031	1.4594 5787	1.4992 8111	1.5401 7381	65
66	1.3898 2486	1.4679 7138	1.5086 5162	1.5504 4164	66
67	1.3967 7399	1.4765 3454	1.5180 8069	1.5607 7792	67
68	1.4037 5785	1.4851 4766	1.5275 6869	1.5711 8310	68
69	1.4107 7664	1.4938 1102	1.5371 1600	1.5816 5766	69
70	1.4178 3053	1.5025 2492	1.5467 2297	1.5922 0204	70
71	1.4249 1968	1.5112 8965	1.5563 8999	1.6028 1672	71
72	1.4320 4428	1.5201 0550	1.5661 1743	1.6135 0217	72
73	1.4392 0450	1.5289 7279	1.5759 0566	1.6242 5885	73
74	1.4464 0052	1.5378 9179	1.5857 5507	1.6350 8724	74
75	1.4536 3252	1.5468 6283	1.5956 6604	1.6459 8782	75
76	1.4609 0069	1.5558 8620	1.6056 3896	1.6569 6107	76
77	1.4682 0519	1.5649 6220	1.6156 7420	1.6680 0748	77
78	1.4755 4622	1.5740 9115	1.6257 7216	1.6791 2753	78
79	1.4829 2395	1.5832 7334	1.6359 3324	1.6903 2172	79
80	1.4903 3857	1.5925 0910	1.6461 5782	1.7015 9053	80
81	1.4977 9026	1.6017 9874	1.6564 4631	1.7129 3446	81
82	1.5052 7921	1.6111 4257	1.6667 9910	1.7243 5403	82
83	1.5128 0561	1.6205 4090	1.6772 1659	1.7358 4972	83
84	1.5203 6964	1.6299 9405	1.6876 9920	1.7474 2205	84
85	1.5279 7148	1.6395 0235	1.6982 4732	1.7590 7153	85
86	1.5356 1134	1.6490 6612	1.7088 6136	1.7707 9868	86
87	1.5432 8940	1.6586 8567	1.7195 4175	1.7826 0400	87
88	1.5510 0585	1.6683 6134	1.7302 8888	1.7944 8803	88
89	1.5587 6087	1.6780 9344	1.7411 0319	1.8064 5128	89
90	1.5665 5468	1.6878 8232	1.7519 8508	1.8184 9429	90
91	1.5743 8745	1.6977 2830	1.7629 3499	1.8306 1758	91
92	1.5822 5939	1.7076 3172	1.7739 5333	1.8428 2170	92
93	1.5901 7069	1.7175 9290	1.7850 4054	1.8551 0718	93
94	1.5981 2154	1.7276 1219	1.7961 9704	1.8674 7456	94
95	1.6061 1215	1.7376 8993	1.8074 2328	1.8799 2439	95
96	1.6141 4271	1.7478 2646	1.8187 1967	1.8924 5722	96
97	1.6222 1342	1.7580 2211	1.8300 8667	1.9050 7360	97
98	1.6303 2449	1.7682 7724	1.8415 2471	1.9177 7409	98
99	1.6384 7611	1.7785 9219	1.8530 3424	1.9305 5925	99
100	1.6466 6849	1.7889 6731	1.8646 1570	1.9434 2965	100

TABLE III.—Amount of 1 at Compound Interest

$$s = (1 + i)^n$$

n	½%	⁷⁄₁₂%	⅝%	⅔%	u
101	1.6549 0183	1.7994 0295	1.8762 6955	1.9563 8585	101
102	1.6631 7634	1.8098 9947	1.8879 9624	1.9694 2842	102
103	1.6714 9223	1.8204 5722	1.8997 9621	1.9825 5794	103
104	1.6798 4969	1.8310 7655	1.9116 6994	1.9957 7499	104
105	1.6882 4894	1.8417 5783	1.9236 1788	2.0090 8016	105
106	1.6966 9018	1.8525 0142	1.9356 4049	2.0224 7403	106
107	1.7051 7363	1.8633 0768	1.9477 3824	2.0359 5719	107
108	1.7136 9950	1.8741 7697	1.9599 1161	2.0495 3024	108
109	1.7222 6800	1.8851 0967	1.9721 6105	2.0631 9377	109
110	1.7308 7934	1.8961 0614	1.9844 8706	2.0769 4840	110
111	1.7395 3373	1.9071 6676	1.9968 9010	2.0907 9472	111
112	1.7482 3140	1.9182 9190	2.0093 7067	2.1047 3335	112
113	1.7569 7256	1.9294 8194	2.0219 2923	2.1187 6491	113
114	1.7657 5742	1.9407 3725	2.0345 6629	2.1328 9000	114
115	1.7745 8621	1.9520 5822	2.0472 8233	2.1471 0927	115
116	1.7834 5914	1.9634 4522	2.0600 7785	2.1614 2333	116
117	1.7923 7644	1.9748 9865	2.0729 5333	2.1758 3282	117
118	1.8013 3832	1.9864 1890	2.0859 0929	2.1903 3837	118
119	1.8103 4501	1.9980 0634	2.0989 4622	2.2049 4063	119
120	1.8193 9673	2.0096 6138	2.1120 6464	2.2196 4023	120
121	1.8284 9372	2.0213 8440	2.1252 6504	2.2344 3784	121
122	1.8376 3619	2.0331 7581	2.1385 4795	2.2493 3409	122
123	1.8468 2437	2.0450 3600	2.1519 1387	2.2643 2965	123
124	1.8560 5849	2.0569 6538	2.1653 6333	2.2794 2518	124
125	1.8653 3878	2.0689 6434	2.1788 9685	2.2946 2135	125
126	1.8746 6548	2.0810 3330	2.1925 1496	2.3099 1882	126
127	1.8840 3880	2.0931 7266	2.2062 1818	2.3253 1828	127
128	1.8934 5900	2.1053 8284	2.2200 0704	2.3408 2040	128
129	1.9029 2629	2.1176 6424	2.2338 8209	2.3564 2587	129
130	1.9124 4092	2.1300 1728	2.2478 4385	2.3721 3538	130
131	1.9220 0313	2.1424 4238	2.2618 9287	2.3879 4962	131
132	1.9316 1314	2.1549 3996	2.2760 2970	2.4038 6928	132
133	1.9412 7121	2.1675 1044	2.2902 5489	2.4198 9507	133
134	1.9509 7757	2.1801 5425	2.3045 6898	2.4360 2771	134
135	1.9607 3245	2.1928 7182	2.3189 7254	2.4522 6789	135
136	1.9705 3612	2.2056 6357	2.3334 6612	2.4686 1635	136
137	1.9803 8880	2.2185 2994	2.3480 5028	2.4850 7379	137
138	1.9902 9074	2.2314 7137	2.3627 2559	2.5016 4095	138
139	2.0002 4219	2.2444 8828	2.3774 9263	2.5183 1855	139
140	2.0102 4340	2.2575 8113	2.3923 5196	2.5351 0734	140
141	2.0202 9462	2.2707 5036	2.4073 0416	2.5520 0806	141
142	2.0303 9609	2.2839 9640	2.4223 4981	2.5690 2145	142
143	2.0405 4808	2.2973 1971	2.4374 8950	2.5861 4826	143
144	2.0507 5082	2.3107 2074	2.4527 2380	2.6033 8924	144
145	2.0610 0457	2.3241 9995	2.4680 5333	2.6207 4517	145
146	2.0713 0959	2.3377 5778	2.4834 7866	2.6382 1681	146
147	2.0816 6614	2.3513 9470	2.4990 0040	2.6558 0492	147
148	2.0920 7447	2.3651 1117	2.5146 1916	2.6735 1028	148
149	2.1025 3484	2.3789 0765	2.5303 3553	2.6913 3369	149
150	2.1130 4752	2.3927 8461	2.5461 5012	2.7092 7591	150

TABLE III.—Amount of 1 at Compound Interest

$$s = (1 + i)^n$$

n	½%	⁷⁄₁₂%	⅝%	⅔%	n
151	2.1236 1276	2.4067 4252	2.5620 6356	2.7273 3775	151
152	2.1342 3082	2.4207 8186	2.5780 7646	2.7455 2000	152
153	2.1449 0197	2.4349 0308	2.5941 8944	2.7638 2347	153
154	2.1556 2648	2.4491 0668	2.6104 0312	2.7822 4896	154
155	2.1664 0462	2.4633 9314	2.6267 1814	2.8007 9729	155
156	2.1772 3664	2.4777 6293	2.6431 3513	2.8194 6927	156
157	2.1881 2282	2.4922 1655	2.6596 5472	2.8382 6573	157
158	2.1990 6344	2.5067 5448	2.6762 7756	2.8571 8750	158
159	2.2100 5875	2.5213 7722	2.6930 0430	2.8762 3542	159
160	2.2211 0905	2.5360 8525	2.7098 3558	2.8954 1032	160
161	2.2322 1459	2.5508 7908	2.7267 7205	2.9147 1306	161
162	2.2433 7566	2.5657 5921	2.7438 1437	2.9341 4448	162
163	2.2545 9254	2.5807 2614	2.7609 6321	2.9537 0544	163
164	2.2658 6551	2.5957 8037	2.7782 1923	2.9733 9681	164
165	2.2771 9483	2.6109 2242	2.7955 8310	2.9932 1945	165
166	2.2885 8081	2.6261 5280	2.8130 5550	3.0131 7425	166
167	2.3000 2371	2.6414 7203	2.8306 3710	3.0332 6208	167
168	2.3115 2383	2.6568 8062	2.8483 2858	3.0534 3883	168
169	2.3230 8145	2.6723 7909	2.8661 3063	3.0738 4038	169
170	2.3346 9686	2.6879 6796	2.8840 4395	3.0943 3265	170
171	2.3463 7034	2.7036 4778	2.9020 6922	3.1149 6154	171
172	2.3581 0219	2.7194 1906	2.9202 0715	3.1357 2795	172
173	2.3698 9270	2.7352 8233	2.9384 5845	3.1566 3280	173
174	2.3817 4217	2.7512 3815	2.9568 2381	3.1776 7702	174
175	2.3936 5088	2.7672 8704	2.9753 0396	3.1988 6153	175
176	2.4056 1913	2.7834 2954	2.9938 9961	3.2201 8728	176
177	2.4176 4723	2.7996 6622	3.0126 1149	3.2416 5519	177
178	2.4297 3546	2.8159 9760	3.0314 4031	3.2632 6623	178
179	2.4418 8414	2.8324 2426	3.0503 8681	3.2850 2134	179
180	2.4540 9356	2.8489 4673	3.0694 5173	3.3069 2148	180
181	2.4663 6403	2.8655 6559	3.0886 3580	3.3289 6762	181
182	2.4786 9585	2.8822 8139	3.1079 3977	3.3511 6074	182
183	2.4910 8933	2.8990 9469	3.1272 6440	3.3735 0181	183
184	2.5035 4478	2.9160 0608	3.1469 1043	3.3959 9182	184
185	2.5160 6250	2.9330 1612	3.1665 7862	3.4186 3177	185
186	2.5286 4281	2.9501 2538	3.1863 6973	3.4414 2265	186
187	2.5412 8603	2.9673 3444	3.2062 8454	3.4643 6546	187
188	2.5539 9246	2.9846 4389	3.2263 2382	3.4874 6123	188
189	2.5667 6242	3.0020 5431	3.2464 8834	3.5107 1097	189
190	2.5795 9623	3.0195 6630	3.2667 7890	3.5341 1571	190
191	2.5924 9421	3.0371 8043	3.2871 9627	3.5576 7649	191
192	2.6054 5668	3.0548 9732	3.3077 4124	3.5813 9433	192
193	2.6184 8397	3.0727 1755	3.3284 1462	3.6052 7029	193
194	2.6315 7639	3.0906 4174	3.3492 1722	3.6293 0543	194
195	2.6447 3427	3.1086 7048	3.3701 4982	3.6535 0080	195
196	2.6579 5794	3.1268 0440	3.3912 1326	3.6778 5747	196
197	2.6712 4773	3.1450 4409	3.4124 0834	3.7023 7652	197
198	2.6846 0397	3.1633 9018	3.4337 3589	3.7270 5903	198
199	2.6980 2699	3.1818 4329	3.4551 9674	3.7519 0609	199
200	2.7115 1712	3.2004 0404	3.4767 9172	3.7769 1880	200

TABLE III.—Amount of 1 at Compound Interest

$$s = (1 + i)^n$$

n	$\frac{3}{4}\%$	$\frac{7}{8}\%$	1%	$1\frac{1}{8}\%$	n
1	1.0075 0000	1.0087 5000	1.0100 0000	1.0112 5000	1
2	1.0150 5625	1 0175 7656	1.0201 0000	1.0226 2656	2
3	1.0226 6917	1.0264 8036	1.0303 0100	1.0341 3111	3
4	1.0303 3919	1.0354 6206	1.0406 0401	1.0457 6509	4
5	1.0380 6673	1.0445 2235	1.0510 1005	1.0575 2994	5
6	1.0458 5224	1.0536 6192	1.0615 2015	1.0694 2716	6
7	1.0536 9613	1.0628 8147	1.0721 3535	1.0814 5821	7
8	1.0615 9885	1.0721 8168	1.0828 5671	1.0936 2462	8
9	1.0695 6084	1.0815 6327	1.0936 8527	1.1059 2789	9
10	1.0775 8255	1.0910 2695	1.1046 2213	1.1183 6958	10
11	1.0856 6441	1.1005 7343	1.1156 6835	1.1309 5124	11
12	1.0938 0690	1.1102 0345	1.1268 2503	1.1436 7444	12
13	1.1020 1045	1.1199 1773	1.1380 9328	1.1565 4078	13
14	1.1102 7553	1.1297 1701	1.1494 7421	1.1695 5186	14
15	1.1186 0259	1.1396 0203	1.1609 6896	1.1827 0932	15
16	1.1269 9211	1.1495 7355	1.1725 7864	1.1960 1480	16
17	1.1354 4455	1.1596 3232	1.1843 0443	1.2094 6997	17
18	1.1439 6039	1.1697 7910	1.1961 4748	1.2230 7650	18
19	1.1525 4009	1.1800 1467	1.2081 0895	1.2368 3611	19
20	1.1611 8414	1.1903 3980	1.2201 9004	1.2507 5052	20
21	1.1698 9302	1.2007 5527	1.2323 9194	1.2648 2146	21
22	1.1786 6722	1.2112 6188	1.2447 1586	1.2790 5071	22
23	1.1875 0723	1.2218 6042	1.2571 6302	1.2934 4003	23
24	1.1964 1353	1.2325 5170	1.2697 3465	1.3079 9123	24
25	1.2053 8663	1.2433 3653	1.2824 3200	1.3227 0613	25
26	1.2144 2703	1.2542 1572	1.2952 5631	1.3375 8657	26
27	1.2235 3523	1.2651 9011	1.3082 0888	1.3526 3442	27
28	1.2327 1175	1.2762 6052	1.3212 9097	1.3678 5156	28
29	1.2419 5709	1.2874 2780	1.3345 0388	1.3832 3989	29
30	1 2512 7176	1.2986 9280	1.3478 4892	1.3988 0134	30
31	1.2606 5630	1.3100 5636	1.3613 2740	1.4145 3785	31
32	1.2701 1122	1.3215 1935	1.3749 4068	1.4304 5140	32
33	1.2796 3706	1.3330 8265	1.3886 9009	1.4465 4398	33
34	1.2892 3434	1.3447 4712	1.4025 7699	1.4628 1760	34
35	1.2989 0359	1.3565 1366	1.4166 0276	1.4792 7430	35
36	1.3086 4537	1.3683 8315	1.4307 6878	1.4959 1613	36
37	1.3184 6021	1.3803 5650	1.4450 7647	1.5127 4519	37
38	1.3283 4866	1.3924 3462	1.4595 2724	1.5297 6357	38
39	1.3383 1128	1.4046 1843	1.4741 2251	1.5469 7341	39
40	1.3483 4861	1.4169 0884	1.4888 6373	1.5643 7687	40
41	1.3584 6123	1.4293 0679	1.5037 5237	1.5819 7611	41
42	1.3686 4969	1.4418 1322	1.5187 8989	1.5997 7334	42
43	1.3789 1456	1.4544 2909	1.5339 7779	1.6177 7079	43
44	1.3892 5642	1.4671 5534	1.5493 1757	1.6359 7071	44
45	1.3996 7584	1.4799 9295	1.5648 1075	1.6543 7538	45
46	1.4101 7341	1.4929 4289	1.5804 5885	1.6729 8710	46
47	1.4207 4971	1.5060 0614	1.5962 6344	1.6918 0821	47
48	1.4314 0533	1.5191 8370	1.6122 2608	1.7108 4105	48
49	1.4421 4087	1.5324 7655	1.6283 4834	1.7300 8801	49
50	1.4529 5693	1.5458 8572	1.6446 3182	1.7495 5150	50

TABLE III.—Amount of 1 at Compound Interest

$$s = (1 + i)^n$$

n	¾%	⅞%	1%	1⅛%	n
51	1.4638 5411	1.5594 1222	1.6610 7814	1.7692 3395	51
52	1.4748 3301	1.5730 5708	1.6776 8892	1.7891 3784	52
53	1.4858 9426	1.5868 2133	1.6944 6581	1.8092 6564	53
54	1.4970 3847	1.6007 0602	1.7114 1047	1.8296 1988	54
55	1.5082 6626	1.6147 1219	1.7285 2457	1.8502 0310	55
56	1.5195 7825	1.6288 4093	1.7458 0982	1.8710 1788	56
57	1.5309 7509	1.6430 9328	1.7632 6792	1.8920 6684	57
58	1.5424 5740	1.6574 7035	1.7809 0060	1.9133 5259	58
59	1.5540 2583	1.6719 7322	1.7987 0960	1.9348 7780	59
60	1.5656 8103	1.6866 0298	1.8166 9670	1.9566 4518	60
61	1.5774 2363	1.7013 6076	1.8348 6367	1.9786 5744	61
62	1.5892 5431	1.7162 4766	1.8532 1230	2.0009 1733	62
63	1.6011 7372	1.7312 6483	1.8717 4443	2.0234 2765	63
64	1.6131 8252	1.7464 1340	1.8904 6187	2.0461 9121	64
65	1.6252 8139	1.7616 9452	1.9093 6649	2.0692 1087	65
66	1.6374 7100	1.7771 0934	1.9284 6015	2.0924 8949	66
67	1.6497 5203	1.7926 5905	1.9477 4475	2.1160 2999	67
68	1.6621 2517	1.8083 4482	1.9672 2220	2.1398 3533	68
69	1.6745 9111	1.8241 6783	1.9868 9442	2.1639 0848	69
70	1.6871 5055	1.8401 2930	2.0067 6337	2.1882 5245	70
71	1.6998 0418	1.8562 3043	2.0268 3100	2.2128 7029	71
72	1.7125 5271	1.8724 7245	2.0470 9931	2.2377 6508	72
73	1.7253 9685	1.8888 5658	2.0675 7031	2.2629 3994	73
74	1.7383 3733	1.9053 8408	2.0882 4601	2.2883 9801	74
75	1.7513 7486	1.9220 5619	2.1091 2847	2.3141 4249	75
76	1.7645 1017	1.9388 7418	2.1302 1975	2.3401 7659	76
77	1.7777 4400	1.9558 3933	2.1515 2195	2.3665 0358	77
78	1.7910 7708	1.9729 5292	2.1730 3717	2.3931 2675	78
79	1.8045 1015	1.9902 1626	2.1947 6754	2.4200 4942	79
80	1.8180 4398	2.0076 3066	2.2167 1522	2.4472 7498	80
81	1.8316 7931	2.0251 9742	2.2388 8237	2.4748 0682	81
82	1.8454 1691	2.0429 1790	2.2612 7119	2.5026 4840	82
83	1.8592 5753	2.0607 9343	2.2838 8390	2.5308 0319	83
84	1.8732 0196	2.0788 2537	2.3067 2274	2.5592 7473	84
85	1.8872 5098	2.0970 1510	2.3297 8997	2.5880 6657	85
86	1.9014 0536	2.1153 6398	2.3530 8787	2.6171 8232	86
87	1.9156 6590	2.1338 7341	2.3766 1875	2.6466 2562	87
88	1.9300 3339	2.1525 4481	2.4003 8494	2.6764 0016	88
89	1.9445 0865	2.1713 7957	2.4243 8879	2.7065 0966	89
90	1.9590 9246	2.1903 7914	2.4486 3267	2.7369 5789	90
91	1.9737 8565	2.2095 4496	2.4731 1900	2.7677 4867	91
92	1.9885 8905	2.2288 7843	2.4978 5019	2.7988 8584	92
93	2.0035 0346	2.2483 8117	2.5228 2869	2.8303 7331	93
94	2.0185 2974	2.2680 5450	2.5480 5698	2.8622 1501	94
95	2.0336 6871	2.2878 9998	2.5735 3755	2.8944 1492	95
96	2.0489 2123	2.3079 1910	2.5992 7293	2.9269 7709	96
97	2.0642 8814	2.3281 1340	2.6252 6565	2.9599 0559	97
98	2.0797 7030	2.3484 8439	2.6515 1831	2.9932 0452	98
99	2.0953 6858	2.3690 3363	2.6780 3349	3.0268 7807	99
100	2.1110 8384	2.3897 6267	2.7048 1383	3.0609 3045	100

TABLE III.—Amount of 1 at Compound Interest

$$s = (1 + i)^n$$

n	$1\frac{1}{4}\%$	$1\frac{3}{8}\%$	$1\frac{1}{2}\%$	$1\frac{3}{4}\%$	n
1	1.0125 0000	1.0137 5000	1.0150 0000	1.0175 0000	1
2	1.0251 5625	1.0276 8906	1.0302 2500	1.0353 0625	2
3	1.0379 7070	1.0418 1979	1.0456 7838	1.0534 2411	3
4	1.0509 4534	1.0561 4481	1.0613 6355	1.0718 5903	4
5	1.0640 8215	1.0706 6680	1.0772 8400	1.0906 1656	5
6	1.0773 8318	1.0853 8847	1.0934 4326	1.1097 0235	6
7	1.0908 5047	1.1003 1256	1.1098 4491	1.1291 2215	7
8	1.1044 8610	1.1154 4186	1.1264 9259	1.1488 8178	8
9	1.1182 9218	1.1307 7918	1.1433 8998	1.1689 8721	9
10	1.1322 7083	1.1463 2740	1.1605 4083	1.1894 4449	10
11	1.1464 2422	1.1620 8940	1.1779 4894	1.2102 5977	11
12	1.1607 5452	1.1780 6813	1.1956 1817	1.2314 3931	12
13	1.1752 6395	1.1942 6656	1.2135 5244	1.2529 8950	13
14	1.1899 5475	1.2106 8773	1.2317 5573	1.2749 1682	14
15	1.2048 2918	1.2273 3469	1.2502 3207	1.2972 2786	15
16	1.2198 8955	1.2442 1054	1.2689 8555	1.3199 2935	16
17	1.2351 3817	1.2613 1843	1.2880 2033	1.3430 2811	17
18	1.2505 7739	1.2786 6156	1.3073 4064	1.3665 3111	18
19	1.2662 0961	1.2962 4316	1.3269 5075	1.3904 4540	19
20	1.2820 3723	1.3140 6650	1.3468 5501	1.4147 7820	20
21	1.2980 6270	1.3321 3492	1.3670 5783	1.4395 3681	21
22	1.3142 8848	1.3504 5177	1.3875 6370	1.4647 2871	22
23	1.3307 1709	1.3690 2048	1.4083 7715	1.4903 6146	23
24	1.3473 5105	1.3878 4451	1.4295 0281	1.5164 4279	24
25	1.3641 9294	1.4069 2738	1.4509 4535	1.5429 8054	25
26	1.3812 4535	1.4262 7263	1.4727 0953	1.5699 8269	26
27	1.3985 1092	1.4458 8388	1.4948 0018	1.5974 5739	27
28	1.4159 9230	1.4657 6478	1.5172 2218	1.6254 1290	28
29	1.4336 9221	1.4859 1905	1.5399 8051	1.6538 5762	29
30	1.4516 1336	1.5063 5043	1.5630 8022	1.6828 0013	30
31	1.4697 5853	1.5270 6275	1.5865 2642	1.7122 4913	31
32	1.4881 3051	1.5480 5986	1.6103 2432	1.7422 1349	32
33	1.5067 3214	1.5693 4569	1.6344 7918	1.7727 0223	33
34	1.5255 6629	1.5909 2419	1.6589 9637	1.8037 2452	34
35	1.5446 3587	1.6127 9940	1.6838 8132	1.8352 8970	35
36	1.5639 4382	1.6349 7539	1.7091 3954	1.8674 0727	36
37	1.5834 9312	1.6574 5630	1.7347 7663	1.9000 8689	37
38	1.6032 8678	1.6802 4633	1.7607 9828	1.9333 3841	38
39	1.6233 2787	1.7033 4971	1.7872 1025	1.9671 7184	39
40	1.6436 1946	1.7267 7077	1.8140 1841	2.0015 9734	40
41	1.6641 6471	1.7505 1387	1.8412 2868	2.0366 2530	41
42	1.6849 6677	1.7745 8343	1.8688 4712	2.0722 6624	42
43	1.7060 2885	1.7989 8396	1.8968 7982	2.1085 3090	43
44	1.7273 5421	1.8237 1999	1.9253 3302	2.1454 3019	44
45	1.7489 4614	1.8487 9614	1.9542 1301	2.1829 7522	45
46	1.7708 0797	1.8742 1708	1.9835 2621	2.2211 7728	46
47	1.7929 4306	1.8999 8757	2.0132 7910	2.2600 4789	47
48	1.8153 5485	1.9261 1240	2.0434 7829	2.2995 9872	48
49	1.8380 4679	1.9525 9644	2.0741 3046	2.3398 4170	49
50	1.8610 2237	1.9794 4464	2.1052 4242	2.3807 8893	50

TABLE III.—Amount of 1 at Compound Interest

$$s = (1 + i)^n$$

n	$1\frac{1}{4}\%$	$1\frac{3}{8}\%$	$1\frac{1}{2}\%$	$1\frac{3}{4}\%$	n
51	1.8842 8515	2.0066 6201	2.1368 2106	2.4224 5274	51
52	1.9078 3872	2.0342 5361	2.1688 7337	2.4648 4566	52
53	1.9316 8670	2.0622 2460	2.2014 0647	2.5070 8046	53
54	1.9558 3249	2.0905 3249	2.2344 2757	2.5518 7012	54
55	1.9802 8070	2.1193 2566	2.2679 4398	2.5965 2785	55
56	2.0050 3420	2.1484 6639	2.3019 6314	2.6419 6708	56
57	2.0300 9713	2.1780 0780	2.3364 9259	2.6882 0151	57
58	2.0554 7335	2.2079 5541	2.3715 3998	2.7352 4503	58
59	2.0811 6676	2.2383 1480	2.4071 1308	2.7831 1182	59
60	2.1071 8135	2.2690 9163	2.4432 1978	2.8318 1628	60
61	2.1335 2111	2.3002 9164	2.4798 6807	2.8813 7306	61
62	2.1601 9013	2.3319 2065	2.5170 6609	2.9317 9709	62
63	2.1871 9250	2.3639 8456	2.5548 2208	2.9831 0354	63
64	2.2145 3241	2.3964 8934	2.5931 4442	3.0343 0785	64
65	2.2422 1407	2.4294 4107	2.6320 4158	3.0884 2574	65
66	2.2702 4174	2.4628 4589	2.6715 2221	3.1424 7319	66
67	2.2986 1976	2.4967 1002	2.7115 9504	3.1974 6647	67
68	2.3273 5251	2.5310 3978	2.7522 6896	3.2534 2213	68
69	2.3564 4442	2.5658 4158	2.7935 5300	3.3103 5702	69
70	2.3858 9997	2.6011 2190	2.8354 5629	3.3682 8827	70
71	2.4157 2372	2.6368 8732	2.8779 8814	3.4272 3331	71
72	2.4459 2027	2.6731 4453	2.9211 5796	3.4872 0990	72
73	2.4764 9427	2.7099 0026	2.9649 7533	3.5482 3607	73
74	2.5074 5045	2.7471 6139	3.0094 4996	3.6103 3020	74
75	2.5387 9358	2.7849 3486	3.0545 9171	3.6735 1098	75
76	2.5705 2850	2.8232 2771	3.1004 1059	3.7377 9742	76
77	2.6026 6011	2.8620 4710	3.1469 1674	3.8032 0888	77
78	2.6351 9336	2.9014 0024	3.1941 2050	3.8697 6503	78
79	2.6681 3327	2.9412 9450	3.2420 3230	3.9374 8592	79
80	2.7014 8494	2.9817 3730	3.2906 6279	4.0063 9192	80
81	2.7352 5350	3.0227 3618	3.3400 2273	4.0765 0378	81
82	2.7694 4417	3.0642 9881	3.3901 2307	4.1478 4260	82
83	2.8040 6222	3.1064 3291	3.4409 7492	4.2204 2984	83
84	2.8391 1300	3.1491 4637	3.4925 8954	4.2942 8737	84
85	2.8746 0191	3.1924 4713	3.5449 7838	4.3694 3740	85
86	2.9105 3444	3.2363 4328	3.5981 5306	4.4459 0255	86
87	2.9469 1612	3.2808 4300	3.6521 2535	4.5237 0584	87
88	2.9837 5257	3.3259 5459	3.7069 0723	4.6028 7070	88
89	3.0210 4948	3.3716 8646	3.7625 1084	4.6834 2093	89
90	3.0588 1260	3.4180 4715	3.8189 4851	4.7653 8080	90
91	3.0970 4775	3.4650 4530	3.8762 3273	4.8487 7496	91
92	3.1357 6085	3.5126 8967	3.9343 7622	4.9336 2853	92
93	3.1749 5786	3.5609 8916	3.9933 9187	5.0199 6703	93
94	3.2146 4483	3.6099 5276	4.0532 9275	5.1078 1645	94
95	3.2548 2789	3.6595 8961	4.1140 9214	5.1972 0324	95
96	3.2955 1324	3.7099 0897	4.1758 0352	5.2881 5429	96
97	3.3367 0716	3.7609 2021	4.2384 4057	5.3806 9699	97
98	3.3784 1600	3.8126 3287	4.3020 1718	5.4748 5919	98
99	3.4206 4620	3.8650 5657	4.3665 4744	5.5706 6923	99
100	3.4634 0427	3.9182 0110	4.4320 4565	5.6681 5594	100

469

TABLE III.—Amount of 1 at Compound Interest

$$s = (1 + i)^n$$

n	2%	$2\frac{1}{4}\%$	$2\frac{1}{2}\%$	$2\frac{3}{4}\%$	n
1	1.0200 0000	1.0225 0000	1.0250 0000	1.0275 0000	1
2	1.0404 0000	1.0455 0625	1.0506 2500	1.0557 5625	2
3	1.0612 0800	1.0690 3014	1.0768 9063	1.0847 8955	3
4	1.0824 3216	1.0930 8332	1.1038 1289	1.1146 2126	4
5	1.1040 8080	1.1176 7769	1.1314 0821	1.1452 7334	5
6	1.1261 6242	1.1428 2544	1.1596 9342	1.1767 6836	6
7	1.1486 8567	1.1685 3901	1.1886 8575	1.2091 2949	7
8	1.1716 5938	1.1948 3114	1.2184 0290	1.2423 8055	8
9	1.1950 9257	1.2217 1484	1.2488 6297	1.2765 4602	9
10	1.2189 9442	1.2492 0343	1.2800 8454	1.3116 5103	10
11	1.2433 7431	1.2773 1050	1.3120 8666	1.3477 2144	11
12	1.2682 4179	1.3060 4999	1.3448 8882	1.3847 8378	12
13	1.2936 0663	1.3354 3611	1.3785 1104	1.4228 6533	13
14	1.3194 7876	1.3654 8343	1.4129 7382	1.4619 9413	14
15	1.3458 6834	1.3962 0680	1.4482 9817	1.5021 9896	15
16	1.3727 8571	1.4276 2146	1.4845 0562	1.5435 0944	16
17	1.4002 4142	1.4597 4294	1.5216 1826	1.5859 5595	17
18	1.4282 4625	1.4925 8716	1.5596 5872	1.6295 6973	18
19	1.4568 1117	1.5261 7037	1.5986 5019	1.6743 8290	19
20	1.4859 4740	1.5605 0920	1.6386 1644	1.7204 2843	20
21	1.5156 6634	1.5956 2066	1.6795 8185	1.7677 4021	21
22	1.5459 7967	1.6315 2212	1.7215 7140	1.8163 5307	22
23	1.5768 9926	1.6682 3137	1.7646 1068	1.8663 0278	23
24	1.6084 3725	1.7057 6658	1.8087 2595	1.9176 2610	24
25	1.6406 0599	1.7441 4632	1.8539 4410	1.9703 6082	25
26	1.6734 1811	1.7833 8962	1.9002 9270	2.0245 4575	26
27	1.7068 8648	1.8235 1588	1.9478 0002	2.0802 2075	27
28	1.7410 2421	1.8645 4499	1.9964 9502	2.1374 2682	28
29	1.7758 4469	1.9064 9725	2.0464 0739	2.1962 0606	29
30	1.8113 6158	1.9493 9344	2.0975 6758	2.2566 0173	30
31	1.8475 8882	1.9932 5479	2.1500 0677	2.3186 5828	31
32	1.8845 4059	2.0381 0303	2.2037 5694	2.3824 2138	32
33	1.9222 3140	2.0839 6034	2.2588 5086	2.4479 3797	33
34	1.9606 7603	2.1308 4945	2.3153 2213	2.5152 5626	34
35	1.9998 8955	2.1787 9356	2.3732 0519	2.5844 2581	35
36	2.0398 8734	2.2278 1642	2.4325 3532	2.6554 9752	36
37	2.0806 8509	2.2779 4229	2.4933 4870	2.7285 2370	37
38	2.1222 9879	2.3291 9599	2.5556 8242	2.8035 5810	38
39	2.1647 4477	2.3816 0290	2.6195 7448	2.8806 5595	39
40	2.2080 3966	2.4351 8897	2.6850 6384	2.9598 7399	40
41	2.2522 0046	2.4899 8072	2.7521 9043	3.0412 7052	41
42	2.2972 4447	2.5460 0528	2.8209 9520	3.1249 0546	42
43	2.3431 8936	2.6032 9040	2.8915 2008	3.2108 4036	43
44	2.3900 5314	2.6618 6444	2.9638 0808	3.2991 3847	44
45	2.4378 5421	2.7217 5639	3.0379 0328	3.3898 6478	45
46	2.4866 1129	2.7829 9590	3.1138 5086	3.4830 8606	46
47	2.5363 4351	2.8456 1331	3.1916 9713	3.5788 7093	47
48	2.5870 7039	2.9096 3961	3.2714 8956	3.6772 8988	48
49	2.6388 1179	2.9751 0650	3.3532 7680	3.7784 1535	49
50	2.6915 8803	3.0420 4640	3.4371 0872	3.8823 2177	50

TABLE III.—Amount of 1 at Compound Interest

$$s = (1 + i)^n$$

n	2%	2¼%	2½%	2¾%	n
51	2.7454 1979	3.1104 9244	3.5230 3644	3.9890 8562	51
52	2.8003 2819	3.1804 7852	3.6111 1235	4.0987 8547	52
53	2.8563 3475	3.2520 3929	3.7013 9016	4.2115 0208	53
54	2.9134 6144	3.3252 1017	3.7939 2491	4.3273 1838	54
55	2.9717 3067	3.4000 2740	3.8887 7303	4.4463 1964	55
56	3.0311 6529	3.4765 2802	3.9859 9236	4.5685 9343	56
57	3.0917 8859	3.5547 4990	4.0856 4217	4.6942 2975	57
58	3.1536 2436	3.6347 3177	4.1877 8322	4.8233 2107	58
59	3.2166 9685	3.7165 1324	4.2924 7780	4.9559 6239	59
60	3.2810 3079	3.8001 3479	4.3997 8975	5.0922 5136	60
61	3.3466 5140	3.8856 3782	4.5097 8449	5.2322 8827	61
62	3.4135 8443	3.9730 6467	4.6225 2910	5.3761 7620	62
63	3.4818 5612	4.0624 5862	4.7380 9233	5.5240 2105	63
64	3.5514 9324	4.1538 6394	4.8565 4464	5.6759 3162	64
65	3.6225 2311	4.2473 2588	4.9779 5826	5.8320 1974	65
66	3.6949 7357	4.3428 9071	5.1024 0721	5.9924 0029	66
67	3.7688 7304	4.4406 0576	5.2299 6739	6.1571 9130	67
68	3.8442 5050	4.5405 1939	5.3607 1658	6.3265 1406	68
69	3.9211 3551	4.6426 8107	5.4947 3449	6.5004 9319	69
70	3.9995 5822	4.7471 4140	5.6321 0286	6.6792 5676	70
71	4.0795 4939	4.8539 5208	5.7729 0543	6.8629 3632	71
72	4.1611 4038	4.9631 6600	5.9172 2806	7.0516 6706	72
73	4.2443 6318	5.0748 3723	6.0651 5876	7.2455 8791	73
74	4.3292 5045	5.1890 2107	6.2167 8773	7.4448 4158	74
75	4.4158 3546	5.3057 7405	6.3722 0743	7.6495 7472	75
76	4.5041 5216	5.4251 5396	6.5315 1261	7.8599 3802	76
77	4.5942 3521	5.5472 1993	6.6948 0043	8.0760 8632	77
78	4.6861 1991	5.6720 3237	6.8621 7044	8.2981 7869	78
79	4.7798 4231	5.7996 5310	7.0337 2470	8.5263 7861	79
80	4.8754 3916	5.9301 4530	7.2095 6782	8.7608 5402	80
81	4.9729 4794	6.0635 7357	7.3898 0701	9.0017 7751	81
82	5.0724 0690	6.2000 0397	7.5745 5219	9.2493 2639	82
83	5.1738 5504	6.3395 0406	7.7639 1599	9.5036 8286	83
84	5.2773 3214	6.4821 4290	7.9580 1389	9.7650 3414	84
85	5.3828 7878	6.6279 9112	8.1569 6424	10.0335 7258	85
86	5.4905 3636	6.7771 2092	8.3608 8834	10.3094 9583	86
87	5.6003 4708	6.9296 0614	8.5699 1055	10.5930 0696	87
88	5.7123 5402	7.0855 2228	8.7841 5832	10.8843 1465	88
89	5.8266 0110	7.2449 4653	9.0037 6228	11.1836 3331	89
90	5.9431 3313	7.4079 5782	9.2288 5633	11.4911 8322	90
91	6.0619 9579	7.5746 3688	9.4595 7774	11.8071 9076	91
92	6.1832 3570	7.7450 6621	9.6960 6718	12.1318 8851	92
93	6.3069 0042	7.9193 3020	9.9384 6886	12.4655 1544	93
94	6.4330 3843	8.0975 1512	10.1869 3058	12.8083 1711	94
95	6.5616 9920	8.2797 0921	10.4416 0385	13.1605 4584	95
96	6.6929 3318	8.4660 0267	10.7026 4395	13.5224 6085	96
97	6.8267 9184	8.6564 8773	10.9702 1004	13.8943 2852	97
98	6.9633 2768	8.8512 5871	11.2444 6530	14.2764 2255	98
99	7.1025 9423	9.0504 1203	11.5255 7693	14.6690 2417	99
100	7.2446 4612	9.2540 4630	11.8137 1635	15.0724 2234	100

TABLE III.—Amount of 1 at Compound Interest

$$s = (1 + i)^n$$

n	3%	3½%	4%	4½%	n
1	1.0300 0000	1.0350 0000	1.0400 0000	1.0450 0000	1
2	1.0609 0000	1.0712 2500	1.0816 0000	1.0920 2500	2
3	1.0927 2700	1.1087 1788	1.1248 6400	1.1411 6613	3
4	1.1255 0881	1.1475 2300	1.1698 5856	1.1925 1860	4
5	1.1592 7407	1.1876 8631	1.2166 5290	1.2461 8194	5
6	1.1940 5230	1.2292 5533	1.2653 1902	1.3022 6012	6
7	1.2298 7387	1.2722 7926	1.3159 3178	1.3608 6183	7
8	1.2667 7008	1.3168 0904	1.3685 6905	1.4221 0061	8
9	1.3047 7318	1.3628 9735	1.4233 1181	1.4860 9514	9
10	1.3439 1638	1.4105 9876	1.4802 4428	1.5529 6942	10
11	1.3842 3387	1.4599 6972	1.5394 5406	1.6228 5305	11
12	1.4257 6089	1.5110 6866	1.6010 3222	1.6958 8143	12
13	1.4685 3371	1.5639 5606	1.6650 7351	1.7721 9610	13
14	1.5125 8972	1.6186 9452	1.7316 7645	1.8519 4492	14
15	1.5579 6742	1.6753 4883	1.8009 4351	1.9352 8244	15
16	1.6047 0644	1.7339 8604	1.8729 8125	2.0223 7015	16
17	1.6528 4763	1.7946 7555	1.9479 0050	2.1133 7681	17
18	1.7024 3306	1.8574 8920	2.0258 1652	2.2084 7877	18
19	1.7535 0605	1.9225 0132	2.1068 4918	2.3078 6031	19
20	1.8061 1123	1.9897 8886	2.1911 2314	2.4117 1402	20
21	1.8602 9457	2.0594 3147	2.2787 6807	2.5202 4116	21
22	1.9161 0341	2.1315 1158	2.3699 1879	2.6336 5201	22
23	1.9735 8651	2.2061 1448	2.4647 1554	2.7521 6635	23
24	2.0327 9411	2.2833 2849	2.5633 0416	2.8760 1383	24
25	2.0937 7793	2.3632 4498	2.6658 3633	3.0054 3446	25
26	2.1565 9127	2.4459 5856	2.7724 6978	3.1406 7901	26
27	2.2212 8901	2.5315 6711	2.8833 6858	3.2820 0956	27
28	2.2879 2768	2.6201 7196	2.9987 0332	3.4296 9999	28
29	2.3565 6551	2.7118 7798	3.1186 5145	3.5840 3649	29
30	2.4272 6247	2.8067 9370	3.2433 9751	3.7453 1813	30
31	2.5000 8035	2.9050 3148	3.3731 3341	3.9138 5745	31
32	2.5750 8276	3.0067 0759	3.5080 5875	4.0899 8104	32
33	2.6523 3524	3.1119 4235	3.6483 8110	4.2740 3018	33
34	2.7319 0530	3.2208 6033	3.7943 1634	4.4663 6154	34
35	2.8138 6245	3.3335 9045	3.9460 8899	4.6673 4781	35
36	2.8982 7833	3.4502 6611	4.1039 3255	4.8773 7846	36
37	2.9852 2668	3.5710 2543	4.2680 8986	5.0968 6049	37
38	3.0747 8348	3.6960 1132	4.4388 1345	5.3262 1921	38
39	3.1670 2698	3.8253 7171	4.6163 6599	5.5658 9908	39
40	3.2620 3779	3.9592 5972	4.8010 2063	5.8163 6454	40
41	3.3598 9893	4.0978 3381	4.9930 6145	6.0781 0094	41
42	3.4606 9589	4.2412 5799	5.1927 8391	6.3516 1548	42
43	3.5645 1677	4.3897 0202	5.4004 9527	6.6374 3818	43
44	3.6714 5227	4.5433 4160	5.6165 1508	6.9361 2290	44
45	3.7815 9584	4.7023 5855	5.8411 7568	7.2482 4843	45
46	3.8950 4372	4.8669 4110	6.0748 2271	7.5744 1961	46
47	4.0118 9503	5.0372 8404	6.3178 1562	7.9152 6849	47
48	4.1322 5188	5.2135 8898	6.5705 2824	8.2714 5557	48
49	4.2562 1944	5.3960 6459	6.8333 4937	8.6436 7107	49
50	4.3839 0602	5.5849 2686	7.1066 8335	9.0326 3627	50

TABLE III.—Amount of 1 at Compound Interest

$$s = (1 + i)^n$$

n	3%	3½%	4%	4½%	n
51	4.5154 2320	5.7803 9930	7.3909 5068	9.4391 0490	51
52	4.6508 8590	5.9827 1327	7.6865 8871	9.8638 6463	52
53	4.7904 1247	6.1921 0824	7.9940 5226	10.3077 3853	53
54	4.9341 2485	6.4088 3202	8.3138 1435	10.7715 8677	54
55	5.0821 4859	6.6331 4114	8.6463 6692	11.2563 0817	55
56	5.2346 1305	6.8653 0108	8.9922 2160	11.7628 4204	56
57	5.3916 5144	7.1055 8662	9.3519 1046	12.2921 6993	57
58	5.5534 0098	7.3542 8215	9.7259 8688	12.8453 1758	58
59	5.7200 0301	7.6116 8203	10.1150 2635	13.4233 5687	59
60	5.8916 0310	7.8780 9090	10.5196 2741	14.0274 0793	60
61	6.0683 5120	8.1538 2408	10.9404 1250	14.6586 4129	61
62	6.2504 0173	8.4392 0793	11.3780 2900	15.3182 8014	62
63	6.4379 1379	8.7345 8020	11.8331 5016	16.0076 0275	63
64	6.6310 5120	9.0402 9051	12.3064 7617	16.7279 4487	64
65	6.8299 8273	9.3567 0068	12.7987 3522	17.4807 0239	65
66	7.0348 8222	9.6841 8520	13.3106 8463	18.2673 3400	66
67	7.2459 2868	10.0231 3168	13.8431 1201	19.0893 6403	67
68	7.4633 0654	10.3739 4129	14.3968 3649	19.9483 8541	68
69	7.6872 0574	10.7370 2924	14.9727 0995	20.8460 6276	69
70	7.9178 2191	11.1128 2526	15.5716 1835	21.7841 3558	70
71	8.1553 5657	11.5017 7414	16.1944 8308	22.7644 2168	71
72	8.4000 1727	11.9043 3624	16.8422 6241	23.7888 2066	72
73	8.6520 1778	12.3209 8801	17.5159 5290	24.8593 1759	73
74	8.9115 7832	12.7522 2259	18.2165 9102	25.9779 8688	74
75	9.1789 2567	13.1985 5038	18.9452 5466	27.1469 9629	75
76	9.4542 9344	13.6604 9964	19.7030 6485	28.3686 1112	76
77	9.7379 2224	14.1386 1713	20.4911 8744	29.6451 9862	77
78	10.0300 5991	14.6334 6873	21.3108 3494	30.9792 3256	78
79	10.3309 6171	15.1456 4013	22.1632 6834	32.3782 9802	79
80	10.6408 9056	15.6757 3754	23.0497 9907	33.8300 9643	80
81	10.9601 1727	16.2243 8£35	23.9717 9103	35.3524 5077	81
82	11.2889 2079	16.7922 4195	24.9306 6267	36.9433 1106	82
83	11.6275 8842	17.3799 7041	25.9278 8918	38.6057 6006	83
84	11.9764 1607	17.9882 6938	26.9650 0475	40.3430 1926	84
85	12.3357 0855	18.6178 5881	28.0436 0494	42.1584 5513	85
86	12.7057 7981	19.2694 8387	29.1653 4914	44.0555 8561	86
87	13.0869 5320	19.9439 1580	30.3319 6310	46.0380 8696	87
88	13.4795 6180	20.6419 5285	31.5452 4163	48.1098 0087	88
89	13.8839 4865	21.3644 2120	32.8070 5129	50.2747 4191	89
90	14.3004 6711	22.1121 7595	34.1193 3334	52.5371 0530	90
91	14.7294 8112	22.8861 0210	35.4841 0668	54.9012 7503	91
92	15.1713 6556	23.6871 1568	36.9034 7094	57.3718 3241	92
93	15.6265 0652	24.5161 6473	38.3796 0978	59.9535 6487	93
94	16.0953 0172	25.3742 3049	39.9147 9417	62.6514 7529	94
95	16.5781 6077	26.2623 2856	41.5113 8594	65.4707 9168	95
96	17.0755 0559	27.1815 1006	43.1718 4138	68.4169 7730	96
97	17.5877 7076	28.1328 6291	44.8987 1503	71.4957 4128	97
98	18.1154 0388	29.1175 1311	46.6946 6363	74.7130 4964	98
99	18.6588 6600	30.1366 2607	48.5624 5018	78.0751 3687	99
100	19.2186 3198	31.1914 0798	50.5049 4818	81.5885 1803	100

TABLE III.—Amount of 1 at Compound Interest

$$s = (1 + i)^n$$

n	5%	5½%	6%	6½%	n
1	1.0500 0000	1.0550 0000	1.0600 0000	1.0650 0000	1
2	1.1025 0000	1.1130 2500	1.1236 0000	1.1342 2500	2
3	1.1576 2500	1.1742 4138	1.1910 1600	1.2079 4963	3
4	1.2155 0625	1.2388 2465	1.2624 7696	1.2864 6635	4
5	1.2762 8156	1.3069 6001	1.3382 2558	1.3700 8666	5
6	1.3400 9564	1.3788 4281	1.4185 1911	1.4591 4230	6
7	1.4071 0042	1.4546 7916	1.5036 3026	1.5539 8655	7
8	1.4774 5544	1.5346 8651	1.5938 4807	1.6549 9567	8
9	1.5513 2822	1.6190 9427	1.6894 7896	1.7625 7039	9
10	1.6288 9463	1.7081 4446	1.7908 4770	1.8771 3747	10
11	1.7103 3936	1.8020 9240	1.8982 9856	1.9991 5140	11
12	1.7958 5633	1.9012 0749	2.0121 9647	2.1290 9624	12
13	1.8856 4914	2.0057 7390	2.1329 2826	2.2674 8750	13
14	1.9799 3160	2.1160 9146	2.2609 0396	2.4148 7418	14
15	2.0789 2818	2.2324 7649	2.3965 5819	2.5718 4101	15
16	2.1828 7459	2.3552 6270	2.5403 5168	2.7390 1067	16
17	2.2920 1832	2.4848 0215	2.6927 7279	2.9170 4637	17
18	2.4066 1923	2.6214 6627	2.8543 3915	3.1066 5438	18
19	2.5269 5020	2.7656 4691	3.0255 9950	3.3085 8691	19
20	2.6532 9771	2.9177 5749	3.2071 3547	3.5236 4506	20
21	2.7859 6259	3.0782 3415	3.3995 6360	3.7526 8199	21
22	2.9252 6072	3.2475 3703	3.6035 3742	3.9966 0632	22
23	3.0715 2376	3.4261 5157	3.8197 4966	4.2563 8573	23
24	3.2250 9994	3.6145 8990	4.0489 3464	4.5330 5081	24
25	3.3863 5494	3.8133 9235	4.2918 7072	4.8276 9911	25
26	3.5556 7269	4.0231 2893	4.5493 8296	5.1414 9955	26
27	3.7334 5632	4.2444 0102	4.8223 4594	5.4756 9702	27
28	3.9201 2914	4.4778 4307	5.1116 8670	5.8316 1733	28
29	4.1161 3560	4.7241 2444	5.4183 8790	6.2106 7245	29
30	4.3219 4238	4.9839 5129	5.7434 9117	6.6143 6616	30
31	4.5380 3949	5.2580 6861	6.0881 0064	7.0442 9996	31
32	4.7649 4147	5.5472 6238	6.4533 8668	7.5021 7946	32
33	5.0031 8854	5.8523 6181	6.8405 8988	7.9898 2113	33
34	5.2533 4797	6.1742 4171	7.2510 2528	8.5091 5950	34
35	5.5160 1537	6.5138 2501	7.6860 8679	9.0622 5487	35
36	5.7918 1614	6.8720 8538	8.1472 5200	9.6513 0143	36
37	6.0814 0694	7.2500 5008	8.6360 8712	10.2786 3603	37
38	6.3854 7729	7.6488 0283	9.1542 5235	10.9467 4737	38
39	6.7047 5115	8.0694 8699	9.7035 0749	11.6582 8595	39
40	7.0399 8871	8.5133 0877	10.2857 1794	12.4160 7453	40
41	7.3919 8815	8.9815 4076	10.9028 6101	13.2231 1938	41
42	7.7615 8756	9.4755 2550	11.5570 3267	14.0826 2214	42
43	8.1496 6693	9.9966 7940	12.2504 5463	14.9979 9258	43
44	8.5571 5028	10.5464 9677	12.9854 8191	15.9728 6209	44
45	8.9850 0779	11.1265 5409	13.7646 1083	17.0110 9813	45
46	9.4342 5818	11.7385 1456	14.5904 8748	18.1168 1951	46
47	9.9059 7109	12.3841 3287	15.4659 1673	19.2944 1278	47
48	10.4012 6965	13.0652 6017	16.3938 7173	20.5485 4961	48
49	10.9213 3313	13.7838 4948	17.3775 0403	21.8842 0533	49
50	11.4673 9979	14.5419 6120	18.4201 5427	23.3066 7868	50

TABLE III.—Amount of 1 at Compound Interest

$$s = (1 + i)^n$$

n	5%	5½%	6%	6½%	n
51	12.0407 6978	15.3417 6907	19.5253 6353	24.8216 1279	51
52	12.6428 0826	16.1855 6637	20.6968 8534	26.4350 1762	52
53	13.2749 4868	17.0757 7252	21.9386 9846	28.1532 9377	53
54	13.9386 9611	18.0149 4001	23.2550 2037	29.9832 5786	54
55	14.6356 3092	19.0057 6171	24.6503 2159	31.9321 6963	55
56	15.3674 1246	20.0510 7860	26.1293 4089	34.0077 6065	56
57	16.1357 8309	21.1538 8793	27.6971 0134	36.2182 6509	57
58	16.9425 7224	22.3173 5176	29.3589 2742	38.5724 5233	58
59	17.7897 0085	23.5448 0611	31.1204 6307	41.0796 6173	59
60	18.6791 8589	24.8397 7045	32.9876 9085	43.7498 3974	60
61	19.6131 4519	26.2059 5782	34.9669 5230	46.5935 7932	61
62	20.5938 0245	27.6472 8550	37.0649 6944	49.6221 6198	62
63	21.6234 9257	29.1678 8620	39.2888 6761	52.8476 0251	63
64	22.7046 6720	30.7721 1994	41.6461 9967	56.2826 9667	64
65	23.8399 0056	32.4645 8654	44.1449 7165	59.9410 7195	65
66	25.0318 9559	34.2501 3880	46.7936 6994	63.8372 4163	66
67	26.2834 9037	36.1338 9643	49.6012 9014	67.9866 6234	67
68	27.5976 6488	38.1212 6074	52.5773 6755	72.4057 9539	68
69	28.9775 4813	40.2179 3008	55.7320 0960	77.1121 7209	69
70	30.4264 2554	42.4299 1623	59.0759 3018	82.1244 6327	70
71	31.9477 4681	44.7635 6163	62.6204 8599	87.4625 5339	71
72	33.5451 3415	47.2255 5751	66.3777 1515	93.1476 1936	72
73	35.2223 9086	49.8229 6318	70.3603 7806	99.2022 1461	73
74	36.9835 1040	52.5632 2615	74.5820 0074	105.6503 5856	74
75	38.8326 8592	55.4542 0359	79.0569 2079	112.5176 3187	75
76	40.7743 2022	58.5041 8479	83.8003 3603	119.8312 7794	76
77	42.8130 3623	61.7219 1495	88.8283 5620	127.6203 1101	77
78	44.9536 8804	65.1166 2027	94.1580 5757	135.9156 3122	78
79	47.2013 7244	68.6980 3439	99.8075 4102	144.7501 4725	79
80	49.5614 4107	72.4764 2628	105.7959 9348	154.1589 0683	80
81	52.0395 1312	76.4626 2973	112.1437 5309	164.1792 3577	81
82	54.6414 8878	80.6680 7436	118.8723 7828	174.8508 8609	82
83	57.3735 6322	85.1048 1845	126.0047 2097	186.2161 9369	83
84	60.2422 4138	89.7855 8347	133.5650 0423	198.3202 4628	84
85	63.2543 5344	94.7237 9056	141.5789 0449	211.2110 6229	85
86	66.4170 7112	99.9335 9904	150.0736 3875	224.9397 8134	86
87	69.7379 2467	105.4299 4698	159.0780 5708	239.5608 6712	87
88	73.2248 2091	111.2285 9407	168.6227 4050	255.1323 2349	88
89	76.8860 6195	117.3461 6674	178.7401 0493	271.7159 2451	89
90	80.7303 6505	123.8002 0591	189.4645 1123	289.3774 5961	90
91	84.7668 8330	130.6092 1724	200.8323 8190	308.1869 9448	91
92	89.0052 2747	137.7927 2419	212.8823 2482	328.2191 4912	92
93	93.4554 8884	145.3713 2402	225.6552 6431	349.5533 9382	93
94	98.1282 6328	153.3667 4684	239.1945 8017	372.2743 6441	94
95	103.0346 7645	161.8019 1791	253.5462 5498	396.4721 9810	95
96	108.1864 1027	170.7010 2340	268.7590 3028	422.2428 9098	96
97	113.5957 3078	180.0895 7969	284.8845 7209	449.6886 7889	97
98	119.2755 1732	189.9945 0657	301.9776 4642	478.9184 4302	98
99	125.2392 9319	200.4442 0443	320.0963 0520	510.0481 4181	99
100	131.5012 5785	211.4686 3567	339.3020 8351	543.2012 7103	100

TABLE III.—Amount of 1 at Compound Interest

$$s = (1 + i)^n$$

n	7%	$7\frac{1}{2}\%$	8%	$8\frac{1}{2}\%$	n
1	1.0700 0000	1.0750 0000	1.0800 0000	1.0850 0000	1
2	1.1449 0000	1.1556 2500	1.1664 0000	1.1772 2500	2
3	1.2250 4300	1.2422 9688	1.2597 1200	1.2772 8913	3
4	1.3107 9601	1.3354 6914	1.3604 8896	1.3858 5870	4
5	1.4025 5173	1.4356 2933	1.4693 2808	1.5036 5669	5
6	1.5007 3035	1.5433 0153	1.5868 7432	1.6314 6751	6
7	1.6057 8148	1.6590 4914	1.7138 2427	1.7701 4225	7
8	1.7181 8618	1.7834 7783	1.8509 3021	1.9206 0434	8
9	1.8384 5921	1.9172 3866	1.9990 0463	2.0838 5571	9
10	1.9671 5136	2.0610 3156	2.1589 2500	2.2609 8344	10
11	2.1048 5195	2.2156 0893	2.3316 3900	2.4531 6703	11
12	2.2521 9159	2.3817 7960	2.5181 7012	2.6616 8623	12
13	2.4098 4500	2.5604 1307	2.7196 2373	2.8879 2956	13
14	2.5785 3415	2.7524 4405	2.9371 9362	3.1334 0357	14
15	2.7590 3154	2.9588 7735	3.1721 6911	3.3997 4288	15
16	2.9521 6375	3.1807 9315	3.4259 4264	3.6887 2102	16
17	3.1588 1521	3.4193 5264	3.7000 1805	4.0022 6231	17
18	3.3799 3228	3.6758 0409	3.9960 1950	4.3424 5461	18
19	3.6165 2754	3.9514 8940	4.3157 0106	4.7115 6325	19
20	3.8696 8446	4.2478 5110	4.6609 5714	5.1120 4612	20
21	4.1405 6237	4.5664 3993	5.0338 3372	5.5465 7005	21
22	4.4304 0174	4.9089 2293	5.4365 4041	6.0180 2850	22
23	4.7405 2986	5.2770 9215	5.8714 6365	6.5295 6092	23
24	5.0723 6695	5.6728 7406	6.3411 8074	7.0845 7360	24
25	5.4274 3264	6.0983 3961	6.8484 7520	7.6867 6236	25
26	5.8073 5292	6.5557 1508	7.3963 5321	8.3401 3716	26
27	6.2138 6763	7.0473 9371	7.9880 6147	9.0490 4881	27
28	6.6488 3836	7.5759 4824	8.6271 0639	9.8182 1796	28
29	7.1142 5705	8.1441 4436	9.3172 7490	10.6527 6649	29
30	7.6122 5504	8.7549 5519	10.0626 5689	11.5582 5164	30
31	8.1451 1290	9.4115 7683	10.8676 6944	12.5407 0303	31
32	8.7152 7080	10.1174 4509	11.7370 8300	13.6066 6279	32
33	9.3253 3975	10.8762 5347	12.6760 4964	14.7632 2913	33
34	9.9781 1354	11.6919 7248	13.6901 3361	16.0181 0360	34
35	10.6765 8148	12.5688 7042	14.7853 4429	17.3796 4241	35
36	11.4239 4219	13.5115 3570	15.9681 7184	18.8569 1201	36
37	12.2236 1814	14.5249 0088	17.2456 2558	20.4597 4953	37
38	13.0792 7141	15.6142 6844	18.6252 7563	22.1988 2824	38
39	13.9948 2041	16.7853 3858	20.1152 9768	24.0857 2865	39
40	14.9744 5784	18.0442 3897	21.7245 2150	26.1330 1558	40
41	16.0226 6989	19.3975 5689	23.4624 8322	28.3543 2190	41
42	17.1442 5678	20.8523 7366	25.3394 8187	30.7644 3927	42
43	18.3443 5475	22.4163 0168	27.3666 4042	33.3794 1660	43
44	19.6284 5959	24.0975 2431	29.5559 7166	36.2166 6702	44
45	21 0024 5176	25.9048 3863	31 9204 4939	39.2950 8371	45
46	22.4726 2338	27.8477 0153	34.4740 8534	42.6351 6583	46
47	24.0457 0702	29.9362 7915	37.2320 1217	46.2591 5492	47
48	25.7289 0651	32.1815 0008	40.2105 7314	50.1911 8309	48
49	27.5299 2997	34.5951 1259	43.4274 1899	54.4574 3365	49
50	29.4570 2506	37.1897 4603	46.9016 1251	59.0863 1551	50

476

TABLE III.—Amount of 1 at Compound Interest

$$s = (1 + i)^n$$

n	7%	7½%	8%	8½%	n
51	31.5190 1682	39.9789 7698	50.6537 4151	64.1086 5233	51
52	33.7253 4799	42.9774 0026	54.7060 4084	69.5578 8778	52
53	36.0861 2235	46.2007 0528	59.0825 2410	75.4703 0824	53
54	38.6121 5092	49.6657 5817	63.8091 2603	81.8852 8444	54
55	41.3150 0148	53.3906 9004	68.9138 5611	88.8455 3362	55
56	44.2070 5159	57.3949 9179	74.4269 6460	96.3974 0398	56
57	47.3015 4520	61.6996 1617	80.3811 2177	104.5911 8332	57
58	50.6126 5336	66.3270 8739	86.8116 1151	113.4814 3390	58
59	54.1555 3910	71.3016 1894	93.7565 4043	123.1273 5578	59
60	57.9464 2683	76.6492 4036	01.2570 6367	133.5931 8102	60
61	62.0026 7671	82.3979 3339	109.3576 2876	144.9486 0141	61
62	66.3428 6408	88.5777 7839	118.1062 3906	157.2692 3253	62
63	70.9868 6457	95.2211 1177	127.5547 3819	170.6371 1729	63
64	75.9559 4509	102.3626 9515	137.7591 1724	185.1412 7226	64
65	81.2728 6124	110.0398 9729	148.7798 4662	200.8782 8041	65
66	86.9619 6153	118.2928 8959	160.6822 3435	217.9529 3424	66
67	93.0492 9884	127.1648 5631	173.5368 1310	236.4789 3365	67
68	99.5627 4976	136.7022 2053	187.4197 5815	256.5796 4301	68
69	106.5321 4224	146.9548 8707	202.4133 3880	278.3889 1267	69
70	113.9893 9220	157.9765 0360	218.6064 0590	302.0519 7024	70
71	121.9686 4965	169.8247 4137	236.0949 1837	327.7263 8771	71
72	130.5064 5513	182.5615 9697	254.9825 1184	355.5831 3067	72
73	139.6419 0699	196.2537 1675	275.3811 1279	385.8076 9678	73
74	149.4168 4047	210.9727 4550	297.4116 0181	418.6013 5100	74
75	159.8760 1931	226.7957 0141	321.2045 2996	454.1824 6584	75
76	171.0673 4066	243.8053 7902	346.9008 9236	492.7879 7543	76
77	183.0420 5451	262.0907 8245	374.6529 6374	534.6749 5335	77
78	195.8549 9832	281.7475 9113	404.6252 0084	580.1223 2438	78
79	209.5648 4820	302.8786 6046	436.9952 1691	629.4327 2195	79
80	224.2343 8758	325.5945 6000	471.9548 3426	682.9345 0332	80
81	239.9307 9471	350.0141 5200	509.7112 2101	740.9839 3610	81
82	256.7259 5034	376.2652 1340	550.4881 1869	803.9675 7067	82
83	274.6967 6686	404.4851 0440	594.5271 6818	872.3048 1418	83
84	293.9255 4054	434.8214 8723	642.0893 4164	946.4507 2338	84
85	314.5003 2838	467.4330 9878	693.4564 8897	1026.8990 3487	85
86	336.5153 5137	502.4905 8119	748.9330 0808	1114.1854 5283	86
87	360.0714 2596	540.1773 7477	808.8476 4873	1208.8912 1633	87
88	385.2764 2578	580.6906 7788	873.5554 6063	1311.6469 6971	88
89	412.2457 7558	624.2424 7872	943.4398 9748	1423.1369 6214	89
90	441.1029 7988	671.0606 6463	1018.9150 8928	1544.1036 0392	90
91	471.9801 8847	721.3902 1447	1100.4282 9642	1675.3524 1025	91
92	505.0188 0166	775.4944 8056	1188.4625 6013	1817.7573 6512	92
93	540.3701 1778	833.6565 6660	1283.5395 6494	1972.2667 4116	93
94	578.1960 2602	896.1808 0910	1386.2227 3014	2139.9094 1416	94
95	618.6697 4784	963.3943 6978	1497.1205 4855	2321.8017 1436	95
96	661.9766 3019	1035.6489 4751	1616.8901 9244	2519.1548 6008	96
97	708.3149 9430	1113.3226 1858	1746.2414 0783	2733.2830 2319	97
98	757.8970 4390	1196.8218 1497	1885.9407 2046	2965.6120 8016	98
99	810.9498 3698	1286.5834 5109	2036.8159 7809	3217.6891 0698	99
100	867.7163 2557	1383.0772 0993	2199.7612 5634	3491.1926 8107	100

TABLE IV.—Present Value of 1 at Compound Interest

$$v^n = (1 + i)^{-n}$$

n	$\frac{1}{4}\%$	$\frac{7}{24}\%$	$\frac{1}{3}\%$	$\frac{5}{12}\%$	n
1	0.9975 0623	0.9970 9182	0.9966 7774	0.9958 5062	1
2	0.9950 1869	0.9941 9209	0.9933 6652	0.9917 1846	2
3	0.9925 3734	0.9913 0079	0.9900 6630	0.9876 0345	3
4	0.9900 6219	0.9884 1791	0.9867 7704	0.9835 0551	4
5	0.9875 9321	0.9855 4341	0.9834 9871	0.9794 2457	5
6	0.9851 3038	0.9826 7726	0.9802 3127	0.9753 6057	6
7	0.9826 7370	0.9798 1946	0.9769 7469	0.9713 1343	7
8	0.9802 2314	0.9769 6996	0.9737 2893	0.9672 8308	8
9	0.9777 7869	0.9741 2875	0.9704 9395	0.9632 6946	9
10	0.9753 4034	0.9712 9580	0.9672 6972	0.9592 7249	10
11	0.9729 0807	0.9684 7110	0.9640 5620	0.9552 9211	11
12	0.9704 8187	0.9656 5460	0.9608 5335	0.9513 2824	12
13	0.9680 6171	0.9628 4630	0.9576 6115	0.9473 8082	13
14	0.9656 4759	0.9600 4617	0.9544 7955	0.9434 4978	14
15	0.9632 3949	0.9572 5418	0.9513 0852	0.9395 3505	15
16	0.9608 3740	0.9544 7030	0.9481 4803	0.9356 3656	16
17	0.9584 4130	0.9516 9453	0.9449 9803	0.9317 5425	17
18	0.9560 5117	0.9489 2682	0.9418 5851	0.9278 8805	18
19	0.9536 6700	0.9461 6717	0.9387 2941	0.9240 3789	19
20	0.9512 8878	0.9434 1554	0.9356 1071	0.9202 0371	20
21	0.9489 1649	0.9406 7191	0.9325 0236	0.9163 8544	21
22	0.9465 5011	0.9379 3627	0.9294 0435	0.9125 8301	22
23	0.9441 8964	0.9352 0857	0.9263 1663	0.9087 9636	23
24	0.9418 3505	0.9324 8881	0.9232 3916	0.9050 2542	24
25	0.9394 8634	0.9297 7696	0.9201 7192	0.9012 7012	25
26	0.9371 4348	0.9270 7300	0.9171 1487	0.8975 3041	26
27	0.9348 0646	0.9243 7690	0.9140 6798	0.8938 0622	27
28	0.9324 7527	0.9216 8864	0.9110 3121	0.8900 9748	28
29	0.9301 4990	0.9190 0820	0.9080 0453	0.8864 0413	29
30	0.9278 3032	0.9163 3556	0.9049 8790	0.8827 2610	30
31	0.9255 1653	0.9136 7068	0.9019 8130	0.8790 6334	31
32	0.9232 0851	0.9110 1356	0.8989 8468	0.8754 1577	32
33	0.9209 0624	0.9083 6416	0.8959 9802	0.8717 8334	33
34	0.9186 0972	0.9057 2247	0.8930 2128	0.8681 6599	34
35	0.9163 1892	0.9030 8847	0.8900 5444	0.8645 6364	35
36	0.9140 3384	0.9004 6212	0.8870 9745	0.8609 7624	36
37	0.9117 5445	0.8978 4341	0.8841 5028	0.8574 0372	37
38	0.9094 8075	0.8952 3231	0.8812 1290	0.8538 4603	38
39	0.9072 1272	0.8926 2881	0.8782 8528	0.8503 0310	39
40	0.9049 5034	0.8900 3288	0.8753 6739	0.8467 7487	40
41	0.9026 9361	0.8874 4450	0.8724 5920	0.8432 6128	41
42	0.9004 4250	0.8848 6365	0.8695 6066	0.8397 6227	42
43	0.8981 9701	0.8822 9030	0.8666 7175	0.8362 7778	43
44	0.8959 5712	0.8797 2444	0.8637 9245	0.8328 0775	44
45	0.8937 2281	0.8771 6604	0.8609 2270	0.8293 5211	45
46	0.8914 9407	0.8746 1508	0.8580 6249	0.8259 1082	46
47	0.8892 7090	0.8720 7153	0.8552 1179	0.8224 8380	47
48	0.8870 5326	0.8695 3539	0.8523 7055	0.8190 7100	48
49	0.8848 4116	0.8670 0662	0.8495 3876	0.8156 7237	49
50	0.8826 3457	0.8644 8520	0.8467 1637	0.8122 8784	50

TABLE IV.—Present Value of 1 at Compound Interest

$$v^n = (1 + i)^{-n}$$

n	$\frac{1}{4}\%$	$\frac{7}{24}\%$	$\frac{1}{3}\%$	$\frac{5}{12}\%$	n
51	0.8804 3349	0.8619 7112	0.8439 0336	0.8089 1735	51
52	0.8782 3790	0.8594 6435	0.8410 9969	0.8055 6084	52
53	0.8760 4778	0.8569 6487	0.8383 0534	0.8022 1827	53
54	0.8738 6312	0.8544 7266	0.8355 2027	0.7988 8956	54
55	0.8716 8391	0.8519 8769	0.8327 4446	0.7955 7467	55
56	0.8695 1013	0.8495 0995	0.8299 7787	0.7922 7353	56
57	0.8673 4178	0.8470 3942	0.8272 2047	0.7889 8608	57
58	0.8651 7883	0.8445 7608	0.8244 7222	0.7857 1228	58
59	0.8630 2128	0.8421 1989	0.8217 3311	0.7824 5207	59
60	0.8608 6911	0.8396 7085	0.8190 0310	0.7792 0538	60
61	0.8587 2230	0.8372 2893	0.8162 8216	0.7759 7216	61
62	0.8565 8085	0.8347 9412	0.8135 7026	0.7727 5236	62
63	0.8544 4474	0.8323 6638	0.8108 6737	0.7695 4591	63
64	0.8523 1395	0.8299 4571	0.8081 7346	0.7663 5278	64
65	0.8501 8848	0.8275 3207	0.8054 8850	0.7631 7289	65
66	0.8480 6831	0.8251 2545	0.8028 1246	0.7600 0620	66
67	0.8459 5343	0.8227 2584	0.8001 4531	0.7568 5265	67
68	0.8438 4382	0.8203 3320	0.7974 8702	0.7537 1218	68
69	0.8417 3947	0.8179 4752	0.7948 3756	0.7505 8474	69
70	0.8396 4037	0.8155 6878	0.7921 9690	0.7474 7028	70
71	0.8375 4650	0.8131 9695	0.7895 6502	0.7443 6874	71
72	0.8354 5786	0.8108 3202	0.7869 4188	0.7412 8008	72
73	0.8333 7442	0.8084 7397	0.7843 2745	0.7382 0423	73
74	0.8312 9618	0.8061 2278	0.7817 2171	0.7351 4114	74
75	0.8292 2312	0.8037 7843	0.7791 2463	0.7320 9076	75
76	0.8271 5523	0.8014 4089	0.7765 3618	0.7290 5304	76
77	0.8250 9250	0.7991 1015	0.7739 5632	0.7260 2792	77
78	0.8230 3491	0.7967 8619	0.7713 8504	0.7230 1536	78
79	0.8209 8246	0.7944 6899	0.7688 2230	0.7200 1529	79
80	0.8189 3512	0.7921 5853	0.7662 6807	0.7170 2768	80
81	0.8168 9289	0.7898 5479	0.7637 2233	0.7140 5246	81
82	0.8148 5575	0.7875 5774	0.7611 8505	0.7110 8959	82
83	0.8128 2369	0.7852 6738	0.7586 5619	0.7081 3901	83
84	0.8107 9670	0.7829 8368	0.7561 3574	0.7052 0067	84
85	0.8087 7476	0.7807 0662	0.7536 2366	0.7022 7453	85
86	0.8067 5787	0.7784 3618	0.7511 1993	0.6993 6052	86
87	0.8047 4600	0.7761 7234	0.7486 2451	0.6964 5861	87
88	0.8027 3915	0.7739 1509	0.7461 3739	0.6935 6874	88
89	0.8007 3731	0.7716 6440	0.7436 5853	0.6906 9086	89
90	0.7987 4046	0.7694 2026	0.7411 8790	0.6878 2493	90
91	0.7967 4859	0.7671 8264	0.7387 2548	0.6849 7088	91
92	0.7947 6168	0.7649 5153	0.7362 7125	0.6821 2868	92
93	0.7927 7973	0.7627 2691	0.7338 2516	0.6792 9827	93
94	0.7908 0273	0.7605 0876	0.7313 8720	0.6764 7960	94
95	0.7888 3065	0.7582 9706	0.7289 5735	0.6736 7263	95
96	0.7868 6349	0.7560 9179	0.7265 3556	0.6708 7731	96
97	0.7849 0124	0.7538 9294	0.7241 2182	0.6680 9359	97
98	0.7829 4388	0.7517 0048	0.7217 1610	0.6653 2141	98
99	0.7809 9140	0.7495 1439	0.7193 1837	0.6625 6074	99
100	0.7790 4379	0.7473 3467	0.7169 2861	0.6598 1153	100

TABLE IV.—Present Value of 1 at Compound Interest

$$v^n = (1 + i)^{-n}$$

n	¼%	⁷⁄₂₄%	⅓%	⁵⁄₁₂%	n
101	0.7771 0104	0.7451 6128	0.7145 4681	0.6570 7372	101
102	0.7751 6313	0.7429 9421	0.7121 7290	0.6543 4727	102
104	0.7732 3006	0.7408 3345	0.7098 0688	0.6516 3214	103
104	0.7713 0180	0.7386 7897	0.7074 4872	0.6489 2827	104
105	0.7693 7836	0.7365 3075	0.7050 9839	0.6462 3562	105
106	0.7674 5971	0.7343 8879	0.7027 5587	0.6435 5415	106
107	0.7655 4584	0.7322 5305	0.7004 2114	0.6408 8380	107
108	0.7636 3675	0.7301 2352	0.6980 9416	0.6382 2453	108
109	0.7617 3242	0.7280 0019	0.6957 7491	0.6355 7630	109
110	0.7598 3284	0.7258 8303	0.6934 6336	0.6329 3905	110
111	0.7579 3799	0.7237 7203	0.6911 5950	0.6303 1275	111
112	0.7560 4787	0.7216 6716	0.6888 6329	0.6276 9734	112
113	0,7541 6247	0.7195 6842	0.6865 7470	0.6250 9279	113
114	0.7522 8176	0.7174 7578	0.6842 9372	0.6224 9904	114
115	0.7504 0575	0.7153 8923	0.6820 2032	0.6199 1606	115
116	0.7485 3441	0.7133 0875	0.6797 5448	0.6173 4379	116
117	0.7466 6774	0.7112 3431	0.6774 9616	0.6147 8220	117
118	0.7448 0573	0.7091 6591	0.6752 4534	0.6122 3123	118
119	0.7429 4836	0.7071 0353	0.6730 0200	0.6096 9086	119
120	0.7410 9562	0.7050 4714	0.6707 6611	0.6071 6102	120
121	0.7392 4750	0.7029 9673	0.6685 3765	0.6046 4168	121
122	0.7374 0399	0.7009 5229	0.6663 1660	0.6021 3279	122
123	0.7355 6508	0.6989 1379	0.6641 0292	0.5996 3431	123
124	0.7337 3075	0.6968 8122	0.6618 9660	0.5971 4620	124
125	0.7319 0100	0.6948 5456	0.6596 9761	0.5946 6842	125
126	0.7300 7581	0.6928 3379	0.6575 0592	0.5922 0091	126
127	0.7282 5517	0.6908 1890	0.6553 2152	0.5897 4365	127
128	0.7264 3907	0.6888 0988	0.6531 4437	0.5872 9658	128
129	0.7246 2750	0.6868 0669	0.6509 7445	0.5848 5966	129
130	0.7228 2045	0.6848 0933	0.6488 1175	0.5824 3286	130
131	0.7210 1791	0.6828 1778	0.6466 5623	0.5800 1613	131
132	0.7192 1986	0.6808 3202	0.6445 0787	0.5776 0942	132
133	0.7174 2629	0.6788 5203	0.6423 6665	0.5752 1270	133
134	0.7156 3720	0.6768 7780	0.6402 3254	0.5728 2593	134
135	0.7138 5257	0.6749 0932	0.6381 0552	0.5704 4906	135
136	0.7120 7239	0.6729 4656	0.6359 8557	0.5680 8205	136
137	0.7102 9664	0.6709 8950	0.6338 7266	0.5657 2486	137
138	0.7085 2533	0.6690 3814	0.6317 6677	0.5633 7745	138
139	0.7067 5843	0.6670 9246	0.6296 6788	0.5610 3979	139
140	0.7049 9595	0.6651 5243	0.6275 7596	0.5587 1182	140
141	0.7032 3785	0.6632 1804	0.6254 9099	0.5563 9351	141
142	0.7014 8414	0.6612 8928	0.6234 1295	0.5540 8483	142
143	0.6997 3480	0.6593 6613	0.6213 4181	0.5517 8572	143
144	0.6979 8983	0.6574 4857	0.6192 7755	0.5494 9615	144
145	0.6962 4921	0.6555 3659	0.6172 2015	0.5472 1609	145
146	0.6945 1292	0.6536 3017	0.6151 6958	0.5449 4548	146
147	0.6927 8097	0.6517 2929	0.6131 2583	0.5426 8429	147
148	0.6910 5334	0.6498 3394	0.6110 8887	0 5404 3249	148
149	0.6893 3001	0.6479 4410	0.6090 5867	0 5381 9003	149
150	0.6876 1098	0.6460 5976	0.6070 3522	0 5359 5688	150

TABLE IV.—Present Value of 1 at Compound Interest

$$v^n = (1 + i)^{-n}$$

n	¼%	⁷⁄₂₄%	⅓%	⁵⁄₁₂%	n
151	0.6858 9624	0.6441 8090	0.6050 1849	0.5337 3299	151
152	0.6841 8578	0.6423 0750	0.6030 0847	0.5315 1833	152
153	0.6824 7958	0.6404 3956	0.6010 0512	0.5293 1286	153
154	0.6807 7764	0.6385 7704	0.5990 0842	0.5271 1654	154
155	0.6790 7994	0.6367 1994	0.5970 1836	0.5249 2934	155
156	0.6773 8647	0.6348 6824	0.5950 3491	0.5227 5121	156
157	0.6756 9723	0.6330 2193	0.5930 5805	0.5205 8211	157
158	0.6740 1220	0.6311 8098	0.5910 8776	0.5184 2202	158
159	0.6723 3137	0.6293 4539	0.5891 2401	0.5162 7089	159
160	0.6706 5473	0.6275 1514	0.5871 6679	0.5141 2869	160
161	0.6689 8228	0.6256 9021	0.5852 1607	0.5119 9538	161
162	0.6673 1399	0.6238 7058	0.5832 7183	0.5098 7091	162
163	0.6656 4987	0.6220 5625	0.5813 3405	0.5077 5527	163
164	0.6639 8989	0.6202 4720	0.5794 0271	0.5056 4840	164
165	0.6623 3406	0.6184 4341	0.5774 7778	0.5035 5027	165
166	0.6606 8235	0.6166 4486	0.5755 5925	0.5014 6085	166
167	0.6590 3476	0.6148 5154	0.5736 4710	0.4993 8010	167
168	0.6573 9129	0.6130 6344	0.5717 4129	0.4973 0798	168
169	0.6557 5191	0.6112 8054	0.5698 4182	0.4952 4447	169
170	0.6541 1661	0.6095 0282	0.5679 4866	0.4931 8951	170
171	0.6524 8540	0.6077 3027	0.5660 6178	0.4911 4308	171
172	0.6508 5826	0.6059 6288	0.5641 8118	0.4891 0514	172
173	0.6492 3517	0.6042 0063	0.5623 0682	0.4870 7566	173
174	0.6476 1613	0.6024 4350	0.5604 3870	0.4850 5460	174
175	0.6460 0112	0.6006 9149	0.5585 7677	0.4830 4192	175
176	0.6443 9015	0.5989 4456	0.5567 2104	0.4810 3760	176
177	0.6427 8319	0.5972 0272	0.5548 7147	0.4790 4159	177
178	0.6411 8024	0.5954 6595	0.5530 2804	0.4770 5387	178
179	0.6395 8129	0.5937 3422	0.5511 9074	0.4750 7439	179
180	0.6379 8632	0.5920 0753	0.5493 5954	0.4731 0313	180
181	0.6363 9533	0.5902 8586	0.5475 3442	0.4711 4005	181
182	0.6348 0831	0.5885 6920	0.5457 1537	0.4691 8511	182
183	0.6332 2525	0.5868 5754	0.5439 0237	0.4672 3828	183
184	0.6316 4613	0.5851 5085	0.5420 9538	0.4652 9953	184
185	0.6300 7096	0.5834 4912	0.5402 9440	0.4633 6883	185
186	0.6284 9971	0.5817 5234	0.5384 9940	0.4614 4614	186
187	0.6269 3238	0.5800 6050	0.5367 1037	0.4595 3142	187
188	0.6253 6895	0.5783 7357	0.5349 2728	0.4576 2465	188
189	0.6238 0943	0.5766 9156	0.5331 5011	0.4557 2580	189
190	0.6222 5380	0.5750 1443	0.5313 7885	0.4538 3482	190
191	0.6207 0204	0.5733 4218	0.5296 1347	0.4519 5168	191
192	0.6191 5416	0.5716 7480	0.5278 5396	0.4500 7637	192
193	0.6176 1013	0.5700 1226	0.5261 0029	0.4482 0883	193
194	0.6160 6996	0.5683 5456	0.5243 5245	0.4463 4904	194
195	0.6145 3362	0.5667 0168	0.5226 1041	0.4444 9697	195
196	0.6130 0112	0.5650 5361	0.5208 7417	0.4426 5258	196
197	0.6114 7244	0.5634 1033	0.5191 4369	0.4408 1585	197
198	0.6099 4757	0.5617 7183	0.5174 1896	0.4389 8674	198
199	0.6084 2650	0.5601 3809	0.5156 9996	0.4371 6522	199
200	0.6069 0923	0.5585 0911	0.5139 8667	0.4353 5125	200

TABLE IV.—Present Value of 1 at Compound Interest

$$v^n = (1 + i)^{-n}$$

n	½%	⁷⁄₁₂%	⅝%	⅔%	n
1	0.9950 2488	0.9942 0050	0.9937 8882	0.9933 7748	1
2	0.9900 7450	0.9884 3463	0.9876 1622	0.9867 9882	2
3	0.9851 4876	0.9827 0220	0.9814 8196	0.9802 6373	3
4	0.9802 4752	0.9770 0302	0.9753 8580	0.9737 7192	4
5	0.9753 7067	0.9713 3688	0.9693 2750	0.9673 2310	5
6	0.9705 1808	0.9657 0361	0.9633 0683	0.9609 1699	6
7	0.9656 8963	0.9601 0301	0.9573 2356	0.9545 5330	7
8	0.9608 8520	0.9545 3489	0.9513 7745	0.9482 3175	8
9	0.9561 0468	0.9489 9907	0.9454 6827	0.9419 5207	9
10	0.9513 4794	0.9434 9534	0.9395 9580	0.9357 1398	10
11	0.9466 1489	0.9380 2354	0.9337 5980	0.9295 1720	11
12	0.9419 0534	0.9325 8347	0.9279 6005	0.9233 6145	12
13	0.9372 1924	0.9271 7495	0.9221 9632	0.9172 4648	13
14	0.9325 5646	0.9217 9780	0.9164 6840	0.9111 7200	14
15	0.9279 1688	0.9164 5183	0.9107 7604	0.9051 3775	15
16	0.9233 0037	0.9111 3686	0.9051 1905	0.8991 4346	16
17	0.9187 0684	0.9058 5272	0.8994 9719	0.8931 8886	17
18	0.9141 3616	0.9005 9923	0.8939 1025	0.8872 7371	18
19	0.9095 8822	0.8953 7620	0.8883 5802	0.8813 9772	19
20	0.9050 6290	0.8901 8346	0.8828 4027	0.8755 6065	20
21	0.9005 6010	0.8850 2084	0.8773 5679	0.8697 6224	21
22	0.8960 7971	0.8798 8816	0.8719 0736	0.8640 0222	22
23	0.8916 2160	0.8747 8525	0.8664 9179	0.8582 8035	23
24	0.8871 8567	0.8697 1193	0.8611 0985	0.8525 9638	24
25	0.8827 7181	0.8646 6803	0.8557 6135	0.8469 5004	25
26	0.8783 7991	0.8596 5339	0.8504 4606	0.8413 4110	26
27	0.8740 0986	0.8546 6782	0.8451 6378	0.8357 6931	27
28	0.8696 6155	0.8497 1118	0.8399 1432	0.8302 3441	28
29	0.8653 3488	0.8447 8327	0.8346 9746	0.8247 3617	29
30	0.8610 2973	0.8398 8395	0.8295 1300	0.8192 7434	30
31	0.8567 4600	0.8350 1304	0.8243 6075	0.8138 4868	31
32	0.8524 8358	0.8301 7038	0.8192 4050	0.8084 5896	32
33	0.8482 4237	0.8253 5581	0.8141 5205	0.8031 0492	33
34	0.8440 2226	0.8205 6915	0.8090 9520	0.7977 8635	34
35	0.8398 2314	0.8158 1026	0.8040 6976	0.7925 0299	35
36	0.8356 4492	0.8110 7897	0.7990 7554	0.7872 5463	36
37	0.8314 8748	0.8063 7511	0.7941 1234	0.7820 4102	37
38	0.8273 5073	0.8016 9854	0.7891 7997	0.7768 6194	38
39	0.8232 3455	0.7970 4908	0.7842 7823	0.7717 1716	39
40	0.8191 3886	0.7924 2660	0.7794 0693	0.7666 0645	40
41	0.8150 6354	0.7878 3092	0.7745 6590	0.7615 2959	41
42	0.8110 0850	0.7832 6189	0.7697 5493	0.7564 8635	42
43	0.8069 7363	0.7787 1936	0.7649 7384	0.7514 7650	43
44	0.8029 5884	0.7742 0317	0.7602 2245	0.7464 9984	44
45	0.7989 6402	0.7697 1318	0.7555 0057	0.7415 5613	45
46	0.7949 8907	0.7652 4923	0.7508 0802	0.7366 4516	46
47	0.7910 3390	0.7608 1116	0.7461 4462	0.7317 6672	47
48	0.7870 9841	0.7563 9884	0.7415 1018	0.7269 2058	48
49	0.7831 8250	0.7520 1210	0.7369 0453	0.7221 0654	49
50	0.7792 8607	0.7476 5080	0.7323 2748	0.7173 2437	50

TABLE IV.—Present Value of 1 at Compound Interest

$$v^n = (1 + i)^{-n}$$

n	½%	⁷⁄₁₂%	⅝%	⅔%	n
51	0.7754 0902	0.7433 1480	0.7277 7886	0.7125 7388	51
52	0.7715 5127	0.7390 0394	0.7232 5849	0.7078 5485	52
53	0.7677 1270	0.7347 1809	0.7187 6620	0.7031 6707	53
54	0.7638 9324	0.7304 5709	0.7143 0182	0.6985 1033	54
55	0.7600 9277	0.7262 2080	0.7098 6516	0.6938 8444	55
56	0.7563 1122	0.7220 0908	0.7054 5606	0.6892 8918	56
57	0.7525 4847	0.7178 2179	0.7010 7434	0.6847 2435	57
58	0.7488 0445	0.7136 5878	0.6967 1985	0.6801 8975	58
59	0.7450 7906	0.7095 1991	0.6923 9239	0.6756 8518	59
60	0.7413 7220	0.7054 0505	0.6880 9182	0.6712 1044	60
61	0.7376 8378	0.7013 1405	0.6838 1796	0.6667 6534	61
62	0.7340 1371	0.6972 4678	0.6795 7064	0.6623 4968	62
63	0.7303 6190	0.6932 0310	0.6753 4970	0.6579 6326	63
64	0.7267 2826	0.6891 8286	0.6711 5499	0.6536 0588	64
65	0.7231 1269	0.6851 8594	0.6669 8632	0.6492 7737	65
66	0.7195 1512	0.6812 1221	0.6628 4355	0.6449 7752	66
67	0.7159 3544	0.6772 6151	0.6587 2651	0.6407 0614	67
68	0.7123 7357	0.6733 3373	0.6546 3504	0.6364 6306	68
69	0.7088 2943	0.6694 2873	0.6505 6898	0.6322 4807	69
70	0.7053 0291	0.6655 4638	0.6465 2818	0.6280 6100	70
71	0.7017 9394	0.6616 8654	0.6425 1248	0.6239 0165	71
72	0.6983 0243	0.6578 4909	0.6385 2172	0.6197 6985	72
73	0.6948 2829	0.6540 3389	0.6345 5574	0.6156 6541	73
74	0.6913 7143	0.6502 4082	0.6306 1440	0.6115 8816	74
75	0.6879 3177	0.6464 6975	0.6266 9754	0.6075 3791	75
76	0.6845 0923	0.6427 2054	0.6228 0501	0.6035 1448	76
77	0.6811 0371	0.6389 9308	0.6189 3666	0.5995 1769	77
78	0.6777 1513	0.6352 8724	0.6150 9233	0.5955 4738	78
79	0.6743 4342	0.6316 0289	0.6112 7188	0.5916 0336	79
80	0.6709 8847	0.6279 3991	0.6074 7516	0.5876 8545	80
81	0.6676 5022	0.6242 9817	0.6037 0203	0.5837 9350	81
82	0.6643 2858	0.6206 7755	0.5999 5232	0.5799 2732	82
83	0.6610 2346	0.6170 7793	0.5962 2591	0.5760 8674	83
84	0.6577 3479	0.6134 9919	0.5925 2264	0.5722 7159	84
85	0.6544 6248	0.6099 4120	0.5888 4238	0.5684 8171	85
86	0.6512 0644	0.6064 0384	0.5851 8497	0.5647 1693	86
87	0.6479 6661	0.6028 8700	0.5815 5028	0.5609 7709	87
88	0.6447 4290	0.5993 9056	0.5779 3817	0.5572 6201	88
89	0.6415 3522	0.5959 1439	0.5743 4849	0.5535 7153	89
90	0.6383 4350	0.5924 5838	0.5707 8111	0.5499 0549	90
91	0.6351 6766	0.5890 2242	0.5672 3589	0.5462 6374	91
92	0.6320 0763	0.5856 0638	0.5637 1268	0.5426 4610	92
93	0.6288 6331	0.5822 1015	0.5602 1136	0.5390 5241	93
94	0.6257 3464	0.5788 3363	0.5567 3179	0.5354 8253	94
95	0.6226 2153	0.5754 7668	0.5532 7383	0.5319 3629	95
96	0.6195 2391	0.5721 3920	0.5498 3734	0.5284 1353	96
97	0.6164 4170	0.5688 2108	0.5464 2220	0.5249 1410	97
98	0.6133 7483	0.5655 2220	0.5430 2828	0.5214 3785	98
99	0.6103 2321	0.5622 4245	0.5396 5543	0.5179 8462	99
100	0.6072 8678	0.5589 8172	0.5363 0353	0.5145 5426	100

TABLE IV.—Present Value of 1 at Compound Interest

$$v^n = (1 + i)^{-n}$$

n	½%	⁷⁄₁₂%	⅝%	⅔%	n
101	0.6042 6545	0.5557 3991	0.5329 7246	0.5111 4660	101
102	0.6012 5915	0.5525 1689	0.5296 6207	0.5077 6152	102
103	0.5982 6781	0.5493 1257	0.5263 7225	0.5043 9886	103
104	0.5952 9136	0.5461 2683	0.5231 0285	0.5010 5847	104
105	0.5923 2971	0.5429 5957	0.5198 5377	0.4977 4020	105
106	0.5893 8279	0.5398 1067	0.5166 2486	0.4944 4391	106
107	0.5864 5054	0.5366 8004	0.5134 1601	0.4911 6945	107
108	0.5835 3288	0.5335 6756	0.5102 2709	0.4879 1667	108
109	0.5806 2973	0.5304 7313	0.5070 5798	0.4846 8543	109
110	0.5777 4102	0.5273 9665	0.5039 0855	0.4814 7559	110
111	0.5748 6669	0.5243 3801	0.5007 7868	0.4782 8701	111
112	0.5720 0666	0.5212 9711	0.4976 6826	0.4751 1955	112
113	0.5691 6085	0.5182 7385	0.4945 7715	0.4719 7306	113
114	0.5663 2921	0.5152 6812	0.4915 0524	0.4688 4741	114
115	0.5635 1165	0.5122 7982	0.4884 5242	0.4657 4246	115
116	0.5607 0811	0.5093 0885	0.4854 1855	0.4626 5808	116
117	0.5579 1852	0.5063 5512	0.4824 0353	0.4595 9411	117
118	0.5551 4280	0.5034 1851	0.4794 0723	0.4565 5044	118
119	0.5523 8090	0.5004 9893	0.4764 2955	0.4535 2693	119
120	0.5496 3273	0.4975 9629	0.4734 7036	0.4505 2344	120
121	0.5468 9824	0.4947 1047	0.4705 2955	0.4475 3984	121
122	0.5441 7736	0.4918 4140	0.4676 0700	0.4445 7600	122
123	0.5414 7001	0.4889 8896	0.4647 0261	0.4416 3179	123
124	0.5387 7612	0.4861 5307	0.4618 1626	0.4387 0708	124
125	0.5360 9565	0.4833 3363	0.4589 4784	0.4358 0173	125
126	0.5334 2850	0.4805 3053	0.4560 9723	0.4329 1563	126
127	0.5307 7463	0.4777 4369	0.4532 6433	0.4300 4864	127
128	0.5281 3396	0.4749 7302	0.4504 4902	0.4272 0063	128
129	0.5255 0643	0.4722 1841	0.4476 5120	0.4243 7149	129
130	0.5228 9197	0.4694 7978	0.4448 7076	0.4215 6108	130
131	0.5202 9052	0.4667 5703	0.4421 0759	0.4187 6929	131
132	0.5177 0201	0.4640 5007	0.4393 6158	0.4159 9598	132
133	0.5151 2637	0.4613 5881	0.4366 3262	0.4132 4104	133
134	0.5125 6356	0.4586 8316	0.4339 2062	0.4105 0434	134
135	0.5100 1349	0.4560 2303	0.4312 2546	0.4077 8577	135
136	0.5074 7611	0.4533 7832	0.4285 4704	0.4050 8520	136
137	0.5049 5135	0.4507 4895	0.4258 8526	0.4024 0252	137
138	0.5024 3916	0.4481 3483	0.4232 4001	0.3997 3760	138
139	0.4999 3946	0.4455 3587	0.4206 1119	0.3970 9033	139
140	0.4974 5220	0.4429 5198	0.4179 9870	0.3944 6059	140
141	0.4949 7731	0.4403 8308	0.4154 0243	0.3918 4827	141
142	0.4925 1474	0.4378 2908	0.4128 2229	0.3892 5325	142
143	0.4900 6442	0.4352 8989	0.4102 5818	0.3866 7541	143
144	0.4876 2628	0.4327 6542	0.4077 0999	0.3841 1465	144
145	0.4852 0028	0.4302 5560	0.4051 7763	0.3815 7084	145
146	0.4827 8635	0.4277 6033	0.4026 6100	0.3790 4389	146
147	0.4803 8443	0.4252 7953	0.4001 6000	0.3765 3366	147
148	0.4779 9446	0.4228 1312	0.3976 7453	0.3740 4006	148
149	0.4756 1637	0.4203 6102	0.3952 0451	0.3715 6297	159
150	0.4732 5012	0.4179 2313	0.3927 4982	0.3691 0229	150

TABLE IV.—Present Value of 1 at Compound Interest

$$v^n = (1 + i)^{-n}$$

n	½%	⁷⁄₁₂%	⅝%	⅔%	n
151	0.4708 9565	0.4154 9939	0.3903 1038	0.3666 5791	151
152	0.4685 5288	0.4130 8970	0.3878 8609	0.3642 2971	152
153	0.4662 2177	0.4106 9398	0.3854 7686	0.3618 1759	153
154	0.4639 0226	0.4083 1216	0.3830 8259	0.3594 2145	154
155	0.4615 9429	0.4059 4416	0.3807 0320	0.3570 4117	155
156	0.4592 9780	0.4035 8988	0.3783 3858	0.3546 7666	156
157	0.4570 1274	0.4012 4926	0.3759 8865	0.3523 2781	157
158	0.4547 3904	0.3989 2221	0.3736 5332	0.3499 9451	158
159	0.4524 7666	0.3966 0866	0.3713 3249	0.3476 7667	159
160	0.4502 2553	0.3943 0853	0.3690 2608	0.3453 7417	160
161	0.4479 8560	0.3920 2174	0.3667 3399	0.3430 8693	161
162	0.4457 5682	0.3897 4821	0.3644 5614	0.3408 1483	162
163	0.4435 3912	0.3874 8786	0.3621 9244	0.3385 5778	163
164	0.4413 3246	0.3852 4062	0.3599 4280	0.3363 1567	164
165	0.4391 3678	0.3830 0642	0.3577 0713	0.3340 8841	165
166	0.4369 5202	0.3807 8517	0.3554 8534	0.3318 7591	166
167	0.4347 7813	0.3785 7681	0.3532 7736	0.3296 7805	167
168	0.4326 1505	0.3763 8125	0.3510 8309	0.3274 9476	168
169	0.4304 6274	0.3741 9843	0.3489 0245	0.3253 2592	169
170	0.4283 2113	0.3720 2826	0.3467 3535	0.3231 7144	170
171	0.4261 9018	0.3698 7068	0.3445 8172	0.3210 3123	171
172	0.4240 6983	0.3677 2562	0.3424 4146	0.3189 0520	172
173	0.4219 6003	0.3655 9299	0.3403 1449	0.3167 9324	173
174	0.4198 6073	0.3634 7273	0.3382 0074	0.3146 9527	174
175	0.4177 7187	0.3613 6477	0.3361 0011	0.3126 1120	175
176	0.4156 9340	0.3592 6904	0.3340 1254	0.3105 4093	176
177	0.4136 2528	0.3571 8546	0.3319 3792	0.3084 8436	177
178	0.4115 6744	0.3551 1396	0.3298 7620	0.3064 4142	178
179	0.4095 1984	0.3530 5447	0.3278 2728	0.3044 1201	179
180	0.4074 8243	0.3510 0693	0.3257 9108	0.3023 9603	180
181	0.4054 5515	0.3489 7127	0.3237 6754	0.3003 9341	181
182	0.4034 3796	0.3469 4741	0.3217 5656	0.2984 0405	182
183	0.4014 3081	0.3449 3529	0.3197 5807	0.2964 2786	183
184	0.3994 3364	0.3429 3483	0.3177 7199	0.2944 6477	184
185	0.3974 4641	0.3409 4598	0.3157 9825	0.2925 1467	185
186	0.3954 6906	0.3389 6866	0.3138 3677	0.2905 7748	186
187	0.3935 0155	0.3370 0281	0.3118 8748	0.2886 5313	187
188	0.3915 4383	0.3350 4837	0.3099 5029	0.2867 4152	188
189	0.3895 9586	0.3331 0525	0.3080 2513	0.2848 4257	189
190	0.3876 5757	0.3311 7341	0.3061 1193	0.2829 5619	190
191	0.3857 2892	0.3292 5277	0.3042 1062	0.2810 8231	191
192	0.3838 0987	0.3273 4326	0.3023 2111	0.2792 2084	192
193	0.3819 0037	0.3254 4484	0.3004 4334	0.2773 7170	193
194	0.3800 0037	0.3235 5742	0.2985 7723	0.2755 3480	194
195	0.3781 0982	0.3216 8095	0.2967 2271	0.2737 1006	195
196	0.3762 2868	0.3198 1536	0.2948 7972	0.2718 9741	196
197	0.3743 5689	0.3179 6059	0.2930 4816	0.2700 9677	197
198	0.3724 9442	0.3161 1657	0.2912 2799	0.2683 0805	198
199	0.3706 4121	0.3142 8325	0.2894 1912	0.2665 3117	199
200	0.3687 9723	0.3124 6057	0.2876 2149	0.2647 6607	200

TABLE IV.—Present Value of 1 at Compound Interest

$$v^n = (1 + i)^{-n}$$

n	¾%	⅞%	1%	1⅛%	n
1	0.9925 5583	0.9913 2590	0.9900 9901	0.9888 7515	1
2	0.9851 6708	0.9827 2704	0.9802 9605	0.9778 7407	2
3	0.9778 3333	0.9742 0276	0.9705 9015	0.9669 9537	3
4	0.9705 5417	0.9657 5243	0.9609 8034	0.9562 3770	4
5	0.9633 2920	0.9573 7539	0.9514 6569	0.9455 9970	5
6	0.9561 5802	0.9490 7102	0.9420 4524	0.9350 8005	6
7	0.9490 4022	0.9408 3868	0.9327 1805	0.9246 7743	7
8	0.9419 7540	0.9326 7775	0.9234 8322	0.9143 9054	8
9	0.9349 6318	0.9245 8761	0.9143 3982	0.9042 1808	9
10	0.9280 0315	0.9165 6765	0.9052 8695	0.8941 5881	10
11	0.9210 9494	0.9086 1724	0.8963 2372	0.8842 1142	11
12	0.9142 3815	0.9007 3581	0.8874 4923	0.8743 7470	12
13	0.9074 3241	0.8929 2273	0.8786 6260	0.8646 4742	13
14	0.9006 7733	0.8851 7743	0.8699 6297	0.8550 2835	14
15	0.8939 7254	0.8774 9931	0.8613 4947	0.8455 1629	15
16	0.8873 1766	0.8698 8779	0.8528 2126	0.8361 1005	16
17	0.8807 1231	0.8623 4230	0.8443 7749	0.8268 0846	17
18	0.8741 5614	0.8548 6225	0.8360 1731	0.8176 1034	18
19	0.8676 4878	0.8474 4709	0.8277 3992	0.8085 1455	19
20	0.8611 8985	0.8400 9624	0.8195 4447	0.7995 1995	20
21	0.8547 7901	0.8328 0917	0.8114 3017	0.7906 2542	21
22	0.8484 1589	0.8255 8530	0.8033 9621	0.7818 2983	22
23	0.8421 0014	0.8184 2409	0.7954 4179	0.7731 3210	23
24	0.8358 3140	0.8113 2499	0.7875 6613	0.7645 3112	24
25	0.8296 0933	0.8042 8748	0.7797 6844	0.7560 2583	25
26	0.8234 3358	0.7973 1101	0.7720 4796	0.7476 1516	26
27	0.8173 0380	0.7903 9505	0.7644 0392	0.7392 9806	27
28	0.8112 1966	0.7835 3908	0.7568 3557	0.7310 7348	28
29	0.8051 8080	0.7767 4258	0.7493 4215	0.7229 4040	29
30	0.7991 8690	0.7700 0504	0.7419 2292	0.7148 9780	30
31	0.7932 3762	0.7633 2594	0.7345 7715	0.7069 4467	31
32	0.7873 3262	0.7567 0477	0.7273 0411	0.6990 8002	32
33	0.7814 7158	0.7501 4104	0.7201 0307	0.6913 0287	33
34	0.7756 5418	0.7436 3424	0.7129 7334	0.6836 1223	34
35	0.7698 8008	0.7371 8388	0.7059 1420	0.6760 0715	35
36	0.7641 4896	0.7307 8947	0.6989 2495	0.6684 8667	36
37	0.7584 6051	0.7244 5053	0.6920 0490	0.6610 4986	37
38	0.7528 1440	0.7181 6657	0.6851 5337	0.6536 9578	38
39	0.7472 1032	0.7119 3712	0.6783 6967	0.6464 2352	39
40	0.7416 4796	0.7057 6171	0.6716 5314	0.6392 3216	40
41	0.7361 2701	0.6996 3986	0.6650 0311	0.6321 2080	41
42	0.7306 4716	0.6935 7111	0.6584 1892	0.6250 8855	42
43	0.7252 0809	0.6875 5500	0.6518 9992	0.6181 3454	43
44	0.7198 0952	0.6815 9108	0.6454 4546	0.6112 5789	44
45	0.7144 5114	0.6756 7889	0.6390 5492	0.6044 5774	45
46	0.7091 3264	0.6698 1798	0.6327 2764	0.5977 3324	46
47	0.7038 5374	0.6640 0792	0.6264 6301	0.5910 8355	47
48	0.6986 1414	0.6582 4824	0.6202 6041	0.5845 0784	48
49	0.6934 1353	0.6525 3853	0.6141 1921	0.5780 0528	49
50	0.6882 5165	0.6468 7835	0.6080 3882	0.5715 7506	50

TABLE IV.—Present Value of 1 at Compound Interest

$$v^n = (1 + i)^{-n}$$

n	$\frac{3}{4}\%$	$\frac{7}{8}\%$	1%	$1\frac{1}{8}\%$	n
51	0.6831 2819	0.6412 6726	0.6020 1864	0.5652 1637	51
52	0.6780 4286	0.6357 0484	0.5960 5806	0.5589 2843	52
53	0.6729 9540	0.6301 9067	0.5901 5649	0.5527 1044	53
54	0.6679 8551	0.6247 2433	0.5843 1336	0.5465 6162	54
55	0.6630 1291	0.6193 0541	0.5785 2808	0.5404 8120	55
56	0.6580 7733	0.6139 3349	0.5728 0008	0.5344 6843	56
57	0.6531 7849	0.6086 0817	0.5671 2879	0.5285 2256	57
58	0.6483 1612	0.6033 2904	0.5615 1365	0.5226 4282	58
59	0.6434 8995	0.5980 9571	0.5559 5411	0.5168 2850	59
60	0.6386 9970	0.5929 0776	0.5504 4962	0.5110 7887	60
61	0.6339 4511	0.5877 6482	0.5449 9962	0.5053 9319	61
62	0.6292 2592	0.5826 6649	0.5396 0358	0.4997 7077	62
63	0.6245 4185	0.5776 1238	0.5342 6097	0.4942 1090	63
64	0.6198 9266	0.5726 0211	0.5289 7126	0.4887 1288	64
65	0.6152 7807	0.5676 3530	0.5237 3392	0.4832 7602	65
66	0.6106 9784	0.5627 1158	0.5185 4844	0.4778 9965	66
67	0.6061 5170	0.5578 3056	0.5134 1429	0.4725 8309	67
68	0.6016 3940	0.5529 9188	0.5083 3099	0.4673 2568	68
69	0.5971 6070	0.5481 9517	0.5032 9801	0.4621 2675	69
70	0.5927 1533	0.5434 4007	0.4983 1486	0.4569 8566	70
71	0.5883 0306	0.5387 2622	0.4933 8105	0.4519 0177	71
72	0.5839 2363	0.5340 5325	0.4884 9609	0.4468 7443	72
73	0.5795 7681	0.5294 2082	0.4836 5949	0.4419 0302	73
74	0.5752 6234	0.5248 2857	0.4788 7078	0.4369 8692	74
75	0.5709 7999	0.5202 7615	0.4741 2949	0.4321 2551	75
76	0.5667 2952	0.5157 6322	0.4694 3514	0.4273 1818	76
77	0.5625 1069	0.5112 8944	0.4647 8726	0.4225 6433	77
78	0.5583 2326	0.5068 5447	0.4601 8541	0.4178 6337	78
79	0.5541 6701	0.5024 5796	0.4556 2912	0.4132 1470	79
80	0.5500 4170	0.4980 9959	0.4511 1794	0.4086 1775	80
81	0.5459 4710	0.4937 7902	0.4466 5142	0.4040 7194	81
82	0.5418 8297	0.4894 9593	0.4422 2913	0.3995 7670	82
83	0.5378 4911	0.4852 4999	0.4378 5063	0.3951 3148	83
84	0.5338 4527	0.4810 4089	0.4335 1547	0.3907 3570	84
85	0.5298 7123	0.4768 6829	0.4292 2324	0.3863 8882	85
86	0.5259 2678	0.4727 3188	0.4249 7350	0.3820 9031	86
87	0.5220 1169	0.4686 3136	0.4207 6585	0.3778 3961	87
88	0.5181 2575	0.4645 6640	0.4165 9985	0.3736 3621	88
89	0.5142 6873	0.4605 3671	0.4124 7510	0.3694 7956	89
90	0.5104 4043	0.4565 4197	0.4083 9119	0.3653 6916	90
91	0.5066 4063	0.4525 8187	0.4043 4771	0.3613 0448	91
92	0.5028 6911	0.4486 5613	0.4003 4427	0.3572 8503	92
93	0.4991 2567	0.4447 6444	0.3963 8046	0.3533 1029	93
94	0.4954 1009	0.4409 0651	0.3924 5590	0.3493 7976	94
95	0.4917 2217	0.4370 8204	0.3885 7020	0.3454 9297	95
96	0.4880 6171	0.4332 9075	0.3847 2297	0.3416 4941	96
97	0.4844 2850	0.4295 3234	0.3809 1383	0.3378 4861	97
98	0.4808 2233	0.4258 0654	0.3771 4241	0.3340 9010	98
99	0.4772 4301	0.4221 1305	0.3734 0832	0.3303 7340	99
100	0.4736 9033	0.4184 5159	0.3697 1121	0.3266 9805	100

TABLE IV.—Present Value of 1 at Compound Interest

$$v^n = (1+i)^{-n}$$

n	$1\frac{1}{4}\%$	$1\frac{3}{8}\%$	$1\frac{1}{2}\%$	$1\frac{3}{4}\%$	n
1	0.9876 5432	0.9864 3650	0.9852 2167	0.9828 0098	1
2	0.9754 6106	0.9730 5696	0.9706 6175	0.9658 9777	2
3	0.9634 1833	0.9598 5890	0.9563 1699	0.9492 8528	3
4	0.9515 2428	0.9468 3986	0.9421 8423	0.9329 5851	4
5	0.9397 7706	0.9339 9739	0.9282 6033	0.9169 1254	5
6	0.9281 7488	0.9213 2912	0.9145 4219	0.9011 4254	6
7	0.9167 1593	0.9088 3267	0.9010 2679	0.8856 4378	7
8	0.9053 9845	0.8965 0571	0.8877 1112	0.8704 1157	8
9	0.8942 2069	0.8843 4596	0.8745 9224	0.8554 4135	9
10	0.8831 8093	0.8723 5113	0.8616 6723	0.8407 2860	10
11	0.8722 7746	0.8605 1899	0.8489 3323	0.8262 6889	11
12	0.8615 0860	0.8488 4734	0.8363 8742	0.8120 5788	12
13	0.8508 7269	0.8373 3400	0.8240 2702	0.7980 9128	13
14	0.8403 6809	0.8259 7682	0.8118 4928	0.7843 6490	14
15	0.8299 9318	0.8147 7368	0.7998 5150	0.7708 7459	15
16	0.8197 4635	0.8037 2250	0.7880 3104	0.7576 1631	16
17	0.8096 2602	0.7928 2120	0.7763 8526	0.7445 8605	17
18	0.7996 3064	0.7820 6777	0.7649 1159	0.7317 7990	18
19	0.7897 5866	0.7714 6020	0.7536 0747	0.7191 9401	19
20	0.7800 0855	0.7609 9649	0.7424 7042	0.7068 2458	20
21	0.7703 7881	0.7506 7472	0.7314 9795	0.6946 6789	21
22	0.7608 6796	0.7404 9294	0.7206 8763	0.6827 2028	22
23	0.7514 7453	0.7304 4926	0.7100 3708	0.6709 7817	23
24	0.7421 9707	0.7205 4181	0.6995 4392	0.6594 3800	24
25	0.7330 3414	0.7107 6874	0.6892 0583	0.6480 9632	25
26	0.7239 8434	0.7011 2823	0.6790 2052	0.6369 4970	26
27	0.7150 4626	0.6916 1847	0.6689 8574	0.6259 9479	27
28	0.7062 1853	0.6822 3771	0.6590 9925	0.6152 2829	28
29	0.6974 9978	0.6729 8417	0.6493 5887	0.6046 4697	29
30	0.6888 8867	0.6638 5615	0.6397 6243	0.5942 4764	30
31	0.6803 8387	0.6548 5194	0.6303 0781	0.5840 2716	31
32	0.6719 8407	0.6459 6985	0.6209 9292	0.5739 8247	32
33	0.6636 8797	0.6372 0824	0.6118 1568	0.5641 1053	33
34	0.6554 9429	0.6285 6546	0.6027 7407	0.5544 0839	34
35	0.6474 0177	0.6200 3991	0.5938 6608	0.5448 7311	35
36	0.6394 0916	0.6116 3000	0.5850 8974	0.5355 0183	36
37	0.6315 1522	0.6033 3416	0.5764 4309	0.5262 9172	37
38	0.6237 1873	0.5951 5083	0.5679 2423	0.5172 4002	38
39	0.6160 1850	0.5870 7850	0.5595 3126	0.5083 4400	39
40	0.6084 1334	0.5791 1566	0.5512 6232	0.4996 0098	40
41	0.6009 0206	0.5712 6083	0.5431 1559	0.4910 0834	41
42	0.5934 8352	0.5635 1253	0.5350 8925	0.4825 6348	42
43	0.5861 5656	0.5558 6933	0.5271 8153	0.4742 6386	43
44	0.5789 2006	0.5483 2979	0.5193 9067	0.4661 0699	44
45	0.5717 7290	0.5408 9252	0.5117 1494	0.4580 9040	45
46	0.5647 1397	0.5335 5612	0.5041 5265	0.4502 1170	46
47	0.5577 4219	0.5263 1923	0.4967 0212	0.4424 6850	47
48	0.5508 5649	0.5191 8050	0.4893 6170	0.4348 5848	48
49	0.5440 5579	0.5121 3860	0.4821 2975	0.4273 7934	49
50	0.5373 3905	0.5051 9220	0.4750 0468	0.4200 2883	50

TABLE IV.—Present Value of 1 at Compound Interest

$$v^n = (1 + i)^{-n}$$

n	$1\frac{1}{4}\%$	$1\frac{3}{8}\%$	$1\frac{1}{2}\%$	$1\frac{3}{4}\%$	n
51	0.5307 0524	0.4983 4003	0.4679 8491	0.4128 0475	51
52	0.5241 5332	0.4915 8079	0.4610 6887	0.4057 0492	52
53	0.5176 8229	0.4849 1323	0.4542 5505	0.3987 2719	53
54	0.5112 9115	0.4783 3611	0.4475 4192	0.3918 6947	54
55	0.5049 7892	0.4718 4820	0.4409 2800	0.3851 2970	55
56	0.4987 4461	0.4654 4829	0.4344 1182	0.3785 0585	56
57	0.4925 8727	0.4591 3518	0.4279 9194	0.3719 9592	57
58	0.4865 0594	0.4529 0770	0.4216 6694	0.3655 9796	58
59	0.4804 9970	0.4467 6468	0.4154 3541	0.3593 1003	59
60	0.4745 6760	0.4407 0499	0.4092 9597	0.3531 3025	60
61	0.4687 0874	0.4347 2749	0.4032 4726	0.3470 5676	61
62	0.4629 2222	0.4288 3106	0.3972 8794	0.3410 8772	62
63	0.4572 0713	0.4230 1461	0.3914 1669	0.3352 2135	63
64	0.4515 6259	0.4172 7705	0.3856 3221	0.3294 5587	64
65	0.4459 8775	0.4116 1731	0.3799 3321	0.3237 8956	65
66	0.4404 8173	0.4060 3434	0.3743 1843	0.3182 2069	66
67	0.4350 4368	0.4005 2709	0.3687 8663	0.3127 4761	67
68	0.4296 7277	0.3950 9454	0.3633 3658	0.3073 6866	68
69	0.4243 6817	0.3897 3568	0.3579 6708	0.3020 8222	69
70	0.4191 2905	0.3844 4949	0.3526 7692	0.2968 8670	70
71	0.4139 5462	0.3792 3501	0.3474 6495	0.2917 8054	71
72	0.4088 4407	0.3740 9126	0.3423 3000	0.2867 6221	72
73	0.4037 9661	0.3690 1727	0.3372 7093	0.2818 3018	73
74	0.3988 1147	0.3640 1210	0.3322 8663	0.2769 8298	74
75	0.3938 8787	0.3590 7483	0.3273 7599	0.2722 1914	75
76	0.3890 2506	0.3542 0451	0.3225 3793	0.2675 3724	76
77	0.3842 2228	0.3494 0026	0.3177 7136	0.2629 3586	77
78	0.3794 7879	0.3446 6117	0.3130 7523	0.2584 1362	78
79	0.3747 9387	0.3399 8636	0.3084 4850	0.2539 6916	79
80	0.3701 6679	0.3353 7495	0.3038 9015	0.2496 0114	80
81	0.3655 9683	0.3308 2609	0.2993 9916	0.2453 0825	81
82	0.3610 8329	0.3263 3893	0.2949 7454	0.2410 8919	82
83	0.3566 2547	0.3219 1263	0.2906 1531	0.2369 4269	83
84	0.3522 2268	0.3175 4637	0.2863 2050	0.2328 6751	84
85	0.3478 7426	0.3132 3933	0.2820 8917	0.2288 6242	85
86	0.3435 7951	0.3089 9071	0.2779 2036	0.2249 2621	86
87	0.3393 3779	0.3047 9971	0.2738 1316	0.2210 5770	87
88	0.3351 4843	0.3006 6556	0.2697 6666	0.2172 5572	88
89	0.3310 1080	0.2965 8748	0.2657 7997	0.2135 1914	89
90	0.3269 2425	0.2925 6472	0.2618 5218	0.2098 4682	90
91	0.3228 8814	0.2885 9652	0.2579 8245	0.2062 3766	91
92	0.3189 0187	0.2846 8214	0.2541 6990	0.2026 9057	92
93	0.3149 6481	0.2808 2085	0.2504 1369	0.1992 0450	93
94	0.3110 7636	0.2770 1194	0.2467 1300	0.1957 7837	94
95	0.3072 3591	0.2732 5468	0.2430 6699	0.1924 1118	95
96	0.3034 4287	0.2695 4839	0.2394 7487	0.1891 0190	96
97	0.2996 9666	0.2658 9237	0.2359 3583	0.1858 4953	97
98	0.2959 9670	0.2622 8594	0.2324 4909	0.1826 5310	98
99	0.2923 4242	0.2587 2843	0.2290 1389	0.1795 1165	99
100	0.2887 3326	0.2552 1916	0.2256 2944	0.1764 2422	100

TABLE IV.—Present Value of 1 at Compound Interest

$$v^n = (1+i)^{-n}$$

n	2%	2¼%	2½%	2¾%	n
1	0.9803 9216	0.9779 9511	0.9756 0976	0.9732 3601	1
2	0.9611 6878	0.9564 7444	0.9518 1440	0.9471 8833	2
3	0.9423 2233	0.9354 2732	0.9285 9941	0.9218 3779	3
4	0.9238 4543	0.9148 4335	0.9059 5064	0.8971 6573	4
5	0.9057 3081	0.8947 1232	0.8838 5429	0.8731 5400	5
6	0.8879 7138	0.8750 2427	0.8622 9687	0.8497 8491	6
7	0.8705 6018	0.8557 6946	0.8412 6524	0.8270 4128	7
8	0.8534 9037	0.8369 3835	0.8207 4657	0.8049 0635	8
9	0.8367 5527	0.8185 2161	0.8007 2836	0.7833 6385	9
10	0.8203 4830	0.8005 1013	0.7811 9840	0.7623 9791	10
11	0.8042 6304	0.7828 9499	0.7621 4478	0.7419 9310	11
12	0.7884 9318	0.7656 6748	0.7435 5589	0.7221 3440	12
13	0.7730 3253	0.7488 1905	0.7254 2038	0.7028 0720	13
14	0.7578 7502	0.7323 4137	0.7077 2720	0.6839 9728	14
15	0.7430 1473	0.7162 2628	0.6904 6556	0.6656 9078	15
16	0.7284 4581	0.7004 6580	0.6736 2493	0.6478 7424	16
17	0.7141 6256	0.6850 5212	0.6571 9506	0.6305 3454	17
18	0.7001 5937	0.6699 7763	0.6411 6591	0.6136 5892	18
19	0.6864 3076	0.6552 3484	0.6255 2772	0.5972 3496	19
20	0.6729 7133	0.6408 1647	0.6102 7094	0.5812 5057	20
21	0.6597 7582	0.6267 1538	0.5953 8629	0.5656 9398	21
22	0.6468 3904	0.6129 2457	0.5808 6467	0.5505 5375	22
23	0.6341 5592	0.5994 3724	0.5666 9724	0.5358 1874	23
24	0.6217 2149	0.5862 4668	0.5528 7535	0.5214 7809	24
25	0.6095 3087	0.5733 4639	0.5393 9059	0.5075 2126	25
26	0.5975 7928	0.5607 2997	0.5262 3472	0.4939 3796	26
27	0.5858 6204	0.5483 9117	0.5133 9973	0.4807 1821	27
28	0.5743 7455	0.5363 2388	0.5008 7778	0.4678 5227	28
29	0.5631 1231	0.5245 2213	0.4886 6125	0.4553 3068	29
30	0.5520 7089	0.5129 8008	0.4767 4269	0.4431 4421	30
31	0.5412 4597	0.5016 9201	0.4651 1481	0.4312 8391	31
32	0.5306 3330	0.4906 5233	0.4537 7055	0.4197 4103	32
33	0.5202 2873	0.4798 5558	0.4427 0298	0.4085 0708	33
34	0.5100 2817	0.4692 9641	0.4319 0534	0.3975 7380	34
35	0.5000 2761	0.4589 6960	0.4213 7107	0.3869 3314	35
36	0.4902 2315	0.4488 7002	0.4110 9372	0.3765 7727	36
37	0.4806 1093	0.4389 9268	0.4010 6705	0.3664 9856	37
38	0.4711 8719	0.4293 3270	0.3912 8492	0.3566 8959	38
39	0.4619 4822	0.4198 8528	0.3817 4139	0.3471 4316	39
40	0.4528 9042	0.4106 4575	0.3724 3062	0.3378 5222	40
41	0.4440 1021	0.4016 0954	0.3633 4695	0.3288 0995	41
42	0.4353 0413	0.3927 7216	0.3544 8483	0.3200 0968	42
43	0.4267 6875	0.3841 2925	0.3458 3886	0.3114 4495	43
44	0.4184 0074	0.3756 7653	0.3374 0376	0.3031 0944	44
45	0.4101 9680	0.3674 0981	0.3291 7440	0.2949 9702	45
46	0.4021 5373	0.3593 2500	0.3211 4576	0.2871 0172	46
47	0.3942 6836	0.3514 1809	0.3133 1294	0.2794 1773	47
48	0.3865 3761	0.3436 8518	0.3056 7116	0.2719 3940	48
49	0.3789 5844	0.3361 2242	0.2982 1576	0.2646 6122	49
50	0.3715 2788	0.3287 2608	0.2909 4221	0.2575 7783	50

TABLE IV.—Present Value of 1 at Compound Interest

$$v^n = (1 + i)^{-n}$$

n	2%	2¼%	2½%	2¾%	n
51	0.3642 4302	0.3214 9250	0.2838 4606	0.2506 8402	51
52	0.3571 0100	0.3144 1810	0.2769 2298	0.2439 7471	52
53	0.3500 9902	0.3074 9936	0.2701 6876	0.2374 4497	53
54	0.3432 3433	0.3007 3287	0.2635 7928	0.2310 9000	54
55	0.3365 0425	0.2941 1528	0.2571 5052	0.2249 0511	55
56	0.3299 0613	0.2876 4330	0.2508 7855	0.2188 8575	56
57	0.3234 3738	0.2813 1374	0.2447 5956	0.2130 2749	57
58	0.3170 9547	0.2751 2347	0.2387 8982	0.2073 2603	58
59	0.3108 7791	0.2690 6940	0.2329 6568	0.2017 7716	59
60	0.3047 8227	0.2631 4856	0.2272 8359	0.1963 7679	60
61	0.2988 0614	0.2573 5801	0.2217 4009	0.1911 2097	61
62	0.2929 4720	0.2516 9487	0.2163 3179	0.1860 0581	62
63	0.2872 0314	0.2461 5635	0.2110 5541	0.1810 2755	63
64	0.2815 7170	0.2407 3971	0.2059 0771	0.1761 8253	64
65	0.2760 5069	0.2354 4226	0.2008 8557	0.1714 6718	65
66	0.2706 3793	0.2302 6138	0.1959 8593	0.1668 7804	66
67	0.2653 3130	0.2251 9450	0.1912 0578	0.1624 1172	67
68	0.2601 2873	0.2202 3912	0.1865 4223	0.1580 6493	68
69	0.2550 2817	0.2153 9278	0.1819 9241	0.1538 3448	69
70	0.2500 2761	0.2106 5309	0.1775 5358	0.1497 1726	70
71	0.2451 2511	0.2060 1769	0.1732 2300	0.1457 1023	71
72	0.2403 1874	0.2014 8429	0.1689 9805	0.1418 1044	72
73	0.2356 0661	0.1970 5065	0.1648 7615	0.1380 1503	73
74	0.2309 8687	0.1927 1458	0.1608 5478	0.1343 2119	74
75	0.2264 5771	0.1884 7391	0.1569 3149	0.1307 2622	75
76	0.2220 1737	0.1843 2657	0.1531 0389	0.1272 2747	76
77	0.2176 6408	0.1802 7048	0.1493 6965	0.1238 2235	77
78	0.2133 9616	0.1763 0365	0.1457 2649	0.1205 0837	78
79	0.2092 1192	0.1724 2411	0.1421 7218	0.1172 8309	79
80	0.2051 0973	0.1686 2993	0.1387 0457	0.1141 4412	80
81	0.2010 8797	0.1649 1925	0.1353 2153	0.1110 8917	81
82	0.1971 4507	0.1612 9022	0.1320 2101	0.1081 1598	82
83	0.1932 7948	0.1577 4105	0.1288 0098	0.1052 2237	83
84	0.1894 8968	0.1542 6997	0.1256 5949	0.1024 0620	84
85	0.1857 7420	0.1508 7528	0.1225 9463	0.0996 6540	85
86	0.1821 3157	0.1475 5528	0.1196 0452	0.0969 9795	86
87	0.1785 6036	0.1443 0835	0.1166 8733	0.0944 0190	87
88	0.1750 5918	0.1411 3286	0.1138 4130	0.0918 7533	88
89	0.1716 2665	0.1380 2724	0.1110 6468	0.0894 1638	89
90	0.1682 6142	0.1349 8997	0.1083 5579	0.0870 2324	90
91	0.1649 6217	0.1320 1953	0.1057 1296	0.0846 9415	91
92	0.1617 2762	0.1291 1445	0.1031 3460	0.0824 2740	92
93	0.1585 5649	0.1262 7331	0.1006 1912	0.0802 2131	93
94	0.1554 4754	0.1234 9468	0.0981 6500	0.0780 7427	94
95	0.1523 9955	0.1207 7719	0.0957 7073	0.0759 8469	95
96	0.1494 1132	0.1181 1950	0.0934 3486	0.0739 5104	96
97	0.1464 8169	0.1155 2029	0.0911 5596	0.0719 7181	97
98	0.1436 0950	0.1129 7828	0.0889 3264	0.0700 4556	98
99	0.1407 9363	0.1104 9221	0.0867 6355	0.0681 7086	99
100	0.1380 3297	0.1080 6084	0.0846 4737	0.0663 4634	100

TABLE IV.—Present Value of 1 at Compound Interest

$$v^n = (1 + i)^{-n}$$

n	3%	3½%	4%	4½%	n
1	0.9708 7379	0.9661 8357	0.9615 3846	0.9569 3780	1
2	0.9425 9591	0.9335 1070	0.9245 5621	0.9157 2995	2
3	0.9151 4166	0.9019 4271	0.8889 9636	0.8762 9660	3
4	0.8884 8705	0.8714 4223	0.8548 0419	0.8385 6134	4
5	0.8626 0878	0.8419 7317	0.8219 2711	0.8024 5105	5
6	0.8374 8426	0.8135 0064	0.7903 1453	0.7678 9574	6
7	0.8130 9151	0.7859 9096	0.7599 1781	0.7348 2846	7
8	0.7894 0923	0.7594 1156	0.7306 9021	0.7031 8513	8
9	0.7664 1673	0.7337 3097	0.7025 8674	0.6729 0443	9
10	0.7440 9391	0.7089 1881	0.6755 6417	0.6439 2768	10
11	0.7224 2128	0.6849 4571	0.6495 8093	0.6161 9874	11
12	0.7013 7988	0.6617 8330	0.6245 9705	0.5896 6386	12
13	0.6809 5134	0.6394 0415	0.6005 7409	0.5642 7164	13
14	0.6611 1781	0.6177 8179	0.5774 7508	0.5399 7286	14
15	0.6418 6195	0.5968 9062	0.5552 6450	0.5167 2044	15
16	0.6231 6694	0.5767 0591	0.5339 0818	0.4944 6932	16
17	0.6050 1645	0.5572 0378	0.5133 7325	0.4731 7639	17
18	0.5873 9461	0.5383 6114	0.4936 2812	0.4528 0037	18
19	0.5702 8603	0.5201 5569	0.4746 4242	0.4333 0179	19
20	0.5536 7575	0.5025 6588	0.4563 8695	0.4146 4286	20
21	0.5375 4928	0.4855 7090	0.4388 3360	0.3967 8743	21
22	0.5218 9250	0.4691 5063	0.4219 5539	0.3797 0089	22
23	0.5066 9175	0.4532 8563	0.4057 2633	0.3633 5013	23
24	0.4919 3374	0.4379 5713	0.3901 2147	0.3477 0347	24
25	0.4776 0557	0.4231 4699	0.3751 1680	0.3327 3060	25
26	0.4636 9473	0.4088 3767	0.3606 8923	0.3184 0248	26
27	0.4501 8906	0.3950 1224	0.3468 1657	0.3046 9137	27
28	0.4370 7675	0.3816 5434	0.3334 7747	0.2915 7069	28
29	0.4243 4636	0.3687 4815	0.3206 5141	0.2790 1502	29
30	0.4119 8676	0.3562 7841	0.3083 1867	0.2670 0002	30
31	0.3999 8715	0.3442 3035	0.2964 6026	0.2555 0241	31
32	0.3883 3703	0.3325 8971	0.2850 5794	0.2444 9991	32
33	0.3770 2625	0.3213 4271	0.2740 9417	0.2339 7121	33
34	0.3660 4490	0.3104 7605	0.2635 5209	0.2238 9589	34
35	0.3553 8340	0.2999 7686	0.2534 1547	0.2142 5444	35
36	0.3450 3243	0.2898 3272	0.2436 6872	0.2050 2817	36
37	0.3349 8294	0.2800 3161	0.2342 9685	0.1961 9921	37
38	0.3252 2615	0.2705 6194	0.2252 8543	0.1877 5044	38
39	0.3157 5355	0.2614 1250	0.2166 2061	0.1796 6549	39
40	0.3065 5684	0.2525 7247	0.2082 8904	0.1719 2870	40
41	0.2976 2800	0.2440 3137	0.2002 7793	0.1645 2507	41
42	0.2889 5922	0.2357 7910	0.1925 7493	0.1574 4026	42
43	0.2805 4294	0.2278 0590	0.1851 6820	0.1506 6054	43
44	0.2723 7178	0.2201 0231	0.1780 4635	0.1441 7276	44
45	0.2644 3862	0.2126 5924	0.1711 9841	0.1379 6437	45
46	0.2567 3653	0.2054 6787	0.1646 1386	0.1320 2332	46
47	0.2492 5876	0.1985 1968	0.1582 8256	0.1263 3810	47
48	0.2419 0880	0.1918 0645	0.1521 9476	0.1208 9771	48
49	0.2349 5029	0.1853 2024	0.1463 4112	0.1156 9158	49
50	0.2281 0708	0.1790 5337	0.1407 1262	0.1107 0965	50

TABLE IV.—Present Value of 1 at Compound Interest

$$v^n = (1 + i)^{-n}$$

n	3%	3½%	4%	4½%	n
51	0.2214 6318	0.1729 9843	0.1353 0059	0.1059 4225	51
52	0.2150 1280	0.1671 4824	0.1300 9672	0.1013 8014	52
53	0.2087 5029	0.1614 9589	0.1250 9300	0.0970 1449	53
54	0.2026 7019	0.1560 3467	0.1202 8173	0.0928 3683	54
55	0.1967 6717	0.1507 5814	0.1156 5551	0.0888 3907	55
56	0.1910 3609	0.1456 6004	0.1112 0722	0.0850 1347	56
57	0.1854 7193	0.1407 3433	0.1069 3002	0.0813 5260	57
58	0.1800 6984	0.1359 7520	0.1028 1733	0.0778 4938	58
59	0.1748 2508	0.1313 7701	0.0988 6282	0.0744 9701	59
60	0.1697 3309	0.1269 3431	0.0950 6040	0.0712 8901	60
61	0.1647 8941	0.1226 4184	0.0914 0423	0.0682 1915	61
62	0.1599 8972	0.1184 9453	0.0878 8868	0.0652 8148	62
63	0.1553 2982	0.1144 8747	0.0845 0835	0.0624 7032	63
64	0.1508 0565	0.1106 1591	0.0812 5803	0.0597 8021	64
65	0.1464 1325	0.1068 7528	0.0781 3272	0.0572 0594	65
66	0.1421 4879	0.1032 6114	0.0751 2762	0.0547 4253	66
67	0.1380 0853	0.0997 6922	0.0722 3809	0.0523 8519	67
68	0.1339 8887	0.0963 9538	0.0694 5970	0.0501 2937	68
69	0.1300 8628	0.0931 3563	0.0667 8818	0.0479 7069	69
70	0.1262 9736	0.0899 8612	0.0642 1940	0.0459 0497	70
71	0.1226 1880	0.0869 4311	0.0617 4942	0.0439 2820	71
72	0.1190 4737	0.0840 0300	0.0593 7445	0.0420 3655	72
73	0.1155 7998	0.0811 6232	0.0570 9081	0.0402 2637	73
74	0.1122 1357	0.0784 1770	0.0548 9501	0.0384 9413	74
75	0.1089 4521	0.0757 6590	0.0527 8367	0.0368 3649	75
76	0.1057 7205	0.0732 0376	0.0507 5353	0.0352 5023	76
77	0.1026 9131	0.0707 2827	0.0488 0147	0.0337 3228	77
78	0.0997 0030	0.0683 3650	0.0469 2449	0.0322 7969	78
79	0.0967 9641	0.0660 2560	0.0451 1970	0.0308 8965	79
80	0.0939 7710	0.0637 9285	0.0433 8433	0.0295 5948	80
81	0.0912 3990	0.0616 3561	0.0417 1570	0.0282 8658	81
82	0.0885 8243	0.0595 5131	0.0401 1125	0.0270 6850	82
83	0.0860 0236	0.0575 3750	0.0385 6851	0.0259 0287	83
84	0.0834 9743	0.0555 9178	0.0370 8510	0.0247 8744	84
85	0.0810 6547	0.0537 1187	0.0356 5875	0.0237 2003	85
86	0.0787 0434	0.0518 9553	0.0342 8726	0.0226 9860	86
87	0.0764 1198	0.0501 4060	0.0329 6852	0.0217 2115	87
88	0.0741 8639	0.0484 4503	0.0317 0050	0.0207 8579	88
89	0.0720 2562	0.0468 0679	0.0304 8125	0.0198 9070	89
90	0.0699 2779	0.0452 2395	0.0293 0890	0.0190 3417	90
91	0.0678 9105	0.0436 9464	0.0281 8163	0.0182 1451	91
92	0.0659 1364	0.0422 1704	0.0270 9772	0.0174 3016	92
93	0.0639 9383	0.0407 8941	0.0260 5550	0.0166 7958	93
94	0.0621 2993	0.0394 1006	0.0250 5337	0.0159 6132	94
95	0.0603 2032	0.0380 7735	0.0240 8978	0.0152 7399	95
96	0.0585 6342	0.0367 8971	0.0231 6325	0.0146 1626	96
97	0.0568 5769	0.0355 4562	0.0222 7235	0.0139 8685	97
98	0.0552 0164	0.0343 4359	0.0214 1572	0.0133 8454	98
99	0.0535 9383	0.0331 8221	0.0205 9204	0.0128 0817	99
100	0.0520 3284	0.0320 6011	0.0198 0004	0.0122 5663	100

TABLE IV.—Present Value of 1 at Compound Interest

$$v^n = (1 + i)^{-n}$$

n	5%	5½%	6%	6½%	n
1	0.9523 8095	0.9478 6730	0.9433 9623	0.9389 6714	1
2	0.9070 2948	0.8984 5242	0.8899 9644	0.8816 5928	2
3	0.8638 3760	0.8516 1366	0.8396 1928	0.8278 4909	3
4	0.8227 0247	0.8072 1674	0.7920 9366	0.7773 2309	4
5	0.7835 2617	0.7651 3435	0.7472 5817	0.7298 8084	5
6	0.7462 1540	0.7252 4583	0.7049 6054	0.6853 3412	6
7	0.7106 8133	0.6874 3681	0.6650 5711	0.6435 0621	7
8	0.6768 3936	0.6515 9887	0.6274 1237	0.6042 3119	8
9	0.6446 0892	0.6176 2926	0.5918 9846	0.5673 5323	9
10	0.6139 1325	0.5854 3058	0.5583 9478	0.5327 2604	10
11	0.5846 7929	0.5549 1050	0.5267 8753	0.5002 1224	11
12	0.5568 3742	0.5259 8152	0.4969 6936	0.4696 8285	12
13	0.5303 2135	0.4985 6068	0.4688 3902	0.4410 1676	13
14	0.5050 6795	0.4725 6937	0.4423 0096	0.4141 0025	14
15	0.4810 1710	0.4479 3305	0.4172 6506	0.3888 2652	15
16	0.4581 1152	0.4245 8109	0.3936 4628	0.3650 9533	16
17	0.4362 9669	0.4024 4653	0.3713 6442	0.3428 1251	17
18	0.4155 2065	0.3814 6590	0.3503 4379	0.3218 8969	18
19	0.3957 3396	0.3615 7906	0.3305 1301	0.3022 4384	19
20	0.3768 8948	0.3427 2896	0.3118 0473	0.2837 9703	20
21	0.3589 4236	0.3248 6158	0.2941 5540	0.2664 7608	21
22	0.3418 4987	0.3079 2567	0.2775 0510	0.2502 1228	22
23	0.3255 7131	0.2918 7267	0.2617 9726	0.2349 4111	23
24	0.3100 6791	0.2766 5656	0.2469 7855	0.2206 0198	24
25	0.2953 0277	0.2622 3370	0.2329 9863	0.2071 3801	25
26	0.2812 4073	0.2485 6275	0.2198 1003	0.1944 9579	26
27	0.2678 4832	0.2356 0450	0.2073 6795	0.1826 2515	27
28	0.2550 9364	0.2233 2181	0.1956 3014	0.1714 7902	28
29	0.2429 4632	0.2116 7944	0.1845 5674	0.1610 1316	29
30	0.2313 7745	0.2005 4402	0.1741 1013	0.1511 8607	30
31	0.2203 5947	0.1901 8390	0.1642 5484	0.1419 5875	31
32	0.2098 6617	0.1802 6910	0.1549 5740	0.1332 9460	32
33	0.1998 7254	0.1708 7119	0.1461 8622	0.1251 5925	33
34	0.1903 5480	0.1619 6321	0.1379 1153	0.1175 2042	34
35	0.1812 9029	0.1535 1963	0.1301 0522	0.1103 4781	35
36	0.1726 5741	0.1455 1624	0.1227 4077	0.1036 1297	36
37	0.1644 3563	0.1379 3008	0.1157 9318	0.0972 8917	37
38	0.1566 0536	0.1307 3941	0.1092 3885	0.0913 5134	38
39	0.1491 4797	0.1239 2362	0.1030 5552	0.0857 7590	39
40	0.1420 4568	0.1174 6314	0.0972 2219	0.0805 4075	40
41	0.1352 8160	0.1113 3947	0.0917 1905	0.0756 2512	41
42	0.1288 3962	0.1055 3504	0.0865 2740	0.0710 0950	42
43	0.1227 0440	0.1000 3322	0.0816 2962	0.0666 7559	43
44	0.1168 6133	0.0948 1822	0.0770 0908	0.0626 0619	44
45	0.1112 9651	0.0898 7509	0.0726 5007	0.0587 8515	45
46	0.1059 9668	0.0851 8965	0.0685 3781	0.0551 9733	46
47	0.1009 4921	0.0807 4849	0.0646 5831	0.0518 2848	47
48	0.0961 4211	0.0765 3885	0.0609 9840	0.0486 6524	48
49	0.0915 6391	0.0725 4867	0.0575 4566	0.0456 9506	49
50	0.0872 0373	0.0687 6652	0.0542 8836	0.0429 0616	50

TABLE IV.—Present Value of 1 at Compound Interest

$$v^n = (1 + i)^{-n}$$

n	5%	5½%	6%	6½%	n
51	0.0830 5117	0.0651 8153	0.0512 1544	0.0402 8747	51
52	0.0790 9635	0.0617 8344	0.0483 1645	0.0378 2861	52
53	0.0753 2986	0.0585 6250	0.0455 8156	0.0355 1982	53
54	0.0717 4272	0.0555 0948	0.0430 0147	0.0333 5195	54
55	0.0683 2640	0.0526 1562	0.0405 6742	0.0313 1638	55
56	0.0650 7276	0.0498 7263	0.0382 7115	0.0294 0505	56
57	0.0619 7406	0.0472 7263	0.0361 0486	0.0276 1038	57
58	0.0590 2291	0.0448 0818	0.0340 6119	0.0259 2524	58
59	0.0562 1230	0.0424 7221	0.0321 3320	0.0243 4295	59
60	0.0535 3552	0.0402 5802	0.0303 1434	0.0228 5723	60
61	0.0509 8621	0.0381 5926	0.0285 9843	0.0214 6218	61
62	0.0485 5830	0.0361 6992	0.0269 7965	0.0201 5229	62
63	0.0462 4600	0.0342 8428	0.0254 5250	0.0189 2233	63
64	0.0440 4381	0.0324 9695	0.0240 1179	0.0177 6745	64
65	0.0419 4648	0.0308 0279	0.0226 5264	0.0166 8305	65
66	0.0399 4903	0.0291 9696	0.0213 7041	0.0156 6484	66
67	0.0380 4670	0.0276 7485	0.0201 6077	0.0147 0877	67
68	0.0362 3495	0.0262 3208	0.0190 1959	0.0138 1105	68
69	0.0345 0948	0.0248 6453	0.0179 4301	0.0129 6812	69
70	0.0328 6617	0.0235 6828	0.0169 2737	0.0121 7664	70
71	0.0313 0111	0.0223 3960	0.0159 6921	0.0114 3346	71
72	0.0298 1058	0.0211 7498	0.0150 6530	0.0107 3565	72
73	0.0283 9103	0.0200 7107	0.0142 1254	0.0100 8042	73
74	0.0270 3908	0.0190 2471	0.0134 0806	0.0094 6518	74
75	0.0257 5150	0.0180 3290	0.0126 4911	0.0088 8750	75
76	0.0245 2524	0.0170 9279	0.0119 3313	0.0083 4507	76
77	0.0233 5737	0.0162 0170	0.0112 5767	0.0078 3574	77
78	0.0222 4512	0.0153 5706	0.0106 2044	0.0073 5751	78
79	0.0211 8582	0.0145 5646	0.0100 1928	0.0069 0846	79
80	0.0201 7698	0.0137 9759	0.0094 5215	0.0064 8681	80
81	0.0192 1617	0.0130 7828	0.0089 1713	0.0060 9090	81
82	0.0183 0111	0.0123 9648	0.0084 1238	0.0057 1916	82
83	0.0174 2963	0.0117 5022	0.0079 3621	0.0053 7010	83
84	0.0165 9965	0.0111 3765	0.0074 8699	0.0050 4235	84
85	0.0158 0919	0.0105 5701	0.0070 6320	0.0047 3460	85
86	0.0150 5637	0.0100 0664	0.0066 6340	0.0044 4563	86
87	0.0143 3940	0.0094 8497	0.0062 8622	0.0041 7430	87
88	0.0136 5657	0.0089 9049	0.0059 3040	0.0039 1953	88
89	0.0130 0626	0.0085 2180	0.0055 9472	0.0036 8031	89
90	0.0123 8691	0.0080 7753	0.0052 7803	0.0034 5569	90
91	0.0117 9706	0.0076 5643	0.0049 7928	0.0032 4478	91
92	0.0112 3530	0.0072 5728	0.0046 9743	0.0030 4674	92
93	0.0107 0028	0.0068 7894	0.0044 3154	0.0028 6079	93
94	0.0101 9074	0.0065 2032	0.0041 8070	0.0026 8619	94
95	0.0097 0547	0.0061 8040	0.0039 4405	0.0025 2224	95
96	0.0092 4331	0.0058 5820	0.0037 2081	0.0023 6831	96
97	0.0088 0315	0.0055 5279	0.0035 1019	0.0022 2376	97
98	0.0083 8395	0.0052 6331	0.0033 1150	0.0020 8804	98
99	0.0079 8471	0.0049 8892	0.0031 2406	0.0019 6060	99
100	0.0076 0449	0.0047 2883	0.0029 4723	0.0018 4094	100

TABLE IV.—Present Value of 1 at Compound Interest

$$v^n = (1 + i)^{-n}$$

n	7%	7½%	8%	8½%	n
1	0.9345 7944	0.9302 3256	0.9259 2593	0.9216 5899	1
2	0.8734 3873	0.8653 3261	0.8573 3882	0.8494 5529	2
3	0.8162 9788	0.8049 6057	0.7938 3224	0.7829 0810	3
4	0.7628 9521	0.7488 0053	0.7350 2985	0.7215 7428	4
5	0.7129 8618	0.6965 5863	0.6805 8320	0.6650 4542	5
6	0.6663 4222	0.6479 6152	0.6301 6963	0.6129 4509	6
7	0.6227 4974	0.6027 5490	0.5834 9040	0.5649 2635	7
8	0.5820 0910	0.5607 0223	0.5402 6888	0.5206 6945	8
9	0.5439 3374	0.5215 8347	0.5002 4897	0.4798 7968	9
10	0.5083 4929	0.4851 9393	0.4631 9349	0.4422 8542	10
11	0.4750 9280	0.4513 4319	0.4288 8286	0.4076 3633	11
12	0.4440 1196	0.4198 5413	0.3971 1376	0.3757 0168	12
13	0.4149 6445	0.3905 6198	0.3676 9792	0.3462 6883	13
14	0.3878 1724	0.3633 1347	0.3404 6104	0.3191 4178	14
15	0.3624 4602	0.3379 6602	0.3152 4170	0.2941 3989	15
16	0.3387 3460	0.3143 8699	0.2918 9047	0.2710 9667	16
17	0.3165 7439	0.2924 5302	0.2702 6895	0.2498 5869	17
18	0.2958 6392	0.2720 4932	0.2502 4903	0.2302 8450	18
19	0.2765 0832	0.2530 6913	0.2317 1206	0.2122 4378	19
20	0.2584 1900	0.2354 1315	0.2145 4821	0.1956 1639	20
21	0.2415 1309	0.2189 8897	0.1986 5575	0.1802 9160	21
22	0.2257 1317	0.2037 1067	0.1839 4051	0.1661 6738	22
23	0.2109 4688	0.1894 9830	0.1703 1528	0.1531 4965	23
24	0.1971 4662	0.1762 7749	0.1576 9934	0.1411 5176	24
25	0.1842 4918	0.1639 7906	0.1460 1790	0.1300 9378	25
26	0.1721 9549	0.1525 3866	0.1352 0176	0.1199 0210	26
27	0.1609 3037	0.1418 9643	0.1251 8682	0.1105 0885	27
28	0.1504 0221	0.1319 9668	0.1159 1372	0.1018 5148	28
29	0.1405 6282	0.1227 8761	0.1073 2752	0.0938 7233	29
30	0.1313 6712	0.1142 2103	0.0993 7733	0.0865 1828	30
31	0.1227 7301	0.1062 5212	0.0920 1605	0.0797 4035	31
32	0.1147 4113	0.0988 3918	0.0852 0005	0.0734 9341	32
33	0.1072 3470	0.0919 4343	0.0788 8893	0.0677 3586	33
34	0.1002 1934	0.0855 2877	0.0730 4531	0.0624 2936	34
35	0.0936 6294	0.0795 6164	0.0676 3454	0.0575 3858	35
36	0.0875 3546	0.0740 1083	0.0626 2458	0.0530 3095	36
37	0.0818 0884	0.0688 4729	0.0579 8572	0.0488 7645	37
38	0.0764 5686	0.0640 4399	0.0536 9048	0.0450 4742	38
39	0.0714 5501	0.0595 7580	0.0497 1341	0.0415 1836	39
40	0.0667 8038	0.0554 1935	0.0460 3093	0.0382 6577	40
41	0.0624 1157	0.0515 5288	0.0426 2123	0.0352 6799	41
42	0.0583 2857	0.0479 5617	0.0394 6411	0.0325 0506	42
43	0.0545 1268	0.0446 1039	0.0365 4084	0.0299 5858	43
44	0.0509 4643	0.0414 9804	0.0338 3411	0.0276 1160	44
45	0.0476 1349	0.0386 0283	0.0313 2788	0.0254 4848	45
46	0.0444 9859	0.0359 0961	0.0290 0730	0.0234 5482	46
47	0.0415 8747	0.0334 0428	0.0268 5861	0.0216 1734	47
48	0.0388 6679	0.0310 7375	0.0248 6908	0.0199 2382	48
49	0.0363 2410	0.0289 0582	0.0230 2693	0.0183 6297	49
50	0.0339 4776	0.0268 8913	0.0213 2123	0.0169 2439	50

TABLE IV.—Present Value of 1 at Compound Interest

$$v^n = (1+i)^{-n}$$

n	7%	7½%	8%	8½%	n
51	0.0317 2688	0.0250 1315	0.0197 4188	0.0155 9852	51
52	0.0296 5129	0.0232 6804	0.0182 7952	0.0143 7651	52
53	0.0277 1148	0.0216 4469	0.0169 2548	0.0132 5024	53
54	0.0258 9858	0.0201 3460	0.0156 7174	0.0122 1221	54
55	0.0242 0428	0.0187 2986	0.0145 1087	0.0112 5549	55
56	0.0226 2083	0.0174 2312	0.0134 3599	0.0103 7372	56
57	0.0211 4096	0.0162 0756	0.0124 4073	0.0095 6104	57
58	0.0197 5791	0.0150 7680	0.0115 1920	0.0088 1201	58
59	0.0184 6533	0.0140 2493	0.0106 6592	0.0081 2167	59
60	0.0172 5732	0.0130 4644	0.0098 7585	0.0074 8541	60
61	0.0161 2834	0.0121 3623	0.0091 4431	0.0068 9900	61
62	0.0150 7321	0.0112 8951	0.0084 6695	0.0063 5852	62
63	0.0140 8711	0.0105 0187	0.0078 3977	0.0058 6039	63
64	0.0131 6553	0.0097 6918	0.0072 5905	0.0054 0128	64
65	0.0123 0423	0.0090 8761	0.0067 2134	0.0049 7814	65
66	0.0114 9928	0.0084 5359	0.0062 2346	0.0045 8815	66
67	0.0107 4699	0.0078 6381	0.0057 6247	0.0042 2871	67
68	0.0100 4392	0.0073 1517	0.0053 3562	0.0038 9743	68
69	0.0093 8684	0.0068 0481	0.0049 4039	0.0035 9210	69
70	0.0087 7275	0.0063 3006	0.0045 7443	0.0033 1069	70
71	0.0081 9883	0.0058 8842	0.0042 3558	0.0030 5133	71
72	0.0076 6246	0.0054 7760	0.0039 2184	0.0028 1228	72
73	0.0071 6117	0.0050 9544	0.0036 3133	0.0025 9196	73
74	0.0066 9269	0.0047 3995	0.0033 6234	0.0023 8891	74
75	0.0062 5485	0.0044 0925	0.0031 1328	0.0022 0176	75
76	0.0058 4565	0.0041 0163	0.0028 8267	0.0020 2927	76
77	0.0054 6323	0.0038 1547	0.0026 6914	0.0018 7030	77
78	0.0051 0582	0.0035 4928	0.0024 7142	0.0017 2377	78
79	0.0047 7179	0.0033 0165	0.0022 8835	0.0015 8873	79
80	0.0044 5962	0.0030 7130	0.0021 1885	0.0014 6427	80
81	0.0041 6787	0.0028 5703	0.0019 6190	0.0013 4956	81
82	0.0038 9520	0.0026 5770	0.0018 1657	0.0012 4383	82
83	0.0036 4038	0.0024 7228	0.0016 8201	0.0011 4639	83
84	0.0034 0222	0.0022 9979	0.0015 5742	0.0010 5658	84
85	0.0031 7965	0.0021 3934	0.0014 4205	0.0009 7381	85
86	0.0029 7163	0.0019 9009	0.0013 3523	0.0008 9752	86
87	0.0027 7723	0.0018 5124	0.0012 3633	0.0008 2720	87
88	0.0025 9554	0.0017 2209	0.0011 4475	0.0007 6240	88
89	0.0024 2574	0.0016 0194	0.0010 5995	0.0007 0267	89
90	0.0022 6704	0.0014 9018	0.0009 8144	0.0006 4762	90
91	0.0021 1873	0.0013 8621	0.0009 0874	0.0005 9689	91
92	0.0019 8012	0.0012 8950	0.0008 4142	0.0005 5013	92
93	0.0018 5058	0.0011 9953	0.0007 7910	0.0005 0703	93
94	0.0017 2952	0.0011 1585	0.0007 2138	0.0004 6731	94
95	0.0016 1637	0.0010 3800	0.0006 6795	0.0004 3070	95
96	0.0015 1063	0.0009 6558	0.0006 1847	0.0003 9696	96
97	0.0014 1180	0.0008 9821	0.0005 7266	0.0003 6586	97
98	0.0013 1944	0.0008 3555	0.0005 3024	0.0003 3720	98
99	0.0012 3312	0.0007 7725	0.0004 9096	0.0003 1078	99
100	0.0011 5245	0.0007 2303	0.0004 5459	0.0002 8644	100

TABLE V.—Amount of Annuity of 1 per Period

$$s_{\overline{n}|i} = \frac{(1 + i)^n - 1}{i}$$

n	¼%	$\frac{7}{24}$%	⅓%	$\frac{5}{12}$%	n
1	1.0000 0000	1.0000 0000	1.0000 0000	1.0000 0000	1
2	2.0025 0000	2.0029 1667	2.0033 3333	2.0041 6667	2
3	3.0075 0625	3.0087 5851	3.0100 1111	3.0125 1736	3
4	4.0150 2502	4.0175 3405	4.0200 4448	4.0250 6952	4
5	5.0250 6258	5.0292 5186	5.0334 4463	5.0418 4064	5
6	6.0376 2523	6.0439 2051	6.0502 2278	6.0628 4831	6
7	7.0527 1930	7.0615 4861	7.0703 9019	7.0881 1018	7
8	8.0703 5110	8.0821 4480	8.0939 5816	8.1176 4397	8
9	9.0905 2697	9.1057 1772	9.1209 3802	9.1514 6749	9
10	10.1132 5329	10.1322 7606	10.1513 4114	10.1895 9860	10
11	11.1385 3642	11.1618 2853	11.1851 7895	11.2320 5526	11
12	12.1663 8277	12.1943 8387	12.2224 6288	12.2788 5549	12
13	13.1967 9872	13.2299 5082	13.2632 0442	13.3300 1739	13
14	14.2297 9072	14.2685 3818	14.3074 1510	14.3855 5913	14
15	15.2653 6520	15.3101 5475	15.3551 0648	15.4454 9896	15
16	16.3035 2861	16.3548 0936	16.4062 9017	16.5098 5520	16
17	17.3442 8743	17.4025 1089	17.4609 7781	17.5786 4627	17
18	18.3876 4815	18.4532 6822	18.5191 8107	18.6518 9063	18
19	19.4336 1727	19.5070 9025	19.5809 1167	19.7296 0684	19
20	20.4822 0131	20.5639 8593	20.6461 8137	20.8118 1353	20
21	21.5334 0682	21.6239 6422	21.7150 0198	21.8985 2942	21
22	22.5872 4033	22.6870 3412	22.7873 8532	22.9897 7330	22
23	23.6437 0843	23.7532 0463	23.8633 4327	24.0855 6402	23
24	24.7028 1770	24.8224 8481	24.9428 8775	25.1859 2054	24
25	25.7645 7475	25.8948 8373	26.0260 3071	26.2908 6187	25
26	26.8289 8619	26.9704 1047	27.1127 8414	27.4004 0713	26
27	27.8960 5865	28.0490 7417	28.2031 6009	28.5145 7549	27
28	28.9657 9880	29.1308 8397	29.2971 7062	29.6333 8622	28
29	30.0382 1330	30.2158 4904	30.3948 2786	30.7568 5867	29
30	31.1133 0883	31.3039 7860	31.4961 4395	31.8850 1224	30
31	32.1910 9210	32.3952 8188	32.6011 3110	33.0178 6646	31
32	33.2715 6983	33.4897 6811	33.7098 0154	34.1554 4090	32
33	34.3547 4876	34.5874 4660	34.8221 6754	35.2977 5524	33
34	35.4406 3563	35.6883 2666	35.9382 4143	36.4448 2922	34
35	36.5292 3722	36.7924 1761	37.0580 3557	37.5966 8268	35
36	37.6205 6031	37.8997 2883	38.1815 6236	38.7533 3552	36
37	38.7146 1171	39.0102 6970	39.3088 3423	39.9148 0775	37
38	39.8113 9824	40.1240 4966	40.4398 6368	41.0811 1945	38
39	40.9109 2673	41.2410 7813	41.5746 6322	42.2522 9078	39
40	42.0132 0405	42.3613 6461	42.7132 4543	43.4283 4199	40
41	43.1182 3706	43.4849 1859	43.8556 2292	44.6092 9342	41
42	44.2260 3265	44.6117 4961	45.0018 0833	45.7951 6548	42
43	45.3365 9774	45.7418 6721	46.1518 1436	46.9859 7866	43
44	46.4499 3923	46.8752 8099	47.3056 5374	48.1817 5358	44
45	47.5660 6408	48.0120 0056	48.4633 3925	49.3825 1088	45
46	48.6849 7924	49.1520 3556	49.6248 8371	50.5882 7134	46
47	49.8066 9169	50.2953 9566	50.7902 9999	51.7990 5581	47
48	50.9312 0842	51.4420 9057	51.9596 0099	53.0148 8521	48
49	52.0585 3644	52.5921 3000	53.1327 9966	54.2357 8056	49
50	53.1886 8278	53.7455 2371	54.3099 0899	55.4617 6298	50

TABLE V.—Amount of Annuity of 1 per Period

$$s_{\overline{n}|i} = \frac{(1 + i)^n - 1}{i}$$

n	$\frac{1}{4}\%$	$\frac{7}{24}\%$	$\frac{1}{3}\%$	$\frac{5}{12}\%$	n
51	54.3216 5449	54.9022 8149	55.4909 4202	56.6928 5366	51
52	55.4574 5862	56.0624 1314	56.6759 1183	57.9290 7388	52
53	56.5961 0227	57.2259 285!	57.8648 3154	59.1704 4503	53
54	57.7375 9252	58.3928 3747	59.0577 1431	60.4169 8855	54
55	58.8819 3650	59.5631 4991	60.2545 7336	61.6687 2600	55
56	60.0291 4135	60.7368 7577	61.4554 2194	62.9256 7902	56
57	61.1792 1420	61.9140 2499	62.6602 7334	64.1878 6935	57
58	62.3321 6223	63.0946 0756	63.8691 4092	65.4553 1881	58
59	63.4879 9264	64.2786 3350	65.0820 3806	66.7280 4930	59
60	64.6467 1262	65.4661 1285	66.2989 7818	68.0060 8284	60
61	65.8083 2940	66.6570 5568	67.5199 7478	69.2894 4152	61
62	66.9728 5023	67.8514 7209	68.7450 4136	70.5781 4753	62
63	68.1402 8235	69.0493 7222	69.9741 9150	71.8722 2314	63
64	69.3106 3306	70.2507 6622	71.2074 3880	73.1716 9074	64
65	70.4839 0964	71.4556 6429	72.4447 9693	74.4765 7278	65
66	71.6601 1942	72.6640 7664	73.6862 7959	75.7868 9184	66
67	72.8392 6971	73.8760 1353	74.9319 0052	77.1026 7055	67
68	74.0213 6789	75.0914 8524	76.1816 7352	78.4239 3168	68
69	75.2064 2131	76.3105 0207	77.4356 1243	79.7506 9806	69
70	76.3944 3736	77.5330 7437	78.6937 3114	81.0829 9264	70
71	77.5854 2345	78.7592 1250	79.9560 4358	82.4208 3844	71
72	78.7793 8701	79.9889 2687	81.2225 6372	83.7642 5860	72
73	79.9763 3548	81.2222 2791	82.4933 0560	85.1132 7634	73
74	81.1762 7632	82.4591 2607	83.7682 8329	86.4679 1500	74
75	82.3792 1701	83.6996 3186	85.0475 1090	87.8281 9797	75
76	83.5851 6505	84.9437 5578	86.3310 0260	89.1941 4880	76
77	84.7941 2797	86.1915 0840	87.6187 7261	90.5657 9109	77
78	86.0061 1329	87.4429 0030	88.9108 3519	91.9431 4855	78
79	87.2211 2857	88.6979 4209	90.2072 0464	93.3262 4500	79
80	88.4391 8139	89.9566 4443	91.5078 9532	94.7151 0436	80
81	89.6602 7934	91.2190 1797	92.8129 2164	96.1097 5062	81
82	90.8844 3004	92.4850 7344	94.1222 9804	97.5102 0792	82
83	92.1116 4112	93.7548 2157	95.4360 3904	98.9165 0045	8?
84	93.3419 2022	95.0282 7313	96.7541 5917	100.3286 5254	84
85	94.5752 7502	96.3054 3893	98.0766 7303	101.7466 8859	85
86	95.8117 1321	97.5863 2980	99.4035 9527	103.1706 3312	86
87	97.0512 4249	98.8709 5659	100.7349 4059	104.6005 1076	87
88	98.2938 7060	100.1593 3021	102.0707 2373	106.0363 4622	88
89	99.5396 0527	101.4514 6159	103.4109 5947	107.4781 6433	89
90	100.7884 5429	102.7473 6169	104.7556 6267	108.9259 9002	90
91	102.0404 2542	104.0470 4149	106.1048 4821	110.3798 4831	91
92	103.2955 2649	105.3505 1203	107.4585 3104	111.8397 6434	92
93	104.5537 6530	106.6577 8436	108.8167 2614	113.3057 6336	93
94	105.8151 4972	107.9688 6956	110.1794 4856	114.7778 7071	94
95	107.0796 8759	109.2837 7877	111.5467 1339	116.2561 1184	95
96	108.3473 8681	110.6025 2312	112.9185 3577	117.7405 1230	96
97	109.6182 5528	111.9251 1381	114.2949 3089	119.2310 9777	97
98	110.8923 0091	113.2515 6206	115.6759 1399	120.7278 9401	98
99	112.1695 3167	114.5818 7912	117.0615 0037	122.2309 2690	99
100	113.4499 5550	115.9160 7626	118.4517 0537	123.7402 2243	100

TABLE V.—Amount of Annuity of 1 per Period

$$s_{\overline{n}|i} = \frac{(1 + i)^n - 1}{i}$$

n	$\frac{1}{4}\%$	$\frac{7}{24}\%$	$\frac{1}{3}\%$	$\frac{5}{12}\%$	n
101	114.7335 8038	117.2541 6482	119.8465 4439	125.2558 0669	101
102	116.0204 1434	118.5961 5613	121.2460 3287	126.7777 0589	102
103	117.3104 6537	119.9420 6159	122.6501 8632	128.3059 4633	103
104	118.6037 4153	121.2918 9260	124.0590 2027	129.8405 5444	104
105	119.9002 5089	122.6456 6062	125.4725 5034	131.3815 5675	105
106	121.2000 0152	124.0033 7713	126.8907 9217	132.9289 7990	106
107	122.5030 0152	125.3650 5365	128.3137 6148	134.4828 5065	107
108	123.8092 5902	126.7307 0172	129.7414 7402	136.0431 9586	108
109	125.1187 8217	128.1003 3294	131.1739 4560	137.6100 4251	109
110	126.4315 7913	129.4739 5891	132.6111 9208	139.1834 1769	110
111	127.7476 5807	130.8515 9129	134.0532 2939	140.7633 4860	111
112	129.0670 2722	132.2332 4176	135.5000 7349	142.3498 6255	112
113	130.3896 9479	133.6189 2205	136.9517 4040	143.9429 8698	113
114	131.7156 6902	135.0086 4391	138.4082 4620	145.5427 4942	114
115	133.0449 5820	136.4024 1912	139.8696 0702	147.1491 7754	115
116	134.3775 7059	137.8002 5951	141.3358 3905	148.7622 9912	116
117	135.7135 1452	139.2021 7693	142.8069 5851	150.3821 4203	117
118	137.0527 9830	140.6081 8328	144.2829 8170	152.0087 3429	118
119	138.3954 3030	142.0182 9048	145.7639 2498	153.6421 0401	119
120	139.7414 1888	143.4325 1049	147.2498 0477	155.2822 7945	120
121	141.0907 7242	144.8508 5532	148.7406 3745	156.9292 8895	121
122	142.4434 9935	146.2733 3698	150.2364 3958	158.5831 6098	122
123	143.7996 0810	147.6999 6754	151.7372 2771	160.2439 2415	123
124	145.1591 0712	149.1307 5912	153.2430 1847	161.9116 0717	124
125	146.5220 0489	150.5657 2383	154.7538 2853	163.5862 3887	125
126	147.8883 0990	152.0048 7386	156.2696 7463	165.2678 4819	126
127	149.2580 3068	153.4482 2141	157.7905 7354	166.9564 6423	127
128	150.6311 7575	154.8957 7872	159.3165 4212	168.6521 1616	128
129	152.0077 5369	156.3475 5807	160.8475 9726	170.3548 3331	129
130	153.3877 7308	157.8035 7178	162.3837 5592	172.0646 4512	130
131	154.7712 4251	159.2638 3220	163.9250 3510	173.7815 8114	131
132	156.1581 7062	160.7283 5171	165.4714 5189	175.5056 7106	132
133	157.5485 6604	162.1971 4274	167.0230 2339	177.2369 4469	133
134	158.9424 3746	163.6702 1774	168.5797 6680	178.9754 3196	134
135	160.3397 9355	165.1475 8920	170.1416 9936	180.7211 6293	135
136	161.7406 4304	166.6292 6967	171.7088 3836	182.4741 6777	136
137	163.1449 9464	168.1152 7171	173.2812 0115	184.2344 7681	137
138	164.5528 5713	169.6056 0792	174.8588 0516	186.0021 2046	138
139	165.9642 3927	171.1002 9094	176.4416 6784	187.7771 2929	139
140	167.3791 4987	172.5993 3346	178.0298 0673	189.5595 3400	140
141	168.7975 9775	174.1027 4818	179.6232 3942	191.3493 6539	141
142	170.2195 9174	175.6105 4786	181.2219 8355	193.1466 5441	142
143	171.6451 4072	177.1227 4529	182.8260 5683	194.9514 3214	143
144	173.0742 5357	178.6393 5330	184.4354 7702	196.7637 2977	144
145	174.5069 3921	180.1603 8475	186.0502 6194	198.5835 7865	145
146	175.9432 0655	181.6858 5254	187.6704 2948	200.4110 1023	146
147	177.3830 6457	183.2157 6961	189.2959 9758	202.2460 5610	147
148	178.8265 2223	184.7501 4893	190.9269 8424	204.0887 4800	148
149	180.2735 8854	186.2890 0353	192.5634 0752	205.9391 1779	149
150	181.7242 7251	187.8323 4646	194.2052 8554	207.7971 9744	150

TABLE V.—Amount of Annuity of 1 per Period

$$s_{n|i} = \frac{(1 + i)^n - 1}{i}$$

n	¼%	⁷⁄₂₄%	⅓%	⁵⁄₁₂%	n
151	183.1785 8319	189.3801 9080	195.8526 3650	209.6630 1910	151
152	184.6365 2965	190.9325 4969	197.5054 7862	211.5366 1501	152
153	186.0981 2097	192.4894 3630	199.1638 3021	213.4180 1758	153
154	187.5633 6627	194.0508 6382	200.8277 0965	215.3072 5932	154
155	189.0322 7469	195.6168 4551	202.4971 3534	217.2043 7290	155
156	190.5048 5538	197.1873 9464	204.1721 2580	219.1093 9112	156
157	191.9811 1752	198.7625 2454	205.8526 9955	221.0223 4691	157
158	193.4610 7031	200.3422 4857	207.5388 7521	222.9432 7336	158
159	194.9447 2298	201.9265 8013	209.2306 7146	224.8722 0366	159
160	196.4320 8479	203.5155 3265	210.9281 0704	226.8091 7118	160
161	197.9231 6500	205.1091 1962	212.6312 0073	228.7542 0939	161
162	199.4179 7292	206.7073 5455	214.3399 7139	230.7073 5193	162
163	200.9165 1785	208.3102 5101	216.0544 3797	232.6686 3256	163
164	202.4188 0914	209.9178 2257	217.7746 1942	234.6380 8520	164
165	203.9248 5617	211.5300 8289	219.5005 3482	236.6157 4389	165
166	205.4346 6831	213.1470 4563	221.2322 0327	238.6016 4282	166
167	206.9482 5498	214.7687 2451	222.9696 4395	240.5958 1633	167
168	208.4656 2562	216.3951 3329	224.7128 7610	242.5982 9890	168
169	209.9867 8968	218.0262 8576	226.4619 1902	244.6091 2515	169
170	211.5117 5665	219.6621 9576	228.2167 9208	246.6283 2983	170
171	213.0405 3605	221.3028 7717	229.9775 1472	248.6559 4788	171
172	214.5731 3739	222.9483 4389	231.7441 0643	250.6920 1433	172
173	216.1095 7023	224.5986 0989	233.5165 8679	252.7365 6439	173
174	217.6498 4415	226.2536 8917	235.2949 7541	254.7896 3340	174
175	219.1939 6876	227.9135 9577	237.0792 9200	256.8512 5688	175
176	220.7419 5369	229.5783 4375	238.8695 5630	258.9214 7045	176
177	222.2938 0857	231.2479 4726	240.6657 8816	261.0003 0991	177
178	223.8495 4309	232.9224 2044	242.4680 0745	263.0878 1120	178
179	225.4091 6695	234.6017 7750	244.2762 3414	265.1840 1041	179
180	226.9726 8987	236.2860 3268	246.0904 8826	267.2889 4379	180
181	228.5401 2159	237.9752 0028	247.9107 8988	269.4026 4772	181
182	230.1114 7130	239.6692 9461	249.7371 5918	271.5251 5875	182
183	231.6867 5058	241.3683 3005	251.5696 1638	273.6565 1358	183
184	233.2659 6745	243.0723 2101	253.4081 8177	275.7967 4905	184
185	234.8491 3237	244.7812 8195	255.2528 7571	277.9459 0218	185
186	236.4362 5520	246.4952 2736	257.1037 1863	280.1040 1010	186
187	238.0273 4584	248.2141 7177	258.9607 3102	282.2711 1014	187
188	239.6224 1420	249.9381 2977	260.8239 3346	284.4472 3977	188
189	241.2214 7024	251.6671 1598	262.6933 4657	286.6324 3660	189
190	242.8245 2392	253.4011 4507	264.5689 9106	288.8267 3842	190
191	244.4315 8523	255.1402 3174	266.4508 8769	291.0301 8316	191
192	246.0426 6419	256.8843 9075	268.3390 5732	293.2428 0892	192
193	247.6577 7085	258.6336 3689	270.2335 2084	295.4646 5396	193
194	249.2769 1528	260.3879 8500	272.1342 9925	297.6957 5669	194
195	250.9001 0756	262.1474 4995	274.0414 1358	299.9361 5568	195
196	252.5273 5783	263.9120 4668	275.9548 8495	302.1858 8966	196
197	254.1586 7623	265.6817 9015	277.8747 3457	304.4449 9753	197
198	255.7940 7292	267.4566 9537	279.8009 8369	306.7135 1835	198
199	257.4335 5810	269.2367 7740	281.7336 5363	308.9914 9135	199
200	259.0771 4200	271.0220 5134	283.6727 6581	311.2789 5589	200

TABLE V.—Amount of Annuity of 1 per Period

$$s_{\overline{n}|i} = \frac{(1 + i)^n - 1}{i}$$

n	½%	7/12%	5/8%	2/3%	n
1	1.0000 0000	1.0000 0000	1.0000 0000	1.0000 0000	1
2	2.0050 0000	2.0058 3333	2.0062 5000	2.0066 6667	2
3	3.0150 2500	3.0175 3403	3.1087 8906	3.0200 4444	3
4	4.0301 0013	4.0351 3631	4.0376 5649	4.0401 7807	4
5	5.0502 5063	5.0586 7460	5.0628 9185	5.0671 1259	5
6	6.0755 0188	6.0881 8354	6.0945 3492	6.1008 9335	6
7	7.1058 7939	7.1236 9794	7.1326 2576	7.1415 6597	7
8	8.1414 0879	8.1652 5284	8.1772 0468	8.1891 7641	8
9	9.1821 1583	9.2128 8349	9.2283 1220	9.2437 7092	9
10	10.2280 2641	10.2666 2531	10.2859 8916	10.3053 9606	10
11	11.2791 6654	11.3265 1396	11.3502 7659	11.3740 9870	11
12	12.3355 6237	12.3925 8529	12.4212 1582	12.4499 2602	12
13	13.3972 4018	13.4648 7537	13.4988 4842	13.5329 2553	13
14	14.4642 2639	14.5434 2048	14.5832 1622	14.6231 4503	14
15	15.5365 4752	15.6282 5710	15.6743 6132	15.7206 3266	15
16	16.6142 3026	16.7194 2193	16.7723 2608	16.8254 3688	16
17	17.6973 0141	17.8169 5189	17.8771 5312	17.9376 0646	17
18	18.7857 8791	18.9208 8411	18.9888 8532	19.0571 9051	18
19	19.8797 1685	20.0312 5593	20.1075 6586	20.1842 3844	19
20	20.9791 1544	21.1481 0493	21.2332 3814	21.3188 0003	20
21	22.0840 1101	22.2714 6887	22.3659 4588	22.4609 2536	21
22	23.1944 3107	23.4013 8577	23.5057 3304	23.6106 6487	22
23	24.3104 0322	24.5378 9386	24.6526 4387	24.7680 6930	23
24	25.4319 5524	25.6810 3157	25.8067 2290	25.9331 8976	24
25	26.5591 1502	26.8308 3759	26.9680 1492	27.1060 7769	25
26	27.6919 1059	27.9873 5081	28.1365 6501	28.2867 8488	26
27	28.8303 7015	29.1506 1005	29.3124 1854	29.4753 6344	27
28	29.9745 2200	30.3206 5558	30.4956 2116	30.6718 6586	28
29	31.1243 9461	31.4975 2607	31.6862 1879	31.8763 4497	29
30	32.2800 1658	32.6812 6164	32.8842 5766	33.0888 5394	30
31	33.4414 1666	33.8719 0233	34.0897 8427	34.3094 4630	31
32	34.6086 2375	35.0694 8843	35.3028 4542	35.5381 7594	32
33	35.7816 6686	36.2740 6045	36.5234 8820	36.7750 9711	33
34	36.9605 7520	37.4856 5913	37.7517 6000	38.0202 6443	34
35	38.1453 7807	38.7043 2548	38.9877 0850	39.2737 3286	35
36	39.3361 0496	39.9301 0071	40.2313 8168	40.5355 5774	36
37	40.5327 8549	41.1630 2630	41.4828 2782	41.8057 9479	37
38	41.7354 4942	42.4031 4395	42.7420 9549	43.0845 0009	38
39	42.9441 2666	43.6504 9562	44.0092 3359	44.3717 3009	39
40	44.1588 4730	44.9051 2352	45.2842 9130	45.6675 4163	40
41	45.3796 4153	46.1670 7007	46.5673 1812	46.9719 9191	41
42	46.6065 3974	47.4363 7798	47.8583 6386	48.2851 3852	42
43	47.8395 7244	48.7130 9018	49.1574 7863	49.6070 3944	43
44	49.0787 7030	49.9972 4988	50.4647 1287	50.9377 5304	44
45	50.3241 6415	51.2889 0050	51.7801 1733	52.2773 3806	45
46	51.5757 8497	52.5880 6575	53.1037 4306	53.6258 5365	46
47	52.8336 6390	53.8948 4959	54.4356 4146	54.9833 5934	47
48	54.0978 3222	55.2092 3621	55.7758 6421	56.3499 1507	48
49	55.3683 2138	56.5312 9009	57.1244 6337	57.7255 8117	49
50	56.6451 6299	57.8610 5595	58.4814 9126	59.1104 1837	50

TABLE V.—Amount of Annuity of 1 per Period

$$s_{\overline{n}|i} = \frac{(1+i)^n - 1}{i}$$

n	½%	⁷⁄₁₂%	⅝%	⅔%	n
51	57.9283 8880	59.1985 7877	59.8470 0058	60.5044 8783	51
52	59.2180 3075	60.5439 0381	61.2210 4434	61.9078 5108	52
53	60.5141 2090	61.8970 7659	62.6036 7586	63.3205 7009	53
54	61.8166 9150	63.2581 4287	63.9949 4884	64.7427 0722	54
55	63.1257 7496	64.6271 4870	65.3949 1727	66.1743 2527	55
56	64.4414 0384	66.0041 4040	66.8036 3550	67.6154 8744	56
57	65.7636 1086	67.3891 6455	68.2211 5822	69.0662 5736	57
58	67.0924 2891	68.7822 6801	69.6475 4046	70.5266 9907	58
59	68.4278 9105	70.1834 9791	71.0828 3759	71.9968 7706	59
60	69.7700 3051	71.5929 0165	72.5271 0532	73.4768 5625	60
61	71.1188 8066	73.0105 2691	73.9803 9973	74.9667 0195	61
62	72.4744 7507	74.4364 2165	75.4427 7723	76.4664 7997	62
63	73.8368 4744	75.8706 3411	76.9142 9459	77.9762 5650	63
64	75.2060 3168	77.3132 1281	78.3950 0893	79.4960 9821	64
65	76.5820 6184	78.7642 0655	79.8849 7774	81.0260 7220	65
66	77.9649 7215	80.2236 6442	81.3842 5885	82.5662 4601	66
67	79.3547 9701	81.6916 3579	82.8929 1046	84.1166 8765	67
68	80.7515 7099	83.1681 7034	84.4109 9115	85.6774 6557	68
69	82.1553 2885	84.6533 1800	85.9385 5985	87.2486 4867	69
70	83.5661 0549	86.1471 2902	87.4756 7585	88.8303 0633	70
71	84.9839 3602	87.6496 5394	89.0223 9882	90.4225 0837	71
72	86.4088 5570	89.1609 4359	90.5787 8882	92.0253 2510	72
73	87.8408 9998	90.6810 4909	92.1449 0625	93.6388 2726	73
74	89.2801 0448	92.2100 2188	93.7208 1191	95.2630 8611	74
75	90.7265 0500	93.7479 1367	95.3065 6698	96.8981 7335	75
76	92.1801 3752	95.2947 7650	96.9022 3303	98.5441 6118	76
77	93.6410 3821	96.8506 6270	98.5078 7198	100.2011 2225	77
78	95.1092 4340	98.4156 2490	100.1235 4618	101.8691 2973	78
79	96.5847 8962	99.9897 1604	101.7493 1835	103.5482 5726	79
80	98.0677 1357	101.5729 8938	103.3852 5159	105.2385 7898	80
81	99.5580 5214	103.1654 9849	105.0314 0941	106.9401 6950	81
82	101.0558 4240	104.7672 9723	106.6878 5572	108.6531 0397	82
83	102.5611 2161	106.3784 3980	108.3546 5482	110.3774 5799	83
84	104.0739 2722	107.9989 8070	110.0318 7141	112.1133 0771	84
85	105.5942 9685	109.6289 7475	111.7195 7061	113.8607 2977	85
86	107.1222 6834	111.2684 7710	113.4178 1792	115.6198 0130	86
87	108.6578 7968	112.9175 4322	115.1266 7928	117.3905 9997	87
88	110.2011 6908	114.5762 2889	116.8462 2103	119.1732 0397	88
89	111.7521 7492	116.2445 9022	118.5765 0991	120.9676 9200	89
90	113.3109 3580	117.9226 8367	120.3176 1310	122.7741 4328	90
91	114.6774 9048	119.6105 6599	122.0695 9818	124.5926 3757	91
92	116.4518 7793	121.3082 9429	123.8325 3317	126.4232 5515	92
93	118.0341 3732	123.0159 2601	125.6064 8650	128.2660 7685	93
94	119.6243 0800	124.7335 1891	127.3915 2704	130.1211 8403	94
95	121.2224 2954	126.4611 3110	129.1877 2408	131.9886 5859	95
96	122.8285 4169	128.1988 2103	130.9951 4736	133.8685 8298	96
97	124.4426 8440	129.9466 4749	132.8138 6703	135.7610 4020	97
98	126.0648 9782	131.7046 6960	134.6439 5370	137.6661 1380	98
99	127.6952 2231	133.4729 4684	136.4854 7841	139.5838 8790	99
100	129.3336 9842	135.2515 3903	138.3385 1265	141.5144 4715	100

503

TABLE V.—Amount of Annuity of 1 per Period

$$s_{\overline{n}|i} = \frac{(1 + i)^n - 1}{i}$$

n	½%	⁷⁄₁₂%	⅝%	⅔%	n
101	130.9803 6692	137.0405 0634	140.2031 2836	143.4578 7680	101
102	132.6352 6875	138.8399 0929	142.0793 9791	145.4142 6264	102
103	134.2984 4509	140.6498 0876	143.9673 9414	147.3836 9106	103
104	135.9699 3732	142.4702 6598	145.8671 9036	149.3662 4900	104
105	137.6497 8701	144.3013 4253	147.7788 6030	151.3620 2399	105
106	139.3380 3594	146.1431 0036	149.7024 7817	153.3711 0415	106
107	141.0347 2612	147.9956 0178	151.6381 1866	155.3935 7818	107
108	142.7398 9975	149.8589 0946	153.5858 5690	157.4295 3537	108
109	144.4535 9925	151.7330 8643	155.5457 6851	159.4790 6560	109
110	146.1758 6725	153.6181 9610	157.5179 2956	161.5422 5937	110
111	147.9067 4658	155.5143 0225	159.5024 1662	163.6192 0777	111
112	149.6462 8032	157.4214 6901	161.4993 0673	165.7100 0249	112
113	151.3945 1172	159.3397 6091	163.5086 7739	167.8147 3584	113
114	153.1514 8428	161.2692 4285	165.5306 0663	169.9335 0074	114
115	154.9172 4170	163.2099 8010	167.5651 7292	172.0663 9075	115
116	156.6918 2791	165.1620 3832	169.6124 5525	174.2135 0002	116
117	158.4752 8704	167.1254 8354	171.6725 3310	176.3749 2335	117
118	160.2676 6348	169.1003 8219	173.7454 8643	178.5507 5618	118
119	162.0690 0180	171.0868 0109	175.8313 9572	180.7410 9455	119
120	163.8793 4681	173.0848 0743	177.9303 4194	182.9460 3518	120
121	165.6987 4354	175.0944 6881	180.0424 0658	185.1656 7542	121
122	167.5272 3726	177.1158 5321	182.1676 7162	187.4001 1325	122
123	169.3648 7344	179.1490 2902	184.3062 1957	189.6494 4734	123
124	171.2116 9781	181.1940 6502	186.4581 3344	191.9137 7699	124
125	173.0677 5630	183.2510 3040	188.6234 9677	194.1932 0217	125
126	174.9330 9508	185.3199 9474	190.8023 9363	196.4878 2352	126
127	176.8077 6056	187.4010 2805	192.9949 0859	198.7977 4234	127
128	178.6917 9936	189.4942 0071	195.2011 2677	201.1230 6062	128
129	180.5852 5836	191.5995 8355	197.4211 3381	203.4638 8103	129
130	182.4881 8465	193.7172 4778	199.6550 1589	205.8203 0690	130
131	184.4006 2557	195.8472 6506	201.9028 5974	208.1924 4228	131
132	186.3226 2870	197.9897 0744	204.1647 5262	210.5803 9189	132
133	188.2542 4184	200.1446 4740	206.4407 8232	212.9842 6117	133
134	190.1955 1305	202.3121 5785	208.7310 3721	215.4041 5625	134
135	192.1464 9062	204.4923 1210	211.0356 0619	217.8401 8396	135
136	194.1072 2307	206.6851 8392	213.3545 7873	220.2924 5185	136
137	196.0777 5919	208.8908 4749	215.6880 4485	222.7610 6820	137
138	198.0581 4798	211.1093 7744	218.0360 9513	225.2461 4198	138
139	200.0484 3872	213.3408 4881	220.3988 2072	227.7477 8293	139
140	202.0486 8092	215.5853 3709	222.7763 1335	230.2661 0148	140
141	204.0589 2432	217.8429 1822	225.1686 6531	232.8012 0883	141
142	206.0792 1894	220.1136 6858	227.5759 6947	235.3532 1688	142
143	208.1096 1504	222.3976 6498	229.9983 1928	237.9222 3833	143
144	210.1501 6311	224.6949 8469	232.4358 0878	240.5083 8659	144
145	212.2009 1393	227.0057 0544	234.8885 3258	243.1117 7583	145
146	214.2619 1850	229.3299 0538	237.3565 8591	245.7325 2100	146
147	216.3332 2809	231.6676 6317	239.8400 6457	248.3707 3781	147
148	218.4148 9423	234.0190 5787	242.3390 6497	251.0265 4273	148
149	220.5069 6870	236.3841 6904	244.8536 8413	253.7000 5301	149
150	222.6095 0354	238.7630 7669	247.3840 1966	256.3913 8670	150

504

TABLE V.—Amount of Annuity of 1 per Period

$$s_{\overline{n}|i} = \frac{(1 + i)^n - 1}{i}$$

n	$\frac{1}{2}\%$	$\frac{7}{12}\%$	$\frac{5}{8}\%$	$\frac{2}{3}\%$	n
151	224.7225 5106	241.1558 6130	249.9301 6978	259.1006 6261	151
152	226.8461 6382	243.5626 0383	252.4922 3334	261.8280 0036	152
153	228.9803 9464	245.9833 8568	255.0703 0980	264.5735 2036	153
154	231.1252 9661	248.4182 8877	257.6644 9923	267.3373 4383	154
155	233.2809 2309	250.8673 9545	260.2749 0235	270.1195 9279	155
156	235.4473 2771	253.3307 8859	262.9016 2049	272.9203 9008	156
157	237.6245 6435	255.8085 5153	265.5447 5562	275.7398 5934	157
158	239.8126 8717	258.3007 6808	268.2044 1035	278.5781 2507	158
159	242.0117 5060	260.8075 2256	270.8806 8791	281.4353 1257	159
160	244.2218 0936	263.3288 9977	273.5736 9221	284.3115 4799	160
161	246.6429 1840	265.8649 8502	276.2835 2779	287.2069 5831	161
162	248.6751 3300	268.4158 6410	279.0102 9983	290.1216 7136	162
163	250.9185 0866	270.9816 2331	281.7541 1421	293.0558 1584	163
164	253.1731 0121	273.5623 4944	284.5150 7742	296.0095 2128	164
165	255.4389 6671	276.1581 2982	287.2932 9666	298.9829 1809	165
166	257.7161 6154	278.7690 5224	290.0888 7976	301.9761 3754	166
167	260.0047 4235	281.3952 0504	292.9019 3526	304.9893 1179	167
168	262.3047 6606	284.0366 7707	295.7325 7235	308.0225 7387	168
169	264.6162 8989	286.6935 5769	298.5809 0093	311.0760 5770	169
170	266.9393 7134	289.3659 3678	301.4470 3156	314.1498 9808	170
171	269.2740 6820	292.0539 0474	304.3310 7551	317.2442 3073	171
172	271.6204 3854	294.7575 5252	307.2331 4473	320.3591 9227	172
173	273.9785 4073	297.4769 7158	310.1533 5189	323.4949 2022	173
174	276.3484 3344	300.2122 5391	313.0918 1033	326.6515 5302	174
175	278.7301 7561	302.9634 9206	316.0486 3415	329.8292 3004	175
176	281.1238 2648	305.7307 7910	319.0239 3811	333.0280 9158	176
177	283.5294 4562	308.5142 0864	322.0178 3773	336.2482 7885	177
178	285.9470 9284	311.3138 7486	325.0304 4921	339.4899 3405	178
179	288.3768 2831	314.1298 7246	328.0618 8952	342.7532 0027	179
180	290.8187 1245	316.9622 9672	331.1122 7633	346.0382 2161	180
181	293.2728 0601	319.8112 4345	334.1817 2806	349.3451 4309	181
182	295.7391 7004	322.6768 0904	337.2703 6386	352.6741 1071	182
183	298.2178 6589	325.5590 9042	340.3783 0363	356.0252 7144	183
184	300.7089 5522	328.4581 8512	343.5056 6803	359.3987 7325	184
185	303.2125 0000	331.3741 9120	346.6525 7845	362.7947 6508	185
186	305.7285 6250	334.3072 0731	349.8191 5707	366.2133 9684	186
187	308.2572 0531	337.2573 3269	353.0055 2680	369.6548 1949	187
188	310.7984 9134	340.2246 6713	356.2118 1134	373.1191 8495	188
189	313.3524 8379	343.2093 1102	359.4381 3516	376.6066 4618	189
190	315.9192 4621	346.2113 6533	362.6846 2351	380.1173 5716	190
191	318.4988 4244	349.2309 3163	365.9514 0241	383.6514 7287	191
192	321.0913 3666	352.2681 1207	369 2385 9867	387.2091 4936	192
193	323.6967 9334	355.3230 0939	372.5463 3991	390.7905 4369	193
194	326.3152 7731	358.3957 2694	375.8747 5454	394.3958 1398	194
195	328.9468 5369	361.4863 6868	379.2239 7175	398.0251 1941	195
196	331.5915 8796	364.5950 3917	382.5941 2158	401.6786 2020	196
197	334.2495 4590	367.7218 4356	385.9853 3484	405.3564 7767	197
198	336.9207 9363	370.8668 8765	389.3977 4318	409.0588 5419	198
199	339.6053 9760	374.0302 7783	392.8314 7907	412.7859 1322	199
200	342.3034 2450	377.2121 2111	396.2866 7582	416.5378 1930	200

TABLE V.—Amount of Annuity of 1 per Period

$$s_{\overline{n}|i} = \frac{(1 + i)^n - 1}{i}$$

n	¾%	⅞%	1%	1⅛%	n
1	1.0000 0000	1.0000 0000	1.0000 0000	1.0000 0000	1
2	2.0075 0000	2.0087 5000	2.0100 0000	2.0112 5000	2
3	3.0225 5625	3.0263 2656	3.0301 0000	3.0338 7656	3
4	4.0452 2542	4.0528 0692	4.0604 0100	4.0680 0767	4
5	5.0755 6461	5.0882 6898	5.1010 0501	5.1137 7276	5
6	6.1136 3135	6.1327 9133	6.1520 1506	6.1713 0270	6
7	7.1594 8358	7.1864 5326	7.2135 3521	7.2407 2986	7
8	8.2131 7971	8.2493 3472	8.2856 7056	8.3221 8807	8
9	9.2747 7856	9.3215 1640	9.3685 2727	9.4158 1269	9
10	10.3443 3940	10.4030 7967	10.4622 1254	10.5217 4058	10
11	11.4219 2194	11.4941 0662	11.5668 3467	11.6401 1016	11
12	12.5075 8636	12.5946 8005	12.6825 0301	12.7710 6140	12
13	13.6013 9325	13.7048 8350	13.8093 2804	13.9147 3584	13
14	14.7034 0370	14.8248 0123	14.9474 2132	15.0712 7662	14
15	15.8136 7923	15.9545 1824	16.0968 9554	16.2408 2848	15
16	16.9322 8183	17.0941 2028	17.2578 6449	17.4235 3780	16
17	18.0592 7394	18.2436 9383	18.4304 4314	18.6195 5260	17
18	19.1947 1849	19.4033 2615	19.6147 4757	19.8290 2257	18
19	20.3386 7888	20.5731 0526	20.8108 9504	21.0520 9907	19
20	21.4912 1897	21.7531 1993	22.0190 0399	22.2889 3519	20
21	22.6524 0312	22.9434 5973	23.2391 9403	23.5396 8571	21
22	23.8222 9614	24.1442 1500	24.4715 8598	24.8045 0717	22
23	25.0009 6336	25.3554 7688	25.7163 0183	26.0835 5788	23
24	26.1884 7059	26.5773 3730	26.9734 6485	27.3769 9790	24
25	27.3848 8412	27.8098 8900	28.2431 9950	28.6849 8913	25
26	28.5902 7075	29.0532 2553	29.5256 3150	30.0076 9526	26
27	29.8046 9778	30.3074 4126	30.8208 8781	31.3452 8183	27
28	31.0282 3301	31.5726 3137	32.1290 9669	32.6979 1625	28
29	32.2609 4476	32.8488 9189	33.4503 8766	34.0657 6781	29
30	33.5029 0184	34.1363 1970	34.7848 9153	35.4490 0769	30
31	34.7541 7361	35.4350 1249	36.1327 4045	36.8478 0903	31
32	36.0148 2991	36.7450 6885	37.4940 6785	38.2623 4688	32
33	37.2849 4113	38.0665 8820	38.8690 0853	39.6927 9829	33
34	38.5645 7819	39.3996 7085	40.2576 9862	41.1393 4227	34
35	39.8538 1253	40.7444 1797	41.6602 7560	42.6021 5987	35
36	41.1527 1612	42.1009 3163	43.0768 7836	44.0814 3417	36
37	42.4613 6149	43.4693 1478	44.5076 4714	45.5773 5030	37
38	43.7798 2170	44.8496 7128	45.9527 2361	47.0900 9549	38
39	45.1081 7037	46.2421 0591	47.4122 5085	48.6198 5906	39
40	46.4464 8164	47.6467 2433	48.8863 7336	50.1668 3248	40
41	47.7948 3026	49.0636 3317	50.3752 3709	51.7312 0934	41
42	49.1532 9148	50.4929 3996	51.8789 8946	53.3131 8545	42
43	50.5219 4117	51.9347 5319	53.3977 7936	54.9129 5879	43
44	51.9008 5573	53.3891 8228	54.9317 5715	56.5307 2957	44
45	53.2901 1215	54.8563 3762	56.4810 7472	58.1667 0028	45
46	54.6897 8799	56.3363 3058	58.0458 8547	59.8210 7566	46
47	56.0999 6140	57.8292 7347	59.6263 4432	61.4940 6276	47
48	57.5207 1111	59.3352 7961	61.2226 0777	63.1858 7097	48
49	58.9521 1644	60.8544 6331	62.8348 3385	64.8967 1201	49
50	60.3942 5732	62.3869 3986	64.4631 8218	66.6268 0002	50

506

TABLE V.—Amount of Annuity of 1 per Period

$$s_{\overline{n}|i} = \frac{(1 + i)^n - 1}{i}$$

n	¾%	⅞%	1%	1⅛%	n
51	61.8472 1424	63.9328 2559	66.1078 1401	68.3763 5152	51
52	63.3110 6835	65.4922 3781	67.7688 9215	70.1455 8548	52
53	64.7859 0136	67.0652 9489	69.4465 8107	71.9347 2332	53
54	66.2717 9562	68.6521 1622	71.1410 4688	73.7439 8895	54
55	67.7688 3409	70.2528 2224	72.8524 5735	75.5736 0883	55
56	69.2771 0035	71.8675 3443	74.5809 8192	77.4238 1193	56
57	70.7966 7860	73.4963 7536	76.3267 9174	79.2948 2981	57
58	72.3276 5369	75.1394 6864	78.0900 5966	81.1868 9665	58
59	73.8701 1109	76.7969 3900	79.8709 6025	83.1002 4923	59
60	75.4241 3693	78.4689 1221	81.6696 6986	85.0351 2704	60
61	76.9898 1795	80.1555 1519	83.4863 6655	86.9917 7222	61
62	78.5672 4159	81.8568 7595	85.3212 3022	88.9704 2966	62
63	80.1564 9590	83.5731 2362	87.1744 4252	90.9713 4699	63
64	81.7576 6962	85.3043 8845	89.0461 8695	92.9947 7464	64
65	83.3708 5214	87.0508 0185	90.9366 4882	95.0409 6586	65
66	84.9961 3353	88.8124 9636	92.8460 1531	97.1101 7672	66
67	86.6336 0453	90.5896 0571	94.7744 7546	99.2026 6621	67
68	88.2833 5657	92.3822 6476	96.7222 2021	101.3186 9621	68
69	89.9454 8174	94.1906 0957	98.6894 4242	103.4585 3154	69
70	91.6200 7285	96.0147 7741	100.6763 3684	105.6224 4002	70
71	93.3072 2340	97.8549 0671	102.6831 0021	107.8106 9247	71
72	95.0070 2758	99.7111 3714	104.7099 3121	110.0235 6276	72
73	96.7195 8028	101.5836 0959	106.7570 3052	112.2613 2784	73
74	98.4449 7714	103.4724 6618	108.8246 0083	114.5242 6778	74
75	100.1833 1446	105.3778 5025	110.9128 4684	116.8126 6579	75
76	101.9346 8932	107.2999 0644	113.0219 7530	119.1268 0828	76
77	103.6991 9949	109.2387 8063	115.1521 9506	121.4669 8487	77
78	105.4769 4349	111.1946 1996	117.3037 1701	123.8334 8845	78
79	107.2680 2056	113.1675 7288	119.4767 5418	126.2266 1520	79
80	109.0725 3072	115.1577 8914	121.6715 2172	128.6466 6462	80
81	110.8905 7470	117.1654 1980	123.8882 3694	131.0939 3960	81
82	112.7222 5401	119.1906 1722	126.1271 1931	133.5687 4642	82
83	114.5676 7091	121.2335 3512	128.3883 9050	136.0713 9481	83
84	116.4269 2845	123.2943 2855	130.6722 7440	138.6021 9801	84
85	118.3001 3041	125.3731 5393	132.9789 9715	141.1614 7273	85
86	120.1873 8139	127.4701 6903	135.3087 8712	143.7495 3930	86
87	122.0887 8675	129.5855 3301	137.6618 7499	146.3667 2162	87
88	124.0044 5265	131.7194 0642	140.0384 9374	149.0133 4724	88
89	125.9344 8604	133.8719 5123	142.4388 7868	151.6897 4739	89
90	127.8789 9469	136.0433 3080	144.8632 6746	154.3962 5705	90
91	129.8380 8715	138.2337 0994	147.3119 0014	157.1332 1494	91
92	131.8118 7280	140.4432 5491	149.7850 1914	159.9009 6361	92
93	133.8004 6185	142.6721 3339	152.2828 6933	162.6998 4945	93
94	135.8039 6531	144.9205 1455	154.8056 9803	165.5302 2276	94
95	137.8224 9505	147.1885 6906	157.3537 5501	168.3924 3776	95
96	139.8561 6377	149.4764 6903	159.9272 9256	171.2868 5269	96
97	141.9050 8499	151.7843 8813	162.5265 6548	174.2138 2978	97
98	143.9693 7313	154.1125 0153	165.1518 3114	177.1737 3537	98
99	146.0491 4343	156.4609 8592	167.8033 4945	180.1669 3989	99
100	148.1445 1201	158.8300 1955	170.4813 8294	183.1938 1796	100

TABLE V.—Amount of Annuity of 1 per Period

$$s_{\overline{n}|i} = \frac{(1+i)^n - 1}{i}$$

n	1¼%	1⅜%	1½%	1¾%	n
1	1.0000 0000	1.0000 0000	1.0000 0000	1.0000 0000	1
2	2.0125 0000	2.0137 5000	2.0150 0000	2.0175 0000	2
3	3.0376 5625	3.0414 3906	3.0452 2500	3.0528 0625	3
4	4.0756 2695	4.0832 5885	4.0909 0338	4.1062 3036	4
5	5.1265 7229	5.1394 0366	5.1522 6693	5.1780 8938	5
6	6.1906 5444	6.2100 7046	6.2295 5093	6.2687 0596	6
7	7.2680 3762	7.2954 5893	7.3229 9419	7.3784 0831	7
8	8.3588 8809	8.3957 7149	8.4328 3911	8.5075 3045	8
9	9.4633 7420	9.5112 1335	9.5593 3169	9.6564 1224	9
10	10.5816 6637	10.6419 9253	10.7027 2167	10.8253 9945	10
11	11.7139 3720	11.7883 1993	11.8632 6249	12.0148 4394	11
12	12.8603 6142	12.9504 0933	13.0412 1143	13.2251 0371	12
13	14.0211 1594	14.1284 7745	14.2368 2960	14.4565 4303	13
14	15.1963 7988	15.3227 4402	15.4503 8205	15.7095 3253	14
15	16.3863 3463	16.5334 3175	16.6821 3778	16.9844 4935	15
16	17.5911 6382	17.7607 6644	17.9323 6984	18.2816 7721	16
17	18.8110 5336	19.0049 7697	19.2013 5539	19.6016 0656	17
18	20.0461 9153	20.2662 9541	20.4893 7572	20.9446 3468	18
19	21.2967 6893	21.5449 5697	21.7967 1636	22.3111 6578	19
20	22.5629 7854	22.8412 0013	23.1236 6710	23.7016 1119	20
21	23.8450 1577	24.1552 6663	24.4705 2211	25.1163 8938	21
22	25.1430 7847	25.4874 0155	25.8375 7994	26.5559 2620	22
23	26.4573 6695	26.8378 5332	27.2251 4364	28.0206 5490	23
24	27.7880 8403	28.2068 7380	28.6335 2080	29.5110 1637	24
25	29.1354 3508	29.5947 1832	30.0630 2361	31.0274 5915	25
26	30.4996 2802	31.0016 4569	31.5139 6896	32.5704 3969	26
27	31.8808 7337	32.4279 1832	32.9866 7850	34.1404 2238	27
28	33.2793 8429	33.8738 0220	34.4814 7867	35.7378 7977	28
29	34.6953 7659	35.3395 6698	35.9987 0085	37.3632 9267	29
30	36.1290 6880	36.8254 8602	37.5386 8137	39.0171 5029	30
31	37.5806 8216	38.3318 3646	39.1017 6159	40.6999 5042	31
32	39.0504 4069	39.8588 9921	40.6882 8801	42.4121 9955	32
33	40.5385 7120	41.4069 5907	42.2986 1233	44.1544 1305	33
34	42.0453 0334	42.9763 0476	43.9330 9152	45.9271 1527	34
35	43.5708 6963	44.5672 2895	45.5920 8789	47.7308 3979	35
36	45.1155 0550	46.1800 2835	47.2759 6921	49.5661 2949	36
37	46.6794 4932	47.8150 0374	48.9851 0874	51.4335 3675	37
38	48.2926 4243	49.4724 6004	50.7198 8538	53.3336 2365	38
39	49.8862 2921	51.1527 0636	52.4806 8366	55.2669 6206	39
40	51.4895 5708	52.8560 5608	54.2678 9391	57.2341 3390	40
41	53.1331 7654	54.5828 2685	56.0819 1232	59.2357 3124	41
42	54.7973 4125	56.3333 4072	57.9231 4100	61.2723 5654	42
43	56.4823 0801	58.1079 2415	59.7919 8812	63.3446 2278	43
44	58.1883 3687	59.9069 0811	61.6888 6794	65.4531 5367	44
45	59.9156 9108	61.7306 2810	63.6142 0096	67.5985 8386	45
46	61.6646 3721	63.5794 2423	65.5684 1398	69.7815 5908	46
47	63.4354 4518	65.4536 4131	67.5519 4018	72.0027 3637	47
48	65.2283 8824	67.3536 2888	69.5652 1929	74.2627 8425	48
49	67.0437 4310	69.2797 4128	71.6086 9758	76.5623 8298	49
50	68.8817 8989	71.2323 3772	73.6828 2804	78.9022 2468	50

TABLE V.—Amount of Annuity of 1 per Period

$$s_{\overline{n}|i} = \frac{(1 + i)^n - 1}{i}$$

n	$1\frac{1}{4}\%$	$1\frac{3}{8}\%$	$1\frac{1}{2}\%$	$1\frac{3}{4}\%$	n
51	70.7428 1226	73.2117 8237	75.7880 7046	81.2830 1361	51
52	72.6270 9741	75.2184 4437	77.9248 9152	83.7054 6635	52
53	74.5349 3613	77.2526 9798	80.0937 6489	86.1703 1201	53
54	76.4666 2283	79.3149 2258	82.2951 7136	88.6782 9247	54
55	78.4224 5562	81.4055 0277	84.5295 9893	91.2301 6259	55
56	80.4027 3631	83.5248 2843	86.7975 4292	93.8266 9043	56
57	82.4077 7052	85.6732 9482	89.0995 0606	96.4686 5752	57
58	84.4378 6765	87.8513 0262	91.4359 9865	99.1568 5902	58
59	86.4933 4099	90.0592 5804	93.8075 3863	101.8921 0405	59
60	88.5745 0776	92.2975 7283	96.2146 5171	104.6752 1588	60
61	90.6816 8910	94.5666 6446	98.6578 7149	107.5070 3215	61
62	92.8152 1022	96.8669 5610	101.1377 3956	110.3884 0522	62
63	94.9754 0034	99.1988 7674	103.6548 0565	113.3202 0231	63
64	97.1625 9285	101.5628 6130	106.2096 2774	116.3033 0585	64
65	99.3771 2526	103.9593 5064	108.8027 7215	119.3386 1370	65
66	101.6193 3933	106.3887 9171	111.4348 1374	122.4270 3944	66
67	103.8895 8107	108.8516 3760	114.1063 3594	125.5695 1263	67
68	106.1882 0083	111.3483 4761	116.8179 3098	128.7669 7910	68
69	108.5155 5334	113.8793 8739	119.5701 9995	132.0204 0124	69
70	110.8719 9776	116.4452 2897	122.3637 5295	135.3307 5826	70
71	113.2578 9773	119.0463 5087	125.1992 0924	138.6990 4653	71
72	115.6736 2145	121.6832 3819	128.0771 9738	142.1262 7984	72
73	118.1195 4172	124.3563 8272	130.9983 5534	145.6134 8974	73
74	120.5960 3599	127.0662 8298	133.9633 3067	149.1617 2581	74
75	123.1034 8644	129.8134 4437	136.9727 8063	152.7720 5601	75
76	125.6422 8002	132.5983 7923	140.0273 7234	156.4455 6699	76
77	128.2128 0852	135.4216 0695	143.1277 8292	160.1833 6441	77
78	130.8154 6863	138.2836 5404	146.2746 9967	163.9865 7329	78
79	133.4506 6199	141.1850 5429	149.4688 2016	167.8563 3832	79
80	136.1187 9526	144.1263 4878	152.7108 5247	171.7938 2424	80
81	138.8202 8020	147.1080 8608	156.0015 1525	175.8002 1617	81
82	141.5555 3370	150.1308 2226	159.3415 3798	179.8767 1995	82
83	144.3249 7787	153.1951 2107	162.7316 6105	184.0245 6255	83
84	147.1290 4010	156.3015 5398	166.1726 3597	188.2449 9239	84
85	149.9681 5310	159.4507 0035	169.6652 2551	192.5392 7976	85
86	152.8427 5501	162.6431 4748	173.2102 0389	196.9087 1716	86
87	155.7532 8945	165.8794 9076	176.8083 5695	201.3546 1971	87
88	158.7002 0557	169.1603 3375	180.4604 8230	205.8783 2555	88
89	161.6839 5814	172.4862 8834	184.1673 8954	210.4811 9625	89
90	164.7050 0762	175.8579 7481	187.9299 0038	215.1646 1718	90
91	167.7638 2021	179.2760 2196	191.7488 4889	219.9299 9798	91
92	170.8608 6796	182.7410 6726	195.6250 8162	224.7787 7295	92
93	173.9966 2881	186.2537 5694	199.5594 5784	229.7124 0148	93
94	177.1715 8667	189.8147 4610	203.5528 4971	234.7323 6850	94
95	180.3862 3151	193.4246 9886	207.6061 4246	239.8401 8495	95
96	183.6410 5940	197.0842 8847	211.7202 3459	245.0373 8819	96
97	186.9365 7264	200.7941 9743	215.8960 3811	250.3255 4248	97
98	190.2732 7980	204.5551 1765	220.1344 7868	255.7062 3947	98
99	193.6516 9580	208.3677 5051	224.4364 9586	261.1810 9866	99
100	197.0723 4200	212.2328 0708	228.8030 4330	266.7517 6789	100

TABLE V.—Amount of Annuity of 1 per Period

$$s_{\overline{n}|i} = \frac{(1 + i)^n - 1}{i}$$

n	2%	2¼%	2½%	2¾%	n
1	1.0000 0000	1.0000 0000	1.0000 0000	1.0000 0000	1
2	2.0200 0000	2.0225 0000	2.0250 0000	2.0275 0000	2
3	3.0604 0000	3.0680 0625	3.0756 2500	3.0832 5625	3
4	4.1216 0800	4.1370 3639	4.1525 1563	4.1680 4580	4
5	5.2040 4016	5.2301 1971	5.2563 2852	5.2826 6706	5
6	6.3081 2096	6.3477 9740	6.3877 3673	6.4279 4040	6
7	7.4342 8338	7.4906 2284	7.5474 3015	7.6047 0876	7
8	8.5829 6905	8.6591 6186	8.7361 1590	8.8138 3825	8
9	9.7546 2843	9.8539 9300	9.9545 1880	10.0562 1880	9
10	10.9497 2100	11.0757 0784	11.2033 8177	11.3327 6482	10
11	12.1687 1542	12.3249 1127	12.4834 6631	12.6444 1585	11
12	13.4120 8973	13.6022 2177	13.7955 5297	13.9921 3729	12
13	14.6803 3152	14.9082 7176	15.1404 4179	15.3769 2107	13
14	15.9739 3815	16.2437 0788	16.5189 5284	16.7997 8639	14
15	17.2934 1692	17.6091 9130	17.9319 2666	18.2617 8052	15
16	18.6392 8525	19.0053 9811	19.3802 2483	19.7639 7948	16
17	20.0120 7096	20.4330 1957	20.8647 3045	21.3074 8892	17
18	21.4123 1238	21.8927 6251	22.3863 4871	22.8934 4487	18
19	22.8405 5863	23.3853 4966	23.9460 0743	24.5230 1460	19
20	24.2973 6980	24.9115 2003	25.5446 5761	26.1973 9750	20
21	25.7833 1719	26.4720 2923	27.1832 7405	27.9178 2593	21
22	27.2989 8354	28.0676 4989	28.8628 5590	29.6855 6615	22
23	28.8449 6321	29.6991 7201	30.5844 2730	31.5019 1921	23
24	30.4218 6247	31.3674 0338	32.3490 3798	33.3682 2199	24
25	32.0302 9972	33.0731 6996	34.1577 6393	35.2858 4810	25
26	33.6709 0572	34.8173 1628	36.0117 0803	37.2562 0892	26
27	35.3443 2383	36.6007 0590	37.9120 0073	39.2807 5467	27
28	37.0512 1031	38.4242 2178	39.8598 C075	41.3609 7542	28
29	38.7922 3451	40.2887 6677	41.8562 9577	43.4984 0224	29
30	40.5680 7921	42.1952 6402	43.9027 0316	45.6946 0830	30
31	42.3794 4079	44.1446 5746	46.0002 7074	47.9512 1003	31
32	44.2270 2961	46.1379 1226	48.1502 7751	50.2698 6831	32
33	46.1115 7020	48.1760 1528	50.3540 3445	52.6522 8969	33
34	48.0338 0160	50.2599 7563	52.6128 8531	55.1002 2765	34
35	49.9944 7763	52.3908 2508	54.9282 0744	57.6154 8391	35
36	51.9943 6719	54.5696 1864	57.3014 1263	60.1999 0972	36
37	54.0342 5453	56.7974 3506	59.7339 4794	62.8554 0724	37
38	56.1149 3962	59.0753 7735	62.2272 9664	65.5839 3094	38
39	58.2372 3841	61.4045 7334	64.7829 7906	68.3874 8904	39
40	60.4019 8318	63.7861 7624	67.4025 5354	71.2681 4499	40
41	62.6100 2284	66.2213 6521	70.0876 1737	74.2280 1898	41
42	64.8622 2330	68.7113 4592	72.8398 0781	77.2692 8950	42
43	67.1594 6777	71.2573 5121	75.6608 0300	80.3941 9496	43
44	69.5026 5712	73.8606 4161	78.5523 2308	83.6050 3532	44
45	71.8927 1027	76.5225 0605	81.5161 3116	86.9041 7379	45
46	74.3305 6447	79.2442 6243	84.5540 3443	90.2940 3857	46
47	76.8171 7576	82.0272 5834	87.6678 8530	93.7771 2463	47
48	79.3535 1927	84.8728 7165	90.8595 8243	97.3559 9556	48
49	81.9405 8966	87.7825 1126	94.1310 7199	101.0332 8544	49
50	84.5794 0145	90.7576 1776	97.4843 4879	104.8117 0079	50

510

TABLE V.—Amount of Annuity of 1 per Period

$$s_{\overline{n}|i} = \frac{(1+i)^n - 1}{i}$$

n	2%	2¼%	2½%	2¾%	n
51	87.2709 8948	93.7996 6416	100.9214 5751	108.6940 2256	51
52	90.0164 0927	96.9101 5661	104.4444 9395	112.6831 0818	52
53	92.8167 3746	100.0906 3513	108.0556 0629	116.7818 9365	53
54	95.6730 7221	103.3426 7442	111.7569 9645	120.9933 9573	54
55	98.5865 3365	106.6678 8460	115.5509 2136	125.3207 1411	55
56	101.5582 6432	110.0679 1200	119.4396 9440	129.7670 3375	56
57	104.5894 2961	113.5444 4002	123.4256 8676	134.3356 2718	57
58	107.6812 1820	117.0991 8992	127.5113 2893	139.0298 5692	58
59	110.8348 4257	120.7339 2169	131.6991 1215	143.8531 7799	59
60	114.0515 3942	124.4504 3493	135.9915 8995	148.8091 4038	60
61	117.3325 7021	128.2505 6972	140.3913 7970	153.9013 9174	61
62	120.6792 2161	132.1362 0754	144.9011 6419	159.1336 8002	62
63	124.0928 0604	136.1092 7221	149.5236 9330	164.5098 5622	63
64	127.5746 6216	140.1717 3083	154.2617 8563	170.0338 7726	64
65	131.1261 5541	144.3255 9477	159.1183 3027	175.7098 0889	65
66	134.7486 7852	148.5729 2066	164.0962 8853	181.5418 2863	66
67	138.4436 5209	152.9158 1137	169.1986 9574	187.5342 2892	67
68	142.2125 2513	157.3564 1713	174.4286 6314	193.6914 2021	68
69	146.0567 7563	161.8969 3651	179.7893 7971	200.0179 3427	69
70	149.9779 1114	166.5396 1758	185.2841 1421	206.5184 2746	70
71	153.9774 6937	171.2867 5898	190.9162 1706	213.1976 8422	71
72	158.0570 1875	176.1407 1106	196.6891 2249	220.0606 2054	72
73	162.2181 5913	181.1038 7705	202.6063 5055	227.1122 8760	73
74	166.4625 2231	186.1787 1429	208.6715 0931	234.3578 7551	74
75	170.7917 7276	191.3677 3536	214.8882 9705	241.8027 1709	75
76	175.2076 0821	196.6735 0941	221.2605 0447	249.4522 9181	76
77	179.7117 6038	202.0986 6337	227.7920 1709	257.3122 2983	77
78	184.3059 9558	207.6458 8329	234.4868 1751	265.3883 1615	78
79	188.9921 1549	213.3179 1567	241.3489 8795	273.6864 9485	79
80	193.7719 5780	219.1175 6877	248.3827 1265	282.2128 7345	80
81	198.6473 9696	225.0477 1407	255.5922 8047	290.9737 2747	81
82	203.6203 4490	231.1112 8763	262.9820 8748	299.9755 0498	82
83	208.6927 5180	237.3112 9160	270.5566 3966	309.2248 3137	83
84	213.8666 0683	243.6507 9567	278.3205 5566	318.7285 1423	84
85	219.1439 3897	250.1329 3857	286.2785 6955	328.4935 4837	85
86	224.5268 1775	256.7609 2969	294.4355 3379	338.5271 2095	86
87	230.0173 5411	263.5380 5060	302.7964 2213	348.8366 1678	87
88	235.6177 0119	270.4676 5674	311.3663 3268	359.4296 2374	88
89	241.3300 5521	277.5531 7902	320.1504 9100	370.3139 3839	89
90	247.1566 5632	284.7981 2555	329.1542 5328	381.4975 7170	90
91	253.0997 8944	292.2060 8337	338.3831 0961	392.9887 5492	91
92	259.1617 8523	299.7807 2025	347.8426 8735	404.7959 4568	92
93	265.3450 2094	307.5257 8645	357.5387 5453	416.9278 3418	93
94	271.6519 2135	315.4451 1665	367.4772 2339	429.3933 4962	94
95	278.0849 5978	323.5426 3177	377.6641 5398	442.2016 6674	95
96	284.6466 5898	331.8223 4099	388.1057 5783	455.3622 1257	96
97	291.3395 9216	340.2883 4366	398.8084 0177	468.8846 7342	97
98	298.1663 8400	348.9448 3139	409.7786 1182	482.7790 0194	98
99	305.1297 1168	357.7960 9010	421.0230 7711	497.0554 2449	99
100	312.2323 0591	366.8465 0213	432.5486 5404	511.7244 4867	100

TABLE V.—Amount of Annuity of 1 per Period

$$s_{\overline{n}|i} = \frac{(1 + i)^n - 1}{i}$$

n	3%	3½%	4%	4½%	n
1	1.0000 0000	1.0000 0000	1.0000 0000	1.0000 0000	1
2	2.0300 0000	2.0350 0000	2.0400 0000	2.0450 0000	2
3	3.0909 0000	3.1062 2500	3.1216 0000	3.1370 2500	3
4	4.1836 2700	4.2149 4288	4.2464 6400	4.2781 9113	4
5	5.3091 3581	5.3624 6588	5.4163 2256	5.4707 0973	5
6	6.4684 0988	6.5501 5218	6.6329 7546	6.7168 9166	6
7	7.6624 6218	7.7794 0751	7.8982 9448	8.0191 5179	7
8	8.8923 3605	9.0516 8677	9.2142 2626	9.3800 1362	8
9	10.1591 0613	10.3684 9581	10.5827 9531	10.8021 1423	9
10	11.4638 7931	11.7313 9316	12.0061 0712	12.2882 0937	10
11	12.8077 9569	13.1419 9192	13.4863 5141	13.8411 7879	11
12	14.1920 2956	14.6019 6164	15.0258 0546	15.4640 3184	12
13	15.6177 9045	16.1130 3030	16.6268 3768	17.1599 1327	13
14	17.0863 2416	17.6769 8636	18.2919 1119	18.9321 0937	14
15	18.5989 1389	19.2956 8088	20.0235 8764	20.7840 5429	15
16	20.1568 8130	20.9710 2971	21.8245 3114	22.7193 3673	16
17	21.7615 8774	22.7050 1575	23.6975 1239	24.7417 0689	17
18	23.4144 3537	24.4996 9130	25.6454 1288	26.8550 8370	18
19	25.1168 6844	26.3571 8050	27.6712 2940	29.0635 6246	19
20	26.8703 7449	28.2796 8181	29.7780 7858	31.3714 2277	20
21	28.6764 8572	30.2694 7068	31.9692 0172	33.7831 3680	21
22	30.5367 8030	32.3289 0215	34.2479 6979	36.3033 7795	22
23	32.4528 8370	34.4604 1373	36.6178 8858	38.9370 2996	23
24	34.4264 7022	36.6665 2821	39.0826 0412	41.6891 9631	24
25	36.4592 6432	38.9498 5669	41.6459 0829	44.5652 1015	25
26	38.5530 4225	41.3131 0168	44.3117 4462	47.5706 4460	26
27	40.7096 3352	43.7590 6024	47.0842 1440	50.7113 2361	27
28	42.9309 2252	46.2906 2734	49.9675 8298	53.9933 3317	28
29	45.2188 5020	48.9107 9930	52.9662 8630	57.4230 3316	29
30	47.5754 1571	51.6226 7728	56.0849 3775	61.0070 6966	30
31	50.0026 7818	54.4294 7098	59.3283 3526	64.7523 8779	31
32	52.5027 5852	57.3345 0247	62.7014 6867	68.6662 4524	32
33	55.0778 4128	60.3412 1005	66.2095 2742	72.7562 2628	33
34	57.7301 7652	63.4531 5240	69.8579 0851	77.0302 5646	34
35	60.4620 8181	66.6740 1274	73.6522 2486	81.4966 1800	35
36	63.2759 4427	70.0076 0318	77.5983 1385	86.1639 6581	36
37	66.1742 2259	73.4578 6930	81.7022 4640	91.0413 4427	37
38	69.1594 4927	77.0288 9472	85.9703 3626	96.1382 0476	38
39	72.2342 3275	80.7249 0604	90.4091 4971	101.4644 2398	39
40	75.4012 5973	84.5502 7775	95.0255 1570	107.0303 2306	40
41	78.6632 9753	88.5095 3747	99.8265 3633	112.8466 8760	41
42	82.0231 9645	92.6073 7128	104.8195 9778	118.9247 8854	42
43	85.4838 9234	96.8486 2928	110.0123 8169	125.2764 0402	43
44	89.0484 0911	101.2383 3130	115.4128 7696	131.9138 4220	44
45	.92.7198 6139	105.7816 7290	121.0293 9204	138.8499 6510	45
46	96.5014 5723	110.4840 3145	126.8705 6772	146.0982 1353	46
47	100.3965 0095	115.3509 7255	132.9453 9043	153.6726 3314	47
48	104.4083 9598	120.3882 5659	139.2632 0604	161.5879 0163	48
49	108.5406 4785	125.6018 4557	145.8337 3429	169.8593 5720	49
50	112.7968 6729	130.9979 1016	152.6670 8366	178.5030 2828	50

TABLE V.—Amount of Annuity of 1 per Period

$$s_{\overline{n}|i} = \frac{(1 + i)^n - 1}{i}$$

n	3%	3½%	4%	4½%	n
51	117.1807 7331	136.5828 3702	159.7737 6700	187.5356 6455	51
52	121.6961 9651	142.3632 3631	167.1647 1768	196.9747 6946	52
53	126.3470 8240	148.3459 4958	174.8513 0639	206.8386 3408	53
54	131.1374 9488	154.5380 5782	182.8453 5865	217.1463 7262	54
55	136.0716 1972	160.9468 8984	191.1591 7299	227.9179 5938	55
56	141.1537 6831	167.5800 3099	199.8055 3991	239.1742 6756	56
57	146.3883 8136	174.4453 3207	208.7977 6151	250.9371 0960	57
58	151.7800 3280	181.5509 1869	218.1496 7197	263.2292 7953	58
59	157.3334 3379	188.9052 0085	227.8756 5885	276.0745 9711	59
60	163.0534 3680	196.5168 8288	237.9906 8520	289.4979 5398	60
61	168.9450 3991	204.3949 7378	248.5103 1261	303.5253 6190	61
62	175.0133 9110	212.5487 9786	259.4507 2511	318.1840 0319	62
63	181.2637 9284	220.9880 0579	270.8287 5412	333.5022 8333	63
64	187.7017 0662	229.7225 8599	282.6619 0428	349.5098 8608	64
65	194.3327 5782	238.7628 7650	294.9683 8045	366.2378 3096	65
66	201.1627 4055	248.1195 7718	307.7671 1567	383.7185 3335	66
67	208.1976 2277	257.8037 6238	321.0778 0030	401.9858 6735	67
68	215.4435 5145	267.8268 9406	334.9209 1231	421.0752 3138	68
69	222.9068 5800	278.2008 3535	349.3177 4880	441.0236 1679	69
70	230.5940 6374	288.9378 6459	364.2904 5876	461.8696 7955	70
71	238.5118 8565	300.0506 8985	379.8620 7711	483.6538 1513	71
72	246.6672 4222	311.5524 6400	396.0565 6019	506.4182 3681	72
73	255.0672 5949	323.4568 0024	412.8988 2260	530.2070 5747	73
74	263.7192 7727	335.7777 8824	430.4147 7550	555.0663 7505	74
75	272.6308 5559	348.5300 1083	448.6313 6652	581.0443 6193	75
76	281.8097 8126	361.7285 6121	467.5766 2118	608.1913 5822	76
77	291.2640 7469	375.3890 6085	487.2796 8603	636.5599 6934	77
78	301.0019 9693	389.5276 7798	507.7708 7347	666.2051 6796	78
79	311.0320 5684	404.1611 4671	529.0817 0841	697.1844 0052	79
80	321.3630 1855	419.3067 8685	551.2449 7675	729.5576 9854	80
81	332.0039 0910	434.9825 2439	574.2947 7582	763.3877 9497	81
82	342.9640 2638	451.2069 1274	598.2665 6685	798.7402 4575	82
83	354.2529 4717	467.9991 5469	623.1972 2952	835.6835 5680	83
84	365.8805 3558	485.3791 2510	649.1251 1870	874.2893 1686	84
85	377.8569 5165	503.3673 9448	676.0901 2345	914.6323 3612	85
86	390.1926 6020	521.9852 5329	704.1337 2839	956.7907 9125	86
87	402.8984 4001	541.2547 3715	733.2990 7753	1000.8463 7685	87
88	415.9853 9321	561.1986 5295	763.6310 4063	1046.8844 6381	88
89	429.4649 5500	581.8406 0581	795.1762 8225	1094.9942 6468	89
90	443.3489 0365	603.2050 2701	827.9833 3354	1145.2690 0659	90
91	457.6493 7076	625.3172 0295	862.1026 6688	1197.8061 1189	91
92	472.3788 5189	648.2033 0506	897.5867 7356	1252.7073 8692	92
93	487.5502 1744	671.8904 2073	934.4902 4450	1310.0792 1933	93
94	503.1767 2397	696.4065 8546	972.8698 5428	1370.0327 8420	94
95	519.2720 2569	721.7808 1595	1012.7846 4845	1432.6842 5949	95
96	535.8501 8645	748.0431 4451	1054.2960 3439	1498.1550 5117	96
97	552.9256 9205	775.2246 5457	1097.4678 7577	1566.5720 2847	97
98	570.5134 6281	803.3575 1748	1142.3665 9080	1638.0677 6976	98
99	588.6288 6669	832.4750 3059	1189.0612 5443	1712.7808 1939	99
100	607.2877 3270	862.6116 5666	1237.6237 0461	1790.8559 5627	100

TABLE V.—Amount of Annuity of 1 per Period

$$s_{\overline{n}|i} = \frac{(1+i)^n - 1}{i}$$

n	5%	5½%	6%	6½%	n
1	1.0000 0000	1.0000 0000	1.0000 0000	1.0000 0000	1
2	2.0500 0000	2.0550 0000	2.0600 0000	2.0650 0000	2
3	3.1525 0000	3.1680 2500	3.1836 0000	3.1992 2500	3
4	4.3101 2500	4.3422 6638	4.3746 1600	4.4071 7463	4
5	5.5256 3125	5.5810 9103	5.6370 9296	5.6936 4098	5
6	6.8019 1281	6.8880 5103	6.9753 1854	7.0637 2764	6
7	8.1420 0845	8.2668 9384	8.3938 3765	8.5228 6994	7
8	9.5491 0888	9.7215 7300	9.8974 6791	10.0768 5648	8
9	11.0265 6432	11.2562 5951	11.4913 1598	11.7318 5215	9
10	12.5778 9254	12.8753 5379	13.1807 9494	13.4944 2254	10
11	14.2067 8716	14.5834 9825	14.9716 4264	15.3715 6001	11
12	15.9171 2652	16.3855 9065	16.8699 4120	17.3707 1141	12
13	17.7129 8285	18.2867 9814	18.8821 3767	19.4998 0765	13
14	19.5986 3199	20.2925 7203	21.0150 6593	21.7672 9515	14
15	21.5785 6359	22.4086 6350	23.2759 6988	24.1821 6933	15
16	23.6574 9177	24.6411 3999	25.6725 2808	26.7540 1034	16
17	25.8403 6636	26.9964 0269	28.2128 7976	29.4930 2101	17
18	28.1323 8467	29.4812 0483	30.9056 5255	32.4100 6738	18
19	30.5390 0391	32.1026 7110	33.7599 9170	35.5167 2176	19
20	33.0659 5410	34.8683 1801	36.7855 9120	38.8253 0867	20
21	35.7192 5181	37.7860 7550	39.9927 2668	42.3489 5373	21
22	38.5052 1440	40.8643 0965	43.3922 9028	46.1016 3573	22
23	41.4304 7512	44.1118 4669	46.9958 2769	50.0982 4205	23
24	44.5019 9887	47.5379 9825	50.8155 7735	54.3546 2778	24
25	47.7270 9882	51.1525 8816	54.8645 1200	58.8876 7859	25
26	51.1134 5376	54.9659 8051	59.1563 8272	63.7153 7769	26
27	54.6691 2645	58.9991 0943	63.7057 6568	68.8568 7725	27
28	58.4025 8277	63.2335 1045	68.5281 1162	74.3325 7427	28
29	62.3227 1191	67.7113 5353	73.6397 9832	80.1641 9159	29
30	66.4388 4750	72.4354 7797	79.0581 8622	86.3748 6405	30
31	70.7607 8988	77.4194 2926	84.8016 7739	92.9892 3021	31
32	75.2988 2937	82.6774 9787	90.8897 7803	100.0335 3017	32
33	80.0637 7084	88.2247 6025	97.3431 6471	107.5357 0963	33
34	85.0669 5938	94.0771 2207	104.1837 5460	115.5255 3076	34
35	90.3203 0735	100.2513 6378	111.4347 7987	124.0346 9026	35
36	95.8363 2272	106.7651 8879	119.1208 6666	133.0969 4513	36
37	101.6281 3886	113.6372 7417	127.2681 1866	142.7482 4656	37
38	107.7095 4580	120.8873 2425	135.9042 0578	153.0268 8259	38
39	114.0950 2309	128.5361 2708	145.0584 5813	163.9736 2995	39
40	120.7997 7424	136.6056 1407	154.7619 6562	175.6319 1590	40
41	127.8397 6295	145.1189 2285	165.0476 8356	188.0479 9044	41
42	135.2317 5110	154.1004 6360	175.9505 4457	201.2711 0981	42
43	142.9933 3866	163.5759 8910	187.5075 7724	215.3537 3195	43
44	151.1430 0559	173.5726 6850	199.7580 3188	230.3517 2453	44
45	159.7001 5587	184.1191 6527	212.7435 1379	246.3245 8662	45
46	168.6851 6366	195.2457 1936	226.5081 2462	263.3356 8475	46
47	178.1194 2185	206.9842 3392	241.0986 1210	281.4525 0426	47
48	188.0253 9294	219.3683 6679	256.5645 2882	300.7469 1704	48
49	198.4266 6259	232.4336 2696	272.9584 0055	321.2954 6665	49
50	209.3479 9572	246.2174 7645	290.3359 0458	343.1796 7198	50

TABLE V.—Amount of Annuity of 1 per Period

$$s_{\overline{n}|i} = \frac{(1 + i)^n - 1}{i}$$

n	5%	5½%	6%	6½%	n
51	220.8153 9550	260.7594 3765	308.7560 5886	366.4863 5066	51
52	232.8561 6528	276.1012 0672	328.2814 2239	391.3079 6345	52
53	245.4989 7354	292.2867 7309	348.9783 0773	417.7429 8108	53
54	258.7739 2222	309.3625 4561	370.9170 0620	445.8962 7485	54
55	272.7126 1833	327.3774 8562	394.1720 2657	475.8795 3271	55
56	287.3482 4924	346.3832 4733	418.8223 4816	507.8117 0234	56
57	302.7156 6171	366.4343 2593	444.9516 8905	541.8194 6299	57
58	318.8514 4479	387.5882 1386	472.6487 9040	578.0377 2808	58
59	335.7940 1703	409.9055 6562	502.0077 1782	616.6101 8041	59
60	353.5837 1788	433.4503 7173	533.1281 8089	657.6898 4214	60
61	372.2629 0378	458.2901 4217	566.1158 7174	701.4396 8187	61
62	391.8760 4897	484.4960 9999	601.0828 2405	748.0332 6120	62
63	412.4698 5141	512.1433 8549	638.1477 9349	797.6554 2317	63
64	434.0933 4398	541.3112 7170	677.4366 6110	850.5030 2568	64
65	456.7980 1118	572.0833 9164	719.0828 6076	906.7857 2235	65
66	480.6379 1174	604.5479 7818	763.2278 3241	966.7267 9430	66
67	505.6698 0733	638.7981 1698	810.0215 0236	1030.5640 3593	67
68	531.9532 9770	674.9320 1341	859.6227 9250	1098.5506 9827	68
69	559.5509 6258	713.0532 7415	912.2001 6005	1170.9564 9365	69
70	588.5285 1071	753.2712 0423	967.9321 6965	1248.0686 6574	70
71	618.9549 3625	795.7011 2046	1027.0080 9983	1330.1931 2901	71
72	650.9026 8306	840.4646 8209	1089.6285 8582	1417.6556 8240	72
73	684.4478 1721	887.6902 3960	1156.0063 0097	1510.8033 0176	73
74	719.6702 0807	937.5132 0278	1226.3666 7903	1610.0055 1637	74
75	756.6537 1848	990.0764 2893	1300.9486 7977	1715.6558 7493	75
76	795.4864 0440	1045.5306 3252	1380.0056 0055	1828.1735 0681	76
77	836.2607 2462	1104.0348 1731	1463.8059 3659	1948.0047 8475	77
78	879.0737 6085	1165.7567 3226	1552.6342 9278	2075.6250 9576	78
79	924.0274 4889	1230.8733 5254	1646.7923 5035	2211.5407 2698	79
80	971.2288 2134	1299.5713 8693	1746.5998 9137	2356.2908 7423	80
81	1020.7902 6240	1372.0478 1321	1852.3958 8485	2510.4497 8106	81
82	1072.8297 7552	1448.5104 4294	1964.5396 3794	2674.6290 1683	82
83	1127.4712 6430	1529.1785 1730	2083.4120 1622	2849.4799 0292	83
84	1184.8448 2752	1614.2833 3575	2209.4167 3719	3035.6960 9661	84
85	1245.0870 6889	1704.0689 1921	2342.9817 4142	3234.0163 4289	85
86	1308.3414 2234	1798.7927 0977	2484.5606 4591	3445.2274 0518	86
87	1374.7584 9345	1898.7263 0881	2634.6342 8466	3670.1671 8652	87
88	1444.4964 1812	2004.1562 5579	2793.7123 4174	3909.7280 5364	88
89	1517.7212 3903	2115.3848 4986	2962.3350 8225	4164.8603 7713	89
90	1594.6073 0098	2232.7310 1660	3141.0751 8718	4436.5763 0164	90
91	1675.3376 6603	2356.5312 2252	3330.5396 9841	4725.9537 6125	91
92	1760.1045 4933	2487.1404 3976	3531.3720 8032	5034.1407 5573	92
93	1849.1097 7680	2624.9331 6394	3744.2544 0514	5362.3599 0485	93
94	1942.5652 6564	2770.3044 8796	3969.9096 6944	5711.9132 9867	94
95	2040.6935 2892	2923.6712 3480	4209.1042 4961	6084.1876 6308	95
96	2143.7282 0537	3085.4731 5271	4462.6505 0459	6480.6598 6118	96
97	2251.9146 1564	3256.1741 7611	4731.4095 3486	6902.9027 5216	97
98	2365.5103 4642	3436.2637 5580	5016.2941 0696	7352.5914 3105	98
99	2484.7858 6374	3626.2582 6237	5318.2717 5337	7831.5098 7406	99
100	2610.0251 5693	3826.7024 6680	5638.3680 5857	8341.5580 1588	100

515

TABLE V.—Amount of Annuity of 1 per Period

$$s_{\overline{n}|i} = \frac{(1+i)^n - 1}{i}$$

n	7%	7½%	8%	8½%	n
1	1.0000 0000	1.0000 0000	1.0000 0000	1.0000 0000	1
2	2.0700 0000	2.0750 0000	2.0800 0000	2.0850 0000	2
3	3.2149 0000	3.2306 2500	3.2464 0000	3.2622 2500	3
4	4.4399 4300	4.4729 2188	4.5061 1200	4.5395 1413	4
5	5.7507 3901	5.8083 9102	5.8666 0096	5.9253 7283	5
6	7.1532 9074	7.2440 2034	7.3359 2904	7.4290 2952	6
7	8.6540 2109	8.7873 2187	8.9228 0336	9.0604 9702	7
8	10.2598 0257	10.4463 7101	10.6366 2763	10.8306 3927	8
9	11.9779 8875	12.2298 4883	12.4875 5784	12.7512 4361	9
10	13.8164 4796	14.1470 8750	14.4865 6247	14.8350 9932	10
11	15.7835 9932	16.2081 1906	16.6454 8746	17.0960 8276	11
12	17.8884 5127	18.4237 2799	18.9771 2646	19.5492 4979	12
13	20.1406 4286	20.8055 0759	21.4952 9658	22.2109 3603	13
14	22.5504 8786	23.3659 2066	24.2149 2030	25.0988 6559	14
15	25.1290 2201	26.1183 6470	27.1521 1393	28.2322 6916	15
16	27.8880 5355	29.0772 4206	30.3242 8304	31.6320 1204	16
17	30.8402 1730	32.2580 3521	33.7502 2569	35.3207 3306	17
18	33.9990 3251	35.6773 8785	37.4502 4374	39.3229 9538	18
19	37.3789 6479	39.3531 9194	41.4462 6324	43.6654 4998	19
20	40.9954 9232	43.3046 8134	45.7619 6430	48.3770 1323	20
21	44.8651 7678	47.5525 3244	50.4229 2144	53.4890 5936	21
22	49.0057 3916	52.1189 7237	55.4567 5516	59.0356 2940	22
23	53.4361 4090	57.0278 9530	60.8932 9557	65.0536 5790	23
24	58.1766 7076	62.3049 8744	66.7647 5922	71.5832 1882	24
25	63.2490 3772	67.9778 6150	73.1059 3995	78.6677 9242	25
26	68.6764 7036	74.0762 0112	79.9544 1515	86.3545 5478	26
27	74.4838 2328	80.6319 1620	87.3507 6836	94.6946 9193	27
28	80.6976 9091	87.6793 0991	95.3388 2983	103.7437 4075	28
29	87.3465 2927	95.2552 5816	103.9659 3622	113.5619 5871	29
30	94.4607 8632	103.3994 0252	113.2832 1111	124.2147 2520	30
31	102.0730 4137	112.1543 5771	123.3458 6800	135.7729 7684	31
32	110.2181 5426	121.5659 3454	134.2135 3744	148.3136 7987	32
33	118.9334 2506	131.6833 7963	145.9506 2044	161.9203 4266	33
34	128.2587 6481	142.5596 3310	158.6266 7007	176.6835 7179	34
35	138.2368 7835	154.2516 0558	172.3168 0368	192.7016 7539	35
36	148.9134 5984	166.8204 7600	187.1021 4797	210.0813 1780	36
37	160.3374 0202	180.3320 1170	203.0703 1981	228.9382 2981	37
38	172.5610 2017	194.8569 1258	220.3159 4540	249.3979 7935	38
39	185.6402 9158	210.4711 8102	238.9412 2103	271.5968 0759	39
40	199.6351 1199	227.2565 1960	259.0565 1871	295.6825 3624	40
41	214.6095 6983	245.3007 5857	280.7810 4021	321.8155 5182	41
42	230.6322 3972	264.6983 1546	304.2435 2342	350.1698 7372	42
43	247.7764 9650	285.5506 8912	329.5830 0530	380.9343 1299	43
44	266.1208 5125	307.9669 9080	356.9496 4572	414.3137 2959	44
45	285.7493 1084	332.0645 1511	386.5056 1738	450.5303 9661	45
46	306.7517 6260	357.9693 5375	418.4260 6677	489.8254 8032	46
47	329.2243 8598	385.8170 5528	452.9001 5211	532.4606 4615	47
48	353.2700 9300	415.7533 3442	490.1321 6428	578.7198 0107	48
49	378.9989 9951	447.9348 3451	530.3427 3742	628.9109 8416	49
50	406.5289 2947	482.5299 4709	573.7701 5642	683.3684 1782	50

TABLE V.—Amount of Annuity of 1 per Period

$$s_{\overline{n}|i} = \frac{(1 + i)^n - 1}{i}$$

n	7%	7½%	8%	8½%	n
51	435.9859 5454	519.7196 9313	620.6717 6893	742.4547 3333	51
52	467.5049 7135	559.6986 7011	671.3255 1044	806.5633 8566	52
53	501.2303 1935	602.6760 7037	726.0315 5128	876.1212 7345	53
54	537.3164 4170	648.8767 7565	785.1140 7538	951.5915 8169	54
55	575.9285 9262	698.5425 3382	848.9232 0141	1033.4768 6613	55
56	617.2435 9410	751.9332 2386	917.8370 5752	1122.3223 9975	56
57	661.4506 4569	809.3282 1564	992.2640 2213	1218.7198 0373	57
58	708.7521 9089	871.0278 3182	1072.6451 4390	1323.3109 8705	58
59	759.3648 4425	937.3549 1920	1159.4567 5541	1436.7924 2095	59
60	813.5203 8335	1008.6565 3814	1253.2132 9584	1559.9197 7673	60
61	871.4668 1019	1085.3057 7851	1354.4703 5951	1693.5129 5775	61
62	933.4694 8690	1167.7037 1189	1463.8279 8827	1838.4615 5916	62
63	999.8123 5098	1256.2814 9029	1581.9342 2733	1995.7307 9169	63
64	1070.7992 1555	1351.5026 0206	1709.4889 6552	2166.3679 0898	64
65	1146.7551 6064	1453.8652 9721	1847.2480 8276	2351.5091 8125	65
66	1228.0280 2188	1563.9051 9450	1996.0279 2938	2552.3874 6165	66
67	1314.9899 8341	1682.1980 8409	2156.7101 6373	2770.3403 9589	67
68	1408.0392 8225	1809.3629 4040	2330.2469 7683	3006.8193 2954	68
69	1507.6020 3201	1946.0651 6093	2517.6667 3497	3263.3989 7255	69
70	1614.1341 7425	2093.0200 4800	2720.0800 7377	3541.7878 8522	70
71	1728.1235 6645	2250.9965 5160	2938.6864 7967	3843.8398 5546	71
72	1850.0922 1610	2420.8212 9296	3174.7813 9805	4171.5662 4318	72
73	1980.5986 7123	2603.3828 8994	3429.7639 0989	4527.1493 7385	73
74	2120.2405 7821	2799.6366 0668	3705.1450 2268	4912.9570 7063	74
75	2269.6574 1869	3010.6093 5218	4002.5566 2449	5331.5584 2163	75
76	2429.5334 3800	3237.4050 5360	4323.7611 5445	5785.7408 8747	76
77	2600.6007 7866	3481.2104 3262	4670.6620 4681	6278.5288 6290	77
78	2783.6428 3316	3743.3012 1506	5045.3150 1056	6813.2038 1625	78
79	2979.4978 3148	4025.0488 0619	5449.9402 1140	7393.3261 4063	79
80	3189.0626 7969	4327.9274 6666	5886.9354 2831	8022.7588 6259	80
81	3413.2970 6727	4653.5220 2666	6358.8902 6258	8705.6933 6591	81
82	3653.2278 6198	5003.5361 7866	6868.6014 8358	9446.6773 0201	82
83	3909.9538 1231	5379.8013 9206	7419.0896 0227	10250.6448 7268	83
84	4184.6505 7918	5784.2864 9646	8013.6167 7045	11122.9496 8686	84
85	4478.5761 1972	6219.1079 8369	8655.7061 1209	12069.4004 1024	85
86	4793.0764 4810	6686.5410 8247	9349.1626 0105	13096.2994 4511	86
87	5129.5917 9946	7189.0316 6366	10098.0956 0914	14210.4848 9794	87
88	5489.6632 2543	7729.2090 3843	10906.9432 5787	15419.3761 1427	88
89	5874.9396 5121	8309.8997 1631	11780.4987 1850	16731.0230 8398	89
90	6287.1854 2679	8934.1421 9504	12723.9386 1598	18154.1600 4612	90
91	6728.2884 0667	9605.2028 5966	13742.8537 0526	19698.2636 5004	91
92	7200.2685 9513	10326.5930 7414	14843.2820 0168	21373.6160 6029	92
93	7705.2873 9679	11102.0875 5470	16031.7445 6181	23191.3734 2542	93
94	8245.6575 1457	11935.7441 2130	17315.2841 2676	25163.6401 6658	94
95	8823.8535 4059	12831.9249 3040	18701.5068 5690	27303.5495 8074	95
96	9442.5232 8843	13795.3193 0018	20198.6274 0545	29625.3512 9510	96
97	10104.4999 1862	14830.9682 4769	21815.5175 9788	32144.5061 5518	97
98	10812.8149 1292	15944.2908 6627	23561.7590 0572	34877.7891 7837	98
99	11570.7119 5683	17141.1126 8124	25447.6997 2617	37843.4012 5853	99
100	12381.6617 9381	18427.6961 3233	27484.5157 0427	41061.0903 6551	100

TABLE VI.—Présent Value of Annuity of 1 per Period

$$a_{\overline{n}|i} = \frac{1 - (1 + i)^{-n}}{i}$$

n	$\frac{1}{4}$%	$\frac{7}{24}$%	$\frac{1}{3}$%	$\frac{5}{12}$%	n
1	0.9975 0623	0.9970 9182	0.9966 7774	0.9958 5062	1
2	1.9925 2492	1.9912 8390	1.9900 4426	1.9875 6908	2
3	2.9850 6227	2.9825 8470	2.9801 1056	2.9751 7253	3
4	3.9751 2446	3.9710 0260	3.9668 8760	3.9586 7804	4
5	4.9627 1766	4.9565 4601	4.9503 8631	4.9381 0261	5
6	5.9478 4804	5.9392 2327	5.9306 1759	5.9134 6318	6
7	6.9305 2174	6.9190 4273	6.9075 9228	6.8847 7661	7
8	7.9107 4487	7.8960 1269	7.8813 2121	7.8520 5969	8
9	8.8885 2357	8.8701 4144	8.8518 1516	8.8153 2915	9
10	9.8638 6391	9.8414 3725	9.8190 8487	9.7746 0164	10
11	10.8367 7198	10.8099 0834	10.7831 4107	10.7298 9374	11
12	11.8072 5384	11.7755 6295	11.7439 9442	11.6812 2198	12
13	12.7753 1555	12.7384 0915	12.7016 5557	12.6286 0280	13
14	13.7409 2414	13.6984 5542	13.6561 3512	13.5720 5257	14
15	14.7042 0264	14.6557 0959	14.6074 4364	14.5115 8762	15
16	15.6650 4004	15.6101 7990	15.5555 9167	15.4472 2418	16
17	16.6234 8133	16.5618 7442	16.5005 8970	16.3789 7843	17
18	17.5795 3250	17.5108 0125	17.4424 4821	17.3068 6648	18
19	18.5331 9950	18.4569 6842	18.3811 7762	18.2309 0438	19
20	19.4844 8828	19.4003 8396	19.3167 8832	19.1511 0809	20
21	20.4334 0477	20.3410 5587	20.2492 9069	20.0674 9352	21
22	21.3799 5488	21.2789 9213	21.1786 9504	20.9800 7653	22
23	22.3241 4452	22.2142 0071	22.1050 1167	21.8888 7289	23
24	23.2659 7957	23.1466 8952	23.0282 5083	22.7938 9831	24
25	24.2054 6591	24.0764 6648	23.9484 2275	23.6951 6843	25
26	25.1426 0939	25.0035 3949	24.8655 3763	24.5926 9884	26
27	26.0774 1585	25.9279 1639	25.7796 0561	25.4865 0506	27
28	27.0098 9112	26.8496 0503	26.6906 3682	26.3766 0254	28
29	27.9400 4102	27.7686 1324	27.5986 4135	27.2630 0668	29
30	28.8678 7134	28.6849 4879	28.5036 2925	28.1457 3278	30
31	29.7933 8787	29.5986 1947	29.4056 1055	29.0247 9612	31
32	30.7165 9638	30.5096 3303	30.3045 9523	29.9002 1189	32
33	31.6375 0262	31.4179 9720	31.2005 9325	30.7719 9524	33
34	32.5561 1234	32.3237 1967	32.0936 1454	31.6401 6122	34
35	33.4724 3126	33.2268 0814	32.9836 6898	32.5047 2486	35
36	34.3864 6510	34.1272 7025	33.8707 6642	33.3657 0109	36
37	35.2982 1955	35.0251 1366	34.7549 1670	34.2231 0481	37
38	36.2077 0030	35.9203 4597	35.6361 2960	35.0769 5084	38
39	37.1149 1302	36.8129 7478	36.5144 1488	35.9272 5394	39
40	38.0198 6336	37.7030 0767	37.3897 8228	36.7740 2881	40
41	38.9225 5697	38.5904 5217	38.2622 4147	37.6172 9009	41
42	39.8229 9947	39.4753 1582	39.1318 0213	38.4570 5236	42
43	40.7211 9648	40.3576 0612	39.9984 7388	39.2933 3013	43
44	41.6171 5359	41.2373 3056	40.8622 6633	40.1261 3788	44
45	42.5108 7640	42.1144 9659	41.7231 8903	40.9554 8999	45
46	43.4023 7047	42.9891 1167	42.5812 5153	41.7814 0081	46
47	44.2916 4137	43.8611 8320	43.4364 6332	42.6038 8461	47
48	45.1786 9463	44.7307 1859	44.2888 3387	43.4229 5562	48
49	46.0635 3580	45.5977 2521	45.1383 7263	44.2386 2799	49
50	46.9461 7037	46.4622 1042	45.9850 8900	45.0509 1582	50

TABLE VI.—Present Value of Annuity of 1 per Period

$$a_{\overline{n}|i} = \frac{1 - (1 + i)^{-n}}{i}$$

n	$\frac{1}{4}\%$	$\frac{7}{24}\%$	$\frac{1}{3}\%$	$\frac{5}{12}\%$	n
51	47.8266 0386	47.3241 8154	46.8289 9236	45.8598 3317	51
52	48.7048 4176	48.1836 4589	47.6700 9205	46.6653 9401	52
53	49.5808 8953	49.0406 1076	48.5083 9739	47.4676 1228	53
54	50.4547 5265	49.8950 8341	49.3439 1767	48.2665 0184	54
55	51.3264 3656	50.7470 7110	50.1766 6213	49.0620 7651	55
56	52.1959 4669	51.5965 8106	51.0066 3999	49.8543 5003	56
57	53.0632 8847	52.4436 2048	51.8338 6046	50.6433 3612	57
58	53.9284 6730	53.2881 9656	52.6583 3268	51.4290 4840	58
59	54.7914 8858	54.1303 1645	53.4800 6580	52.2115 0046	59
60	55.6523 5769	54.9699 8730	54.2990 6890	52.9907 0584	60
61	56.5110 7999	55.8072 1623	55.1153 5106	53.7666 7800	61
62	57.3676 6083	56.6420 1035	55.9289 2133	54.5394 3035	62
63	58.2221 0557	57.4743 7673	56.7397 8870	55.3089 7627	63
64	59.0744 1952	58.3043 2244	57.5479 6216	56.0753 2905	64
65	59.9246 0800	59.1318 5451	58.3534 5065	56.8385 0194	65
66	60.7726 7631	59.9569 7996	59.1562 6311	57.5985 0814	66
67	61.6186 2974	60.7797 0580	59.9564 0842	58.3553 6078	67
68	62.4624 7355	61.6000 3900	60.7538 9543	59.1090 7296	68
69	63.3042 1302	62.4179 8652	61.5487 3299	59.8596 5770	69
70	64.1438 5339	63.2335 5529	62.3409 2989	60.6071 2798	70
71	64.9813 9989	64.0467 5224	63.1304 9490	61.3514 9672	71
72	65.8168 5774	64.8575 8427	63.9174 3678	62.0927 7680	72
73	66.6502 3216	65.6660 5824	64.7017 6423	62.8309 8103	73
74	67.4815 2834	66.4721 8103	65.4834 8595	63.5661 2216	74
75	68.3107 5146	67.2759 5945	66.2626 1058	64.2982 1292	75
76	69.1379 0670	68.0774 0035	67.0391 4676	65.0272 6596	76
77	69.9629 9920	68.8765 1050	67.8131 0308	65.7532 9388	77
78	70.7860 3411	69.6732 9670	68.5844 8812	66.4763 0924	78
79	71.6070 1657	70.4677 6569	69.3533 1042	67.1963 2453	79
80	72.4259 5169	71.2599 2422	70.1195 7849	67.9133 5221	80
81	73.2428 4458	72.0497 7901	70.8833 0082	68.6274 0467	81
82	74.0577 0033	72.8373 3675	71.6444 8587	69.3384 9426	82
83	74.8705 2402	73.6226 0413	72.4031 4206	70.0466 3326	83
84	75.6813 2072	74.4055 8781	73.1592 7780	70.7518 3393	84
85	76.4900 9548	75.1862 9442	73.9129 0146	71.4541 0846	85
86	77.2968 5335	75.9647 3060	74.6640 2139	72.1534 6898	86
87	78.1015 9935	76.7409 0294	75.4126 4591	72.8499 2759	87
88	78.9043 3850	77.5148 1803	76.1587 8329	73.5434 9633	88
89	79.7050 7581	78.2864 8243	76.9024 4182	74.2341 8720	89
90	80.5038 1627	79.0559 0268	77.6436 2972	74.9220 1212	90
91	81.3005 6486	79.8230 8532	78.3823 5520	75.6069 8300	91
92	82.0953 2654	80.5880 3685	79.1186 2645	76.2891 1168	92
93	82.8881 0628	81.3507 6377	79.8524 5161	76.9684 0995	93
94	83.6789 0900	82.1112 7253	80.5838 3882	77.6448 8955	94
95	84.4677 3966	82.8695 6959	81.3127 9616	78.3185 6218	95
96	85.2546 0315	83.6256 6138	82.0393 3172	78.9894 3950	96
97	86.0395 0439	84.3795 5432	82.7634 5354	79.6575 3308	97
98	86.8224 4827	85.1312 5480	83.4851 6964	80.3228 5450	98
99	87.6034 3967	85.8807 6919	84.2044 8802	80.9854 1524	99
100	88.3824 8346	86.6281 0386	84.9214 1663	81.6452 2677	100

519

TABLE VI.—Present Value of Annuity of 1 per Period

$$a_{\overline{n}|i} = \frac{1 - (1 + i)^{-n}}{i}$$

n	¼%	⁷⁄₂₄%	⅓%	⁵⁄₁₂%	n
101	89.1595 8450	87.3732 6514	85.6359 6344	82.3023 0049	101
102	89.9347 4763	88.1162 5935	86.3481 3635	82.9566 4777	102
103	90.7079 7768	88.8570 9280	87.0579 4323	83.6082 7991	103
104	91.4792 7948	89.5957 7177	87.7653 9195	84.2572 0818	104
105	92.2486 5784	90.3323 0252	88.4704 9034	84.9034 4381	105
106	93.0161 1755	91.0666 9131	89.1732 4621	85.5469 9795	106
107	93.7816 6339	91.7989 4436	89.8736 6735	86.1878 8175	107
108	94.5453 0014	92.5290 6788	90.5717 6150	86.8261 0628	108
109	95.3070 3256	93.2570 6806	91.2675 3641	87.4616 8258	109
110	96.0668 6539	93.9829 5109	91.9609 9977	88.0946 2163	110
111	96.8248 0338	94.7067 2312	92.6521 5927	88.7249 3437	111
112	97.5808 5126	95.4283 9028	93.3410 2255	89.3526 3171	112
113	98.3350 1372	96.1479 5870	94.0275 9726	89.9777 2450	113
114	99.0872 9548	96.8654 3448	94.7118 9098	90.6002 2354	114
115	99.8377 0123	97.5808 2372	95.3939 1131	91.2201 3959	115
116	100.5862 3564	98.2941 3246	96.0736 6578	91.8374 8338	116
117	101.3329 0338	99.0053 6678	96.7511 6194	92.4522 6558	117
118	102.0777 0911	99.7145 3269	97.4264 0727	93.0644 9681	118
119	102.8206 5747	100.4216 3621	98.0994 0927	93.6741 8767	119
120	103.5617 5308	101.1266 8335	98.7701 7538	94.2813 4869	120
121	104.3010 0058	101.8296 8009	99.4387 1304	94.8859 9036	121
122	105.0384 0457	102.5306 3237	100.1050 2964	95.4881 2315	122
123	105.7739 6965	103.2295 4616	100.7691 3256	96.0877 5747	123
124	106.5077 0040	103.9264 2738	101.4310 2916	96.6849 0367	124
125	107.2396 0139	104.6212 8194	102.0907 2677	97.2795 7209	125
126	107.9696 7720	105.3141 1573	102.7482 3269	97.8717 7301	126
127	108.6979 3237	106.0049 3464	103.4035 5420	98.4615 1666	127
128	109.4243 7144	106.6937 4451	104.0566 9857	99.0488 1324	128
129	110.1489 9894	107.3805 5120	104.7076 7303	99.6336 7290	129
130	110.8718 1939	108.0653 6053	105.3564 8478	100.2161 0576	130
131	111.5928 3730	108.7481 7831	106.0031 4101	100.7961 2189	131
132	112.3120 5716	109.4290 1032	106.6476 4888	101.3737 3131	132
133	113.0294 8345	110.1078 6235	107.2900 1552	101.9489 4401	133
134	113.7451 2065	110.7847 4016	107.9302 4806	102.5217 6994	134
135	114.4589 7321	111.4596 4947	108.5683 5358	103.0922 1899	135
136	115.1710 4560	112.1325 9603	109.2043 3915	103.6603 0104	136
137	115.8813 4224	112.8035 8553	109.8382 1181	104.2260 2590	137
138	116.5898 6758	113.4726 2368	110.4699 7859	104.7894 0335	138
139	117.2966 2601	114.1397 1613	111.0996 4646	105.3504 4314	139
140	118.0016 2196	114.8048 6856	111.7272 2242	105.9091 5496	140
141	118.7048 5981	115.4680 8660	112.3527 1341	106.4655 4847	141
142	119.4063 4395	116.1293 7588	112.9761 2636	107.0196 3330	142
143	120.1060 7875	116.7887 4201	113.5974 6817	107.5714 1902	143
144	120.8040 6858	117.4461 9058	114.2167 4572	108.1209 1517	144
145	121.5003 1778	118.1017 2717	114.8339 6586	108.6681 3126	145
146	122.1948 3071	118.7553 5734	115.4491 3545	109.2130 7674	146
147	122.8876 1168	119.4070 8663	116.0622 6128	109.7557 6103	147
148	123.5786 6502	120.0569 2057	116.6733 5015	110.2961 9353	148
149	124.2679 9503	120.7048 6467	117.2824 0882	110.8343 8356	149
150	124.9556 0601	121.3509 2444	117.8894 4404	111.3703 4044	150

TABLE VI.—Present Value of Annuity of 1 per Period

$$a_{\overline{n}|i} = \frac{1 - (1 + i)^{-n}}{i}$$

n	¼%	7/24%	⅓%	5/12%	n
151	125.6415 0226	121.9951 0534	118.4944 6254	111.9040 7343	151
152	126.3256 8804	122.6374 1284	119.0974 7100	112.4355 9176	152
153	127.0081 6762	123.2778 5240	119.6984 7612	112.9649 0463	153
154	127.6889 4525	123.9164 2944	120.2974 8454	113.4920 2117	154
155	128.3680 2519	124.5531 4937	120.8945 0290	114.0169 5051	155
156	129.0454 1166	125.1880 1761	121.4895 3781	114.5397 0171	156
157	129.7211 0889	125.8210 3954	122.0825 9587	115.0602 8383	157
158	130.3951 2109	126.4522 2052	122.6736 8363	115.5787 0585	158
159	131.0674 5246	127.0815 6591	123.2628 0764	116.0949 7674	159
160	131.7381 0719	127.7090 8105	123.8499 7443	116.6091 0543	160
161	132.4070 8946	128.3347 7125	124.4351 9050	117.1211 0081	161
162	133.0744 0346	128.9586 4184	125.0184 6233	117.6309 7172	162
163	133.7400 5332	129.5806 9809	125.5997 9638	118.1387 2699	163
164	134.4040 4321	130.2009 4529	126.1791 9909	118.6443 7539	164
165	135.0663 7727	130.8193 8870	126.7566 7687	119.1479 2566	165
166	135.7270 5962	131.4360 3355	127.3322 3612	119.6493 8641	166
167	136.3860 9439	132.0508 8509	127.9058 8322	120.1487 6662	167
168	137.0434 8567	132.6639 4853	128.4776 2451	120.6460 7460	168
169	137.6992 3758	133.2752 2907	129.0474 6633	121.1413 1907	169
170	138.3533 5419	133.8847 3189	129.6154 1499	121.6345 0858	170
171	139.0058 3959	134.4924 6216	130.1814 7677	122.1256 5166	171
172	139.6566 9785	135.0984 2564	130.7456 5795	122.6147 5680	172
173	140.3059 3302	135.7026 2567	131.3079 6478	123.1018 3246	173
174	140.9535 4914	136.3050 6917	131.8684 0347	123.5868 8705	174
175	141.5995 5027	136.9057 6066	132.4269 8025	124.0699 2898	175
176	142.2439 4042	137.5047 0522	132.9837 0128	124.5509 6658	176
177	142.8867 2361	138.1019 0794	133.5385 7275	125.0300 0817	177
178	143.5279 0385	138.6973 7389	134.0916 0079	125.5070 6204	178
179	144.1674 8514	139.2911 0811	134.6427 9152	125.9821 3643	179
180	144.8054 7146	139.8831 1564	135.1921 5106	126.4552 3956	180
181	145.4418 6679	140.4734 0151	135.7396 8549	126.9263 7961	181
182	146.0766 7510	141.0619 7071	136.2854 0086	127.3955 6471	182
183	146.7099 0035	141.6488 2825	136.8293 0322	127.8628 0299	183
184	147.3415 4649	142.2339 7909	137.3713 9860	128.3281 0253	184
185	147.9716 1744	142.8174 2821	137.9116 9300	128.7914 7136	185
186	148.6001 1715	143.3991 8055	138.4501 9241	129.2529 1749	186
187	149.2270 4952	143.9792 4105	138.9869 0277	129.7124 4891	187
188	149.8524 1848	144.5576 1463	139.5218 3005	130.1700 7357	188
189	150.4762 2791	145.1343 0618	140.0549 8016	130.6257 9936	189
190	151.0984 8170	145.7093 2062	140.5863 5901	131.0796 3418	190
191	151.7191 8375	146.2826 6280	141.1159 7248	131.5315 8586	191
192	152.3383 3790	146.8543 3760	141.6438 2643	131.9816 6223	192
193	152.9559 4803	147.4243 4986	142.1699 2672	132.4298 7106	193
194	153.5720 1799	147.9927 0442	142.6942 7917	132.8762 2010	194
195	154.1865 5161	148.5594 0611	143.2168 8958	133.3207 1707	195
196	154.7995 5272	149.1244 5971	143.7377 6375	133.7633 6965	196
197	155.4110 2516	149.6878 7004	144.2569 0743	134.2041 8550	197
198	156.0209 7273	150.2496 4187	144.7743 2639	134.6431 7224	198
199	156.6293 9923	150.8097 7996	145.2900 2635	135.0803 3746	199
200	157.2363 0846	151.3682 8907	145.8040 1302	135.5156 8872	200

TABLE VI.—Present Value of Annuity of 1 per Period

$$a_{\overline{n}|i} = \frac{1 - (1 + i)^{-n}}{i}$$

n	½%	₇⁄₁₂%	⅝%	⅔%	n
1	0.9950 2488	0.9942 0050	0.9937 8882	0.9933 7748	1
2	1.9850 9938	1.9826 3513	1.9814 0504	1.9801 7631	2
3	2.9702 4814	2.9653 3733	2.9628 8699	2.9604 4004	3
4	3.9504 9566	3.9423 4034	3.9382 7279	3.9342 1196	4
5	4.9258 6633	4.9136 7723	4.9076 0029	4.9015 3506	5
6	5.8963 8441	5.8793 8084	5.8709 0712	5.8624 5205	6
7	6.8620 7404	6.8394 8385	6.8282 3068	6.8170 0535	7
8	7.8229 5924	7.7940 1875	7.7796 0813	7.7652 3710	8
9	8.7790 6392	8.7430 1781	8.7250 7640	8.7071 8917	9
10	9.7304 1186	9.6865 1315	9.6646 7220	9.6429 0315	10
11	10.6770 2673	10.6245 3669	10.5984 3200	10.5724 2035	11
12	11.6189 3207	11.5571 2016	11.5263 9205	11.4957 8180	12
13	12.5561 5131	12.4842 9511	12.4485 8837	12.4130 2828	13
14	13.4887 0777	13.4060 9291	13.3650 5676	13.3242 0028	14
15	14.4166 2465	14.3225 4473	14.2758 3281	14.2293 3802	15
16	15.3399 2502	15.2336 8160	15.1809 5186	15.1284 8148	16
17	16.2586 3186	16.1395 3432	16.0804 4905	16.0216 7035	17
18	17.1727 6802	17.0401 3354	16.9743 5931	16.9089 4405	18
19	18.0823 5624	17.9355 0974	17.8627 1733	17.7903 4177	19
20	18.9874 1915	18.8256 9320	18.7455 5759	18.6659 0242	20
21	19.8879 7925	19.7107 1404	19.6229 1438	19.5356 6466	21
22	20.7840 5896	20.5906 0220	20.4948 2174	20.3996 6688	22
23	21.6756 8055	21.4653 8745	21.3613 1353	21.2579 4723	23
24	22.5628 6622	22.3350 9938	22.2224 2338	22.1105 4361	24
25	23.4456 3803	23.1997 6741	23.0781 8473	22.9574 9365	25
26	24.3240 1794	24.0594 2079	23.9286 3079	23.7988 3475	26
27	25.1980 2780	24.9140 8862	24.7737 9457	24.6346 0406	27
28	26.0676 8936	25.7637 9979	25.6137 0889	25.4648 3847	28
29	26.9330 2423	26.6085 8307	26.4484 0635	26.2895 7464	29
30	27.7940 5397	27.4484 6702	27.2779 1935	27.1088 4898	30
31	28.6507 9997	28.2834 8006	28.1022 8010	27.9226 9766	31
32	29.5032 8355	29.1136 5044	28.9215 2060	28.7311 5662	32
33	30.3515 2592	29.9390 0625	29.7356 7265	29.5342 6154	33
34	31.1955 4818	30.7595 7540	30.5447 6785	30.3320 4789	34
35	32.0353 7132	31.5753 8566	31.3488 3761	31.1245 5088	35
36	32.8710 1624	32.3864 6463	32.1479 1315	31.9118 0551	36
37	33.7025 0372	33.1928 3974	32.9420 2550	32.6938 4653	37
38	34.5298 5445	33.9945 3828	33.7312 0546	33.4707 0848	38
39	35.3530 8900	34.7915 8736	34.5154 8369	34.2424 2564	39
40	36.1722 2786	35.5840 1396	35.2948 9062	35.0090 3209	40
41	36.9872 9141	36.3718 4487	36.0694 5652	35.7705 6168	41
42	37.7982 9991	37.1551 0676	36.8392 1145	36.5270 4803	42
43	38.6052 7354	37.9338 2612	37.6041 8529	37.2785 2453	43
44	39.4082 3238	38.7080 2929	38.3644 0774	38.0250 2437	44
45	40.2071 9640	39.4777 4248	39.1199 0831	38.7665 8050	45
46	41.0021 8547	40.2429 9170	39.8707 1634	39.5032 2566	46
47	41.7932 1937	41.0038 0287	40.6168 6096	40.2349 9238	47
48	42.5803 1778	41.7602 0170	41.3583 7114	40.9619 1296	48
49	43.3635 0028	42.5122 1380	42.0952 7566	41.6840 1949	49
50	44.1427 8635	43.2598 6460	42.8276 0314	42.4013 4387	50

TABLE VI.—Present Value of Annuity of 1 per Period

$$a_{\overline{n}|i} = \frac{1 - (1 + i)^{-n}}{i}$$

n	½%	⁷⁄₁₂%	⅝%	⅔%	n
51	44.9181 9537	44.0031 7940	43.5553 8201	43.1139 1775	51
52	45.6897 4664	44.7421 8335	44.2786 4050	43.8217 7260	52
53	46.4574 5934	45.4769 0144	44.9974 0671	44.5249 3967	53
54	47.2213 5258	46.2073 5853	45.7117 0853	45.2234 5000	54
55	47.9814 4535	46.9335 7933	46.4215 7370	45.9173 3444	55
56	48.7377 5657	47.6555 8841	47.1270 2976	46.6066 2362	56
57	49.4903 0505	48.3734 1020	47.8281 0410	47.2913 4796	57
58	50.2391 0950	49.0870 6898	48.5248 2396	47.9715 3771	58
59	50.9841 8855	49.7965 8889	49.2172 1636	48.6472 2289	59
60	51.7255 6075	50.5019 9394	49.9053 0818	49.3184 3334	60
61	52.4632 4453	51.2033 0800	50.5891 2614	49.9851 9868	61
62	53.1972 5824	51.9005 5478	51.2686 9679	50.6475 4835	62
63	53.9276 2014	52.5937 5787	51.9440 4650	51.3055 1161	63
64	54.6543 4839	53.2829 4073	52.6152 0149	51.9591 1749	64
65	55.3774 6109	53.9681 2668	53.2821 8781	52.6083 9486	65
66	56.0969 7621	54.6493 3888	53.9450 3137	53.2533 7238	66
67	56.8129 1165	55.3266 0040	54.6037 5788	53.8940 7852	67
68	57.5252 8522	55.9999 3413	55.2583 9293	54.5305 4158	68
69	58.2341 1465	56.6693 6287	55.9089 6191	55.1627 8965	69
70	58.9394 1756	57.3349 0925	56.5554 9010	55.7908 5064	70
71	59.6412 1151	57.9965 9579	57.1980 0258	56.4147 5229	71
72	60.3395 1394	58.6544 4488	57.8365 2431	57.0345 2215	72
73	61.0343 4222	59.3084 7877	58.4710 8006	57.6501 8756	73
74	61.7257 1366	59.9587 1959	59.1016 9447	58.2617 7572	74
75	62.4136 4543	60.6051 8934	59.7283 9201	58.8693 1363	75
76	63.0981 5466	61.2479 0988	60.3511 9703	59.4728 2811	76
77	63.7792 5836	61.8869 0297	60.9701 3370	60.0723 4581	77
78	64.4569 7350	62.5221 9021	61.5852 2604	60.6678 9319	78
79	65.1313 1691	63.1537 9310	62.1964 9792	61.2594 9654	79
80	65.8023 0538	63.7817 3301	62.8039 7309	61.8471 8200	80
81	66.4699 5561	64.4060 3118	63.4076 7512	62.4309 7549	81
82	67.1342 8419	65.0267 0874	64.0076 2745	63.0109 0281	82
83	67.7953 0765	65.6437 8667	64.6038 5337	63.5869 8954	83
84	68.4530 4244	66.2572 8585	65.1963 7602	64.1592 6114	84
85	69.1075 0491	66.8672 2705	65.7852 1840	64.7277 4285	85
86	69.7587 1135	67.4736 3089	66.3704 0338	65.2924 5979	86
87	70.4066 7796	68.0765 1789	66.9519 5367	65.8534 3687	87
88	71.0514 2086	68.6759 0845	67.5298 9185	66.4106 9888	88
89	71.6929 5608	69.2718 2283	68.1042 4034	66.9642 7041	89
90	72.3312 9958	69.8642 8121	68.6750 2146	67.5141 7590	90
91	72.9664 6725	70.4533 0363	69.2422 5735	68.0604 3964	91
92	73.5984 7487	71.0389 1001	69.8059 7004	68.6030 8574	92
93	74.2273 3818	71.6211 2017	70.3661 8141	69.1421 3815	93
94	74.8530 7282	72.1999 5379	70.9229 1320	69.6776 2068	94
95	75.4756 9434	72.7754 3047	71.4761 8703	70.2095 5696	95
96	76.0952 1825	73.3475 6967	72.0260 2438	70.7379 7049	96
97	76.7116 5995	73.9163 9075	72.5724 4658	71.2628 8460	97
98	77.3250 3478	74.4819 1294	73.1154 7487	71.7843 2245	98
99	77.9353 5799	75.0441 5539	73.6551 3030	72.3023 0707	99
100	78.5426 4477	75.6031 3712	74.1914 3384	72.8168 6132	100

TABLE VI.—Present Value of Annuity of 1 per Period

$$a_{\overline{n}|i} = \frac{1 - (1 + i)^{-n}}{i}$$

n	½%	7⁄12%	5⁄8%	⅔%	n
101	79.1469 1021	76.1588 7702	74.7244 0630	73.3280 0792	101
102	79.7481 6937	76.7113 9392	75.2540 6838	73.8357 6944	102
103	80.3464 3718	77.2607 0648	75.7804 4062	74.3401 6830	103
104	80.9417 2854	77.8068 3331	76.3035 4348	74.8412 2677	104
105	81.5340 5825	78.3497 9288	76.8233 9724	75.3389 6697	105
106	82.1234 4104	78.8896 0355	77.3400 2210	75.8334 1088	106
107	82.7098 9158	79.4262 8359	77.8534 3812	76.3245 8032	107
108	83.2934 2446	79.9598 5115	78.3636 6521	76.8124 9699	108
109	83.8740 5419	80.4903 2428	78.8707 2319	77.2971 8242	109
110	84.4517 9522	81.0177 2093	79.3746 3174	77.7786 5801	110
111	85.0266 6191	81.5420 5895	79.8754 1043	78.2569 4503	111
112	85.5986 6856	82.0633 5606	80.3730 7868	78.7320 6458	112
113	86.1678 2942	82.5816 2991	80.8676 5583	79.2040 3764	113
114	86.7341 5862	83.0968 9803	81.3591 6108	79.6728 8505	114
115	87.2976 7027	83.6091 7785	81.8476 1349	80.1386 2751	115
116	87.8583 7838	84.1184 8671	82.3330 3204	80.6012 8559	116
117	88.4162 9690	84.6248 4182	82.8154 3557	81.0608 7970	117
118	88.9714 3970	85.1282 6033	83.2948 4280	81.5174 3015	118
119	89.5238 2059	85.6287 5926	83.7712 7235	81.9709 5708	119
120	90.0734 5333	86.1263 5554	84.2447 4271	82.4214 8052	120
121	90.6203 5157	86.6210 6602	84.7152 7226	82.8690 2036	121
122	91.1645 2892	87.1129 0742	85.1828 7926	83.3135 9636	122
123	91.7059 9893	87.6018 9638	85.6475 8188	83.7552 2815	123
124	92.2447 7505	88.0880 4946	86.1093 9814	84.1939 3523	124
125	92.7808 7070	88.5713 8308	86.5683 4597	84.6297 3696	125
126	93.3142 9920	89.0519 1361	87.0244 4320	85.0626 5259	126
127	93.8450 7384	89.5296 5731	87.4777 0753	85.4927 0122	127
128	94.3732 0780	90.0046 3032	87.9281 5655	85.9199 0185	128
129	94.8987 1422	90.4768 4873	88.3758 0776	86.3442 7334	129
130	95.4216 0619	90.9463 2851	88.8206 7852	86.7658 3442	130
131	95.9418 9671	91.4130 8554	89.2627 8610	87.1846 0371	131
132	96.4595 9872	91.8771 3561	89.7021 4768	87.6005 9969	132
133	96.9747 2509	92.3384 9442	90.1387 8030	88.0138 4072	133
134	97.4872 8865	92.7971 7758	90.5727 0092	88.4243 4507	134
135	97.9973 0214	93.2532 0060	91.0039 2638	88.8321 3084	135
136	98.5047 7825	93.7065 7892	91.4324 7342	89.2372 1604	136
137	99.0097 2960	94.1573 2787	91.8583 5868	89.6396 1856	137
138	99.5121 6875	94.6054 6270	92.2815 9869	90.0393 5616	138
139	100.0121 0821	95.0509 9857	92.7022 0988	90.4364 4649	139
140	100.5095 6041	95.4939 5056	93.1202 0857	90.8309 0709	140
141	101.0045 3772	95.9343 3364	93.5356 1100	91.2227 5536	141
142	101.4970 5246	96.3721 6272	93.9484 3330	91.6120 0861	142
143	101.9871 1688	96.8074 5261	94.3586 9148	91.9986 8402	143
144	102.4747 4316	97.2402 1804	94.7664 0147	92.3827 9867	144
145	102.9599 4344	97.6704 7364	95.1715 7910	92.7643 6952	145
146	103.4427 2979	98.0982 3397	95.5742 4010	93.1434 1340	146
147	103.9231 1422	98.5235 1350	95.9744 0010	93.5199 4706	147
148	104.4011 0868	98.9463 2663	96.3720 7163	93.8939 8712	148
149	104.8767 2505	99.3666 8765	96.7672 7913	94.2655 5010	149
150	105.3499 7518	99.7846 1078	97.1600 2895	94.6346 5239	150

524

TABLE VI.—Present Value of Annuity of 1 per Period

$$a_{\overline{n}|i} = \frac{1 - (1 + i)^{-n}}{i}$$

n	½%	⁷⁄₁₂%	⅝%	⅔%	n
151	105.8208 7082	100.2001 1017	97.5503 3933	95.0013 1029	151
152	106.2894 2371	100.6131 9987	97.9382 2542	95.3655 4000	152
153	106.7556 4548	101.0238 9385	98.3237 0228	95.7273 5759	153
154	107.2195 4774	101.4322 0601	98.7067 8488	96.0867 7904	154
155	107.6811 4203	101.8381 5017	99.0874 8808	96.4438 2021	155
156	108.1404 3983	102.2417 4005	99.4658 2666	96.7984 9687	156
157	108.5974 5257	102.6429 8931	99.8418 1532	97.1508 2468	157
158	109.0521 9161	103.0419 1152	100.2154 6864	97.5008 1919	158
159	109.5046 6827	103.4385 2019	100.5868 0113	97.8484 9586	159
160	109.9548 9380	103.8328 2872	100.9558 2721	98.1938 7003	160
161	110.4028 7940	104.2248 5046	101.3225 6120	98.5369 5695	161
162	110.8486 3622	104.6145 9866	101.6870 1734	98.8777 7178	162
163	111.2921 7534	105.0020 8652	102.0492 0978	99.2163 2956	163
164	111.7335 0780	105.3873 2715	102.4091 5258	99.5526 4523	164
165	112.1726 4458	105.7703 3357	102.7668 5971	99.8867 3364	165
166	112.6095 9660	106.1511 1874	103.1223 4505	100.2186 0955	166
167	113.0443 7473	106.5296 9555	103.4756 2241	100.5482 8760	167
168	113.4769 8978	106.9060 7680	103.8267 0550	100.8757 8236	168
169	113.9074 5251	107.2802 7523	104.1756 0795	101.2011 0828	169
170	114.3357 7365	107.6523 0349	104.5223 4330	101.5242 7972	170
171	114.7619 6383	108.0221 7417	104.8669 2502	101.8453 1095	171
172	115.1860 3366	108.3898 9979	105.2093 6648	102.1642 1614	172
173	115.6079 9369	108.7554 9278	105.5496 8098	102.4810 0939	173
174	116.0278 5442	109.1189 6552	105.8878 8172	102.7957 0466	174
175	116.4456 2629	109.4803 3029	106.2239 8183	103.1083 1586	175
176	116.8613 1969	109.8395 9933	106.5579 9436	103.4188 5678	176
177	117.2749 4496	110.1967 8478	106.8899 3229	103.7273 4115	177
178	117.6865 1240	110.5518 9874	107.2198 0848	104.0337 8257	178
179	118.0960 3224	110.9049 5322	107.5476 3576	104.3381 9457	179
180	118.5035 1467	111.2559 6015	107.8734 2684	104.6405 9061	180
181	118.9089 6982	111.6049 3142	108.1971 9438	104.9409 8402	181
182	119.3124 0778	111.9518 7882	108.5189 5094	105.2393 8807	182
183	119.7138 3859	112.2968 1411	108.8387 0900	105.5358 1593	183
184	120.1132 7222	112.6397 4894	109.1564 8100	105.8302 8070	184
185	120.5107 1863	112.9806 9492	109.4722 7925	106.1227 9536	185
186	120.9061 8769	113.3196 6359	109.7861 1603	106.4133 7285	186
187	121.2996 8925	113.6566 6640	110.0980 0351	106.7020 2598	187
188	121.6912 3308	113.9917 1477	110.4079 5379	106.9887 6750	188
189	122.0808 2894	114.3248 2002	110.7159 7893	107.2736 1007	189
190	122.4684 8650	114.6559 9342	111.0220 9086	107.5565 6626	190
191	122.8542 1543	114.9852 4619	111.3263 0147	107.8376 4557	191
192	123.2380 2530	115.3125 8945	111.6286 2258	108.1168 6941	192
193	123.6199 2567	115.6380 3429	111.9290 6592	108.3942 4111	193
194	123.9999 2604	115.9615 9171	112.2276 4315	108.6697 7590	194
195	124.3780 3586	116.2832 7265	112.5243 6586	108.9434 8597	195
196	124.7542 6454	116.6030 8801	112.8192 4558	109.2153 8338	196
197	125.1286 2143	116.9210 4859	113.1122 9374	109.4854 8015	197
198	125.5011 1585	117.2371 6516	113.4035 2173	109.7537 8819	198
199	125.8717 5707	117.5514 4842	113.6929 4085	110.0203 1937	199
200	126.2405 5430	117.8639 0899	113.9805 6234	110.2850 8543	200

TABLE VI.—Present Value of Annuity of 1 per Period

$$a_{\overline{n}|i} = \frac{1 - (1 + i)^{-n}}{i}$$

n	¾%	⅞%	1%	1⅛%	n
1	0.9925 5583	0.9913 2590	0.9900 9901	0.9888 7515	1
2	1.9777 2291	1.9740 5294	1.9703 9506	1.9667 4923	2
3	2.9555 5624	2.9482 5570	2.9409 8521	2.9337 4460	3
4	3.9261 1041	3.9140 0813	3.9019 6555	3.8899 8230	4
5	4.8894 3961	4.8713 8352	4.8534 3124	4.8355 8200	5
6	5.8455 9763	5.8204 5454	5.7954 7647	5.7706 6205	6
7	6.7946 3785	6.7612 9323	6.7281 9453	6.6953 3948	7
8	7.7366 1325	7.6939 7098	7.6516 7775	7.6097 3002	8
9	8.6715 7642	8.6185 5859	8.5660 1758	8.5139 4810	9
10	9.5995 7958	9.5351 2624	9.4713 0453	9.4081 0690	10
11	10.5206 7452	10.4437 4348	10.3676 2825	10.2923 1832	11
12	11.4349 1267	11.3444 7929	11.2550 7747	11.1666 9302	12
13	12.3423 4508	12.2374 0202	12.1337 4007	12.0313 4044	13
14	13.2430 2242	13.1225 7945	13.0037 0304	12.8863 6880	14
15	14.1369 9495	14.0000 7876	13.8650 5252	13.7318 8509	15
16	15.0243 1261	14.8699 6656	14.7178 7378	14.5679 9514	16
17	15.9050 2492	15.7323 0885	15.5622 5127	15.3948 0360	17
18	16.7791 8107	16.5871 7111	16.3982 6858	16.2124 1395	18
19	17.6468 2984	17.4346 1820	17.2260 0850	17.0209 2850	19
20	18.5080 1969	18.2747 1445	18·0455 5297	17.8204 4845	20
21	19.3627 9870	19.1075 2361	18.8569 8313	18.6110 7387	21
22	20.2112 1459	19.9331 0891	19.6603 7934	19.3929 0371	22
23	21.0533 1473	20.7515 3300	20.4558 2113	20.1660 3580	23
24	21.8891 4614	21.5628 5799	21.2433 8726	20.9305 6693	24
25	22.7187 5547	22.3671 4547	22.0231 5570	21.6865 9276	25
26	23.5421 8905	23.1644 5647	22.7952 0366	22.4342 0792	26
27	24.3594 9286	23.9548 5152	23.5596 0759	23.1735 0598	27
28	25.1707 1251	24.7383 9060	24.3164 4316	23.9045 7946	28
29	25.9758 9331	25.5151 3319	25.0657 8530	24.6275 1986	29
30	26.7750 8021	26.2851 3823	25.8077 0822	25.3424 1766	30
31	27.5683 1783	27.0484 6417	26.5422 8537	26.0493 6233	31
32	28.3556 5045	27.8051 6894	27.2695 8947	26.7484 4236	32
33	29.1371 2203	28.5553 0998	27.9896 9255	27.4397 4522	33
34	29.9127 7621	29.2989 4422	28.7026 6589	28.1233 5745	34
35	30.6826 5629	30.0361 2809	29.4085 8009	28.7993 6460	35
36	31.4468 0525	30.7669 1757	30.1075 0504	29.4678 5127	36
37	32.2052 6576	31.4913 6810	30.7995 0994	30.1289 0114	37
38	32.9580 8016	32.2095 3467	31.4846 6330	30.7825 9692	38
39	33.7052 9048	32.9214 7179	32.1630 3298	31.4290 2044	39
40	34.4469 3844	33.6272 3350	32.8346 8611	32.0682 5260	40
41	35.1830 6545	34.3268 7335	33.4996 8922	32.7903 7340	41
42	35.9137 1260	35.0204 4446	34.1581 0814	33.3254 6195	42
43	36.6389 2070	35.7079 9947	34.8100 0806	33.9435 9649	43
44	37.3587 3022	36.3895 9055	35.4554 5352	34.5548 5438	44
45	38.0731 8136	37.0652 6944	36.0945 0844	35.1593 1212	45
46	38.7823 1401	37.7350 8743	36.7272 3608	35.7570 4536	46
47	39.4861 6774	38.3990 9535	37.3536 9909	36.3481 2891	47
48	40.1847 8189	39.0573 4359	37.9739 5949	36.9326 3674	48
49	40.8781 9542	39.7098 8212	38.5880 7871	37.5106 4202	49
50	41.5664 4707	40.3567 6047	39.1961 1753	38.0822 1708	50

TABLE VI.—Present Value of Annuity of 1 per Period

$$a_{\overline{n}|i} = \frac{1 - (1 + i)^{-n}}{i}$$

n	¾%	⅞%	1%	1⅛%	n
51	42.2495 7525	40.9980 2772	39.7981 3617	38.6474 3345	51
52	42.9276 1812	41.6337 3256	40.3941 9423	39.2063 6188	52
53	43.6006 1351	42.2639 2324	40.9843 5072	39.7590 7232	53
54	44.2685 9902	42.8886 4757	41.5686 6408	40.3056 3394	54
55	44.9316 1193	43.5079 5298	42.1471 9216	40.8461 1514	55
56	45.5896 8926	44.1218 8647	42.7199 9224	41.3805 8358	56
57	46.2428 6776	44.7304 9465	43.2871 2102	41.9091 0613	57
58	46.8911 8388	45.3338 2369	43.8486 3468	42.4317 4896	58
59	47.5346 7382	45.9319 1939	44.4045 8879	42.9485 7746	59
60	48.1733 7352	46.5248 2716	44.9550 3841	43.4596 5633	60
61	48.8073 1863	47.1125 9198	45.5000 3803	43.9650 4952	61
62	49.4365 4455	47.6952 5847	46.0396 4161	44.4648 2029	62
63	50.0610 8640	48.2728 7085	46.5739 0258	44.9590 3119	63
64	50.6809 7906	48.8454 7296	47.1028 7385	45.4477 4407	64
65	51.2962 5713	49.4131 0826	47.6266 0777	45.9310 2009	65
66	51.9069 5497	49.9758 1984	48.1451 5621	46.4089 1975	66
67	52.5131 0667	50.5336 5040	48.6585 7050	46.8815 0284	67
68	53.1147 4607	51.0866 4228	49.1669 0149	47.3488 2852	68
69	53.7119 0677	51.6348 3745	49.6701 9949	47.8109 5527	69
70	54.3046 2210	52.1782 7752	50.1685 1435	48.2679 4094	70
71	54.8929 2516	52.7170 0374	50.6618 9539	48.7198 4270	71
72	55.4768 4880	53.2510 5699	51.1503 9148	49.1667 1714	72
73	56.0564 2561	53.7804 7781	51.6340 5097	49.6086 2016	73
74	56.6316 8795	54.3053 0638	52.1129 2175	50.0456 0708	74
75	57.2026 6794	54.8255 8253	52.5870 5124	50.4777 3259	75
76	57.7693 9746	55.3413 4575	53.0564 8637	50.9050 5077	76
77	58.3319 0815	55.8526 3520	53.5212 7364	51.3276 1510	77
78	58.8902 3141	56.3594 8966	53.9814 5905	51.7454 7847	78
79	59.4443 9842	56.8619 4762	54.4370 8817	52.1586 9317	79
80	59.9944 4012	57.3600 4721	54.8882 0611	52.5673 1092	80
81	60.5403 8722	57.8538 2623	55.3348 5753	52.9713 8286	81
82	61.0822 7019	58.3433 2216	55.7770 8666	53.3709 5957	82
83	61.6201 1930	58.8285 7215	56.2149 3729	53.7660 9104	83
84	62.1539 6456	59.3096 1304	56.6484 5276	54.1568 2674	84
85	62.6838 3579	59.7864 8133	57.0776 7600	54.5432 1557	85
86	63.2097 6257	60.2592 1321	57.5026 4951	54.9253 0588	86
87	63.7317 7427	60.7278 4457	57.9234 1535	55.3031 4549	87
88	64.2499 0002	61.1924 1097	58.3400 1520	55.6767 8169	88
89	64.7641 6875	61.6529 4768	58.7524 9030	56.0462 6126	89
90	65.2746 0918	62.1094 8965	59.1608 8148	56.4116 3041	90
91	65.7812 4981	62.5620 7152	59.5652 2919	56.7729 3490	91
92	66.2841 1892	63.0107 2765	59.9655 7346	57.1302 1992	92
93	66.7832 4458	63.4554 9210	60.3619 5392	57.4835 3021	93
94	67.2786 5467	63.8963 9861	60.7544 0982	57.8329 0997	94
95	67.7703 7685	64.3334 8065	61.1429 8002	58.1784 0294	95
96	68.2584 3856	64.7667 7140	61.5277 0299	58.5200 5235	96
97	68.7428 6705	65.1963 0375	61.9086 1682	58.8579 0096	97
98	69.2236 8938	65.6221 1028	62.2857 5923	59.1919 9106	98
99	69.7009 3239	66.0442 2333	62.6591 6755	59.5223 6446	99
100	70.1746 2272	66.4626 7492	63.0288 7877	59.8490 6251	100

TABLE VI.—Present Value of Annuity of 1 per Period

$$a_{\overline{n}|i} = \frac{1 - (1 + i)^{-n}}{i}$$

n	$1\tfrac{1}{4}\%$	$1\tfrac{3}{8}\%$	$1\tfrac{1}{2}\%$	$1\tfrac{3}{4}\%$	n
1	0.9876 5432	0.9864 3650	0.9852 2167	0.9828 0098	1
2	1.9631 1538	1.9594 9346	1.9558 8342	1.9486 9875	2
3	2.9265 3371	2.9193 5237	2.9122 0042	2.8979 8403	3
4	3.8780 5798	3.8661 9222	3.8543 8465	3.8309 4254	4
5	4.8178 3504	4.8001 8962	4.7826 4497	4.7478 5508	5
6	5.7460 0992	5.7215 1874	5.6971 8717	5.6489 9762	6
7	6.6627 2585	6.6303 5140	6.5982 1396	6.5346 4139	7
8	7.5681 2429	7.5268 5712	7.4859 2508	7.4050 5297	8
9	8.4623 4498	8.4112 0308	8.3605 1732	8.2604 9432	9
10	9.3455 2591	9.2835 5421	9.2221 8455	9.1012 2291	10
11	10.2178 0337	10.1440 7320	10.0711 1779	9.9274 9181	11
12	11.0793 1197	10.9929 2054	10.9075 0521	10.7395 4969	12
13	11.9301 8466	11.8302 5454	11.7315 3222	11.5376 4097	13
14	12.7705 5275	12.6562 3136	12.5433 8150	12.3220 0587	14
15	13.6005 4592	13.4710 0504	13.3432 3301	13.0928 8046	15
16	14.4202 9227	14.2747 2754	14.1312 6405	13.8504 9677	16
17	15.2299 1829	15.0675 4874	14.9076 4931	14.5950 8282	17
18	16.0295 4893	15.8496 1651	15.6725 6089	15.3268 6272	18
19	16.8193 0759	16.6210 7671	16.4261 6837	16.0460 5673	19
20	17.5993 1613	17.3820 7320	17.1686 3879	16.7528 8130	20
21	18.3696 9495	18.1327 4792	17.9001 3673	17.4475 4919	21
22	19.1305 6291	18.8732 4086	18.6208 2437	18.1302 6948	22
23	19.8820 3744	19.6036 9012	19.3308 6145	18.8012 4764	23
24	20.6242 3451	20.3242 3193	20.0304 0537	19.4606 8565	24
25	21.3572 6865	21.0350 0067	20.7196 1120	20.1087 8196	25
26	22.0812 5299	21.7361 2890	21.3986 3172	20.7457 3166	26
27	22.7962 9925	22.4277 4737	22.0676 1746	21.3717 2644	27
28	23.5025 1778	23.1099 8508	22.7267 1671	21.9869 5474	28
29	24.2000 1756	23.7829 6925	23.3760 7558	22.5916 0171	29
30	24.8889 0623	24.4468 2540	24.0158 3801	23.1858 4934	30
31	25.5692 9010	25.1016 7734	24.6461 4582	23.7698 7650	31
32	26.2412 7418	25.7476 4719	25.2671 3874	24.3438 5897	32
33	26.9049 6215	26.3848 5543	25.8789 5442	24.9079 6951	33
34	27.5604 5644	27.0134 2089	26.4817 2849	25.4623 7789	34
35	28.2078 5822	27.6334 6080	27.0755 9458	26.0072 5100	35
36	28.8472 6737	28.2450 9080	27.6606 8431	26.5427 5283	36
37	29.4787 8259	28.8484 2496	28.2371 2740	27.0690 4455	37
38	30.1025 0133	29.4435 7579	28.8050 5163	27.5862 8457	38
39	30.7185 1983	30.0306 5430	29.3645 8288	28.0946 2857	39
40	31.3269 3316	30.6097 6996	29.9158 4520	28.5942 2955	40
41	31.9278 3522	31.1810 3079	30.4589 6079	29.0852 3789	41
42	32.5213 1874	31.7445 4332	30.9940 5004	29.5678 0135	42
43	33.1074 7530	32.3004 1264	31.5212 3157	30.0420 6522	43
44	33.6863 9536	32.8487 4243	32.0406 2223	30.5081 7221	44
45	34.2581 6825	33.3896 3495	32.5523 3718	30.9662 6261	45
46	34.8228 8222	33.9231 9108	33.0564 8983	31.4164 7431	46
47	35.3806 2442	34.4495 1031	33.5531 9195	31.8589 4281	47
48	35.9314 8091	34.9686 9081	34.0425 5365	32.2938 0129	48
49	36.4755 3670	35.4808 2941	34.5246 8339	32.7211 8063	49
50	37.0128 7574	35.9860 2161	34.9996 8807	33.1412 0946	50

528

TABLE VI.—Present Value of Annuity of 1 per Period

$$a_{\overline{n}|i} = \frac{1 - (1 + i)^{-n}}{i}$$

n	1¼%	1⅜%	1½%	1¾%	n
51	37.5435 8099	36.4843 6164	35.4676 7298	33.5540 1421	51
52	38.0677 3431	36.9759 4243	35.9287 4185	33.9597 1913	52
53	38.5854 1660	37.4608 5566	36.3829 9690	34.3584 4633	53
54	39.0967 0776	37.9391 9178	36.8305 3882	34.7503 1579	54
55	39.6016 8667	38.4110 3998	37.2714 6681	35.1354 4550	55
56	40.1004 3128	38.8764 8826	37.7058 7863	35.5139 5135	56
57	40.5930 1855	39.3356 2344	38.1338 7058	35.8859 4727	57
58	41.0795 2449	39.7885 3114	38.5555 3751	36.2515 4523	58
59	41.5600 2419	40.2352 9582	38.9709 7292	36.6108 5526	59
60	42.0345 9179	40.6760 0081	39.3802 6889	36.9639 8552	60
61	42.5033 0054	41.1107 2829	39.7835 1614	37.3110 4228	61
62	42.9662 2275	41.5395 5935	40.1808 0408	37.6521 3000	62
63	43.4234 2988	41.9625 7396	40.5722 2077	37.9873 5135	63
64	43.8749 9247	42.3798 5101	40.9578 5298	38.3168 0723	64
65	44.3209 8022	42.7914 6832	41.3377 8618	38.6405 9678	65
66	44.7614 6195	43.1975 0266	41.7121 0461	38.9588 1748	66
67	45.1965 0563	43.5980 2975	42.0808 9125	39.2715 6509	67
68	45.6261 7840	43.9931 2429	42.4442 2783	39.5789 3375	68
69	46.0505 4656	44.3828 5997	42.8021 9490	39.8810 1597	69
70	46.4696 7562	44.7673 0946	43.1548 7183	40.1779 0267	70
71	46.8836 3024	45.1465 4448	43.5023 3678	40.4696 8321	71
72	47.2924 7431	45.5206 3573	43.8446 6677	40.7564 4542	72
73	47.6962 7093	45.8896 5300	44.1819 3771	41.0382 7560	73
74	48.0950 8240	46.2536 6511	44.5142 2434	41.3152 5857	74
75	48.4889 7027	46.6127 3994	44.8416 0034	41.5874 7771	75
76	48.8779 9533	46.9669 4445	45.1641 3826	41.8550 1495	76
77	49.2622 1761	47.3163 4471	45.4819 0962	42.1179 5081	77
78	49.6416 9640	47.6610 0588	45.7949 8485	42.3763 6443	78
79	50.0164 9027	48.0009 9224	46.1034 3335	42.6303 3359	79
80	50.3866 5706	48.3363 6719	46.4073 2349	42.8799 3474	80
81	50.7522 5389	48.6671 9328	46.7067 2265	43.1252 4298	81
82	51.1133 3717	48.9935 3221	47.0016 9720	43.3663 3217	82
83	51.4699 6264	49.3154 4484	47.2923 1251	43.6032 7486	83
84	51.8221 8532	49.6329 9122	47.5786 3301	43.8361 4237	84
85	52.1700 5958	49.9462 3055	47.8607 2218	44.0650 0479	85
86	52.5136 3909	50.2552 2125	48.1386 4254	44.2899 3099	86
87	52.8529 7688	50.5600 2096	48.4124 5571	44.5109 8869	87
88	53.1881 2531	50.8606 8653	48.6822 2237	44.7282 4441	88
89	53.5191 3611	51.1572 7401	48.9480 0234	44.9417 6355	89
90	53.8460 6035	51.4498 3873	49.2098 5452	45.1516 1037	90
91	54.1689 4850	51.7384 3524	49.4678 3696	45.3578 4803	91
92	54.4878 5037	52.0231 1738	49.7220 0686	45.5605 3860	92
93	54.8028 1518	52.3039 3823	49.9724 2055	45.7597 4310	93
94	55.1138 9154	52.5809 5016	50.2191 3355	45.9555 2147	94
95	55.4211 2744	52.8542 0484	50.4622 0054	46.1479 3265	95
96	55.7245 7031	53.1237 5324	50.7016 7541	46.3370 3455	96
97	56.0242 6698	53.3896 4561	50.9376 1124	46.5228 8408	97
98	56.3202 6368	53.6519 3155	51.1700 6034	46.7055 3718	98
99	56.6126 0610	53.9106 5998	51.3990 7422	46.8850 4882	99
100	56.9013 3936	54.1658 7914	51.6247 0367	47.0614 7304	100

TABLE VI.—Present Value of Annuity of 1 per Period

$$a_{\overline{n}|i} = \frac{1 - (1 + i)^{-n}}{i}$$

n	2%	2¼%	2½%	2¾%	n
1	0.9803 9216	0.9779 9511	0.9756 0976	0.9732 3601	1
2	1.9415 6094	1.9344 6955	1.9274 2415	1.9204 2434	2
3	2.8838 8327	2.8698 9687	2.8560 2356	2.8422 6213	3
4	3.8077 2870	3.7847 4021	3,7619 7421	3.7394 2787	4
5	4.7134 5951	4.6794 5253	4.6458 2850	4.6125 8186	5
6	5.6014 3089	5.5544 7680	5.5081 2536	5.4623 6678	6
7	6.4719 9107	6.4102 4626	6.3493 9060	6.2894 0806	7
8	7.3254 8144	7.2471 8461	7.1701 3717	7.0943 1441	8
9	8.1622 3671	8.0657 0622	7.9708 6553	7.8776 7826	9
10	8.9825 8501	8.8662 1635	8.7520 6393	8.6400 7616	10
11	9.7868 4805	9.6491 1134	9.5142 0871	9.3820 6926	11
12	10.5753 4122	10.4147 7882	10.2577 6460	10.1042 0366	12
13	11.3483 7375	11.1635 9787	10.9831 8497	10.8070 1086	13
14	12.1062 4877	11.8959 3924	11.6909 1217	11.4910 0814	14
15	12.8492 6350	12.6121 6551	12.3813 7773	12.1566 9892	15
16	13.5777 0931	13.3126 3131	13.0550 0266	12.8045 7315	16
17	14.2918 7188	13.9976 8343	13.7121 9772	13.4351 0769	17
18	14.9920 3125	14.6676 6106	14.3533 6363	14.0487 6661	18
19	15.6784 6201	15.3228 9590	14.9788 9134	14.6460 0157	19
20	16.3514 3334	15.9637 1237	15.5891 6229	15.2272 5213	20
21	17.0112 0916	16.5904 2775	16.1845 4857	15.7929 4612	21
22	17.6580 4820	17.2033 5232	16.7654 1324	16.3434 9987	22
23	18.2922 0412	17.8027 8955	17.3321 1048	16.8793 1861	23
24	18.9139 2560	18.3890 3624	17.8849 8583	17.4007 9670	24
25	19.5234 5647	18.9623 8263	18.4243 7642	17.9083 1795	25
26	20.1210 3576	19.5231 1260	18.9506 1114	18.4022 5592	26
27	20.7068 9780	20.0715 0376	19.4640 1087	18.8829 7413	27
28	21.2812 7236	20.6078 2764	19.9648 8866	19.3508 2640	28
29	21.8443 8466	21.1323 4977	20.4535 4991	19.8061 5708	29
30	22.3964 5555	21.6453 2985	20.9302 9259	20.2493 0130	30
31	22.9377 0152	22.1470 2186	21.3954 0741	20.6805 8520	31
32	23.4683 3482	22.6376 7419	21.8491 7796	21.1003 2623	32
33	23.9885 6355	23.1175 2977	22.2918 8094	21.5088 3332	33
34	24.4985 9172	23.5868 2618	22.7237 8628	21.9064 0712	34
35	24.9986 1933	24.0457 9577	23.1451 5734	22.2933 4026	35
36	25.4888 4248	24.4946 6579	23.5562 5107	22.6699 1753	36
37	25.9694 5341	24.9336 5848	23.9573 1812	23.0364 1609	37
38	26.4406 4060	25.3629 9118	24.3486 0304	23.3931 0568	38
39	26.9025 8883	25.7828 7646	24.7303 4443	23.7402 4884	39
40	27.3554 7924	26.1935 2221	25.1027 7505	24.0781 0106	40
41	27.7994 8945	26.5951 3174	25.4661 2200	24.4069 1101	41
42	28.2347 9358	26.9879 0390	25.8206 0683	24.7269 2069	42
43	28.6615 6233	27.3720 3316	26.1664 4569	25.0383 6563	43
44	29.0799 6307	27.7477 0969	26.5038 4945	25.3414 7507	44
45	29.4901 5987	28.1151 1950	26.8330 2386	25.6364 7209	45
46	29.8923 1360	28.4744 4450	27.1541 6962	25.9235 7381	46
47	30.2865 8196	28.8258 6259	27.4674 8255	26.2029 9154	47
48	30.6731 1957	29.1695 4777	27.7731 5371	26.4749 3094	48
49	31.0520 7801	29.5056 7019	28.0713 6947	26.7395 9215	49
50	31.4236 0589	29.8343 9627	28.3623 1168	26.9971 6998	50

530

TABLE VI.—Present Value of Annuity of 1 per Period

$$a_{\overline{n}|i} = \frac{1 - (1 + i)^{-n}}{i}$$

n	2%	2¼%	2½%	2¾%	n
51	31.7878 4892	30.1558 8877	28.6461 5774	27.2478 5400	51
52	32.1449 4992	30.4703 0687	28.9230 8072	27.4918 2871	52
53	32.4950 4894	30.7778 0623	29.1932 4948	27.7292 7368	53
54	32.8382 8327	31.0785 3910	29.4568 2876	27.9603 6368	54
55	33.1747 8752	31.3726 5438	29.7139 7928	28.1852 6879	55
56	33.5046 9365	31.6602 9768	29.9648 5784	28.4041 5454	56
57	33.8281 3103	31.9416 1142	30.2096 1740	28.6171 8203	57
58	34.1452 2650	32.2167 3489	30.4484 0722	28.8245 0806	58
59	34.4561 0441	32.4858 0429	30.6813 7290	29.0262 8522	59
60	34.7608 8668	32.7489 5285	30.9086 5649	29.2226 6201	60
61	35.0596 9282	33.0063 1086	31.1303 9657	29.4137 8298	61
62	35.3526 4002	33.2580 0573	31.3467 2836	29.5997 8879	62
63	35.6398 4316	33.5041 6208	31.5577 8377	29.7808 1634	63
64	35.9214 1486	33.7449 0179	31.7636 9148	29.9569 9887	64
65	36.1974 6555	33.9803 4405	31.9645 7705	30.1284 6605	65
66	36.4681 0348	34.2106 0543	32.1605 6298	30.2953 4409	66
67	36.7334 3478	34.4357 9993	32.3517 6876	30.4577 5581	67
68	36.9935 6351	34.6560 3905	32.5383 1099	30.6158 2074	68
69	37.2485 9168	34.8714 3183	32.7203 0340	30.7696 5522	69
70	37.4986 1929	35.0820 8492	32.8978 5698	30.9193 7247	70
71	37.7437 4441	35.2881 0261	33.0710 7998	31.0650 8270	71
72	37.9840 6314	35.4895 8691	33.2400 7803	31.2068 9314	72
73	38.2196 6975	35.6866 3756	33.4049 5417	31.3449 0816	73
74	38.4506 5662	35.8793 5214	33.5658 0895	31.4792 2936	74
75	38.6771 1433	36.0678 2605	33.7227 4044	31.6099 5558	75
76	38.8991 3170	36.2521 5262	33.8758 4433	31.7371 8304	76
77	39.1167 9578	36.4324 2310	34.0252 1398	31.8610 0540	77
78	39.3301 9194	36.6087 2675	34.1709 4047	31.9815 1377	78
79	39.5394 0386	36.7811 5085	34.3131 1265	32.0987 9685	79
80	39.7445 1359	36.9497 8079	34.4518 1722	32.2129 4098	80
81	39.9456 0156	37.1147 0004	34.5871 3875	32.3240 3015	81
82	40.1427 4663	37.2759 9026	34.7191 5976	32.4321 4613	82
83	40.3360 2611	37.4337 3130	34.8479 6074	32.5373 6850	83
84	40.5255 1579	37.5880 0127	34.9736 2023	32.6397 7469	84
85	40.7112 8999	37.7388 7655	35.0962 1486	32.7394 4009	85
86	40.8934 2156	37.8864 3183	35.2158 1938	32.8364 3804	86
87	41.0719 8192	38.0307 4018	35.3325 0671	32.9308 3994	87
88	41.2470 4110	38.1718 7304	35.4463 4801	33.0227 1527	88
89	41.4186 6774	38.3099 0028	35.5574 1269	33.1121 3165	89
90	41.5869 2916	38.4448 9025	35.6657 6848	33.1991 5489	90
91	41.7518 9133	38.5769 0978	35.7714 8144	33.2838 4905	91
92	41.9136 1895	38.7060 2423	35.8746 1604	33.3662 7644	92
93	42.0721 7545	38.8322 9754	35.9752 3516	33.4464 9776	93
94	42.2276 2299	38.9557 9221	36.0734 0016	33.5245 7202	94
95	42.3800 2254	39.0765 6940	36.1691 7089	33.6005 5671	95
96	42.5294 3386	39.1946 8890	36.2626 0574	33.6745 0775	96
97	42.6759 1555	39.3102 0920	36.3537 6170	33.7464 7956	97
98	42.8195 2505	39.4231 8748	36.4426 9434	33.8165 2512	98
99	42.9603 1867	39.5336 7968	36.5294 5790	33.8846 9598	99
100	43.0983 5164	39.6417 4052	36.6141 0526	33.9510 4232	100

TABLE VI.—Present Value of Annuity of 1 per Period

$$a_{\overline{n}|i} = \frac{1 - (1 + i)^{-n}}{i}$$

n	3%	3½%	4%	4½%	n
1	0.9708 7379	0.9661 8357	0.9615 3846	0.9569 3780	1
2	1.9134 6970	1.8996 9428	1.8860 9467	1.8726 6775	2
3	2.8286 1135	2.8016 3698	2.7750 9103	2.7489 6435	3
4	3.7170 9840	3.6730 7921	3.6298 9522	3.5875 2570	4
5	4.5797 0719	4.5150 5238	4.4518 2233	4.3899 7674	5
6	5.4171 9144	5.3285 5302	5.2421 3686	5.1578 7248	6
7	6.2302 8296	6.1145 4398	6.0020 5467	5.8927 0094	7
8	7.0196 9219	6.8739 5554	6.7327 4487	6.5958 8607	8
9	7.7861 0892	7.6076 8651	7.4353 3161	7.2687 9050	9
10	8.5302 0284	8.3166 0532	8.1108 9578	7.9127 1818	10
11	9.2526 2411	9.0015 5104	8.7604 7671	8.5289 1692	11
12	9.9540 0399	9.6633 3433	9.3850 7376	9.1185 8078	12
13	10.6349 5533	10.3027 3849	9.9856 4785	9.6828 5242	13
14	11.2960 7314	10.9205 2028	10.5631 2293	10.2228 2528	14
15	11.9379 3509	11.5174 1090	11.1183 8743	10.7395 4573	15
16	12.5611 0203	12.0941 1681	11.6522 9561	11.2340 1505	16
17	13.1661 1847	12.6513 2059	12.1656 6885	11.7071 9143	17
18	13.7535 1308	13.1896 8173	12.6592 9697	12.1599 9180	18
19	14.3237 9911	13.7098 3742	13.1339 3940	12.5932 9359	19
20	14.8774 7486	14.2124 0330	13.5903 2634	13.0079 3645	20
21	15.4150 2414	14.6979 7420	14.0291 5995	13.4047 2388	21
22	15.9369 1664	15.1671 2484	14.4511 1533	13.7844 2476	22
23	16.4436 0839	15.6204 1047	14.8568 4167	14.1477 7489	23
24	16.9355 4212	16.0583 6760	15.2469 6314	14.4954 7837	24
25	17.4131 4769	16.4815 1459	15.6220 7994	14.8282 0896	25
26	17.8768 4242	16.8903 5226	15.9827 6918	15.1466 1145	26
27	18.3270 3147	17.2853 6451	16.3295 8575	15.4513 0282	27
28	18.7641 0823	17.6670 1885	16.6630 6322	15.7428 7351	28
29	19.1884 5459	18.0357 6700	16.9837 1463	16.0218 8853	29
30	19.6004 4135	18.3920 4541	17.2920 3330	16.2888 8854	30
31	20.0004 2849	18.7362 7576	17.5884 9356	16.5443 9095	31
32	20.3887 6553	19.0688 6547	17.8735 5150	16.7888 9086	32
33	20.7657 9178	19.3902 0818	18.1476 4567	17.0228 6207	33
34	21.1318 3668	19.7006 8423	18.4111 9776	17.2467 5796	34
35	21.4872 2007	20.0006 6110	18.6646 1323	17.4610 1240	35
36	21.8322 5250	20.2904 9381	18.9082 8195	17.6660 4058	36
37	22.1672 3544	20.5705 2542	19.1425 7880	17.8622 3979	37
38	22.4924 6159	20.8410 8736	19.3678 6423	18.0499 9023	38
39	22.8082 1513	21.1024 9987	19.5844 8484	18.2296 5572	39
40	23.1147 7197	21.3550 7234	19.7927 7388	18.4015 8442	40
41	23.4123 9997	21.5991 0371	19.9930 5181	18.5661 0949	41
42	23.7013 5920	21.8348 8281	20.1856 2674	18.7235 4975	42
43	23.9819 0213	22.0626 8870	20.3707 9494	18.8742 1029	43
44	24.2542 7392	22.2827 9102	20.5488 4129	19.0183 8305	44
45	24.5187 1254	22.4954 5026	20.7200 3970	19.1563 4742	45
46	24.7754 4907	22.7009 1813	20.8846 5356	19.2883 7074	46
47	25.0247 0783	22.8994 3780	21.0429 3612	19.4147 0884	47
48	25.2667 0664	23.0912 4425	21.1951 3088	19.5356 0654	48
49	25.5016 5693	23.2765 6450	21.3414 7200	19.6512 9813	49
50	25.7297 6401	23.4556 1787	21.4821 8462	19.7620 0778	50

TABLE VI.—Present Value of Annuity of 1 per Period

$$a_{\overline{n}|i} = \frac{1 - (1 + i)^{-n}}{i}$$

n	3%	3½%	4%	4½%	n
51	25.9512 2719	23.6286 1630	21.6174 8521	19.8679 5003	51
52	26.1662 3999	23.7957 6454	21.7475 8193	19.9693 3017	52
53	26.3749 9028	23.9572 6043	21.8726 7493	20.0663 4466	53
54	26.5776 6047	24.1132 9510	21.9929 5667	20.1591 8149	54
55	26.7744 2764	24.2640 5323	22.1086 1218	20.2480 2057	55
56	26.9654 6373	24.4097 1327	22.2189 1940	20.3330 3404	56
57	27.1509 3566	24.5504 4760	22.3267 4943	20.4143 8664	57
58	27.3310 0549	24.6864 2281	22.4295 6676	20.4922 3602	58
59	27.5058 3058	24.8177 9981	22.5284 2957	20.5667 3303	59
60	27.6755 6367	24.9447 3412	22.6234 8997	20.6380 2204	60
61	27.8403 5307	25.0673 7596	22.7148 9421	20.7062 4118	61
62	28.0003 4279	25.1858 7049	22.8027 8289	20.7715 2266	62
63	28.1556 7261	25.3003 5796	22.8872 9124	20.8339 9298	63
64	28.3064 7826	25.4109 7388	22.9685 4927	20.8937 7319	64
65	28.4528 9152	25.5178 4916	23.0466 8199	20.9509 7913	65
66	28.5950 4031	25.6211 1030	23.1218 0961	21.0057 2165	66
67	28.7330 4884	25.7208 7951	23.1940 4770	21.0581 0684	67
68	28.8670 3771	25.8172 7489	23.2635 0740	21.1082 3621	68
69	28.9971 2399	25.9104 1052	23.3302 9558	21.1562 0690	69
70	29.1234 2135	26.0003 9664	23.3945 1498	21.2021 1187	70
71	29.2460 4015	26.0873 3975	23.4562 6440	21.2460 4007	71
72	29.3650 8752	26.1713 4275	23.5156 3885	21.2880 7662	72
73	29.4806 6750	26.2525 0508	23.5727 2966	21.3283 0298	73
74	29.5928 8106	26.3309 2278	23.6276 2468	21.3667 9711	74
75	29.7018 2628	26.4066 8868	23.6804 0834	21.4036 3360	75
76	29.8075 9833	26.4798 9244	23.7311 6187	21.4388 8383	76
77	29.9102 8964	26.5506 2072	23.7799 6333	21.4726 1611	77
78	30.0099 8994	26.6189 5721	23.8268 8782	21.5048 9579	78
79	30.1067 8635	26.6849 8281	23.8720 0752	21.5357 8545	79
80	30.2007 6345	26.7487 7567	23.9153 9185	21.5653 4493	80
81	30.2920 0335	26.8104 1127	23.9571 0754	21.5936 3151	81
82	30.3805 8577	26.8699 6258	23.9972 1879	21.6207 0001	82
83	30.4665 8813	26.9275 0008	24.0357 8730	21.6466 0288	83
84	30.5500 8556	26.9830 9186	24.0728 7240	21.6713 9032	84
85	30.6311 5103	27.0368 0373	24.1085 3116	21.6951 1035	85
86	30.7098 5537	27.0886 9926	24.1428 1842	21.7178 0895	86
87	30.7862 6735	27.1388 3986	24.1757 8694	21.7395 3009	87
88	30.8604 5374	27.1872 8489	24.2074 8745	21.7603 1588	88
89	30.9324 7936	27.2340 9168	24.2379 6870	21.7802 0658	89
90	31.0024 0714	27.2793 1564	24.2672 7759	21.7992 4075	90
91	31.0702 9820	27.3230 1028	24.2954 5923	21.8174 5526	91
92	31.1362 1184	27.3652 2732	24.3225 5695	21.8348 8542	92
93	31.2002 0567	27.4060 1673	24.3486 1245	21.8515 6499	93
94	31.2623 3560	27.4454 2680	24.3736 6582	21.8675 2631	94
95	31.3226 5592	27.4835 0415	24.3977 5559	21.8828 0030	95
96	31.3812 1934	27.5202 9387	24.4209 1884	21.8974 1655	96
97	31.4380 7703	27.5558 3948	24.4431 9119	21.9114 0340	97
98	31.4932 7867	27.5901 8308	24.4646 0692	21.9247 8794	98
99	31.5468 7250	27.6233 6529	24.4851 9896	21.9375 9612	99
100	31.5989 0534	27.6554 2540	24.5049 9900	21.9498 5274	100

TABLE VI.—Present Value of Annuity of 1 per Period

$$a_{\overline{n}|i} = \frac{1 - (1 + i)^{-n}}{i}$$

n	5%	5½%	6%	6½%	n
1	0.9523 8095	0.9478 6730	0.9433 9623	0.9389 6714	1
2	1.8594 1043	1.8463 1971	1.8333 9267	1.8206 2642	2
3	2.7232 4803	2.6979 3338	2.6730 1195	2.6484 7551	3
4	3.5459 5050	3.5051 5012	3.4651 0561	3.4257 9860	4
5	4.3294 7667	4.2702 8448	4.2123 6379	4.1556 7944	5
6	5.0756 9206	4.9955 3031	4.9173 2433	4.8410 1356	6
7	5.7863 7340	5.6829 6712	5.5823 8144	5.4845 1977	7
8	6.4632 1276	6.3345 6599	6.2097 9381	6.0887 5096	8
9	7.1078 2168	6.9521 9525	6.8016 9227	6.6561 0419	9
10	7.7217 3493	7.5376 2583	7.3600 8705	7.1888 3022	10
11	8.3064 1422	8.0925 3633	7.8868 7458	7.6890 4246	11
12	8.8632 5164	8.6185 1785	8.3838 4394	8.1587 2532	12
13	9.3935 7299	9.1170 7853	8.8526 8296	8.5997 4208	13
14	9.8986 4094	9.5896 4790	9.2949 8393	9.0138 4233	14
15	10.3796 5804	10.0375 8094	9.7122 4899	9.4026 6885	15
16	10.8377 6956	10.4621 6203	10.1058 9527	9.7677 6418	16
17	11.2740 6625	10.8646 0856	10.4772 5969	10.1105 7670	17
18	11.6895 8690	11.2460 7447	10.8276 0348	10.4324 6638	18
19	12.0853 2086	11.6076 5352	11.1581 1649	10.7347 1022	19
20	12.4622 1034	11.9503 8249	11.4699 2122	11.0185 0725	20
21	12.8211 5271	12.2752 4406	11.7640 7662	11.2849 8333	21
22	13.1630 0258	12.5831 6973	12.0415 8172	11.5351 9562	22
23	13.4885 7388	12.8750 4240	12.3033 7898	11.7701 3673	23
24	13.7986 4179	13.1516 9895	12.5503 5753	11.9907 3871	24
25	14.0939 4457	13.4139 3266	12.7833 5616	12.1978 7672	25
26	14.3751 8530	13.6624 9541	13.0031 6619	12.3923 7251	26
27	14.6430 3362	13.8980 9991	13.2105 3414	12.5749 9766	27
28	14.8981 2726	14.1214 2172	13.4061 6428	12.7464 7668	28
29	15.1410 7358	14.3331 0116	13.5907 2102	12.9074 8984	29
30	15.3724 5103	14.5337 4517	13.7648 3115	13.0586 7591	30
31	15.5928 1050	14.7239 2907	13.9290 8599	13.2006 3465	31
32	15.8026 7667	14.9041 9817	14.0840 4339	13.3339 2925	32
33	16.0025 4921	15.0750 6936	14.2302 2961	13.4590 8850	33
34	16.1929 0401	15.2370 3257	14.3681 4114	13.5766 0892	34
35	16.3741 9429	15.3905 5220	14.4982 4636	13.6869 5673	35
36	16.5468 5171	15.5360 6843	14.6209 8713	13.7905 6970	36
37	16.7112 8734	15.6739 9851	14.7367 8031	13.8878 5887	37
38	16.8678 9271	15.8047 3793	14.8460 1916	13.9792 1021	38
39	17.0170 4067	15.9286 6154	14.9490 7468	14.0649 8611	39
40	17.1590 8635	16.0461 2469	15.0462 9687	14.1455 2687	40
41	17.2943 6796	16.1574 6416	15.1380 1592	14.2211 5199	41
42	17.4232 0758	16.2629 9920	15.2245 4332	14.2921 6149	42
43	17.5459 1198	16.3630 3242	15.3061 7294	14.3588 3708	43
44	17.6627 7331	16.4578 5063	15.3831 8202	14.4214 4327	44
45	17.7740 6982	16.5477 2572	15.4558 3209	14.4802 2842	45
46	17.8800 6650	16.6329 1537	15.5243 6990	14.5354 2575	46
47	17.9810 1571	16.7136 6386	15.5890 2821	14.5872 5422	47
48	18.0771 5782	16.7902 0271	15.6500 2661	14.6359 1946	48
49	18.1687 2173	16.8627 5139	15.7075 7227	14.6816 1451	49
50	18.2559 2546	16.9315 1790	15.7618 6064	14.7245 2067	50

TABLE VI.—Present Value of Annuity of 1 per Period

$$a_{\overline{n}|i} = \frac{1 - (1 + i)^{-n}}{i}$$

n	5%	5½%	6%	6½%	n
51	18.3389 7663	16.9966 9943	15.8130 7607	14.7648 0814	51
52	18.4180 7298	17.0584 8287	15.8613 9252	14.8026 3675	52
53	18.4934 0284	17.1170 4538	15.9069 7408	14.8381 5658	53
54	18.5651 4556	17.1725 5486	15.9499 7554	14.8715 0852	54
55	18.6334 7196	17.2251 7048	15.9905 4297	14.9028 2490	55
56	18.6985 4473	17.2750 4311	16.0288 1412	14.9322 2996	56
57	18.7605 1879	17.3223 1575	16.0649 1898	14.9598 4033	57
58	18.8195 4170	17.3671 2393	16.0989 8017	14.9857 6557	58
59	18.8757 5400	17.4095 9614	16.1311 1337	15.0101 0852	59
60	18.9292 8952	17.4498 5416	16.1614 2771	15.0329 6574	60
61	18.9802 7574	17.4880 1343	16.1900 2614	15.0544 2793	61
62	19.0288 3404	17.5241 8334	16.2170 0579	15.0745 8021	62
63	19.0750 8003	17.5584 6762	16.2424 5829	15.0935 0255	63
64	19.1191 2384	17.5909 6457	16.2664 7009	15.1112 7000	64
65	19.1610 7033	17.6217 6737	16.2891 2272	15.1279 5305	65
66	19.2010 1936	17.6509 6433	16.3104 9314	15.1436 1789	66
67	19.2390 6606	17.6786 3917	16.3306 5390	15.1583 2666	67
68	19.2753 0101	17.7048 7125	16.3496 7349	15.1721 3770	68
69	19.3098 1048	17.7297 3579	16.3676 1650	15.1851 0583	69
70	19.3426 7665	17.7533 0406	16.3845 4387	15.1972 8247	70
71	19.3739 7776	17.7756 4366	16.4005 1308	15.2087 1593	71
72	19.4037 8834	17.7968 1864	16.4155 7838	15.2194 5158	72
73	19.4321 7937	17.8168 8970	16.4297 9093	15.2295 3200	73
74	19.4592 1845	17.8359 1441	16.4431 9899	15.2389 9718	74
75	19.4849 6995	17.8539 4731	16.4558 4810	15.2478 8468	75
76	19.5094 9519	17.8710 4010	16.4677 8123	15.2562 2974	76
77	19.5328 5257	17.8872 4180	16.4790 3889	15.2640 6549	77
78	19.5550 9768	17.9025 9887	16.4896 5933	15.2714 2299	78
79	19.5762 8351	17.9171 5532	16.4996 7862	15.2783 3145	79
80	19.5964 6048	17.9309 5291	16.5091 3077	15.2848 1826	80
81	19.6156 7665	17.9440 3120	16.5180 4790	15.2909 0917	81
82	19.6339 7776	17.9564 2768	16.5264 6028	15.2966 2832	82
83	19.6514 0739	17.9681 7789	16.5343 9649	15.3019 9843	83
84	19.6680 0704	17.9793 1554	16.5418 8348	15.3070 4078	84
85	19.6838 1623	17.9898 7255	16.5489 4668	15.3117 7538	85
86	19.6988 7260	17.9998 7919	16.5556 1008	15.3162 2101	86
87	19.7132 1200	18.0093 6416	16.5618 9630	15.3203 9531	87
88	19.7268 6857	18.0183 5466	16.5678 2670	15.3243 1485	88
89	19.7398 7483	18.0268 7645	16.5734 2141	15.3279 9516	89
90	19.7522 6174	18.0349 5398	16.5786 9944	15.3314 5086	90
91	19.7640 5880	18.0426 1041	16.5836 7872	15.3346 9564	91
92	19.7752 9410	18.0498 6769	16.5883 7615	15.3377 4239	92
93	19.7859 9438	18.0567 4662	16.5928 0769	15.3406 0318	93
94	19.7961 8512	18.0632 6694	16.5969 8839	15.3432 8937	94
95	19.8058 9059	18.0694 4734	16.6009 3244	15.3458 1161	95
96	19.8151 3390	18.0753 0553	16.6046 5325	15.3481 7992	96
97	19.8239 3705	18.0808 5833	16.6081 6344	15.3504 0368	97
98	19.8323 2100	18.0861 2164	16.6114 7494	15.3524 9172	98
99	19.8403 0571	18.0911 1055	16.6145 9900	15.3544 5232	99
100	19.8479 1020	18.0958 3939	16.6175 4623	15.3562 9326	100

TABLE VI.—Present Value of Annuity of 1 per Period

$$a_{\overline{n}|i} = \frac{1 - (1 + i)^{-n}}{i}$$

n	7%	7½%	8%	8½%	n
1	0.9345 7944	0.9302 3256	0.9259 2593	0.9216 5899	1
2	1.8080 1817	1.7955 6517	1.7832 6475	1.7711 1427	2
3	2.6243 1604	2.6005 2574	2.5770 9699	2.5540 2237	3
4	3.3872 1126	3.3493 2627	3.3121 2684	3.2755 9666	4
5	4.1001 9744	4.0458 8490	3.9927 1004	3.9406 4208	5
6	4.7665 3966	4.6938 4642	4.6228 7966	4.5535 8717	6
7	5.3892 8940	5.2966 0132	5.2063 7006	5.1185 1352	7
8	5.9712 9851	5.8573 0355	5.7466 3894	5.6391 8297	8
9	6.5152 3225	6.3788 8703	6.2468 8791	6.1190 6264	9
10	7.0235 8154	6.8640 8096	6.7100 8140	6.5613 4806	10
11	7.4986 7434	7.3154 2415	7.1389 6426	6.9689 8439	11
12	7.9426 8630	7.7352 7827	7.5360 7802	7.3446 8607	12
13	8.3576 5074	8.1258 4026	7.9037 7594	7.6909 5490	13
14	8.7454 6799	8.4891 5373	8.2442 3698	8.0100 9668	14
15	9.1079 1401	8.8271 1974	8.5594 7869	8.3042 3658	15
16	9.4466 4860	9.1415 0674	8.8513 6916	8.5753 3325	16
17	9.7632 2299	9.4339 5976	9.1216 3811	8.8251 9194	17
18	10.0590 8691	9.7060 0908	9.3718 8714	9.0554 7644	18
19	10.3355 9524	9.9590 7821	9.6035 9920	9.2677 2022	19
20	10.5940 1425	10.1944 9136	9.8181 4741	9.4633 3661	20
21	10.8355 2733	10.4134 8033	10.0168 0316	9.6436 2821	21
22	11.0612 4050	10.6171 9101	10.2007 4366	9.8097 9559	22
23	11.2721 8738	10.8066 8931	10.3710 5895	9.9629 4524	23
24	11.4693 3400	10.9829 6680	10.5287 5828	10.1040 9700	24
25	11.6535 8318	11.1469 4586	10.6747 7619	10.2341 9078	25
26	11.8257 7867	11.2994 8452	10.8099 7795	10.3540 9288	26
27	11.9867 0904	11.4413 8095	10.9351 6477	10.4646 0174	27
28	12.1371 1125	11.5733 7763	11.0510 7849	10.5664 5321	28
29	12.2776 7407	11.6961 6524	11.1584 0601	10.6603 2554	29
30	12.4090 4118	11.8103 8627	11.2577 8334	10.7468 4382	30
31	12.5318 1419	11.9166 3839	11.3497 9939	10.8265 8416	31
32	12.6465 5532	12.0154 7757	11.4349 9944	10.9000 7757	32
33	12.7537 9002	12.1074 2099	11.5138 8837	10.9678 1343	33
34	12.8540 0936	12.1929 4976	11.5869 3367	11.0302 4279	34
35	12.9476 7230	12.2725 1141	11.6545 6822	11.0877 8137	35
36	13.0352 0776	12.3465 2224	11.7171 9279	11.1408 1233	36
37	13.1170 1660	12.4153 6953	11.7751 7851	11.1896 8878	37
38	13.1934 7345	12.4794 1351	11.8288 6899	11.2347 3620	38
39	13.2649 2846	12.5389 8931	11.8785 8240	11.2762 5457	39
40	13.3317 0884	12.5944 0866	11.9246 1333	11.3145 2034	40
41	13.3941 2041	12.6459 6155	11.9672 3457	11.3497 8833	41
42	13.4524 4898	12.6939 1772	12.0066 9867	11.3822 9339	42
43	13.5069 6167	12.7385 2811	12.0432 3951	11.4122 5197	43
44	13.5579 0810	12.7800 2615	12.0770 7362	11.4398 6357	44
45	13.6055 2159	12.8186 2898	12.1084 0150	11.4653 1205	45
46	13.6500 2018	12.8545 3858	12.1374 0880	11.4887 6686	46
47	13.6916 0764	12.8879 4287	12.1642 6741	11.5103 8420	47
48	13.7304 7443	12.9190 1662	12.1891 3649	11.5303 0802	48
49	13.7667 9853	12.9479 2244	12.2121 6341	11.5486 7099	49
50	13.8007 4629	12.9748 1157	12.2334 8464	11.5655 9538	50

TABLE VI.—Present Value of Annuity of 1 per Period

$$a_{\overline{n}|i} = \frac{1 - (1 + i)^{-n}}{i}$$

n	7%	7½%	8%	8½%	n
51	13.8324 7317	12.9998 2472	12.2532 2652	11.5811 9390	51
52	13.8621 2446	13.0230 9276	12.2715 0604	11.5955 7041	52
53	13.8898 3594	13.0447 3745	12.2884 3152	11.6088 2066	53
54	13.9157 3453	13.0648 7205	12.3041 0326	11.6210 3287	54
55	13.9399 3881	13.0836 0191	12.3186 1413	11.6322 8835	55
56	13.9625 5964	13.1010 2503	12.3320 5012	11.6426 6208	56
57	13.9837 0059	13.1172 3258	12.3444 9085	11.6522 2311	57
58	14.0034 5850	13.1323 0938	12.3560 1005	11.6610 3513	58
59	14.0219 2383	13.1463 3431	12.3666 7597	11.6691 5680	59
60	14.0391 8115	13.1593 8075	12.3765 5182	11.6766 4221	60
61	14.0553 0949	13.1715 1698	12.3856 9613	11.6835 4121	61
62	14.0703 8270	13.1828 0649	12.3941 6309	11.6898 9973	62
63	14.0844 6981	13.1933 0836	12.4020 0286	11.6957 6012	63
64	14.0976 3534	13.2030 7755	12.4092 6190	11.7011 6140	64
65	14.1099 3957	13 2121 6516	12.4159 8324	11.7061 3954	65
66	14.1214 3885	13.2206 1875	12.4222 0671	11.7107 2769	66
67	14.1321 8584	13.2284 8256	12.4279 6917	11.7149 5639	67
68	14.1422 2976	13.2357 9773	12.4333 0479	11.7188 5382	68
69	14.1516 1660	13.2426 0254	12.4382 4518	11.7224 4592	69
70	14.1603 8934	13.2489 3260	12.4428 1961	11.7257 5661	70
71	14.1685 8817	13.2548 2102	12.4470 5519	11.7288 0793	71
72	14.1762 5063	13.2602 9862	12.4509 7703	11.7316 2021	72
73	14.1834 1180	13.2653 9407	12.4546 0836	11.7342 1218	73
74	14.1901 0449	13.2701 3402	12.4579 7071	11.7366 0109	74
75	14.1963 5933	13.2745 4327	12.4610 8399	11.7388 0284	75
76	14.2022 0498	13.2786 4490	12.4639 6665	11.7408 3211	76
77	14.2076 6821	13.2824 6038	12.4666 3579	11.7427 0241	77
78	14.2127 7403	13.2860 0965	12.4691 0721	11.7444 2618	78
79	14.2175 4582	13.2893 1130	12.4713 9557	11.7460 1492	79
80	14.2220 0544	13.2923 8261	12.4735 1441	11.7474 7919	80
81	14.2261 7331	13.2952 3964	12.4754 7631	11.7488 2874	81
82	14.2300 6851	13.2978 9734	12.4772 9288	11.7500 7257	82
83	14.2337 0889	13.3003 6962	12.4789 7489	11.7512 1896	83
84	14.2371 1111	13.3026 6941	12.4805 3230	11.7522 7554	84
85	14.2402 9076	13.3048 0875	12.4819 7436	11.7532 4935	85
86	14.2432 6239	13.3067 9884	12.4833 0959	11.7541 4686	86
87	14.2460 3962	13.3086 5008	12.4845 4592	11.7549 7407	87
88	14.2486 3516	13.3103 7217	12.4856 9066	11.7557 3647	88
89	14.2510 6099	13.3119 7411	12.4867 5061	11.7564 3914	89
90	14.2533 2794	13.3134 6429	12.4877 3205	11.7570 8677	90
91	14.2554 4667	13.3148 5050	12.4886 4079	11.7576 8365	91
92	14.2574 2680	13.3161 4000	12.4894 8221	11.7582 3378	92
93	14.2592 7738	13.3173 3954	12.4902 6131	11.7587 4081	93
94	14.2610 0690	13.3184 5538	12.4909 8269	11.7592 0812	94
95	14.2626 2327	13.3194 9338	12.4916 5064	11.7596 3882	95
96	14.2641 3390	13.3204 5896	12.4922 6911	11.7600 3578	96
97	14.2655 4570	13.3213 5717	12.4928 4177	11.7604 0164	97
98	14.2668 6514	13.3221 9272	12.4933 7201	11.7607 3884	98
99	14.2680 9826	13.3229 6997	12.4938 6297	11.7610 4962	99
100	14.2692 5071	13.3236 9290	12.4943 1757	11.7613 3606	100

TABLE VII.—Periodic Rent of Annuity Whose Present Value is 1

$$\frac{1}{a_{\overline{n}|i}} = \frac{i}{1-(1+i)^{-n}} \qquad \left[\frac{1}{s_{\overline{n}|i}} = \frac{1}{a_{\overline{n}|i}} - i\right]$$

n	¼%	⁷⁄₂₄%	⅓%	⁵⁄₁₂%	n
1	1.0025 0000	1.0029 1667	1.0033 3333	1.0041 6667	1
2	0.5018 7578	0.5021 8856	0.5025 0139	0.5031 2717	2
3	0.3350 0139	0.3352 7967	0.3355 5802	0.3361 1496	3
4	0.2515 6445	0.2518 2557	0.2520 8680	0.2526 0958	4
5	0.2015 0250	0.2017 5340	0.2020 0444	0.2025 0693	5
6	0.1681 2803	0.1683 7219	0.1686 1650	0.1691 0564	6
7	0.1442 8928	0.1445 2866	0.1447 6824	0.1452 4800	7
8	0.1264 1035	0.1266 4620	0.1268 8228	0.1273 5512	8
9	0.1125 0462	0.1127 3777	0.1129 7118	0.1134 3876	9
10	0.1013 8015	0.1016 1117	0.1018 4248	0.1023 0596	10
11	0.0922 7840	0.0925 0772	0.0927 3736	0.0931 9757	11
12	0.0846 9370	0.0849 2163	0.0851 4990	0.0856 0748	12
13	0.0782 7595	0.0785 0274	0.0787 2989	0.0791 8532	13
14	0.0727 7510	0.0730 0093	0.0732 2716	0.0736 8082	14
15	0.0680 0777	0.0682 3279	0.0684 5825	0.0689 1045	15
16	0.0638 3642	0.0640 6076	0.0642 8557	0.0647 3655	16
17	0.0601 5587	0.0603 7964	0.0606 0389	0.0610 5387	17
18	0.0568 8433	0.0571 0761	0.0573 3140	0.0577 8053	18
19	0.0539 5722	0.0541 8008	0.0544 0348	0.0548 5191	19
20	0.0513 2288	0.0515 4537	0.0517 6844	0.0522 1630	20
21	0.0489 3947	0.0491 6166	0.0493 8445	0.0498 3183	21
22	0.0467 7278	0.0469 9471	0.0472 1726	0.0476 6427	22
23	0.0447 9455	0.0450 1625	0.0452 3861	0.0456 8531	23
24	0.0429 8121	0.0432 0272	0.0434 2492	0.0438 7139	24
25	0.0413 1298	0.0415 3433	0.0417 5640	0.0422 0270	25
26	0.0397 7312	0.0399 9434	0.0402 1630	0.0406 6247	26
27	0.0383 4736	0.0385 6847	0.0387 9035	0.0392 3645	27
28	0.0370 2347	0.0372 4450	0.0374 6632	0.0379 1239	28
29	0.0357 9093	0.0360 1188	0.0362 3367	0.0366 7974	29
30	0.0346 4059	0.0348 6149	0.0350 8325	0.0355 2936	30
31	0.0335 6449	0.0337 8536	0.0340 0712	0.0344 5330	31
32	0.0325 5569	0.0327 7653	0.0329 9830	0.0334 4458	32
33	0.0316 0806	0.0318 2889	0.0320 5067	0.0324 9708	33
34	0.0307 1620	0.0309 3703	0.0311 5885	0.0316 0540	34
35	0.0298 7533	0.0300 9618	0.0303 1803	0.0307 6476	35
36	0.0290 8121	0.0293 0208	0.0295 2399	0.0299 7090	36
37	0.0283 3004	0.0285 5094	0.0287 7291	0.0292 2003	37
38	0.0276 1843	0.0278 3938	0.0280 6141	0.0285 0875	38
39	0.0269 4335	0.0271 6434	0.0273 8644	0.0278 3402	39
40	0.0263 0204	0.0265 2308	0.0267 4527	0.0271 9310	40
41	0.0256 9204	0.0259 1315	0.0261 3543	0.0263 8352	41
42	0.0251 1112	0.0253 3229	0.0255 5466	0.0260 0303	42
43	0.0245 5724	0.0247 7848	0.0250 0095	0.0254 4961	43
44	0.0240 2855	0.0242 4987	0.0244 7246	0.0249 2141	44
45	0.0235 2339	0.0237 4479	0.0239 6749	0.0244 1675	45
46	0.0230 4022	0.0232 6170	0.0234 8451	0.0239 3409	46
47	0.0225 7762	0.0227 9920	0.0230 2213	0.0234 7204	47
48	0.0221 3433	0.0223 5600	0.0225 7905	0.0230 2929	48
49	0.0217 0915	0.0219 3092	0.0221 5410	0.0226 0468	49
50	0.0213 0099	0.0215 2287	0.0217 4618	0.0221 9711	50

TABLE VII.—Periodic Rent of Annuity Whose Present Value is 1

$$\frac{1}{a_{\overline{n}|i}} = \frac{i}{1 - (1 + i)^{-n}} \qquad \left[\frac{1}{s_{\overline{n}|i}} = \frac{1}{a_{\overline{n}|i}} - i \right]$$

n	¼%	⁷⁄₂₄%	⅓%	⁵⁄₁₂%	n
51	0.0209 0886	0.0211 3085	0.0213 5429	0.0218 0557	51
52	0.0205 3184	0.0207 5393	0.0209 7751	0.0214 2916	52
53	0.0201 6906	0.0203 9126	0.0206 1499	0.0210 6700	53
54	0.0198 1974	0.0200 4205	0.0202 6592	0.0207 1830	54
55	0.0194 8314	0.0197 0557	0.0199 2958	0.0203 8234	55
56	0.0191 5858	0.0193 8113	0.0196 0529	0.0200 5843	56
57	0.0188 4542	0.0190 6810	0.0192 9241	0.0197 4593	57
58	0.0185 4308	0.0187 6588	0.0189 9035	0.0194 4426	58
59	0.0182 5101	0.0184 7394	0.0186 9856	0.0191 5287	59
60	0.0179 6869	0.0181 9175	0.0184 1652	0.0188 7123	60
61	0.0176 9564	0.0179 1883	0.0181 4377	0.0185 9888	61
62	0.0174 3142	0.0176 5474	0.0178 7984	0.0183 3536	62
63	0.0171 7561	0.0173 9906	0.0176 2432	0.0180 8025	63
64	0.0169 2780	0.0171 5139	0.0173 7681	0.0178 3315	64
65	0.0166 8764	0.0169 1136	0.0171 3695	0.0175 9371	65
66	0.0164 5476	0.0166 7863	0.0169 0438	0.0173 6156	66
67	0.0162 2886	0.0164 5286	0.0166 7878	0.0171 3639	67
68	0.0160 0961	0.0162 3376	0.0164 5985	0.0169 1788	68
69	0.0157 9674	0.0160 2102	0.0162 4729	0.0167 0574	69
70	0.0155 8996	0.0158 1439	0.0160 4083	0.0164 9971	70
71	0.0153 8902	0.0156 1359	0.0158 4021	0.0162 9952	71
72	0.0151 9368	0.0154 1840	0.0156 4518	0.0161 0493	72
73	0.0150 0370	0.0152 2857	0.0154 5553	0.0159 1572	73
74	0.0148 1887	0.0150 4389	0.0152 7103	0.0157 3165	74
75	0.0146 3898	0.0148 6415	0.0150 9147	0.0155 5253	75
76	0.0144 6385	0.0146 8916	0.0149 1666	0.0153 7816	76
77	0.0142 9327	0.0145 1974	0.0147 4641	0.0152 0836	77
78	0.0141 2708	0.0143 5270	0.0145 8056	0.0150 4295	78
79	0.0139 6511	0.0141 9089	0.0144 1892	0.0148 8177	79
80	0.0138 0721	0.0140 3313	0.0142 6135	0.0147 2464	80
81	0.0136 5321	0.0138 7929	0.0141 0770	0.0145 7144	81
82	0.0135 0298	0.0137 2922	0.0139 5781	0.0144 2200	82
83	0.0133 5639	0.0135 8278	0.0138 1156	0.0142 7620	83
84	0.0132 1330	0.0134 3985	0.0136 6881	0.0141 3391	84
85	0.0130 7359	0.0133 0030	0.0135 2944	0.0139 9500	85
86	0.0129 3714	0.0131 6400	0.0133 9333	0.0138 5935	86
87	0.0128 0384	0.0130 3086	0.0132 6038	0.0137 2685	87
88	0.0126 7357	0.0129 0076	0.0131 3046	0.0135 9740	88
89	0.0125 4625	0.0127 7360	0.0130 0349	0.0134 7088	89
90	0.0124 2177	0.0126 4928	0.0128 7936	0.0133 4721	90
91	0.0123 0004	0.0125 2770	0.0127 5797	0.0132 2629	91
92	0.0121 8096	0.0124 0879	0.0126 3925	0.0131 0803	92
93	0.0120 6446	0.0122 9245	0.0125 2310	0.0129 9234	93
94	0.0119 5044	0.0121 7860	0.0124 0944	0.0128 7915	94
95	0.0118 3884	0 0120 6716	0.0122 9819	0.0127 6837	95
96	0.0117 2957	0.0119 5805	0.0121 8928	0.0126 5992	96
97	0.0116 2257	0.0118 5121	0 0120 8263	0.0125 5374	97
98	0.0115 1776	0.0117 4657	0.0119 7818	0.0124 4976	98
99	0.0114 1508	0.0116 4405	0.0118 7585	0.0123 4790	99
100	0.0113 1446	0.0115 4360	0.0117 7559	0.0122 4811	100

TABLE VII.—Periodic Rent of Annuity Whose Present Value is 1

$$\frac{1}{a_{\overline{n}|i}} = \frac{i}{1 - (1 + i)^{-n}} \qquad \left[\frac{1}{s_{\overline{n}|i}} = \frac{1}{a_{\overline{n}|i}} - i\right]$$

n	¼%	⁷⁄₂₄%	⅓%	⁵⁄₁₂%	n
101	0.0112 1584	0.0114 4515	0.0116 7734	0.0121 5033	101
102	0.0111 1917	0.0113 4864	0.0115 8103	0.0120 5449	102
103	0.0110 2439	0.0112 5403	0.0114 8660	0.0119 6054	103
104	0.0109 3144	0.0111 6124	0.0113 9401	0.0118 6842	104
105	0.0108 4027	0.0110 7024	0.0113 0320	0.0117 7809	105
106	0.0107 5083	0.0109 8096	0.0112 1413	0.0116 8948	106
107	0.0106 6307	0.0108 9337	0.0111 2673	0.0116 0256	107
108	0.0105 7694	0.0108 0741	0.0110 4097	0.0115 1727	108
109	0.0104 9241	0.0107 2305	0.0109 5680	0.0114 3358	109
110	0.0104 0942	0.0106 4023	0.0108 7417	0.0113 5143	110
111	0.0103 2793	0.0105 5891	0.0107 9306	0.0112 7079	111
112	0.0102 4791	0.0104 7906	0.0107 1340	0.0111 9161	112
113	0.0101 6932	0.0104 0064	0.0106 3518	0.0111 1386	113
114	0.0100 9211	0.0103 2360	0.0105 5834	0.0110 3750	114
115	0.0100 1625	0.0102 4792	0.0104 8285	0.0109 6249	115
116	0.0099 4172	0.0101 7355	0.0104 0868	0.0108 8880	116
117	0.0098 6846	0.0101 0046	0.0103 3579	0.0108 1639	117
118	0.0097 9646	0.0100 2863	0.0102 641€	0.0107 4524	118
119	0.0097 2567	0.0099 5801	0.0101 9374	0.0106 7530	119
120	0.0096 5608	0.0098 8859	0.0101 2451	0.0106 0655	120
121	0.0095 8764	0.0098 2032	0.0100 5645	0.0105 3896	121
122	0.0095 2033	0.0097 5318	0.0099 8951	0.0104 7251	122
123	0.0094 5412	0.0096 8715	0.0099 2367	0.0104 0715	123
124	0.0093 8899	0.0096 2219	0.0098 5892	0.0103 4288	124
125	0.0093 2491	0.0095 5828	0.0097 9521	0.0102 7965	125
126	0̄.0092 6186	0.0094 9540	0.0097 3253	0.0102 1745	126
127	0.0091 9981	0.0094 3352	0.0096 7085	0.0101 5625	127
128	0.0091 3873	0.0093 7262	0.0096 1015	0.0100 9603	128
129	0.0090 7861	0.0093 1267	0.0095 5040	0.0100 3677	129
130	0.0090 1942	0.0092 5366	0.0094 9159	0.0099 7844	130
131	0.0089 6115	0.0091 9556	0.0094 3368	0.0099 2102	131
132	0.0089 0376	0.0091 3834	0.0093 7667	0.0098 6449	132
133	0.0088 4725	0.0090 8200	0.0093 2053	0.0098 0883	133
134	0.0087 9159	0.0090 2651	0.0092 6524	0.0097 5403	134
135	0.0087 3675	0.0089 7186	0.0092 1079	0.0097 0005	135
136	0.0086 8274	0.0089 1801	0.0091 5715	0.0096 4689	136
137	0.0086 2952	0.0088 6497	0.0091 0430	0.0095 9453	137
138	0.0085 7707	0.0088 1270	0.0090 5223	0.0095 4295	138
139	0.0085 2539	0.0087 6119	0.0090 0093	0.0094 9213	139
140	0.0084 7446	0.0087 1043	0.0089 5037	0.0094 4205	140
141	0.0084 2425	0.0086 6040	0.0089 0054	0.0093 9271	141
142	0.0083 7476	0.0086 1109	0.0088 5143	0.0093 4408	142
143	0.0083 2597	0.0085 6247	0.0088 0301	0.0092 9615	143
144	0.0082 7787	0.0085 1454	0.0087 5528	0.0092 4890	144
145	0.0082 3043	0.0084 6728	0.0087 0822	0.0092 0233	145
146	0.0081 8365	0.0084 2067	0.0086 6182	0.0091 5641	146
147	0.0081 3752	0.0083 7471	0.0086 1607	0.0091 1114	147
148	0.0080 9201	0.0083 2938	0.0085 7094	0.0090 6650	148
149	0.0080 4712	0.0082 8467	0.0085 2643	0.0090 2247	149
150	0.0080 0284	0.0082 4056	0.0084 8252	0.0089 7905	150

TABLE VII.—Periodic Rent of Annuity Whose Present Value is 1

$$\frac{1}{a_{\overline{n}|i}} = \frac{i}{1 - (1 + i)^{-n}} \qquad \left[\frac{1}{s_{\overline{n}|i}} = \frac{1}{a_{\overline{n}|i}} - i\right]$$

n	¼%	⁷⁄₂₄%	⅓%	⁵⁄₁₂%	n
151	0.0079 5915	0.0081 9705	0.0084 3921	0.0089 3623	151
152	0.0079 1605	0.0081 5412	0.0083 9648	0.0088 9398	152
153	0.0078 7351	0.0081 1176	0.0083 5432	0.0088 5231	153
154	0.0078 3153	0.0080 6995	0.0083 1273	0.0088 1119	154
155	0.0077 9010	0.0080 2870	0.0082 7167	0.0087 7063	155
156	0.0077 4921	0.0079 8798	0.0082 3116	0.0087 3060	156
157	0.0077 0885	0.0079 4780	0.0081 9118	0.0086 9110	157
158	0.0076 6900	0.0079 0813	0.0081 5171	0.0086 5211	158
159	0.0076 2966	0.0078 6896	0.0081 1275	0.0086 1364	159
160	0.0075 9082	0.0078 3030	0.0080 7429	0.0085 7566	160
161	0.0075 5246	0.0077 9212	0.0080 3631	0.0085 3817	161
162	0.0075 1459	0.0077 5442	0.0079 9882	0.0085 0116	162
163	0.0074 7719	0.0077 1720	0.0079 6180	0.0084 6462	163
164	0.0074 4025	0.0076 0844	0.0079 2524	0.0084 2855	164
165	0.0074 0377	0.0076 4413	0.0078 8913	0.0083 9293	165
166	0.0073 6773	0.0076 0826	0.0078 5347	0.0083 5775	166
167	0.0073 3213	0.0075 7284	0.0078 1825	0.0083 2302	167
168	0.0072 9695	0.0075 3784	0.0077 8346	0.0082 8871	168
169	0.0072 6220	0.0075 0327	0.0077 4909	0.0082 5482	169
170	0.0072 2787	0.0074 6911	0.0077 1513	0.0082 2135	170
171	0.0071 9394	0.0074 3536	0.0076 8158	0.0081 8829	171
172	0.0071 6042	0.0074 0201	0.0076 4844	0.0081 5563	172
173	0.0071 2728	0.0073 6905	0.0076 1568	0.0081 2336	173
174	0.0070 9454	0.0073 3648	0.0075 8332	0.0080 9147	174
175	0.0070 6217	0.0073 0429	0.0075 5133	0.0080 5997	175
176	0.0070 3018	0.0072 7248	0.0075 1972	0.0080 2884	176
177	0.0069 9855	0.0072 4103	0.0074 8847	0.0079 9808	177
178	0.0069 6729	0.0072 0994	0.0074 5759	0.0079 6768	178
179	0.0069 3638	0.0071 7921	0.0074 2706	0.0079 3763	179
180	0.0069 0582	0.0071 4883	0.0073 9688	0.0079 0794	180
181	0.0068 7560	0.0071 1879	0.0073 6704	0.0078 7858	181
182	0.0068 4572	0.0070 8908	0.0073 3754	0.0078 4957	182
183	0.0068 1617	0.0070 5971	0.0073 0838	0.0078 2088	183
184	0.0067 8695	0.0070 3067	0.0072 7954	0.0077 9253	184
185	0.0067 5805	0.0070 0195	0.0072 5102	0.0077 6449	185
186	0.0067 2947	0.0069 7354	0.0072 2281	0.0077 3677	186
187	0.0067 0120	0.0069 4545	0.0071 9492	0.0077 0936	187
188	0.0066 7323	0.0069 1766	0.0071 6734	0.0076 8226	188
189	0.0066 4557	0.0068 9017	0.0071 4005	0.0076 5546	189
190	0.0066 1820	0.0068 6298	0.0071 1307	0.0076 2895	190
191	0.0065 9112	0.0068 3608	0.0070 8637	0.0076 0274	191
192	0.0065 6434	0.0068 0947	0.0070 5996	0.0075 7681	192
193	0.0065 3783	0.0067 8314	0.0070 3384	0.0075 5117	193
194	0.0065 1160	0.0067 5708	0.0070 0799	0.0075 2580	194
195	0.0064 8565	0.0067 3131	0.0069 8242	0.0075 0071	195
196	0.0064 5997	0.0067 0581	0.0069 5711	0.0074 7589	196
197	0.0064 3455	0.0066 8057	0.0069 3208	0.0074 5133	197
198	0.0064 0939	0.0066 5559	0.0069 0730	0.0074 2704	198
199	0.0063 8450	0.0066 3087	0.0068 8278	0.0074 0300	199
200	0.0063 5985	0.0066 0640	0.0068 5852	0.0073 7922	200

TABLE VII.—Periodic Rent of Annuity Whose Present Value is 1

$$\frac{1}{a_{\overline{n}|i}} = \frac{i}{1-(1+i)^{-n}} \qquad \left[\frac{1}{s_{\overline{n}|i}} = \frac{1}{a_{\overline{n}|i}} - i\right]$$

n	½%	7/12%	⅝%	⅔%	n
1	1.0050 0000	1.0058 3333	1.0062 5000	1.0066 6667	1
2	0.5037 5312	0.5043 7924	0.5046 9237	0.5050 0554	2
3	0.3366 7221	0.3372 2976	0.3375 0865	0.3377 8762	3
4	0.2531 3279	0.2536 5644	0.2539 1842	0.2541 8051	4
5	0.2030 0997	0.2035 1357	0.2037 6558	0.2040 1772	5
6	0.1695 9546	0.1700 8594	0.1703 3143	0.1705 7709	6
7	0.1457 2854	0.1462 0986	0.1464 5082	0.1466 9198	7
8	0.1278 2886	0.1283 0351	0.1285 4118	0.1287 7907	8
9	0.1139 0736	0.1143 7698	0.1146 1218	0.1148 4763	9
10	0.1027 7057	0.1032 3632	0.1034 6963	0.1037 0321	10
11	0.0936 5903	0.0941 2175	0.0943 5358	0.0945 8572	11
12	0.0860 6643	0.0865 2675	0.0867 5742	0.0869 8843	12
13	0.0796 4224	0.0801 0064	0.0803 3039	0.0805 6052	13
14	0.0741 3609	0.0745 9295	0.0748 2198	0.0750 5141	14
15	0.0693 6436	0.0698 1999	0.0700 4845	0.0702 7734	15
16	0.0651 8937	0.0656 4401	0.0658 7202	0.0661 0049	16
17	0.0615 0579	0.0619 5966	0.0621 8732	0.0624 1546	17
18	0.0582 3173	0.0586 8499	0.0589 1239	0.0591 4030	18
19	0.0553 0253	0.0557 5532	0.0559 8252	0.0562 1027	19
20	0.0526 6645	0.0531 1889	0.0533 4597	0.0535 7362	20
21	0.0502 8163	0.0507 3383	0.0509 6083	0.0511 8843	21
22	0.0481 1380	0.0485 6585	0.0487 9281	0.0490 2041	22
23	0.0461 3465	0.0465 8663	0.0468 1360	0.0470 4123	23
24	0.0443 2061	0.0447 7258	0.0449 9959	0.0452 2729	24
25	0.0426 5186	0.0431 0388	0.0433 3096	0.0435 5876	25
26	0.0411 1163	0.0415 6376	0.0417 9094	0.0420 1886	26
27	0.0396 8565	0.0401 3793	0.0403 6523	0.0405 9331	27
28	0.0383 6167	0.0388 1415	0.0390 4159	0.0392 6983	28
29	0.0371 2914	0.0375 8186	0.0378 0946	0.0380 3789	29
30	0.0359 7892	0.0364 3191	0.0366 5969	0.0368 8832	30
31	0.0349 0304	0.0353 5633	0.0355 8430	0.0358 1316	31
32	0.0338 9453	0.0343 4815	0.0345 7633	0.0348 0542	32
33	0.0329 4727	0.0334 0124	0.0336 2964	0.0338 5898	33
34	0.0320 5586	0.0325 1020	0.0327 3883	0.0329 6843	34
35	0.0312 1550	0.0316 7024	0.0318 9911	0.0321 2898	35
36	0.0304 2194	0.0308 7710	0.0311 0622	0.0313 3637	36
37	0.0296 7139	0.0301 2698	0.0303 5636	0.0305 8680	37
38	0.0289 6045	0.0294 1649	0.0296 4614	0.0298 7687	38
39	0.0282 8607	0.0287 4258	0.0289 7250	0.0292 0354	39
40	0.0276 4552	0.0281 0251	0.0283 3271	0.0285 6406	40
41	0.0270 3631	0.0274 9379	0.0277 2429	0.0279 5595	41
42	0.0264 5622	0.0269 1420	0.0271 4499	0.0273 7697	42
43	0.0259 0320	0.0263 6170	0.0265 9278	0.0268 2509	43
44	0.0253 7541	0.0258 3443	0.0260 6583	0.0262 9847	44
45	0.0248 7117	0.0253 3073	0.0255 6243	0.0257 9541	45
46	0.0243 8894	0.0248 4905	0.0250 8106	0.0253 1439	46
47	0.0239 2733	0.0243 8798	0.0246 2032	0.0248 5399	47
48	0.0234 8503	0.0239 4624	0.0241 7890	0.0244 1292	48
49	0.0230 6087	0.0235 2265	0.0237 5563	0.0239 9001	49
50	0.0226 5376	0.0231 1611	0.0233 4943	0.0235 8416	50

TABLE VII.—Periodic Rent of Annuity Whose Present Value is 1

$$\frac{1}{a_{\overline{n}|i}} = \frac{i}{1 - (1+i)^{-n}} \qquad \left[\frac{1}{s_{\overline{n}|i}} = \frac{1}{a_{\overline{n}|i}} - i\right]$$

n	½%	7/12%	5/8%	2/3%	n
51	0.0222 6269	0.0227 2563	0.0229 5928	0.0231 9437	51
52	0.0218 8675	0.0223 5027	0.0225 8425	0.0228 1971	52
53	0.0215 2507	0.0219 8919	0.0222 2350	0.0224 5932	53
54	0.0211 7686	0.0216 4157	0.0218 7623	0.0221 1242	54
55	0.0208 4139	0.0213 0671	0.0215 4171	0.0217 7827	55
56	0.0205 1797	0.0209 8390	0.0212 1925	0.0214 5618	56
57	0.0202 0598	0.0206 7251	0.0209 0821	0.0211 4552	57
58	0.0199 0481	0.0203 7196	0.0206 0801	0.0208 4569	58
59	0.0196 1392	0.0200 8170	0.0203 1809	0.0205 5616	59
60	0.0193 3280	0.0198 0120	0.0200 3795	0.0202 7639	60
61	0.0190 6096	0.0195 2999	0.0197 6709	0.0200 0592	61
62	0.0187 9796	0.0192 6762	0.0195 0508	0.0197 4429	62
63	0.0185 4337	0.0190 1366	0.0192 5148	0.0194 9108	63
64	0.0182 9681	0.0187 6773	0.0190 0591	0.0192 4590	64
65	0.0180 5789	0.0185 2946	0.0187 6800	0.0190 0837	65
66	0.0178 2627	0.0182 9848	0.0185 3739	0.0187 7815	66
67	0.0176 0163	0.0180 7449	0.0183 1376	0.0185 5491	67
68	0.0173 8366	0.0178 5716	0.0180 9680	0.0183 3835	68
69	0.0171 7206	0.0176 4622	0.0178 8622	0.0181 2816	69
70	0.0169 6657	0.0174 4138	0.0176 8175	0.0179 2409	70
71	0.0167 6693	0.0172 4239	0.0174 8313	0.0177 2586	71
72	0.0165 7289	0.0170 4901	0.0172 9011	0.0175 3324	72
73	0.0163 8422	0.0168 6100	0.0171 0247	0.0173 4600	73
74	0.0162 0070	0.0166 7814	0.0169 1999	0.0171 6391	74
75	0.0160 2214	0.0165 0024	0.0167 4246	0.0169 8678	75
76	0.0158 4832	0.0163 2709	0.0165 6968	0.0168 1440	76
77	0.0156 7908	0.0161 5851	0.0164 0147	0.0166 4659	77
78	0.0155 1423	0.0159 9432	0.0162 3766	0.0164 8318	78
79	0.0153 5360	0.0158 3436	0.0160 7808	0.0163 2400	79
80	0.0151 9704	0.0156 7847	0.0159 2256	0.0161 6889	80
81	0.0150 4439	0.0155 2650	0.0157 7096	0.0160 1769	81
82	0.0148 9552	0.0153 7830	0.0156 2314	0.0158 7027	82
83	0.0147 5028	0.0152 3373	0.0154 7895	0.0157 2649	83
84	0.0146 0855	0.0150 9268	0.0153 3828	0.0155 8621	84
85	0.0144 7021	0.0149 5501	0.0152 0098	0.0154 4933	85
86	0.0143 3513	0.0148 2060	0.0150 6696	0.0153 1570	86
87	0.0142 0320	0.0146 8935	0.0149 3608	0.0151 8524	87
88	0.0140 7431	0.0145 6115	0.0148 0826	0.0150 5781	88
89	0.0139 4837	0.0144 3588	0.0146 8337	0.0149 3334	89
90	0.0138 2527	0.0143 1347	0.0145 6134	0.0148 1170	90
91	0.0137 0493	0.0141 9380	0.0144 4205	0.0146 9282	91
92	0.0135 8724	0.0140 7679	0.0143 2542	0.0145 7660	92
93	0.0134 7213	0.0139 6236	0.0142 1137	0.0144 6296	93
94	0.0133 5950	0.0138 5042	0.0140 9982	0.0143 5181	94
95	0.0132 4930	0.0137 4090	0.0139 9067	0.0142 4308	95
96	0.0131 4143	0.0136 3372	0.0138 8387	0.0141 3668	96
97	0.0130 3583	0.0135 2880	0.0137 7933	0.0140 3255	97
98	0.0129 3242	0.0134 2608	0.0136 7700	0.0139 3062	98
99	0.0128 3115	0.0133 2549	0.0135 7679	0.0138 3082	99
100	0.0127 3194	0.0132 2696	0.0134 7865	0.0137 3308	100

TABLE VII.—Periodic Rent of Annuity Whose Present Value is 1

$$\frac{1}{a_{\overline{n}|i}} = \frac{i}{1 - (1 + i)^{-n}} \qquad \left[\frac{1}{s_{\overline{n}|i}} = \frac{1}{a_{\overline{n}|i}} - i\right]$$

n	½%	7/12%	5/8%	⅔%	n
101	0.0126 3473	0.0131 3045	0.0133 8251	0.0136 3735	101
102	0.0125 3947	0.0130 3587	0.0132 8832	0.0135 4357	102
103	0.0124 4611	0.0129 4319	0.0131 9602	0.0134 5168	103
104	0.0123 5457	0.0128 5234	0.0131 0555	0.0133 6162	104
105	0.0122 6481	0.0127 6238	0.0130 1687	0.0132 7334	105
106	0.0121 7679	0.0126 7594	0.0129 2992	0.0131 8680	106
107	0.0120 9045	0.0125 9029	0.0128 4465	0.0131 0194	107
108	0.0120 0575	0.0125 0628	0.0127 6102	0.0130 1871	108
109	0.0119 2264	0.0124 2385	0.0126 7897	0.0129 3708	109
110	0.0118 4107	0.0123 4298	0.0125 9848	0.0128 5700	110
111	0.0117 6102	0.0122 6361	0.0125 1950	0.0127 7842	111
112	0.0116 8242	0.0121 8571	0.0124 4198	0.0127 0131	112
113	0.0116 0526	0.0121 0923	0.0123 6588	0.0126 2562	113
114	0.0115 2948	0.0120 3414	0.0122 9118	0.0125 5132	114
115	0.0114 5506	0.0119 6041	0.0122 1783	0.0124 7838	115
116	0.0113 8195	0.0118 8799	0.0121 4579	0.0124 0675	116
117	0.0113 1013	0.0118 1686	0.0120 7504	0.0123 3641	117
118	0.0112 3956	0.0117 4698	0.0120 0555	0.0122 6732	118
119	0.0111 7021	0.0116 7832	0.0119 3727	0.0121 9944	119
120	0.0111 0205	0.0116 1085	0.0118 7018	0.0121 3276	120
121	0.0110 3505	0.0115 4454	0.0118 0425	0.0120 6724	121
122	0.0109 6918	0.0114 7936	0.0117 3945	0.0120 0284	122
123	0.0109 0441	0.0114 1528	0.0116 7575	0.0119 3955	123
124	0.0108 4072	0.0113 5228	0.0116 1314	0.0118 7734	124
125	0.0107 7808	0.0112 9033	0.0115 5157	0.0118 1618	125
126	0.0107 1647	0.0112 2940	0.0114 9102	0.0117 5604	126
127	0.0106 5586	0.0111 6948	0.0114 3148	0.0116 9690	127
128	0.0105 9623	0.0111 1054	0.0113 7292	0.0116 3875	128
129	0.0105 3755	0.0110 5255	0.0113 1531	0.0115 8154	129
130	0.0104 7981	0.0109 9550	0.0112 5864	0.0115 2527	130
131	0.0104 2298	0.0109 3935	0.0112 0288	0.0114 6992	131
132	0.0103 6704	0.0108 8410	0.0111 4800	0.0114 1545	132
133	0.0103 1197	0.0108 2972	0.0110 9400	0.0113 6185	133
134	0.0102 5775	0.0107 7619	0.0110 4086	0.0113 0910	134
135	0.0102 0436	0.0107 2349	0.0109 8854	0.0112 5719	135
136	0.0101 5179	0.0106 7161	0.0109 3703	0.0112 0609	136
137	0.0101 0002	0.0106 2052	0.0108 8633	0.0111 5578	137
138	0.0100 4902	0.0105 7021	0.0108 3640	0.0111 0625	138
139	0.0099 9879	0.0105 2067	0.0107 8723	0.0110 5749	139
140	0.0099 4930	0.0104 7187	0.0107 3881	0.0110 0947	140
141	0.0099 0055	0.0104 2380	0.0106 9111	0.0109 6218	141
142	0.0098 5250	0.0103 7644	0.0106 4414	0.0109 1560	142
143	0.0098 0516	0.0103 2978	0.0105 9786	0.0108 6972	143
144	0.0097 5850	0.0102 8381	0.0105 5226	0.0108 2453	144
145	0.0097 1252	0.0102 3851	0.0105 0734	0.0107 8000	145
146	0.0096 6719	0.0101 9386	0.0104 6307	0.0107 3613	146
147	0.0096 2250	0.0101 4986	0.0104 1944	0.0106 9291	147
148	0.0095 7844	0.0101 0649	0.0103 7645	0.0106 5031	148
149	0.0095 3500	0.0100 6373	0.0103 3407	0.0106 0833	149
150	0.0094 9217	0.0100 2159	0.0102 9230	0.0105 6695	150

TABLE VII.—Periodic Rent of Annuity Whose Present Value is 1

$$\frac{1}{a_{\overline{n}|i}} = \frac{i}{1 - (1 + i)^{-n}} \qquad \left[\frac{1}{s_{\overline{n}|i}} = \frac{1}{a_{\overline{n}|i}} - i\right]$$

n	½%	⁷⁄₁₂%	⅝%	⅔%	n
151	0.0094 4993	0.0099 8003	0.0102 5112	0.0105 2617	151
152	0.0094 0827	0.0099 3905	0.0102 1052	0.0104 8597	152
153	0.0093 6719	0.0098 9865	0.0101 7049	0.0104 4633	153
154	0.0093 2666	0.0098 5880	0.0101 3102	0.0104 0726	154
155	0.0092 8668	0.0098 1950	0.0100 9209	0.0103 6873	155
156	0.0092 4723	0.0097 8074	0.0100 5370	0.0103 3074	156
157	0.0092 0832	0.0097 4251	0.0100 1584	0.0102 9327	157
158	0.0091 6992	0.0097 0479	0.0099 7850	0.0102 5632	158
159	0.0091 3203	0.0096 6758	0.0099 4166	0.0102 1988	159
160	0.0090 9464	0.0096 3087	0.0099 0532	0.0101 8394	160
161	0.0090 5774	0.0095 9464	0.0098 6947	0.0101 4848	161
162	0.0090 2131	0.0095 5890	0.0098 3410	0.0101 1350	162
163	0.0089 8536	0.0095 2362	0.0097 9919	0.0100 7899	163
164	0.0089 4987	0.0094 8881	0.0097 6475	0.0100 4494	164
165	0.0089 1483	0.0094 5445	0.0097 3076	0.0100 1134	165
166	0.0088 8024	0.0094 2053	0.0096 9722	0.0099 7819	166
167	0.0088 4608	0.0093 8705	0.0096 6411	0.0099 4547	167
168	0.0088 1236	0.0093 5400	0.0096 3143	0.0099 1318	168
169	0.0087 7906	0.0093 2138	0.0095 9918	0.0098 8131	169
170	0.0087 4617	0.0092 8917	0.0095 6733	0.0098 4986	170
171	0.0087 1369	0.0092 5736	0.0095 3589	0.0098 1881	171
172	0.0086 8161	0.0092 2595	0.0095 0486	0.0097 8816	172
173	0.0086 4992	0.0091 9494	0.0094 7421	0.0097 5791	173
174	0.0086 1862	0.0091 6431	0.0094 4395	0.0097 2803	174
175	0.0085 8770	0.0091 3406	0.0094 1407	0.0096 9854	175
176	0.0085 5715	0.0091 0418	0.0093 8456	0.0096 6942	176
177	0.0085 2697	0.0090 7468	0.0093 5542	0.0096 4066	177
178	0.0084 9715	0.0090 4553	0.0093 2664	0.0096 1226	178
179	0.0084 6769	0.0090 1673	0.0092 9821	0.0095 8422	179
180	0.0084 3857	0.0089 8828	0.0092 7012	0.0095 5652	180
181	0.0084 0979	0.0089 6018	0.0092 4238	0.0095 2917	181
182	0.0083 8136	0.0089 3241	0.0092 1498	0.0095 0215	182
183	0.0083 5325	0.0089 0497	0.0091 8791	0.0094 7546	183
184	0.0083 2547	0.0088 7786	0.0091 6116	0.0094 4909	184
185	0.0082 9802	0.0088 5107	0.0091 3473	0.0094 2305	185
186	0.0082 7087	0.0088 2459	0.0091 0862	0.0093 9732	186
187	0.0082 4404	0.0087 9843	0.0090 8282	0.0093 7189	187
188	0.0082 1752	0.0087 7257	0.0090 5732	0.0093 4678	188
189	0.0081 9129	0.0087 4701	0.0090 3212	0.0093 2196	189
190	0.0081 6537	0.0087 2174	0.0090 0722	0.0092 9743	190
191	0.0081 3973	0.0086 9677	0.0089 8260	0.0092 7320	191
192	0.0081 1438	0.0086 7208	0.0089 5828	0.0092 4925	192
193	0.0080 8931	0.0086 4767	0.0089 3423	0.0092 2558	193
194	0.0080 6452	0.0086 2355	0.0089 1046	0.0092 0219	194
195	0.0080 4000	0.0085 9969	0.0088 8696	0.0091 7907	195
196	0.0080 1576	0.0085 7610	0.0088 6374	0.0091 5622	196
197	0.0079 9178	0.0085 5278	0.0088 4077	0.0091 3363	197
198	0.0079 6806	0.0085 2972	0.0088 1807	0.0091 1130	198
199	0.0079 4459	0.0085 0691	0.0087 9562	0.0090 8923	199
200	0.0079 2138	0.0084 8436	0.0087 7343	0.0090 6741	200

TABLE VII.—Periodic Rent of Annuity Whose Present Value is 1

$$\frac{1}{a_{\overline{n}|i}} = \frac{i}{1 - (1+i)^{-n}} \qquad \left[\frac{1}{s_{\overline{n}|i}} = \frac{1}{a_{\overline{n}|i}} - i\right]$$

n	¾%	⅞%	1%	1⅛%	n
1	1.0075 0000	1.0087 5000	1.0100 0000	1.0112 5000	1
2	0.5056 3200	0.5065 7203	0.5075 1244	0.5084 5323	2
3	0.3383 4579	0.3391 8361	0.3400 2211	0.3408 6130	3
4	0.2547 0501	0.2554 9257	0.2562 8109	0.2570 7058	4
5	0.2045 2242	0.2052 8049	0.2060 3980	0.2068 0034	5
6	0.1710 6891	0.1718 0789	0.1725 4837	0.1732 9034	6
7	0.1471 7488	0.1479 0070	0.1486 2828	0.1493 5762	7
8	0.1292 5552	0.1299 7190	0.1306 9029	0.1314 1071	8
9	0.1153 1929	0.1160 2868	0.1167 4037	0.1174 5432	9
10	0.1041 7123	0.1048 7538	0.1055 8208	0.1062 9131	10
11	0.0950 5094	0.0957 5111	0.0964 5408	0.0971 5984	11
12	0.0874 5148	0.0881 4860	0.0888 4879	0.0895 5203	12
13	0.0810 2188	0.0817 1669	0.0824 1482	0.0831 1626	13
14	0.0755 1146	0.0762 0453	0.0769 0117	0.0776 0138	14
15	0.0707 3639	0.0714 2817	0.0721 2378	0.0728 2321	15
16	0.0665 5879	0.0672 4965	0.0679 4460	0.0686 4363	16
17	0.0628 7321	0.0635 6346	0.0642 5806	0.0649 5698	17
18	0.0595 9766	0.0602 8756	0.0609 8205	0.0616 8113	18
19	0.0566 6740	0.0573 5715	0.0580 5175	0.0587 5120	19
20	0.0540 3063	0.0547 2042	0.0554 1532	0.0561 1531	20
21	0.0516 4543	0.0523 3541	0.0530 3075	0.0537 3145	21
22	0.0494 7748	0.0501 6779	0.0508 6371	0.0515 6525	22
23	0.0474 9846	0.0481 8921	0.0488 8584	0.0495 8833	23
24	0.0456 8474	0.0463 7604	0.0470 7347	0.0477 7701	24
25	0.0440 1650	0.0447 0843	0.0454 0675	0.0461 1144	25
26	0.0424 7693	0.0431 6959	0.0438 6888	0.0445 7479	26
27	0.0410 5176	0.0417 4520	0.0424 4553	0.0431 5273	27
28	0.0397 2871	0.0404 2300	0.0411 2444	0.0418 3299	28
29	0.0384 9723	0.0391 9243	0.0398 9502	0.0406 0498	29
30	0.0373 4816	0.0380 4431	0.0387 4811	0.0394 5953	30
31	0.0362 7352	0.0369 7068	0.0376 7573	0.0383 8866	31
32	0.0352 6634	0.0359 6454	0.0366 7089	0.0373 8535	32
33	0.0343 2048	0.0350 1976	0.0357 2744	0.0364 4349	33
34	0.0334 3053	0.0341 3092	0.0348 3997	0.0355 5763	34
35	0.0325 9170	0.0332 9324	0.0340 0368	0.0347 2299	35
36	0.0317 9973	0.0325 0244	0.0332 1431	0.0339 3529	36
37	0.0310 5082	0.0317 5473	0.0324 6805	0.0331 9072	37
38	0.0303 4157	0.0310 4671	0.0317 6150	0.0324 8589	38
39	0.0296 6893	0.0303 7531	0.0310 9160	0.0318 1773	39
40	0.0290 3016	0.0297 3780	0.0304 5560	0.0311 8349	40
41	0.0284 2276	0.0291 3169	0.0298 5102	0.0305 8069	41
42	0.0278 4452	0.0285 5475	0.0292 7563	0.0300 0709	42
43	0.0272 9338	0.0280 0493	0.0287 2737	0.0294 6064	43
44	0.0267 6751	0.0274 8039	0.0282 0441	0.0289 3949	44
45	0.0262 6521	0.0269 7943	0.0277 0505	0.0284 4197	45
46	0.0257 8495	0.0265 0053	0 0272 2775	0.0279 6652	46
47	0.0253 2532	0.0260 4228	0.0267 7111	0.0275 1173	47
48	0.0248 8504	0.0256 0338	0.0263 3384	0.0270 7632	48
49	0.0244 6292	0.0251 8265	0.0259 1474	0.0266 5910	49
50	0.0240 5787	0.0247 7900	0.0255 1273	0.0262 5898	50

TABLE VII.—Periodic Rent of Annuity Whose Present Value is 1

$$\frac{1}{a_{\overline{n}|i}} = \frac{i}{1 - (1+i)^{-n}} \qquad \left[\frac{1}{s_{\overline{n}|i}} = \frac{1}{a_{\overline{n}|i}} - i\right]$$

n	¾%	⅞%	1%	1⅛%	n
51	0.0236 6888	0.0243 9142	0.0251 2680	0.0258 7494	51
52	0.0232 9503	0.0240 1899	0.0247 5603	0.0255 0606	52
53	0.0229 3546	0.0236 6084	0.0243 9956	0.0251 5149	53
54	0.0225 8938	0.0233 1619	0.0240 5658	0.0248 1043	54
55	0.0222 5605	0.0229 8430	0.0237 2637	0.0244 8213	55
56	0.0219 3478	0.0226 6449	0.0234 0823	0.0241 6592	56
57	0.0216 2496	0.0223 5611	0.0231 0156	0.0238 6116	57
58	0.0213 2597	0.0220 5858	0.0228 0573	0.0235 6726	58
59	0.0210 3727	0.0217 7135	0.0225 2020	0.0232 8366	59
60	0.0207 5836	0.0214 9390	0.0222 4445	0.0230 0985	60
61	0.0204 8873	0.0212 2575	0.0219 7800	0.0227 4534	61
62	0.0202 2795	0.0209 6644	0.0217 2041	0.0224 8969	62
63	0 0199 7560	0.0207 1557	0.0214 7125	0.0222 4247	63
64	0.0197 3127	0.0204 7273	0.0212 3013	0.0220 0329	64
65	0.0194 9460	0.0202 3754	0.0209 9667	0.0217 7178	65
66	0.0192 6524	0.0200 0968	0.0207 7052	0.0215 4758	66
67	0.0190 4286	0.0197 8879	0.0205 5136	0.0213 3037	67
68	0 0188 2716	0.0195 7459	0.0203 3888	0.0211 1985	68
69	0.0186 1785	0.0193 6677	0.0201 3280	0.0209 1571	69
70	0.0184 1464	0.0191 6506	0.0199 3282	0.0207 1769	70
71	0.0182 1728	0.0189 6921	0.0197 3870	0.0205 2552	71
72	0.0180 2554	0.0187 7897	0.0195 5019	0.0203 3896	72
73	0.0178 3917	0.0185 9411	0.0193 6706	0.0201 5779	73
74	0.0176 5796	0.0184 1441	0.0191 8910	0.0199 8177	74
75	0.0174 8170	0.0182 3966	0.0190 1609	0.0198 1072	75
76	0.0173 1020	0.0180 6967	0.0188 4784	0.0196 4442	76
77	0.0171 4328	0.0179 0426	0.0186 8416	0.0194 8269	77
78	0.0169 8074	0.0177 4324	0.0185 2488	0.0193 2536	78
79	0.0168 2244	0.0175 8645	0.0183 6984	0.0191 7226	79
80	0.0166 6821	0.0174 3374	0.0182 1885	0.0190 2323	80
81	0.0165 1790	0.0172 8494	0.0180 7180	0.0188 7812	81
82	0.0163 7136	0.0171 3992	0.0179 2851	0.0187 3678	82
83	0.0162 2847	0.0169 9854	0.0177 8886	0.0185 9908	83
84	0.0160 8908	0.0168 6067	0.0176 5273	0.0184 6489	84
85	0.0159 5308	0.0167 2619	0.0175 1998	0.0183 3409	85
86	0.0158 2034	0.0165 9497	0.0173 9050	0.0182 0654	86
87	0.0156 9076	0.0164 6691	0.0172 6417	0.0180 8215	87
88	0.0155 6423	0.0163 4190	0.0171 4089	0.0179 6081	88
89	0.0154 4064	0.0162 1982	0.0170 2056	0.0178 4240	89
90	0.0153 1989	0.0161 0060	0.0169 0306	0.0177 2684	90
91	0.0152 0190	0.0159 8413	0.0167 8832	0.0176 1403	91
92	0.0150 8657	0.0158 7031	0.0166 7624	0.0175 0387	92
93	0.0149 7382	0.0157 5908	0.0165 6673	0.0173 9629	93
94	0.0148 6356	0.0156 5033	0.0164 5971	0.0172 9119	94
95	0.0147 5571	0.0155 4401	0.0163 5511	0.0171 8851	95
96	0.0146 5020	0.0154 4002	0.0162 5284	0.0170 8816	96
97	0.0145 4696	0.0153 3829	0.0161 5284	0.0169 9007	97
98	0.0144 4592	0.0152 3877	0.0160 5503	0.0168 9418	98
99	0.0143 4701	0.0151 4137	0.0159 5936	0.0168 0041	99
100	0.0142 5017	0.0150 4604	0.0158 6574	0.0167 0870	100

TABLE VII.—Periodic Rent of Annuity Whose Present Value is 1

$$\frac{1}{a_{\overline{n}|i}} = \frac{i}{1 - (1+i)^{-n}} \qquad \left[\frac{1}{s_{\overline{n}|i}} = \frac{1}{a_{\overline{n}|i}} - i \right]$$

n	1¼%	1⅜%	1½%	1¾%	n
1	1.0125 0000	1.0137 5000	1.0150 0000	1.0175 0000	1
2	0.5093 9441	0.5103 3597	0.5112 7792	0.5131 6295	2
3	0.3417 0117	0.3425 4173	0.3433 8296	0.3450 6746	3
4	0.2578 6102	0.2586 5243	0.2594 4478	0.2610 3237	4
5	0.2075 6211	0.2083 2510	0.2090 8932	0.2106 2142	5
6	0.1740 3381	0.1747 7877	0.1755 2521	0.1770 2256	6
7	0.1500 8872	0.1508 2157	0.1515 5616	0.1530 3059	7
8	0.1321 3314	0.1328 5758	0.1335 8402	0.1350 4292	8
9	0.1181 7055	0.1188 8906	0.1196 0982	0.1210 5813	9
10	0.1070 0307	0.1077 1737	0.1084 3418	0.1098 7534	10
11	0.0978 6839	0.0985 7973	0.0992 9384	0.1007 3038	11
12	0.0902 5831	0.0909 6764	0.0916 7999	0.0931 1377	12
13	0.0838 2100	0.0845 2903	0.0852 4036	0.0866 7283	13
14	0.0783 0515	0.0790 1246	0.0797 2332	0.0811 5562	14
15	0.0735 2646	0.0742 3351	0.0749 4436	0.0763 7739	15
16	0.0693 4672	0.0700 5388	0.0707 6508	0.0721 9958	16
17	0.0656 6023	0.0663 6780	0.0670 7966	0.0685 1623	17
18	0.0623 8479	0.0630 9301	0.0638 0578	0.0652 4492	18
19	0.0594 5548	0.0601 6457	0.0608 7847	0.0623 2061	19
20	0.0568 2039	0.0575 3054	0.0582 4574	0.0596 9122	20
21	0.0544 3748	0.0551 4884	0.0558 6550	0.0573 1464	21
22	0.0522 7238	0.0529 8507	0.0537 0331	0.0551 5638	22
23	0.0502 9666	0.0510 1080	0.0517 3075	0.0531 8796	23
24	0.0484 8665	0.0492 0235	0.0499 2410	0.0513 8565	24
25	0.0468 2247	0.0475 3981	0.0482 6345	0.0497 2952	25
26	0.0452 8729	0.0460 0635	0.0467 3196	0.0482 0269	26
27	0.0438 6677	0.0445 8763	0.0453 1527	0.0467 9079	27
28	0.0425 4863	0.0432 7134	0.0440 0108	0.0454 8151	28
29	0.0413 2228	0.0420 4689	0.0427 7878	0.0442 6424	29
30	0.0401 7854	0.0409 0511	0.0416 3919	0.0431 2975	30
31	0.0391 0942	0.0398 3798	0.0405 7430	0.0420 7005	31
32	0.0381 0791	0.0388 3850	0.0395 7710	0.0410 7812	32
33	0.0371 6786	0.0379 0053	0.0386 4144	0.0401 4779	33
34	0.0362 8387	0.0370 1864	0.0377 6189	0.0392 7363	34
35	0.0354 5111	0.0361 8801	0.0369 3363	0.0384 5082	35
36	0.0346 6533	0.0354 0438	0.0361 5240	0.0376 7507	36
37	0.0339 2270	0.0346 6394	0.0354 1437	0.0369 4257	37
38	0.0332 1983	0.0339 6327	0.0347 1613	0.0362 4990	38
39	0.0325 5365	0.0332 9931	0.0340 5463	0.0355 9399	39
40	0.0319 2141	0.0326 6931	0.0334 2710	0.0349 7209	40
41	0.0313 2063	0.0320 7078	0.0328 3106	0.0343 8170	41
42	0.0307 4906	0.0315 0148	0.0322 6426	0.0338 2057	42
43	0.0302 0466	0.0309 5936	0.0317 2465	0.0332 8666	43
44	0.0296 8557	9.0304 4257	0.0312 1038	0.0327 7810	44
45	0.0291 9012	0.0299 4941	0.0307 1976	0.0322 9321	45
46	0.0287 1675	0.0294 7836	0.0302 5125	0.0318 3043	46
47	0.0282 6406	0.0290 2799	0.0298 0342	0.0313 8836	47
48	0.0278 3075	0.0285 9701	0.0293 7500	0.0309 6569	48
49	0.0274 1563	0.0281 8424	0.0289 6478	0.0305 6124	49
50	0.0270 1763	0.0277 8857	0.0285 7168	0.0301 7391	50

TABLE VII.—Periodic Rent of Annuity Whose Present Value is 1

$$\frac{1}{a_{\overline{n}|i}} = \frac{i}{1 - (1 + i)^{-n}} \qquad \left[\frac{1}{s_{\overline{n}|i}} = \frac{1}{a_{\overline{n}|i}} - i \right]$$

n	$1\frac{1}{4}\%$	$1\frac{3}{8}\%$	$1\frac{1}{2}\%$	$1\frac{3}{4}\%$	n
51	0.0266 3571	0.0274 0900	0.0281 9469	0.0298 0269	51
52	0.0262 6897	0.0270 4461	0.0278 3287	0.0294 4665	52
53	0.0259 1653	0.0266 9453	0.0274 8537	0.0291 0492	53
54	0.0255 7760	0.0263 5797	0.0271 5138	0.0287 7672	54
55	0.0252 5145	0.0260 3418	0.0268 3018	0.0284 6129	55
56	0.0249 3739	0.0257 2249	0.0265 2106	0.0281 5795	56
57	0.0246 3478	0.0254 2225	0.0262 2341	0.0278 6606	57
58	0.0243 4303	0.0251 3287	0.0259 3661	0.0275 8503	58
59	0.0240 6158	0.0248 5380	0.0256 6012	0.0273 1430	59
60	0.0237 8993	0.0245 8452	0.0253 9343	0.0270 5336	60
61	0.0235 2758	0.0243 2455	0.0251 3604	0.0268 0172	61
62	0.0232 7410	0.0240 7344	0.0248 8751	0.0265 5892	62
63	0.0230 2904	0.0238 3076	0.0246 4741	0.0263 2455	63
64	0.0227 9203	0.0235 9612	0.0244 1534	0.0260 9821	64
65	0.0225 6268	0.0233 6914	0.0241 9094	0.0258 7952	65
66	0.0223 4065	0.0231 4949	0.0239 7386	0.0256 6813	66
67	0.0221 2560	0.0229 3682	0.0237 6376	0.0254 6372	67
68	0.0219 1724	0.0227 3082	0.0235 6033	0.0252 6596	68
69	0.0217 1527	0.0225 3122	0.0233 6329	0.0250 7459	69
70	0.0215 1941	0.0223 3773	0.0231 7235	0.0248 8930	70
71	0.0213 2941	0.0221 5009	0.0229 8727	0.0247 0985	71
72	0.0211 4501	0.0219 6806	0.0228 0779	0.0245 3600	72
73	0.0209 6600	0.0217 9140	0.0226 3368	0.0243 6750	73
74	0.0207 9215	0.0216 1991	0.0224 6473	0.0242 0413	74
75	0.0206 2325	0.0214 5336	0.0223 0072	0.0240 4570	75
76	0.0204 5910	0.0212 9157	0.0221 4146	0.0238 9200	76
77	0.0202 9953	0.0211 3435	0.0219 8676	0.0237 4284	77
78	0.0201 4435	0.0209 8151	0.0218 3645	0.0235 9806	78
79	0.0199 9341	0.0208 3290	0.0216 9036	0.0234 5748	79
80	0.0198 4652	0.0206 8836	0.0215 4832	0.0233 2093	80
81	0.0197 0356	0.0205 4772	0.0214 1019	0.0231 8828	81
82	0.0195 6437	0.0204 1086	0.0212 7583	0.0230 5936	82
83	0.0194 2881	0.0202 7762	0.0211 4509	0.0229 3406	83
84	0.0192 9675	0.0201 4789	0.0210 1784	0.0228 1223	84
85	0.0191 6808	0.0200 2153	0.0208 9396	0.0226 9375	85
86	0.0190 4267	0.0198 9843	0.0207 7333	0.0225 7850	86
87	0.0189 2041	0.0197 7847	0.0206 5584	0.0224 6636	87
88	0.0188 0119	0.0196 6155	0.0205 4138	0.0223 5724	88
89	0.0186 8490	0.0195 4756	0.0204 2984	0.0222 5102	89
90	0.0185 7146	0.0194 3641	0.0203 2113	0.0221 4760	90
91	0.0184 6076	0.0193 2799	0.0202 1516	0.0220 4690	91
92	0.0183 5271	0.0192 2222	0.0201 1182	0.0219 4882	92
93	0.0182 4724	0.0191 1902	0.0200 1104	0.0218 5327	93
94	0.0181 4425	0.0190 1829	0.0199 1273	0.0217 6017	94
95	0.0180 4366	0.0189 1997	0.0198 1681	0.0216 6944	95
96	0.0179 4540	0.0188 2397	0.0197 2321	0.0215 8101	96
97	0.0178 4941	0.0187 3022	0.0196 3186	0.0214 9480	97
98	0.0177 5560	0.0186 3866	0.0195 4268	0.0214 1074	98
99	0.0176 6391	0.0185 4921	0.0194 5560	0.0213 2876	99
100	0.0175 7428	0.0184 6181	0.0193 7057	0.0212 4880	100

TABLE VII.—Periodic Rent of Annuity Whose Present Value is 1

$$\frac{1}{a_{\overline{n}|i}} = \frac{i}{1 - (1 + i)^{-n}} \qquad \left[\frac{1}{s_{\overline{n}|i}} = \frac{1}{a_{\overline{n}|i}} - i\right]$$

n	2%	2¼%	2½%	2¾%	n
1	1.0200 0000	1.0225 0000	1.0250 0000	1.0275 0000	1
2	0.5150 4950	0.5169 3758	0.5188 2716	0.5207 1825	2
3	0.3467 5467	0.3484 4458	0.3501 3717	0.3518 3243	3
4	0.2626 2375	0.2642 1893	0.2658 1788	0.2674 2059	4
5	0.2121 5839	0.2137 0021	0.2152 4686	0.2167 9832	5
6	0.1785 2581	0.1800 3496	0.1815 4997	0.1830 7083	6
7	0.1545 1196	0.1560 0025	0.1574 9543	0.1589 9747	7
8	0.1365 0980	0.1379 8462	0.1394 6735	0.1409 5795	8
9	0.1225 1544	0.1239 8170	0.1254 5689	0.1269 4095	9
10	0.1113 2653	0.1127 8768	0.1142 5876	0.1157 3972	10
11	0.1021 7794	0.1036 3649	0.1051 0596	0.1065 8629	11
12	0.0945 5960	0.0960 1740	0.0974 8713	0.0989 6871	12
13	0.0881 1835	0.0895 7686	0.0910 4827	0.0925 3252	13
14	0.0826 0197	0.0840 6230	0.0855 3653	0.0870 2457	14
15	0.0778 2547	0.0792 8852	0.0807 6646	0.0822 5917	15
16	0.0736 5013	0.0751 1663	0.0765 9899	0.0780 9710	16
17	0.0699 6984	0.0714 4039	0.0729 2777	0.0744 3186	17
18	0.0667 0210	0.0681 7720	0.0696 7008	0.0711 8063	18
19	0.0637 8177	0.0652 6182	0.0667 6062	0.0682 7802	19
20	0.0611 5672	0.0626 4207	0.0641 4713	0.0656 7173	20
21	0.0587 8477	0.0602 7572	0.0617 8733	0.0633 1941	21
22	0.0566 3140	0.0581 2821	0.0596 4661	0.0611 8640	22
23	0.0546 6810	0.0561 7097	0.0576 9638	0.0592 4410	23
24	0.0528 7110	0.0543 8023	0.0559 1282	0.0574 6863	24
25	0.0512 2044	0.0527 3599	0.0542 7592	0.0558 3997	25
26	0.0496 9923	0.0512 2134	0.0527 6875	0.0543 4116	26
27	0.0482 9309	0.0498 2188	0.0513 7687	0.0529 5776	27
28	0.0469 8967	0.0485 2525	0.0500 8793	0.0516 7738	28
29	0.0457 7836	0.0473 2081	0.0488 9127	0.0504 8935	29
30	0.0446 4992	0.0461 9934	0.0477 7764	0.0493 8442	30
31	0.0435 9635	0.0451 5280	0.0467 3900	0.0483 5453	31
32	0.0426 1061	0.0441 7415	0.0457 6831	0.0473 9263	32
33	0.0416 8653	0.0432 5722	0.0448 5938	0.0464 9253	33
34	0.0408 1867	0.0423 9655	0.0440 0675	0.0456 4875	34
35	0.0400 0221	0.0415 8731	0.0432 0558	0.0448 5645	35
36	0.0392 3285	0.0408 2522	0.0424 5158	0.0441 1132	36
37	0.0385 0678	0.0401 0643	0.0417 4090	0.0434 0953	37
38	0.0378 2057	0.0394 2753	0.0410 7012	0.0427 4764	38
39	0.0371 7114	0.0387 8543	0.0404 3615	0.0421 2256	39
40	0.0365 5575	0.0381 7738	0.0398 3623	0.0415 3151	40
41	0.0359 7188	0.0376 0087	0.0392 6786	0.0409 7200	41
42	0.0354 1729	0.0370 5364	0.0387 2876	0.0404 4175	42
43	0.0348 8993	0.0365 3364	0.0382 1688	0.0399 3871	43
44	0.0343 8794	0.0360 3901	0.0377 3037	0.0394 6100	44
45	0.0339 0962	0.0355 6805	0.0372 6752	0.0390 0693	45
46	0.0334 5342	0.0351 1921	0.0368 2676	0.0385 7493	46
47	0.0330 1792	0.0346 9107	0.0364 0669	0.0381 6358	47
48	0.0326 0184	0.0342 8233	0.0360 0599	0.0377 7158	48
49	0.0322 0396	0.0338 9179	0.0356 2348	0.0373 9773	49
50	0.0318 2321	0.0335 1836	0.0352 5806	0.0370 4092	50

TABLE VII.—Periodic Rent of Annuity Whose Present Value is 1

$$\frac{1}{a_{\overline{n}|i}} = \frac{i}{1 - (1+i)^{-n}} \qquad \left[\frac{1}{s_{\overline{n}|i}} = \frac{1}{a_{\overline{n}|i}} - i \right]$$

n	2%	2¼%	2½%	2¾%	n
51	0.0314 5856	0.0331 6102	0.0349 0870	0.0367 0014	51
52	0.0311 0909	0.0328 1884	0.0345 7446	0.0363 7444	52
53	0.0307 7392	0.0324 9094	0.0342 5449	0.0360 6297	53
54	0.0304 5226	0.0321 7654	0.0339 4799	0.0357 6491	54
55	0.0301 4337	0.0318 7489	0.0336 5419	0.0354 7953	55
56	0.0298 4656	0.0315 8530	0.0333 7243	0.0352 0612	56
57	0.0295 6120	0.0313 0712	0.0331 0204	0.0349 4404	57
58	0.0292 8667	0.0310 3977	0.0328 4244	0.0346 9270	58
59	0.0290 2243	0.0307 8268	0.0325 9307	0.0344 5153	59
60	0.0287 6797	0.0305 3533	0.0323 5340	0.0342 2002	60
61	0.0285 2278	0.0302 9724	0.0321 2294	0.0339 9767	61
62	0.0282 8643	0.0300 6795	0.0319 0126	0.0337 8402	62
63	0.0280 5848	0.0298 4704	0.0316 8790	0.0335 7866	63
64	0.0278 3855	0.0296 3411	0.0314 8249	0.0333 8118	64
65	0.0276 2624	0.0294 2878	0.0312 8463	0.0331 9120	65
66	0.0274 2122	0.0292 3070	0.0310 9398	0.0330 0837	66
67	0.0272 2316	0.0290 3955	0.0309 1021	0.0328 3236	67
68	0.0270 3173	0.0288 5500	0.0307 3300	0.0326 6285	68
69	0.0268 4665	0.0286 7677	0.0305 6206	0.0324 9955	69
70	0.0266 6765	0.0285 0458	0.0303 9712	0.0323 4218	70
71	0.0264 9446	0.0283 3816	0.0302 3790	0.0321 9048	71
72	0.0263 2683	0.0281 7728	0.0300 8417	0.0320 4420	72
73	0.0261 6454	0.0280 2169	0.0299 3568	0.0319 0311	73
74	0.0260 0736	0.0278 7118	0.0297 9222	0.0317 6698	74
75	0.0258 5508	0.0277 2554	0.0296 5358	0.0316 3560	75
76	0.0257 0751	0.0275 8457	0.0295 1956	0.0315 0878	76
77	0.0255 6447	0.0274 4808	0.0293 8997	0.0313 8633	77
78	0.0254 2576	0.0273 1589	0.0292 6463	0.0312 6806	78
79	0.0252 9123	0.0271 8784	0.0291 4338	0.0311 5382	79
80	0.0251 6071	0.0270 6376	0.0290 2605	0.0310 4342	80
81	0.0250 3405	0.0269 4350	0.0289 1248	0.0309 3674	81
82	0.0249 1110	0.0268 2692	0.0288 0254	0.0308 3361	82
83	0.0247 9173	0.0267 1387	0.0286 9608	0.0307 3389	83
84	0.0246 7581	0.0266 0423	0.0285 9298	0.0306 3747	84
85	0.0245 6321	0.0264 9787	0.0284 9310	0.0305 4420	85
86	0.0244 5381	0.0263 9467	0.0283 9633	0.0304 5397	86
87	0.0243 4750	0.0262 9452	0.0283 0255	0.0303 6667	87
88	0.0242 4416	0.0261 9730	0.0282 1165	0.0302 8219	88
89	0.0241 4370	0.0261 0291	0.0281 2353	0.0302 0041	89
90	0.0240 4602	0.0260 1126	0.0280 3809	0.0301 2125	90
91	0.0239 5101	0.0259 2224	0.0279 5523	0.0300 4460	91
92	0.0238 5859	0.0258 3577	0.0278 7486	0.0299 7038	92
93	0.0237 6868	0.0257 5176	0.0277 9690	0.0298 9850	93
94	0.0236 8118	0.0256 7012	0.0277 2126	0.0298 2887	94
95	0.0235 9602	0.0255 9078	0.0276 4786	0.0297 6141	95
96	0.0235 1313	0.0255 1366	0.0275 7662	0.0296 9605	96
97	0.0234 3242	0.0254 3868	0.0275 0747	0.0296 3272	97
98	0.0233 5383	0.0253 6578	0.0274 4034	0.0295 7134	98
99	0.0232 7729	0.0252 9489	0.0273 7517	0.0295 1185	99
100	0.0232 0274	0.0252 2594	0.0273 1188	0.0294 5418	100

TABLE VII.—Periodic Rent of Annuity Whose Present Value is 1

$$\frac{1}{a_{\overline{n}|i}} = \frac{i}{1 - (1 + i)^{-n}} \qquad \left[\frac{1}{s_{\overline{n}|i}} = \frac{1}{a_{\overline{n}|i}} - i \right]$$

n	3%	3½%	4%	4½%	n
1	1.0300 0000	1.0350 0000	1.0400 0000	1.0450 0000	1
2	0.5226 1084	0.5264 0049	0.5301 9608	0.5339 9756	2
3	0.3535 3036	0.3569 3418	0.3603 4854	0.3637 7336	3
4	0.2690 2705	0.2722 5114	0.2754 9005	0.2787 4365	4
5	0.2183 5457	0.2214 8137	0.2246 2711	0.2277 9164	5
6	0.1845 9750	0.1876 6821	0.1907 6190	0.1938 7839	6
7	0.1605 0635	0.1635 4449	0.1666 0961	0.1697 0147	7
8	0.1424 5639	0.1454 7665	0.1485 2783	0.1516 0965	8
9	0.1284 3386	0.1314 4601	0.1344 9299	0.1375 7447	9
10	0.1172 3051	0.1202 4137	0.1232 9094	0.1263 7882	10
11	0.1080 7745	0.1110 9197	0.1141 4904	0.1172 4818	11
12	0.1004 6209	0.1034 8395	0.1065 5217	0.1096 6619	12
13	0.0940 2954	0.0970 6157	0.1001 4373	0.1032 7535	13
14	0.0885 2634	0.0915 7073	0.0946 6897	0.0978 2032	14
15	0.0837 6658	0.0868 2507	0.0899 4110	0.0931 1381	15
16	0.0796 1085	0.0826 8483	0.0858 2000	0.0890 1537	16
17	0.0759 5253	0.0790 4313	0.0821 9852	0.0854 1758	17
18	0.0727 0870	0.0758 1684	0.0789 9333	0.0822 3690	18
19	0.0698 1388	0.0729 4033	0.0761 3862	0.0794 0734	19
20	0.0672 1571	0.0703 6108	0.0735 8175	0.0768 7614	20
21	0.0648 7178	0.0680 3659	0.0712 8011	0.0746 0057	21
22	0.0627 4739	0.0659 3207	0.0691 9881	0.0725 4565	22
23	0.0608 1390	0.0640 1880	0.0673 0906	0.0706 8249	23
24	0.0590 4742	0.0622 7283	0.0655 8683	0.0689 8703	24
25	0.0574 2787	0.0606 7404	0.0640 1196	0.0674 3903	25
26	0.0559 3829	0.0592 0540	0.0625 6738	0.0660 2137	26
27	0.0545 6421	0.0578 5241	0.0612 3854	0.0647 1946	27
28	0.0532 9323	0.0566 0265	0.0600 1298	0.0635 2081	28
29	0.0521 1467	0.0554 4538	0.0588 7993	0.0624 1461	29
30	0.0510 1926	0.0543 7133	0.0578 3010	0.0613 9154	30
31	0.0499 9893	0.0533 7240	0.0568 5535	0.0604 4345	31
32	0.0490 4662	0.0524 4150	0.0559 4859	0.0595 6320	32
33	0.0481 5612	0.0515 7242	0.0551 0357	0.0587 4453	33
34	0.0473 2196	0.0507 5966	0.0543 1477	0.0579 8191	34
35	0.0465 3929	0.0499 9835	0.0535 7732	0.0572 7045	35
36	0.0458 0379	0.0492 8416	0.0528 8688	0.0566 0578	36
37	0.0451 1162	0.0486 1325	0.0522 3957	0.0559 8402	37
38	0.0444 5934	0.0479 8214	0.0516 3192	0.0554 0169	38
39	0.0438 4385	0.0473 8775	0.0510 6083	0.0548 5567	39
40	0.0432 6238	0.0468 2728	0.0505 2349	0.0543 4315	40
41	0.0427 1241	0.0462 9822	0.0500 1738	0.0538 6158	41
42	0.0421 9167	0.0457 9828	0.0495 4020	0.0534 0868	42
43	0.0416 9811	0.0453 2539	0.0490 8989	0.0529 8235	43
44	0.0412 2985	0.0448 7768	0.0486 6454	0.0525 8071	44
45	0.0407 8518	0.0444 5343	0.0482 6246	0.0522 0202	45
46	0.0403 6254	0.0440 5108	0.0478 8205	0.0518 4471	46
47	0.0399 6051	0.0436 6919	0.0475 2189	0.0515 0734	47
48	0.0395 7777	0.0433 0646	0.0471 8065	0.0511 8858	48
49	0.0392 1314	0.0429 6167	0.0468 5712	0.0508 8722	49
50	0.0388 6550	0.0426 3371	0.0465 5020	0.0506 0215	50

TABLE VII.—Periodic Rent of Annuity Whose Present Value is 1

$$\frac{1}{a_{\overline{n}|i}} = \frac{i}{1 - (1 + i)^{-n}} \qquad \left[\frac{1}{s_{\overline{n}|i}} = \frac{1}{a_{\overline{n}|i}} - i \right]$$

n	3%	3½%	4%	4½%	n
51	0.0385 3382	0.0423 2156	0.0462 5885	0.0503 3232	51
52	0.0382 1718	0.0420 2429	0.0459 8212	0.0500 7679	52
53	0.0379 1471	0.0417 4100	0.0457 1915	0.0498 3469	53
54	0.0376 2558	0.0414 7090	0.0454 6910	0.0496 0519	54
55	0.0373 4907	0.0412 1323	0.0452 3124	0.0493 8754	55
56	0.0370 8447	0.0409 6730	0.0450 0487	0.0491 8105	56
57	0.0368 3114	0.0407 3245	0.0447 8932	0.0489 8506	57
58	0.0365 8848	0.0405 0810	0.0445 8401	0.0487 9897	58
59	0.0363 5593	0.0402 9366	0.0443 8836	0.0486 2221	59
60	0.0361 3296	0.0400 8862	0.0442 0185	0.0484 5426	60
61	0.0359 1908	0.0398 9249	0.0440 2398	0.0482 9462	61
62	0.0357 1385	0.0397 0480	0.0438 5430	0.0481 4284	62
63	0.0355 1682	0.0395 2513	0.0436 9237	0.0479 9848	63
64	0.0353 2760	0.0393 5308	0.0435 3780	0.0478 6115	64
65	0.0351 4581	0.0391 8826	0.0433 9019	0.0477 3047	65
66	0.0349 7110	0.0390 3031	0.0432 4921	0.0476 0608	66
67	0.0348 0313	0.0388 7892	0.0431 1451	0.0474 8765	67
68	0.0346 4159	0.0387 3375	0.0429 8578	0.0473 7487	68
69	0.0344 8618	0.0385 9453	0.0428 6272	0.0472 6745	69
70	0.0343 3663	0.0384 6095	0.0427 4506	0.0471 6511	70
71	0.0341 9266	0.0383 3277	0.0426 3253	0.0470 6759	71
72	0.0340 5404	0.0382 0973	0.0425 2489	0.0469 7465	72
73	0.0339 2053	0.0380 9160	0.0424 2190	0.0468 8606	73
74	0.0337 9191	0.0379 7816	0.0423 2334	0.0468 0159	74
75	0.0336 6796	0.0378 6919	0.0422 2900	0.0467 2104	75
76	0.0335 4849	0.0377 6450	0.0421 3869	0.0466 4422	76
77	0.0334 3331	0.0376 6390	0.0420 5221	0.0465 7094	77
78	0.0333 2224	0.0375 6721	0.0419 6939	0.0465 0104	78
79	0.0332 1510	0.0374 7426	0.0418 9007	0.0464 3434	79
80	0.0331 1175	0.0373 8489	0.0418 1408	0.0463 7069	80
81	0.0330 1201	0.0372 9894	0.0417 4127	0.0463 0995	81
82	0.0329 1576	0.0372 1628	0.0416 7150	0.0462 5197	82
83	0.0328 2284	0.0371 3676	0.0416 0463	0.0461 9663	83
84	0.0327 3313	0.0370 6025	0.0415 4054	0.0461 4379	84
85	0.0326 4650	0.0369 8662	0.0414 7909	0.0460 9334	85
86	0.0325 6284	0.0369 1576	0.0414 2018	0.0460 4516	86
87	0.0324 8202	0.0368 4756	0.0413 6370	0.0459 9915	87
88	0.0324 0393	0.0367 8190	0.0413 0953	0.0459 5522	88
89	0.0323 2848	0.0367 1868	0.0412 5758	0.0459 1325	89
90	0.0322 5556	0.0366 5781	0.0412 0775	0.0458 7316	90
91	0.0321 8508	0.0365 9919	0.0411 5995	0.0458 3486	91
92	0.0321 1694	0.0365 4273	0.0411 1410	0.0457 9827	92
93	0.0320 5107	0.0364 8834	0.0410 7010	0.0457 6331	93
94	0.0319 8737	0.0364 3594	0.0410 2789	0.0457 2991	94
95	0.0319 2577	0.0363 8546	0.0409 8738	0.0456 9799	95
96	0.0318 6619	0.0363 3682	0.0409 4850	0.0456 6749	96
97	0.0318 0856	0.0362 8995	0.0409 1119	0.0456 3834	97
98	0.0317 5281	0.0362 4478	0.0408 7538	0.0456 1048	98
99	0.0316 9886	0.0362 0124	0.0408 4100	0.0455 8385	99
100	0.0316 4667	0.0361 5927	0.0408 0800	0.0455 5839	100

TABLE VII.—Periodic Rent of Annuity Whose Present Value is 1

$$\frac{1}{a_{\overline{n}|i}} = \frac{i}{1 - (1+i)^{-n}} \qquad \left[\frac{1}{s_{\overline{n}|i}} = \frac{1}{a_{\overline{n}|i}} - i\right]$$

n	5%	5½%	6%	6½%	n
1	1.0500 0000	1.0550 0000	1.0600 0000	1.0650 0000	1
2	0.5378 0488	0.5416 1800	0.5454 3689	0.5492 6150	2
3	0.3672 0856	0.3706 5407	0.3741 0981	0.3775 7570	3
4	0.2820 1183	0.2852 9449	0.2885 9149	0.2919 0274	4
5	0.2309 7480	0.2341 7644	0.2373 9640	0.2406 3454	5
6	0.1970 1747	0.2001 7895	0.2033 6263	0.2065 6831	6
7	0.1728 1982	0.1759 6442	0.1791 3502	0.1823 3137	7
8	0.1547 2181	0.1578 6401	0.1610 3594	0.1642 3730	8
9	0.1406 9008	0.1438 3946	0.1470 2224	0.1502 3803	9
10	0.1295 0458	0.1326 6777	0.1358 6796	0.1391 0469	10
11	0.1203 8889	0.1235 7065	0.1267 9294	0.1300 5521	11
12	0.1128 2541	0.1160 2923	0.1192 7703	0.1225 6817	12
13	0.1064 5577	0.1096 8426	0.1129 6011	0.1162 8256	13
14	0.1010 2397	0.1042 7912	0.1075 8491	0.1109 4048	14
15	0.0963 4229	0.0996 2560	0.1029 6276	0.1063 5278	15
16	0.0922 6991	0.0955 8254	0.0989 5214	0.1023 7757	16
17	0.0886 9914	0.0920 4797	0.0954 4480	0.0989 0633	17
18	0.0855 4622	0.0889 1992	0.0923 5654	0.0958 5461	18
19	0.0827 4501	0.0861 5006	0.0896 2086	0.0931 5575	19
20	0.0802 4259	0.0836 7933	0.0871 8456	0.0907 5640	20
21	0.0779 9611	0.0814 6478	0.0850 0455	0.0886 1333	21
22	0.0759 7051	0.0794 7123	0.0830 4557	0.0866 9120	22
23	0.0741 3682	0.0776 6965	0.0812 7848	0.0849 6078	23
24	0.0724 7090	0.0760 3580	0.0796 7900	0.0833 9770	24
25	0.0709 5246	0.0745 4935	0.0782 2672	0.0819 8148	25
26	0.0695 6432	0.0731 9307	0.0769 0435	0.0806 9480	26
27	0.0682 9186	0.0719 5228	0.0756 9717	0.0795 2288	27
28	0.0671 2253	0.0708 1440	0.0745 9255	0.0784 5305	28
29	0.0660 4551	0.0697 6857	0.0735 7961	0.0774 7440	29
30	0.0650 5144	0.0688 0539	0.0726 4891	0.0765 7744	30
31	0.0641 3212	0.0679 1665	0.0717 9222	0.0757 5393	31
32	0.0632 8042	0.0670 9519	0.0710 0234	0.0749 9665	32
33	0.0624 9004	0.0663 3469	0.0702 7293	0.0742 9924	33
34	0.0617 5545	0.0656 2958	0.0695 9843	0.0736 5610	34
35	0.0610 7171	0.0649 7493	0.0689 7386	0.0730 6226	35
36	0.0604 3446	0.0643 6635	0.0683 9483	0.0725 1332	36
37	0.0598 3049	0.0637 9993	0.0678 5743	0.0720 0534	37
38	0.0592 8423	0.0632 7217	0.0673 5812	0.0715 3480	38
39	0.0587 6462	0.0627 7991	0.0668 9377	0.0710 9854	39
40	0.0582 7816	0.0623 2034	0.0664 6154	0.0706 9373	40
41	0.0578 2229	0.0618 9090	0.0660 5886	0.0703 1779	41
42	0.0573 9471	0.0614 8927	0.0656 8342	0.0699 6842	42
43	0.0569 9333	0.0611 1337	0.0653 3312	0.0696 4352	43
44	0.0566 1625	0.0607 6128	0.0650 0606	0.0693 4119	44
45	0.0562 6173	0.0604 3127	0.0647 0050	0.0690 5968	45
46	0.0559 2820	0.0601 2175	0.0644 1485	0.0687 9743	46
47	0.0556 1421	0.0598 3129	0.0641 4768	0.0685 5300	47
48	0.0553 1843	0.0595 5854	0.0638 9766	0.0683 2506	48
49	0.0550 3965	0.0593 0230	0.0636 6356	0.0681 1240	49
50	0.0547 7674	0.0590 6145	0.0634 4429	0.0679 1393	50

TABLE VII.—Periodic Rent of Annuity Whose Present Value is 1

$$\frac{1}{a_{\overline{n}|i}} = \frac{i}{1 - (1+i)^{-n}} \qquad \left[\frac{1}{s_{\overline{n}|i}} = \frac{1}{a_{\overline{n}|i}} - i\right]$$

n	5%	5½%	6%	6½%	n
51	0.0545 2867	0.0588 3495	0.0632 3880	0.0677 2861	51
52	0.0542 9450	0.0586 2186	0.0630 4617	0.0675 5553	52
53	0.0540 7334	0.0584 2130	0.0628 6551	0.0673 9382	53
54	0.0538 6438	0.0582 3245	0.0626 9602	0.0672 4267	54
55	0.0536 6686	0.0580 5458	0.0625 3696	0.0671 0137	55
56	0.0534 8010	0.0578 8698	0.0623 8765	0.0669 6923	56
57	0.0533 0343	0.0577 2900	0.0622 4744	0.0668 4563	57
58	0.0531 3626	0.0575 8006	0.0621 1574	0.0667 2999	58
59	0.0529 7802	0.0574 3959	0.0619 9200	0.0666 2177	59
60	0.0528 2818	0.0573 0707	0.0618 7572	0.0665 2047	60
61	0.0526 8627	0.0571 8202	0.0617 6642	0.0664 2564	61
62	0.0525 5183	0.0570 6400	0.0616 6366	0.0663 3684	62
63	0.0524 2442	0.0569 5258	0.0615 6704	0.0662 5367	63
64	0.0523 0365	0.0568 4737	0.0614 7615	0.0661 7577	64
65	0.0521 8915	0.0567 4800	0.0613 9066	0.0661 0280	65
66	0.0520 8057	0.0566 5413	0.0613 1022	0.0660 3442	66
67	0.0519 7757	0.0565 6544	0.0612 3454	0.0659 7034	67
68	0.0518 7986	0.0564 8163	0.0611 6330	0.0659 1029	68
69	0.0517 8715	0.0564 0242	0.0610 9625	0.0658 5400	69
70	0.0516 9915	0.0563 2754	0.0610 3313	0.0658 0124	70
71	0.0516 1563	0.0562 5675	0.0609 7370	0.0657 5177	71
72	0.0515 3633	0.0561 8982	0.0609 1774	0.0657 0539	72
73	0.0514 6103	0.0561 2652	0.0608 6505	0.0656 6190	73
74	0.0513 8953	0.0560 6665	0.0608 1542	0.0656 2112	74
75	0.0513 2161	0.0560 1002	0.0607 6867	0.0655 8287	75
76	0.0512 5709	0.0559 5645	0.0607 2463	0.0655 4699	76
77	0.0511 9580	0.0559 0577	0.0606 8315	0.0655 1335	77
78	0.0511 3756	0.0558 5781	0.0606 4407	0.0654 8178	78
79	0.0510 8222	0.0558 1243	0.0606 0724	0.0654 5217	79
80	0.0510 2962	0.0557 6948	0.0605 7254	0.0654 2440	80
81	0.0509 7963	0.0557 2884	0.0605 3984	0.0653 9834	81
82	0.0509 3211	0.0556 9036	0.0605 0903	0.0653 7388	82
83	0.0508 8694	0.0556 5395	0.0604 7998	0.0653 5094	83
84	0.0508 4399	0.0556 1947	0.0604 5261	0.0653 2941	84
85	0.0508 0316	0.0555 8683	0.0604 2681	0.0653 0921	85
86	0.0507 6433	0.0555 5593	0.0604 0249	0.0652 9026	86
87	0.0507 2740	0.0555 2667	0.0603 7956	0.0652 7247	87
88	0.0506 9228	0.0554 9896	0.0603 5795	0.0652 5577	88
89	0.0506 5888	0.0554 7273	0.0603 3757	0.0652 4010	89
90	0.0506 2711	0.0554 4788	0.0603 1836	0.0652 2540	90
91	0.0505 9689	0.0554 2435	0.0603 0025	0.0652 1160	91
92	0.0505 6815	0.0554 0207	0.0602 8318	0.0651 9864	92
93	0.0505 4080	0.0553 8096	0.0602 6708	0.0651 8649	93
94	0.0505 1478	0.0553 6097	0.0602 5190	0.0651 7507	94
95	0.0504 9003	0.0553 4204	0.0602 3758	0.0651 6436	95
96	0.0504 6648	0.0553 2410	0.0602 2408	0.0651 5431	96
97	0.0504 4407	0.0553 0711	0.0602 1135	0.0651 4487	97
98	0.0504 2274	0.0552 9101	0.0601 9935	0.0651 3601	98
99	0.0504 0245	0.0552 7577	0.0601 8803	0.0651 2769	99
100	0.0503 8314	0.0552 6132	0.0601 7736	0.0651 1988	100

TABLE VII.—Periodic Rent of Annuity Whose Present Value is 1

$$\frac{1}{a_{\overline{n}|i}} = \frac{i}{1-(1+i)^{-n}} \qquad \left[\frac{1}{s_{\overline{n}|i}} = \frac{1}{a_{\overline{n}|i}} - i\right]$$

n	7%	7½%	8%	8½%	n
1	1.0700 0000	1.0750 0000	1.0800 0000	1.0850 0000	1
2	0.5530 9179	0.5569 2771	0.5607 6923	0.5646 1631	2
3	0.3810 5166	0.3845 3763	0.3880 3351	0.3915 3925	3
4	0.2952 2812	0.2985 6751	0.3019 2080	0.3052 8789	4
5	0.2438 9069	0.2471 6472	0.2504 5645	0.2537 6575	5
6	0.2097 9580	0.2130 4489	0.2163 1539	0.2196 0708	6
7	0.1855 5322	0.1888 0032	0.1920 7240	0.1953 6922	7
8	0.1674 6776	0.1707 2702	0.1740 1476	0.1773 3065	8
9	0.1534 8647	0.1567 6716	0.1600 7971	0.1634 2372	9
10	0.1423 7750	0.1456 8593	0.1490 2949	0.1524 0771	10
11	0.1333 5690	0.1366 9747	0.1400 7634	0.1434 9293	11
12	0.1259 0199	0.1292 7783	0.1326 9502	0.1361 5286	12
13	0.1196 5085	0.1230 6420	0.1265 2181	0.1300 2287	13
14	0.1143 4494	0.1177 9737	0.1212 9685	0.1248 4244	14
15	0.1097 9462	0.1132 8724	0.1168 2954	0.1204 2046	15
16	0.1058 5765	0.1093 9116	0.1129 7687	0.1166 1354	16
17	0.1024 2519	0.1060 0003	0.1096 2943	0.1133 1198	17
18	0.0994 1260	0.1030 2896	0.1067 0210	0.1104 3041	18
19	0.0967 5301	0.1004 1090	0.1041 2763	0.1079 0140	19
20	0.0943 9293	0.0980 9219	0.1018 5221	0.1056 7097	20
21	0.0922 8900	0.0960 2937	0.0998 3225	0.1036 9541	21
22	0.0904 0577	0.0941 8687	0.0980 3207	0.1019 3892	22
23	0.0887 1393	0.0925 3528	0.0964 2217	0.1003 7193	23
24	0.0871 8902	0.0910 5008	0.0949 7796	0.0989 6975	24
25	0.0858 1052	0.0897 1067	0.0936 7878	0.0977 1168	25
26	0.0845 6103	0.0884 9961	0.0925 0713	0.0965 8016	26
27	0.0834 2573	0.0874 0204	0.0914 4809	0.0955 6025	27
28	0.0823 9193	0.0864 0520	0.0904 8891	0.0946 3914	28
29	0.0814 4865	0.0854 9811	0.0896 1854	0.0938 0577	29
30	0.0805 8640	0.0846 7124	0.0888 2743	0.0930 5058	30
31	0.0797 9691	0.0839 1628	0.0881 0728	0.0923 6524	31
32	0.0790 7292	0.0832 2599	0.0874 5081	0.0917 4247	32
33	0.0784 0807	0.0825 9397	0.0868 5163	0.0911 7588	33
34	0.0777 9674	0.0820 1461	0.0863 0411	0.0906 5984	34
35	0.0772 3396	0.0814 8291	0.0858 0326	0.0901 8937	35
36	0.0767 1531	0.0809 9447	0.0853 4467	0.0897 6006	36
37	0.0762 3685	0.0805 4533	0.0849 2440	0.0893 6799	37
38	0.0757 9505	0.0801 3197	0.0845 3894	0.0890 0966	38
39	0.0753 8647	0.0797 5124	0.0841 8513	0.0886 8193	39
40	0.0750 0914	0.0794 0031	0.0838 6016	0.0883 8201	40
41	0.0746 5962	0.0790 7663	0.0835 6149	0.0881 0737	41
42	0.0743 3591	0.0787 7789	0.0832 8684	0.0878 5576	42
43	0.0740 3590	0.0785 0201	0.0830 3414	0.0876 2512	43
44	0.0737 5769	0.0782 4710	0.0828 0152	0 0874 1363	44
45	0.0734 9957	0.0780 1146	0.0825 8728	0.0872 1961	45
46	0.0732 5996	0.0777 9353	0.0823 8991	0.0870 4154	46
47	0.0730 3744	0.0775 9190	0.0822 0799	0.0868 7807	47
48	0.0728 3070	0.0774 0527	0.0820 4027	0.0867 2795	48
49	0.0726 3853	0.0772 3247	0.0818 8557	0.0865 9005	49
50	0.0724 5985	0.0770 7241	0.0817 4286	0.0864 6334	50

TABLE VII.—Periodic Rent of Annuity Whose Present Value is 1

$$\frac{1}{a_{\overline{n}|i}} = \frac{i}{1 - (1+i)^{-n}} \qquad \left[\frac{1}{s_{\overline{n}|i}} = \frac{1}{a_{\overline{n}|i}} - i \right]$$

n	7%	7½%	8%	8½%	n
51	0.0722 9365	0.0769 2411	0.0816 1116	0.0863 4688	51
52	0.0721 3901	0.0767 8668	0.0814 8959	0.0862 3983	52
53	0.0719 9509	0.0766 5927	0.0813 7735	0.0861 4139	53
54	0.0718 6110	0.0765 4112	0.0812 7370	0.0860 5087	54
55	0.0717 3633	0.0764 3155	0.0811 7796.	0.0859 6761	55
56	0.0716 2011	0.0763 2991	0.0810 8952	0.0858 9101	56
57	0.0715 1183	0.0762 3559	0.0810 0780	0.0858 2053	57
58	0.0714 1093	0.0761 4807	0.0809 3227	0.0857 5568	58
59	0.0713 1689	0.0760 6683	0.0808 6247	0.0856 9599	59
60	0.0712 2923	0.0759 9142	0.0807 9795	0.0856 4106	60
61	0.0711 4749	0.0759 2140	0.0807 3830	0.0855 9049	61
62	0.0710 7127	0.0758 5638	0.0806 8314	0.0855 4393	62
63	0.0710 0019	0.0757 9600	0.0806 3214	0.0855 0107	63
64	0.0709 3388	0.0757 3992	0.0805 8497	0.0854 6160	64
65	0.0708 7203	0.0756 8782	0.0805 4135	0.0854 2526	65
66	0.0708 1431	0.0756 3942	0.0805 0100	0.0853 9179	66
67	0.0707 6046	0.0755 9446	0.0804 6367	0.0853 6097	67
68	0.0707 1021	0.0755 5268	0.0804 2914	0.0853 3258	68
69	0.0706 6331	0.0755 1386	0.0803 9719	0.0853 0643	69
70	0.0706 1953	0.0754 7778	0.0803 6764	0.0852 8234	70
71	0.0705 7866	0.0754 4425	0.0803 4029	0.0852 6016	71
72	0.0705 4051	0.0754 1308	0.0803 1498	0.0852 3972	72
73	0.0705 0490	0.0753 8412	0.0802 9157	0.0852 2089	73
74	0.0704 7164	0.0753 5719	0.0802 6989	0.0852 0354	74
75	0.0704 4060	0.0753 3216	0.0802 4984	0.0851 8756	75
76	0.0704 1160	0.0753 0889	0.0802 3128	0.0851 7284	76
77	0.0703 8453	0.0752 8726	0.0802 1410	0.0851 5927	77
78	0.0703 5924	0.0752 6714	0.0801 9820	0.0851 4677	78
79	0.0703 3563	0.0752 4844	0.0801 8349	0.0851 3526	79
80	0.0703 1357	0.0752 3106	0.0801 6987	0.0851 2465	80
81	0.0702 9297	0.0752 1489	0.0801 5726	0.0851 1487	81
82	0.0702 7373	0.0751 9986	0.0801 4559	0.0851 0586	82
83	0.0702 5576	0.0751 8588	0.0801 3479	0.0850 9756	83
84	0.0702 3897	0.0751 7288	0.0801 2479	0.0850 8990	84
85	0.0702 2329	0.0751 6079	0.0801 1553	0.0850 8285	85
86	0.0702 0863	0.0751 4955	0.0801 0696	0.0850 7636	86
87	0.0701 9495	0.0751 3910	0.0800 9903	0.0850 7037	87
88	0.0701 8216	0.0751 2938	0.0800 9168	0.0850 6485	88
89	0.0701 7021	0.0751 2034	0.0800 8489	0.0850 5977	89
90	0.0701 5905	0.0751 1193	0.0800 7859	0.0850 5508	90
91	0.0701 4863	0.0751 0411	0.0800 7277	0.0850 5077	91
92	0.0701 3888	0.0750 9684	0.0800 6737	0.0850 4679	92
93	0.0701 2978	0.0750 9007	0.0800 6238	0.0850 4312	93
94	0.0701 2128	0.0750 8378	0.0800 5775	0.0850 3974	94
95	0.0701 1333	0.0750 7793	0.0800 5347	0.0850 3663	95
96	0.0701 0590	0.0750 7249	0.0800 4951	0.0850 3375	96
97	0.0700 9897	0.0750 6743	0.0800 4584	0.0850 3111	97
98	0.0700 9248	0.0750 6272	0.0800 4244	0.0850 2867	98
99	0.0700 8643	0.0750 5834	0.0800 3930	0.0850 2642	99
100	0.0700 8076	0.0750 5427	0.0800 3638	0.0850 2435	100

TABLE VIII.—Values of $(1+i)^{1/p}$

p	$\frac{1}{4}\%$	$\frac{7}{24}\%$	$\frac{1}{3}\%$	$\frac{5}{12}\%$	$\frac{1}{2}\%$
2	1.0012 4922	1.0014 5727	1.0016 6528	1.0020 8117	1.0024 9688
3	1.0008 3264	1.0009 7128	1.0011 0988	1.0013 8696	1.0016 6390
4	1.0006 2441	1.0007 2837	1.0008 3229	1.0010 4004	1.0012 4766
6	1.0004 1623	1.0004 8552	1.0005 5479	1.0006 9324	1.0008 3160
12	1.0002 0809	1.0002 4273	1.0002 7735	1.0003 4656	1.0004 1571

p	$\frac{7}{12}\%$	$\frac{2}{3}\%$	$\frac{3}{4}\%$	$\frac{7}{8}\%$	1%
2	1.0029 1243	1.0033 2780	1.0037 4299	1.0043 6547	1.0049 8756
3	1.0019 4068	1.0022 1730	1.0024 9378	1.0029 0820	1.0033 2228
4	1.0014 5515	1.0016 6252	1.0018 6975	1.0021 8036	1.0024 9068
6	1.0009 6987	1.0011 0804	1.0012 4611	1.0014 5304	1.0016 5977
12	1.0004 8482	1.0005 5387	1.0006 2286	1.0007 2626	1.0008 2954

p	$1\frac{1}{8}\%$	$1\frac{1}{4}\%$	$1\frac{3}{8}\%$	$1\frac{1}{2}\%$	$1\frac{3}{4}\%$
2	1.0056 0927	1.0062 3059	1.0068 5153	1.0074 7208	1.0087 1205
3	1.0037 3602	1.0041 4943	1.0045 6249	1.0049 7521	1.0057 9963
4	1.0028 0081	1.0031 1046	1.0034 1992	1.0037 2909	1.0043 4658
6	1.0018 6627	1.0020 7257	1.0022 7865	1.0024 8452	1.0028 9562
12	1.0009 3270	1.0010 3575	1.0011 3868	1.0012 4149	1.0014 4677

p	2%	$2\frac{1}{4}\%$	$2\frac{1}{2}\%$	$2\frac{3}{4}\%$	3%
2	1.0099 5049	1.0111 8742	1.0124 2284	1.0136 5675	1.0148 8916
3	1.0066 2271	1.0074 4444	1.0082 6484	1.0090 8390	1.0099 0163
4	1.0049 6293	1.0055 7815	1.0061 9225	1.0068 0522	1.0074 1707
6	1.0033 0589	1.0037 1532	1.0041 2392	1.0045 3168	1.0049 3862
12	1.0016 5158	1.0018 5594	1.0020 5984	1.0022 6328	1.0024 6627

p	$3\frac{1}{2}\%$	4%	$4\frac{1}{2}\%$	5%	$5\frac{1}{2}\%$
2	1.0173 4950	1.0198 0390	1.0222 5242	1.0246 9508	1.0271 3193
3	1.0115 3314	1.0131 5941	1.0147 8046	1.0163 9636	1.0180 0713
4	1.0086 3745	1.0098 5341	1.0110 6499	1.0122 7224	1.0134 7518
6	1.0057 5004	1.0065 5820	1.0073 6312	1.0081 6485	1.0089 6340
12	1.0028 7090	1.0032 7374	1.0036 7481	1.0040 7412	1.0044 7170

p	6%	$6\frac{1}{2}\%$	7%	$7\frac{1}{2}\%$	8%
2	1.0295 6302	1.0319 8837	1.0344 0804	1.0368 2207	1.0392 3048
3	1.0196 1282	1.0212 1347	1.0228 0912	1.0243 9981	1.0259 8557
4	1.0146 7385	1.0158 6828	1.0170 5853	1.0182 4460	1.0194 2655
6	1.0097 5880	1.0105 5107	1.0113 4026	1.0121 2638	1.0129 0946
12	1.0048 6755	1.0052 6169	1.0056 5415	1.0060 4492	1.0064 3403

TABLE IX.—Values of $s_{\frac{1}{p}|i} = \dfrac{(1+i)^{1/p} - 1}{i}$

p	$\frac{1}{4}\%$	$2\frac{7}{4}\%$	$\frac{1}{3}\%$	$\frac{5}{12}\%$	$\frac{1}{2}\%$
2	0.4996 8789	0.4996 3595	0.4995 8403	0.4994 8025	0.4993 7656
3	0.3330 5594	0.3330 0978	0.3329 6365	0.3328 7144	0.3327 7932
4	0.2497 6597	0.2497 2703	0.2496 8811	0.2496 1032	0.2495 3261
6	0.1664 9332	0.1664 6448	0.1664 3566	0.1663 7805	0.1663 2050
12	0.0832 3800	0.0832 2214	0.0832 0629	0.0831 7461	0.0831 4297

p	$\frac{7}{12}\%$	$\frac{2}{3}\%$	$\frac{3}{4}\%$	$\frac{7}{8}\%$	1%
2	0.4992 7295	0.4991 6943	0.4990 6600	0.4989 1101	0.4987 5621
3	0.3326 8728	0.3325 9532	0.3325 0346	0.3323 6581	0.3322 2835
4	0.2494 5498	0.2493 7742	0.2492 9994	0.2491 8385	0.2490 6793
6	0.1662 6301	0.1662 0558	0.1661 4821	0.1660 6226	0.1659 7644
12	0.0831 1136	0.0830 7978	0.0830 4824	0.0830 0099	0.0829 5381

p	$1\frac{1}{8}\%$	$1\frac{1}{4}\%$	$1\frac{3}{8}\%$	$1\frac{1}{2}\%$	$1\frac{3}{4}\%$
2	0.4986 0160	0.4984 4719	0.4982 9297	0.4981 3893	0.4978 3143
3	0.3320 9109	0.3319 5401	0.3318 1712	0.3316 8042	0.3314 0758
4	0.2489 5218	0.2488 3660	0.2487 2117	0.2486 0593	0.2483 7592
6	0.1658 8986	0.1658 0518	0.1657 1975	0.1656 3445	0.1654 6423
12	0.0829 0627	0.0828 5968	0.0828 1273	0.0827 6585	0.0826 7231

p	2%	$2\frac{1}{4}\%$	$2\frac{1}{2}\%$	$2\frac{3}{4}\%$	3%
2	0.4975 2469	0.4972 1870	0.4969 1346	0.4966 0897	0.4963 0522
3	0.3311 3548	0.3308 6412	0.3305 9350	0.3303 2362	0.3300 5447
4	0.2481 4658	0.2479 1789	0.2476 8985	0.2474 6247	0.2472 3573
6	0.1652 9452	0.1651 2531	0.1649 5662	0.1647 8843	0.1646 2073
12	0.0825 7907	0.0824 8611	0.0823 9345	0.0823 0108	0.0822 0899

p	$3\frac{1}{2}\%$	4%	$4\frac{1}{2}\%$	5%	$5\frac{1}{2}\%$
2	0.4956 9993	0.4950 9757	0.4944 9811	0.4939 0153	0.4933 0780
3	0.3295 1834	0.3289 8510	0.3284 5470	0.3279 2714	0.3274 0237
4	0.2467 8417	0.2463 3516	0.2458 8868	0.2454 4469	0.2450 0317
6	0.1642 8684	0.1639 5492	0.1636 2496	0.1632 9692	0.1629 7080
12	0.0820 2568	0.0818 4349	0.0816 6243	0.0814 8248	0.0813 0362

p	6%	$6\frac{1}{2}\%$	7%	$7\frac{1}{2}\%$	8%
2	0.4927 1690	0.4921 2880	0.4915 4348	0.4909 6090	0.4903 8106
3	0.3268 8037	0.3263 6113	0.3258 4460	0.3253 3076	0.3248 1960
4	0.2445 6410	0.2441 2746	0.2436 9321	0.2432 6135	0.2428 3184
6	0.1626 4657	0.1623 2422	0.1620 0372	0.1616 8505	0.1613 6821
12	0.0811 2584	0.0809 4914	0.0807 7351	0.0805 9892	0.0804 2538

TABLE X.—Values of $\dfrac{1}{s_{\frac{1}{p}|i}} = \dfrac{i}{(1+i)^{1/p}-1}$ $\left[\dfrac{1}{a_{\frac{1}{p}|i}} = \dfrac{1}{s_{\frac{1}{p}|i}} + i\right]$

p	$\frac{1}{4}\%$	$\frac{7}{24}\%$	$\frac{1}{3}\%$	$\frac{5}{12}\%$	$\frac{1}{2}\%$
2	2.0012 4922	2.0014 5727	2.0016 6528	2.0020 8117	2.0024 9688
3	3.0024 9861	3.0029 1478	3.0033 3087	3.0041 6282	3.0049 9446
4	4.0037 4805	4.0043 7235	4.0049 9654	4.0062 4459	4.0074 9221
6	6.0062 4696	6.0072 8756	6.0083 2795	6.0104 0824	6.0124 8788
12	12.0137 4384	12.0160 3328	12.0183 2234	12.0228 9946	12.0274 7526

p	$\frac{7}{12}\%$	$\frac{2}{3}\%$	$\frac{3}{4}\%$	$\frac{7}{8}\%$	1%
2	2.0029 1243	2.0033 2780	2.0037 4300	2.0043 6547	2.0049 8756
3	3.0058 2579	3.0066 5682	3.0074 8755	3.0087 3306	3.0099 7789
4	4.0087 3940	4.0099 8616	4.0112 3249	4.0131 0118	4.0149 6891
6	6.0145 6684	6.0166 4513	6.0187 2276	6.0218 3795	6.0249 5163
12	12.0320 4968	12.0366 2270	12.0411 9435	12.0480 4930	12.0549 0119

p	$1\frac{1}{8}\%$	$1\frac{1}{4}\%$	$1\frac{3}{8}\%$	$1\frac{1}{2}\%$	$1\frac{3}{4}\%$
2	2.0056 0927	2.0062 3059	2.0068 5153	2.0074 7208	2.0087 1205
3	3.0112 2203	3.0124 6549	3.0137 0827	3.0149 5037	3.0174 3253
4	4.0168 3567	4.0187 0147	4.0205 6648	4.0224 3021	4.0261 5513
6	6.0280 9600	6.0311 7452	6.0342 8372	6.0373 9144	6.0436 0242
12	12.0618 1437	12.0685 9580	12.0754 3856	12.0822 7820	12.0959 4852

p	2%	$2\frac{1}{4}\%$	$2\frac{1}{2}\%$	$2\frac{3}{4}\%$	3%
2	2.0099 5049	2.0111 8742	2.0124 2284	2.0136 5675	2.0148 8916
3	3.0199 1199	3.0223 8875	3.0248 6282	3.0273 3422	3.0298 0294
4	4.0298 7623	4.0335 9356	4.0373 0709	4.0410 1686	4.0447 2289
6	6.0498 0747	6.0560 0662	6.0621 9991	6.0683 8735	6.0745 6894
12	12.1096 0670	12.1232 5281	12.1368 8697	12.1505 0916	12.1641 1941

p	$3\frac{1}{2}\%$	4%	$4\frac{1}{2}\%$	5%	$5\frac{1}{2}\%$
2	2.0173 4950	2.0198 0390	2.0222 5241	2.0246 9508	2.0271 3193
3	3.0347 3244	3.0396 5138	3.0445 5985	3.0494 5791	3.0543 4565
4	4.0521 2375	4.0595 0975	4.0668 8103	4.0742 3769	4.0815 7982
6	6.0869 1473	6.0992 3739	6.1115 3716	6.1238 1418	6.1360 6860
12	12.1913 0435	12.2184 4211	12.2455 3306	12.2725 7753	12.2995 7585

p	6%	$6\frac{1}{2}\%$	7%	$7\frac{1}{2}\%$	8%
2	2.0295 6301	2.0319 8837	2.0344 0804	2.0368 2207	2.0392 3048
3	3.0592 2313	3.0640 9043	3.0689 4762	3.0737 9477	3.0786 3195
4	4.0889 0752	4.0962 2091	4.1035 2009	4.1108 0514	4.1180 7618
6	6.1483 0059	6.1605 1031	6.1726 9791	6.1848 6355	6.1970 0737
12	12.3265 2834	12.3534 3534	12.3802 9716	12.4071 1409	12.4338 8648

TABLE XI.—Values of $a_{\frac{1}{p}|i} = \dfrac{1 - (1+i)^{-1/p}}{i}$

p	$\frac{1}{4}\%$	$\frac{7}{24}\%$	$\frac{1}{3}\%$	$\frac{5}{12}\%$	$\frac{1}{2}\%$
2	0.4990 6445	0.4989 0890	0.4987 5346	0.4984 4291	0.4981 3278
3	0.3327 7886	0.3326 8665	0.3325 9451	0.3324 1040	0.3322 2652
4	0.2496 1011	0.2495 4527	0.2494 8047	0.2493 5099	0.2492 2167
6	0.1664 2405	0.1663 8370	0.1663 4337	0.1662 6279	0.1661 8230
12	0.0832 2068	0.0832 0194	0.0831 8322	0.0831 4580	0.0831 0842

p	$\frac{7}{12}\%$	$\frac{2}{3}\%$	$\frac{3}{4}\%$	$\frac{7}{8}\%$	1%
2	0.4978 2308	0.4975 1381	0.4972 0496	0.4967 4249	0.4962 8098
3	0.3320 4289	0.3318 5949	0.3316 7633	0.3314 0203	0.3311 2825
4	0.2490 9251	0.2489 6351	0.2488 3468	0.2486 4172	0.2484 4912
6	0.1661 0192	0.1660 2162	0.1659 4143	0.1658 2131	0.1657 0141
12	0.0830 7108	0.0830 3379	0.0829 9654	0.0829 4075	0.0828 8506

p	$1\frac{1}{8}\%$	$1\frac{1}{4}\%$	$1\frac{3}{8}\%$	$1\frac{1}{2}\%$	$1\frac{3}{4}\%$
2	0.4958 2042	0.4953 6080	0.4949 0213	0.4944 4440	0.4935 3176
3	0.3308 5501	0.3305 8228	0.3303 1009	0.3300 3841	0.3294 9662
4	0.2482 5688	0.2480 6500	0.2478 7346	0.2476 8230	0.2473 0101
6	0.1655 8084	0.1654 6225	0.1653 4299	0.1652 2395	0.1649 8649
12	0.0828 2901	0.0827 7395	0.0827 1854	0.0826 6322	0.0825 5287

p	2%	$2\frac{1}{4}\%$	$2\frac{1}{2}\%$	$2\frac{3}{4}\%$	3%
2	0.4926 2285	0.4917 1765	0.4908 1613	0.4899 1828	0.4890 2406
3	0.3289 5689	0.3284 1922	0.3278 8360	0.3273 5001	0.3268 1843
4	0.2469 2113	0.2465 4264	0.2461 6554	0.2457 8981	0.2454 1546
6	0.1647 4987	0.1645 1409	0.1642 7915	0.1640 4503	0.1638 1173
12	0.0824 4290	0.0823 3331	0.0822 2408	0.0821 1523	0.0820 0674

p	$3\frac{1}{2}\%$	4%	$4\frac{1}{2}\%$	5%	$5\frac{1}{2}\%$
2	0.4872 4645	0.4854 8311	0.4837 3386	0.4819 9854	0.4802 7696
3	0.3257 6129	0.3247 1208	0.3236 7070	0.3226 3706	0.3216 1108
4	0.2446 7084	0.2439 3161	0.2431 9770	0.2424 6905	0.2417 4561
6	0.1633 4759	0.1628 8668	0.1624 2897	0.1619 7442	0.1615 2300
12	0.0817 9086	0.0815 7643	0.0813 6344	0.0811 5185	0.0809 4167

p	6%	$6\frac{1}{2}\%$	7%	$7\frac{1}{2}\%$	8%
2	0.4785 6896	0.4768 7437	0.4751 9301	0.4735 2474	0.4718 6939
3	0.3205 9265	0.3195 8169	0.3185 7811	0.3175 8183	0.3165 9276
4	0.2410 2731	0.2403 1409	0.2396 0589	0.2389 0266	0.2382 0435
6	0.1610 7468	0.1606 2940	0.1601 8715	0.1597 4789	0.1593 1159
12	0.0807 3287	0.0805 2544	0.0803 1937	0.0801 1463	0.0799 1123

TABLE XII.—American Experience Table of Mortality

Age x	Number living l_x	Number of deaths d_x	Yearly probability of dying q_x	Yearly probability of living p_x	Age x	Number living l_x	Number of deaths d_x	Yearly probability of dying q_x	Yearly probability of living p_x
10	100,000	749	0.007 490	0.992 510	53	66,797	1,091	0.016 333	0.983 667
11	99,251	746	0.007 516	0.992 484	54	65,706	1,143	0.017 396	0.982 604
12	98,505	743	0.007 543	0.992 457	55	64,563	1,199	0.018 571	0.981 429
13	97,762	740	0.007 569	0.992 431	56	63,364	1,260	0.019 885	0.980 115
14	97,022	737	0.007 596	0.992 404	57	62,104	1,325	0.021 335	0.978 665
15	96,285	735	0.007 634	0.992 366	58	60,779	1,394	0.022 936	0.977 064
16	95,550	732	0.007 661	0.992 339	59	59,385	1,468	0.024 720	0.975 280
17	94,818	729	0.007 688	0.992 312	60	57,917	1,546	0.026 693	0.973 307
18	94,089	727	0.007 727	0.992 273	61	56,371	1,628	0.028 880	0.971 120
19	93,362	725	0.007 765	0.992 235	62	54,743	1,713	0.031 292	0,968 708
20	92,637	723	0.007 805	0.992 195	63	53,030	1,800	0.033 943	0.966 057
21	91,914	722	0.007 855	0.992 145	64	51,230	1,889	0.036 873	0.963 127
22	91,192	721	0.007 906	0.992 094	65	49,341	1,980	0.040 129	0.959 871
23	90,471	720	0.007 958	0.992 042	66	47,361	2,070	0.043 707	0.956 293
24	89,751	719	0.008 011	0.991 989	67	45,291	2,158	0.047 647	0.952 353
25	89,032	718	0.008 065	0.991 935	68	43,133	2,243	0.052 002	0.947 998
26	88,314	718	0.008 130	0.991 870	69	40,890	2,321	0.056 762	0.943 238
27	87,596	718	0.008 197	0.991 803	70	38,569	2,391	0.061 993	0.938 007
28	86,878	718	0.008 264	0.991 736	71	36,178	2,448	0.067 665	0.932 335
29	86,160	719	0.008 345	0.991 655	72	33,730	2,487	0.073 733	0.926 267
30	85,441	720	0.008 427	0.991 573	73	31,243	2,505	0.080 178	0.919 822
31	84,721	721	0.008 510	0.991 490	74	28,738	2,501	0.087 028	0.912 972
32	84,000	723	0.008 607	0.991 393	75	26,237	2,476	0.094 371	0.905 629
33	83,277	726	0.008 718	0.991 282	76	23,761	2,431	0.102 311	0.897 689
34	82,551	729	0.008 831	0.991 169	77	21,330	2,369	0.111 064	0.888 936
35	81,822	732	0.008 946	0.991 054	78	18,961	2,291	0.120 827	0.879 173
36	81,090	737	0.009 089	0.990 911	79	16,670	2,196	0.131 734	0.868 266
37	80,353	742	0.009 234	0.990 766	80	14,474	2,091	0.144 466	0.855 534
38	79,611	749	0.009 408	0.990 592	81	12,383	1,964	0.158 605	0.841 395
39	78,862	756	0.009 586	0.990 414	82	10,419	1,816	0.174 297	0.825 703
40	78,106	765	0.009 794	0.990 206	83	8,603	1,648	0.191 561	0.808 439
41	77,341	774	0.010 008	0.989 992	84	6,955	1,470	0.211 359	0.788 641
42	76,567	785	0.010 252	0.989 748	85	5,485	1,292	0.235 552	0.764 448
43	75,782	797	0.010 517	0.989 483	86	4,193	1,114	0.265 681	0.734 319
44	74,985	812	0.010 829	0.989 171	87	3,079	933	0.303 020	0.696 980
45	74,173	828	0.011 163	0.988 837	88	2,146	744	0.346 692	0.653 308
46	73,345	848	0.011 562	0.988 438	89	1,402	555	0.395 863	0.604 137
47	72,497	870	0.012 000	0.988 000	90	847	385	0.454 545	0.545 455
48	71,627	896	0.012 509	0.987 491	91	462	246	0.532 466	0.467 534
49	70,731	927	0.013 106	0.986 894	92	216	137	0.634 259	0.365 741
50	69,804	962	0.013 781	0.986 219	93	79	58	0.734 177	0.265 823
51	68,842	1,001	0.014 541	0.985 459	94	21	18	0.857 143	0.142 857
52	67,841	1,044	0.015 389	0.984 611	95	3	3	1.000 000	0.000 000

TABLE XIII.—Commutation Columns, American Experience, $3\frac{1}{2}\%$

Age x	D_x	N_x	C_x	M_x	$\ddot{a}_x = \dfrac{N_x}{D_x} = 1 + a_x$	$A_x = \dfrac{M_x}{D_x}$
10	70891.9	1575 535.	513.02	17612.9	22.2245	0.24845
11	67981.5	1504 643.	493.69	17099.9	22.1331	0.25154
12	65189.0	1436 662.	475.08	16606.2	22.0384	0.25474
13	62509.4	1371 473.	457.16	16131.1	21.9403	0.25806
14	59938.4	1308 963.	439.91	15674.0	21.8385	0.26151
15	57471.6	1249 025.	423.88	15234.1	21.7329	0.26507
16	55104.2	1191 553.	407.87	14810.2	21.6236	0.26877
17	52832.9	1136 449.	392.47	14402.3	21.5102	0.27260
18	50653.9	1083 616.	378.15	14009.8	21.3926	0.27658
19	48562.8	1032 962.	364.36	13631.7	21.2707	0.28070
20	46556.2	984 400.	351.07	13267.3	21.1443	0.28497
21	44630.8	937 843.	338.73	12916.3	21.0134	0.28940
22	42782.8	893 213.	326.82	12577.5	20.8779	0.29399
23	41009.2	850 430.	315.33	12250.7	20.7375	0.29873
24	39307.1	809 421.	304.24	11935.4	20.5922	0.30364
25	37673.6	770 114.	293.55	11631.1	20.4417	0.30873
26	36106.1	732 440.	283.62	11337.6	20.2858	0.31401
27	34601.5	696 334.	274.03	11054.0	20.1244	0.31947
28	33157.4	661 732.	264.76	10779.9	19.9573	0.32512
29	31771.3	628 575.	256.16	10515.2	19.7843	0.33097
30	30440.8	596 804.	247.85	10259.0	19.6054	0.33702
31	29163.5	566 363.	239.797	10011.2	19.4202	0.34328
32	27937.5	537 199.	232.331	9771.37	19.2286	0.34976
33	26760.5	509 262.	225.406	9539.04	19.0304	0.35646
34	25630.1	482 501.	218.683	9313.64	18.8256	0.36339
35	24544.7	456 871.	212.158	9094.96	18.6138	0.37055
36	23502.5	432 327.	206.383	8882.80	18.3949	0.37795
37	22501.4	408 824.	200.757	8676.41	18.1688	0.38560
38	21539.7	386 323.	195.798	8475.66	17.9354	0.39349
39	20615.5	364 783.	190.945	8279.86	17.6946	0.40163
40	19727.4	344 167.	186.684	8088.91	17.4461	0.41003
41	18873.6	324 440.	182.493	7902.23	17.1901	0.41869
42	18052.9	305 566.	178.828	7719.74	16.9262	0.42762
43	17263.6	287 513.	175.422	7540.91	16.6543	0.43681
44	16504.4	270 250.	172.679	7365.49	16.3744	0.44628
45	15773.6	253 745.	170.127	7192.81	16.0867	0.45600
46	15070.0	237 972.	168.345	7022.68	15.7911	0.46600
47	14392.1	222 902.	166.872	6854.34	15.4878	0.47626
48	13738.5	208 510.	166.047	6687.47	15.1770	0.48677
49	13107.9	194 771.	165.982	6521.42	14.8591	0.49752
50	12498.6	181 663.	166.424	6355.44	14.5346	0.50849
51	11909.6	169 165.	167.315	6189.01	14.2041	0.51967
52	11339.5	157 255.	168.602	6021.70	13.8679	0.53104

TABLE XIII.—Commutation Columns, American Experience, $3\frac{1}{2}\%$

Age x	D_x	N_x	C_x	M_x	$\ddot{a}_x = \dfrac{N_x}{D_x}$ $= 1 + a_x$	$A_x = \dfrac{M_x}{D_x}$
53	10787.4	145916.	170.234	5853.09	13.5264	0.54258
54	10252.4	135128.	172.317	5682.86	13.1801	0.55430
55	9733.40	124876.	174.646	5510.54	12.8296	0.56615
56	9229.60	115142.	177.325	5335.90	12.4753	0.57813
57	8740.17	105913.	180.167	5158.57	12.1179	0.59022
58	8264.44	97172.6	183.140	4978.41	11.7579	0.60239
59	7801.82	88908.2	186.340	4795.27	11.3958	0.61463
60	7351.65	81106.4	189.604	4608.93	11.0324	0.62692
61	6913.44	73754.7	192.909	4419.32	10.6683	0.63924
62	6486.75	66841.3	196.117	4226.41	10.3043	0.65155
63	6071.27	60354.5	199.109	4030.30	9.9410	0.66383
64	5666.85	54283.3	201.887	3831.19	9.5791	0.67607
65	5273.33	48616.4	204.457	3629.30	9.2193	0.68824
66	4890.55	43343.1	206.522	3424.84	8.8626	0.70030
67	4518.65	38452.5	208.021	3218.32	8.5097	0.71223
68	4157.82	33933.9	208.903	3010.30	8.1615	0.72401
69	3808.32	29776.1	208.858	2801.40	7.8187	0.73560
70	3470.67	25967.7	207.881	2592.54	7.4820	0.74698
71	3145.43	22497.1	205.639	2384.66	7.1523	0.75813
72	2833.42	19351.6	201.851	2179.02	6.8298	0.76904
73	2535.75	16518.2	196.436	1977.17	6.5141	0.77972
74	2253.57	13982.5	189.491	1780.73	6.2046	0.79018
75	1987.87	11728.9	181.253	1591.24	5.9002	0.80048
76	1739.39	9741.03	171.940	1409.99	5.6002	0.81062
77	1508.63	8001.63	161.889	1238.05	5.3039	0.82064
78	1295.73	6493.00	151.265	1076.16	5.0111	0.83054
79	1100.65	5197.27	140.089	924.894	4.7220	0.84032
80	923.338	4096.62	128.880	784.805	4.4368	0.84997
81	763.234	3173.29	116.959	655.925	4.1577	0.85940
82	620.465	2410.05	104.488	538.966	3.8843	0.86865
83	494.995	1789.59	91.6152	434.478	3.6154	0.87774
84	386.641	1294.59	78.9564	342.862	3.3483	0.88677
85	294.610	907.951	67.0490	263.906	3.0819	0.89578
86	217.598	613.342	55.8566	196.857	2.8187	0.90468
87	154.383	395.744	45.1992	141.000	2.5634	0.91332
88	103.963	241.361	34.8243	95.8011	2.3216	0.92149
89	65.6231	137.398	25.0993	60.9768	2.0937	0.92920
90	38.3047	71.7747	16.8224	35.8775	1.8738	0.93664
91	20.1869	33.4700	10.3854	19.0551	1.6580	0.94393
92	9.1189	13.2831	5.5881	8.6697	1.4567	0.95074
93	3.2224	4.1642	2.2858	3.0815	1.2923	0.95630
94	0.8276	0.9418	0.6854	0.7958	1.1380	0.96152
95	0.1142	0.1142	0.1104	0.1104	1.0000	0.96618

INDEX

565